FABIANISM IN THE POLITICAL LIFE OF BRITAIN, 1919–1931

This dissertation was conducted under the direction of Professor John T. Farrell, as major professor, and was approved by Professor Friedrich Engel-Janosi, and the Reverend Wilfred Parsons, S.J., as readers.

FABIANISM IN THE POLITICAL LIFE OF BRITAIN, 1919-1931

A DISSERTATION

Submitted to the Faculty of the Graduate School of Arts
and Sciences of the Catholic University of America
in Partial Fulfillment of the Requirements for
the Degree of Doctor of Philosophy

BY

Sister M. Margaret Patricia McCarran, Ph.D.

OF THE

Sisters of the Holy Names

SECOND EDITION

PUBLISHED BY

The Heritage Foundation, Inc.

75 East Wacker Drive, Chicago 1, Ill.

TABLE OF CONTENTS

List of Abbreviations

ADA	Americans for Democratic Action
CWS	Cooperative Wholesale Society
FN	*Fabian News*
FQ	*Fabian Quarterly*
FRD	Fabian Research Department
FSAR	*Fabian Society Annual Report*
IFTU	The International Federation of Trade Unions
ILO	International Labor Organisation
ILP	Independent Labour Party
LSE	London School of Economics
LYB	*Labour Year Book*
NCWC	National Catholic Welfare Council
NEP	New Economic Plan
NFRB	New Fabian Research Bureau of 1932
NS	*The New Statesman*
NUR	National Union of Railwaymen
QA	*Quadragesimo Anno*
SDA	Students for Democratic Action
S.S.I.P.	("Zip") Socialist Society for Information and Propaganda
TUC	The Trade Unions Congress
TUGC	The Trade Unions General Council
TVA	Tennessee Valley Authority
WFTU	The World Federation of Trade Unions

Spelling

The British spelling of labor, Labor, and words ending in "ization" is used in quotations and close paraphrasing.

PREFACE

Fabianism represents the predominating type of Socialism in England. In general, it may be said to be a mentality which certains persons, members of the Fabian Society of London, exemplify either as publicists, lecturers, and politicians, or as an anonymous cohort of devoted workers for Social Democracy. This mentality is collectivist in social theory and monistic in philosophy. The Socialism professed by the Fabian Society is gradualist, not catastrophic; political, not direct-actionist.

The present study picks up the thread of Fabian history at a point after World War I, when the *Basis* was revised and plans laid during the war by Fabians for steps-leading-to-socialism were translated into action. The *Basis* proclaimed it the objective of the Society to bring about Socialism by research, education, permeation and penetration. Fabian " research" was to provide propaganda toward socialism. Finding the times characterized by reform movement already a century old and originating in natural justice, Fabians permeated and penetrated the national labor element as well as all that the English guild-socialists termed "the Movement." They shaped the Labour Party and assumed command thereof. By extending the boundaries of the term " labour " to include all who work at anything, they politicized a centre and, indoctrinating it with " socialist faith," produced a social religion secular in spirit. The rise to power and the grappling with political realities strengthened the hand of Fabian leadership, i.e. of the Intellectuals, to the despair of trade unionists and the disgust of " pure socialists " or " sentimental socialists " such as the Clydesiders who, to that point, had provided the Labour Party with its most spirited history and with its leader, Ramsay Mac-Donald. " Education " toward Fabian ends embraced alike liberal economics and the struggling cooperative movement.

Notwithstanding the peculiarities of the " third party," in the area of domestic politics, Conservatives put the far-reaching influence of English Social Democracy (a term interchangeable with

Fabian Socialism) to uses conducive to some Tory ends, notably the acceptance of the Dawes Report leading to the Anglo-German commercial treaty of 1925. Looking toward a German-British-Russian trade axis Fabian opinion in regard to Germany embraced Social Democracy and rejected the Centre; and at the level of the International Labour Organisation, it headed and reformed the Second International while opposing the Third. Nevertheless Fabians, holding out the incentive of trade to English workmen, maintained within the Party unbroken loyalty to the Russian Revolution and seconded Russia's aspirations to hegemony of the Straits. Defeat of the Labour Government in 1924 induced Fabian preoccupation with the semantics of " freedom "—as distinguished from " liberty." The electorate had exhibited fear that English liberties were threatened by socialism.

In 1929, under circumstances strikingly parallel with 1924, and under even greater Fabian influence, the Labour Party again assumed office. In the ensuing impasse, the British Constitution, dependent as it is upon Party Government, endured its greatest stress. This occurred at the point of balance of the forces of populace, Parliament, and prerogative: The Liberal Party was in eclipse and the Independent Labour Party (a socialist society rather than a political party) was helplessly involved with Fabianism. Labour's Left, feeling cheated, was demanding that Socialism be enacted into law and that the Cabinet be ruled by Parliament through the Labour Party's Consultative Committee. Dictatorship stood in the offing. The prerogative was invoked—to the extreme chagrin of certain Fabians—and the King's " favorite " set up a National Government. It is almost symbolical that at this point, the founders of the Fabian Society journeyed to the U.S.S.R. They took with them the mental picture of all they would see there.

Fabian Socialism demonstrated in the time span of 1919–1931 at least, that it advocates Statism and is averse to republicanism, that it intends to capture and to bring under its aegis labor, socialist thought, and international socialism. It showed itself of set purpose, monistic. In its own preachment, reform, welfare—any dynamism arising from Natural Law and tending toward commonweal—will not ever constitute Socialism. The Fabian cooperation with such a dynamic must be temporary and undertaken for pragmatic reasons because the dualistic concept of social order inherent in the Natural Law is abhorrent to those who fashion an artificial construct called Social Democracy and make themselves the spokesmen for a world clamant—they assert—for a purely secular way of life.

The study was undertaken in an attitude of sympathy for ostensible Fabian ideals and with respect for the high character of many Fabians.

The writer acknowledges the debt of gratitude this thesis owes to the major professor, Professor John T. Farrell, and to the readers, Professor Friedrich Engel-Janosi, and the Reverend Wilfred Parsons, S.J. The writer wishes also to thank her religious community, the Sisters of the Holy Names, for the opportunity given for study. To her father and mother much is owed for many special kinds of help including most of the printing costs. The daughters of the late renowned Senator Newlands of Nevada made the plan to print possible in the first place and gave great encouragement. The Library of Congress has supplied facilities and helpful associations, especially that with Dr. David Baumgardt, Consultant in Philosophy. For fine typescript thanks are due Miss Marjorie Pence. Assistance with the index was given most efficiently by Mrs. Leola Benedict.

Quotations have been used with the permission of the publishers credited herein.

For high standards of workmanship, for kindly interest and for fairness and cooperation thanks are due the York Composition Company.

FABIANISM IN THE POLITICAL LIFE OF BRITAIN
1919 1931

INTRODUCTION

"The Fabian Society consists of Socialists," as the first line of the *Basis* on the flyleaf of many a Fabian Tract declares. A Society which bears the heritage of Benthamite radicalism, it rose with strange genius in the 1880's, did effective work in the political life of Britain in the *fin de siecle* and up to 1914, permeated the reform movements [1] of the times with Socialism, and survived the war. Revivified, it flourishes today as an agency for research, toward penetration and permeation of all societary orders with Socialism which it holds as a creed. There follows a brief sketch of its origins and early ideological patterns.

In 1883 Thomas Davidson,[2] a Scotland-born American citizen, together with a few of his associates in the *Nuova Vita,* a cultural association, joined another group, friends of Edward R. Pease, in the latter's rooms in London.[3] The *Nuova Vita* was a nascent society whose objective was Progress, cultural, ethical, and individual. Pease, a psychical researcher and a member of the Stock Exchange, had heard of Davidson from the writer, Frank Pod-

---

[1] Helen Merrell Lynd, *England in the Eighteen-Eighties* (London: Oxford University Press, 1945), p. 405. Webb always referred to Robert Owen as the genitor of Fabian and workingmen's socialism, as if abandonment of Owen's non-political ideal was a temporary aberration. Furthermore, early Fabians were steeped in J. S. Mill's *Political Economy.*

[2] The Founder of the movement was a sort of benign comet in the London sky out of America. Cf. William Knight, "Memorials of Thomas Davidson," in *The Wandering Scholar* (Boston: Ginn and Company, 1907). In this volume as contributors of Memorials appear the names of Percival Chubb, Felix Adler, Havelock Ellis, William James, Wyndham R. Dunstan, and others. Davidson was a Rosminian philosopher and *persona grata* (*ibid.,* p. 126) as "visiting student" at the court of Leo XIII. Cf. also, Morris Cohen, "Thomas Davidson," *The Encyclopedia of the Social Sciences,* III:10. "He tried to establish a religious basis for democracy . . . pluralistic, individualistic . . . subjectivistic." (The titles alone of Rosmini's works indicate the rise of the idea of State intervention for Social Justice.)

[3] Edward R. Pease, *The History of the Fabian Society,* 2nd Edition (London: The Fabian Society, 1925).

more, when both were on an excursion connected with spiritism. Pease and Podmore arranged a joint meeting of the two groups at which Davidson read his paper, " The New Life." [4]   At a second meeting the novelist Hubert Bland appeared. He was destined to perennial treasureship up to his conversion to Catholicism. At the third meeting, by previous arrangement, a resolution expressing common agreement upon their aim to reconstitute society, " to secure the general welfare and happiness," was unanimously adopted; but the organization discovered no other unanimity. Whether the methods to be adopted toward the agreed ends should be material or spiritual could not be decided. At best a sort of philosophical monism emerged; their ends should be material and their means secular. Among the members, Percival Chubb, Havelock Ellis, and William Clarke stood for forming an " Order." Sharing the ethical and cultural bent of Davidson, they actually planned a " common life " like that lived by religious; but by the fifth meeting, the material side advocating life in the world had won. Adopting a socialist creed, they resolved to live in the world, pursuing their avocations and joining other societies. It was Podmore's idea that in allusion to the tactics of Hannibal's patient vanquisher, the Society so formed should be called Fabian. The aforesaid resolution concerning the aim to reconstitute society now became the basis of their organization. A plan was formulated to penetrate civic and social units and to find means to disseminate contemporary social ideas, concentrating on concrete objectives rather than on doctrines. The twin organization, *Nuova Vita,* or The Fellowship of the New Life, existed independently until 1898. [5]   Ramsay MacDonald, J. F. Oakshott, Corrie Grant,

---

[4] The *Index* Association of Boston published Davidson's New York Lecture to the Fellowship of the New Life, *The Moral Aspects of the Economic Question* (Boston, 1886). The Fabians, it would seem, were slow to grasp his point of dissent with them: " There are few more curious examples of the irony of human nature than this, that, while men are everywhere shouting and struggling for individual liberty and independence, they are quietly submitting to a division of labor [economics divided from culture] whose infallible tendency is to render them helpless cogs in the great economic machine, creatures without liberty and without independence " (p. 3).

[5] Davidson held a Summer School of the Cultural Sciences at Keene, New York, in the Adirondacks; he also carried on the Educational Alliance on the lower east side of New York, and lectured to his group called " The

Havelock Ellis and his wife, were identified with it and wrote for its organ, *Seedtime*.

Between 1884 and 1886, much transpired to give the Society character: It learned that of " two socialisms " it was distinguished from H. M. Hyndman's Social Democratic Federation in that it eschewed violence or militant action; that while it had in view the advance of Socialism in England, it intended to become part of the world socialist movement in order to re-shape it. Fabianism encouraged the Marxist SDF while it also absorbed the preachments of Henry George, who had lectured in London in 1881. On March 16, 1884, Bernard Shaw, because he was a member of the Zetetical (debating) Society, in search of a debate, as he himself relates, appeared among the Fabians. He was already a follower of Hyndman and a devoté of *Das Kapital*. James Lecky had introduced him to the Zetetical devotees of Phonetics exercised in discussion of Mill, Darwin, Spencer, Huxley, Malthus, and Ingersoll. On September 5, Shaw contributed the second great Fabian Tract, "A Manifesto,"—not to be the last. Henceforth, Shaw was the soul of the organization as Sidney and Beatrice Webb were later to be the brain. Shaw responded to this student's suggestion that such was the relationship that he, indeed, discovered the genius of Sidney Webb and brought him to the languishing Society but that Webb did more than any other to bring out Bernard Shaw, the born actor.[6] Histories, lecture courses, tracts, even the Webbs' famous *Trade Unionism* as later

---

Breadwinners." At Glenmore Summer School, T. H. Green, John Dewey, W. J. Potter, W. T. Harris, H. D. Lloyd, Brother Agarias [sic], A. N. Alcott, and others lectured. Cf. Knight, *op. cit.,* pp. 55 ff. Among the students was Morris Cohen.

Fabianism has never stood alone, and this has been its strength rather than its weakness. It appears like a plant grown as a perfect entity by chemurgy but always needing something upon which to climb the contours of which it would alter materially. In 1889, for example, it stood with the Progressives and offered the London Programme; in 1907, it lent guiding principles to the Metropolitan Radical Federation. These small beginnings patterned the experience of the Society in connection with the William Morris followers, the Hyndman Federation, the ILP, the Labour Representation Committee, and the Labour Party.

[6] Since letters received from Fabians will not be published, no further documentation will be possible.

their tract on " the new [Russian] civilisation," were enlivened by
a contribution from Shaw. Pease says that the platform was
" unqualified Shaw," and that although they had set out to recon-
struct society, they did not know how to go about it. The manifesto clarified some principles but did not suggest means. The
Fabians groped in the same blind way as most of their contemporaries [7] to find a science in the social studies, for they believed
" science " must be the key to perfect action. The one unifying
tenet was the monistic approach to the problem of society, and
Fabians, according to their Shavian *Manifesto,* stood for " spreading " their opinions and discussing " consequences." (It is important to note that they did not pretend to know what consequences to
expect in advance.) Ten underscored items in the ensuing brief
statement of the platform indicate characteristic points of future
agitation: *Wealth* enjoyed was dishonor; forgone, misery. All
must labor. Access to *Land* and *Capital* was the individual's
birthright independent of any other private person's will; " farming out " Land and Capital had created *Class.* Nationalization of
Land was a public duty. Capital's presumed encouragement to
Invention had been discredited by nineteenth century experience.
Competition made inevitable the practices of adulteration, dis-
honesty, and inhumanity; but it secured for the public the most
satisfactory products; hence, the *State* should compete with every
business—and, operate upon a non-profit basis. *Taxes* should be
direct, and no " proceeds " should be held back to replenish the
public treasury. Exhibiting what was to be a characteristic note,
family and fiscal matters were mingled. The State should compete

---

[7] At this time Nationalist Clubs were rising in every direction in the
United States. They were based on the socialistic nationalization plans of
Edward Bellamy, novelized in his *Looking Backward,* and *Equality.* The
organ of the American Fabian Society founded by W. D. P. Bliss, *The
American Fabian,* upon completing its fifth year, ceased to appear and passed
its editorial torch to the Bellamy societies in January, 1900. Cf. *The American Fabian,* V :2 (January, 1900) ; in the Library of Congress, HX1.A3,
7–11, no more published.

Clydesiders, too, were reading Bellamy while Londoners read George. This
is easily verified in the lives of Kirkwood, MacDonald, Tillett. A Fabian,
W. A. Peacock, said in *The Clarion,* I :7 (January, 1929), 9, that Blatchford's *Merrie England* had more influence toward Socialism than Morris'
News From Nowhere or George's *Progress and Poverty.*

especially with *Parents,* ensuring children against tyranny while seeing to it that they be provided with a happy home. (The State should compete in and with the home.) The sexes should have equal political rights since men no longer needed protection from *Women.*[8] No privileges should appertain to relatives of distinguished public servants. "The State should secure a liberal *Education* and an equal share in the National Industry to each of its units."[9] Finally, this platform declared that the established Government had no right to be called the State. Better a civil war than another century of such suffering as the preceding century had brought![10] In January 1885, Shaw led the Society into public notice when he represented it at the meeting of the Industrial Remuneration Conference, at which Arthur J. Balfour, in an address, compared Henry George and Karl Marx to the disparagement of the former, while Shaw in some agreement with both George and Marx said that all landlords were burglars.[11] So we see that early the attitudes on family, State, and property were set within a frame of reference of materialism.

In March of 1885, a generation before the creation of the famous Royal Commission on the Poor Law which occasioned Mrs. Webb's emergence into active leadership, the Society set up a committee to study poor law administration. When joiners

---

[8] The jocular quality of these early writings passed over to *The Clarion* rollicking with the rallying cry, "Boots and Spurs!" Margaret Cole characterizes her own life in "the movement" and in "Zip," the organization preceding the New Fabian Research Bureau, as "fun and games in Politics." She excoriates Shaw, however, as a mere mountebank. Cf. her *Growing Up Into Revolution* (London: Longmans Sons and Company, 1949).

[9] Pease, *op. cit.,* pp. 2 f.

[10] Pease wrote in 1924 that Shaw had remained consistently devoted to these principles. This attitude toward the Government sprang from an unqualified conviction that it represented and served *only* the moneyed class.

[11] Cf. Pease, *op. cit.,* pp. 2 f. Balfour made one with this group much as Asquith, Lloyd George and Haldane consorted with the Webbs in the early days of agitation. In fact, Balfour was appointed by Webb in 1924, to head an investigating committee. (*Ibid.*) Shaw wrote his equation into a play in 1918, *Heartbreak House,* where the burglar and the businessman perish together in an air raid by jumping into a cache-trench full of the explosive inventions of the old "navigator." The latter had advised all present to "learn navigation," meaning, of course, to learn tactics of social control.

came, there was sympathetic work laid out for them. In May of the same year, Sidney Webb, Sydney Olivier, both of the Colonial Office, and Harold Cox, M.P., editor of the *Edinburgh Review,* joined the Fabian Society. Mrs. Annie Besant had joined in April. A disciple of Malthus, she was a friend of the professed atheist, Charles Bradlaugh. A year later, Graham Wallas joined, and William Clarke, who had dropped out came back, bringing to the aggregate thought, however late, attraction toward the feeling of the American transcendentalists and a devotion to Mazzini. Wide diversity of membership opinion increased with every meeting. The Fabian group outgrew Podmore's dwelling and delighted themselves, among other places, in Mrs. Charlotte M. Wilson's " simplified " menage.[12] This hostess remained with the Society all her life but her energies were devoted to the Anarchistic Movement headed by Prince Kropotkin. She edited *Freedom,* from which we shall have occasion to quote criticism of Webb-Shaw Socialism. Among the Fabians there were some respectable elderly ladies and many university-trained young persons.

Thus it appears the Society had acquired its type-set by 1890. The seven essayists were now within the fold: Shaw, Webb, Olivier, Wallas, Mrs. Besant, Clarke, and Bland. Webb and Pease went to America in 1888, returning in 1889 in time to help Shaw get out the first edition of *Fabian Essays in Socialism.* Shaw's work as editor was meticulous. Pease called it " excellent." The Prefaces to succeeding editions make Fabian-Socialist ideological history. Especially noteworthy, however, is the edition of 1948 with a " Postscript " by Shaw appraising the Society.[13]

They were to devote themselves to research, education, penetration, permeation. Already " penetration " as well as " research "

---

[12] It was to become characteristic of Fabian women to do, or insist all women should do, all their own housework. In 1949 an exposition of this principle was made in *FN* where Fabian women showed no sympathy whatever with the servantless middle class women who were complaining of overwork. Cf. *FN,* 60:5 (May, 1949). Mrs. Cole gives as the reason for limiting her family the political and social services she felt called upon to perform. However, the Cole menage uses all the servants found necessary in upper middle-class domestic arrangements. Cf. Margaret Cole, *Growing Up Into Revolution,* pp. 103–105.

[13] Cf. *Infra,* pp. 651 f., where this is discussed.

had commenced.[14] The Socialism which Shaw inculcated in 1889 was built upon a democracy which from the Lincolnian formula, dropped the phrase " by the people." Shaw had been through " Bloody Sunday " in 1887.[15] He had marched to Trafalgar Square with the demonstrators protesting infringement of free speech. The experience, he declared, taught him how Napoleons and Cromwells are made and what produces bludgeons and barricades.[16] He had come definitely to the conclusion that the people must be governed by carefully selected leaders.[17] William Morris, who had been through that experience with Shaw and Annie Besant, agreed with Shaw.[18] For them, government was " education " in the sense of governess-ing. In 1889, Webb, Wallas, and Olivier were permeating the Fabians themselves with Positivism, London variety.[19] All members were expected to be cognizant of the tenets of Ricardo, Jevons, Cairnes, and Marshall.[20] All of them knew their John Stuart Mill. However, Webb alone knew and was the first to announce that Mill had died a Socialist.[21] In

---

[14] Mrs. Mary Agnes Hamilton, *Sidney and Beatrice Webb* (Boston: Houghton Mifflin Company, 1933), pp. 34 f.

[15] Cf. Francis Williams, *Fifty Years' March* (London: Odhams, 1950), pp. 61 f.

[16] Cf. G. B. Shaw, " Sixty Years of Fabianism " in *Fabian Essays* (London: Allen and Unwin, 1948), p. 207. He later claimed the Society rescued Socialism and Communism " from the barricades " and from the " pseudo-democracy of the Party System." He admired Cromwell.

[17] Cf. Francis Williams, *Fifty Years' March* (London: Odhams, 1948), p. 129; also, Hesketh Pearson, *Bernard Shaw* (London: Collins, 1942), pp. 81 f.

[18] Pease's *History*, unless otherwise indicated, is the source of the story up to 1915 as outlined here.

[19] Cf. Helen M. Lynd, *op. cit.*, p. 405. Shaw attributed the inclusion of Positivism and the resultant State-aided Capitalism to Olivier's influence, particularly. Cf. G. B. Shaw, " Fabian Failures and Successes," *Fabian Quarterly*, 41 (April, 1944), 2. For the position of Cairnes and Mill, et al., in British thought, see Lynd, *op. cit.*, pp. 35, 99, 105.

[20] The best description of the intellectual climate of early Fabianism comes from Shaw, again. Cf. Pease, *op. cit.*, Appendix I, " Memoranda by Bernard Shaw," pp. 273 f, where one reads, " Mill's *Essay on Liberty* was much more the Bible of English Individualism than *Das Kapital* ever was of English Socialism." Also, " Cairnes denunciation of the idle consumers of rent and interest was frequently quoted and Marshall's *Economics of Industry* was put into our book boxes as a textbook." *Ibid.*, p. 273.

[21] Both Pease and Shaw in the former's *History*, pp. 21 and 274 respec-

the person of Webb was gathered the legacy of Owen, Bentham, and Mill. He was to train the new electorate in " municipal " action.[22] Typified by the work of Webb, Susan Lawrence, Herbert Morrison and A. Emil Davies, the effectiveness of Fabians in reorganizing London would make a special study and produce a specimen of their methods.[23]

Through the 1890's the pattern of growth was the same as in the preceding decade—growth through the small political unit, the municipality, and within its historical structure; in other words, not in creating new patterns but in bursting through the old was the Fabian plant-like extension into the socio-political fabric of British life, to take place. Municipal ownership of some utilities was already well-advanced. The Fabians of the 1890's pointed out that municipal management was more desirable than control of all industry by a centralized state, while they taught that Fabian Socialism was to come by ballots, not by revolution. Although they agitated concerning the business of London, London was a difficult place to begin. A village would accept " municipalisation " without an ideological struggle. Londoners wondered if monopolistic graft were not preferable to Socialism with its submergence of the individual. If Mill had died a Socialist he had not burnt his books. If the boroughs were Benthamite in sentiment, in London it was Mill. To resolve the ideological conflict prag-

tively, show that Webb cites Mill often against Mill's followers, to illustrate the failure of Mill to undo the individualistic teaching of Mill's *Political Economy*. " It is probably due to Webb more than any other disciple that it is now generally known that Mill died a Socialist. . . . The only other prominent Socialist who can be claimed by Mill as a convert was, rather unexpectedly, William Morris . . . as Mill had clearly given his verdict against the evidence [in stating that the worst evils of Communism are but dust compared with the evils of Commercialism]."

[22] Lansbury, a " pure " Socialist, turned away from municipal action as he moved in ideology toward Lenin's Communism and Internationalism. But as a front-bencher, he became more Fabian; he worked with strict Fabians in their Commonwealth Group headed by W. G. Pole. Cf. George Lansbury, *My Life* (London: Constable and Company, 1928), *passim*.

[23] But it does not follow that what can be done with the assent of the electorate on a small scale is feasible on an international or even on a national scale. Pease shows the relation of municipalization to socialism and the difference between provincial town municipalization and that of London which the Fabians developed. Cf. Pease, *op. cit.*, pp. 82 f.

matically, Sidney Webb brought out *Facts for Londoners*. Meanwhile, the Reverend S. D. Headlam produced his *Christian Socialism*. Fabians approved the latter's conclusions but rejected his premises; so henceforth their Social Gospel need not be Christian and Mill and Bentham were reconciled in Webb. Although their activity was focused on decentralized political entities,[24] *Facts for Londoners* became " Facts for England " on the way to becoming facts for the world—not just for Leeds or for Manchester.

Following the Dock Strike, which the Society viewed almost as a laboratory experiment,[25] there appeared " Tract No. 9." It was meant to be a parliament bill legislating an eight-hour day *when feasible*. (The spirit of gradualism appears.) They had demonstrated sympathy with workmen without conniving with the principle of direct action and they concretized the problem in a bid for legislation on hours of labor.

The *Essays* went on their successful way. In them Shaw explained the " Economic Basis " and the hoped-for " Transition " to Social Democracy. He grafted Jevons' system onto Ricardo's as found in Henry George. Clarke previsioned the growth of Trusts in the twentieth century placing himself squarely among those who welcomed simplification as a means toward State control. Trustification might be deplored, but as a means to nationalization it offered a method ready to hand. The *Essays* slighted

---

[24] Cf. Martin Ray Adams, *Studies in the Literary Backgrounds of English Radicalism* (Lancaster, Pa.: Franklin and Marshall College Studies, 1947). This shows the hundred years' connection of " liberal " thought with French Revolutionary ideology, and the link is tangible—Parr to Bentham. In Fabianism there is a concretizing and emergence out of literary backgrounds of liberal socio-economic agitation, exemplified in the breach with Davidson. Shaw wrote that " the fellow " returned but once and got short shrift from the Society he founded.

[25] Individuals like Mrs. Besant, but not the Society officially, worked with and for the Dockers, and Tom Mann, a Fabian, relied on members as friends. By 1906, Mann had joined himself with those who lined up with Lloyd George to " dish the Webbs." He did not acquiesce in Beatrice's plan to make " our little home " the center of intellectual leadership of Labour. The turning point is shown exactly on page 116 of Beatrice Webb's *Our Partnership* (New York: Longmann and Sons Company, 1948). Cf. also, *Ibid.*, pp. 460 and 122.

the rising Trade Unionism and disparaged Cooperatives. Pease, the idealist, thought in 1924 that Annie Besant's "puerile" essay, untouched as it was by Shaw—unlike the other essays—had been the farthest afield with its design for state industries for the unemployed: besides the social care it provided, here was a method likely to lead to the State's superseding private enterprise in industry.[26] Bland's "The Outlook" foresaw the time when Liberal and Tory would be united against "the dispossessed." Pease was hesitant in 1924 to declare that Bland's foreboding would never materialize. In the 1890's, fortified by a brilliant lecture series in which the dry periods of Webb on the Eight-Hour Bill, of Bernard Bosanquet on Individualism and its social antithesis, of Mrs. Besant on the School Board,[27] were vivified by Olivier on Zola, Robert Morris on Gothic Architecture, Sergei Stepniak on Tolstoi, Bland on Socialist Novels, and Shaw on Ibsen, the Fabians launched a campaign of propaganda for reform and a drive into Tory and Union preserves for membership. The drive was spearheaded by the *Essays*.

As to organization and growth: Henry M. Hutchinson, M.P., financed the "Lancashire Campaign." Fabians reached and preached to the working-class liberals, and procured collaboration from S.D.F. everywhere, as also from Cooperatives and Radical Clubs; but especially was assistance forthcoming from the Cooperative Union and the National Reform Union. Local Fabian Societies sprang up.[28] But these were absorbed into the Inde-

---

[26] Pease could not foresee, as England was undergoing a temporary reaction to the near-victory of 1919–1924, that his hope for 1928–1929 would be deferred to 1945. Pease at 92 assisted in the Jubilee of the Labour Party. Cf. The broadsheet, *The Labour Press Service* (London Labour Party publication issued free to the Labour Press), December 1949, p. 4.

[27] They were admittedly ignorant articles but they did the movement no harm. Indeed they served to attract the attention of uncritical persons to elements in society usually taken for granted or overlooked. This sharpened attention gave new aspects to familiar things and raised questions which Fabians answered with socialism in such a way as to produce the social stratification they were beginning to devise.

[28] Cf. Williams, *op. cit.*, Index, p. 381. He gives the Society the credit denied it by other writers of Trade Union mentality.

Cf. also, Mrs. Cole's *Growing Up Into Revolution*, p. 207. The locals were revived by her efforts.

pendent Labour Party (founded in 1893), which incorporated the ideas but disagreed with the methods of Fabianism. The process of absorption was later reversed. After this campaign, Annie Besant, converted to Buddhistic Theosophy,[29] detached herself, her political machine and press, and her power to put into effective words the thought of others, from the Society. (She later returned.) But these were days of too rapid growth to miss even a colorful member. And Fabians created other means of publicizing their views. In March, 1891, *Fabian News* was founded with Bland and Pease as editors. The *Annual Reports* had been published since 1890. In 1895 Oxford acquired a Fabian local unit. There were four University groups by 1900, and some colonial units.[30] The year 1891 was marked by the resignation of Webb from Civil Service to be elected by his own party, the Progressives, to the London County Council. It also marked the success of the "Newcastle Programme,"[31] achieved by infiltration into editorial offices of newspapers (Massingham in *The Star*, then and later in the *Daily Chronicle*, and Webb in both), and the mutual recognition of their respective talents by Sidney Webb and Beatrice Potter, one of eight daughters of an indulgent father who left them an inheritance in Canadian railway stock.

C. R. Attlee's *The Labour Party in Perspective* (London: Gollanz, 1937) also outlines the preparations made in the composition of English social thought from Owen through Bentham and Mill to Morris.

[29] Shaw had given her a book on Theosophy, to review for *Contemporary Review* at the bitter end of their notorious liaison.

[30] By 1924 all the university locals had become Labour Clubs. Cf. *FSAR* (1924), 8. (*Fabian Society Annual Reports* are designated *FSAR*, hereafter.)

[31] A program to placate Liberals, the "Newcastle Programme" was Gladstonian regarding Ireland, free traders, Little Englanders and the new imperialists. Fabians endorsed it to "permeate" the Liberal Party and promote housing schemes, then called "socialist." Cf. Lynd, *op. cit.*, pp. 226 f. Pease, *op. cit.*, pp. 111 f, has Shaw's story of how he and "Mr. Beale" moved the programme at a meeting of about ten Fabians and how the Press reported it as a "revolutionary break-away."

It was in 1892 that the ILP was "set up" in *The Clarion* offices. Cf. R. B. Suthers, "Birth of *The Clarion*," *Labour Press Service* (December, 1949), p. 7. He "set up" seven chairs he had borrowed to seat the men who met to form the Manchester ILP a year before the National ILP was created in Bradford.

By 1892, London liberalism was sufficiently penetrated with Fabianism that J. Keir Hardie could be elected to Parliament as an Independent Labour Candidate. A new *Election Manifesto* by Shaw had already forecast the idea of a Labour Party but had advised support at present for those candidates of either party who favored the working classes. In the confusion caused by antipathies involving Liberal Unionism or Home Rule the Fabian project prospered. When the air cleared it was discovered that the Liberal Party was captive to Fabianism; even the Liberal Party's peculiar Leasehold Enfranchisement Association had been cut away from it. " Pure " Socialists like L. MacNeill Weir, author of *The Tragedy of Ramsay MacDonald,* and George Lansbury, the father of " Poplarism " (a term for the system of " outdoor " poor relief Lansbury inaugurated in Poplar), detested cooperation with Liberals. *The Clarion,* which claims to have laid down the plan for creating the Labour Party and capturing " the Movement " for Socialism in its office in 1892, likewise protested against partnership with the Liberals. It was Socialist Blatchford whose famous " fourth clause " kept the ILP free from political entanglements, especially with Liberals. Despite the design to keep ILP out of politics, to accent Socialist-labor's independence, and preserve it free to inculcate Socialism, " pure " Socialists and gradualists continued to permeate liberalism. Webb, foreseeing that the solution of the Irish question was likely to be postponed, said the striking outcome of the election was " the defeat of mere Gladstonianism "; the election had a " collectivist complexion." The Liberals were destined for defeat, Webb warned, unless they devoted themselves to raising the living standard of the degraded populations: In the present state of Parliament legislative measures were hopeless; it would be well to give " Home Rule " to London. In the words reported in *Fabian News,* he pointed out how the Government might achieve reforms without " appealing to a busy House of Commons to pass special bills." [32] The Budget was the key; they could shift five or six millions in duties on the breakfast table onto " those who received rent and interest." [33] Among other reforms, he urged the eight-

---

[32] *Fabian News,* II :10 (December, 1892), Vols. 1–13.

[33] *Ibid.* These are points to bear in mind when considering the great debate

hour day for Government employees, and a minimum wage. The election of 1892, concerning which these words of Webb are a commentary, is a very important marker in Fabian progress. After that there was always a Fabian on the London County Council cooperating with the Labour Bench and with the Trade Union Progressive Party led by John Burns until its demise in 1914. Socialists like Snowden and Lansbury disapproved of this cooperation with Trade Unionism and with the Progressive Party, respectively. Yet they remained Fabians, being pragmatists.

As the Society grew, its developing methods furnished interesting and instructive data. Selected items from the record to be found in the London Fabian Society's *Fabian News,* specifically the volume for 1891–1903, give evidence of this method. Under "What Members are Doing" [34] Bruce Wallace, an honorary minister of a Congregational Church,[35] held a conference every Sunday afternoon. The religious service lasted fifteen minutes; then came a lecture, questions and reply, and "Keir Hardie, J. W. Martin, H. B. Holding, Ben Tillett, and other Fabians, are among the lecturers." Further on, Tom Mann, it was reported, had been appointed Secretary to the London Reform Union, "founded on the 28th of October by a number of M.P.'s, L.C.C.'s, and others.

---

of the election of 1923, "Protection." Only vaguely the ideas of British Socialists were shaping toward "control" of trade by "cooperative" world buying. The constitutional feature of this suggestion is important: Webb here suggested rule by administrative boards and bureaus. In 1932, he will be found to be severely critical of rule by "acts in council." In 1950, rule by decree would be the accepted mode of administration. Cf. Marguerite A. Sieghart, *Government by Decree* (London: Stevens, Stevens and Sons, Ltd., 1950).

[34]*Fabian News,* II:9 (November, 1892). Parallel usage arises in U. S. today.

[35]A characteristic list of Protestant ministers who were very prominent Fabians and publicists or members of Parliament would include besides Arthur Henderson (MacDonald also filled a pulpit on occasion), John Clifford and S. D. Headlam (both deceased, 1923), Clifford Allen and William Mellor whose great activity is noted by Mrs. Cole, *op. cit.* (eight references in index), James Adderly, G. C. Binyon (who like Clifford wrote to identify Christianity and Socialism), Ramsden Balmforth, James Kerr, M.P., J. C. Hamilton, I. Massingham and Ben Spoor, M.P. (ordained but not practicing), Henry Carter, Richard Lee, C. Jenkinson, and the chairman of the Canterbury House of Laymen, as well as Lord Paramoor, editor of the *Laws of the Church and Clergy.*

Sidney Webb is a member of the Executive Committee." [36]
Under "Fabian Organizer in Lancashire," W. H. Utley (the
father of Freda Utley) ". . . . will be glad if members of the F. S.
who can arrange lectures for Cooperative Societies, Liberal Clubs,
etc., in the North will communicate with him through the London
Office." Throughout 1891–1892, the activities of W. S. de Mattos,
a convinced collectivist, were notable—lecturing, campaigning, and
recruiting. The same article on what members were doing showed
anxiety and underlined the conviction that gradualism was in
order: "Many Fabian Societies seem to be in danger of neglecting
the educational work, which should be their principal object, in
order to devote themselves exclusively to working as a political
party." [37] The locals in "the provinces" were to tend to their
social knitting.

Penetration in churches, in *ad hoc* committees, by itinerant lecturers to specified groups, went forward. The locals were properly
corrected. Under "Local Fabian Societies" in the supplement
of 1892,[38] nine typical activities appeared as follows: 1) The
Fabians joined with the Trades Council in a joint manifesto aimed
at "free and efficient education"—this was at Ashton-Under-
Lyne; 2) in Clifton and Bristol they worked with strikers. The
fact that this activity was in behalf of the girls engaged in con-
fectionary work and the alum workers shows the inclusiveness
and detail of the Society's evolving plan. Continuously thereafter
the organizing of women workers went on, as a glance at *Fabian
News* will show. 3) It was notable that women members opened
French language or elocution classes (shades of the Zetetical
Society!) which lent themselves to Fabian techniques. 4) Glasgow's local group imitated Webb's *Facts for Londoners* with
Facts for Glasgow. This illustrates the point in the Marxist criticism that Fabianism was "gas-and-water socialism." It also illus-

---

[36] In 1896 Fabians had tried to permeate the International Socialist Workers and Trade Union Congress, held in London. They inculcated their policy
of "political toleration," yet cooperated in the expulsion of the Anarchists.
Pragmatic and eclectic as they were, they were typically British.

[37] The ILP became the politicizing agency, the fateful decision to go into
politics having been made in 1892. But Fabians made up about two-thirds of
the membership of ILP.

[38] *FN*, Supplement (December, 1892).

trates Glasgow's tendency to seek independence from London. 5) In Glasgow, as in the initial plans in London, music and literature sections were formed—a " spiritual " endeavor. 6) At Hull they took up " the unemployment question " and action was to have been taken by the Labour Members of the Town Council " in the direction of an immediate proceeding *with necessary public works.*" [39] 7) Bad news from Manchester had to be faced: The Society there was already moribund because it had adopted a rule excluding any official of Conservative, Liberal, Liberal Union, or National League Parties. The local was chided for its lack of insight into the meaning of " penetration." 8) Election returns were listed showing ILP and Fabian Society acting together; defeats and successes in contests for Parliamentary seats. 9) As ever, there is evidence of work within another group's framework: It was reported that the Liberal Party had broken a promise that the Labour Party should have the next vacancy for Halifax; the Fabians appealed for money and announced, " The best known London Fabians have promised to aid with their persuasive oratory, and the Liberals will learn once more that Fabians will fight whenever they are not allowed to permeate." [40] Furthermore, Fabians invaded upper bourgeois literature: H. W. Massingham, Shaw, and Webb formed a symposium in the *Fortnightly Review* on " What Mr. Gladstone Ought To Do." [41] William Clarke wrote for *The Contemporary,* "The Limits of Collectivism." [42] It was apparent that Gladstone, the Tory-hearted " Liberal," epitomized that liberalism which Fabians were in the act of scrapping. " Collectivism " was the replacement which they offered; it was not Marxian but English. They did not say but

---

[39] *Idem.* Italics inserted.

[40] *FN,* II :12, p. 46. Whereas Locals might be warned to eschew political activities, the London parent Society acted in a political manner, freely.

[41] *Ibid.,* p. 47.

[42] He also wrote " The Fabian Society " in the *New England Magazine,* X :1 (March, 1894), pp. 89–99 : " No visitor to the British Capital will mingle long in the political life of London before he will hear of the Fabian Society." He lists (*ibid.,* p. 90) " Miss Willard, one of America's reformers " as a member. Written for New England the article stressed the cultural and religious attainments of its members. The sentence quoted above is as true of 1950 as of 1894.

they were soon to exemplify that for them only Socialism would do, nor as yet did they give great emphasis to the abolition of Capitalism; but they were set for total social control of the economic order through the political.

There is a tendency in telling the story of Fabianism to note prominent or recurrent writers but an idea of the momentum of the movement is lost by so doing. New names of writers, lecturers, members, appear in each issue of *Fabian News*. Obituaries note the passing of efficient workers known to the Society but never theretofore to fame in print. This is important; there were great leaders and able followers. They formed an "Order" in the sense of being at least like a religious "congregation," whether they said so or not.[43] Work which bore fruit in 1906 was commenced in 1893. "The Strange Death of Liberal England"[44] is perhaps not too strange or inexplicable when one knows that Sidney Webb supplied the intimate knowledge of each department and Bernard Shaw the devastating prose, which manifested in the pages of *Fortnightly* the fact that the Liberal Government were not, as Campbell-Bannerman had hoped they would be, "the best employers of labour in the country."[45] The third party was scarcely in the field when it began to undermine both other parties and to tend toward becoming the One-Party. H. M. Massingham of the *Daily Chronicle* revolted against Fabianism and turned bitterly upon the Fabians.[46] He returned to the fold, however.

Pease and Shaw came very near being excluded from the Bradford Convention of 1893 which created the national ILP—designed to capture Labour for Socialism—but they insisted on re-

---

[43] There is an accidental relation of the Fabian "Order" to Plato's concept of the consecration of political leaders to the people's interests.

[44] George Dangerfield, *The Strange Death of Liberal England*, overlooks Fabianism and R. C. K. Ensor, himself a Fabian, says their influence is overrated. Cf. Lynd, *op. cit.*, p. 402. The correctness of the estimate is open to doubt.

[45] This is the expression of Mr. Campbell-Bannerman cited in Pease, *op. cit.*, p. 114. We must use the plural form for "Government," as in British usage.

[46] He returned to write for the *NS* when already there were rumors in *NS* that it was to acquire *The Nation*, in 1923. In fact, he came back earlier. Cf. Beatrice Webb, *Our Partnership* (New York: Longmans Green) 1948, p. 333.

maining. Permeation of ILP went on with a will until the Labour Representation Committee, designed to free Trade Unions from ILP domination in 1900, formed the outright political party in 1903.[47] Trying to make themselves heard in Parliament, the Trade Unions lent themselves to manipulation by Fabians, and to inoculation with socialism from both ILP and Fabian societies. ILP and the Fabian Society had been over-represented on the L.R.C. by a construction given the constitution of the Trade Union Congress; and the Fabians, having the stronger political bent took the ascendency when the Party was formed. There was a fringe of voters of the Liberal ticket who thought primarily of labor—of workers. Fabians induced a slow "growing up" in Socialism among Liberals as in the unions. Although everyone spoke of the Liberal Party as dead after 1895, in 1905, the Liberals were back in office. Then, when the Ministry was formed, every member was found to have perused Webb's "Intercepted Letter" which had appeared on their desks embodying the Trade Union standards of hours and wages, urging graduated and differentiated income taxes and compulsory arbitration in labor disputes,[48] also proposing wages boards for agriculture.[49]

The Liberals were in office but they were no longer free. It had been very difficult to persuade the Liberal Party to adopt a reform platform as Mrs. Webb narrates in *Our Partnership*.[50] But now, in place of the party, stood the plan, and, activating the party machine, there was the bourgeois confidence throughout England

---

[47] The ILP, it is said, absorbed the personnel of most local Fabian Societies. "Absorption" sometimes in reverse became "permeation." A typical case in point is that of Ben Turner. Cf. *About Myself, 1863–1950* (London: Humphrey Toulman, 1930), p. 166. Turner's local Fabian Society became ILP but he deplores (p. 162) ILP antagonism toward the leaders (mostly Fabians) and its peculiar social ethics (birth control, etc.). He also detested Fabian collaboration with Liberals.

[48] This was an "error" Fabianism recovered from earlier than its United States exponents did. Fabians have always stood for party or government control of Trade Unions. "Governance" would be a better word than control, implying an inner control. Mechanically, or as an apparatus, the unions are autonomous.

[49] This is important. Agriculture as a way of life is remote from the thinking of State-planning advocates of industrial democracy.

[50] Beatrice Webb, *Our Partnership*, p. 296.

in the mitigated "socialism" of Lloyd George.[51] In the race to capture Trade Unionism for the "Movement" or for Socialism, the Fabians had overtaken ILP because two-thirds of the ILP membership were Fabians, according to Pease.

The ensuing years of Conservative Government passed in research and education rather than permeation on the part of Fabians. The Society became an information bureau by publishing a study of the Local Government Act of 1894 (30,000 copies), and also one on the Workmen's Compensation Act of 1897 (120,000 copies). Making the best of existent legislation, they disclosed ways of developing better housing and means of increasing actual "compensation"—in other words, to make the law work. Meantime, they developed their unique device, the book-box circulating library. The Society numbered many barristers and solicitors and profited by their free services, as an occasional obituary notice in the *Fabian News* indicates, and as the life story of Sir Henry Slesser demonstrates.[52] The numerous editions and steady sales of tracts describing the workings of the London County Council, London Vestries, Metropolitan Borough Councils and local housing authorities, signify the permeation of the new bourgeoisie with socio-political education, and the rising habit of laying history under tribute. Fabianism may not claim to have created the demand for such education; but the perspicacity which gauged it and supplied it was to their credit. Political Science, once taught as the fruit of thought found in Plato, Hobbes, Bentham, and Mill, must now instruct voters in the means of using

---

[51] Much has been said of the drab and mirthless statistics of "Webbism." (Dean Inge is known to have complained that under Fabianism they would all die of boredom.) Shaw bluffed uproariously when he launched into Jevons' economics (Pease, *op. cit.*, p. 276); together they had all but sung "To Your Tents, O Israel"; Sidney was "rollicking" when he wrote the "Letter" of 1906. At least it can be said that when they relaxed they were most effective: Jevons' system fastened upon Ricardo's formed the nearest approach to an economic platform which Fabianism had until they adopted Marshall and Keynes. "To Your Tents" was an indictment of Liberal Government, a summons and a plan to put candidates in the field to stand for Trade Unions. The "Letter" concretized or cast into political projects partial Fabian objectives.

[52] Cf. Rt. Hon. Sir Henry Slesser, *Judgment Reserved* (London: Hutchinson and Company, 1941).

government to deal with strikes, trusts, tramways, wages and poverty. So, when the Fabians in the person of Sidney Webb acquired a legacy from Henry Hutchinson, the sponsor of the Lancashire campaign to develop Fabian locals, and when later they received one also from his daughter, they, Sidney Webb acting as sole agent, founded the London School of Economics and Political Science. The mind of the school was Sidney Webb. Designedly, it was not a Fabian project but was cut off as a separate entity to proceed upon its own course toward " the best science which could be obtained." Its history and influence afford material for another study. It boasts famous teachers besides the Webbs—Tawney, Beveridge (the latter's father-in-law), and Laski—all Fabians. Suffice it to say that in a generation from its foundation it was supplying many new Fabians as well as the old members with youthful " brains and political science," in Shaw's words; and *The Clarion* was to note in 1929 that the "New Fabians" were graduates of this school, pupils of Laski and bed-fellows of Communists. Harold Laski, Fabian teacher and pub-licist, preached the aim of " Society's New High Priests " to har-monize " the experts " and " plain men," and " harness " effort to " the profounder idealism of ordinary men and women " [53] and his proteges from the University of London also were welcomed to the Society and the Party by *The Clarion*.[54]

Nothing more exciting than J. Ramsay MacDonald's demand-ing the recall of Tract No. 70 in which Shaw had talked of Fabians " throwing their weight " in elections (ILP wanted slower political action), than Olivier's going to Jamaica as Colonial Secre-tary,[55] than Shaw's becoming Vestryman for St. Pancras, and Wallas' being elected to the School Board, occurred in the years 1894 to 1898. But each of these items had a far-reaching sig-nificance: MacDonald's anti-Shaw spirit was to persist until 1931

---

[53] *The Clarion,* II:12 (December, 1930), 349. For such expressions Laski is said to have a " spiritual " trait. He wrote to this student that he deplored being compared with Berdyaev as a reviewer whom she cited had done, and that he was a neo-Marxist and no mystic.

[54] *Ibid.,* II:6 (June, 1930), 175.

[55] He stayed there until 1913 when he became Secretary of the Board of Agriculture. In 1924, he was Minister for India. It is important as far as space will allow, to note the positions of public trust held by Fabians.

and after. Olivier, as Lord Olivier, was to advance from the West Indies to India. The Shaw story needs no re-telling. Professor Wallas was to have an historic quarrel with Webb [56] over State aid to Catholic schools, and to project other of his ideas far into the formation of early twentieth century thought, and into the American thought-stream.

The Society had been surprised by the Boer War. The ILP stood out immediately against the war, consistently with their common Socialism, but the Fabians, acting in the Society's defense, in self-preservation evaded the issue. But discussion created an hiatus between the " Old Gang," as the Webb-Shaw coterie was called, and the "left wing." Both the MacDonalds resigned, although daughter Ishbel was again to be found active in the Society in the 1920's. Mrs. Pankhurst, J. F. Green, G. N. Barnes, Pete Curran, Walter Crane (he had designed the cover for the first edition of Fabian Essays), H. S. Salt, G. Hobson, and Will Crooks stayed with the group—at least for a while longer. Shaw wrote *Fabianism and Empire* to explain their view.[57] The Webbs then agreed with the "Limps" (Liberal Imperialists, namely, Haldane, the Asquiths and Grey, among others). They were not against the war. Seeing no more liberalism in Dutch farmers than in mining companies, they were beginning to evolve theories about letting natives and native law be as found. Fabians were working to penetrate the "Limps" and to turn certain Tories and TUC people toward Socialism, and the war brought no abatement of their efforts.

Two clear effects of discussion about the Boer War were important: First, the conscious purpose of the Fabians to make the working class pay less attention to Party matters than to their own social condition—to induce them to leave politics to the Party; second, the calling forth of another of Shaw's succinct manifestos expressive of the Fabian consensus on Socialism and British Im-

---

[56] Beatrice writes in *Our Partnership,* p. 340, " Sidney thinks the Education Bill [ensuing one of 1906 reversing 1902 which placed expenses for denominational schools upon local authorities] a harsh measure. . . . [But] as we belong neither to the Church [sic] nor to the Catholics, we have no place in either of the movements of the country against it."

[57] Margaret Cole, *Beatrice Webb,* pp. 84 f.

perialism.[58] The thesis of this document was startlingly original—prescinding from the spirit of law under which the Papal Bulls of the sixteenth century had been written. It was realistic and, from one point of view, just: No nation any more than an individual has the right to use its territory without reference to the interests of its neighbours; the very comprehensive right to trade includes right to stable government which might be supplied by the interested nation if a native government fails; the value of a state lies not in romantic nationalism but in the quality of its civilization; and a Great Power is charged with the interests of civilization.[59] Responsible imperialism must take the place of World Federation in the case, for example, of the African gold mines—which should " in theory" be internationalized. Realistically, Shaw stated that China was being partitioned because " The state which obstructs international civilization will have to go." In the light of what is to follow, tracing Fabian behaviour regarding Germany as it affected home politics, it is very important to note that Shaw insisted that German State organization of foreign trade in contrast with British *laissez-faire* proved—according to this Fabian document—that the application of State Socialism to the *consular service* was possible (i.e., a commonwealth of world co-operatives might be geared at the consular level); and to think otherwise was to doubt the *survival of Britain* in the age of Powers. The italicized words spell fascism and imperialism.[60]

---

[58] Pease, *op. cit.,* p. 135. Shaw developed principles later embodied in the League Mandates and United Nations Trusteeships. Not " aggression" but a sort of international "eminent domain" covers his ideas on the "white man's burden." Cf. Lord Olivier, *Imperial Trusteeship,* Fabian Tract No. 230, 1929. Here Trusteeship aims at leaving intact the native political order and social-economic practices, *e.g.,* in land ownership. Fabian literature on the subject leaves blank the question of industrializing colonial populations, developing private property and suffrage. Cf. H. Finer, *The TVA; Lessons for International Application,* (Montreal: for ILO), 1944.

[59] An interesting parallel is found in Burckhardt, who speaks in *Force and Freedom* (New York: Pantheon Books, 1943), p. 117, of the " sovereign right of civilization to conquer and subdue barbarism which must . . . bow to the moral principles of the civilized state."

[60] Pease, *op. cit.,* p. 138. Shaw's thought is always in advance of Fabian conclusions and Socialist implications. Lansbury's advocacy of these principles together with the idea of boycotting states which did not adhere to

There followed an advocacy of universal military training, a living wage, super-annuation grants, grants in aid for housing, new educational machinery; and then, " The moral of it all is that what the British Empire wants most urgently in its government is not Conservatism, not Liberalism, not Imperialism, but brains and political science."

The Society devoted itself to Education which was suffering from the incrustation of its non-conformist history and the unreflecting approval of Gladstonian Liberals; and Sidney Webb almost singlehandedly produced the plan and the bill which Arthur Balfour got through Parliament.[61] It provided for the control of all elementary schools by *local* authorities.   Only in 1906 was the State feeding of school children begun.   It is indicative of the working policy of Fabianism that they opposed as impracticable the feeding program sponsored by the Social Democratic Federation until they had won on the point of local control.

In 1907, a plan for raising election funds was successfully laid. This was the nearest approach to innovation at the time when H. G. Wells [62] was agitating to remodel the Fabian Society along more militant Socialist lines.   Hitherto only a few Fabians like

---

Conventions on conditions of labor was an echo of the Commonwealth Labour Group founded by Fabians H. Guest, Tom Johnston, Harry Snell and advised by E. F. Wise, " the expert adviser to the Russian Cooperatives " toward " a scientific system of controlling all imports."   Cf. Lansbury, *op. cit.,* pp. 269–272.

[61] Cf. Margaret Cole, *Beatrice Webb* (London: Longmann Green and Company, 1945), p. 83.   Sidney Webb lost his place in the inner councils of the Liberal Party because he advocated the " dual system " which the Liberals believed favored Roman Catholic schools.   Webb stood for " variety " and the " door open to new and unthought of experiments " and he judged from the United States' pattern of parochial schools that non-support would not close them.

[62] Cf. " The Episode of Mr. Wells," Pease, *op. cit.,* Chapter IX, pp. 163–184.   Lewis L. Lorwin states in *Labor and Internationalism* (New York: The Macmillan Company, 1929), p. 65, that " the Fabian Society was founded by Sidney Webb, George Bernard Shaw, and H. G. Wells."   He is in slight error on this point.   Cf. *Labour Press Service* (London: Labour Party, December, 1949) which commemorates the foundation of the Party as of 1900, taking the Labour Representation Committee as the root of *the Party.* Everything in this news service tends to glorify ILP and to relegate the Fabian Society to an inconspicuous corner of the Party's history.

Will Crooks, for Labour, and Sir L. G. Chiozza Money, a Liberal (then a member of the Fabian Executive Committee), had been elected to Parliament, having been given the Society's special assistance. Mr. Arthur Henderson, a Fabian and Secretary of the Labour Party Executive, became Chairman of the Party in the House of Commons. Politics and learning were brought together by Fabians.

In 1904, Graham Wallas had dropped his membership in the Society but not from the faculty of the LSE. He maintained his friendship with members and again lectured to the Society in 1922. He disagreed on tariffs with Shaw, and on education with Webb. Active younger members included Henry W. Macrosty who wrote the bill adopted as the " Eight Hour Law," and Henry Slesser who drafted many labor measures. Macrosty also wrote studies on state arbitration, the living wage, monopolies, and trust control and was a member of the Royal Economics Society. In his project for the revival of agriculture he anticipated the Liberal Government's reforms which were interrupted by war in 1914. Land development and Poor Law reforms were agitated by Mr. Lansbury of Poplar and he had for collaborator Joseph Fels, the famous American soap maker and Single Taxer.[63] Lansbury's [64] ardour for redevelopment of marginal lands and rehabilitation of urban unemployed was admirable. He called himself " a Capitalist, a Socialist propagandist and a talking Christian." His daughter Daisy married Raymond Postgate.[65] There was also Joseph F. Oakshott, formerly of the Fellowship of the New Life,

---

[63] Cf. Lansbury, *op. cit.,* pp. 10 and 99–109. The Fabian effort to capture Fels or some of his money is told in Beatrice's *Our Partnership,* p. 291, edited by Barbara Drake (her niece) and Margaret Cole. The story was told this student by the American historian, Miss Elizabeth Kite, who was Mrs. Mary Fels' companion and one of the " dowdy Americans " as Beatrice describes them—to former Quakeress Kite's amusement. The latter became a Catholic after seeing Shaw's *Candida* that year, 1904. Fels was listed as a Fabian in *Fabian News* of the time. He preferred working with Lansbury.

[64] Lansbury, *op. cit.,* p. 13.

[65] Lansbury was invidiously critical of Fabian intellectuals in 1928. They had kept him out of office in 1924 on account of his " Poplarism " which he explains convincingly in his *Autobiography (ibid.,* pp. 129–169). But in 1929 he was on the front bench in Parliament and working closely with Fabians.

and John W. Martin who transferred his activities to New York.[66]

The Fabians mixed sociological drives and political issues. Listing Fabian interests, e.g., milk, liquor, pensions, pawnshops, bakeries, slaughterhouses, fire insurance, transportation, all of which were studied with a view to municipalization, there must not be omitted their rebuke administered to victims of the Malthusian phobia. They proved statistically that the birth rate in Britain was dropping (six out of 120 marriages practised no family restriction) on account of voluntary family limitation. It was one of two projects Fabians boasted most about in their history. (The other was the Poor Law Minority Report of 1909.) Although the research was made among themselves and probably represents a middle-class cross section only, its importance is obvious. Socialist and self-admitted Capitalist Lansbury for one raised a very large family. Fabian Ben Turner writing *About Myself* [67] expostulates against the Socialist habit of mixing these social matters with Trade Union politics or Party programmes. But under the Socialist creed of Fabians, any protestants who appear need not form a new church. It was Fabian practice to evade responsibility on the part of the Society by notice that the Fabian Tracts represented their author's views, and not official views of the Society, but nothing in their history indicates they could have published a Catholic response on the birth control question.

To close the discussion on developments of the Fabian third decade there follows a list of names of some members acquired by the close of this period. These several famous names are to be found in Pease's *History of the Fabian Society*. The accent upon literary pursuits and interest in the humanities is obvious:

> Aylmer Maude, Arnold Bennett, Laurence Irving, Edgar Jepson, Reginald Bray, Stanton Coit, H. H. Fyfe, A. R. Orage (*The New Age*), G. M. Trevelyan, R. C. K. Ensor, Edward Garnett, G. B. Clark, Constance Smedley, Mr. and Mrs. Philip Snowden, George Lansbury, Herbert Trench, Jerome K. Jerome, Edwin Pugh, Spencer Pryse, A. C. Brock, Mrs. G. B. Shaw, and Holbrook Jackson.

[66] Pease, *op. cit.*, p. 138.
[67] Cf. Ben Turner, *op. cit.*, p. 162.

Among the activated groups of the time, "Nursery," Biology, Local Government, and Arts, the most important wz· the Women's Group. Backing Mrs. Pankhurst were Mrs. C. M. Wilson, Mrs. Bernard Shaw, Mrs. Pember Reeves, Emma Brooke, and others like Millicent Murbley, Doctor Letitia Fairfield, May Morris and Professor Edith Morley.[68] Not only Suffrage but Women's Rights, equal wages for women and men, and related problems figured on the agenda of the Women's Group.

The Society was going through a period of exuberance and stress. From 1906 to 1914, organizational planning came to a head, only to be stopped by the war. Local groups and university groups annually sent delegates to the Conference of Fabian Societies. The principal stress felt in this Pan-Fabian gathering was the position of this Society of Socialists in relation to the Parties called Labour and Liberal. The Webbs had returned from a world tour in 1912 with money from a steel firm in Bombay to found the Social Science Department of the London School of Economics, and with plans for creating an independent Socialist Party from the Fabian nucleus.[69] What was envisioned

---

[68] *FN*, XIX :9 (August, 1908) lists 13 Fabian women who had gone to jail "for the Suffrage Cause." That Beatrice Potter Webb repudiated Mrs. Pankhurst's movement in its early stages, 1889, represented a stage in the conflict of civilization taking place in her, the conservative and bourgeois against the new Socialism. That she repudiated this error has significance because of other matters which she did not repudiate. Beatrice did not join the Society until 1893. In 1908 she wanted to lead the "Nursery," not to be reckoned with the "Old Gang," and in 1912 she was elected to the Executive. Cf. Margaret Cole, *op. cit.*, p. 35. Beatrice calls her anti-suffragist action "my false step" in her autobiography, *My Apprenticeship* (London: Longmann Green and Company, 1926), p. 341. The tendency of Beatrice Potter Webb to follow as a religion something that she decided to like is evidenced in her partiality for "old" Fabians against the new "young men" in 1912–1915. It throws light on her affection for Russia in 1932. It will not be inapropos perhaps to mention here her concern with political ethics, a concern which did not trouble Sidney. Cf. Keith Hutchinson, "Apostles of the Fabian Dream," a review of Beatrice Webb's *Our Partnership*, edited by Margaret Cole and Barbara Drake, in The New York Times Book Review, LIII :113 (March 28, 1948). "He [Sidney] did what he thought was right with none of the qualms that Beatrice suffered when zeal for the cause led her to slip below her own high standards of political morality."

[69] Margaret Cole, *Beatrice Webb*, p. 110.

was the capture of the Labour Movement for Socialism and for a " new order " (Webb's) through politics. The war in 1914 interrupted their two tentative plans which were, first, to affiliate the Labour Party and the British Socialist Party; and second, to create the Joint Socialist Council by which Sidney Webb hoped to solve the terminological difficulties found among British, French, and Belgian Socialists. Ten years later this hope remained unfulfilled. Pease wrote again in 1924: " The project for Socialist Unity therefore awaits the happy time when war shall have ceased "; the war of Socialist semantics had not ceased. Incidentally, only the ILP, of all the English Socialistic groups, as in the case of the Boer War, criticized the prosecution of World War I.

The year 1906 had witnessed the aroused interest of Mrs. Beatrice Webb, a member since 1893. Wells and the Suffragists seemed to challenge her. She lectured upon her own upbringing in the " Faith I Hold," a series in which Hobson and several others participated, but her first great contribution was made in 1909, after the findings of the Poor Law Commission made necessary the famous Minority Report. To judge by the account given by Edward Pease, this supplied the bridge between the palliative measures recently adopted to relieve the distress of unemployment, and the distant attainment of perfect Socialism. Supplying a bridge to an ill-defined Socialism was an element of many future patterns made by Fabians. Mrs. Webb created a separate organization in The National Committee to Prevent Destitution.[70] Such a committee could glean assistance from organizations which would have no truck with Socialism. This demonstrates the fact that the Webbs cared not by what doctrinaire logic or absence of philosophy an end was gained. A remark of G. B. Shaw is appropriate and significant here: " The Webbs [had] no time for

---

[70] Cf. M. A. Hamilton, *Sidney and Beatrice Webb* (Boston: Houghton Mifflin Company, 1933), p. 199. They " roped in " persons whose names disguised the Labour Party backing and the steps to Socialism: Balfour, Churchill, Gilbert Murray, Sir Oliver Lodge. They failed because of John Burns and the Liberals but the roads were made ready for Socialists to travel into the Labour Party and along with it.

The Committee to Prevent Destitution used bicyclists to deliver literature; *The Clarion* did likewise up to its last expiring.

argybargy as between Marx's Hegelian metaphysics and Max Eastman's Cartesian materialism." [71] Fabianism was then headed into its storm and stress period.[72]

In 1912 Mrs. Webb founded Fabian Research. It embodied in an agency the methods and objectives of Beatrice. She had a genius for the grubbing research which was to be the work of this agency. In 1915 she tried to rescue the Research Committee from the Guild Socialism and Syndicalism with which it had become infiltrated. After the war it became the Labour Research Department which a little later became Communist.[73] In the war years and some time after, the "young cuckoos," as Mrs. Cole terms them, Margaret Postgate (later Mrs. Cole), G. D. H. Cole, Raymond Postgate and other well-known young Socialists worked in the Fabian headquarters. Impudent youngsters, they still moved in awe and in fear of "the Great Ones," the Webbs and Mr. Pease.[74]

---

[71] Bernard Shaw, "Essay on the Webbs," in Sidney and Beatrice Webb's *The Truth About Soviet Russia* (London: Longmann Green and Company, 1942), p. 14.

[72] A very interesting reaction of Fabianism upon Americans is found in *Fabian Anarchism, A Fragmentary Exposition of Mutualism, Communism, and Freeland* by Alexander Horr, editor of *Freeland,* published by Freeland Publishing Company, 1814 Webster Street, San Francisco, California (January, 1911). The author and founder is an anarchist who borrowed a *tone* of Fabianism for his Spencer-based philosophy and Kropotkin-based anarchism.

[73] Margaret Cole, *Growing Up Into Revolution,* p. 121. When the New Fabian Research Bureau was formed in 1932 Mrs. Webb gave it her blessing. Having renounced gradualism in 1932 and resigned in 1936, she was willing, nevertheless, to lend the name Fabian to the new organization, N.F.R.B., which later rejoined and rejuvenated the old Society. Those who imagine the Society was moribund by 1930 overlook the fact that with characteristic zeal *The Clarion* trumpeted "Fabians to the Rescue" when "Zip," the Society for Socialist Inquiry and Propaganda, was formed in 1931. Cf. "Reporters Notebook," *The Clarion,* III:7 (July, 1931), p. 195.

[74] Cf. Mrs. Cole, *Growing Up Into Revolution,* p. 71. The literary erudition of these young persons was remarkable as a perusal of this book will show. The correlation between a very high and worldly literacy and ideological Socialism is demonstrated often. When this literacy becomes spiritual in a religious sense, it leaves Socialism behind, as witness Bland, Slesser, Knox, and Chesterton. Of her sister, Mary Playne, Beatrice wrote "presently she will be a veritable saint. Will she end in the Catholic

In 1913 Shaw, the Webbs, and D. H. Harben founded the *New Statesman,* extant as the *New Statesman and Nation.*[75]   Again, like the London School of Economics, it was a separate entity, although it published prominent Fabians' viewpoints.   Its editors-in-chief have been to date: Webb to 1922; Clifford Sharp to 1931; Kingsley Martin having for colleague R. S. Crossman—all Fabians.   (Serial Record reports that no editors' names are given.) Robert Dell, correspondent from Germany in the 1920's and as consistent a contributor as Bensusan or Lloyd, was a former member of the Fabian Executive.   Supplements bearing the reports of Committees of Inquiry upon Land problems and Rural Development and upon the Control of Industry (studies of many a suggested or experimental method) were published by this organ. Pease tells of a storm of criticism arising over " control of industry," noisy with counter-proposals.   It was comparable with the Wells episode of a decade before.   Fabians played a large part in warding off from English Socialism George Sorel's syndicalism. Sorel's followers argued for organization of the state on the basis of Trade Unions (basing the franchise not upon the home and geography but upon the shop and economics) ; and, while working for collective bargaining and against the " servile state," syndicalists urged control of industry by Producers (i.e., workmen) rather than by Consumers, to whom, they asserted, Capitalists truckled. Syndicalists thus opposed two things which by now were clearly Fabian-approved, consumer cooperatives and state agency in behalf of consumers.

However, these were not the Fabian Society's only opponents. Hilaire Belloc, suspicious that the " Servile State " was implied in the *Minority Report,* carried into the fray his ideal of the self-sufficient producer, the peasant.   Belloc foresaw that " industrial democracy " would destroy agriculture as a way of life.   Then Tom Mann, nominally a Fabian, came back from Australia and captured about all the working class attention with his fervid new proletarianism   heightening   the   self-consciousness   of   Trade

---

Church?" Cf. *Our Partnership,* p. 340.   On this page, also, Beatrice speaks of the need for " an Order " to give society light and leadership.

[75] Massingham joined the *NS* staff in 1923.   *The Nation* was incorporated with the *NS* in 1931.

Unionism. Thus, during the years 1910–1915, Fabianism had to meet the impact of several attacks upon its program while, presaging the conflicts of incongruities of 1931, militant Suffragists and South Wales miners made demands upon the Labour Party which would have wrecked its program of cooperation with the Liberals for Irish Home Rule had it yielded. Syndicalism together with the new Guild Socialism advocated by A. R. Orage and G. D. H. Cole, who were connected with the *New Age* and the Oxford Fabian local respectively, stood out against the idea of a Labour Party. Orage and Cole also urged a " reform " of the Fabian *Basis*. This was done after the War. Cole left the Society in 1915 although he continued to work in the Fabian Research Bureau until after the War, and in the 1920's he wrote for the *New Statesman*. In the 1930's and 1940's he is found back in the fold.[76] Another famous socialist, S. G. Hobson, left the Society in 1910, fighting with his native Quaker intuition and his platonic political idealism for a genuine Socialist Party. Trade Unionism and Fabianism had, he said, rejected the " larger concept of industrial democracy." [77] Fabianism withstood the stress, fastened as it was upon the growing Labour Party. But the movement lost the " spiritual " Russian contact it might have had in Hobson—a

[76] G. D. H. Cole, *Fabian Socialism* (London: George Allen and Unwin, Ltd., 1942). Shaw answered a query of the present writer regarding Guild Socialism to the effect that it was no longer a schism since he, Shaw, had demonstrated that it was not hostile to but an integral part of Fabianism. Mrs. G. D. H. Cole remarked in a reply to this student that Guild Socialism never was orthodox. To compare Cole's *Fabian Socialism* with his commentary on the Labour Party's manifesto of 1949, *Labour's Second Term*, Tract No. 273, ". . . written for the Fabian Society . . . and offered for discussion to the Labour Movement," is to find no satisfactory definition of Socialism and to find Cole verbosely critical of deviations from " only Socialism will do" but arriving at the same conclusions that the compromisers have perforce accepted already. Cole's writings appeared in both the *NS* and the *New Age,* in the 1920's; he was the author of numerous articles on industrial questions and the Labour Party's programme for Unemployment. His return to the Fabian Society, his dalliance with Mosleyism and final joining with Bevin against Mosley, are hailed by *The Clarion,* " G. D. H. Cole States a Comeback," 26 n.s. (June, 1926), 14.

[77] S. G. Hobson, *Pilgrim to the Left* (New York: Longmans Green and Company, 1938), p. 40. Hobson had caught the (North) Russian reform ideal.

sort of eastern " mystique "—as well as the earthy practical feeling found in Guild Socialism and evoked from the western Middle Ages. Fabianism supplied the anomalous bridge between Trade Unionism and a Socialistic new order, as Mrs. Webb later stated.

Edwin Pease found Fabianism in 1915 to be " the dominant principle in political progress." [78] Still collectivist, it had not lost its identity in any other movement. It hated the " idle rich," the anarchy of competition, the " insidious " licensed monopoly. It aimed to abolish poverty by the " reconstruction of society." *Why Are So Many Poor?* was still the theme song. The evident class partisanship needs no further demonstration. There was revolt in some circles hardly to be called reaction: e.g., in *Freedom*,[79] a London monthly, we read:

> It were tragedy to throw off the slavery of capitalism only to rush . . . into the slavery of Fabian Bureaucracy. The frightful mess that Webbism would make of life under its system of a modified state capitalism is a disaster one does not care to think of. No more poetry, no more romance, no more cakes and ale under the regime of these tight-lipped superior nonentities. Just as their industrial organization would make us obedient machine-like agglomerations of soulless units, so their marriage market would reduce us to the likeness of marionettes, whose strings would be pulled by eugenic cranks. . . .

The rest is unquotable here, and Rabelaisian regarding Shaw. It illustrates the antagonism Fabianism aroused in those who tried to resist being managed and the juxtaposition if not fusion of politics and social problems usually found in Fabian Socialism and here reflected in the words of critics. The range of Fabian energies embraced family relations and relations within the family of nations, equally.

In the light of present-day developments, it must be noted that in 1916 there appeared as a Fabian Society publication the work of L. S. Woolf, *International Government*.[80] Fabians following

---

[78] Pease, *op. cit.,* p. 255.

[79] " What is Slavery," *Freedom,* XXVIII:301 (May, 1914), 33.

[80] L. S. Woolf, *International Government* (New York: Brentano's, 1916).

the Socialist ethic, stood for pacifism but compromised on total draft for total war; and by professed internationalism they advocated a supranational government, one which must invest the vacuum found where international anomy had dissolved forces governing brotherly relations among sovereign states. The plan in Woolf's book bears comparison with Wilson's League of Nations and with the present United Nations organization. Possibly it has greater likeness to the latter. After 1919, through the date span of this study there was always a Fabian in the person of Stephan Sanders, C. Delisle Burns, or Philip Noel-Baker in the International Labour Organization or in the League of Nations secretariat at Geneva. The deliberately anonymous *International Labour* [*sic*] *Organisation* of 1931, published by Allen and Unwin, is, judging from internal criticism, the work of some of these persons, here mentioned.

Having traced the story of Fabianism and illustrated its main characteristics, we turn to sketch the frame-work in which its action is particularly to be studied, the political scene in Britain, 1919–1931.

Subtitle: Two reports prepared by the Fabian Research Department with an introduction by George Bernard Shaw, together with a project by a Fabian Committee for a Supranational Authority that will prevent war.

For the Fabian Socialists, the supranational government of "one world" replaced that concept of the brotherhood of nations which is inherent in Natural Law (cf. Pius XII, *Christmas Message of 1944*. Washington: NCWC, p. 9, where reference is made to the natural-law basis of society of nations and the "equal right of its own sovereignty" belonging to each State). Since Fabian philosophy abscinds from the Natural Law, it may be said to produce anomy because it dissolves the basis of adhesion of States in brotherhood; the divine basis discernible in Natural Law is replaced by an artificial device, "sovereign equality" in a supranational world. For a modern meaning of anomy cf. Sebastian de Grazia, *The Political Community: A Study of Anomy* (University of Chicago Press, 1948).

CHAPTER I

THE FIELD AND THE PLAYERS FOR "FUN AND GAMES IN POLITICS"

A. The Political Background, 1919–1931

British political life to all outward appearance from 1919 to 1931 can be described in simple outline.[1] The Coalition Government headed by Lloyd George had won the war and the ensuing " Coupon Election " gave the Prime Minister a very large and unwieldy majority. Certain social problems lay within everyone's purview;[2] recession and concentrated new wealth on one hand, and demobilisation, together with the dispersal of large numbers of Government workers on the other, coincided with early but not unprecedented strikes in the coal mines and railways. People knew that peace conferences were going on, that Germany was trying to shape herself into the pattern of the Weimar Republic and that Russia was in the hands of revolutionary leaders who were not the idealists of 1917, and that Greeks and Turks were at war. There was great surprise, however, when " Chanak," in 1922, rocked the Cabinet.[3] The ensuing election produced the first Conservative Government in sixteen years. It cleared the political air and revealed the presence of a new power in the person of Stanley Baldwin, who became Chancellor of the Exchequer under Bonar Law, while Lloyd George, Austen Chamberlain, Balfour, and Birkenhead were relegated to temporary inactivity. Lord Curzon then in the Foreign Office, would, it seemed, become the successor to the ailing Prime Minister, Bonar Law. Labour, led by MacDonald, for whom J. R. Clynes[4] had stepped aside, stood

---

[1] John Alfred Spender, *A Short History of Our Times* (London: Cassell and Company, 1934), pp. 225–309.

[2] Sidney and Beatrice Webb, *History of Trade Unions* (Revised Edition Extending to 1920) (London: Longmans Green and Company, 1920), p. 645.

[3] Winston S. Churchill, *The Aftermath,* being a sequel to *The World Crisis* (London: The Macmillan Company, 1941), pp. 409–438.

[4] Cf. Mary Agnes Hamilton, *Arthur Henderson* (London: William Heine-

34

in official Opposition. The English people found Tory leadership acceptable. It was a stabilizing force, so its aversion to "surrender" to the Irish coupled with its favoring of Turkish nationalism was overlooked. The tax-burdened and nervous populace was relieved to be rid of Lloyd George's empiricism, war scares, and scandals. Bonar Law achieved a measure of success, for the Germans paid in fifty millions of pounds in 1922 on their Reparations debt (although somewhat less was paid the next year). The English learned that French troops had been dispatched to the Ruhr, also that the Prime Minister was opposed to this action taken by Poincaré.

Bonar Law had to resign in May and Stanley Baldwin became Prime Minister. In October, the latter exhibited conscientious scruples regarding Protection which resulted in an election to get a mandate from the people on the matter. It was still the style for any one with pretensions to liberalism to vote for free trade. To the uncritical observer this circumstance ensured Baldwin's defeat yet produced the most surprising event of the decade, the election of a Labour Government. In a sense, the people did not elect a Labour Government; the too few elected liberals divided into warring camps, and there were too few free trade conservatives. In spite of the fears suggested to the English mind, fears which were derived from the uncertain knowledge of Russian affairs and of German waverings, and from such British manifestations of radicalism as were embodied in "the Clydesiders," [5] Asquith the

---

mann, 1938), pp. 229 f; also, J. R. Clynes, P.C., M.P., D.C.L., *Memoirs* I, 1869–1924, pp. 330–333, and II, 1924–1937 (London: Hutchinson and Company, 1937). J. R. Clynes, "half-Irish and wholly Lancastrian," had been Labour leader in Parliament 1920–1922. He had begun life as a "piecer." He formed a Piecers' union, 1885–1888, and became, through the initial fame of his "Piecer" letters, president of the National Union of General and Municipal Workers. He brought to his leadership a knowledge of Carlyle, Emerson, Ruskin, but most of all experience of the rise of Kerr Hardie, and discipleship of Burns, Crooks, Gillett, Morris and Shaw. During the War he had headed the Ministry of Food Control. His Socialism was an unarticulated religion of humanitarianism.

[5] Cf. Mary Agnes Hamilton, *Arthur Henderson*, p. 231. Led by "boss" Baillie John Wheatley and James Maxton, an Irish and Scottish group which Mrs. Hamilton characterized as pro-Soviet, class-war agitators, the "Clydesiders" supported MacDonald, then, and later repudiated him.

Liberal leader was known [6] to have stated that it would be unconstitutional not to permit Labour to form a Government. The winter of 1923 furnished any Government which might ensue with the results of the financial statesmanship of Balfour [7] who in 1922, in place of the ailing Curzon, had issued the " Balfour Note " on the basis of which Baldwin, in the winter of 1922, had achieved the agreement with Washington on war debts, whereby British credit was saved. Wisely or not, the idea of connecting debts and reparations had thus been formulated in the British view. The unemployment problem impressed the public more than the fact of Curzon's limping off to a sinecure leadership of the Tories in the House of Lords.[8] But the public failed to perceive the connection between the settlement in Washington which had linked the real (debts) with the hypothetical (reparations), and evoked the reactionary proposal to revert to Protection. It seemed that a Labour Government was accepted as the result merely of the tally. It was indeed to be another short-lived Government. Yet notable success in the field of foreign affairs marked by the adoption of the Dawes Plan and preparation for the Commercial Treaty fell to Labour's lot.

In 1924, because the fear of Bolshevism had become more real, Labour could not hold its position in the election which a vote of censure precipitated. Conservatives came back with " safeguarding " tariffs under Baldwin. Churchill deserted the Liberals and took a place in the Cabinet. Balfour returned to the Government along with Austen Chamberlain and Lord Birkenhead. Asquith, still a Liberal failed to get a seat in Parliament by being adopted

---

[6] J. A. Spender and Cyril Asquith, *The Life of Herbert Henry Asquith, Lord Oxford and Asquith* (London: Hutchinson and Company, 1932), pp. 342–346.

[7] Blanche E. C. Dugdale, *Arthur James Balfour* (London: Hutchinson and Company, 1936), II, p. 315.

[8] The shattering of Lord Curzon's life's ambition came when Baldwin became Prime Minister. Cf. The Earl of Ronaldshay (Lawrence John Lumley Dundas, 2nd Marquis of Zetland), *The Life of Lord Curzon* (London: Ernest Benn, 1928), III, pp. 349–365. A principle formulated since Salisbury's premiership was thus exemplified: The Prime Minister must lead in Commons. Labour leaders insisted upon its application in Curzon's case. Asquith had faced it squarely too. Cf. Spender and Asquith, *op. cit.*, p. 51.

by Paisley. It seemed like old England again. The Dawes Plan and its sequel, the Commercial Treaty with Germany, paved the way to Locarno. Few people understood that creditor nations were borrowing to postpone the disruption of trade, and were buying currencies to pay debtor nations. Tariffs were reappearing, as a result of which all the world's gold became magnetized at two poles, America and France. The only constructive measure attributable to the Labour Government, the Wheatley Housing Act, amended, went into effect. The people of Britain had at last been given something they had been promised before the "coupon" election: two and one-half million working class houses were begun. In 1925, Winston Churchill, implementing full reaction on the economic side, by his first budget as Chancellor of the Exchequer, brought about the return to the gold standard, the resumption of the policy of basing sterling upon gold, and the allowance of the export of gold. The pound gained in international trade but exports, especially coal, were curtailed. The Government maintained equilibrium by subsidies to the coal mining industry. These subsidies were stopped in 1926. The great Strike in 1926 was the result, to all appearances, of an effort to reduce wages and increase hours of labour. There had been talk of the possibility of a General Strike ever since the Dock Strike in 1908, and especially during the Railway Strike of 1911; and in 1921 a General Strike had nearly come to pass.[9] Now a new power entered the press and parlance—TUC, it was called after being once named, the Trade Union Council. Every element involved in the Strike shared a common fear, that of Revolution.[10] It was all over in nine days. Popular reliance upon public authority grew appreciably—approaching dependence, while sections of the Liberal Party developed schism, and Lloyd George and Asquith parted for good. The coal miners remained out, to return to work, terribly defeated, in 1927. The same Government prepared legislation to deal with labor problems which was passed

---

[9] Cf. J. H. Thomas, *My Story* (London: Hutchinson and Company, 1937), pp. 31 f.

[10] The Webbs, *op. cit.*, p. 672, had written in 1920 that such a strike could result only from a reactionary Parliament's "fishing up" from the "legal armoury" something like an injunction, and that such a General Strike must mean "revolution" in the continental sense.

in 1927 and did not show political effects until Stanley Baldwin's Government was defeated in the regular election of 1929.

Meantime, certain social measures, implemented by " de-rating " designed for poor law reform, went into operation under the disparate direction of Neville Chamberlain [11] and Winston Churchill. Publishing his theory that the general interest would be served if industry and agriculture were relieved of taxation, Churchill put through his scheme to de-rate all agriculture and reduce by three-fourths the rates on all industry, the Exchequer to compensate local administrations to the extent of twenty-two million pounds total annually. Chamberlain's Local Government Bill meantime set up Councils in place of the old Board of Guardians in an effort to unify administration and humanize the Poor Laws. At this time the public was less aware of the differences between Churchill and Chamberlain than of those between Lloyd George and Asquith.[12]

During the same years, 1927 and 1928, public feeling was stirred by the introduction of a bill for modification of the Prayer Book. The British public learned how far secularism had advanced and in what quarters. It was noted that the Lords approved the changes which would have legalized the position of Anglo-Catholics while Commons evinced Protestant feeling which, by its illiberalism, created a new non-conformity.[13]

An election fell due in 1929. The public was aware of differences between Churchill and Joynson-Hicks, of Trade Union resentment against the Trades Disputes Act of 1927, of increasing unemployment, of a spirit of " safety first " in a world in which fascism had announced a slogan of " living dangerously." A Labour Government was elected. MacDonald and the colleagues of the Labour Government of 1924 came back. Almost simultaneously the American stock market crashed. The new Govern-

---

[11] Cf. Keith Graham Feiling, *The Life of Neville Chamberlain* (London: The Macmillan Company, 1946), pp. 149–197, where the different positions taken by the two leaders, N. Chamberlain and Churchill, are shown. Cf. also, " Mr. Churchill and the Ratepayers " in *NS*, XXXI (May 5, 1928), 113 f.

[12] A. J. Sylvester, *The Real Lloyd George* (London: Cassell and Company, 1947), pp. 146–159.

[13] *NS*, XXX (March 24, 1928), 748 f. Cf. also, H. Slesser, *Judgment Reserved,* pp. 129–136 and 232–235.

ment found itself headed toward abandoning free trade and again going off the gold standard.

Although Asquith had stated in 1923 that Labour had long been independent of the Liberal Party, the Parliamentary Labour Party, numbering 287 in the House of Commons, found itself again dependent upon Liberal support against Conservatives numbering 261. Early, upon the matter of a Coal Export Bill, came one critical moment which passed and served only as warning when, on the matter of the amendment of the Trade Union Bill of 1927, Liberal opposition checked action. An Education Bill raising the school-leaving age and subsidizing parents of those who would elect to remain longer in school than was customary for their class, failed of passage in the House of Lords. Immediate and pressing were the problems of getting funds for Unemployment Insurance and for balancing the Budget. In 1930, Philip Snowden, Chancellor of the Exchequer, revealed a deficit of 47 million pounds, created by the charges made upon the Exchequer because of the de-rating begun in Churchill's administration. The public now found itself bearing new kinds of taxation; for Snowden managed to raise 30 million pounds by beer and income taxes, super-taxes and death duties. By 1931, the Exchequer was borrowing to meet Unmployment Insurance, while the Minister of Labour, Miss Bondfield, seeking a stop-gap fund of 25 million pounds, admitted a million pounds deficit weekly. Snowden managed to raise 20 million by petrol taxes and through the " dollar exchange " account; and he asked payers of income and super-taxes to remit three-fourths in January instead of the usual half. By 1931 the desperation of the financial situation created a schism in the Cabinet. Philip Snowden and his chief, Ramsay MacDonald, took a stand for economies and for keeping expenditures within the limits of feasible taxation; the rest of the Cabinet, including the powerful Arthur Henderson, thought that the occasion should be used to bring the banks under public control. Alarm had been spread by the publication of the report of the May Committee, a body hitherto unnoticed which had been set up on the suggestion of Liberals in Parliament. Their forecast of 125 million pounds' deficit in the next budget resulted in bank withdrawals and forced the Bank of England to ask help from the United States Federal Reserve and the Bank of France.

MacDonald resigned on August 24, and on the next day formed a Coalition Cabinet. The Labour Party was not to regain control for fourteen years. The British public was ever after aware, however, that the forces creating a Labour Party were extant, needing only coalescence to become formidable. From this point until the eve of Munich, Baldwin and MacDonald shared power.[14]

We turn now to a description of the position and spirit of Fabianism as of c. 1919: its own *Basis,* its work on the new Trade Unions Organization and the new Labour Constitution, followed by a discussion of the Fabian Plan, a blueprint for British Socialism. Then, the significance of its action within the political structure shown above will become apparent.

As to the Fabian Society, it emerged from World War I having shocked and shaken off those of its sentimental Socialists who were pacifists. The War had tested its principle of political action; the Labour Party had gone into coalition to assist in the nationalization of industries and total mobilization of men and materials so as to be able to point out their unique thesis that what could be done for war in the way of raising money for public expenditures was possible in peace time. As in the Boer War, so in World War I (and World War II),[15] the Society took a position which compromised its Socialist tenets but was true to its permeating practice and its long view. The Party, the Trade Unions, the Socialist Societies, especially the Independent Labour Party, and the Cooperatives claimed the attention of Fabians after the War. Like the living creatures flying to and fro among the elders in the apocalyptic vision, Fabians were external to but active among all these parts of the Labour Movement. Each part by reason of its immaturity provided an opportunity to the Fabians to inoculate it with their peculiar Socialism which was monistic,

---

[14] Cf. Rt. Hon. Viscount Samuel (Herbert L. Samuel), *Grooves of Change: A Book of Memoirs* (Indianapolis: The Bobbs-Merrill Company, 1946), especially, " Home Secretary Again, 1931–1932," pp. 257–271.

[15] Written by individuals of the " Socialist Clarity Group," *Labour's Next Step* (London: Fabian Society, 1940) shows the Fabian's concerted will to use the position of Labour in Coalition in World War II to undermine the Government in order to effect a programme of " social democracy " after the war, everywhere, " for purposes that the mass of the people desires." They argue that only a Labour Government will do.

gradualistic and stoic. For all their activity, they were patient people. Their symbol was, and is, the plodding turtle. Their motto reads: "I wait long. When I strike, I strike hard." In what follows we shall see the long slow waiting to strike while infiltrating the elements of political life of Great Britain.

B. Post War Fabians and Their Basis

By deliberate choice a section of the bourgeois intelligentsia called itself "Labour"; thus it beaconed to the working class— beaconed with hand and finger to English workers and signaled with a lantern of Socialism to the Continent. Leaving it to the psychologist to trespass where Veblen found his specimens of "invidious" reaction, history merely shows that this was done. In the following section there is a brief survey of the membership of the Society and its *Basis*.

In the Society, membership in which was gained by being sponsored and elected, several professions were represented: The financial fraternity by A. Emil Davies;[16] medical, by Captain Haden Guest, Doctors Letitia Fairfield and Ethel Bentham; barristers, by many such as H. H. Slesser but none more promising than Clement Attlee and C. M. Lloyd;[17] historians, by F. E.

---

[16] Chairman of several investment trusts, historian of the LCC, editor of the *Treasure Book of Knowledge,* according to *Who's Who,* 1931, and *FN,* XXXIV:8 (August, 1923). Some Fabians contributed to the first-named work, namely, J. L. Cohen, Dorothy Evans, F. W. Galton, Frank Rutter, Ernest Davies.

[17] Cf. Clement R. Attlee, *The Labour Party in Perspective* (London: Victor Gollancz, 1937). His opening sentences in Chapter I are characteristic: "Some thirty years ago, when I was a young barrister just down from Oxford, I engaged in various forms of social work in East London [Toynbeeism]. The conditions of the people led me to study their causes and to reconsider the assumptions of the social class to which I belonged. I became an enthusiastic convert to Socialism. I joined the Fabian Society and the Independent Labour Party and became a member of my Trade Union, the National Union of Clerks. For many years, I worked as a rank and file member of the movement, taking my share of the work of branch activities and propaganda meetings at street corners. I shared the hopes and disappointments incidental to Socialist work in what was then a very backward area." H. H. Slesser (Schloesser) was the legal authority for Fabians on Trade Unions Law. Cf. *FN,* XXIX (February, 1918). Also, cf. his

Green, R. C. K. Ensor, R. H. Tawney and Gilbert Slater;[18] statisticians and economists by Mrs. Frances Wood and C. H.

Judgment Reserved. Lloyd served a long time. Cf. Cole, "Lloyd, Charles Mostyn," *FN,* 57:5 (May, 1946). The notice of Lloyd's death is here given in full because it is highly characteristic of Fabian appraisal of colleagues. G. D. H. Cole signed it under date of May, 1946. "Charles Mostyn Lloyd's death in February, 1946, has taken away a Fabian who was rightly loved. He was one of the most genuine Socialists and one of the best friends I have known. Joining the Fabian Society at Oxford in 1900, he remained faithful to it for the rest of his life, serving on the Executive for a number of years, and always enthusiastically ready to do for it what needed doing rather than what he would have preferred to do. That was Mostyn Lloyd's way; he served the Socialist movement, and never asserted his own claims. [Religiousness is a notable characteristic.] After Oxford he went to live first at Toynbee Hall and then in Bethnal Green, and was called to the *Bar.* The *Webbs* soon claimed him and his first big job was on the staff of the National Committee for the Prevention of Destitution, formed by the Webbs to push the Poor Law Minority Report of 1909. Before that he had married Theo Reeves, who shared his work. [A typical case of intra-sect marriage. The Pember-Reeves were Fabians.] They went on living in Bethnal Green, where they played an active part in the ILP. Mostyn Lloyd refused to label himself as "Progressive." He fought—and lost—as "Labour" [this evinced ILP mentality; the Progressives were a Webb faction which vanished] because he felt his duty was to the Socialist movement. In 1914 war claimed him, of his own accord; he was wounded on the Somme, and was thereafter employed in training officers. After the war he took up double duty [in the London School of Economics and as assistant editor of the *NS*]. He wrote . . . on *Trade Unionism;* the rest of his writings, including some excellent tracts on *Local Government* for the Fabian Society, are scattered largely in the *NS* . . . he effaced himself, doing jobs for the cause, and not bothering about fame or money . . . an idealist cynic, with a great sense of humor; a friend who understood *friendship;* and admirable teacher. . . ." [Repetitiousness is characteristic of Cole.] The italics inserted indicate the characteristics and the habitat, as it were, of many a Fabian. The London School of Economics is not a Fabian Society appurtenance. It was founded by Sidney Webb with moneys from a bequest. Its first president was not a Socialist. It represents the conviction of Fabians that academic freedom in pursuit of truth will bring science to its proper ends. A letter from A. E. Davies, LCC, to the writer confirms this view and also the view that the *NS* may be considered a genuine Fabian organ. *NS* is an organ of Fabianism if not a Fabian organ; LSE turned out many social democrats, if not Fabians.

[18] Cf. R. H. Tawney, *The British Labour Movement* (New Haven: The Institute of Political Publications of Williams College of Williamstown, Massachusetts, 1925).

Clapham; the literary fraternity by Aylmer Maude and Patrick
Braybrooke; the military, by Brigadier General C. B. Thomson,
Major Graham Pole, Captain Basil Hall; engineering, by H. H.
Pearsall; architecture and city planning, by Raymond Unwin;
publishing, by George Standring; [19] novelists and publicists, by
Rebecca West on the staff of the *New Republic* (U.S.) [20] and
Clifford Sharp of the *New Statesman;* theatre, by Herbert Trench
and St. John Ervine; academicians, by Professor Edith Morley;
economists, by Hugh Dalton and W. A. Robson; social scientists,
by Michael Oakeshott and Ernest Barker; [21] ecclesiastical art by
Reverend Percy Dearmer; poetry by Mrs. Jessie Duncan West-
brook, Maurice Hewlett and Edward Carpenter (Rupert Brooke
had been killed in the war) ; philosophy, by C. E. M. Joad; peers,
by Viscount Haldane,[22] Lord Parmoor, and Lord Henry Bentick;

[19] Victor Gollancz was shortly to become their publisher as well as a
member.

[20] Contributor to the *NS* and *The Clarion*, Miss West wrote even then for
the *New Republic,* and in 1931, was "visiting critic" to the *New York
Herald Tribune.* Cf. *Who's Who, 1931.* This is a far from unusual case
in point of "penetration" of the United States.

[21] Cf. Michael Oakeshott, *The Social and Political Doctrines of Contemporary Europe* (Cambridge: The University Press; New York: The Macmillan Company, 1942). This was first published in 1938. The American
edition bears prefaces by Frederic A. Ogg and Ernest Barker.

[22] Richard Burdon Haldane, *An Autobiography* (London: Hodder and
Staughton, 1929), p. 93. He was very intimate with the Webbs, but differed
with Fabianism on Imperial Federation. His philosophy, a synthesis of
Fichte, Hegel and Kant, with Goethe—in " Relativity "—made Haldane sym-
pathetic with the best in German culture. It precluded exaggerated nationalis-
tic positivism. Cf. R. Metz, " Richard Burdon Haldane," *Die Philosophischen
Stromungen der Geganwer in Grosbrittannen,* pp. 294-295. " Die neue Zutage
gefördete Wissenshaft ist nichts anderes als eine neue Erfüllung der
Hegelschen Lehre" (p. 248). At this time Harold Laski was sifting
Marxianism into the Fabian leaven. Pease reviewed in *FN,* XXXIII:10
(October, 1922), Laski's *Karl Marx: A Study,* which had been printed by
the Fabian Society . He pointed out that the theory of value was all anybody
in England paid any attention to in 1892, but that since the war " Mr. Laski
sees in Marx the Prophet of Revolution." Mr. Pease, surely with tongue in
cheek, wrote, " This is the aspect of Marxianism [Laski's remark and assumption that a generation which had seen the doctrine supported by machine guns is not likely to belittle the revolutionary's as a method of the
proletariat's gaining power], which interests readers nowadays and for this
reason, if for no other, Mr. Laski's essay should be a best seller."

organizers, by Tom Mann, J. H. Thomas of the Railways and Ben Cooper of the Cigar Makers Association;[23] university men, by Sidney Ball, up to his death in June, 1918, don of St. John's and founder of the Social Club which sponsored Fabian Lecturers.[24] Stephen Sanders was Fabian Secretary, destined to great service in the ILO as deputy Chief of Administrative Service. Women's names, destined to loom large, were already prominent: Margaret Bondfield, devoted to Trade Unionism; Susan Lawrence and Ellen Wilkinson, Labour Party politicians; the dynamic organizer, Miss Mary MacArthur (her husband, C. W. Anderson, died before 1920). Besides the members there were the friends, those who were joined in their friendship for the Webbs, like Herbert Samuel, Sidney Buxton, Kate Courtney and Lord Parmoor (Cripps); or by connection with the ILP, like Philip Snowden, formerly of the Temperance movement, who detested Trade Unionism. (Mrs. Snowden was a very prominent Fabian. They had been introduced at a Fabian Society meeting.)[25] Again, the

---

[23] *FN*, XXXI:2 (February, 1920). "Obituary."

[24] Cf. Herbert Louis Samuel (Viscount Samuel, P.C., G.D.B., G.B.E., Hon. D.C.L. [Oxford], Hon. Fellow of Balliol), *Grooves of Change, op. cit.,* p. 27. "Return to Politicis: 1926–1931," p. 233, and on through "Resignation: 1932," ending on p. 271, are pertinent pages. Samuel who did not join the Society wrote of those he met in the Grosvenor Road House of the Webbs: Haldane, H. G. Wells, Creighton, Bishop of London, William Pember Reeves from the New Zealand Government, Shaw, Wallas, and later Charles Trevelyan, brother of the poet and historian. He describes his last visit to them, when, aged 85 and 83, Beatrice and Sidney rejoiced in his sympathy with them regarding "the new civilisation"; and he recalls the conversation about Trevelyan's angry reaction to Well's *The New Machiavelli,* which they had found amusing at the time of its publication. Beatrice's last letter to Samuel spoke of Trevelyan's adherence to the Soviet ideal and his "austere life." A certain H. W. Samuels is named as serving as chairman for lectures under Fabian auspices often in *FN;* e.g., the March, 1918, issue (*FN*, XXIX:4) mentions his presiding at a meeting of the Women's Fabian Group. He was an M.P., 1923–24 and 1929–31.

Cf. Ronald Knox, *A Spiritual Aenead* (Westminster: Newman Book Company, 1948) tells of his belonging to the Oxford Fabian Society in undergraduate days. But Knox had become a Catholic by 1919.

[25] ILP was showing signs of developing two mentalities; the scientific and the sentimental, exemplified by Pethick-Lawrence and Jenny Lee, for examples.

Society had its globe trotting lecturers, more like missionaries, such as Samuel K. Ratcliffe, the London representative of the *New Republic* (U.S.) reporting about observations made not only in America but in India. And there were reporters back from Russia like George Lansbury and Julius West.[26] In general, its membership was not drawn from the laboring classes, save for the rising organizers who had to show membership in a socialist society in order to take their places in the Labour and Socialist International. The large and luminous names were those of men and women in the height of careers: Besides the Webbs, Shaw and Lord Olivier, there were Arthur Henderson, Lord Ponsonby,[27] Arthur Greenwood,[28] Harold Laski, Edwin R. Pease and Bertrand Russell,[29] and Beatrice Webb's nephews, Malcolm and H. T. Muggeridge and Stafford Cripps.[30] Margaret and Raymond Postgate (disowned by their father) and G. D. H. Cole were then serving in the Fabian Research Bureau, which, in 1920, was undergoing infiltration by Communists. H. G. Wells was at loggerheads with the Old Gang—not with the Society itself.[31] Graham Wallas was gone but not in any sense forgotten.

Starting in 1919, a new impulse was given to the intellectual efforts exerted by Fabians. Several historical books appeared or were re-issued or re-emphasized: Sidney and Beatrice Webb's

---

[26] Né Rappaport. Cf. *FN*, XXX:1 (January, 1919), "The Death of Julius West."

[27] His last contest as a Liberal was in 1918. M.P. in 1920–1922 as Labour member, Ponsonby was the only notable musician (except Sir Thomas Beecham) among Fabians; a member of the Council of the Royal Society of Music. The Fabian utopia held a vision of free concerts.

[28] Greenwood gave six lectures on local government. Cf. *FN*, XXI:2 (1920).

[29] Cf. "Subject Groups: Fabian Nursery," *FN*, XXIX:5 (April, 1918). A resolution was passed and "forwarded to the Trades Councils, Universities, and individuals" expressing approval of the work done by Bertrand Russell "in the cause of truth and freedom."

[30] Stephen H. Hobhouse was not attached to Fabianism. Cf. his *Margaret Hobhouse and Her Family* (Rochester: The Stanhope Press, 1934).

[31] H. G. Wells, *After Democracy* (London: Watts and Company, 1932), p. 11. Wells, addressing the Liberal Summer School in 1932, acknowledged his too early insistence on international mindedness and on an elite or "Samurai" as of c. 1910 when he had broken with the Fabians. The Samurai idea was little different from "the experts" or "the elite" in Fabian schemes.

History of Trade Unionism, brought down to date with the railway strike included, and the place of Trade Unions in the state "emphasized," [32] had a new edition, as did their *Industrial Democracy.* The history was sold to members at a reduction. Union members and WEA [33] members were given special rates. A cheap edition of Fabian H. Duncan Hall's *The British Commonwealth of Nations* was arranged for members, and the same arrangement, also with Methuen and Company, was made for Max Beer's *History of British Socialism;* [34] likewise a special edition of *The Village Labourer, 1760–1832* by Fabians J. L. and B. Hammond. Evangelical support for Fabian ethics came from such publications as that of the Reverend Gilbert C. Binyon, *The Christian Faith and The Social Revolution.* The author was a Fabian and the publication was made through the SPCK.[35] Special emphasis was given to the cheap edition of J. M. Keynes, *Economic Consequences of the Peace,* orders limited to Trade Unions, Socialist and Labour bodies, and Cooperative Organizations. The volume is almost symbolical of the intermingling of liberal economics with Socialist economic thought at the level of the *Economic Journal,* the organ of the Royal Society of Economists whose lists, as we shall see further on, included many Fabians. Remembering the fate of "made" constitutions and the historicism of the Webbs, it is surprising to learn that there was published by Longmans, Green and Company, *A Constitution for the Socialist Commonwealth of Great Britain,* by Mrs. Sidney Webb. Sidney Webb's *Toward Social Democracy,* described as a

---

[32] Webb, *History of Trade Unionism,* pp. 643–649.

[33] Workingmen's Education Association was not precisely "doctrinaire" as was its predecessor, the Worker's Educational Society of London. It was heavily infiltrated with Fabian teachers. Its "Programme" was listed in Webb's bibliography for his Tutorial Class. Cf. Lorwin, *Labor and Internationalism* (New York: Macmillan and Company, 1929), p. 23.

[34] E. R. Pease, in his review of this book, found fault with the inadequate treatment of the part played by G. B. Shaw in promoting Socialism. "A thousand people have heard Shaw's characters talk Socialism on the stage for every one who has read a Socialistic book or attended a Socialistic meeting." *FN,* XXI:11 (November, 1920).

[35] *FN,* XXXI:12 (December, 1920). (SPCK, the Society for the Promotion of Christian Knowledge. Much is indicated by the names of the publishers which cannot be evaluated here.)

study of social evolution during the past three-quarters of the century, was reprinted from the *Cambridge Modern History*.[36] There was evidence of " gradual transformation, both of opinion and of institutions from an essentially Individualistic to an essentially Collectivistic basis . . . ," as Webb said, lecturing October 17, 1919, at Essex Hall upon "Fabian Essays in Socialism: Thirty Years After." He then announced the reprinting of *Fabian Essays* with emendations to supply their two omissions: " failure to think internationally," and failure to grasp the idea of local bodies as associations of consumers. (The latter idea projected the contrast between Municipal Socialism and State Socialism, and only apparently lent sympathy to the cooperative idea. However, the discussion furthered the movement toward socialism because to categorize little towns as " local bodies, associations of consumers " is to subtract some political element from the idea or concept of " town," and to give the idea an exponent of Socialism or Sovietism.) The essayists thus corrected again their previously acknowledged " errors " regarding Trade Unionism and Cooperatives. " Equality " and " justice " as of old conveyed no " metaphysical nonsense "—equality of opportunity was meant and " the sense of justice of the community," [37] *i.e.*, " fair shares " and " industrial democracy." The attack on the future was launched with great books. It is too soon to point out how erudition was used to justify bold generalizations unwarranted by the data.

---

[36] This had first appeared as a Fabian Tract in 1902. In 1901, Leo XIII's *Graves de Communi* had rejected the terminology " social democracy " on the grounds of its monistic implications, while describing it exactly as Fabians do. " It aims at putting all government in the hands of the people, reducing all ranks to the same level, abolishing all distinction of class, and finally introducing community of goods . . . the right of ownership is to be abrogated. . . . There is nothing in common between Social and Christian Democracy." Cf. *Christian Democracy* (New York: Paulist Press) 1941, p. 6.

[37] Cf. J. H. Thomas, *My Story* (London: Hutchinson and Company, 1937), p. 16. " It was not equality I wanted but equality of opportunity." This was Trade Union mentality. Also, cf. Sidney Webb, *Fabian Tract No. 188*. " It is vital to our character that nothing should be done that would outrage, not justice, as to which there is no abstract definition of validity, but the sense of justice of the community," p. 9. This evinced the pragmatism of a British Socialist.

The *New Basis* of the Fabian Society was confirmed on December 12, 1919, having been moved May 23.[38]   A brief comparison with the old *Basis* is revealing: Both *Bases* stated, " The Fabian Society consists of Socialists," a statement which meant something more positive in 1919 than in 1887; then Fabians had not been partial to the special notes of Socialism except for a nod to the Marxian theory of value for they had been Ricardians primarily, and later they had followed Jevons; and as for economic determinism in history, it was as little regarded as the notion of " comrade." In 1919 they embraced both economic determinism and the appellation of comrade, especially in speaking of Continental Socialists. Both *Bases* declared the aim of the Society to be an equitable sharing by the " whole people " (not indeed " all the people ") of the nation's advantages, natural and acquired, by *means* of " emancipation " of Land and Industrial Capital and the vesting of such in the community. The old *Basis* had said " individual and class ownership " was destined to be destroyed; the new omitted " and class." The old had been an adaptation of pure or doctrinaire Socialism; the new was a summary of political socialistic beliefs, because the middle class, now in 1919, held more individually owned property than in 1887.   The *New Basis* toned down the tenet that the Socialist State should dissolve *all* ownership.   Shaw's fine hand had been detectible in the unscientific but literary old form which defined rent as " the price paid for permission to use the earth, as well as for the advantage of superior soils and sites." The new form, more Webbian, would meet " extinction of private property in land with equitable consideration of established expectations and due provision as to the tenure of the home and the homestead "; that is, the *Basis* of 1919 allowed compensation for expropriated property and permitted ownership of a house and lot (not to mention royalties for writings).   As in the old *Basis,* nationalization of " only such industries as can be conducted socially " should be accomplished—" constitutionally."   Again, in

---

[38] *FN,* XXXI:1 (January, 1920).   Both *Bases* are given in Pease, *History of Fabian Society.*   Italics in quotations inserted.   The names, for what it would be worth in the organization, of those who opposed the motion to confirm were printed.   Webb, Shaw, and William Stephen Sanders supported confirmation.   Later, the Labour Party developed a principle of expulsion of dissenters.   It was possible to expel from the Society a Fabian, once elected, also.

the new *Basis,* in place of the harangue about the worker's obtaining " leave to earn " from the " proprietary class," the contemporary fusion of hand and brain workers was recognized in the dignified statement that the " governing consideration " in regulation was the " common good," instead of private profit, which was to be subordinated to it. It read that " in the regulation of production, distribution and service," private profit was not to be the " governing principle." (It cannot be asserted that private profit was outlawed, although when Fabians wrote for the International they advocated nationalizing all property and all professions.) This distinguished Fabians from the " pure " or " sentimental " Socialists. In the old *Basis,* no compensation, only relief, was to be given for expropriated properties; the new *Basis* undertook compensation. If two characteristics of the old *Basis,* namely the idea of adding Rent and Interest to the reward of Labour, and the disapproval of " the idle class now living on the labour of others," were not expressed in the new, these elements were not lost to view. This will appear later on when the economic basis of 1919, the Capital Levy, is discussed, and Webb's *National Finance and a Levy on Capital: What Labour Intends,* and his *How to Pay for the War,* are examined. The new *Basis* incorporated the information previously given in advertising descriptions of the Society that it was a constituent body of the Labour Party and it added " and of the International Socialist Congress "; also " it takes part freely in all constitutional . . . movements which *can* be guided towards its own objects." [39] It seems necessary to quote entirely its " direct business ":

> (a) The propaganda of Socialism in its application to current problems; (b) investigation and discovery in social, industrial, political and economic relations; (c) the working out of Socialist principles in legislation and administrative reconstruction; (d) the publication of the results of its investigations and their practical lessons.

[39] Italics inserted. The egotism of Fabians shown in their candidly appraising all movements in the light of their own objectives, is something to be noted. Fabians gave attention to all liberal ideas (even though the Webbs were poor listeners) and had no doubts about their own capacity to evaluate them. Margaret Hobhouse wrote in 1901 : " The Sidney Webbs are here, very clever, very conceited. . . ." Cf. Stephen Hobhouse, *op. cit.,* p. 162.

Equal citizenship of men and women, added to the old *Basis* in 1907, was now amplified by the expression by the Society of its belief that citizenship should not be qualified by sex, race, or creed. The new *Basis* spoke of " discovery " in various " relations " where the old *Basis* had spoken of the aim to disseminate knowledge as to the relations of the individual and society under economic, ethical, political aspects.   That collective entities were to supply the fields for discovery of relations is indicated ; in the new *Basis*, the individual has disappeared because Individualism is no longer a problem.[40]   Indeed, mention of " ethical " social aims is not made in the new *Basis*.   And still a definition of Socialism is lacking.   It was good strategy for Fabians not to define Socialism if they hoped to have the cooperation of European and Russian socialists as well as domestic Trade Unionists.

In connection with the new *Basis*, the attitude toward Continental Socialists of the British gradualists is an aid to understanding the new understatements.   In the *Labour Year Book, 1919,* under " The Attitude of the Socialist and Labour Parties during the War," the Socialist Parties of every European country were tabulated.   The effects of an hypothetical unanimity were contemplated.   Socialism was demonstrably conceived as an universal " religion " and " faith." [41]   Socialists in England attempted to do what religion did not do, that is, bring into existence a thing of one-party and one-world.   In this frame of mind the inclusion of an article by the Belgian Socialist and Internationalist Camille Huysman in the British Labour Party's *Year Book* was an acceptable thing.[42]

The most important changes besides the new dignity in diction

[40] *Socialism and Individualism* by Sidney Webb, Bernard Shaw, Sidney Ball and Sir Oliver Lodge.   This was *Fabian Socialist Series No. 3,* reprinted in New York by John Lane Company, 1911.

[41] In Richard V. Burke, " A Conception of Ideology for Historians " in *The Journal of the History of Ideas,* X :2, April 1949, 183–198, note 38, the support of Benedette Croce and Pareto is cited for the idea that the " isms " are " religions."   Beatrice Webb deplored " creed-wars."   (She often tried to escape the conclusions of the Socialist propositions.)   She advocated " the religion of scientific humanism."   Where the governing forces of natural law holding together human institutions are, to all intents and purposes dissolved, socialism offers itself as a replacement.

[42] Cf. *Labour Year Book, 1919,* p. 43.

and the more scientific tone, are the notion of compensation for expropriation and the transfer into a Socialistic order (perhaps the state) of specific industries rather than expropriation of Industrial Capital outright. Shaw named this " State-Aided Capitalism." As long as the Fabian *Basis* would be in operation and Fabians in control of a Government there should be no full abolition of Capitalism; only those industries which can be socially controlled should be expropriated.[43] How the Fabian *Basis* and the utterances of Socialists belonging to the Labour Party were not always consonant is to be seen as this study progresses.

---

[43] " Social control " which can be ethical control is mistakenly equated with State Control. State Control in a republic, means Party Control. Nationalization of a very few basic industries under Party Control conduces to control of all business through taxation to support expropriated businesses. If the Party be Sociaist, the stage is set for Socialism —— a creed.

CHAPTER II

FABIANS AND THE RISE OF THE LABOUR PARTY

A. Ideological Education

In the ensuing chapter is indicated Fabian penetration into the ideological area supporting a Labour Party to set a creed; into the area of resurgent union organizing to propagandize for the Party; into the hinterlands to exercise the Party in political action. By a fluke almost symbolical, the marks of Fabian penetration into the lowly cooperatives revealed Fabian permeation high into the realms of so-called " liberal " economics.

Fabians were at once active and speculative. Arthur Henderson, J. P. Middleton, Barbara Wootton and A. Lockhurst Scott might be out in the hustings marshalling the voters into Labour ranks but the indoctrination of the leadership went on fervidly in London town, under the apparently inexhaustible Webb. The first step in the reconstituting of the Party was the laying down of a set of quasi-philosophical principles. The Society issued a prospectus for a " Tutorial Class on the Policy and Principles of the Labour Party." [1] To be conducted by Sidney Webb at either Tothill Street or the Central Hall, the class would cover a six-part syllabus and read eight books: Henderson's *Aims of Labour,* Webb's *Toward Social Democracy,* the *Labour Year Book,* A. W. Humphrey's *History of Labour Representation,* Mrs. Webb's *Case for the National Minimum,* the FRD's *How to Pay for the War* (edited by Sidney Webb), and Sidney and Beatrice Webb's *The Prevention of Destitution,* Woolf's *International Government,* and the *Education Programme of the Workers' Education Association.* The class was arranged by the Fabian Society, and—indicative that this was not precisely a laborers' set-up—10s 6d was charged for tuition. In the light of the fact that this course was to furnish an exposition of the " policy and principles "

---

[1] This broadsheet was found appended to the volume of the *FN* which covers 1916–1920 in the Library of Congress collection.

of the Party, said to be a political party, it is surprising to read under Section IV of the syllabus, " Music, Literature, Drama, and Art. Religion." There was nothing to warrant inclusion of the arts and religion to be found in Section I which purported to show how the principles of the Party were adduced from its history: Labour Representation in Parliament,[2] the ILP, the LRC, the effects of the Taff Vale and the Osborne judgments. Although the elections of 1906 and 1910 are listed, it is not shown that even though "the constitution of the Labour Party and its successive transformations " followed these elections it was by sequence and not as generic growth. Indeed, these elections had demonstrated that a democratic drive toward the attainment of the commonweal could have thriven within the old framework of parties. The body of persons and organizations bent on reform might never without an extraneous impulsion have been transformed into the One-Party.[3] The spark which precipitated the peculiar party was Socialism which now ordained that the " essential principles of Labour Party Policy " should run along the line of economics and sociology to invade by consequence the area of religion. All this is visible in this syllabus for a tutorial class in " Labour Party " policy and principles.

Under " The Policy of the National Minimum " and " The Control of the Environment " are to be observed two of Mr. Webb's "abysses ": " The abyss involved in unmitigated individualism " and " the abyss involved in unfettered competition and the wage system "—they form but one abyss in reality, human fallibility, an area which was to be filled up by Socialism; and this not only in Webb's teaching but in Laski's, Robson's and

---

[2] It is interesting to note that the third party took its rise in this special or unique representation, not, however, by evolving but by being induced to evolve something new—not by working within the traditional framework of politics, but by lending itself to the creation of a new social element.

[3] This term, One-Party, is one we will have occasion to use through the study, to stand for the instrument which the Movement created to express its will and which embodied the meaning, totalitarian. It aimed to embrace in a political apparatus all who labor by hand or by brain. It might better be named the " All-Party." Young Fabians writing in *The Clarion* at the end of the 1920's will be found to declare that in the future society must be divided between those who are Labour and those who are "damnably otherwise."

the Fraser symposists', all of which will appear in a further treatment.

So many are the reforms listed as objectives under Sections II and IV, where the abysses are found, that the element of Socialism in which they occur is easily disregarded: Factory legislation, sanitation, education, housing, infant care, scientific research— few would boggle at these propositions indeed; corrected individualism and moderated competition which produced these ends would be universally welcomed. Yet the theme which ran through Webb's every utterance, as expressed in his presidential address to the Party Conference of 1923 and as propounded to the Managers [4] (discussed at length elsewhere) was: Only Socialism can do it. Webb exposed the basic assumption of professing Socialists, *i.e.,* individualism and competition as elements of Capitalism could not possibly be made to include responsibility for the good of society even by removing blemishes and invoking morality. "Profit," for Fabians, was separated from community gain; they rejected the concept that private savings increase community national assets. The responsibility for the common good was something to be taken over by Socialism which, unlike a proper religion, absorbed the State. The Socialist State is the State of the One-Party rule.

Against the inference that liberty to act individualistically in the matter of the wage system was to disappear, Trade Unionists might have been expected to struggle. But the Tutorial Class was not exactly a school for Trade Union men. The union organizations had been injected with Socialism since 1894 through ILP in which, in 1919, two-thirds of the members were Fabians, according to Edward Pease. Thus the unions had been prepared to be brought under the One-Party aegis. The story of their struggle to assert themselves independently is the theme for another study.[5] The rank and file of Trade Unionists would

---

[4] Cf. Sidney Webb, *The Root of Labour Unrest* (London: Fabian Society, 1920).

[5] That they have struggled is apparent from Cole's works in *Fabian Socialism* of 1943, p. 163, where he outlines his "New Unionism": "I want the Socialist body [elsewhere he notes that the Fabian Society is the only extant Socialist body] to carry [it] into the Trade Union Movement." Cole has splendid ideas about attaining freedom through the Shop Council from the

have no quarrel with the proposition that unmitigated individualism (Webb's phrase) should be mitigated and unfettered competition be at least controlled; and mere Trade Unionism, once it exchanged self-activity (the term " Direct Action " has taken on the meaning of violence) for political representation, asked that the law should remove inequities arising from human imperfection. But according to the principles of the Tutorial Class private ownership, competition and the wage system were to be extinguished, and in the Webb system these economic relationships were to be absorbed by Socialism (through Parliament, of course) replacing avowedly with simple ethics the theological impulsion (i.e., Charity) in individuals and association. (We shall see in another connection that the young Fraser Group under Harold Laski's guidance held that Socialism should do for civilization what the Church had done for Europe after the barbarian invasions. These students had come to think of Charity as a dole not as a Theological Virtue and an energizing force in organization.) Socialism, according to the tutor, was to be the new civilization. What Sidney Webb taught of religion in the 1920's was set forth by Fabian Mrs. Mary Agnes Hamilton, in her *Sidney and Beatrice Webb.* He stood averse to any profession of secularism, as such. By freedom of religion, however, his students must needs come to comprehend religion as " liberated " by being ejected

---

large stratifications which Webbism fostered. Cf. Cole, *Fabian Socialism,* pp. 152–163. His insistence on Socialism to carry the " New Unionism " into the Trade Union Movement has the effect of assuring the One-Party ideal among the liberated workers. The difference between the Coles and the Webbs is still what it was; 1943 and 1950, as in 1920. Cole returned and cooperated with Fabianism to assure the " carrying in " of Socialism, when, as he properly conceives without so stating it, the monolithic state disappears. Cole's ideas are sublimely consonant with the doctrine of " free association " and might be thought anti-Marxist because he adheres to the idea of collaboration of workers and management at the works-council and shop-council level. But management is State and Party management in his fore-vision. Previously he had written in *The Clarion* that there must be no alliance between worker organizations and owners, as will be shown elsewhere. And his whole system is precipitated in fluid Socialism as animating spirit and ideal. He declares that the whole ideal is " ethical " (*ibid.,* p. 164), (but, most certainly non-theological), and he uses metaphors drawn from New Testament history which show that he identifies himself and Socialism with the Christian religion which he otherwise treats as a myth (*ibid.,* p. 29).

from the field of economics and social planning. Socio-economics having subverted the political art to economic and social ends would invest the State which, in those realms which constitute the domain of " Caesar," lies outside the surveillance of the Church, and would make religion " free." Furthermore, Webb thought of religion as an emotion.[6] The " abyss " of the wage system was to be filled in by the " spirit " (Webb's term) which guided the unions and the Party. It would be strange or unusual to take note of such matters in an ordinary history of a political party, but it is necessary to do so in the case of the Fabian-led Labour Party because on the agenda of Webb's tutorial classes in Labour Party principles stood " Religion." Those elements which were integregated in Webb's Tutorial Class to educate Labour politicians cannot be separated in an honest evaluation.

Section III of the syllabus destroyed the last pretence to there being a mere political party in the thing Webb was creating. Never a stick was wielded, a stone thrown, a barricade raised, nor even a shout in the streets; yet here was "the revolt of the masses." The syllabus read: " Why Democracy cannot stop at political organization, but must include control of industry and commerce." Since by Democracy Webb did not mean State, or purely political government, but the politicizing of social orderings,[7] *i. e.,* unions, cooperatives, social agencies in local government and the like, within the Party, here was the subversion of order. This ideological revolt of the masses consisted in the submerging of civil order in social order, the subversion of political science to the sole role of service to socio-economic ends; in a

---

[6] In present day currency, the collapse of that earthly trinity, republicanism, capitalism and religion (which last, because in a real republic God is the source of authority, can collaborate with government) is represented by the new semantics—" dynamic democracy," meaning politicized social elements; and " decadent governments," meaning Republics which recoil from Statism.

[7] In the discussion of Pigou's criticism of the Webbs' *Consumer Cooperative Movement,* which showed an engineer's model of the communistic order as outlined in the Webb's thought, we have shown in another place what the syllabus meant here by " The sharing of Democratic Control between the Vocational Organizations and the Government [which represents] both the present generation of Consumers and the permanent interests of the State." *Infra* p. 102.

word, The Revolution. The thing called *res publica* is now defined as " Control of material, processes, product, profit, and price "; and " *res privata* " rises to the surface of national configuration. The base of the triangle representing societary order is now broadly extended across the top; and what was hitherto the top-most peak, the angle marked State, is pointing, but momentarily before subsiding in annihilation, perilously at the bottom.[8] The monolithic State is an annihilated State wherein the political is consumed in the economic and social. The trinity of arts, political, economic and societary, having lost differentiation have become unitarian " Democracy " wherein the Party calling itself the People and investing the area of the State invades the private juridical order.

There was one bright young man who grasped Webb's ulti-mates. At the time, in the 1920's, G. D. H. Cole did not see beyond the monolith of Statism as he was later to see. For this reason, as a Guild Socialist, he remained aloof from the Society (even while the Webbs, esteeming his talents, endured his daring to differ and his impertinence); but he worked, up to 1924, for the Fabian Research Department [9] which had been founded by Beatrice Webb, and he returned to the Society in 1929, meantime devoting himself to the education of young radicals in Oxford, most of whom, like Gaitskell and Horrabin, joined the Society

---

[8] Cf. Cole, *Fabian Socialism*, pp. 120 ff. " Democracy means that the people have power, and not merely the formal right to say who shall have it." (He applied the Shop Council plan to the civil order and he confused power and authority. In a Democracy people designate who shall bear authority. He confused social and political democracy.) Cole's power to synthesize immobilizes his thought often, e.g., " Nazi and Communist totalitarianism . . . are not in the least the same in any essential particular. But they both rest in the knowledge that voting does not make a democracy [not an essential particular?] and that he who places his reliance on universal suffrage is building upon quicksand." Aside from the characteristic con-tradiction, Cole says Soviet Russia is a democracy because the " whole community owns the vital instruments of production . . . is trying to be a classless society . . . giving everybody an equal chance. . . ."

[9] In 1920 this Department had become the Labour Research Department but was not yet Communist. It had moved about 1919 to Labour Party Headquarters. Cole quarrelled with the Communists over their obnoxious methods.

with him in the 1930's. He had married, by then, Margaret Postgate, a colleague in the Department. The Coles developed their
" New Unionism " and " Shop Councils " under a principle of
collaboration of management (not capital) and labor, while they
differed from the Webbs who urged stratification and non-alliance.
But the difference was only apparent. The latter pair prepared
the monolithic State which was really a State in which political life
had disappeared (unless " the permanent interests of the State "
should restore the non-Socialist *status quo*—a contradiction they
were perfectly capable of containing in their preachment) and
they had no plan beyond the One-Party or Order, to rule over the
outcropped socio-economic mounds (Councils, Soviets or Zemst-
vos) in the societary terrain upon which the shadow of the monolith lay. These Cole was preparing to invest with his " New
Unionism." The Coles and the Webbs held a common faith in
Socialism and the One-Party.[10] Cole foresaw in the 1920's the
disappearance of the political State, and he was to prepare to warn
against its perpetuation as the "Servile State." Beyond Statism
where Webb merely stopped short, and beyond " joint consultation," *i.e.*, the meeting of representatives of vocational groups with
government agencies, Cole saw that " Industrial Democracy means
much more than ' joint consultation ' . . . [it means] to seek out
deliberately functions of workshop control that can be transferred
to the workers themselves." [11] And another young Fabian destined

---

[10] For the Webbs the monolithic State would harden and perdure; for the
Coles it would form a chimera and disappear; for Marx it would " wither ";
for Stalin it was a temporary tower of steel. Cf. Margaret Cole, *Growing
Up Into Revolution*, pp. 94–102. She declared here that she had no objection
to Communism as such, only to taking orders from Moscow.

[11] Cole, *Labour's Second Term*, p. 10. Cole in 1949 wants to see this
council system principle at work in the armed services; and he considers it
to be working in the field of agriculture, where he equates farmers, for
whom the Government has been " solicitous " to give a " sense of managing
their own affairs " [sic], with the factory workers. Certainly Cole should
be credited with the intelligence to know that farmers differ in the matter
of proprietorship from wage earners; yet he is asking that the Government
which has nationalized industries induce in workers a sentiment which will
have the same value as proprietorship. Where papal doctrine encourages
wage earners to aspire to proprietorship of land, Cole treats the farmer as
a (future) mere wage earner. Cf. Leo XIII, *Rerum Novarum, passim.*

to greatness also descried the societary terrain beyond the monolith:[12]   Twelve years after his *Labour in Perspective* appeared, Clement Attlee was to re-state: " Socialism is not just State Capitalism.   The taking over of an industry is not an end in itself—it is a means of attaining freedom."   " Freedom " meant the breakup into Councils, and other subsidiary groups.   His book expounding the Socialism of a Fabian is a complete restatement again in 1949, as twelve years before, of the points Webb exposed in the tutorial syllabus of 1920.   It preaches total nationalization of land, industry and labor,[13] and of course the abolition of Capitalism.   Attlee believes Capitalism might be abolished without State ownership of *all* industry.   He suggests worker ownership and worker control—under the Party.   What was the definition of the " Freedom " Attlee envisioned is not discoverable except by going back to Cole:

The first principle of soundness in an economic system

[12] Clement Attlee, *Labour in Perspective and Twelve Years Later* (Lon don: Victor Gollancz, 1949), pp. 99 and 193 f.

[13] *Ibid.*   Attlee argues that the " terror " of " socialistic " practices such as that of taking over the Post Office—something which seems nothing but right to Americans—is passing away; he does not obscure the truth that the Socialist Government means to nationalize all and not selected industries. Attlee and Cole do not advocate that the State should repress evil doers in commerce and industry by law, should see to it that public conveyors and purveyors, licensed and regulated, maintain service and goods in full supply at fair prices, and should develop for the people such enterprise or construction (like TVA) as are needed by or are too onerous for private capital. All that Webb, his students, and his colleagues say is said in such language as to signal to Continental Socialism—especially that which they would develop into " Social Democracy "—assent and comradeship; and this more especially with that Socialism toward which it is believed Russian Communism is a transition.   Cf. the *Memoirs* of George Lansbury, pp. 223–264, but especially pp. 244 and 261; also of Ben Turner, pp. 211–231.   Cf. also Cole, *Fabian Socialism,* pp. 45 and 116 f., and the whole of the brochure by the Webbs, *Is Russian Sovietism a New Civilization?*, which they answer affirmatively.   It is this writer's contention that the Webbs and Shaw learned nothing new in Russia but only found articulation for what was inherent in their thought.   Pius XI in *Divini Redemptoris* (1937) begins with a reference to the " new civilization."   He answers the Webbs directly, all but naming them, by describing the new barbarism.   He also refers to the conditions in Russia and Eastern Europe which he uniquely deprecated in 1924.   Cf. Pius XI, *op. cit.,* p. 4 f.

is that it should use all the available resources of man power to work upon the gifts of nature up to the point at which men prefer having more leisure to having more material wealth.[14]

Although this translates total mobilization, the note of genuine freedom rings in the advocacy of the Works Council and the Shop Council, " not as a meeting place for rival representatives of two ' sides ' but as a body representing every grade and group in the factory as partners in the common adventure of making it a success " ; [15] and Cole's New Unionism had the same quality.   But this " freedom " tone is muffled; it is not the true tone of liberty. In Cole's conception these Councils were presupposed to exist in a Socialist, One-Party world,[16] where private ownership of the means of production was abolished, specifically.   Such was the indoctrination on the speculative side which Webb in the Tutorial Classes and Attlee and Cole from the Oxford milieu, supplied to the young leaders of the Party.

The Webbs did everything, suffered much insolence, to keep young Cole in the ranks of Labour.   In this writer's opinion, he symbolizes their own tendency toward the acceptance they were to come to make of the " new civilization," U.S.S.R.

The policy and principles set forth in Section V of the Tutorial

---

[14] Cole, *Fabian Socialism,* p. 68.   His capital-less world leaves no adventure—save perhaps the sweepstakes; Cole's leisured universe is one wherein *homo economicus* must needs be perfected or be doomed to provide the materials for endless mystery stories—unless, forsooth, the printers should come to prefer their leisure to printing.

[15] *Ibid.,* p. 69.

[16] *Ibid.,* p. 141.   Cole carries his concept of free association over into local government, which should be made into " the small neighborhood group of dwellers in, say, a block of flats or a single street or group of small streets . . . a civic centre in miniature . . . [with] its civic restaurant, and . . . some one to whom the members can turn for advice in any of the troubles in life. . . ."   (Baby sitters and games for grown-ups as well as children should be available, too.)   This absurd ordering by blueprint of what develops, at least in America, from the natural association of people " in the block " assumes importance only when it is recalled that the inspiriting reason and permanent ideal was Socialism, Mr. Cole's " Socialist faith."   By inspecting and categorizing ordinary societary phenomena, social scientists like Cole affix to these a coefficient altogether artificial.   In such coefficients, and by manipulating them in series, they concatenate Socialism.

Class syllabus on " National Finance " were consonant with the liberal economics of the day and might have been found in the *Economic Journal,* the organ of the Royal Society of Economists, where Webb and Keynes, Pigou and W. A. Robson (Fabians) were associated; where the names of Haldane, Balfour and Alfred Marshall mingled with Bastable, Beveridge and Tawney (Fabians). Snowden's budgets were to be filled with the same details as Webb set down in his syllabus: "Application [of " developed faculty " and advanced knowledge] to the problems of the budget, re-graduation of Income Tax and Death Duties, the Conscription of Wealth"; but there was added thereto the characteristic note of British Socialism as Fabians developed it: "The Standard of Life " was " No cake until all have bread." This aphorism was as economically absurd as the silly words ascribed to the queen whose memory it evoked. That Webb meant to teach that society should exhibit no wealth until all had competence; that he would teach that nothing accrued to society from the advances made by the more successful unless all made the same advance immediately, could be inferred from the slogan. Of course, Webb meant nothing more than that his State would provide no luxuries until it had saturated the area of human material needs with middle-class standardized goods. On the other hand, the intention may have been simply to attract to his school for guidance the posturing young men who, in the 1920's, fancied themselves the guillotiners of a symbolic Marie Antoinette. Mr. Laski's students had a preoccupation with the French Revolution.[17] He also was tutoring the Labour Party.

The reader will experience some surprise to find that the next topic, Section VI, reads: " The Britannic Alliance and Internationalism." (However, it will be recalled that " Democracy " was to assume control of *commerce.*) Reproduced here, the content of the course needs no comment except that the uses of internationalism will come up again:

> The silent Transformation of the British Empire into a Britannic Alliance. Why there will be no " Imperial " Parliament. The Constitutional Machinery of the

---

[17] Cf. *FAR* (1933), p. 6. Laski's *Socialist Tradition in the French Revolution,* like his essay on Karl Marx, " continue[d] to sell well."

Britannic Alliance. The Abandonment of Cosmopolitanism in favor of Internationalism, and what this implies in Foreign Relations, Tariff Policy and the establishment of a Supernational Authority.[18]

That a step in the technique of creating a cooperative commonwealth of States bound together by "internationalism" was the setting up of Fabian Societies abroad and the encouraging of Labor parties in foreign countries was something not set forth in the syllabus.[19] The outline involved imperialism because Socialist headquarters must constitute imperial headquarters at least during the transformation or transition.[20] The answer to Professor Pigou's question as to where the capital for large enterprise involving great risk in cooperation would be found, lies in

---

[18] Fabian Harold Laski, to whom in the 1920's Arthur Henderson (in another example of the toleration of impudence for the sake of capturing young talent) apologized for misunderstanding him, and who was thus re-joined with the Party's new activity, prolific writer as he always was, produced in 1949 *Socialism as Internationalism* (London: Fabian Society and Gollancz, 1949). Pointing out the implication to Trade Unions and professional groups that their private national interests must be sacrificed, he shows that Socialism implies the separation of Nation from State. The first goes on on cultural lines; the latter goes out to meet other States and be merged in one world, ending all sovereignty. Laski's suggestions presuppose a condition of international anomy. Having repealed the natural law as a basis for international relations, Laski and his followers substitute an artificial basis.

[19] *FSAR* always carried a paragraph on the affiliated Fabian Societies in Japan, India, America (Laider's "Industrial Democracy"), and Germany. Cf. Cole, *Labour's Second Term,* Fabian Tract 273 (London: Fabian Society and Victor Gollancz, 1949), p. 16. "We must keep on trying to reach out across the iron curtain for means of re-establishing Socialist comradeship. . . ." Cf. also, Mark Starr, *Labour Politics in U.S.A.;* foreword by Margaret Cole (London: Fabian Publications and Victor Gollancz, 1949). The author is Educational Director of the International Ladies' Garment Workers Union, U.S.A., Chairman of Queens County Liberal Party. Starr feels that the organization called "Americans for Democratic Action" has fallen short of the hopes that it would "play the role of the Fabian Society" and "formulate long term goals and a philosophy for the new political alignment that is in formation" (p. 42). It is doubtful that Fabians have never deviated from their assigned role of mere formulators.

[20] In the "transition," America would provide the capital. The ensuing thoughts indicate the reasons for ADA's unsympathetic attitude toward Spain at present. Spain's unions cannot be world-amalgamated.

the process of "transformation" from "Cosmopolitanism" wherein differentiated nations subsisted together in mutual understanding, into "Internationalism." Where anomy resulting from the dissolving of national allegiance would also dissolve international relations—in the old and well-understood meaning of the term—Fabians would substitute Socialism as the cohesive force among nations. And it follows that those nations whose economic systems were consonant or could be made consonant with "internationalist" ideals would be cherished and favored and all others would be fought—if only by means of political boycott—until they should conform. Shaw pointed out the logical conclusion to Webb's propositions and was so consistent as to advocate that headquarters be not in London but in Geneva [21] in his 1929 tract for the Society, *The League of Nations* (Fabian Tract 226) wherein he advocated abolishing all the political apparatus of the League save Albert Thomas's ILO office which he equated with "Vatican."

Thus the "philosophy" of the intelligentsia, leaders of the rising Labour Party, was promulgated while the prosy business of penetrating committees went on at the county and borough levels. Trade Unionism presented a middle ground between the ideological camp and the field where the Party took its stand. That Fabian organizers were not agreed on unionizing methods may have been detrimental to the union movement. It is possible that the Webb-Cole argument, by offering alternatives, obscured the real goal of unionism and prevented trade union organization from developing its own character.[22] In any case in organizing or in

---

[21] Cole found that the destruction on the Continent during World War II affords "larger opportunities for the building of an international Socialist order." Cf. *Fabian Socialism* (1943), p. 52. His last sentence in *Fabian Socialism* salutes and singles out for cooperation abroad parties banded under "Social Democracy."

[22] Cf. Leo XIII, Pope, *Rerum Novarum* (Washington, D.C.: NCWC, 1942), pp. 32–35, where the ideal free associations of workingmen are described. They are differentiated by "temperament of each people"; they care for their own sick, needy or aged; they allow no wide difference in their offices such as to create discord; they settle disputes between themselves and employers (or groups of employers) before their own tribunals, "men of the same body" (employer-employee body); they disburse their funds

writing about it, Fabian work served to stimulate interest in organization and in politics and to bring industrial workers into the Party. A large contribution to organizing energy was made by Fabian women; and the Party gained the women's vote.

In 1920, the Webbs, taking tendencies, which they believed they had foreseen in 1894, for positive trends to be recorded as history, wrote:

> To the new school of Trade Unionists the nationalisation or municipalisation of industry, or its assumption by consumers' cooperation, is a necessary preliminary to the partnership of Labour in its government. What they are after is to alter, not only the status of the manual worker, but also the status of the employer who is the director of industry; they wish them both to become agents of the community; they desire that the manual workers and brain workers alike should be inspired, not by the greed of gain made by profit or price, but by the desire to produce the commodities and services needed by the community in return for a sufficient livelihood, and the personal freedom and personal responsibility which they believe should spring from vocational self-government.[23]

No doubt, "vocational self-government" is the bridge built from Guild-Socialism to State-Socialism. Just above this quoted passage the Webbs had described the Trade Unionist of 1920 as objecting to any sort of partnership with Capitalists or shareholders since this involved leaving Rent and Interest to proprietors. They feared that any such cooperation was destined "irretrievably [to] break up the solidarity of the manual working class." (Yet, as "agents of the community" they should have a status confused with employers.) That the Webb presentation of the unionist view was not history but hope is borne out by the story of the years that followed. They presented their scheme rather than current history. The position to be occupied by the

---

according to individual needs and provide religious benefits and educational opportunities.

[23] Sidney and Beatrice Webb, *History of Trade Unionism*, p. 673. The principle contained in this quotation means the defeat of the papal principle of subsidiarity. Government collaboration in the industry council does not imply Government absorption of either labor or ownership.

Labour Party " in the passionate support of public ownership "
toward carrying out the scheme was described in 1920:

> [As] . . . the result of successive attacks upon the
> very existence of Trade Unionism . . . there has been
> growing up a distinct political organisation of the Trade
> Union Movement, aiming at securing the acceptance by
> the electorate, as a whole, of a definitely Socialistic policy
> in the administration of both home and foreign affairs.
> [This is the] formation of a Labour Party, ready for the
> the carrying into effect of the new ideas. . . .[24]

It is abundantly clear that it was intended that the political force
within Trade Unionism was to be captured by the Party ostensibly
for the protection of the principle of unionism, actually to compass the movement and the membership for Fabian ends. The
Independent Labour Party, a mere Socialist society, would be
asked to confine itself to promulgating Socialism in working men's
ranks. The Labour Party, like Beatrice's Poor Law Commission,
could recruit its members from non-Socialists even, those who
would shy away from the ILP but who were nevertheless labor-
minded. Trade Unionism itself sought only to avail itself of the
political action of the Labour Party and yet preserve its own
identity. There can be no doubt that the above statement of the
historians of the movement was in this case propaganda.

B. Fabians in Trade Unionism: For the Party

The Webbs and their fellow Fabians had been beforehand in
capturing the Trade Unions for the Labour Party. Before the
war, Trade Unionists usually voted Liberal. Before the war's
end the area of industrial organization was appropriated by
Fabians to anchor thereon a part of Labour Party machinery. The
Webb method was to stratify workers-by-hand into big national
amalgams. They stressed a sort of non-intercourse between the
" professional groups," *i.e.,* the unionized workers and unionized
owners or employers. They rivalled the Communists in trying to
infiltrate Trade Councils, those local organizations where, in a
given municipality, local civil authority was represented among

---

[24] *Ibid.,* p. 676.

representatives of workers and owners in councils, with the aim to promote local production and to set local wage scales. Communists won these over for the most part.[25]   But national Trade Unions rapidly developed into large amalgamations and affiliated with the Labour Party under Fabian tutelage, which, as has been suggested, took advantage of war conditions to begin the work of building the Party.

Under " Research Department " in the *Fabian News,* February, 1918, Fabians read:

> The Parliamentary committee of the Trade Union Congress has decided to co-operate with the Committee of Enquiry into Trades Councils and local Labour Parties, and has appointed F. Bramley and G. H. Stuart-Bunning [Fabian] as its representatives on that Committee. It will be remembered that the Labour Party appointed A. Peters [in closest collaboration with Henderson] and Sidney Webb to act in a similar capacity. The Committee of which Egerton P. Wake [Fabian successor to Peters in the Henderson party machine] is the chairman, will issue the full questionnaire to Trades Councils and L.R.C.'s [Labour Representation Committees] immediately after the Labour Party Conference.[26]

Two commitees each show at least one Fabian member named if only in second place.   The Enquiry was a Fabian-Labour device to develop the Party.   This is an admirable example of " penetration " by interlocking committee membership.   The Fabians took over the leadership in each section.   Under " Organization of Trade Councils and Local Labour Parties," [27] Fabians learned that then G. H. Stuart-Bunning (Fabian, for TUC), later to figure

[25] Cf. Margaret Cole, *Growing Up Into Revolution,* p. 100.   These reminiscences show that Cole's anti-Webb period accounts for her not knowing much about political work going on at the time.   She did not realize how Mr. Cole's talent was being used when she reports " dull " industrial organizing meetings as the only events that occurred in the period.   Cf. her *Growing Up,* p. 92, where she notes that the Labour Conference of 1918 reorganized the Party and gave it "a real [Socialist] Policy."   The Conference was greeted by Russian Communists through Litvinov.

[26] *FN,* XXIX:3 (February, 1918).

[27] *FN,* XXIX:4 (March, 1918).

prominently on the international labor scene, had presided and that G. D. H. Cole (*Fabian News* never treated him as an ex-Fabian) had represented the Fabian Research Department (it had not yet gone Left and into the Labour Party domicile) when the *joint meeting* heard D. Carmichael of the London Trades Council and John Baker of the Iron and Steel Trade Conference. (This was doubtless a little group destined for amalgamation.) Here we see the Party joining the TUC to survey the possibilities of increasing assimilation of Trade Councils and local Labour Parties by both TUC and the Party, each represented by Fabians.

These instances show the methods of penetration. Another technique toward Party development was to encourage stratification. Back in 1917, at the sixth conference on Restoration of Trade Union Conditions held in Fabian Hall,[28] Mrs. Webb had taken occasion to allude to a current report that President Wilson had suggested repealing the Sherman Anti-Trust Law to allow, as Mr. Ernest Benn also proposed, Capitalists to meet in agreements aimed at increased productivity and to replace competition with collaboration (liable under the Sherman Act to be termed "collusion").[29] She contrived to give the American proposition a pejorative meaning by recalling old chartered companies and saying that state-aided monopolies were not new. She was distinctly not in favor of any cooperation of Trade-Union-with-employer-groups if this involved partnership with Capitalism on the basis of the present wage system; she feared the loss of working-class solidarity as the possible result of their succumbing to the "temptation" for employers and employees to unite, even on a question of tariff. Collaboration of workers' and employers' groups was thus rejected with little reserve, because it impeded the aim to increase the stratification of workers throughout the social fabric. This was expected to produce a bloc vote. Mrs. Webb said the

---

[28] *FN*, XXVIII:5 (April, 1917). England has no anti-trust laws and English businessmen make agreements on prices which it is customary to keep as gentlemen's agreements even if it means supporting a weak and unnecessary competitor. Cf. B. M. Anderson, *Economics and the Public Welfare* (Toronto: D. van Nostrand, 1949), p. 163.

[29] This reference may indicate the anticipation of the Webb-Pomerene Act of 1918, allowing combinations, specifically in exporting businesses, for price fixing and order allotment.

only advantage to workingmen in entering any association of employers and employees, besides mere recognition of their unions, might be to bring about compulsory Trade Unionism. She was emphatically suspicious of any permanent association of Capital and Labor. This may not seem consonant with the expressed Fabian policy of opposing class warfare which appears in Sidney Webb's thought; yet Beatrice was permeating the unions with Socialist " classlessness." Inherent in her principles was the proposition that Capitalism must disappear and the owner be replaced by management, under State Planning. After stratification, came the elimination of the Capitalist, the mobilization of industry through the Party. The Party was to inspirit the State and the Party was to be made up of workers by brain as well as workers by hand [30]—all persons. Beatrice Webb stressed vocational associations, but her use of the term " vocational group " did not connote a perpendicular order, where collaboration of workers and owners looked toward mutual benefit and the common good through production, as it did in its matrix in Guild Socialism. It meant instead, the conquest of one group, the Capitalists, by the others—by all persons who worked organized with their colleagues in horizontal lines. It is very significant that the series of Conferences on Restoring Trade Union Conditions was held in Fabian Hall and that the conferences heard Beatrice Webb and other Fabians. The leaders of Trade Unions believed that Fabian Socialists aimed to " restore Trade Union conditions," conditions which depend upon sound Capitalism; but in the above set of principles propounded by Beatrice Webb lay the reason for the Fabian rejection of the Whitley Council system based upon capital-labor-government collaboration, and the warping of the unions into the Party instead.

Along with assisting and encouraging the big national amalgams of Trade Union groups, the Webbs were writing over again their *History of Trade Unionism*, 1666–1920, with references from which transition was made to this section. E. R. Pease reviewed it when it was re-issued specially for WEA and TUC in 1920.

---

[30] Margaret Cole, *Beatrice Webb* (London: Longmans Green and Company, 1945), pp. 35 and 123. This was not one of Beatrice's " mistakes." It led her to her love of the U.S.S.R.

This founding Fabian's succinct observations will serve to show the increasingly clear articulation of the relations of the Party to the unions affiliated with it and united under TUC.

> Their criticism of the latter [Trades Unions Congress] is severe; but not, we think, unjustified. The Parliamentary Committee has lacked inspiration; it has not made the best of its great opportunity; and its constituents have neither expected great things of it, nor provided the income and organisation necessary for expansion. *The Labour Party has necessarily taken over most of the work* [political] which the Congress used to do, yet the Congress has neither abandoned its political business, nor attempted the *co-ordination of Trade Union activities in the industrial sphere,* a work which is urgently required and which no other body can properly undertake.[31]

The italics supplied indicate the two separated functions assigned to the Party and the TUC respectively, and the excerpt indicates the part the Fabians played in outlining these spheres of industrial and political action. They must be credited with the shunting off of the effectiveness of Communist subversion which gained ground only in small or ill-defined areas. However, the unions lost the right to exercise political activity on their own. Here a Fabian shows them their proper sphere—their own corner. Pease indicated that " political business " had better belong to the Party. Fabians would help with both the political business of the Party and the coordination of Trade Union activities in the industrial sphere. The challenge in this criticism was met by steady growth in Trade Union organization, growth which continued until the TUC plunged itself, with no effort to prevent or stay it on the part of Fabians, into another debacle similar to that known as " Taff Vale," when in 1926 it made a direct attempt to coerce Parliament or the Government. Incidentally, Pease termed " a piece of anthropomorphism more appropriate for a propagandist speech than for serious history " the statement made

---

[31] *FN*, XXXI:5 (May, 1920). (Italics are inserted.) Cf. also, Gannett and Catherwood, *Industrial and Labour Relations in Great Britain: A Symposium* (New York: published by authors, 1939). The Appendix provides descriptive documents on Whitley Councils, p. 349.

by the Webbs that in the Taff Vale case " the Capitalists " [32] regarded the temporary crippling of the Trade Union Movement as
well worth all it might cost them.[33]   Here was an old Fabian
clinging to a Fabian ideal, somewhat repelled by the strategic
pragmatism of the Webbs—in this case, an appeal to an anthropomorphic mentality.   Unionization and Trade Union Congresses
were, for the Webbs, means to political power; they assisted the
ill-shaped and poorly-grounded unions to consolidate their organization at the time when it was believed such unions were doomed
to extinction in " professionalism," by encouraging the growth of
TUC and the amalgamations and by establishing the pattern of
affiliation of all with the Party.   The *Labour Year Book* of 1919
is a monument to this policy, and to Fabian penetration.

Interesting indications of Fabian activity shaping the growth of
the Trade Union Movement and of the latter's being warped to
the Labour Party, can be gleaned from accounts of the Fabian
Women's Group.   *Women and The Labour Party,* a publication
listed in the flyleaf of the *Labour Year Book* of 1919, had for its
authors Mrs. Sidney Webb, Margaret L. Davies, Mary Mac-
Arthur, Margaret McMillan and Rebecca West.   The introduction
was by Marion Phillips and the foreword by Arthur Henderson,
kindly but firm " Uncle Arthur."   All were Fabians, boasting the
patronage of Henderson, the close friend of Mary MacArthur.
Later on these women were given Cole's assistance as assigned
scribe and organizer—he had a knack for getting himself
" adored," Margaret says.   Working women were intimately
affected by the change-over from war production to peace, since
they were marked for replacement earlier than men as demobiliza-
tion was slowed down.   They were most active in forwarding
unionization.   Women unionizers tended to be Fabians first and
workers' organizers second; *vice versa* as regards male organizers.
As far back as December, 1917, the project of compiling a history
of " Women in Trade Unions " was adopted by the Fabian

---

[32] *Ibid.*, XXXI:5 (May, 1920).   Pease might well have noted that the
whole of the section on Trade Unionism of the 1920's is pure propaganda.

[33] *Ibid.*   The sentiment was possibly something Sidney did not change in
a part Beatrice had written.   Pease's remark contributes weight to the
observation made in the preceding pages to the effect that social science was
put under levy for propaganda by Fabian researchers.

Women and Mrs. Webb's niece, Barbara Drake,[34] was charged with the report.[35] This charge coincided or was arranged to coincide with the Fabian Research Conference which opened December 12, 1917, on " The Legal Position of Trade Unions," a field which utilized the brilliant legal skill of Fabian Henry Slesser.[36] Following this, two groups, named Fabian Research Department (mixed) and Fabian Women's Group (from the industrial section) had a *joint meeting* under the slogan, " Equal Pay for Equal Work," in January, 1918. The Fabian Research Department also lent its assistance to the *joint committee* of the Labour Party and the Trade Unions Congress (TUC) Parliamentary Committee to assist, it so happened, in codifying the amendments proposed by them to the Workmen's Compensation Act. Here we have Fabians working with a committee of TUC which they later decreed should desist from political action and we note also the device of the " joint committee " or the coincident meeting.[37] These ramifications are typical of the elaboration of Fabian methods. The Women's Group and the Research Department met again in conference in June, 1918,[38] to exchange views and experiences. Five speakers from various Unions, including the Fabian and politician, Ellen C. Wilkinson of the Union of Co-operative Employers, were heard. They came eventually to the conclusion that women should be admitted to union membership on the same footing as men, among other reasons, in order not to depress the wage scale. Cole, of the Research Department, though not presiding and present only as an observer, nevertheless assumed authority to announce and arrange for future meetings and the Fabian Research Depart-

---

[34] At that time and still a close personal friend of Margaret Postgate, now Mrs. Cole.

[35] *FN*, XXIX :1 (December, 1917). She brought in the Report in November, 1920.

[36] *Ibid.* The legal work done for the unions by Fabian Henry Slesser was very valuable to them. Cf. Slesser, *op. cit.,* p. 47, and *LYB,* 1916.

[37] In March, 1918, the Fabian Research Department reported that with the affiliation of the London Trade Council and the Cooperative Union about a hundred organizations had affiliated with this Department. Mrs. Cole says they had spent a great deal of money in industrial rather than political work. Cf. her *Growing Up Into Revolution,* p. 94. The Communists later gained this Department but in the end lost the Movement to the Fabians.

[38] *FN*, XXIX :7 (June, 1918).

ment took over the secretarial responsibility for these functions.[39]

When the Fabian Women's Group met in January, 1919,[40] they were reminded by Dr. Letitia Fairfield, recently released from administrative work for the Government during the war, that opposition to women in industry and in local government came not only from men but from married women; so "Study Circles" were devised to educate the opposition. Among the Fabian women there arose the question of "class." Professor Edith Morley raised the question as to whether they, as middle-class women and forming so small a body of Socialist women, should not direct their activities toward encouraging the organization of women in professions. As Socialists they should study to eliminate inequalities and increase education among themselves in order to penetrate social circles, but they should not dictate, she thought, to any other part of the community, and should leave to industrial organizations the problems arising from women in industry. These Fabian women, Doctor Fairfield and Professor Morley, represented in their speeches two classes and two points of view. The latter's had the merit of faintly suggesting that women get out of industry. At this time of increasing unemployment Fabians were contributing to the increase of the number of unemployed men by insisting on women's rights in industry. The effect sought was to stratify this social segment and to bring it into the Party; these Party members were aware that the "woman in the home" is lost to politics and is an unaccountable voter. It was natural that women should raise the question of "class." Fabians resolved their doubts.

By October, 1920,[41] when faced with unemployment and the lapse of Part 3 of the Industrial Courts Act, there was no question that women and men should not belong to the same unions, and the question as to class among the women had been settled by

---

[39] This meant work for the "Young Cuckoos" in Mr. Pease's menage. These over-educated children worked late and long under the critical eye of P. Arnot, N. Ewer, and other young Guild Socialists. Sometimes in order to have a week-end off, they had to hide from the "Great Ones" who thought only of work, as M. Cole tells in her *Growing Up.*

[40] *FN,* XXX:2 (February, 1919).

[41] *FN,* XXXI:11 (November, 1920).

May, 1920,[42] in the National Labour Party (Women's) Conference. Then, while excising the idea of separate unions for women, Fabians also abated the women's agitation over class distinction. The Party was clearly the great end and rationale:

> . . . the stupid distinctions, which still exist in the mind of some people, between middle-class and working-class women may be eliminated, and insomuch as that all are members of the Labour Party, and therefore, workers, they are all of one class working for the same object—the reconstitution of society.[43]

Tremendously interesting as exemplifying technique is the fact that although organized Fabian women were not eligible to participate in the last mentioned conference, the names of those women who were active in it were to be found in lists of Fabian Women. Not as delegates but as observers and representatives of the Society went Barbara Drake and Mrs. Stephen Sanders, among others. The chair was filled at times by two Trade Union and Co-operative women who were at the same time prominent Fabians, Miss Mary MacArthur (Mrs. Anderson) and Miss Susan Lawrence. Miss Margaret Bondfield reported from the Washington (Eight-Hour) Conference, one of the first landmarks in the history of the ILO which was the creation of " Amsterdam " and " Berne," as Lorwin shows; and Mrs. Drake moved a resolution regarding education which outlined what actually became the future law on that subject. So from outside the Conference as well as from vantage points within the Conference, Fabian women infiltrated to bring the Conference in under the aegis of the Labour Party and to point out to conferees the peculiar kind of classlessness which Fabian Socialism inculcated.

Our intention in discussing the interweaving of unionizing and

---

[42] *FN*, XXXI :5 (May, 1920).

[43] *Ibid.* Characteristic of the British approach to the class question was the idea of one-class. It veiled the realities of class-struggle and put English Socialism on the side of " Berne " and Amsterdam (minus-IFTU) against the Third International gestating in Europe. Cf. Lorwin, *op. cit.,* pp. 174– 339. Fabians had indoctrinated Bernstein who now was fairly reconciled with Kautsky. Cf. *FN*, XIV :10 (October, 1904), where W. S. reviews R. C. K. Ensor.

politicizing activities is to illustrate Fabian effectiveness, not indeed to trace the rise of Trade Union consolidation after the war. We may, however, point out two balancing, even contradictory, elements: The first, political Socialism, was an incipient threat to Trade Unionism; the second, " Labour," amalgamated the associated workers by hand and brain into one class exclusive only of organized owners, constituting a threat to social order. When a new direction was indicated by the announcement of conferences on " Women in the Home," it showed the sensitiveness of Fabians to social change, and the effect of growing unemployment. By now, however, women, whether industrially employed or at home, had been won to the Party as supporters and voters. Fabian literature followed these Party women into the home. When industrial organizing apparatus became obsolete, it was scrapped or consolidated. Women who had worked through the war remained attached to the Party. When the Fabian Women's Group affiliated with the Joint Standing Committee of Industrial Women's Organization, January, 1921, Barbara Drake addressed them to advocate breaking down the " barrier between workers by hand and workers by brain," rather than on organizational or industrial questions. She was didactic: either professionalism or vocationalism would preserve class; to obliterate class was to develop the Party.

By this time, unemployment and housing had become the proximate problems; Trade Union activities had slowed down and the General Election was in preparation. It was to result in the Labour Party's finding itself His Majesty's Loyal Opposition. While the Fabian women kept up the agitation for " equal pay for equal work," their group attracted thought toward cooperative stores, education, and birth control; [44] meantime, Trade Unionism marked time as National Guildsmen and the Webbs disputed styles of organization, and industry failed to absorb all the workers. But the Fabians' work, mixing the working women of all classes in the Party which embraced all workers had so far been well done. Even though there were two schools of thought in Fabianism—Cole with his " anarchy " substituting " consumer interest " for the State, and the Webbs with their Statism substituting socio-

---

[44] *FN*, XXXIV:10 (October, 1923).

economic interests for the regal science of politics—both schools inhered in the Party. The discussion satisfied the intellectuals with the feeling of a sense of free thought. In the Party, Webb's creed was the "spirit" called Socialism: Cole's was a Socialistic set of "principles of justice as applying to the economic order" (which excluded Charity in the theological aspect of Charity). That stratification was encouraged to obviate the Capitalist and to hasten the subjugation of a social segment, namely, the Trade Unions to the Party, was unstated but implied in all that can be learned of Fabian activities.

In spite of the fact that Mrs. Webb disagreed with Cole on "worker control," both of them agreed about the nature of the Party—a way to unite all who worked and all who had received a tincture of Socialism to induce them to vote for measures laying the groundwork for Socialism. Cole said in defiance of Mrs. Webb's refusal to place the term consumers in place of the State in the Socialist system then evolving:

> I am an unrepentant "vocationalist," believing that the basis of any effective organisation of industry for the service of the consumer must be self-government of industry, so far as its actual management is concerned, by those who work in it by hand and brain. This does not mean complete control of each industry by the producers, but the actual direction by them of the processes of production—the policy of industry being determined jointly by the representatives of consumers and producers—that is by the *will of the community*, or at least by the nearest approach to it which it is possible to secure by a representative system.[45]

The words "will of the community" put Cole back into the Statism he believed he was evading. He then proceeded as a Guild Socialist to mark the "limits" of Trade Unions as they stood; he said they lacked representation of a sufficient number of grades, were wrongly organized, were unimbued with the right spirit to assume the responsibility of solving industrial problems.

---

[45] Syllabus of a lecture, *FN*, November, 1921. Italics are inserted. The volumes 32–35 are bound in L.C. system, together and made to include as an appendix, the syllabi appertaining to the years thus included, in this case 1921–1924. There is therefore no pagination.

They might, he thought, supply a basis for such things as " Building Guilds," which he believed were the groups best equipped to assume responsibility for industrial administration.   The contemporary " vice " of " Professionalism," as described, excoriated by Graham Wallas in his *Our Social Heritage,* was mainly " protective," said Cole, and was lodged in a social system " based upon economic injustice."   " The basis of any good social transformation must be a recognition of certain fundamental principles of justice as applying to the economic order."   Of course, Cole's " principles," meant Socialist belief and the " right spirit " regarding property.   Except for the omission of a scholastic term, " the common good," with its connotations of hierarchical order and collaboration of classes in charity, Cole defined an industrial-social structure giving the illusion of being one capable of producing " social justice."   Here was the bridge from the Guild system to State Socialism, on the way toward the Cooperative Commonwealth, it seemed.   This the Webbs acknowledged in the *History of Trade Unionism.*[46]   This is why the Webbs absorbed so many shocks of lese-majesty from young Cole concerning whom a partisan of the Webbs once moved in meeting: " Resolved that Mr. Cole be a cad! "   Already in 1921, he was expressing their long view. His " Just Price " is really price-fixing and regulation of wages; his " consumer " is the public.   At best his professionally grouped owners are mere recipients of directives from " the community," ultimately, the Party.   His view on professionalism is dialectical:

---

[46] In the Webbs' *History of Trade Unionism,* p. 660, we read: " The bridge between the old conception of Trade Unionism and the new was built by a fresh group of Socialists, who called themselves National Guildsmen. This group of able thinkers, largely drawn from the universities, accepted from those whom we may call the Communal Socialists the idea of the ownership of the instruments of production by the representatives of the citizen-consumers but proposed to vest the management in national associations of the producers in each industry—organizations which they declared ought to include not merely the present wage earners, but all the workers by hand and brain."   The Webbs' antagonism (especially Mrs. Webb's), toward Guild Socialism is apparent in the note which appears on the same page; fully objective, it yet disparaged the movement.   Leo XIII made a bridge out of the medieval guild system into modern associations and thereby created Christian Corporatism.   Cf. *Rerum Novarum* (NCWC: 1942), p. 29.

Professionalism under conditions based on these principles will be a very different thing from the professionalism of today.   A cooperative relation of producer and
consumer, the economic process, will be substituted for
the present antagonism.   With the recognition of those
fundamental principles, of which the greatest are the
" Just Price," and functional self-government, professionalism becomes never a perfect—but the best available
instrument for the administration of industry and
service.[47]

This was the kind of expression, these the ill-articulated concepts
which drew into the ranks of the Labour Party not only Socialists
but many other right meaning persons who adopted a sort of
eclecticism among Acquinan and papal principles.   These were
the days when Anglo-Catholic Henry Slesser could win an election
preaching St. Thomas and Pius XI, as Sir Henry has narrated in
his *Judgment Reserved*.   Cole did not persist in his unrepentant
vocationalism.   The Webbs built a bridge from guildism to Fabian
Socialism and Cole walked over it, leaving Slesser, Belloc and
Chesterton on the other side.

The Party created by all this work and expanding energy did
not necessarily satisfy its creators.   It did permeate society with
Socialism, but it was not the Order of their dreams.   The Party
had to go into the political arena where the slings and arrows of
political fortune became too outrageous.   From 1919 to 1922
politics absorbed activities and ideological differences took care of
themselves.

C.   Fabians in The Hustings

After 1872, voters no longer stood forth to be counted " on the
hustings " while crowds or mobs shouted approval or disapproval.
The hustings became, as of older times still, the " council " or the

---

[47] Cole, Syllabus of a lecture, *FN* (November, 1921).   Compare David
Kirkwood, *My Life of Revolt* (London: Harrap and Company, 1935),
passim.   This autobiography of an ILP Clydesider brings out the difference
between the shop-steward mentality and that of the William Gallacher type
of Communist by illustrating real " vocationalism."   It depicts the religious
emotion marking the Scots' Socialism, exemplifies the non-miscibility of the
ILP spirit and the politicized British Trade Unionism, as well as the in-
compatibility of the " intellectuals " with the worker realists.

" confab " under the roof of some store or drawing room or
" pub." The " smoke-filled " rooms in the constituencies, in
societies and clubs now brought " politics " back into the *hus-
things*.[48]

Having seen the ideological laboratory set up in the Class which
tutored Labour Party principles and having found the pattern of
penetration used to create a Party permeated with Fabian principles, we turn now to the story of the development of the Party
in the hustings, that is, in local political party councils and in
suffragan hinterlands.

It is not the purpose here to narrate British Labour's rise to
power.[49] A few lines from the *Labour Year Book* of 1919 indicate Fabian tentacles in the Party:

The New Party Constitution, based on Sidney Webb's *Labour
and the New Social Order,* was printed in four sections: Rules for
single and undivided boroughs, for county constituencies, for local
parties, and for divided boroughs. The Party was much more like
a fraternity in organization than any American political party.
The party-fraternity formed an elite; the electorate which voted
Labour was less rigid and less reliable, but it possessed great
malleability and amenity—qualities traceable to its sensitive social
conscience.

The *LYB,* 1919, advertised 23 Labour Party Leaflets. Anonymous except for those written by the Webbs, it is safe to say they
were written by Fabians. They comprised matters discussed over
and over again in Fabian circles. The " Capital Levy " was missing. It was good Socialism but not good politics.

---

[48] Incidentally, the responsibility of voters to " the mob " before the hustings
guaranteed a measure of control by public opinion overlooked by those who
argued for widened franchise in 1832, 1867, and 1870.

[49] It has been well done by Professor Carl Brand, *British Labour's Rise
to Power* (Stanford University, California, 1941), in which is shown the
effectiveness of a program of international organization in amalgamating
Labour forces and producing a Party. The nucleus which developed the
Party during the War was formed by three Fabian documents. Leonard
Woolf's *International Government: Two Reports* (New York: Brentano,
1916) " prepared for the Fabian Research Department with an introduction
by Bernard Shaw, together with a project by a Fabian Committee for a
supernational authority that will prevent war "; also, the *Memorandum on
War Aims,* and Webb's *Labour and the New Social Order.* Cf. *NS,* 12
(January 4, 1914), p. 274.

G. D. H. Cole and J. S. Middleton (Henderson's henchman in organizational work) were the joint editors of the *LYB*, 1919. Henderson in his foreword called it the work of " Labour's Civil Service." It is noteworthy that by the time England attained to a paid Parliament she acquired a counter-parliament of unpaid public servants.

Of the 42 contributors to *LYB*, 1919, this student finds only three or four she cannot identify as Fabians, either at the time or later on. Some of the Fabian names were: R. P. Arnot, A. L. Bacherach, C. D. Burns, Wilfred Brown, G. D. H. Cole, M. I. Cole, E. Davies, W. Gillies, A. Henderson, John Hodge, J. F. Horrabin, J. Katz, Barbara Keen, J. J. Mallon, Sir John Maynard, J. W. Dixon, Monica Ewer, Marion Phillips, R. W. Postgate, E. C. Reckitt, M. B. Reckitt, H. P. Rathbone, H. H. Slesser, G. H. Stuart-Bunning, R. H. Tawney, H. Tracey, S. Webb, B. Webb, H. G. Wells, Barbara Wootton—names which appear extremely often in innumerable connections in the Party and the Unions as well as the Society.[50]

Channeling the forces and concretizing the Party structure was the work of one man more than any other, a political genius in the practical use of this term, the Wesleyan minister, Arthur Henderson. Alone he could never have been so successful; but his labors spearheaded the activities of the Fabian Society in this field. Closely associated as Party organizers were the Fabians, Doctor Marian Phillips, Barbara Wootton, Margaret Bondfield, the organizer of women in industry; also Arthur Greenwood, James Middleton, A. Lockhurst Scott, and Herbert Morrison. All were listed consistently as Fabians except Scott who is listed as such only once.

In December, 1917,[51] the Rt. Hon. Arthur Henderson, M.P.,

---

[50] Most of these were colleagues in the FRD. Cole and Wells will be called Fabians; Wells' obituary claims him for the spirit of the Society and Cole came back in 1929. While Cole was out of the Society he continued his usual occupations of working for the Party. Wells and Cole, like Wallas, resented the Webbs rather than dissented from the Society. However, the dissent hinged upon the kind of social order they envisioned rather than a definition of Socialism; later the dissent was resolved by Cole's finding it was all a matter of timing—after the monolithic state the breakup into subsidiary councils—" Freedom."

[51] *FN*, XXIX:2 (January, 1918). For Henderson's Party organizing cf. M. A. Hamilton, *Arthur Henderson*, (London: Heineman, 1938), pp. 220–226.

had spoken almost prophetically: Perhaps a group system should come after the War but it would not last long and would not be such as existed on the Continent. " The hand and brain workers and the adherents of democracy will come together, perhaps under the Labour Party name "; against them, he thought, more strongly organized than ever before, stood the Capitalists. (The Whitley Council system was built on professional organizations of owners and of " men "—Baldwin's word.)[52] Henderson had conceived of a highly disciplined force, the political machine, which could " get down to the roots." The new electorate had increased from eight to over sixteen million and included only two million new male voters; the rest consisted of five million married women mostly wives of working men and one million unmarried women, many of them working women. From 1917 to 1919 this electoral segment was canvassed in the interests of the Labour Party by candidates whose expenses were paid by the Party, and who were supplied with a packet of literature. Labour organizers insisted it should be arranged that all elections be completed in one day, and " We must run enough candidates to secure that the new electors do not joint other parties because Labour is not in the field "; not the old 78, but 560 were needed. Although the Party intended to

---

[52] Cf. Frank E. Gannett and B. F. Catherwood, editors, *Industrial and Labour Relations in Great Britain: A Symposium* (New York: F. Gannett, publisher, 1939), pp. 349–362, for documents on Whitley Councils. The book has articles by Miss Bondfield, Mr. Clynes, and Michael Tracey, an historian of the Labour Movement. A chart on p. 359 shows the relation of the Trade Councils to the National Labour Council. The General Council of the TUC maintains a committee of Joint Consultation with Trades Councils which are local bodies, as well as a position in an advisory capacity with Trade Boards. We have seen the Fabian effectiveness in bringing the Trades Councils into the Labour Party (local and national). Cf. also, " Conferences on the Whitley Report," *FN,* XXIX :2 (January, 1919). Cole and Fred Bramley and Stuart-Bunning voted against mere "Welfare Committees," " single round table organisation," " substituting of shop-bargaining for collective bargaining." They were against any peace in industry which was merely an individual plant's peace and not applicable on a national scale. " Be democratic but be careful " was said to spell the doom of shop-steward, or work-shop and local ordering. The Whitley Report shows Trade Unionism in a stage of flux and shop-stewardism half developed. The Fabian answer was the Labour Party and its substructure, national Trade Unionism.

develop a constituency system, the customary machinery must be kept, that which consisted in a federation of Trade Unions, Trade Councils, local Labour Parties, Socialist Societies and Cooperative Societies:

> . . . it is our only means of securing the money needed by a political party. . . . We cannot create baronetcies and peerages.[53] We must therefore graft the new constituency system upon the old federation of organisations. . . . We can only run the country if our men are drawn from ranks as wide as the new constitution, that is from all classes and occupations.[54]

He was not far wrong when he said: ". . . in ten years, the Cooperatives, the Trades Union Congress and the Labour Party will become the biggest party in the country." [55]

From 1919 to 1922 the Party increased in strength numerically and by local organisation in the constituencies; and it had assumed a viewpoint and position regarding its international responsibility which was uniquely the work of Arthur Henderson. He had been a Fabian since 1912, a Labour leader since 1910, and president of the iron founders since 1909. If the Labour Party as a political force was his creation, the Trade Unions' assumption of a place in the state was his work. The National Industrial Conference of 1919 came to pass because he, having been in the government of Lloyd George, persuaded the Trade Union representatives to meet with the employer representatives. It was he who brought in young G. D. H. Cole to write up the memorable report advocating the Eight-Hour Act, the Minimum Wage Commission, the National Industrial Council. He had the disappointment of seeing the prognostications of Smillie, Thomas and Bevin proved true: the Government failed to carry out the promise which had brought the two groups together; [56] and the intellectual leadership of labor

---

[53] They did create peerages in 1924, 1929 and on a large scale in 1945.

[54] *FN*, XXIX:2 (January, 1918).

[55] *Ibid.* Results appeared in *Ibid.*, XXX:1 (January, 1919).

[56] Mary Agnes Hamilton, *Arthur Henderson* (London: Heineman, 1938), p. 215. These men were the leaders of the Miners, Railwaymen, Transport Unions, respectively. This "Triple Alliance" had professed cynicism regarding Lloyd George's promises. Henderson's "disappointment" was hardly unexpected by him. The fact that the Conference came about and

gave scant support to a conciliar system.   Not only did Henderson
use the old federation of labor system, he worked with the system
of the Whitley Councils, at least as a sort of experiment, with the
result that unionism, as well as Party formation, received clearer
articulation than either had before the War.   Fabians used
Whitley Councils for the piers of " the bridge between the old
conception of Trade Unionism and the new." [57]   Henderson
linked the Trade Unions and the Labor elements to the Labour
Party and at the same time kept the latter from subversion under
the repeated attempts of Communists to unite with the Labour
Party.   " He could organize anything from an electoral campaign
to a Red Army," [58] and he developed Labour as a political party.
It was he who placed Labour in its new relationship with Socialist
and Labor international organization.   He also saved from
oblivion the inspiring leader who was MacDonald, " because
MacDonald had the higher intellectual qualities and the informed
knowledge he could not claim." [59]   And he it was who recognized
the aptitude of the young Arthur Greenwood.[60]   Arthur Greenwood, a Fabian, was secretary of the Joint Committee on Relations
between Employers and Employed (Whitley Committee).

---

cast ideas into the stream of public opinion was a political potential.   For
Henderson's purposes it was not necessary for the Government to have been
expected to carry out the program devised by the Conference.   The Alliance
leaders were naively forthright.   The intellectuals who detested professionalism did not quarrel with any method which forwarded the Party.

[57] Cf. Webb, *History of Trade Unionism*, p. 660.

[58] Hamilton, *op. cit.*, p. 219.   The foundation for this remark was furnished
by Julius West (né Rappaport) who, reporting back from Russia, in 1917,
credited to Henderson's influence on Skobeler and Tseretelli the partial
success of the last named two, in establishing order in Russia in 1917—just
before the Bolsheviks captured the Revolution.   *FN*, XXXVIII:9 (August,
1917), " Report of Our Delegate to Russia."

[59] *Ibid.*, pp. 220 f.

[60] *Ibid.*   " He made what had been, in the main, a class organization, with
idealism vivid on its wings but opportunism dominant at its center, into a
national organisation united in principle and animated, more and more
thoroughly, by idea.   Moreover, he created a working and effective instrument of practical democracy."   Mrs. Hamilton is the author of biographies
of the Webbs and of MacDonald.   Her book on Henderson can be taken for
a Fabian document and an original source of Fabian thought.   Sometimes she
seems to try to furnish doctrinaire Socialism where Henderson the " foreman " appeared to lack it.

Meantime, it was the ILP which withered on the vine. At the beginning of the War, its members numbered about 30,000, six times the Fabian membership.[61] It was perfectly obvious that the organization which had furnished leadership such as that of Mac-Donald, Snowden, Keir Hardie, Will Crooks, Margaret Bondfield, William Anderson, Mary MacArthur, was nevertheless marked for extinction in 1919.[62] Fabians intended the Labour Party to do the political work of Socialists and they removed this function from ILP as well as from TUC. Furthermore, the ILP doomed itself to failure because of its adherence to the " Two and a Half " International. Whether it advocated revolution in sympathy with and imitation of the Bolsheviks is disputable. Fabian Mrs. Hamilton and Clydesider David Kirkwood hold opposite views on this point.

The *New Statesman,* on April 10, 1920,[63] upbraided the ILP for its international preoccupations; the editor reproved its lack of imagination and its inability to sympathize with Russia without trying to imitate Russian methods. While praising MacDonald's appeal against revolution—he had recognized that not a single person at a recent conference was in favor of violence—the weekly criticized the leader's negative attitude and recalled the ILP to its function to restate its Socialism in terms of the conditions which existed in the country at the time, to " frame a clear national policy, industrial as well as political." The Fabian plan was the very exemplification of this advice. Fabians had their own uses for internationalism, too.

That the connection between the ILP and the Fabian Society rested on the pre-war basis was shown by the fact that when, in April 1918, *The Abolition of the Poor Law, Tract 185,* was reprinted and the expense was divided among several agencies, one was the Joint Committee of the Fabian Society and the ILP. Out-

---

[61] In 1945, only three ILP members were elected; in 1950, not one.

[62] The policy advanced by Fabians at the Nottingham Conference, January, 1918, of admitting to membership in the Labour Party individuals who were not Socialists, who were merely left of Liberalism, contributed to the disintegration of ILP. Cf. Margaret Cole, *op. cit.,* pp. 135 f. ILP was divided internally anyway: Christian Socialists of the Clyde and doctrinaires who tended toward the Third International. Cf. Lorwin, *op. cit.,* pp. 138 and 166 f.

[63] *NS,* XV (April 10, 1920), p. 3.

side of committee connections there were personal ones. W. C. Anderson, who died in 1919, had been chairman of this Committee since 1911 and as *Fabian News* of March 1919 observed "though more closely identified with ILP than with our Society . . . [Anderson] was always willing to act with us, and only a year ago lectured to us in 'Rebuilding the International.'" But the link was to become more tenuous and the ILP was to furnish more propaganda "generals" than political "soldiers" as the decade wore on.

Henderson did not confuse Socialism and Bolshevism, but he remained loyal to the Russian experiment. In 1919, at the time when the agenda was concerned with collective control of resources and increased production, Henderson had, in answer to a challenge, introduced the exiled Kerensky to the Conference. In this he had manifested his gift of acute perception as he marked the difference between the "ideal" Socialism of Kerensky and the imperial totalitarianism masquerading as Socialism that was Bolshevism. Nevertheless he bore fealty to the communist-socialism at the core of Leninism. In 1920 and 1921, the Labour Party rejected the application for affiliation with the Labour Party of the newly formed Communist Party. This rejection was brought about by Henderson who understood the Bolshevik double meaning in the use of the words by which they claimed fellowship, like "unity" and "real Trade Unions." [64] What "Uncle Arthur" meant by unity was shown when, in 1919, the Labour Party adopted a resolution that all individuals and every organization constituting the Party must accept the constitution. The constitution was Webb's *Labour and the New Social Order*. Nevertheless, the way was not closed to individual Communist agitators entering as representatives of Trade Unions or of local Labour parties.

We recall the fact that Labour's New Constitution was the embodiment of Sidney Webb's *Labour and the New Social Order;* but a constitution could not create a party. Looked at from the point of view of Arthur Henderson, the Party can be seen assuming its now familiar character and emerging from a stormy period in 1919, rather stronger than weaker for having shed that segment

---

[64] Hamilton, *op. cit.,* pp. 200 ff.

of ILP which joined the Two-and-a-Half International of Adler
and Longuet and the " pacifists " like Clifford Allen who wanted
the revolution now.   The Society ·vas fully aware of the rising
power of political Labour, as its *Report* of 1919 shows. They had
seen the apparent strength of the Coalition for what it was—unwieldy and vulnerable, a heavy foam of sentiment and fear, created
by the wily manipulation of the arch-politician, Lloyd George,
beneath which was a heavier mass of an opposite kind, a ground
swell of popular forces.   Henderson had agreed with Lloyd George
that the election of 1918 should be held.   He benefited by the
winnowing when the Coalition with its " Coupons " garnered all
the forces outside of Labour.   He was to agree again in 1922 when
Labour came in as the Opposition and he was to precipitate the
election of 1923 when Labour formed a Government.[65]   Party
strength by experience and the exercise of being a Party, was
what he sought and what was attained.[66]   But it surprised even
Henderson and Webb to learn how early they might take over the
Government. Henderson was often favored by the " rightness "
of circumstances, as for instance when, regardless of what the
international results were, he gauged the sentiment of the people
regarding Ireland accurately and capitalized upon it to garner
Labour strength.   Working-class detestation of the system of
reprisals and all that " Black-and-Tan " signified, gave the growing Labour Party weight and force.[67]

So we see that the Labour Party was largely the work of a man
who was a Fabian.   Its constitution was a Fabian document; its

---

[65] *Ibid.,* pp. 32 ff.

[66] Beatrice Webb foresaw the effects in Labour Party growth of Lloyd
George's Bismarck-like policies (calling all opposition unpatriotic) and she
wrote in a letter to the Editor of the *NS,* November 30, 1918 : " The National
Liberals, until 1870 the most powerful party in the Reichstag—a party which
had loyally supported the war with France—were wiped out in the following
years.   The Social Democrat Party, . . . rapidly grew in power and became
the only organized opposition to autocracy.   The moral is obvious."

[67] Attlee, *op. cit.,* p. 28.   " It may be noted as a factor in building the
British Labour movement on broad foundations that so many of the
adherents of the Catholic faith in Britain come from Ireland, where a creed
of political and economic revolt has been inculcated into a Catholic population.   The British Labour movement owes much to these men and
women. . . ."

fusion with Trade Unions and industrial workers' organizations was a skilled Fabian " bridge."

Depression, unemployment and deterioration of various unions meant only gain to the Party. The controls set over industry by the Government during the war were removed in March, 1919, rather than on the intended date in August. When Fabian Arthur Greenwood made his special Conference Report, *Unemployment: A Labour Party,* in 1921, it was apparent that unemployment was eroding socialistic idealism.[68] An international policy of reciprocity in trade and the re-creation of Continental markets was advocated. By 1922, the Trade Union movement was flagging. It stood to lose more than the Labour Party, which, of course, was to miss the funds which the unions supplied, but to gain adherents from labor's discontent. The unions had all they could do after 1922 to exercise a little collective bargaining. With scant concern evinced by Fabians, the Whitley Councils waned. Its agitation for Trade Unionism had supplied the Labour Party with an appeal which, even though it lost its efficacy among the unions, was to infuse and sustain rank and file workmen as such: The Party envisioned that *workers should share in the management of industry* whether owned by private capital or assumed by the state. The Party would have to face the decisions as to ownership, and encompass within itself the rapidly growing cooperative movement. For all decisions there was Fabian leadership with its empiricism and gradualness. The Party would soon have to cope with the renewal of " direct action " and the political strike. And here again Fabians would manage to mix the unmiscible.

---

[68] Cf. B. M. Anderson, *op. cit.* p. 162, " Britain demonstrated [in the 1920's] what the present writer believes to be a universal economic ' law,' namely, that any country can have heavy unemployment if it is willing and able to pay for it. . . . [The United States had recovered industrially, 1922–1923, by the operation of the law of supply and demand.] England, on the contrary, had had no such favorable change in her labor situation. When her wages failed to resume their prewar relationship to prices, it was due primarily to the strength of the Trade Unions, which forcibly held union wages above the level which supply and demand would have dictated, with the result that there was heavy chronic unemployment." On the next page Anderson says that businessmen and bankers were reluctant to let wages seek a level proportionate to the drop in wholesale prices—" the poor beggars get so little," expressed their attitude.

By 1923, Fabianism in the person of Arthur Henderson, who was seconded to the point of identity by the *New Statesman*,[69] had produced a perfected party system whose force alert Tories would insist upon testing prematurely or preventively as part of their struggle with it.   Henderson had freed his leader from

[69] Cf. *NS*, XII (January 4, 1919), 273, " from a Labour Correspondent." This article pointed out the fact that " if the Labour Party were represented according to its strength [not an argument for proportional representation was meant], it would have 150 instead of 60 . . . and Mr. Lloyd George's majority . . . would be only in tens. . . . The distance the Labour Party has still to cover is far smaller than it appears."   Reiterating the programs: To rule out particularism and sectarian self-righteousness, to convince a majority of the voting electorate of the rightness of its opinions, not to join in the Government, for, " In vain is the snare set twice."   Liberal Sir Leo Chiozzo-Money (long a Fabian) had resigned from the Cabinet.   Barnes and Roberts were outside the Party now.   The perspicuity of "the Correspondent" was remarkable: The Coalition would not allow Lloyd George to act consistently with pre-election promises.   H. J. Thomas and J. R. Clynes, leaders of the Opposition, would keep before the electorate the views of Labour, which were in part as follows:

1) Taxation according to ability to pay not by mouths rather than means; 2) 300,000 new cottages, not left to speculative builders and with rising rents; 3) reorganization of local public health services, rather than a nominal ministry of health; 4) abolition of the Poor Law, not just the Boards of Guardians; 5) abolition of compulsory military conscription, rather than a reimposed form of perpetual camps; 6) restoration of Trade Union Conditions (" to which the nation is so solemnly pledged "); 7) compelling Capitalists' combinations to sell at prices brought down to legitimate expenses of production; 8) abandonment of any design to repress revolutions in Russia and elsewhere; 9) an effective League of Nations, "a real supernational authority imposing the world's will to peace on our own as well as . . . other governments," rather than a mere league of allies.   The *NS* veered away from Socialist propaganda, in terminology.

The *NS* was not a Labour Party organ, nor did it mention expropriation then; but later, in March (*ibid.,* p. 960) it did so.   It is remarkable that at the election of 1918, with the great Labour gains, not only did the Asquith Liberals go into eclipse but Henderson, Webb, J. J. Mallon, R. MacDonald, R. H. Tawney, Clement Attlee, and others, strong Labour men, were defeated. The *NS* pointed to the need for better central planning (knowing their constituencies).   Mary Agnes Hamilton thought Henderson, for example, had been too busy working for others.   However, it is possible that the popular mind allowed the fear of radicalism to overtake the preeminent Socialist figures and overlooked, if it did not approve outright, the fundamental structural growth of the Party.

entanglements with radical elements; and MacDonald, aided in every way by a young Fabian, Herbert Morrison, was ready to assume the Government, having been leader in Opposition since 1922, when he had replaced the Trade Unionist, J. R. Clynes.

The testing came soon. Shaw, when they were hastily preparing by a series of lectures to learn how to govern, pointed out to Fabians that the ultimate need for those governing was a governable people. " Can Anyone Govern? " he answered with ". . . people cannot govern themselves, and will not let anyone else govern them beyond a point which stops very short of the minimum of regulation needed in a modern industrial state. . . ." He pointed far ahead beyond Pease and Webb and Cole to the real final cause of their being as Socialists: To capture power, lodge it in an elite. With mirthful cynicism, he added, knowing that the possibly eternal state of " transition " involved a compromise with their ideals:

> What the people want is an assurance that the Labour Party, if returned to power, will misgovern as Mr. Winston Churchill's party misgoverns, but with an outlook slightly more modern than that of King Henry VIII. Once reassure the electorate on that point, and they will give Mr. Henderson a turn when they are tired of Mr. Lloyd George.[70]

Of course, for Fabian Shaw this was special pleading—his idea of setting up a panel from which the people might elect parliaments, boards, and the like governing bodies. It is not difficult to discern in his proposal the outline of the Fabian Society, drawing, as he suggested in his project for choosing government. officials, its own strength from among those who had local municipal and industrial experience, and itself setting up a panel from which a preponderant number of government officials was eventually drawn. The Shavian idea had some affinity with the Webb proposal to create a body based upon " functional representation," which involved committees of experts in economic questions grouped like satellites revolving about the Mother Parliament. As set forth in the *Constitution for a Socialist British Commonwealth,* the aim was to supplement if not to supersede Parliament,

---

[70] *Fabian News,* Vols. 32–35, in L. C. collection, p. 5 of inserted Syllabus.

But, typified by the above quotation from the wily Shaw, the concept of "Labour" which Shaw, the Webbs, and the *New Statesman* wished disseminated at the time was that of just another political party.   They were covering up the Socialism of which they boasted—as one would bank a fire.   The ruse seemed successful in 1922, when the electorate increased the Party's power and rejected its outstanding leaders.

The Fabian R. H. Tawney, summarizing the history of British Labour, remarked in 1925:

> From the time the movement began to return to politics in the nineties, down to the explicit affirmation of the Socialist objective in the Constitution of 1918, the acceptance of Socialist ideas by nearly all of the more active spirits and by the steadily increasing proportion of all sections of society, had been the single most impressive fact of English politics.[71]

He thus makes the direct connection between the political expert and the ideologist, Henderson to Webb.   Fabian Socialists went directly into politics as laborites.

Members of the Fabian Society, automatically members of the Labour Party, were asked to give their names through the Society to the local Labour Parties if they were willing to stand for Parliament.   Circumstances favored putting more and more management of the Party into the hands of the London Fabians. Any Fabian residing in a constituency where there was no local Labour Party might join the Westminster Labour Party "Central Branch," whose secretary was at 25 Tothill Street (Fabian address), and he would be transferred to the proper local when it should be formed.[72]   The "active spirits" set out to "capture power."   For this they needed a fiscal policy and a platform.

National Finance and a Levy on Capital: What the Labour Party Intends.[73] took the position that foreign relations, consti-

---

[71] Tawney, *The British Labour Movement* (New Haven: Yale University Press, 1924), pp. 150 f.

[72] *FN*, XXIX:5 (April, 1918).

[73] It is not our intention to explain the plan here, but to make some observations upon it.   There is an arcane conflict between political Labour and Socialist ideology.   Cf. Sidney Webb, *National Finance and a Levy on*

tutional changes, and social reforms must become subservient to
the question of National Finance. The national debt absorbed
all other interests. It was assumed by Mr. Webb that sharp class
conflict must evolve from the divergent interests of those who live
by *producing* through hand or brain, and those who live by *own-
ing*. Labour, he said, faced the issue with no intent to raise class
bitterness only to ask the electorate to decide how to meet a
national debt of ten thousand million pounds, and not to leave the
problem to a practically autocratic Cabinet and Chancellor of
Exchequer. He insisted Labour must struggle to capture political
power in order to cope with the debt. (Confusion of the meanings of "Labour Party" and "labor" is inherent in Webb's
statement.)

It is quite clear the Socialist idea was to utilize the war debt in
order to capture political and social power. There are indications
of this in the document. For example, a not too subtle contradiction was involved in defining Labour's ends:—Austerity was defined without being mentioned; "the nation must forego its fat,"
but "We want a rich and prosperous Exchequer, not a starved
and bankrupt one." An autocratic Cabinet was to be replaced by
a rich Exchequer. Furthermore, the Fabian document boasted
that Socialists in Britain had no "wild" money schemes, none
whatsoever, no "silver," no "Labour Notes" [sic], no "repudiation." They were for sound money and meant to deal with real
wealth only, wherever it could be found. Income taxes were to
continue (lowered, no doubt) but the principle of "equal sacrifice" could not be applied by mere income taxes. You had to find
a way to afflict Standard Oil [74] as sharply as the struggling doctor
or the great dame who had not earned the living bestowed upon
her widowhood in stocks and bonds.[75] *What the Labour Party*

Capital: What the Labour Party Intends (London: The Fabian Society,
1919). This was a lecture given in King's Hall in May, 1918, and again in
Liverpool in November. Neither the Webbs nor Shaw believed in the
"votes-for-everybody" slogan. Here the appeal to the electorate is a campaigning device. Cf. "Postscript" to *Fabian Essays* (London: Allen and
Unwin, 1948), p. 222.

[74] One asks why the American company was singled out and not, for
instance, Shell Oil. Likewise, the document is blatant about conscripting
wealth and silent about conscription of labor.

[75] The equal status of women was being agitated in Fabian Women's

Intends restated, with a less constructive attitude, *How to Pay for the War* [76] which had set forth the extent of "nationalisation" the Fabian Research Department proposed in 1916: Development of the Post Office, not as a mere service or as a supplementary agency where private business did not care to invest, but as a source of revenue and a government monopoly; railway and canal (and docks) transport were to be developed into public services for the profit of the Exchequer; coal to be nationalized for cheaper and wider distribution; a state insurance department was to be set up along with the "revolution" in income tax adjustment and the Capital Levy. The dual purpose of the Capital Levy is explicit in this document: Primarily for repayment of the debt, as "literally a part of National Defence," owners must cede ten percent of their "capital value" that is, of their fortune. And with a captivating romanticism (a Shavian touch, it would seem), the motivation was given, "in order to secure the rest against being held for ransom by a conquerer, not to say looted by an invader." Labour Party control of the Debt meant control of the Exchequer and the reduction of the moneyed or the stock-owning classes to Labour control:

> Every owner of property . . . must be called upon to make a statement of all his property, and to realize one-tenth of its value for the State, whether by selling such portions of it, or by finding the equivalent out of his already severely taxed income, in return for the concession of being allowed to retain his lands, houses and securities intact. *We may as well make this colossal sacri-*

circles. The story of this movement would make a rewarding study, especially in connection with the two bills of disparate philosophical information recently before the Congress of the United States.

[76] Sidney Webb, editor, and R. P. Arnot, J. Bacon, G. P. Blizard, Emil Davies, W. Gillies, J. W. Nixon, and "a large number of friends in different branches of administration who have lent their help on points within their own experience, but whose names cannot conveniently be recorded," *How to Pay for the War: Being Ideas Offered to the Chancellor of the Exchequer by the Fabian Research Department,* published by the Fabian Society at the Fabian Bookshop, 25 Tothill Street, Westminster, and by Allen and Unwin, London, 1916. The "Great One" edited the work supervised by the exacting Arnot and turned out by the young workers in "the Movement" numbering Margaret Postgate and G. D. H. Cole. Mrs. Webb warned Margaret to mind her work and not have ideas about G. D. H.

*fice as easy as we can by calling up only 1 percent in each
of the ten years* [after the Peace].[77]

Then, there was a purpose secondary to mere debt paying; this
was the liquidation of large savings: Since the hope is not
always realized that the rich will usefully invest incomes (to reap
the "reward of abstinence," a principle here rejected with scorn
by Socialists), the State should not depend upon them.   In an
expression lacking consonance with that Christian thinking which
considers that the rich make a contribution to society and that
their savings enrich national assets, Arnot, Davies, Gillies and
others agreed that " such large savings by a wealthy class have an
inherent evil; they increase and perpetuate a functionless, tribute-
levying class of *rentiers*, which is already a dangerous element in
the State." [78]   The *rentiers* could have felt but little security after
the sacrifice of a tenth of their fortunes (not " incomes " which
were taxed separately from " fortunes ").

It is not our purpose to evaluate this Fabian scheme nor to
worry out their contrivance for future care for the encouragement
of the fine arts and the finding of new capital.   (The State, of
course, would provide new capital for investment and stimulation
for creative work.)   There was a core in this philosophical hodge-
podge which almost symbolically centered upon coal.   The principles of production for need, of the " just price," of distributive
justice to producers and equitable reward for entrepreneurs in the
coal-producing industry, were continuously asserted in Fabian
writings which concomitantly reported deplorable conditions in the
coal fields.   Socialism, deprived of the coal question, would have

---

[77] *Ibid.*, p. 264.   The emphasis is original.   The admission of the idea of
converting the capital levy into a surtax is an admission of Fabian doubt as
to whether their objective was a rich Exchequer or to liquidate a class.

[78] *Ibid.*, p. 270.   While pretending to save the ninety percent rights of
this group, their hidden purpose was to eliminate them.   Shaw evaluates the
matter as of 1949 as follows: " In England . . . I am being beggared by
surtaxes called Capital Levies to humbug the Labour Left (which ought to
know better)."   Cf. G. B. Shaw, " Ireland Eternal and External," *The
Atlantic Monthly*, Vol. 183 (February, 1949), pp. 63–64.   That outside the
" direct actionists " there was a " left" to " humbug " is evinced by the fact
of Fabian Shaw's continued faith in Labour.   In the same article, he opines
that Ireland will be united by the North [sic] when a Labour Government
comes to power there.

lacked one of its more potent arguments. It loomed large in the life of English people, and evoked many of the Socialist slogans without dissent. It exemplified better than any other industry the demand for production for need and not for price, and for wages to enable the miners, termed in Socialist parlance the "producers," to raise their living standard, hence their right to have a voice in the policy of the operators—owners. According to the Fabian spokesmen, the *political power* held by owners should be gained for themselves by producers, and the effort to do so was countenanced with the assumption that more would thus accrue to "the community." From the pattern created by the coal mining dilemma came the pattern for the monolithic State; for

> . . . every accession of capital value should be shared with the Government, which was long since declared to be—though our Chancellors of the Exchequer seem habitually to forget it—the sleeping partner in every undertaking, and the *only righteous heir to every increment due to the progress of the nation in population and wealth.*[79]

Although Webb speaks of sharing increment with the State, the concurrent drive for "nationalisation" left no doubt that expropriation was envisioned. The British utilitarian did not speculate about a "withering" State—Fabians knew that the Labour Party possessed as its dowry from the Trade Unions a new check upon the executive, the Partner-Government. It was not yet time to emphasize the point that the Party intended to control services by substituting for owners, the State. The power of labor (not the Party) might one day excel that of the State. That would depend upon the relations of indigenous Trade Unions and the Socialistic Labour Party. It was not discussed. But the "inevitability" of gradualism was understood. In any case, Webb's hearers and readers could have no excuse for not comprehending that Fabians intended to abolish Capitalism. They might also have reasoned that the fate of trade unionism was dubious.

---

[79] *The Capital Levy, Fabian Tract 188*, p. 13. Italics are inserted. It is not highly pertinent to ascertain here if the Coalitionists had really subscribed to this doctrine in their platforms. It is denied by Spender that nationalization of the mines was promised. "Rationalisation" was the burden of the Sankey Report; and "amalgamation" of the Samuel Report.

It should be recalled that the Fabian Society's best gift to the Labour Party, Sidney Webb, became a member of the Party Executive during the war. The above-mentioned statement about the Capital Levy came out during the war. In 1923, as Chairman of the Annual Conference of the Labour Party, Webb delivered the address which appeared as *Fabian Tract 207, The Labour Party on the Threshold*.[80] Benign, jovial, almost pseudo-papal, the future Lord Passfield intended to produce a harmonious unity and to fit the new party into the political scheme of things without arousing fears. Anyone could see that no party could digest " direct actionists " and " inevitable gradualists," but the Fabian Society which boasted it had " no orthodoxy "[81] would try to do so. In June, 1923, Webb drew the attention of the Conference to the curve which Labour returns produced: 62,698 votes in 1900; 323,195 in 1906; 505,690 in 1910; two and a quarter million in 1918; four and one-quarter million in 1922. A clear majority was indicated for 1926. Questions arose: Could Labour supply the responsible leadership? Did Labour have a foreign policy? One question was not spoken: Could Labour present a united front? Webb, however, answered this one succinctly: Although unlike the Liberals and Unionists, labor leaders had no " years of success in the making of profit " to their credit, in the Consumers' Cooperative Movement (wooing these by faint praises) and " the highly complicated work of Trade Unions" they had shown business training and experience. On the other hand, from Liberal Unionist benches had come the " most egregious blunders in Political Economy," and the Treasury had evinced no genius in finance or law or " knowledge of international affairs or in that instinctive wisdom we call statesmanship." Untrammeled by the demand for documentation Webb went on. From forty years' scrutiny, he said he could predict that Labour would be at least as competent as the contemporary ministers. These last had produced " immoral treaties " of peace and here after five years, they had achieved no organization of Europe as a commercial whole, no unified Continental transport system. They ignored

---

[80] Sidney Webb, *The Labour Party on the Threshold* (London: Fabian Bookshop, June, 1923).

[81] Cf. Clement Attlee, *op. cit.*, p. 30.

economics and morality. He implied that Labour Party politicans were above reproach at least on the scale of values where morality means "nature of things." "I confess to the simple faith that morality, like economics, is part of the nature of things . . . whenever we fail to take into account the nature of things our calculations . . . are brought to nought."[82] He had not spoken the underlying truth that British Socialism meant to become the planning centre for the distribution of the raw materials of the world, and that its trade union members were to contribute their self-sacrifice to the cause.[83] This criticism of ministers seemed designed to furnish guidance to future Labourites in office, to act "not on what we presume to be our own rights but on what we discern to be the common interests of the world," for nations are "in a very real sense members of one another." The Labour Party stood, he said, for a policy of mutual service, not a policy of the deliberate pursuit of profit for self. So a united front of workers-by-hand-and-by-brain was to be developed on the level of international affairs, and it called for self-effacement on the part of organized workers.

On foreign policy, Labour was ready with several studied proposals to reassert English leadership and to warn France against a single further step in her "fatal aggression policy"; to accept the willing reparations offered by Germans for mines and buildings (the ILP of Glasgow rejected all reparations) and compensation for damage by German bombs and torpedoes (there was a large segment of Labour which was adamant against any cooperation with the Germans who had submarined merchant-men); to make a real league of nations which would function with the effectiveness of the International Postal Union; with some little deference to political particularism, to work for unhampered intercommunication by suppressing passports and customs.

---

[82] Webb's philosophy was explained in terms of "the nature of things" and his best witness was always "any instructed person."

[83] Cf. G. D. N. Worswick, *The Raw Materials Controls* (London: Fabian Society, 1943), a pamphlet; also, H. Laski, *Socialism as Internationalism* (London: Fabian Research Society and Victor Gallancz, 1949). He would separate state and nation and create "functional federalism," and he would demand ever so gently that Trade Unions and professional groups surrender national interests (self-interest) even as states should surrender sovereignty.

Should the League become efficient as the Postal Union, it was most reasonable to demand "a unified railway and canal administration from Astrachan to Algeciras"; to urge upon governments "a common policy of education in internationalism, instead of the false history and economics taught in the name of patriotism." [84]

This was a platform which Trade Unions were not likely to invent without guidance or the Fabian inspiration of the Labour Party. It introduced a dream into economics, that dull regent science usurper of the realm of regal politics. Since the rest of the program, purely domestic, interested Labour men of all ranks and was explosive to the point where Webb must apply the brakes of "gradualism"—there was "reaction" on all sides in 1923, and a wage-war—the Fabian thesis connected the national debt and the wage-war. The debt problem, however, lay partly in the international field. "I am not sure," said the chairman, "that there may not be some truth in the suggestion that it is not so much national particularism as the *private interest of international Capitalism* that is today the main obstacle to such a foreign policy as I have outlined." [85]   Webb substituted, really, "the private

---

[84] It does not seem to have occurred to any "instructed person," as Webb would say, to reflect that patriotism is a part of the "nature of things" coming under the cardinal virtue of Justice.

[85] In 1931, the moral picture of the financial or economic world was described by the Supreme Pontiff in *QA*, more clearly than by Webb in 1923. (Cf. *On Reconstructing the Social Order* [Washington: NCWC, 1942], p. 38.)   Pius XI marks the degradation of free enterprise—its transformation into economic dictatorship: 1) supplanting the free market, 2) allowing itself to become absorbed in ambition for power, 3) reducing the supreme arbitress, the queenly State to slavery, having induced her to become partial to economic aims to the neglect of all other proper aims. The Pope thus describes that evil which Webb calls "national particularism" when depicting internal national decay. The Pontiff marks out in the international sphere, two "streams from the one fountainhead," greedy individualism: 1) "economic imperialism" (States which are bound in thrall to monopolies wage economic wars against other States) and 2) "a no less deadly and accursed internationalism of finance whose country is where profit is."

Webb seems to see the same picture. He proposes to invest the two "streams" with Socialism. Under this Socialism, the State should become servile to economic ends favoring at first, her own nationals; and then she

interest of international [Socialism] " to bridge the gap from foreign to domestic issues. Then he went on to remind his listeners of a selected group of facts: There was the wave of wage reductions and unemployment; there was retrenchment in social services and reluctance on the part of government to expend moneys on Housing, Education, the Trade Boards Act, and the like. The situation was the work of the " Geddes Ax." It was currently asserted that high taxes necessitated these repressions. This, according to Webb, meant that the poor and ill and the wage earners were to be " made to pay for the war." (This was as bad as his anthropomorphic use of the term " capitalist " noted above.) The Labour Party, he declared:

> . . . must go on asserting that there can be no financial security, indeed no complete restoration of industrial prosperity in this country, so long as one million pounds have to be taken out of the product of labour each work-ing day, before either wages are paid or profit is made, merely to pay interest on the war debt.[86]

The Fabian proposal was restated—the Capital Levy. In 1919, the Fabians entertained a notion that perhaps £100 might be ex-

---

should sally forth to reduce other States and bring them under the yoke of Socialistic imperialism. It is intended that this should be a happy condition of things; and a cartoonist might be inspired to sketch the elfish figure of Webb high on some " fountainhead" dropping a harmless dye into the headwaters of both " streams " to indicate that their beds are preempted for Socialism when the waters of capitalism shall have dried up.

Without an understanding of the above point, it is impossible to see the consistency of the Socialist stand against internationalization of the Ruhr—in 1919 and in 1950. Developing the doctrine of his predecessor, Pius XII points out the danger that the " working class" may make the same " mis-takes " as capital in " withdrawing . . . the management of means of pro-duction from the personal responsibility of the private owner [individual or company] and transferring this management to the responsibility of collective, nameless groups . . . [a situation to which] a Socialist mentality would accommodate itself very easily. . . . The same danger arises when one insists that paid workers in an enterprise should have the right of economic co-management, especially when the exercise of this right depends . . . on organizations managed outside the enterprise." Cf. Text of Papal address to Congresses of Social Studies and Christian Social Union, NCWC News Service release June 5, 1950.

[86] *Fabian Tract 207,* pp. 8 f.

empted from the Capital Levy; now, in 1923, a War Debt Redemption Levy on fortunes above £5,000 was suggested "graduated according to ability to pay." No graduation had been outlined in the 1919 plan. In 1923, the absolute attitude toward a Capital Levy was being modified for political purposes. Yet, such a levy was the "indispensable step to any stable economic order in this country." It is remarkable how succinct and polite, how notably elevated into the realm of the "secondary passions," as Lord Olivier had said in the *Essays* ("Moral"), was this suggestive appeal to the "have-nots" against the "haves," in an ugly era.

The economics in this argument was simply erroneous. Underneath the argument was the assumption of judgment that the wealthy intended to retain their "power over other people's lives" as well as their riches, and so they stood in the way of social reform.[87] The assumption of the right of the working class to appropriate fortunes and eliminate a class was not made here as in the plan of 1919. And before the conclusion of his statement of aims, in 1923, Webb had changed the class-levelling proposal to some proposals for surtaxes. Done in the interest of gradualism, this indicates that socialist-labor's adventure across the boundaries of social and into political life was affecting the Labour Party's principles. A socialist society could expound class-levelling doctrine careless of results; but a political party must have the votes—if it is to win office—of the *rentier* class, which might be induced to accept surtaxes to "pay for the war" but could not be expected to endorse a levy designed to eliminate their class.

Webb proclaimed that in the face of the bankruptcy of the "governing class" which he declared had no programme and no solution for the triple problems of rising trustification, the influence of wealth on the press—a "sinister" dominance—and unemployment, the Labour Party offered the "luxury" of a program consistent with principles. To repeat, his *Labour and the New Social Order* had expounded both programme and principles

---

[87] *Fabian Tract 188*, p. 7. It was admitted that the numbers of the wealthy class hardly changed. Some became richer and the *individuals* making up the group changed.

but the lecturer knew well that within the ranks of those who made up the annual conference there were those who disputed the " inevitability of gradualness "; there were irresponsible persons whose emotions sprang from some particular grievance, dabblers in the theory of violent revolution, strivers for power beyond legal restraints; there were authoritarians who would wipe out local government, and syndicalists who would destroy centralized authority.   The self-interest or class-interest which would tear apart a party made up of workers " of hand and brain " had to be canalized.[88]   There must be a united Labour Party.   Like Karl Marx, writing the " Inaugural Address " for the warring factions in the first International, to supply common ground,[89] Webb found a few common propositions if not principles upon which to base his party as it came face to face with its destiny. Misappropriating a biblical phrase, as Fabians often do, Webb ended the speech which became Tract 207, appealing to " the spirit that giveth life."   He said this was the spirit of *faith* in their proposals, " spirit," in his readers to meet opponents in debate, " spirit . . . in which . . . we give our own lives," " in fellowship " and " for fellowship."   He concluded, " We must remember that the founder of British Socialism was not Karl Marx but Robert Owen, and that Robert Owen preached not class-war but " the ancient doctrine of human brotherhood . . ." and he cited in confirmation William Morris' *Dream of John Ball,* " fellowship is heaven . . . that shall live . . . while many a man's life upon the earth . . . . shall wane."   It is doubtful if listeners touched by this rhapsodic peroration (the lulling repetitious cadences have here been elided) recalled that the argument indicated that " vocational organisation," was made synonymous with " industrial democracy " and indicated not less but more government;[90] that it meant the development of Consumers'

---

[88] There was no word for splinter parties then, save " groups." Each of these splinter potentials will appear further on in connection with the political scene.

[89] Lorwin, *op. cit.,* pp. 36–40.

[90] The confusion of terms here causes the peculiar waywardness which characterized the Fabian philosophical gait up to the Webbs' trip to Russia in 1932.   They habitually confused " government" and " society "; and they saw no problem in a quasi-syndicalism in industry and a State in which

Cooperatives as widely as possible as an integral part of Socialism; that it meant greater power for Trade Councils, and more bureaucracy in Whitehall in connection with mines and rails and especially electricity, " in the name of freedom." To lodge power in councils and bureaus seemingly means no abuse of authority, but Tract 207 prepared for the era of government by decree. Webb made politically adroit reference to the recent violation of *habeas corpus* in the case of conscientious objectors and the Labour Party's fight against Irish deportations. He cleverly pointed out the inadvisability of violence as it was currently demonstrated not in England, where it was just as endemic, but in America (they had read about " goons "), and in Italy, where " property," he said, was " against the popular cause." With no violence, no undue civil restraint, there must also be no lack of research and " inspiring vision." But—he applied the brake of gradualism—there must be on Labour's part no commitment " to new or additional projects, or *to the details of reforms,* if these belong more appropriately to a *stage of greater freedom and less responsibility.*" This was a warning to the ILP not to demand Socialism now. Then came an encouraging word to these ardent fighters: " The whole nation has been imbibing Socialism without realizing it! It is now time for the subconscious to rise into consciousness . . ." in a united spirit.[91] It was clear that on the threshold of power Labour's principal problem was self-unity, and details of reform must await better opportunity. Webb supplied the Party with a mystique.

We have not analyzed *Labour and the New Social Order.* It supplied working ideas to functional documents like the Address of 1923. Webb himself put it to work, flattering the ego of Labour's would-be leaders, anchoring chauvinism (anti-French) in political international idealism which he justified by the promise of international economic ameliorations, preparing British Socialism to assume leadership by invoking " spirit," so as to appeal to

government was not the creature of Society but Society itself. The Cooperative means social action at the level of economic interest of the community. That the monolithic, planning State could tolerate independent cooperatives is impossible. They batten in the margins of Capitalism or of industrial democracy, unless the latter is politicized.

[91] Webb, *Fabian Tract 207,* p. 12. Italics are inserted.

the invidious (with a warning to move slowly). "Spirit" he defined as infused Socialism, something needed to fuse its heterogeneous sections and to make it acceptable to the masses, some of whom were hysterical after the war and prone to dabble in spiritism;[92] some again were frustrated by Manchester Economics and edging toward syndicalism; and the rest, mentally parched by Positivism, were preparing political measures to produce dreams of great socio-economic developments on the international level. "It calls for warmth in politics," Webb said, "for none of the cynicism that saps the life of leisure." The "still undeveloped Science of Society" must be developed by research and dissemination of all the science that exists.[93] No Labour Party, the great Fabian asserted, can govern save with the best Political Science of its time; it cannot of its nature be plutocratic and use pretended solutions of social problems merely to further its political triumph—referring to liberal Tories; nor autocratic and force the adoption of its whims—referring to the fanatical Socialists. Unchanging in policy, it must perpetually develop finer measures as means to Labour's ends, those of democratic cooperation, production unlimited by price and profit, equality in education. "If Law is the Mother of Freedom, Science, to the Labour Party, must be the Parent of Law."[94] There can be no doubt that Mr. Webb knew full well, as his hearers did not, that the "transition" during which "Science" ruled before its offspring, Law, could come to power and produce Freedom, would be long and would be accompanied by eclipse of economic liberty.

---

[92] Cf. Hobhouse, *op. cit.*, p. 280. Pelmanism also was advertised in the *NS*, notably by L'Estrange Malone. (*NS*, 13, *passim*.) Mrs. Hobhouse was Beatrice Webb's sister. She inspired the latter to devote attention to prison reforms because of the sad experience of conscientious objectors during the war.

[93] There should be no misgivings regarding the controls which the science of society would produce. A check on the sociological executive was to be found in the political legislative. This might be checkmated by the TUC, but all would be unified, all checkmates cancelled out, in *the Party* which would be Socialist, comprising *all* who labor by hand or brain.

[94] The idea of social amelioration by legislative measures, *i.e.*, "progress" through "telic" action, was very old by this date among American sociologists. Cf. H. W. Schneider, *History of American Philosophy* (New York: Columbia University Press, 1946).

The events of 1931 would underscore the meaning of " transition." But in 1923, it satisfied an unhappy mass of voters to hear of science, law and freedom.[95]

D. Penetration into High Economics and The Lowly Cooperatives

" Workers by brain " were drawn into the Labour Party about the same time that a great myth arose, the myth that research, especially the Webbs' (and Dalton's) research, produced an infallible guide to " Law " created by " Science." The Webbs had adopted Veblen's denigration of the "leisure classes "; and in the early 1920's they met and mingled with the prophets of the new economics spontaneously generating in a London where Marx was too faintly praised to be condemned.

So it came about that the penetration of the area co-opted by Cooperation signalized the permeation of economics by utilizing the field occupied by Keynesian liberal economics. A. C. Pigou reviewed in the *Economic Journal, The Consumer Co-Operative Movement,* by Sidney and Beatrice Webb, March, 1922.[96] Even though he probably did not intend to be so, Professor Pigou was devastating. He revealed an immense gap in the philosophy of Webbism although he made obeisance dutifully toward the kiosk of secular Socialism in which the image of the Webbs was enshrined.[97]

---

[95] A study of the disappearance of the numerous splinter Socialist societies, seen in a comparison of, for example, the *LYB,* 1916, with that of 1931, would supply a typical example of Fabian penetration and amalgamation.

[96] A. C. Pigou, " Mr. and Mrs. Webb on Consumers' Co-operation," *The Economic Journal,* XXXII (March, 1922), 53–57. The list of editors and contributors to this organ of the Royal Economics Society is at least one-third Fabian. The book was to serve to warp cooperatives into the Labour Party. The review serves to illustrate the more real warping in of contemporary economists while it gives a brief picture of the planned institution which even the Webbs must have thought Utopian but calculated to snare the cooperative movement (Owenism) into the Labour Party. The method here is a little complicated but necessary for brevity: (1) Pigou's review is very serviceable to picture the Soviet machinery visible under the Webbs' prose; (2) it is criticized as it is reported to show penetration and important effects of the presence of Fabianism in fields where economics and politics meet.

[97] This figure of speech is not overdrawn. It recalls the Wellsian Samurai

Pigou spoke of the Webbs' service to social science which, he remarked, economists even of opposing schools respected, at the very moment in which he revealed an unbridgeable chasm between the work and objective truth or science: Clear arrangement, lucid narrative, mastery of detail, he commends—then, boldness of generalization. Should not boldness of generalization be replaced in this sequence by " careful interpretation of data " if science is to emerge from the use of method? This is the chasm; and it is a description of the method of the great Fabians—data piled upon data critically evaluated, followed by bold generalizations having scant relation to the data.[98] There is another gap between the data attached to its appended conclusions and the real value of the work: " It is not necessary to agree with the author's conclusions or analyses [and Pigou does not] in order to recognize the high service that they have rendered, and are still rendering to social science." Certainly, it can be agreed that science in its narrow sense is served by accumulated and categorized data. But the fallacious implication here is that " social science " gains from work in which the conclusions and analyses are not warranted by the data—something which is a philosophical absurdity unless social science is itself a misnomer for a method which allows its adherents to proceed by the seven league boots of Spencer and ignore his " dropped stitches." [99] (Both figures are those of James McCosh concerning Spencer who was Beatrice's only philosophical tutor.)

Without categorizing, Pigou revealed three tendencies in the Webbs' thought moving toward sovietism: 1) Their absolute

and Wallas' admiring conception of the Japanese attitude of looking to military generals for " that unbought effort of the mind by which alone man becomes at once the servant and the master of nature." Cf. G. Wallas, *Human Nature in Politics,* Third Edition (New York: A. Knopf, 1921), p. 214.

[98] Cf. Margaret Cole, *Growing Up Into Revolution,* pp. 156–166, where she notes the deception of those who steered her visitation of U.S.S.R., marks the sordid features of communized life of which she disapproves, then launches into the boldest generalizations, all commendatory. Objectivity having been simulated to perfection, the gap between the conclusion and the data is unnoticeable.

[99] Cf. James McCosh, *Herbert Spencer's Philosophy as Culminated in His Ethics* (New York: Scribner's, 1885), p. 19.

distinction between production for use and production for profit which Pigou considered " plausible " but " in the main illusory," and which conditioned their omission of the consumers' cooperatives of Irish and Continental farmers from their study; 2) their contradictions about democracy—they find that constitutionally the cooperative movement grows more democratic because admission of large numbers of persons is not precluded by any shareholding but is favored by individual capacity, *i.e.,* capacity got from purchasing, and they evince belief that complete democracy of ownership and control is becoming possible at the same time that they praise the condition whereby permanent salaried officers replace elected committeemen. Then they find growing between this hired executive and the yeasty growth of numbers of cooperators, " a characteristic organ of British political democracy, the representative assembly," [100] at a place intermediate between the electorate and the executive.[101] They find it desirable that the Cooperative Union which summons and manages the Cooperative Congresses should become " explicitly a federation of consumers' societies only, instead of embracing, as it now does, association of workers organized as producers," a possible reference to their basic principle that Trade Unions should separate from consumers' societies. Pigou, on the other hand, holds that consumers' associations should frankly ally themselves with producers' organizations, these " weak but socially valuable forms of work people's effort."

All these dichotomies—of profit from its social reference, of masses from elective executives, of producers' from consumers' organizations—would not make a soviet system of thought without being fitted into the apparatus which the Webbs envisioned. This apparatus Pigou described without giving his opinion of it: They fix the " two-fold form of voluntary association " (cooperative commonwealth) together with the " obligatory association of citizens " (Pigou thinks this means Local Government; it could

---

[100] The history of American independence shows that for this assembly to acquire democratic control, or control for the democracy, may take a revolution.

[101] In Soviet history, this " assembly " stage is one upon which the party line is delivered from executive to masses, because of the ubiquitous party.

mean State) into "organic connection" (this cannot mean con-
tiguity or juxtaposition but functional potentiality), with the
"equally ubiquitous organisation of the producers by hand or by
brain." (Pigou thinks this means "Trade Unions and Professional Associations"; it must mean the Party, otherwise it could
not be singular and "ubiquitous"; and besides, in the Webbs'
apparatus the people are all in one or the other of the Cooperative
sectors already.) The relationship which the Webbs assign to
these three constructs is not that of free associations of cooperators subordinated along with their local civil authority to the State
whose surveillance is properly limited, but they envision a mesh-
ing of cooperative society and civic order under the Party through
its "organic connection." It is the Party which mobilizes the
"producers by hand and by brain" and activates the whole
through the civil or "involuntary association" (local commissar)
intergeared with the twinned but separated "voluntary association" represented in "assembly"—or in two assemblies.
The Webbs in modest understatement said that perhaps in this
constitution was to be found the obliteration of Capitalism at
last. They hid an intermediate step in the formula: This set-up
was to "contribute *the greater part* of the New Social Order that
is destined very largely to supersede the present Capitalistic system." [102] In that intermediate step was the great deception for,
as Shaw pointed out, the Fabians' Socialism was destined never to
produce real or ultimate Socialism, and he used the figure of
parallel lines which seemed to meet but never should. [103]

Professor Pigou pointed out some elementary assumptions with
which he found himself in disagreement with the authors of *The
Consumers' Co-operative Movement*. In the gap between this
body of assumptions and reality, possibly, may be discovered the
meaning of the otherwise silly words "very largely" in the above

---

[102] We have seen in another place how Edward Pease noted the anthro-
pomorphousness of the Webbs' criteriology and their propagandistic tendency.
The writer was about to remark upon the integrity of purpose thus evinced
in Pease but recalled that it was he who, to Shaw's chagrin, "roped in" the
Trade Unions to get their money in order to elect Fabians to Parliament.

[103] Cf. Shaw, "Postscript" to *Fabian Essays,* Jubilee Edition (London:
Allen and Unwin, 1948), p. 222. Lenin and Stalin admitted postponing *real*
Communism.

quotation. There is the hidden step in the formula. There were four main assumptions: 1) The possibility of finding adequate capital under voluntary cooperation where there is large risk; 2) the assumption that there is no danger that the State may inhibit experiment; 3) the assumption that increased production from cooperation could result without the existence of a " fringe of private producers upon whom the variable part of the demand could be thrown "; and 4) the assumption that all economists then conceded that Capitalists abstract in the form of rent all but the worst of the instruments of production. Pigou also found highly debatable their conclusion that the highest possible amount of the highest possible development of individual personality is the only reason for the effort to create ideal socio-economic constructs and for their mesh-geared ordination—" this machinery." But he conceded the usefulness of exposing the nature of cooperation, i.e., their " practical intention," and the value of their well-timed " emphasis," whatever that means. The best that could have been said was that the work served an exploratory aim; the worst, that it propagandized Soviet socio-political machinery and irresponsibly left to fate the human materials which did not fit into the three-gear mechanism, in which the State as well as Capitalism has ceased to exist. Pigou represents the liberal mind which, for the sake of the by-products, tolerated both an anthropomorphic interpretation of life and propaganda for a Socialistic order. It was the Fabians' best service to the cause of British Socialism that they were well received in highly respectable circles such as the *Economic Journal* served.

The Party secured anchorage in lofty and lowly organization, in wide sympathies with workers and narrow schools of indoctrination. That it was ready as a party to take its place in the old two-party field was due to the work of the Fabians. That it was, unlike a real political party, a Socialist party, based upon a secular creed, put a burden of anomalism upon the Labour Party which destroyed its political character. The ensuing struggle to keep faith with its plighted membership brings this out.

CHAPTER III

THE FABIAN LEADERSHIP OF LABOUR IN OPPOSITION, 1922

A. Some Underlying Considerations

The most important fact about the Government of 1922 is that it produced the election of 1923 which gave the forces called " Labour " political experience and served to release the impasse in Europe. The event synchronized with the European dynamic in such a way as to raise doubt that it was merely fortuitous that England had a Labour Government during nine months of 1924. The elected Tory regime of 1922 was balked by Opposition which was a new thing, " Labour," and not a mere second party in basic agreement but at odds on detail; this new Party had an ideological core which faced the problems of trade with post Versailles Europe from a viewpoint which might be called " international." This special difference between " Labour " and any other merely political party was something not easily seen, since the Opposition was controlled from within by the Asquith Liberals. Nevertheless, as Tories contemplated the Opposition they discerned in it two elements at work and interacting upon each other, the intelligentsia of the Labour Party and the working men.

Labour elements divided in another way, too: Fabian Socialism *vs* Clydeside Socialism; but this segmentation was criss-crossed by Fabians found on both sides wherever ILP (a Socialist society and not properly a party) extended itself. The criss-cross was the means of ILP's demise, as the sequel shows. To politicians seeing from the Tory viewpoint, and taking note of the Asquith dilemma, it was becoming clear as 1923 dawned that Fabian permeation was constructing a " Party " out of incongruous parts, something which presented the aspect of a real political party at home, and which would be acceptable to the Left abroad, even as the harbinger of such tidings as the Dawes plan, upon which Fabians, especially those whose heads were in the Keynesian

107

clouds of the Royal Economic Society, agreed along with the Tories.

In presenting the following picture of Labour in Opposition it is intended to point out the two extremes in the Party, Fabian Socialism and Clydeside Socialism and in between the ILP which Fabianism permeated and liquidated, first as a political then even as a Socialist society, while it tamed the Clydesiders who would have been what they were regardless of being Socialists or of voting Labour. These were persons who accepted the promise if not the discipline which the rising Labour Party offered through Fabian spokesmen. They were to express their disappointment more vocally than other disappointed persons. They were not subdued in 1924, nor in 1931. A good bit of detail follows regarding differences in the Labour Party and is given in order to show the impression a Tory Government received. At the end of this period comes a mysterious episode; Baldwin precipitated an election no one wanted and one of which Labour did not care to accept the results. If the decision so to proceed came to Baldwin from the facts of the condition and ideological burden of Labour, that condition and ideological burden is indicated in the following presentation. We should see, as the Bonar Law-Baldwin Ministry saw, the Fabians emerging to articulate the Party, revise the type of men holding offices, mark out the lines of leadership of opposition, and reach out to discipline the ideological pursuits; while they themselves were approaching a brand of Socialism acceptable to " respectable " persons and fully " rescued from the barricades." [1] Regardless of its " acceptability," even of its nearness to a Christian idea in some points of its philosophy, Fabians insisted on the name of Socialism for their " spirit." [2]

---

[1] Cf. Shaw, " Postscript " in *Fabian Essays,* Jubilee Edition, p. 207.

[2] There stood a direct rejection of the use of the terms Socialist and " social democracy " in Pope Leo's *Graves de Communi* of 1901 and it was to be reiterated while describing this apparent " acceptability " by Pius XI's *Quadragesimo Anno* in 1931. Cf. *Christian Democracy* (New York: Paulist Press, 1941), p. 6, and *On Reconstructing the Social Order* (Washington, D. C.: NCWC, 1942), p. 40. When Socialism has refined its definition of itself to the point where between Socialism and Christianity there lies only the difference of the philosophic concept regarding the relation of men to society, having forsworn the class-war and the denial of the right to own

B. MacDonald Accepted: Clydesiders Placed Under Tutelage

It is necessary to show how Fabians were constrained to take MacDonald for leader. We see them suggesting realignments of parties—then in coalition—and trying to get rid of the " tired " leadership of trade unionists. Fabian determination met its match in the Glasgow and Clydeside backers of MacDonald; but eventually Fabianism prevailed by assuming the direction of MacDonald. In the ensuing section are noted, first, the circumstances surrounding the selection of Ramsay MacDonald as leader; second, the uneasiness which MacDonald's supporters caused Fabians; third, the opposition within the Opposition, made up of characters quite different from typical English socialists. Some differences between Fabians and Clydesiders lay in the area of religious and economic ideals. The Clydeside socialists represented a type destined for oblivion under the sway of Fabian socialism, but the uneasiness they created was to be an important factor in the future collapse of Labour. It is as important to distinguish between Fabian socialism and Clydeside socialism as to distinguish between Fabianism and continental Christian socialism, or between Fabianism and Communism. Fabianism insists upon its own view of " social democracy." (The word " insist " recurs in their literature.)

To make sure all those who were designated " Labour " came under their aegis, the Fabian intellectual leadership not only had to extract the Labour Party from coalition but had to assert its predominance over the rival socialist society, ILP, which had made Labour's history since 1893. In ILP were mixed many socialists who were also Fabians, and a group of working men and skilled craftsmen from the Beardmore works on the Clyde River in Scotland. The latter boasted of MacDonald's fellowship and insisted on his claim to leadership.

First of all, seeking to differentiate the old parties, the *New Statesman* [3] explained the coalition's longevity with a rhetorical

---

property, then, said the Pope, let Socialists become Christians; let not Christians become Socialists.

[3] *NS,* 20 (October 14, 1922), 33.

question: " Why should the panic stricken puppets in Parliament hasten their return to political oblivion?" Editorially, the *NS* encouraged party differentiation: " Destroy parties and you get the profoundly irresponsible legislature we have at present." This was a recital of political science, made only for pragmatic purposes; it was not indicative of the actual Fabian dilemma—its inherent drive toward an Order while it sought to make a Party. The *NS* was not sure that an election was then in the making; but it pointed out to all that the ground-swell of Labour was detectable, that " tired " Labourites should be replaced, and that its choice for leader was Henderson. The next issue [4] noted the resignation of this " worst of all possible governments " and the inevitability of a general election, prophesying that no political party would achieve a majority. Coalition, the *NS* declared, had led to futility but " coalescence " would be necessary in the new Parliament. It was already foreseen that a Lab-Lib Government must procure Clydeside cooperation. In the next Parliament Labour would be stronger; its defeated " intellectuals "—" a deplorable term "—would be elected. But, " its rank and file will still consist . . . of overworked Trade Union officials, [possessed nonetheless of] as much real ability as any other party in the house." Actually this term " intellectual " was not obnoxious to Fabians and the rating of ability of Trade Union leaders was lowered in Socialists' regard by this estimate. To be as able as any other party was not, in Fabian estimation, to be very able. The term " overworked " applied equally to Fabians, yet their present exercise was but preparing them to assume charge in Parliament. The leadership, according to the *NS*, should be accorded Mr. Arthur Henderson, the former Wesleyan Minister, now the party builder, a Fabian and internationalist. Even Lloyd George, *NS* recalled, had acknowledged Henderson's prestige by quoting him on reparations. The Prime Minister's " inimitable impudence " in making use of Henderson's hedged words— " restitution for *devastation* and wrong doing *outside legal warfare*" (italics inserted)—was cleverly used by the *NS* to point up its own candidate for Party and Opposition leadership [5] while the

---

[4] *NS*, 20 (October 21, 1922), 61.
[5] *NS*, 19 (June 3, 1922), 224.

particular citation served to forecast and smooth over a difference of opinion on reparations in Labour's ranks. Henderson and MacDonald differed openly on this point. But now Henderson failed of re-election to Parliament, so the Fabian hope to have Clynes replaced by Henderson was deferred. With congratulations to the Party along with the reminder that the business of Opposition was opposing, the *NS* accepted the handsome ILP-backed MacDonald, whose opponent had been the unprepossessing Mr. Clynes [6] who had headed the Party in the years of Mac-Donald's eclipse as a pacifist. Forthwith *NS* declared the House of Commons had been " dead," dead for eight years. The challenging editor expected signs of life to emanate from the Labour leadership. This was but making the best of things, for Fabians did not like MacDonald personally—even though, apart from his pacifism, he was then a Fabian in all but membership in the society. The undesirable feature for the *NS* editor lay in the fact that at the time McDonald's socialism was in apparent harmony with that of Glasgow; also in that the ILP attachment to him was deeply sentimental.

Anyone reading *NS* or *Fabian News* must have received a marked impression that the Labour leadership was ill at ease, and was fighting an inner force. The pressing for a real Opposition represented, of course, the beginning of a new urgency for the reviving of independent activity, not of Labour members of Parliament indeed, but of the Labour Party in Parliament. There was little place for the free play of individual talents. Save in the outstanding cases of Henry Slesser, Josiah Wedgwood, and Lord Mamhead,[7] there must be no solo work; and Glasgow had a solo group. As matters had stood since 1903 the Cabinet was a

---

[6] *NS*, 20 (November 25, 1922), 221. It is fairly certain Baldwin and Bonar Law were aware of the Labour ground-swell. It was predictable that the head of the first war coalition, Asquith, would lead his liberals in support rather of Labour than of conservative elements. One real need of the country was the reestablishing of a balanced and steady trade with Europe. Fabians who were closer to these above-named leaders than Clydesiders saw that MacDonald's was the character most acceptable to them. Henderson always had trouble getting himself elected. Politicians of both sides took into consideration personality, appearance, and sentiment.

[7] Cf. Slesser, *op. cit.*, 143–153.

dictatorship which obtained from the Party in Parliament ratification of its actions. For Labour to form such a cabinet there was as yet no unanimity as to leaders; neither was there yet a Party agreed upon Socialism. Not only did the Clydesiders dissent from the Party, the leaders in the political branch dissented from each other, as a glance at the state of affairs between MacDonald and Snowden shows.

The conflict of personalities between MacDonald and Snowden made the ascendency of the former politically reasonable. Clydesider David Kirkwood describes in *My Life of Revolt* [8] the tension between Mr. MacDonald and Mr. Snowden, while he shows in every line the insistence of the Scottish Socialists upon " their man's " primacy in Labour politics. Both were then members of ILP although they were not on speaking terms with each other. MacDonald was more Fabian than Snowden, who nevertheless was a closer friend to the Webbs and also to the Buxton, Scurr, and Cripps families. MacDonald was in all but name and privilege a peer. This comes out in the description of his relations with the sardonic Snowden. Kirkwood had seen the " incorruptible Democrat " who was Snowden (later a viscount) behave with silent animosity toward his leader, one who remained a commoner to the end, although he was one whom peers considered " one of us." Kirkwood who recorded the denouement of their unhappy alliance, in 1932, saw that both these leaders had a wider outlook than most of the Party leaders or any of the Trade Union

---

[8] David Kirkwood, M.P., J.P., *My Life of Revolt* (London: Harrap and Company, 1935), p. 218. Reluctantly, the ILP, that of Scotland especially, had laid aside " pure socialism " for political action; but it had kept its radical objectives, which became well illustrated in Kirkwood's life. These objectives were the immediate and particular interests of Glasgow and the Clyde men. These men, born in the ship and munitions building towns and bred to the machines, were perfectionists as engineers, and fundamentalists as to human rights. They insisted upon the recognition of free manhood in each laborer, and were adamant in the pursuit of independent and frugal economic security for their families—not for a " proletariat." An examination of Kirkwood's principles shows they believed in " vocational " ordering and collaboration of capital and labor at the shop level. The British Trade Unions, which they distrusted, exemplified a class-strata where the workers were bound together by a single interest, the economic, and now were becoming politicized under Fabian guidance.

politicians; also, that within both minds Trade Union sensibilities and ILP principles clashed. Yet the fervent Clydesider never disputed the right of MacDonald to political ascendency or the right of Snowden to leadership in finance.

It was a quasi-religious attitude which induced Clydesiders' adherence to MacDonald and acceptance of Snowden. They were the Christian Socialists of Great Britain. MacDonald's was a quasi-religious Socialism and he had a talent for political oratory which he often exercised in a pulpit. Snowden was likewise a man of evangelical Socialist convictions, which he had developed while working in temperance societies. He retained throughout his life a candid detestation of Trade Unionism.[9] ILP did not hold this against him—a significant point. (In 1929 it was principally the trade unions who backed MacDonald.) While MacDonald was an ex-member of the Fabian Society,[10] Snowden was not very active in it after the war—owing to his poor health—but he expressed admiration for the Society and presided as chairman at lectures under their auspices.[11] His monetary principles, Fabian in every characteristic, were based on the idea that wealth was expropriation and he professed to believe that taxes should be imposed for " reform "; but his later budgets were to be such that they might have been written by members of the Royal Economics Society,[12] a point in which again he represented the Fabian rather than the Clydeside-ILP attitude. In most respects Snowden should have been the chosen leader; save for his terseness of speech and impatience with folly he might have been. In any case, he did not have the European contacts which Henderson and MacDonald enjoyed.

It was Philip Snowden who later revealed that a bargain had been made between MacDonald and Henderson. When the former should become Chairman of the Parliamentary Labour

---

[9] Cf. Snowden, *Autobiography,* I (London: Nicholson and Watson, 1934), p. 534. Snowden traces the rise of the socialistic Labour Party to the old temperance societies.

[10] Mrs. Webb for one thought it well; for he could act better in a larger sphere. Cf. *Our Partnership,* pp. 188 and 192 f.

[11] *FN*, XXXIV:2 (February, 1923).

[12] Cf. Snowden, *Labour and National Finance* (London: Leonard Parsons, 1920).

Party, the latter would become Secretary of the Party outside Parliament, the post carrying with it the Secretaryship of the International.[13] This was so much more important to Fabians fighting the Third International for a world ascendency of Social Democracy that acceptance of MacDonald as Parliamentary leader was but a small sacrifice. Besides, the Webbs saw in MacDonald the natural figurehead.

Glasgow-born Mary Agnes Hamilton, who wrote an adulatory biography of MacDonald in 1929, considers that it was Henderson who reconstituted the leadership of MacDonald. Henderson recognized the need to free MacDonald's name from the obloquy his pacifism had earned. Thus also he would bring the men of Clyde into the Party orbit. These had soured toward Henderson when he had come to Glasgow with Lloyd George to enforce the Munitions Act, an occasion when he had exhibited no real grasp of their problems. Henderson, although he warned the Clydesiders that they would regret selecting MacDonald as leader, himself set an example of great loyalty. He repudiated MacDonald only when he lay dying, in 1935. Mrs. Hamilton once heard him say he would have been willing to play second fiddle to MacDonald all his life. Although ILP Kirkwood was even then disgusted with the fact that MacDonald, after the war, had harangued Soldiers-Sailors-and-Workmen's Councils in a manner to out-Bolshevik the Bolsheviks, he conceded that as of 1922 " we were MacDonald's men." The "Bolshevik" ferment passed away, but it is very possible that Henderson foresaw the break up of the Party or that MacDonald threatened it if he were not chosen leader. Once chosen, MacDonald was gallantly supported by the *NS*.

In the same week that it accepted MacDonald with such grace as it could muster, the *NS* brought a very valuable analysis of the political situation to its readers, thereby providing Tory and Liberal readers with a good picture of the political field Labour sought to invest. It also accounted succinctly for the selection of MacDonald as leader of the Opposition: [14] It was demanded by ILP. It was a fact that Labour had succeeded best where its candidates had had the most clear-cut policy, and that was in ILP

---

[13] Cf. Snowden, *An Autobiography,* I, p. 220.
[14] *NS,* 20 (November, 1923), 222.

strongholds. The *NS* might have added that these were in industrial sections economically depressed and politically problematical.
It would not have been wise to point out the work of Fabians like
Ben Tillett and Ben Turner, Pethick-Lawrence or the Scurrs, the
Clarion writers, and all the " Northern " Fabians in ILP who
spoke for this " clear-cut policy." The ILP wanted Scotsman
MacDonald as a leader, the *NS* stated, not Clynes who had not of
late been so active as MacDonald in the ILP. Labour members
would never, said the *NS*, have elected MacDonald head of the
Party in place of Clynes except for the fact that the ILP demanded recognition on account of its election successes.

The *NS*, having consented to reject a " tired " Trade Unionist
in favor of an ILP Socialist, now had to divest the latter of his
ILP-ism. The Scottish ILP-ers appreciated the consistency with
Socialist principles which MacDonald's pacifism had demonstrated. Now *NS* would wipe out this record: " The election
showed that the *chasse aux renards* is over. The pacifists have
come back to Parliament, and their leader is the leader of the
Opposition." The motivation for the use of the near-epithet
" pacifist " is discernible. It served as a warning to ILP. Pacifism was unpopular and Fabians had a good record for war
service. It is patent that the Fabians, knowing their history, expected recalcitrance from the ILP men of Glasgow who had
shown they were independent thinkers. Equally important was
their already acknowledged success in elections. The only Clydesider who was not elected, Rosslyn Mitchell, who later defeated
Asquith at Paisley, was but narrowly defeated by Bonar Law in
central Glasgow. To dub them " pacifist," as the *NS* did, was to
seek to induce their aspiring to a more popular mode of behaviour.
Pease, writing in February 1922, in *FN*, said:

> The anti-militarism of the Socialist International
> Congress has never rung quite true. It was based on
> the thoroughly unsound contention that all modern wars
> have been instigated by capitalists with a view to profit.[15]

Obviously bringing the ILP into line, Pease said that the public

---

[15] E.R.P. (reviewer), " J. Keir Hardie: A Biography by William Stewart,"
FN, XXXIII:2 (February, 1922).

had come to think of ILP as pacifist first and Socialist secondarily. It is easily seen that Fabians had much to do if they were to rectify Socialist thinking on international relations, and they were beginning on the ILP. Thus, by a clever use of what is today called " smear " technique, the *NS,* which professed to desire that people would not take ILP members for wicked pacifists, intended by calling attention to the record to place the Clydesiders under tutelage. Tutelage was not confined to the group. Beginning with the campaign of 1922, MacDonald had for amanuensis one of the most perfectly cast Fabians, Herbert Morrison, and the story of the young Morrison's service to MacDonald in campaigns and policy making has never been written. It forms the direct link with the Fabian Society.[16]

So Clydesiders elected MacDonald as leader of the Parliamentary Labour Party and the Opposition. Yet followers of Snowden and the Trade Union men had stood by Clynes; and social relations among divisions of the Labour Party were markedly antagonistic. It was not merely a token of self-sacrificing fidelity that Clynes, replacing the absent MacDonald, presided at the Party's night rally following the caucus. MacDonald had appeared distinctly in ill-health before the balloting; but he rallied remarkably and threw off every appearance of depression immediately he was chosen. No one reports ill-health as the reason for his nonappearance. Some of his Scotch supporters who professed great simplicity of life and evaded social contacts were absent. His absence was conspicuous but eloquent of his dilemma: His more ardent supporters would be absent; his temporarily silent critics would be in charge of proceedings. He must in future placate the sedate and wise and not alienate his intractable friends. Kirkwood's group would have been unbearably uncomfortable with Fabians managing them.[17] In any case, Clynes could pull more groups together by a common denominator than MacDonald; the " Little Piecer " could include in his follow-

[16] Cf. Hamilton, *Henderson,* pp. 200, 262, 266.

[17] Ellen Terry had been invited by Shaw to come to London where she would be " rich with Mrs. Webb to arrange you!" Cf. Hamilton, *Sidney and Beatrice Webb,* p. 267. Mrs. Webb was managing M.P.'s wives and others in her Half-Circle Clubs which were designed to inculcate Society manners. *Ibid.,* p. 268.

ing the Fabian ILP section as well as the trade unionists; and even though London Fabians thought him inept, they respected him. MacDonald stayed away; yet he was no longer an ILP man, even though they did not denounce him formally until 1928. Herbert Morrison who wrote his election speeches and election-eered at his elbow had already built a bridge for him out of Soldier-and-Worker-Councils to a Socialism acceptable to Fabians.

From a classification of Labour members of Parliament, we see the narrow crevasses of Party sectionalism which MacDonald's Government would one day fail to bridge. Battle lines were drawn in Parliament where there were ten Fabians; some of them ILP, also. These, with their backs to the obstreperous Clyde-siders, who called themselves ILP and were counted as " Labour," seemed to fear they were associated with Communists; whereas only a few, like Gallacher, were really " Bolsheviks." The strategy of the intellectual Party management was to draw as many ILP-ers toward their point of view as possible. As if for a game of " dare-base " the teams separated. The Fabian managers had already taken the first " prisoner," MacDonald.

To examine the Fabian-managed side: The Fabians were found among the one hundred and forty-two new members (there had been only seventy-eight Labour members in the last Parliament) making up a Labour Party in Commons, which also included four Cooperators and four converted Liberals. Among the two dozen new Labourites, these last converts to Labour along with six pacifists, now reappearing, had been Members before the war. This meant heightened convictions, less resistant radicalism, and more parliamentary skill at the Party's service. There was a size-able group of forty-seven miners, of whom only two were Liberals. There were thirty-two members of ILP claiming ad-herents in the political hinterlands. This meant there were votes to be gained by skillful handling. Metal workers and a few from the less skilled workers were to be found. The " intellectual " section (we use the quotation marks as the *NS* did) had " grown considerably "; professional men included

> . . . three K.C.'s, two doctors, two ministers of religion, three professors, and six or so other teachers. At least four of the Labour members are employers.

(Of course, the *NS* did not list Fabians as such.) Debating ability was ample. The Fabian editor saw a challenge in the presence of so many ILP members and his observation served as a warning against divisiveness; for he recalled in monitory wise the "Parliamentary incapacity" of the Labour group in the former Parliament, and remarked that the few "intellectuals" formed a well-knit and experienced group, each member of which had a wide following. He was suggesting something which we examine here more specifically—the picture of the intelligentsia (Fabian) against the rest, and their striving to bring the rest under Party discipline. Early Fabian interest in medical, administrative, journalistic, educational, industrial, military, agricultural, ethical, and organizational lines was represented by these Fabians in Parliament. Only one of the Fabian M.P.'s was not in the current *Who's Who*, D. Adams. As Councillor, he had made a study of the medical profession or at least had made a speech upon its relationship to rate-paying hospitals.[18] Clement Attlee, then Mayor of Stepney, was a lecturer in social science at the London School of Economics. He had joined the Fabians and the ILP in 1908, and was now to be parliamentary private secretary to MacDonald. Noel-Buxton, son of Sir Thomas F. Buxton, third Baronet, had travelled with his brother (C. R. Buxton, who married a daughter of Sir Gladwyn Jebb, was later a Fabian and an M.P., also) into the Far East and Russia, and had changed from Liberal to Labour Party in his 1910–1918 term in Parliament. William Graham, a Scot, had been in Parliament also since 1918. An economist-journalist, student of forensic medicine and administrative law, he had taught WEA classes. He was destined to do yeoman service in the treasury department. Arthur Greenwood, also an economist and WEA lecturer, was secretary to the Labour Party Advisory Committee (1920–1921) and a member of the "Whitley Committee." George Lansbury, editor of the *Daily Herald,* a national Labour paper, was a member of ILP, had worked on Poor Law reform ("signed the Minority Report" was a badge of honour), had served on the LCC.[19] Henry Snell, a son

---

[18] *FN,* XXXIII :9 (September, 1922).
[19] One of his daughters was Mrs. Ernest Thurtle. Thurtle had been in Parliament before, was not re-elected in 1922, but came back in 1929. His

of agricultural workers, had gone to Parliament in 1920, and had been in LCC since 1919. He was a member of the Executive Committee of both the Labour Party and Fabian Society and a prime mover in American as well as British Ethical Societies.[20] James Stewart was a Glasgow Town Councillor, the only one who was both Clydesider and Fabian. He was identified as a barber and in his capacity of Councillor, was a " Tribune of the People." Ben Tillett, ILP as well as Fabian, had been instrumental in amalgamating Dock, Wharf, and Riverside unions with the General Workers' Union of Great Britain and Ireland; later, with the Transport workers. He had strong views on the Ruhr question and on Russia. He had lately advocated internationalizing the Ruhr when the Party's policy was averse to it; and the *NS* had then insisted that labor spokesmen's " reports," if they involved the Party, should be edited.[21] He was secretary of the Political and International Departments of the Union. The " International Department " was probably the reason for his being a Fabian. He had to belong to a socialist society in order to be admitted to the Labour and Socialist International. Otherwise he was hardly one with whom an Aylmer Maude, a Percival Chubb, a St. John Ervine, or a Bertrand Russell associated. A member of LCC, he was the historian of Dock and Transport workers movements. Sidney Webb,[22] having been elected from a coal mining district where he had campaigned with " research " for implement by getting out a brochure on the story of coal, was by this time Lecturer (honorary) in Political Economy at the City of London College and at the Working Men's College, also Professor (honorary) of Public Administration in the London School of Economics, and an unpaid member of the Faculty and Board of

---

chief interest was " Military discipline and Democracy." And he was London agent for *The Nation* (U.S.).

[20] " Recreations: none," in *Who's Who,* indicates much. A stern puritanism followed many of these English Socialists out of the non-conformist chapels which they abandoned. Cf. Lord Henry Snell, *Men, Movements and Myself* (London: J. M. Dent and Sons, 1936), especially " Religion: Doubts and Appreciation," pp. 126–135. Snell professed atheism.

[21] Cf. *NS,* 20 (April 21, 1923), 33.

[22] Cole once said, " The worst of Webb is that he is permanent." Camille Huysmans called him " L'eminence grise." Cf. Beatrice Webb, *Our Partnership* (London: Longmans Green and Company, 1948), p. 7.

Studies in Economics of London University. He had served up to 1921 on the Central Committee on the Profiteering Act. Webb, inaudible when he read a speech, was highly articulate on many issues. He had already built his monument in better than bronze in London town. Mrs. Hamilton writes of

> . . . the creation of that great network of civic services in London, which are now taken for granted by Londoners, few of whom realize how much of their daily comfort and convenience they owe to him, how much of the opportunities available to their children.[23]

Henderson and other prominent Labourites who had been defeated in the general election won in by-elections and returned to Parliament.

With this leadership, Fabianism possessed inner contacts with the Independent Labour Party, a voice in the Trade Unions Council (Tillett), and a mouthpiece in the Workingmen's Educational Association; and it piped back into the Parilamentary Labour Party the ideas given fluency in the London School of Economics. Besides the Parliamentary foothold, Fabians of Sidney Webb's Progressive Party had a special place in the government of London. This made for greater prestige for those in Parliament and increased the inferior feeling induced in Clydesiders. Even ILP Lansbury attested that the Webbs always gave the impression no one could possibly be as wise as they appeared to be. Fabians had long been prominent on the LCC, *e.g.*, Alderman A. E. Davies, Herbert Morrison, H. Snell. In April, 1922, a " disappointing " election in London saw only the Fabians Susan Lawrence and H. Snell of the Labour Party, and S. D. Headlams and W. J. Pincombe of the Progressives, elected to the London County Council (LCC), together with the Alderman, A. E. Davies and G. M. Gillett. A typical example of political pene-

---

[23] Hamilton, *Sidney and Beatrice Webb* (Boston and New York: Houghton Mifflin Company, 1933), p. 111. Webb had done all these things in the days when he did not believe in the politicizing of trade unions and cooperatives— only in sectional organizations and municipalization. He then had his own little splinter party, the Progressives, in London. Its story prefigures the Liberal Party of New York, one of whose chairmen (for Queens) is Mark Starr, whose Fabian pamphlet, *Labour Politics in U.S.A.* (London: Fabian Publications and Victor Gollancz, 1949), bears a preface by Margaret Cole.

tration: A Fabian, Mrs. Walter Baker, was appointed Justice of the Peace for London County.[24] Into this Fabian company MacDonald passed. He was to remain ill-at-ease among them. He continued to be the idol of the Clydebank hustings until 1927. But his radical connections with ILP had already been cut. Without being a Fabian he was henceforth to do the work of Fabians.

Because it will delineate the effect of Fabianism on the idealism of ILP and the devices by which the Party was recruited, to the disillusionment of some " sentimental Socialists," some space is given here to the group from Glasgow: A description of the group serves to elucidate Fabianism by contrast, and to demonstrate the fate of a local group of Socialists which does not fall into English-directed stratification. The Clydebank men of ILP, although given a fearsome reputation as " Communists," or as " pacifists," were really only laboring men, highly intelligent and specially skilled. Once, faced as they believed with a menace to their freedom, they fought against Lloyd George's Munitions Act; now they faced a menace to their craft and livelihood in shutdowns and unemployment. They were fighting not for their " men " like Trade Union leaders, but for their fellows. Kirkwood, the typical one, had been a socialist ever since reading Bellamy's *Looking Backward,* in 1892, and he had joined ILP because, after some efforts to get results on the purely social level, he had become convinced of the need for political action. He, like his fellows, set his face as a most hard rock against making a profession of Trade Union leadership and against accepting the rewards thereunto appertaining. His position, as go-between and trouble-shooter in the Beardmore works at Parkhead, outside Glasgow, stemming from his office as head of a shop steward union, created, and furnished for us, a near-ideally complete picture of the participation of labor in management. When Sir William Beardmore, owner of the vast Clydeside foundries, shipyards, and munitions works, being ill-advised, forbade Kirkwood's free access to his office or to any place other than Kirkwood's

---

[24] *FN,* XXXIII :4 (April, 1922). In the 1920's the names of at least 23 Justices of the Peace occur in *FN* lists of whom a few may be listed here: David Adams, Maurice Eschwege, George Thomas, G. Burgneay, George M. Gillett, Henry J. May, Lilian Dawson, Marion Phillips, Mrs. C. D. Rackam, A. G. Walkden.

own shop, it brought on the strike for which Kirkwood was arrested. At that time he pleaded successfully with certain groups, like the electricians, to return to work lest harm come to the machinery by their absence. When, later, Tom Gallacher, the "one unbending Communist in Scotland," proposed ousting Beardmore and replacing him with Kirkwood, it was the latter's turn to denounce such a procedure and to exemplify what Kirkwood considered the genuine Socialistic ordering in contrast to a Communistic proletarian ordering. He states on this occasion very clearly his belief in management's right to manage and the owner's right to render economic decisions. He himself represented the ideal shop-steward. (The reader will need to recall the type when the discussion of Fabian attitudes toward certain Fabian writings comes up in the 1929–1931 period.) He was unashamed of his station and unwilling to cross social lines while dealing rightfully with economic matters. Once, when Henderson and Lloyd George, among others in a delegation, invited Kirkwood to join them at dinner, Beardmore remarked in effect: "He won't go to dinner with you; he won't even take a cigar from me." It is easily seen this type of Labour Party politician was different from and a problem to the Fabian intelligentsia. Yet the votes of Kirkwood's fellows, even more than their acquiescence, were definitely needed to constitute a Parliamentary Labour Party.

The group as described individually by Kirkwood, who emphasizes his own ebullience, raucousness, and rough fair-play, comprised John Wheatley, a "Catholic Socialist," cool and fearless, a born intellectual leader; James Maxton of the "wooing" voice, saint-and-martyr, and political gipsy—all things for all his fellows; "Jimmy" Stewart, small, sober—the barber-tribune of Glasgow (listed as a Fabian); Neil MacLean, full of fire without fury; Tom Johnston, his head full of facts;[25] George Hardie, the brother of the founder of ILP, an engineer-chemist; George Buchanan, a pattern maker known to poverty; James Welsh, a miner and poet whose maiden speech described, although without rancour, the glorious scene in the House of Lords the day of

[25] Johnston was to rise to fame in MacDonald's Government of 1924 and 1931 and to stand by him after the debacle of 1931. After 1924, he is listed as a Fabian. Cf. Mrs. Cole, *Growing Up Into Revolution,* p. 62, for the present day description of Kirkwood.

convening Parliament in contrast with the depressing scenes of economic decay that very day upon the banks of the Clyde; John Muir, [26] heroic and a gentleman; " Bob " Smillie, representing an English constituency, an Irishman reared in Scotland, who later, because he feared he might compromise his principles, refused a Cabinet position, when his fellow Clydesider, Wheatley, became Minister of Health to stand the gaff for the Party in the matter of housing. Smillie and Wheatley came near being invited to become Fabians, as the record of reports on lectures indicates. Johnston did become a Fabian. Wheatley, Maxton, Johnston and Kirkwood were free of British Trade Union influence such as Scotsmen mistrusted. " Breathing the noble spirit of the Covenant " expressed in the 124th Psalm, these men held a formal religious dedication service before their departure, with their sworn principles inscribed like a testament, for London and Parliament.[27] Distinguished by a strong religious bent and a sense of brotherhood, they were teetotalers and non-smokers, and, for Scotsmen, tolerant on religious matters. Kirkwood, Maxton, Stewart, Johnston, and Muir had been in jail during the war— not for pacifism! The eleven had met together frequently for months before the election discussing the " ifs " of parliamentary contingencies.[28] They adopted Parnell's and O'Connell's tactics, and made themselves very obnoxious to those Fabian leaders who hated " scenes." Their chief weapon was the " scene." It is simply wrong to call them either Bolsheviks or " pacifists."

In *My Life of Revolt*, Kirkwood gives the platform they espoused. It had few marks of their peculiar Socialism and primitive " Keynesianism " but in it the straightforwardness of their characters stood clear. The economic proposals in it were to form the point of division between their uncompromising attitude and Fabian policy. In contrast with Fabian irenicism they were absolutely opposed to war indemnities and German reparations.

---

[26] He, a single man, had gone to prison for a seditious publication during the war rather than expose the responsible man who had a family.

[27] Kirkwood, *op. cit.*, p. 192. Emanuel Shinwell was associated with them at this time. Cf. *Ibid.*, p. 171. He is found in the Fabian sector with Mosley, later. At present, Kirkwood is a Privy Councillor, along with Buchanan, and is one of the mellowest members of the House of Commons, according to Mrs. Cole.

[28] Kirkwood, *op. cit.*, pp. 188 ff.

These things threatened their jobs. Along with urging " houses suitable to enshrine the spirit of home " they advocated means " to purge industry of the curse of unhealthy workshops, restore wages to the level of adequate maintenance, eradicate the corrupting effect of monopoly and avarice," and to charge social benefits to " those best able to bear it." [29] Although they seemed to confuse graduated income taxes and excess profits taxes, they declared that they intended to conquer unemployment by the Capital Levy. The Levy, inculcated by Webb, Pethick-Lawrence, Dalton and others, was now, in 1922 and 1923, to be evaded as poor politics. The straight-forward ones did not understand. Their economic precepts were simply expressed:

> . . . everyone is afraid to spend, rich and poor. They are banking their money instead of spending it. . . . We could spend thousands of millions in a war, and if another war broke out we should do it again. Why not spend money in a war against poverty? After the Napoleonic Wars there was a shortage. The trouble then was scarcity. Today the trouble is abundance. . . . [The workers demand] power to buy back what is produced.[30]

They should be credited with an early advertence to " abundance " as an element in the economic dilemma. But they were not committed to the abolition of Capitalism. In Kirkwood's words, speaking of the softening of class lines:

> This improvement [the nearer approach of the artisan to the middle class which does not stop at clothes, houses, food, and entertainment; and the fact that class distinctions were fast losing their importance as social criteria] has taken place in the capitalistic society. . . . I have never accepted the theory of a " dying Capitalism." [Yet that very year there was a Fabian lecture series on " Dying Capitalism."] So long as a capitalist society can adjust its laws and its conventions to meet the developing sense of justice and reason of the people, it will continue. . . . In fact, capitalism is surviving only in the measure of its acceptance of a Socialist outlook.[31]

---

[29] Kirkwood, *op. cit.*, pp. 192 f.

[30] *Ibid.*, pp. 259 f. (A conversation with the Prince of Wales which Kirkwood reported.)

[31] *Ibid.*, p. 266. This was not Socialism nor Social Democracy. It had no

It is clear he did not endorse the aim of those advocates of the Capital Levy who marked the employer and *rentier* class for extinction.   Clydesiders were not root and branch anti-capitalists. The Labour men believed, said Kirkwood, in the British people.[32] They expected opinion to support their cause, and looked for fair play even when they were stubborn, as often they were, according to Kirkwood's autobiography.   Political action was secondary with them.   They thought in terms of a societary impulsion— Democracy as a way of living, not as a political system.   They had convictions about the Capital Levy much as it was inculcated by Snowden and Pethick-Lawrence.   They stood for it even while Fabians were for dropping it as a matter of expediency;[33] when, for example, Clifford Sharp authored the article on " Labour Finance " which straddled the issue: Wise or not, he wrote, the Capital Levy should be studied not indignantly condemned; but it would not work without psychological preparation and the consent of the business community, nor without the support of the leading banks, against the determined opposition of the City, not even if passed by five hundred M.P.'s.   The Scotsmen must have seemed impervious to reason or immune to nuance, when Mostyn Lloyd contributed " The Capital Levy and the Level of Prices," which ran counter to the loyally held views of the northerners: As a chief issue in the General Election, Lloyd said, there could hardly be a " worse subject."   (Clearly, the Labour Party was then meeting terrible criticism of a plank in their platform better forgotten in days of industrial depression and times of amorphous party formation.)   Bonar Law, Lloyd said, appealing to the central Glasgow constituencies, had admitted favoring it in 1917 and he was now calling it " lunacy."   Mr. Lloyd hoped the banks would not be too tardy in recognizing the need to control inflation as they

---

affinity to preachments of Marx, Buonarroti, or Babeuf. It embodied much Christian sociality. Cf. Harold Laski, *The Socialist Tradition in the French Revolution* (London: Fabian Society and Allen and Unwin, 1930), a Fabian pamphlet which searches out secular socialism from the skein of social thought.

[32] In 1945 the Conference Program was entitled, *Labour Believes in Britain*.

[33] Cf. " Labour Finance," *NS*, 20 (November 4, 1922), 129.

had retarded the arrival of " dear money " to head off the boom of 1919. " The City " had then opposed "the only possible means by which the post-war boom could have been prevented from getting out of hand." Labour must needs drop the issue but others might be found to adopt it:

> . . . The Capital Levy may prove to be the quickest way of stabilizing prices in this country and preparing the way for the restoration of a free gold market. We believe the banks will sooner or later endorse it as a sound and necessary remedy. It will not be imposed by a Labour Government, for the probability is that a Conservative or Liberal Government will have been forced to adopt it before a Labour Government comes into power.[34]

The Clydesiders were behind the times. They were marked for isolation in the impotency of mere protest; while in the cleavage between its intellectuals and its workingmen lay the cause of ILP'S eventual disappearance.

The Fabian view of the levy was sophisticated beyond any of the conceptions of ILP of Clydeside, for whom the levy suggested itself simply as a means of war against unemployment. Fabians saw it as a means of state finance which, they averred, would spare industry some of the heavier burdens of surtaxes or would spare the lower middle classes some income taxes; meanwhile it should take from the wealthy not their surplus but their capital. It had been reported in June, 1922, that Fabian Pethick-Lawrence (ILP), introducing Fabian Hugh Dalton at an Essex Hall lecture in March, had said Labour alone had " a practical proposal for remedying the present state of affairs "; and that was the Capital Levy, upon which Dalton lectured. Dalton was then reported to have said the levy, falling mostly upon 300,000 wealthy people, would have two effects neither of which, being doctrinaire and class-conscious concepts, characterized Clydeside ideology: First, " removal of the psychological obstacles which prevent all from doing their best and, secondly, a large sum of money would be released for social expenditure." It should be observed that these objectives lay outside the announced purpose of war-debt payment as Webb explained it, and beyond the Clydebank purpose of financing industrial development for employment and security.

---

[34] *NS,* 20 (November 11, 1922), 167 f.

It can be concluded that when the Fabian publicists dropped the Capital Levy from the campaign platform in November, besides running counter to the socialists of the Beardmore works, they betrayed other Fabians, like Dalton and Pethick-Lawrence, and minimized their own major premises. They preserved for English ends, the appeal to class feeling which such discussions stirred up. Pethick-Lawrence and Dalton remained with the compromising Fabians; the workingmen clung to their principles and stood apart, to demonstrate that the Clydesiders' attitude toward class was one of preferring their own. Yet the control of the semantics of the Capital Levy gave Fabian control over the obstreperous and sentimental socialists, while it brought ILP intellectuals into the English camp. In the ascendency of Fabianism, ILP was submerged. Class forged the irenic Fabian attitude into a policy—socialism eventually. The leader whom Fabians were constrained to accept was to be repudiated by ILP, but when the debacle of 1931 came, it was not to be caused by the men of Clyde, but by men of the " Socialism now " school. The collapse evoked from a leading Oxford-type Fabian the exclamation that some Fabians were so glad " to get rid of MacDonald " that the extent of the damage done the Labour movement escaped their early notice.

In spite of jettisoning a major plank, Labour did not expect to capture the Government so early as it did. Snowden thought it would take a decade. How then could a desperate party man like that head of a shattered Liberalism, Asquith, schooled in knowledge of Fabian technique, fail to note the chink in Labour's armour? He held the balance of power in the Opposition and he could envision—as doubtless some Tories envisioned—the advantage to orthodox politics to be gained by bringing to a premature accession to power the new force in politics, Labour. Before coming to this story, however, there is more to be said of the new Opposition. We have seen the success of Fabians in compassing an intra-party force.

C. Fabians and the Others in Opposition

In November, 1922, Fabians expected only a short-lived Parliament. And they laid plans for a Lab-Lib Opposition, in spite of the opposition of Socialist purists. Actually, they won enough seats to constitute the Opposition without Liberal help. In any case, the Society was discovered to be in a position of great power in the Party itself and in relation to the national equilibrium, at a culminating point in permeation.

The Fabian Executive in April, 1923,[35] was a list of now familiar names: W. J. Bassett-Lowke (who ran advertisements in the *NS* for handsome model railway locomotives), Mrs. A. E. Corner *vice* Clement Attlee (resigned), A. E. Davies, LCC (who wrote " The City " in each *NS* issue), Mrs. Boyd Dawson (who wrote as an authority on cooperatives), Dr. F. Lawson Dodd (secretary of the Fabian Society); also, the niece of Mrs. Sidney Webb, Mrs. Barbara Drake (educationist and organizer, the historian of women's Trade Union movements), Dr. Letitia Fairfield (a name faithfully recurrent), F. W. Galton (he was trained in Fabian research while acting as a secretary to Mrs. Webb), Dr. L. Haden Guest, Hubert Humphreys, H. L. Laski, Miss A. Susan Lawrence, LCC (a spirited organizer, she had been jailed in Poplar), Captain C. M. Lloyd (a stalwart of the *NS* out of whom the spirit had been crushed by too many meetings, according to Mrs. Cole), J. H. Macrae-Gibson (the authority on Whitley Councils seen from within) replacing Chiozza-Money, resigned; and the list included Professor Edith Morley, Edward R. Pease, S. K. Ratcliffe, Harry Snell, M.P., LCC., R. H. Tawney, Sidney Webb, M.P., and Mrs. Sidney Webb. A busy Fabian of the Executive Committee, Mrs. Corner, for example, was chairman of the Fabian Women's Group, member of the Fabian Nursery Executive, had served on the standing Joint Committee of Women's Industrial Organizations; and the significance of these penetrating connections is obvious, and characteristic: This lady, from three vantage points in Fabianism—the organizational, the Women's, the Youths'—touched every outside association for bettering women's industrial status. She almost symbolized the Fabians' work of bringing the new electorate—the women—into the Labour Party and making them Socialists. No workingmen were on the Fabian Executive.

To complete the setting showing the position of the leaders of H.M.'s loyal Opposition, it is notable—and Fabians observed it—

---

[35] *FN,* XXXIV:4 (April, 1923).

that there were four Cooperators among the Labourites. In an early chapter, the philosophy by which the cooperatives were warped into the Party was discussed. Here it is a question of warping into the Party the social segment represented by four Cooperative Party men listed as " Labour." The Society had, as we have seen before, a plan for Cooperatives too. But it did not envision a Cooperative Party. In 1922, Sidney and Beatrice Webb had brought out their book, *The Cooperative Movement,* which was reviewed in *Fabian News* and, as we have seen, by Pigou in the *Economic Journal.* Fabianism's examination and categorizing of any movement meant, inevitably, the attempt to politicize it. The CWA was a rising social movement to be captured for the Labour Party and permeated with Socialism. The Fabian reviewer, W. A. Robson, like Pigou, a member of the Royal Society of Economics, threw light upon the internal impulsion of the Webb book on Cooperation, naming it the drive for " a larger development " to be made possible for the life of the whole body of its members rather than a " purely materialistic [sic] organisation based on an indirect form of economic self-interest." In other words, they should be Socialistic and participate in political action within the larger Party. (Contemporary *NS* editorials remarked upon the unattractive appearance of cooperative stores, the dusty jam jars in poorly arranged shelves, the cheap, ugly boots.) Robson thought that the Webbs intended to complete their bookshelf on the New Order by linking the Trade Union movement with the Cooperatives, " particularly as regards the use of Direct Action "; he showed how they warned the Cooperatives of their faults at the same time that they made " devastating " reply to the Guild Socialists. The only great difficulty was pointed out by the reviewer with humor: the " hired man " (wage maker) had to become " self-conscious " and acquire " a clear vision of the part to be played by each in the manifestations of democratic self-government." So, Robson remarked, we had but to wait for the " hired man " and what-should-be would evolve from what was.[36] This reviewer's humorous criticism was as reverent nevertheless as Pigou's if somewhat sharper:

> By about the middle of the volume the paraphernalia is
> prepared and the stage is set for one of those remarkable

[36] It is unnecessary to make a comprehensive examination of the Coopera-

feats of political legerdemain which we have now learned
to expect from Mr. and Mrs. Webb wherever the most
exciting democratic institutions are produced as though
by magic from utterly unpromising material.[37]

W. A. R.'s review was as hilarious as a Shaw play. It is significant that he stated positively that the Webbs were not sure
whether the Cooperative movement could be linked into the
" larger development " by voluntary conviction or by a policed
welfare state. He hoped that in any case the Webbs had seen to
it that none of the " developments " crossed each other, for
example, Trade Unions and Peasant Cooperatives. (As has been
said, they omitted consideration of the Irish and Continental cooperative systems.)

Six meetings were announced following the appearance of the
printed handbook on the cooperative movement which its authors
would explain at each meeting. Represented as part of the attack
on unemployment, such activity had its political uses. In the first
Labour Cabinet, the leader of the Cooperators, A. V. Alexander,
was Mr. Webb's Parliamentary Private Secretary. The four
Cooperators were the object of more Fabian attention, propor-
tionately, than the forty-seven miners.

So we see the formation of the ranks of Opposition. As to that
which was opposed, the *NS* listed the year's problems in a dreary
Christmas editorial: " Cannes, Genoa, . . . Anatolia . . . Chanak
. . . unemployment." To be discussed in the following Chapter,
the list shows a preoccupation with Continental problems. Under

---

tive system. By using the comments of Robson, an eminent economist, it is
possible to learn the method by which the Webbs approached cooperativism
with the purpose of warping it into the Party. The position of communal
charity or mutual self-help in Cooperatives, the original spiritual factor, is
replaced by a new " spiritual " element, political democracy.

[37] *FN*, XXXIII:6 (June, 1922). We have remarked this phenomenon of
Webb thought patterns, above. Robson's corroboration is valuable. Again,
here is a Fabian criticizing the pontiffs of Fabianism. Pease had pointed out
the anthropomorphism employed in their propaganda (the term " the Capitalists " used undifferentiatedly) ; now Robson marks their philosophical
legerdemain; we have noted in another place their writing " history " from *a
priori* philosophy, or wishful thinking, especially in their treatment of the
Trade Unionism of the 1920's.

"unemployment" there was to go on and on the search and research for a principle controlling full employment in total industrial democracy. Even the agitation of research offered a springboard into power. Only the Kirkwood back-benchers, because theirs was a little world, clung to a "capital levy," the need for purchasing power and spending to dissolve over-production, and the urgency of increasing production. The rest, politicians of both camps, the electorate, and the mongers of Socialist philosophy had uses for "unemployment." And the Webbs, with prescience if not with wisdom (which would have devised a radical correction like Benedictinism with its agricultural-liturgical solution and would have sought means of giving purchasing power to Oriental masses to encourage British production), were to state this very clearly, but not until 1928, when commenting on the liquidation of the antique, if not ancient, Poor Law.

Labour in Opposition took *NS* advice and did a good bit of "opposing" so that the "Cannes, Genoa, Chanak" formula was significant of the helplessness of the Tory Government at the moment when relief was coming to Europe in the shape of the Dawes plan, and when there was needed a voice of assent to rise on the Left. It is possible that Tories saw the rift in Labour's ranks. (Certainly the dialectical Labour Party arguments had given European Socialists, and others, a chance to draw their own conclusions.) The Opposition of 1922 had a record on Ireland, on France, on Germany and on Russia which showed the "Cannes, Genoa, Chanak, unemployment" formula to be a taunt about clumsy politics. The injection of the word "unemployment" could only bring to Conservative minds the thought of the "root of unrest." The phrase did not mean "the cause of unrest." It meant that a growing force was, from beneath the surface of the political life of Britain, undermining the foundations of order as Conservatives knew it. To the problem of "unemployment" and "unrest," Socialists answered "nationalisation." No such response could rise without raising another on the Continent. The public silence of Fabians concerning the Orient was eloquent.

CHAPTER IV

LABOUR ON THE THRESHOLD, PART 1

A. " NATIONALISATION "

" Labour Unrest " provided the material for education toward the idea of " nationalisation." " Nationalisation " was a plank in the Party's platform. The Party had begun to act as an independent political entity. A few observations show how the Party gathered its forces from " rank " at the same time that it gathered forces in certain " files "; for we have seen how it fomented itself in tutorial school and industrial organization, in the hustings, and in the enclaves of theoretical economics. The Fabians used " unrest " to convince " instructed persons " regarding " nationalisation "; thus they invaded the political life of Britain proper. " Nationalisation " had to be discussed by Churchill and Lloyd George, not to speak of Haldane and Chiozza-Money. But apart from the domestic value of the agitation the publicized drive for nationalisation of means of production and of natural resources signalled unanimity to Socialists on the Continent; for such matters were given currency in the Studies and Reports published by the International Labor Organization.[1] Domestic politics were agitated by questions of foreign policy. At a certain point, facing stalemate on reparations and economic stabilization on the Continent, Mr. Baldwin asked for a mandate on " Protection," with timing which was, to say the least, providential. For one thing, the idea of protection was as far " right " as nationalisation or the Capital Levy was " left." In this present chapter, we discuss the use of " nationalisation " and of " unrest "; and in that following, of continental policy, and of a list of conference failures. In each of these chapters, " Labour on the Threshold," we leave the situation of Labour in Opposition in 1922 to take a Tory's eye view of these four kinds of political agitation from 1918 to 1923,

---

[1] Cf. especially the important Series A of *Studies and Reports of the International Labour Organization.* By way of sampling Cf. Nos. 4, 6, 18, 19, 24, all of which insist on nationalization.

then we return to a review of co-terminous domestic politics where
the root of unrest was pressing against the political fabric of the
nation, if not of the world.   The aim is to try to see the cause of
the Baldwin challenge, " Protection "; that is, to mark the effect
of Fabianism at this point in British political life.   The challenge
was thrown down at the moment best calculated to put Labour
prematurely into power in England and at the same time to give a
desirable direction to the current of continental policy.

Labour had, by 1923, a record on " nationalisation " as the
answer to " unrest," and on foreign policy as an appeal to Socialism, which gave the Government pause.   Since our purpose is to
show the dilemma Fabians created, we run down the gamut of data
on each of the above items from 1920 (even 1918) to 1923.   Labour
was poised on a fulcrum of power, balancing East and West, in
1922.   Historians have asked why Baldwin was not content to
leave them in Opposition, but risked an election as the barometer
of their prestige was rising.   The writer believes the reason was
something more sapient than the mere aim to " forestall the forestaller," Lloyd George.

When Labour formed a Government in the last days of 1923, it
reaped what the Fabians had sowed in 1918.   Then, at the war's
end, Labour members had withdrawn from the Coalition.   In a
sense, this action redeemed the constitutional practice of Opposition.   A two-party system was preserved at the time when un-
ilateral " loyalty " was urged by Lloyd George and the Coalitionists.   It was clear in 1918 that Labour meant to undermine the
Government and allow none of the reforms Lloyd George's
machine was capable of producing to materialize until the new
order should transpire under Socialism.   " Onyx " wrote in the
NS that " one meets men of all parties who feel " that the Coalition
is unstable and " impudent "; yet " Onyx " thought the Government should delay the election until the soldiers returned.   A
" mandate " was being asked for Mr. George, to achieve, the
electorate knew not what.   Lloyd George had ideas on " reconstruction " resembling his land and insurance schemes before the
war.   Again, " Onyx " had talked to " a very experienced
observer " who believed the Party was growing: " last week it
would have got twenty [seats], this week, thirty, next week, forty,

the week after that, fifty." [2]   (The psychological effect of this dinning was doubtless the reason for its use.)   It was averred that disgust and cynicism met the older parties everywhere.

> It is certain that in all classes—from the agricultural labourers to the more enlightened sections of the prosperous and professional classes—there is a general trend toward the Labour Party, which has a programme, wants to change England and knows the kind of change it wants. [3]

The editors of the *NS* and Sidney Webb himself, in a letter to the editor, [4] inveighed against the " Bolshevism " [sic] of the Coalition, calling it a " pledge-bound " party and a " conscript " motley collection backing something which was " not even a policy " but a man who was as " near to a chameleon " as a man could be.   Webb stressed the aim of Labour to safeguard parliamentarianism: Those who were afraid of " bolshevism " would be well advised not to teach the British workman to give up the House of Commons as a hopeless institution removed completely out of their reach.   The best antidote to an outbreak of Workmen's-and-Soldiers'-Councils (there were current horror stories coming out of Russia and Germany into *NS* pages) seemed to the editor to be an independent Labour Party in Parliament.   Compared with the Coalitionists, Labour had taken " the manlier and franker course " in consulting the electorate because " we hold as indispensable that consciousness of consent [5] which is the basis of British Government " and this, it was promised, would be borne out by the constitutional historian of the future. [6]   (It was being

---

[2] Onyx, " Observations," *NS,* XII (November 23, 1918), 155.   The " experienced observer " quoted is Webb, as Francis Williams' *Fifty Years' March* reveals.

[3] *Ibid.*

[4] This was tantamount to writing oneself a letter, as it were; it is not more unusual than the meeting " Onyx " contrived with the " experienced observer." In 1913, upon acquiring the *NS,* Webb and Shaw announced that they would be responsible for the greater number of unsigned articles.   According to the letter received from A. Emil Davies, the latter and Cole, among others, were also responsible.   Cf. *NS,* XII (November 23, 1919), 155 f.

[5] " Consciousness of consent " was one of Webb's semantic devices.

[6] Sidney Webb, " Correspondence," *NS,* XII (November 23, 1918), 155 f.

made to seem that the electorate had only the choice between " constitutional " Socialism and Bolshevism.)

Fabians re-stated the desirability of a two-party system—one of the old parties must disappear. And they used a " red scare " of their own, while proclaiming the constitutionality of Labour's aims and its deference to British traditional feeling. By hurling the epithets " pledge-bound " and " conscript " at their opponents, Fabian Labour publicists aimed to allay readers' fears that Labour was " pledge-bound " to conscript coal mines and other forms of wealth. Fabians in the *NS* gave every reassurance that its confiscations should be unbloody and constitutional.

Fabians aimed to " change England " constitutionally, using Party Government and the House of Commons. They had to explain to critics of the Labour Party the rule of Labour's constitution that its members stood " committed." Onyx wrote:

> . . . as a fact, this terrible " Constitution " [of the Labour Party] merely demands in the vaguest possible language that a member should in a general way act in accordance with the resolutions of the Party Conferences.

John Burns, who had refused to join the Party, alleged vehemently that no free man could belong to it. That was a pity, said the *NS*, since he possessed a " legendary fame." However, no inconsistency was noted when Webb averred on the next page:

> It seems to me that his [Lloyd George's] Coalition Compact, now exposed to all, ought to enable us to understand better the reason why the Labour Party Conference refused to *renew the permission* [given only for the prosecution of the war] to Labour Party Members of Parliament to hold office in a Ministry dominated by persons of quite opposite policies and opinions than those of Labour Members.[7]

Undeniably, Party members were committed to the Party policy. Fabians were trying to make it palatable. " Pledge-bound " was a less desirable epithet than a " vague " directive to follow Party

---

[7] *Ibid.*, p. 155. Since the Osborn Judgment, Labour candidates did not sign a Party pledge; but discipline held them to the Conference resolutions.

Conference resolutions. The use of the technique of hurling upon opponents the epithet most truly characteristic of the hurler has been noted before in regard to the ILP although this antedates that instance. Exactly at this juncture, George Barnes was expelled from the Labour Party for remaining in the Cabinet.[8]

If " nationalisation " was an element of the Conference resolutions, the incidence of strikes served the purposes of a campaign. The election prognosticated for 1919 did not transpire but a series of strikes helped to underscore the domestic project for " reconstruction " based on retaining such " nationalisation " as had been used during the war, and disregarding the self-sacrificing motivation which patriotism and peril evoked. The Fabians reiterated constantly the alleged promise of ministers to nationalize coal and rails. The Government, so Mr. Churchill declared at Dundee in answer to a question, " had decided on the Nationalisation of the Railways." But, said *NS*, Churchill had " blurted " the truth, after Labour had refused to be " bought " by his scheme substituting mere " control " for nationalisation. He said that the word " expropriation " was something the " Right Wing " of the Coalition detested.[9] So *NS* foretold that by January, 1919, Churchill who had given some lip-service to nationalization would be said to have expressed before election, what was only his own opinion. If Churchill said nationalize, he meant only control and after election he would not even mean that—according to *NS*. In any case if the Government offered " control " in place of " nationalisation " the argument served the purposes of Party-gathering, and that was even better suited to its ends than would be the election Labour prognosticated.

Fabians promulgated a doctrine of guilt, of failure and of de-

---

[8] An experienced Labour leader, G. N. Barnes, continued with Lloyd George to the end and contributed much to the "Labour Chapter" in the League Covenant creating ILO. He went to the Conferences representing Labour but no longer a member of the Labour Party. Lloyd George wrote an introduction to Barnes' *From Workshop to War Cabinet* (London: Herbert Jenkins, 1924) in which he quoted the autobiographer as saying: " Labour is as yet the victim of crude phrases and nebulous theories" risking being " overridden and misrepresented by ill-balanced persons from outside its ranks," p. ix.

[9] *NS*, XII (December 7, 1918), 190.

cadence, then offered salvation in " nationalisation." It took effect
in many earnest minds.   A "young radical," [10] as the *NS* described Sir Leo Chiozza Money, who had created a noticeable stir
by his resignation from the Government and adherence to the
Labour Party policy of the day—abstention from ministerial
office—lectured to the Society, " asserting that the war on its
industrial side had been won on Fabian principles." [11]   Also,
convinced by the success of war-time " nationalisation," Lord
Haldane joined the Labour Party.   An internationally recognized
philosopher, he had been persecuted during the war for his sympathy with German culture.   He had long been associated with
Tawney, Laski, Webb and other Fabians in the Workingmen's
Education Association,[12] an estimable force in politicizing social
aims through learning.   As to Haldane, he was a trustee in a
group formed in 1919 to administer the great endowment for

---

[10] *NS*, XII (November 23, 1918), 155.

[11] *Annual Report of the Work of the Fabian Society, No. 36, adopted May
1919*, p. 10.   The assertion continued, emphasizing that reconstruction was
proceeding incredibly, but mainly along Fabian-advocated lines, the " chief
step" being that women were to sit in Parliament.   In three other matters,
decisions had been reached and awaited embodiment in legislation: (1)
Abolition of the Poor Law wherein the " personal work " of the Webbs had
become " collectively " the Society's assisted by many members through the
National Committee; (2) the "true radical programme " of 1887 pushed by
M. Cunningham, F. Galton, A. E. Davies, was to nationalise the railways;
(3) miners had chosen three Fabians among their representatives—L. Chiozza
Money, R. G. Tawney, Sidney Webb.   They had convinced the Government
that mines should not be " left to mismanagement and profiteering."   This
was interpreted to mean " nationalisation " by the reporter.

This *Report* showed that in furtherance of its work the Society, thanks to
Pease, whose war-time replacement of Sanders had now terminated, was well
off and able to proceed toward its main objective, the development of the
Party.

[12] Such an association could be so powerful only in a country where general
education for workingmen ended at adolescence.   Supplementary adult education then became a specialization which further stratified society by the neglect
of the humanities—except that kind of history which stressed economic determinism—and by emphasis of economics, politics, and institutional sociology.
(How habitual the attendance at WEA classes had become is measurable
from a remark of Sidney Webb, in the *Root of Labour Unrest*, which is
discussed elsewhere, where he suggests that to miss such a WEA class might
be an inconvenience comparable with disturbing the dinner hour caused by a
foreman's peremptory order to " stop tonight "—work overtime.)

adult education made by Sir Ernest Cassel. The group included Asquith and Balfour, H. A. L. Fisher, Sir Gilbert Murray, Miss Philippa Fawcett and Sidney Webb.[13] Haldane had not far to go when he joined the Labour Party because he had approved " nationalisation " during the war; he was following the workman whom he had taught. G. D. H. Cole, supposed to be an ex-Fabian but still working with the *NS,* and with the Webbs and Henderson, extended the meaning of " nationalisation " to include other industries than coal mining. He linked railways with the housing problem and in proposing a Ministry of Transport, declared that nationalized transport was " the Pivot of Reconstruction." [14] The writer of " Observations " in the *NS* in February, 1919, remarked upon the rumor that Labour was " angry " with Lloyd George, but proceeded to show that if by what was quoted as his statement, on the occasion when " fighting for his life," he had given the impression that he stood for nationalization of mines, or the " whole programme," he really had meant " Nothing—nothing whatever." Thus by these light ironies and a gentle insistence, Fabians drove toward a mode of expropriation seemingly impossible, and refused to let Lloyd George steal their thunder. They had concluded that only Labour and not the rest of the Government which they had penetrated, stood firm on whatever was intended by the term " nationalisation."

The strikes of 1919 brought out some peculiarities of Fabian thinking besides the opportunity to make earnest young men and old philosophers feel guilty. " Sardonyx " was found in February, 1919, writing as if the current strikes were failures for which he had no regret. But, he added, as if to incite:

> If Labour knew the ins and outs of the game which it is playing with a sort of heavyweight amateurishness, it would at once engage a first-rate journalist or two at adequate salaries to write manifestos. But Labour is not yet astute enough to do this.[15]

The self-criticism is like something Shaw might write, especially

---

[13] Cf. *NS,* XII (February 15, 1929), 411.

[14] G. D. H. Cole, " The Pivot of Reconstruction," *NS,* XII (January 25, 1919), 345 f.

[15] Sardonyx, " Observations," *NS,* XII (February 8, 1919), 395.

with the reference to salaries and manifestos; but the import
suggests Labour's preference for fluidity.   The well-named
" Sardonyx," after saying that the Clyde strikers were admitting
the ineptitude of their strike, added: " It remains to be seen
whether or not [the employer's] estimate of the men as mere
sheep following a Bolshevist wether was even passably correct."
Whatever this synthesis of opposite attitudes meant, it conveyed
an invitation to the dissatisfied workers to let themselves be
guided by the Party.   That the Fabian purpose was to use, although not to foment strikes, for the purpose of agitation for
nationalization was clear from the long editorial on March 1,
1919, in the *NS*.[16]   In view of a threatened strike one month
hence, it appealed to fear.   The whole tone of the editorial is an
appeal to the electorate to seek the guidance of " Labour."   It
declared that if to coerce labor, the Government were to use the
powers at its command (residual war powers), it would " fire the
heather."   Thus brandishing a threat, the *NS* marked out the
social segments which Fabians aimed to direct.   It declared that
should the Government use its war powers

> . . . the whole Cooperative Movement would be up in
> arms, the Trade Union Movement would be stirred to
> its depths.   No one can feel sure (we feel reluctantly
> compelled to say this) what view would be taken by
> soldiers, who are today only citizens in uniform, of their
> duty in the matter.

Presuming to speak for CWS, TUC, and the soldiers—there
was some fear of soldier-and-worker-councils—and capitalizing
on the subversion to Communism then going forward, the editor
defined the proper function of the Statutory Royal Commission
as one designed principally to deal with wages and hours, perhaps
to survey the cost of expropriation and the " enormous profits of
the owners."   That was all.   The question of " nationalisations "
was not a " justiciable " issue.   In other words, while seeming
to threaten revolt if the alleged promise to nationalize coal was
repudiated, and if the Government should use reactionary methods
to prevent an ensuing strike, Fabians advised the Commission on
how to evade the issue.   Reiterating the assumption that the

---

[16] " The Issue of Nationalisation," *NS*, XII (March 1, 1919), 460 f.

Government had committed itself three months before to the principle of nationalizing the railways, the editorial argued for taking over the mines. It pointed out the fact that the system had proved profitable in "two widely contrasted social experimenters—Germany and New Zealand "—no mention of Russia. There was no example of a nation as large as Great Britain experimenting with nationalization.

When the Coal Commission made its reports, a *NS* editor [17] wrote that "had Mr. Justice Sankey and his colleagues plumped for nationalisation, scarcely a dog would have barked." Interpreting the "third report" (the coal commission reported in three sequential but differing reports), this editor equated the findings to endorsement of "nationalisation," which, he said, was "the only alternative" to waste, maldistribution, and monopoly. The Commission had "significantly, boggled at the word 'nationalisation.'" (There was a little boom in 1919 and the strike, reaction to which was to "fire the heather," was postponed until 1920 when it again collapsed on "Black Friday.")

Whether the Sankey Reports endorsed "nationalisation" was always afterward disputed. The article in the *NS* was not documented with citations from the Reports such as a reliable publication should have been expected to furnish. It prophesied that Lloyd George would rush over from Paris when the strike transpired, to add to his laurels by doing what he had known for long was unavoidable; for it was known he was "not opposed to nationalisation though unable to persuade Lord Curzon and the rest of his odd team that they are living in the year 1919." [18] It is not impossible that the *NS* was hereby offering a hopeful suggestion to the Prime Minister.

The strange practice of sloganizing an all-embracing idea like nationalization when only the nationalizing of certain industries was meant had its reason in the uses of psychology, never explained but quite apparent. Nationalization was not Socialism but an indispensable step toward it. Real Socialism, as professed

---

[17] The use of the expression "unbiased and instructed opinion" is a hint of internal evidence which suggests Sidney Webb was the author. "The Coal Situation," *NS*, XII (March 22, 1919), 540.

[18] *Ibid.*

on the Continent, and by Fabians when at Geneva or reporting through ILO, meant the "transformation" from ownership and control by capitalists to "ownership and control by the community, of all the industries and services essential for the satisfaction of the people's needs." [19] Englishmen could feel fortunate that only a few public services were destined for expropriation, at least for the present.

The reiteration of aims of nationalization was a necessary part of the preparation for assuming government. It was known that Labour was rising to power. If it were not to fail in its principal aims, it must command a majority convinced of the desirability of its major objectives, or resigned to their inevitableness. Blatchford of *The Clarion* always said that the way to get Socialism was to make Socialists. Indoctrination did not proceed at a rate fast enough to complete the ideological conversion of the electorate before power was thrust upon the Labour Party as Opposition in in 1922 and as H. M.'s Government in 1923. The Capital Levy and Poor Law Reform were forgotten until the election of 1923 when it had to be admitted they were not part of the current programme.

To ascertain the significance among Continental Socialists of publicizing this Socialist attitude toward "nationalisation" and the uses of "unrest," the reader has but to peruse the *Studies and Reports of the International Labour Office, Series A*. The tenor of all these Reports (ILO only publishes them without assuming further responsibility), if for samples numbers 3, 4, 6, and 13 are scanned, maintains sympathy toward the Russian revolution and regret for "reaction" in Hungary (reaction against Bela Kun), advocacy of socialization as a necessary *step* toward Socialism, and the abolition of private ownership of land, means of production, means of distribution, and "natural wealth." (In

---

[19] Also cf. for instance, ILO *Reports* Serie A, no. 6, Webb's "Report" of October 1920. He stated that "immediately the phenomenon of wages appears, as soon as work in production is exacted for the benefit of a third person, society has a right to intervene." This report of the meeting of the Labour and Socialist International of 1920 is a mild statement. The various reports run the gamut from Largo Caballero's "Manifesto" (No. 1), to "The Programme and Organisation of the Christian Trade Unions of Germany"—the only one against class-war and nationalization (No. 21).

England, later, banks and banking began to be included). Doubts about the basic principle of contract wages—some Socialists proposed the idea of equality of labor and capital in economic decisions, while others demanded worker control—and steadfast adherence to the aim of nationalization of *all groups and professions,* appear over and over again in the Reports of various organizations, filed with ILO. Number 3, for example, is " Annual Meeting of the Trade Union Congress 1920 "; number 4 is " International Congress of Workers in the Food and Drink Trades "; number 6 is " The Labour and Socialist International of October 1920 " (it was written by Webb as " Reporter," and he whose Fabian *Basis* allowed " tenure " of a " homestead," rebuked the Russian peasants for their revolt against Bolshevism) ; and number 13 is " The Miners Strike in Great Britain." Characteristic tenets of Labor-plus-Socialism are to be found in these Reports, very potently set forth. All Socialists used ILO as an international bulletin board. The meeting and matching, of the Catholic and the Socialist ethic at the ILO level and the conquest of the agency by Christian principles would make a stirring story.[20] It is a phenomenon which must be noted, although it cannot be developed here. All we need to note here is that Socialists in Britain were not talking to themselves. That socialized industries would provide financial support for a Party in power was not noted.

B. " Unrest "

There were other uses of " unrest." Fabians penetrated though they failed to permeate with Socialism a Government-sponsored project created to deal with employment.

There met in April, 1919, the Industrial Conference called by

[20] Cf. especially number 21 in Series A, ILO *Studies and Reports* also *The International Labour Organization: The First Decade* (London: Allen and Unwin, 1931) p. 359 f, where the permeation and penetration of Catholic principles through to the top level of ILO official philosophy is illustrated, whereas, number 1 in the ILO Series A which documents the capture of the workingmen's movements in Spain by the Communists and bears among others, the signature of Largo Caballero, might instead have set the pattern for the capture of the workers of the world for communism.

the Government and addressed by the Prime Minister.[21]   (We have seen the part played by Henderson, and the abstention of the Triple Alliance).   It set up a Joint Committee of employers and Trade Union representatives which reported in March.   This committee called for an Eight Hour Act and a National Minimum Wage; [22] for the recognition of Trade Unions, for " public works and orders "—admittedly, a " drastic policy " but thought necessary for times of depression.   Besides sick pay, old age pensions, and education, the Report on this Industrial Conference advocated a National Industrial Council of four hundred elected by Trade Unions and by employers' associations and implemented with a Standing Executive Committee.   There had been no dissent in

---

[21] A complete account is found in Mrs. Agnes Hamilton's *Arthur Henderson*, pp. 210–215. It is highly illustrative of the struggle between the forces gathered in free associations like the Trade Unions, and "the programme." Mrs. Hamilton shows the elements at work: (1) British Trade itself under control, by means of the overdraft system, of combines and banking trusts; (2) amalgamation of unions which she calls " a movement less marked and less lasting"; (3) the potential of industrial pressure for "reconstruction in the economic field"; (4) the shaping up of an idea of some sort of "parliament of industry" latent in (a) Henderson's hope and (b) the Webbs' projected *Constitution* embodying " functional representation " together with (c) the movement for Industrial Councils, sponsored by I. H. Whitley; (5) the Government's efforts to forestall " direct action." When nothing was done by the Government to implement their findings, the Conference dissolved in protest in the Fall of 1921.

Although "Whitley Councils" had the backing of at least one Fabian who was also a civil servant, John Macrae-Gibson, his views were criticized adversely by W. A. Robson in *FN,* XXXIII (September 9, 1922) who said the author of *The Whitley System in the Civil Service* had not allowed his Fabianism "to shine through" the "adulation" of Whitleyism, else his faith had not been so "fervid" and "without misgivings." It is safe to say Fabianism rejected the Whitley Council system; although the system involves equality of labor and management at the industry council level—an ideal of social justice based on charity, which does not gainsay the owners' right to make final economic decisions at the plant level.

[22] The method had already been exemplified when in October, 1918, the National Liberal Federation, meeting at Manchester, had adopted a programme full of amendments by constituent associations based upon *Labour and the New Social Order.* These amendments involved nationalization "in flat contradiction of the official proposals," the Webbian "breaking up of the Poor Law," and "prevention of unemployment" substituted (by Asquith) for "provision for unemployment." Cf. *NS,* XII (October 5, 1918), 3.

the Conference until the " Memorandum on the Causes and Remedies for Labour Unrest " was appended to the Report by two
Fabians, Henderson and Cole, " in behalf of the workers' side." [23]
As the *NS* interpreted it, this section called the attention of
Lloyd George to the promised " new social order " and restated
the Labour Party programme: Nationalisation, Capital Levy,
Housing. The Memorandum insisted there was a " breakdown of
the existing capitalist system of industrial organisation " and that
it required the questioning of the whole basis of industry (not just
a few key industries) to discover a better motive than private gain
to serve " as the foundation of a democratic system." Thus, the
Report was set forth editorially in the *NS*,[24] which in this case
supplied documentation. The Fabian periodical restated the
Labour Party's programme of post-war reconstruction, which it
claimed was incorporated into the Report which was to be adopted
by the Industrial Conference. The attempt to incorporate the
memorandum of Cole and Henderson in the end caused the
failure of any accomplishment by the Conference. On the other
hand, Cole's " Memorandum on Procedure," which had furnished
the agenda for the joint committee, was, according to Mrs.
Hamilton,[25] the one effective agency of the Conference. Only one
immediate matter, continuance of the Wages Act (temporary
regulation) was all that resulted in the way of Government action.
There was an agreement upon some few points but it was nulli-
fied by the fact, known in advance to the *NS* reporter, that
" neither the official chairman nor the employers could well be
expected to agree " upon the " Memorandum on the Causes and
Remedies for Labour Unrest." [26] Apparent unanimity on the
Report was negated by the impossibility of agreement on the
appended document.

[23] Hamilton, *op. cit.,* p. 213.

[24] *NS,* XII (March 29, 1919), 565.

[25] Hamilton, Henderson, pp. 210 ff.

[26] The editor of the *NS* warned employers in Parliament to take heed to
the action of employers in the Conference in adopting a position of unanimity
upon the Report. Of course, the Parliament then sitting was the result of
the " Coupon" election. But it was misleading to speak of unanimity; the
Cole memorandum destroyed it.

When Cole's *Self-Government in Industry* was reviewed by Pease in
FN, XXIX:3 (February, 1918) the latter described Cole's projected system
with approval and said Cole's " bad manners " should be " condoned."

It is clear that the Socialists were not bent upon remedying present evils, but upon " transition " in the social order, looking toward a changed England. They made for the Conference its only effective instrument and then created for it the stumbling block upon which it fell. It is very important to record that Fabians wrecked the first attempt to create the Industry Council system in England.

" Labour Unrest " persisted during the boom which started after mid-1919. Profits accumulated but unemployment increased. The coal mines might be struck, but scarcity meant better prices and more profits. The industrial " little Englanders " had no such global interests as the planners of international cooperativism. The forces of " reaction " capitalized on a restricted market and the Socialistic forces capitalized upon the " unrest." By 1920 the causes of unrest changed, especially in the matter of coal. German reparations paid in coal threatened to destroy the British market. The miners were locked out in February of 1920.[27]

Men like J. H. Thomas [28] and J. R. Clynes,[29] sought, we might say, in the political-action surf created by Fabianism, tell the story of the strikes of 1919–1921 from the viewpoint of the needs of their " men," their followers who relied upon them to get a decent livelihood out of the industrial scheme which after mid-1919 produced high profits, but which early in 1920 was checked by the dilemma of German reparations and lost markets. It will be recalled that unionists were advised by Webb to accept " willing " German reparations, and that only Clydesiders of all the Labour Party contingents stood out against any reparations.

Thomas, a former railway engineer, had assisted in the formation of the " Triple Alliance," a combination of Railway workers, Transport workers,[30] and Miners. He is to be found the chairman of a lecture by Bernard Shaw under Fabian auspices in 1918. The " Triple Alliance " had been created in April, 1920, when the

---

[27] Cf. ILO *Studies and Reports*, Series A, No. 13, where the whole episode is clearly narrated.

[28] J. H. Thomas, *My Story* (London: Hutchinson and Company, 1937), pp. 62–73.

[29] J. R. Clynes, *Memoirs*, Vol. I, 1869–1924 (London: Hutchinson and Company, 1937).

[30] *NS*, XII (March 30, 1918), 628. Thomas of the " roped-in " NUR chairing a lecture by Shaw is a most interesting spectacle.

miners in conference had approached the other unions seeking cooperation and support in a projected strike. There was at the time much public apprehension of the power of such a combination but Thomas thought that " so long as that Alliance held the balance without taking advantage of its strength, the country would be rid of strikes and lock-outs "; and so he agreed to cooperate. The miners, led by Frank Hodges, a Fabian associate and Herbert Smith, a spirited but illiterate man, were to test Thomas' delicately kept balance severely. The Government ceased to control coal six months earlier than warranted under the wartime powers because the owners wished to negotiate new contracts. Labour insisted that this had produced a " lock-out "; so a general strike was set for Friday, April 15, 1920. At the ultimate point of compromise after both sides had been heard by the members of Commons, the miners repudiated Frank Hodges, their spokesman, who had offered a point of agreement in his presentation of their position. Instead they followed Herbert Smith [31] and refused to settle. The other two unions felt that the miners had rejected a reasonable means of saving their friends (the Railway men would have had to provide seventy percent of the cost of the strike, according to Clynes).[32] The miners had been difficult, too, in the matter of keeping " safety men " in the pits. Thomas and his NUR accepted agreement. The leftist element called the day " Black Friday " ever afterward, because the general strike which they had intended to precipitate did not materialize. Clynes was severely blamed. J. H. Thomas was vilified to his dying day.[33] Thomas sued *The Communist* and won

---

[31] Cf. Sylvester, *The Real Lloyd George,* p. 53, in which Mr. Smith's illiteracy is exemplified: " Well it's these 'ere ums . . . first the referendum, then the maximum, then the minimum, now the datum, and what I say is 'b'um' ! " He showed himself utterly unlearned regarding art, also, on this occasion. The Fabians who wrote in *NS* pages about " *Chasse aux renards* " and used the term " *sans phrase,*" needed special techniques to handle the shrewd Mr. Smith.

[32] Clynes, *op. cit.,* p. 319.

[33] Cf. Raymond Lonergan (a pen name used by the editor), " Lonergan's Comment," in *Labor, A National Weekly Newspaper* (Saturday, January 29, 1949). " ' Jimmy' Thomas died last week in poverty and obscurity. In his day he was one of the outstanding leaders of the British Labor movement. . . . On the occasion of the famous general strike [threatened], following

£2,000 damages. Funds for the payment came into England by way of Russian gems smuggled in as chocolates.[34] The Left never forgave Thomas.[35] Their methods were execrable in 1922, when he represented labor in the Balfour mission to Washington.[36] Their hatred followed him to the end of his life. Fabians whose general line he had followed, albeit on his own judgment, gave Thomas little encouragement. Yet it was he who was to introduce at the First International Trade Congress in 1921, the resolution that

> . . . to govern a country and to claim to direct the workers' International are two things different and irreconcilable; that it is inadmissible that the chiefs of a government even communist [sic], should be at the same time the chiefs of the workers' International.[37]

Back in July, 1919, the *NS* had approved " direct action " [38] for the present, unreformed, day; that is, while the House of Lords remained to check Commons where Fabians intended to express the popular will, so called: [39] but in general, the *NS* took an official

---

World War I, he 'ran out' on the other unions and the movement collapsed. . . . He 'ran out' on the Labor Party in 1931, and with Ramsay Mac-Donald, formed a coalition government. . . . Thomas 'ran out' once more." The commentator wrote a story of a budget secret revealed, a friend's enriching *himself,* and Thomas being " kicked out " by Stanley Baldwin. Lonergan had not read the autobiographies of the leaders, evidently. His story has the slant of the Thomas-hating Left. The paper in which it was printed, *Labor,* is as of 1950 markedly pro-British-Labour, pro-Fair-Deal, violently anti-Chinese-Nationalist. The organ of the Railway Brotherhoods, it is backed by A. F. of L. It uses toward employers unchristian terms of disrespect.

[34] Clynes, *op. cit.,* p. 321. There was quite a bit of newspaper (and *NS*) comment at the time about the ethics of using Russian jewelry (imperial family jewels) to pay Russian bills. The *NS* favored using them, of course.

[35] Lately, July, 1950, NUR endorsed the Communist inspired Stockholm Petition against the use of the A-bomb. The Left seems to have gained strength since the days when it kept up a nuisance heckling against Thomas.

[36] Cf. Thomas, *op. cit.,* pp. 62–73.

[37] Cf. ILO *Studies and Reports,* Series A, No. 18 (Geneva), March, 1921, p. 25.

[38] " Direct Action," *NS,* XIII (July, 1909), 336 f.

[39] It was the contention of Mr. Webb (seconded by Shaw, Laski and usually

stand against " direct action " and the political strike, unless the Government should rule, in some hypothetical case, against the interests of the entire working class.   The Fabian attitude deprived Thomas in 1920 of any real support.   The *NS* in an article of July, 1919, had treated Clynes, who opposed the current plan for a general strike, in the same way.   The general strike was not approved Fabianism, but it could be tolerated.   It would not be possible in the new order, save as revolt.

Even as workmen failed to realize that the new order meant the nationalization of unions, so did employers, managers and foremen fail to grasp their part in the envisioned order.   They saw that Trade Unions with the potential of the general strike and the Labour Party with the potential to nationalize were only means to an end in the great plan which was Fabianism, which persistently proffered, together with the vision of a new industrial state, Fabian leadership.   The Plan was delineated in an address by Sidney Webb " to a representative private gathering of Employers, Managers, and Foremen in 1919 " and was reproduced with bibliography, and with special reference to the earlier pamphlet, *The Works Manager Today*, by the lecturer.   Entitled *The Root*

---

the *NS*) that the House of Lords was obsolete.   Webb declared it had been a " second Chamber " since 1832.   The effect of attempts to revive its claims to be a separate " Estate " in 1910–1911 had " definitely settled that whatever else they may desire, the people of the country will not tolerate the revival of any separate ' Estate ' of persons or classes who are to be privileged to enforce, against the opinion of the majority of the nation, any *views of their own order.*"   The italics inserted suggest the counter-charge that Labour was becoming an estate with a proper view and order of its own.   That Webb voiced " the people " is open to question but illustrative of Socialist technique.   Webb's standpoint was that a second Chamber must not be a rival to the House of Commons.   Review and delay, the only instruments left to the House of Lords, insured, he said, against unjust treatment of property owners who, *not* represented in Lords, must " trust " in " the people " with the assurance that any serious innovation shall obtain a considered judgment.   Cf. Sidney Webb, *The Reform of the House of Lords, Fabian Tract No. 183* (London: Fabian Society, 1917), p. 6.

Nevertheless in the *NS*, XIX (July, 1922), 406 f, Clifford Sharp's " The Proposed Suicide of the House of Lords " counseled leaving well enough alone, since the Lords were showing themselves capable of learning and the contemporary House of Commons was more " reactionary " than the House of Lords.

of Labour Unrest, it was published as *Fabian Tract No. 196* in
November, 1920. (" Black Friday " occurred on April 15, 1920.)

There was a pattern in this speech delivered in 1919 and published in November, 1920, which exemplified perfectly the Fabian
thesis. If it had been understood, there would have been no reason
for surprise when in 1932 the Webbs and Shaw found in Russia
the Order of their dreams. The chronological position of this
Tract is important. Strikes in 1919 were aimed at getting a share
for the workers in the rising profits of industry. Then came a
change in 1921, profits from coal must come from domestic trade
and an economy of scarcity. " Nationalisation " at first seemed
easy to project, by educing argument from the success of its war-
time exemplification; then as rugged self-interest necessarily increased in intensity, it gained sharper cogency. " Production for
need " took on the meaning of production for global need, and
State planning.

The above mentioned speech of Webb straddled two objectives;
for therein was a dual plan. Reform to which all could assent, and
a new order called industrial democracy to which all were invited
to make the *transition,* because " it is coming and we must find a
way of introducing it successfully without upsetting the machine."
Studying the speech, one looks in vain for " the root " of unrest.
Although occurring in the title, the term is not defined. One
might conclude that unrest is the root capable of overturning " the
machine," the force which Fabianism intended to direct.

Webb flattered the industrial leaders : " The sphere of the brain
working professional will be a great one " in this new adaptation
of " the old constitutional ideal of democracy," which will be made
by " putting ourselves in tune with the universe and pulling with
the stream." Unhistorical and romantic, the phrases have a spell-
binding appeal regardless of the mixed figures. That the workingman's mind was " inscrutable " and might not even be judged
by the programmes to which he gave assent, was an honest statement based on the practice of Fabians of capturing conferences,
like the two cited above. Webb knew well how assent was elicited
for ready-made programmes by the Committee system. Webb
was " going to try to describe . . . the ideas which he [the work-
man] is scarcely conscious of himself." The reform platform
which he offered rings in modern ears as something very familiar;

demand for higher wages indicative not altogether of rising living costs but of rising profits, never so large in aggregate in the British empire as that day; [40] a six-hour day for all, for " every healthy adult." (Webb quipped that this was " a terrible consummation . . . for certain people. When we hear of it in Russia, we think the end of the world has come.") He explained that " partnership in industry " was asked by workingmen, not profit sharing. His grey eminence was somewhat unceremonious: " I cannot stop to prove that, but I am expressing the workman's point of view." Proposals for profit sharing stamp " the man who makes them as an ignoramus." Proceeding with the reform programme, Webb answered affirmatively the question put by *Fabian Tract No. 170: Profit Sharing: A Fraud and a Failure?*, by E. R. Pease: Webb's worker seeks not ownership, save " as a member of the community in a sense which I will afterward explain "; not a share in the profits, for the workman does not think that profits (as distinguished from the wage of management) ought to exist; but " he wants to be admitted on equal terms as a partner in the management and direction of the concern. What he objects to is the autocracy, the arbitrary power, to which he is asked to submit." We have a class giving orders and " another class passing its whole existence in receiving them "; the workman does not object to the unjust distribution of the world's wealth " at the moment " but the unjust distribution of the world's *power*. Therefore, Webb argued, " philanthropy," such as welfare, good housing, and the like, was a " manifestation of power " and did not placate the laborer's resentment. Under philanthropy workers were treated like cared-for horses on a " fodder basis." [41]

There is a thin fissure in logic formed by putting side by side the philosophy of power and the needed reform in attitude toward

---

[40] It was the time for employers to consider the propriety of increasing the share of labor in industry's reward; it was the time also for workingmen to recall that savings on the part of employers now meant a pool of national assets upon which their future employment rested. It was the time for Government to see that savings were not put to uses which would defeat both sides. Webb asked for Socialism. The National Industrial Conference had been defeated by the Socialist " Memorandum."

[41] For the expression " fodder basis," Webb credited Ernest Bevin. It appears in the ILO Report, Series A, No. 3, as R. Smillie's expression.

workingmen.   The historian need only record it.   " Fodder "
philanthropy was rejected but a hiring room comparable to the
directors' Board Room, baths and lockers so that a workman left
the premises " fit to enter his wife's parlour " [42] was not " fodder "
because it should be based upon " equality."   The motivation for
profit-sharing and welfare projects is fraud and love of power;
for reception rooms and free baths, it is equality.   This is Webb's
dialectic equation.   This was the affirmation of a power-capturing
drive.   At the same time it forswore " Reform " and adhered to
the formula, " only Socialism can bring them together."

Contrary to the foundational principle of ILO that labor is not
a commodity, Webb described an hypothetical condition and in so
doing he made it appear that only under Socialism could the ill-
effects of the concept of labor as a commodity be abolished.
Actually he made the contemporary employer a slave-owner and
then skipping the stage of desirable human relations between
employer and worker, turned the latter into the owner of a
" quantum " offered for sale, saying,

> . . . the employer imagines that he has bought the whole
> time and energy of the workmen and that his claim upon
> him can be indefinitely extended beyond normal working
> hours, the normal pace, or the normal intensity of effort.
> [This is] the view of the slave owner . . . so long as we
> cling to the capitalistic system . . . there must be some
> . . . mutual engagement in which one party buys and the
> other sells certain definite, clear-cut services with a
> precisely fixed quantum.[43]

In the mind of the workingman as Webb interpreted it, there
was no objection to the high salaries of managers, only to the idea
that they belonged to a different class.   But he affirmed that the
workingmen did object to the existence of the " idle " shareholder,

---

[42] Webb, *The Root of Labour Unrest, Fabian Tract No. 196* (London:
Fabian Society, 1920), p. 9.   Albert Thomas, head of the ILO, had expressed
the psychological effects Webb struggled with, in his stated belief that the
change in attitude made official in the ILO Charter, that Labour is no longer
to be considered a commodity, "achieved a genuine social revolution."   Cf.
Monica Curtis (translator).   *Albert Thomas: International Social Policy*
(ILO: Geneva), 1948, p. 73.

[43] *Ibid.*, p. 8.

royalty owner, " tribute " collecting landlord. How unnecessarily
great was the sum a shareholder received in order to induce saving
no one could compute, Webb said, but the system should be
abolished. " They flatter themselves that they contribute the
capital, on which, of course, we are dependent to keep our business going." The value of this observation must be measured
while taking cognizance of the fact that Webb was a civil service
clerk, a London County Councilman, a Labour Party executive
committeeman, a lecturer at the LSE, the future Lord Passfield,
and one who never owned a business.[44] His theoretic knowledge
must necessarily lack the insight which experience provides.

The managers were told that the workman whose mind was
here portrayed had learned economics while the employing class
had despised the economist. The workman intended to alter the
present state of things using " as a rule " democracy, but a
democracy very different from that understood in America and
England as of 1920. No longer " equality of opportunity," it
now meant " that no control over others shall be exercised by
individuals, but only by the community." (The word community " can be nothing but a Webbian euphemism. It means the
State.) As to " democracy," no longer meaning that it shall be
open to anyone to become Prime Minister, democracy now meant
that the Prime Minister shall execute the will of the people. (This
euphemism meant the rule of the Party.) The workman in
Webb's mind did not want an equal chance to become a million-
aire, but " he wants that which concerns all to be decided by all."
(Some of the current complaints about Cole's ideas concerned the
fact that the system he proposed called for everlastingly electing
and holding meetings.) Webb admitted that the application of
these principles was difficult, that " our suggestions " were
" crude." The " long road " was to be taken *gradually* but success
was inevitable " if we adapt ourselves."

Certain facts challenge Webb's interpretation of the workingman's mind. It is very noticeable that the workmen who became
articulate, many of whom were drawn into the Fabian Society, or

---

[44] Cf. Margaret Cole, *Sidney and Beatrice Webb*, pp. 149 f. Passfield
Corners became the domicile of the Webbs after they had advertised for a
country place out of earshot of cocks or dogs.

into the company of Fabians, demonstrated great pride in the possibility or attainment of Ministerial or Cabinet rank, and boasted with becoming restraint of their association with royalty. One has but to peruse the autobiographies of G. N. Barnes, J. H. Thomas, J. R. Clynes, even David Kirkwood, Ben Tillett, Ben Turner—real workers who came into political power by the Trade Unions way—to see that labor leaders thought of Government as something regal and authority as something divine, bestowed upon designated persons. Even if "divine" and "spiritual" came to have agnostic and monistic connotations as in the case of Henry Snell, they did not confuse "community" with "State." Also, the only Fabian who could afford ease but who embraced an "austere," that is, a servantless life, was Charles Trevelyan. Webbs, Coles, Shaws, Lansburys—all lived in circumstances of upper class ease and on royalties, stock, or profits of industry. Webb's workingman was a robot made from his own drab concepts.

The new democracy must produce new forms for social institutions. In the pamphlet discussed above, *The Root of Labour Unrest,* reference was given to *A Constitution for the Socialist Commonwealth of Great Britain,* by Sidney and Beatrice Webb, where the outline sketched for the employers of 1919 was treated in "elaborate" if "tentative" detail. If the employers could not envision Utopia, they must at least have felt that they had seen Chalot.[45] The vision was as follows: Individual ownership, gradually giving way to collective ownership, would assume many forms on three levels, State, Local, and, to give a name, "popular," not to say Party. The State was to run the nationalized industries and services, canals, rails and coal.[46] The local governments were to run "many other services by which we live," and consumers' cooperatives "which already operate far more successfully than any capitalistic enterprise that I ever heard of" would handle the great mass of commodities which we consume. The functionless shareholder and landlord was to be eliminated, but

---

[45] Edward Bellamy's *Looking Backward,* and his *Equality,* were already three and four decades old, respectively.

[46] Little is said of banks at this date, and nothing about steel. Cooperatives, as has been seen, were coming in for their share of overhauling by the Webbs.

. . . we do not get rid of management. And in this connection the *workman is still very much at sea.* As I have often tried to explain, even with the most complete democracy, and the utmost equality, management, in a sense, autocracy, remains indispensable as ever.[47]

The foreman could be an autocrat if he represented the community; but to give and receive orders under an owner's system was intolerable autocracy and creative of class! The manager was compared to an orchestral conductor whose "beat is law," because "we must have coordination and control." That this picture is superimposed upon the real workman's view is patent in the declaration: "the workers have only the vaguest idea of what the management or direction of an enterprise really is." Yet, since they were intellectually and morally as competent as ordinary directors of companies, let them, Webb advised, be consulted through their Works Committee and admitted to the Board of Directors.

Enough has been cited to show that Webb's Socialism is dogmatic; his political structure vague; his philosophy utilitarian; his psychology unreal; his utterances contradictory.

Furthermore, as "an instructed person," the lecturer should have known better than to say, "Personal autocracy has been banished from the throne, the castle, and the altar," confusing men and offices, or "that men were advancing rapidly in education and common-sense," confusing the acquired and the endowed. Envisioning the new order, he asked "Where will authority go?" and again with confusion, this time of authority and competence, the former London County Councillor told the story of the Council's decision to build a bridge and their need to call in an engineer and entrust the work to this *expert,* leaving themselves with the residual "authority" to choose its color.[48]

---

[47] Webb, *The Root of Labour Unrest,* p. 11. Italics inserted.

[48] After offering this example of the socialist's reliance upon the expert, the planner of the socialist commonwealth exclaimed about the "chaotic conditions" and inefficiency in the engineering shops of "this country and every other country." Cf. Beatrice Webb, *Partnership,* edited by Barbara Drake and Margaret I. Cole (New York: Longmans, Green and Company, 1948), p. 5. Webb had acquired a reputation of omniscience and omnipresence.

Authority, he said, was to be found with the expert.[49] This sort
of thinking lacks even the legerdemain which Robson found in
Webb's constructs, and to discover it increases the amazement
aroused by Professor Pigou's deference for Webbian writings.

The question came up as to who the manager was to be, that
person permissively the autocrat without "personal autocracy."
(Webb did not show how he could be other than a Party man and
bureaucrat.)   It was not readily to be expected that present
officers might qualify. Webb told the assemblage of managers
a story bearing his point and answer. To an old Major-General
who had expostulated with the Councillor regarding some Socialist suggestions, "I cannot run an army that way," Webb rejoined, "If you cannot, perhaps somebody else can, and even run
it better."

Before the managers, Webb propounded his new principles.
He confused political science and physical science to produce
this effect: "Measurement" and "publicity" will transform industry [50] Capitalism, he said, had introduced science into the
mechanical processes but not into "its business organisation,"
so the latter must be measured (planned) and all processes and
organization made public. Webb slipped Socialism into the
formula in place of principle; then he implied that the political arm
would see to the introduction of the new principles into business.

> It is apparently to be left to Socialism to apply science
> to the organisation of production and distribution, in-
> dustry by industry, from the standpoint of supplying,
> to the uttermost, the consumers' needs.[51]

This was where Webb made a bid for employers' collaboration.
(Although he said nothing about joining the Party, he voiced the
"only Socialism" formula.)   "The sphere of the brain-working
professional will be a great one." Once the new principles were
applied, management would be dependent upon *reports* of dis-
interested experts, but actual decision would be arrived at in
committees. The experienced owner's alarm was allayed by the

---

[49] Webb, *The Root of Labour Unrest*, p. 13.

[50] The confusion of psychology and system is notable—organization was to
rectify human behaviour.

[51] Webb, *The Root of Labour Unrest*, p. 14.

information that "nearly all our present industry is managed" by committees—(under the system in which Webb had averred earlier, "the failure of Capitalism is egregious").[52] Mr. Webb's dialecticism was unmatched even by Harold Laski's. Both could speak on two platforms, or on two levels at one time in such a way that hearers might draw conclusions from one to the premises of the other.

To show the effort of Fabianism to create and control the pattern and the future, it must be noted that in summarizing "the conception of what is at the bottom of the new spirit in industry" i.e., "Unrest," it was said that "the demand of the workman [was] for a partnership on the direction [of industry] . . . with the technicians and managers of all grades, with the community as owner." It was also said that "the workers have only the vaguest idea of what the management or direction of an enterprise really is." This is perfectly consistent with the Fabian proffer of expert leadership. The picture of the world after transition was completed with the offer of reward to compliant businessmen. Webb said precisely, it was "just this transformation of business by Measurement and Publicity . . . which would enable businessmen to become professional men and gentlemen instead of mere shopkeepers." Searching for *the method of transition,* one scans the text for the word "by" and finds instead a description in summary of the transition already made. That it was to be made by a social order taking over political power and the subsuming of all wealth by the State, was evident; but this remained unsaid. How Socialism was to effect the transition was not stated.[53]

Fabians made a large contribution to the thought stream of effectual reform. They pointed up the fact of the recognition by the employers of a "new spirit" and dared to advance the idea of an eight-hour or even of a six-hour day; they exposed the (not incorrigible) weaknesses of profit-sharing and the likelihood that love of power lurked in paternalism and "brotherliness" if

---

[52] *Ibid.,* p. 13. Listeners could hardly have overlooked the inconsistency.

[53] Even so, the principal character in Bellamy's *Equality* awoke to find himself in marble halls. The transition had been made, and the device saved the author great labor.

there was lacking that respect which is defined as equality and
based upon liberty; they demanded absolute reciprocity in contracts and they underscored good manners based upon respect
for workmen; above all, they served to explore industrial society
for some practical system for bringing the workmen into the
management of industry [54] where a point of collaboration might
be grounded, and they revived the fundamental proposition that
production should be based upon need, and goods not kept in scarce
supply for profit.   To have contributed these ideas in force
and order—even a mistaken order—was to have achieved what
should not have been left undone.   Even in almost equating
profits with waste, as Webb did (he called profits "lubrica-
tion" of which too much constituted waste), the great Fabian
effected a re-definition of the place of profit in production.   No
other agency of society drew the attention of the world to
the need for scientific economic thought and the workmen's
progress therein so effectively and immediately.   Even under
critical examination, the driving spirit of men who seemingly
give themselves totally for their fellowmen, evokes profound
attention and sympathetic accord to the point where necessary disagreement is distasteful.   It must be said that much of
the contribution was by-product and accidental to the substance
of Fabianism.   It cannot be maintained with exactitude that
hunger for power was absent even from the Fabian impulsion;
else the Socialists would have accepted " Reform " and encouraged the subsidiary functioning of industry councils toward
freedom from State and Party interference; they would have
used their " religion " of Socialism to rectify motivation, raising

---

[54] Pius XII has recently restated management's right to manage and the
owner's or employer's right to make economic decisions (without prejudice
to any arrangement *by contract* for labor's participation in management even
on plant or company level).   On a level higher than the plant or company
level, that is, that of " occupation groups " in Industry Councils, Benjamin L.
Masse says Pius XII " vindicated for workers a position of equality with
management."   Cf. B. J. Masse, S. J., " Labor's Right in Management,"
America, 83 (July 15, 1950), 395.   Masse might have restated the papal
warning against extraneous control of the worker-representatives by unions
gone political or debased ideologically from the *raison d'être* of proper
unionism.

it from social justice to creative Charity without which social justice may become mere regimentation.

A decade later, some of the confusion of political and economic sciences was corrected by a rather keen statement of Mr. Harold Laski in *The Limitations of the Expert,* a Fabian Tract. He reinstated the " plain man " and the politician in their proper sphere and warned of a chasm opening between ruler and ruled. Political heads were necessary, he said, " to tell the civil service what the public will not stand." Scientific invention bears a potential of malignancy as well as of beneficence.

> The danger which confronts us is the quite fatal one that, by the increase of complexity in civilization, we may come to forget the humanity of men. A mental climate so perverted as this would demonstrate at a stroke the fragility of our social institutions. For it would reveal an abyss between rulers and subjects which no amount of technical ingenuity could bridge. The material power that our experts multiply brings with it no system of values. . . . Government by experts would . . . mean, after a time, government in the interests of experts.[55]

Laski's conclusions were striking: " No body of experts is wise enough, or good enough, to be charged with the destiny of mankind . . . they are saved from disaster only by the need of deference to the plain man's common sense." This is so because the expert is in danger of sacrificing in himself the whole to the part. We may be faced with deliberate choice of the kind of civilization we want. We will succeed only by " harnessing " to the choice " the profounder idealism of ordinary men and women." True

[55] H. J. Laski, *The Limitations of the Expert* (London: Fabian Society, 1931), *Fabian Tract No. 235*, pp. 13 f. Noteworthy in the extreme is the use of civilization by Mr. Laski. A year later, the Webbs had found the " new civilisation" that they had sought in Fabianism. Lansbury visited the U.S.S.R. in 1920. He descried Fabianism there and pointed it out to Lenin who admitted it. In 1921 NEP was begun but was "not understood" by the Trade Unions, until some time in 1922. It was promulgated in 1923 and became official, 1924. Shaw told Stalin in 1932 that on Lenin's tomb should be inscribed "inevitability of gradualness." Cf. "The Trade Union Movement in Soviet Russia," *ILO Reports and Studies,* Series A, No. 26 (Geneva, 1927), p. 120.

to Fabian ideals, Laski said this could be done "by supplying knowledge" and by affording opportunity to procure a share in the benefits of this civilization.[56] Laski seemed always to sense that the transition would be fateful and demanding of courage. Yet he advanced no farther spiritually than the ideal of political wisdom based on the "profounder idealism of ordinary men and women."

Both Laski and Webb were to learn that at the point of transition there stood the royal prerogative which could deflect the current. But in 1920, in the face of post-war reaction, Webb placed his faith in experts, and by 1931 Laski, having seen one failure of Socialists to govern, looked for the return of the political man to guide the expert. In the second debacle he turned against the prerogative.

Current perplexity over the industrial situation became the screen upon which Fabian leadership projected the picture of Socialism. Their outline of reform was valuable but they refused to recognize in anyone save Socialists the ability to perform the transformation. On the other hand, their own thinking grew more and more "idealistic" so that when their call to govern came, Socialist thought and Fabian leadership ran too far in advance of the political guard to effect even the primary domestic reforms the Party had advocated. Strange to say, in spite of their ill-balanced domestic agitation the Party's advance to power was accelerated by the stand which Fabians took upon issues of foreign policy. The refusal to be concrete on domestic issues and to accept reforms must have made Baldwin [57] and his party well aware of the international implications in the Socialist propaganda.

---

[56] *Ibid.*

[57] Stanley Baldwin's son, Oliver, was by now a full-fledged Socialist and Fabian. We find him in Parliament in 1929, and writing "Why I Am Labour," *The Clarion*, 25 n. s. May, 1929, p. 9.

CHAPTER V

LABOUR ON THE THRESHOLD, PART 2

A. The Uses of " Foreign Policy "

Labour had arrived at the threshold of power, in Opposition, and the politicians whom it opposed were confronted with a dilemma. If they looked back in the Fall of 1922 to 1918, Tories and Liberals recalled something about the nature of the new party. It boasted of having a " foreign policy." When they looked abroad, it was to see a political and commercial impasse on the Continent. The Tory majority—the Liberal Party had gone into eclipse with the resignation of Lloyd George—sought trade with Europe with a view to profit—and the increase of national assets. Labour too sought trade, but Labour was imbued with a different " spirit "; their international objective, the " cooperative common-wealth " of nations, embraced an Anglo-Russo-German axis, as the current project which they promised to create under Socialism. The Conservative Party recalling Labour Party attitudes from 1918 to the year now ending in failure, 1922, and taking measure of their foe in domestic politics learned that there was a certain likeness in their respective aims. It was possible that Labour in office might set free the arrested economic forces on the Continent.

Our sights are on the peak of power, 1924. In the background lie the " Coupon " elections of 1918 which reaffirmed the Coalition, and the election of 1922, which dissolved the Coalition. That of 1923 is about to bring Labour into power.

What the Fabians, informed as they were by Lord Keynes' *Economic Consequences of the Peace,* considered the failure of the Versailles treaties, moved them toward " reconstruction " of England and of the world. The first step toward reconstruction was nationalization *everywhere.* They maintained a steady drive toward the consummation of this " reconstruction " under the Socialistic ideal on the Continent. Sometimes they stood for " self-determination," again for mandates ; sometimes against inter-

160

vention, again for outright intervention: The line was chosen not on eclecticism entirely, but upon a principle of relationship. Where, in unlike situations, there was a common coefficient of social democracy to be found or planted, there Fabianism fastened its interest.   Most often it seemed to have a policy which was the counterpart of the Government's; but the " spirit " was different.[1]

Before Labour found itself in the powerful position of H. M.'s Loyal Opposition it had begun to express itself in the field of international politics for two main reasons: 1) To rally persons of like persuasion to the Party, since after 1919 individuals might join the Party without belonging to a union or to a Socialist society, and 2) to signal like-mindedness to Socialists on the Continent, whom British Socialists hoped eventually to lead into a peaceful regime of " social democracy."   After the Party came into Opposition, Labour continued to express its dissatisfaction, apparently more to affect the domestic political scene than to glean a following.   But the effect was to alter foreign affairs.   In the following discussion the dates of some of the data descriptive of Fabians' attitudes on France and Germany run beyond 1922 but the views are consistent with those of 1920 and are cited to show the problem which the Tories confronted in the new political

---

[1] Cf. *Fabian Tract No. 196* (November, 1929), p. 7. " Social Democracy " is a redundant term. Democracy is a social thing. To collect and organize the political coefficients from democratic units creates a republican form of government wherein, after election, the parties become unanimous in accepting the majority decision designating the person or persons to bear authority " under God."

Fabians supported the Government in the Boer War and went into coalition in World Wars I and II; and as of today, into collaboration along with all Socialists, Progressives and Liberals in the United States in the Korean " police action."   Although outside the scope of this study, it is possible to state that in all these junctures their " collaboration " has been dictated by the project to bring into the liberated areas " dynamic democracy."   This means politicized social units or Socialism.   What spokesmen for this ethos termed " medieval " at one time and " fascist " later, they now name " decadent."   This description is being applied to republics, such as that headed by Syngman Rhee.   Although " medieval " and " fascist " have been terms applied to the Church and " decadent " to republics, one of the reasons for the term " decadent " in Fabian thought is the possible and demonstrable collaboration of Church and State in republics—not in " social democracies " where " Church " is isolated from the unity of the body politic.

force called Labour. In other words, finding Labour in Opposition in 1922, we look a year or so back and a year forward to learn what one in Mr. Baldwin's place could have known of their attitudes when he dropped the electric spark of " Protection " into the compounded political confusion of late 1923. There had to be some concise differentiations and the " Plymouth plunge " was designed to precipitate such. The effects were not visible until 1925, after an episode of Labour Government.

Having in mind the policy of favoring what was best calculated to lead to Socialism by way of a Labour Government, the *NS* and lecturers reported in *Fabian News* continued a volley of blame upon the Government. For the situation in Ireland, the weakness in France, the reparations problem in Germany, the intervention in Russia, and the debacle (or so it appeared) in the Straits, there was a Fabian opinion pejorative of the Government's prestige. In the short account which follows it is clear that the " foreign policy " of the *NS* was opportunistic. Expediencies relative to the Labour Party's growth, as well as the effort to appeal to a kind of Socialist " centre " on the Continent, governed it. In seeking the reasons for Baldwin's action in precipitating an election on the strange issue, " Protection," the effect of these attitudes of Labour upon the handicapped Tories must be considered.

To examine but five points of foreign policy: The tone of the *NS* in 1921 was highly critical of the Government in Irish matters. Without any warmth of feeling for the Irish people, it contented itself with analysis of Irish internal forces and criticism of the reprisal-earning action of the Coalition. It described the bloody situation, blamed the Government for reprisals, allowed a letter writer to blame the Church for the Irish Republican Army (IRA) and appealed to the English voters. After the drafting of the Anglo-Irish Treaty, the *NS* revealed the activity of an Irish Labour Party and engaged in sharp criticism of de Valera. It seemed in quest of a non-republican compromise. On February 5, 1921,[2] the telling phrase of a speech by de Valera was pointed out by " an Irish correspondent "; " The British Dominions have had conceded to them all the rights that Irish Republicans

---

[2] XX (February 5, 1921), 519.

demand." The correspondent asked that Englishmen should convince the Irish majority who agreed with de Valera that they were wrong; but the *NS* editor pointed up internal conflict when he praised the Sinn Fein leader for his courage in the face of graver dangers than Lloyd George had yet faced in his Irish policy, since many Sinn Feiners would find the leader's idea unpalatable. Although he had not "abandon[ed] his favorite Shibboleth [Republicanism]", a basal point of compromise might be found (in Dominion status); here was "a Sinn Feiner on the bridge." The English Prime Minister was said to have no remaining reason for refusing to negotiate and no excuse for using Black-and-Tans in order to hold Ireland by ties no tighter than those of Canada and Australia. Then on March 19, 1921, "an Irish Correspondent" was allowed to tell his story without comment. "Irish Churches" had asked for a truce during St. Patrick's festival week, but the British Government had taken the occasion to execute six Irishmen, thereby solidifying IRA resistance: Let GHQ proceed to kill and capture Republicans, even keep IRA "on the run," it would not settle the Irish problem.[3] The British official practice of a "no quarter" policy must, by evoking an equal intransigence in IRA, have the effect of arousing *English voters* as it aroused Irishmen.[4] A letter signed H. C-H.,[5] which blamed the Church for its alleged silence regarding IRA, was printed in answer to one sent in a week before by Alfred Ollivant[6] which had accused the Government of "political" use of the ceremonial burial of victims of the IRA. The editor believed both letter writers represented a large number of Englishmen, but that Alfred Ollivant's view (Fabian)[7] represented the spirit which had "made and sustained that unique political phenomenon, the British Empire"; for Ollivant had noted how the people and all save subservient officials absented themselves from what he considered an "obscene ceremony." He thought the English people resented the use of the

---

[3] XX (March 19, 1921), 691 f.

[4] XVI (March 5, 1921), 631 f.

[5] "An Obscene Ceremony," *NS*, XVI (December 11, 1920), 305.

[6] *NS*, XVI (December 4, 1920), 260.

[7] The editor thanked his God that the Government was not made up of real Englishmen, but Welshmen. The *NS* often stooped to impugn the nationality of H. M.'s Ministers.

reprisal-murder victims to further repeal of the " Promise " then pending in Lords. (This was the promise to liberate Ireland given on the outbreak of the war and now threatened with repudiation.) This decent attitude of the *NS* was the Fabian voice shepherding Irish sympathizers in England into the Labour Party and offering something—not republicanism, but a *modus vivendi* without " force "; to be accompanied, it was hoped, by rising Labour leadership.

In October, 1922, the efforts of the Labour leader in Ireland, Mr. Johnson, to attain peace at the price of accepting the Treaty of December, 1921, were praised and de Valera's Republicanism was called " fanaticism." [8] When Irish Labour took " direct action " and struck against sending supplies to Poland in her war with Russia, having at first thought to gain the cooperation of English Railway workers, the *NS* sided with Irish Labour even after English workers had withdrawn their boycott. The Fabian purpose was perhaps merely to point up the nascent Irish labor movement a little more clearly. When the Irish Government tried to turn public opinion by seeing to it that the rail strike caused hardship, the *NS* looked to the return from America of John Larkin to convince de Valera of the reality of the Irish Labour movement. (Later, Larkin and Larkinism were excoriated.) [9] Such data indicate the objective of the *NS*'s interest in Irish affairs. *NS* dictated a compromising policy. It sought out, as a single strand in the mesh of Irish forces, an Irish Labour Party trend. It sought among a shocked majority in England a local Labour Party vote.

But Fabians took an even more direct hand. In November, 1920,[10] a " Peace with Ireland Council " was formed under the presidency of a Fabian, Lord Henry Bentinck. Fabians figured prominently on it: Mr. Oswald Mosley, secretary (soon to be a Fabian if not yet elected), Mr. G. D. H. Cole, and Mr. Ben Tillett. (Among others were the liberal or progressive persons, J. A. Spender and Professor Gilbert Murray, experienced in Mrs. Webb's Poor Law, or Destitution, Committee). The *NS*

---

[8] *NS*, XX (October 7, 1922), 3.

[9] *NS*, XXII (October 27, 1923), 67.

[10] *NS*, XVI (November 12, 1920), 153.

asked for contributions to support this Council's relief work in Ireland. The attempt to form a contact with the Irish at the level of social relief was significant. Another attempt was made at the political level. When the proposal for a Parliamentary commission failed, in the same week of November, 1920, a group of representatives sent by the Labour Party visited Ireland to find a basis for settling the dispute; four Fabians were among those delegated, General Thomson, Arthur Henderson, Arthur Greenwood,[11] F. W. Jowett, John Robert Clynes. Ambiguously enough, they found it "impossible . . . to hope for any composure in Ireland until that country had been placed on the same footing of self-government as England enjoyed." This meant, of course, not a republic but dominion status under England's King. They warned furthermore that "a great and powerful country can be held at bay by bands of citizen-soldiers patriotically inspired." The committee had full *NS* approval for the recommendation of a thorough judicial inquiry—as "the Labour Party demands."[12]

This is the eyewitness account of Clynes who, although frequently associated with Fabians, was first of all a Labour Party man and one ably supported by the Irish in Manchester. In his energetic person he symbolized the position of Fabians on the Irish question even better than the consistent reporting of the *NS*. His was an Irish electorate and he had connections with the Party, the unions, and the Fabians. He had worked with General Thomson, a Fabian, to arrange some kind of peace with the Irish, but lacking the cooperation of the Cabinet, had failed. His labor union viewpoint is accentuated by the naivety with which he used words then coming into use and long since part of Socialist parlance, such for example as "citizen-soldiers." How often he presided at Fabian lectures or spoke under Fabian auspices is not mentioned in his two volumes of *Memoirs* but the *Fabian News* witnesses to the fact that he did at least once.[13] Although a Trade Union man, he was always close to the political side of the move-

---

[11] Hamilton, *Henderson,* pp. 206 f. Greenwood wrote the report at Henderson's suggestion.

[12] *NS,* XVI (January 1, 1921).

[13] *FN,* Vols. 32–35 in L.C. bound collection (1921–1924), Appendix Syllabi have been bound into L.C. collection by years, and are best identified this way. There is no pagination.

ment and he professed Socialism even with cant. The Irish question was a vital one to rank-and-file union men, Labour Party voters since 1919, *en bloc*.

Capitalizing on the Irish question, Henderson and Arthur Greenwood travelled together on a " large-scale series of most impressive demonstrations held all over the country," as Mrs. Hamilton relates:

> The response, everywhere, was tremendous. It was made abundantly plain that the Government policy, and especially this Black-and-Tan regime of terror was detestable to the majority of the nation. The officially inspired Press tried to "blanket" [sic] the meetings, but they undoubtedly had their influence in causing the complete change of front Mr. Lloyd George had to execute before the year was out. . . .[14]

It was characteristic of Henderson to go to the people with his cause—teaching and rallying them into the Party, while the *NS* kept before the union heads and local government leaders, as well as the dissatisfied electorate, the sordid story. The ferment of Irish agitation [15] was a never-to-be-forgotten experience in Labour Party history and in the history of the collapse of Lloyd George Liberalism.

By the end of 1922, Fabians had set their pattern of behaviour. They did not support republicanism; they refused support to their own Government; they sought contact with a labor tangent; they used the publicity of emissaries and enquiries to build " Labour " at home.

As was said above, after Labour came into Opposition the gain in opposing H. M.'s Government was found in its stymie-ing effect on the Tories. The *NS* attitude toward France was built upon sympathy for what was thought to be the Trade Union view; again with the aim to build the Party. However, as the story of Cannes, Genoa and Chanak will show, the Fabian-inspired wrath with France proved a boon to the baffled Government which would not officially express its disgust with its ally in the sacrosanct

---

[14] Cf. of Hamilton *op. cit.*, p. 207.

[15] Cf. Churchill, *The Aftermath*, p. 278, for the new recruit to Conservatism's views on the relationship of the Irish to the French problem.

Entente. To France for her neurotic, even " demented," action in the Ruhr was imputed blame, in the pages of the *NS,* for arousing the angry nationalism which precipitated fascism in Germany, bringing one more nation into the list—indiscriminately as it was given—Hungary, Italy, Spain, now Germany, all countries where, in the *NS* view, the democratic processes had been destroyed.[16] At one time, the *NS* threatened war with France, " our enemies again as they have been for a thousand years." Saying that vital British interests were involved which no British Government could long ignore, the *NS* spoke boldly,

> . . . the destruction of German industry is something which Great Britain cannot and will not tolerate. We shall be obliged to take a hand in this *new war* as in all European wars which involve *the issue of hegemony.*[17]

This epitomizes the attitude of the Fabian statesman in regard to France from 1920 to 1923. However, on the eve of election, when Baldwin fell, the *NS* was at pains to state it had never advocated war with France. Lloyd George, as later Bonar Law, received sharp criticism, the latter especially for his handling of the question of French occupation of the Ruhr. The *NS*'s policy toward France was based upon its sympathetic attitude toward Germany and its horror of French hegemony. But the Government itself, although traditionally seeking " equality " in the balance of power on the Rhine, was currently informed by a francophobe policy. It is pointed out by a student of Anglo-French relations [18]

---

[16] *NS,* XV (August 14, 1920), 514. Clynes, *op. cit.,* p. 335, said: " Before the French soldiers marched out of the ruined German industrial belt, France had forged . . . the iron swastika of Nazi-ism." His backward glance is inaccurate. The whole Stresemann era is overlooked by him.

[17] *NS,* XIII (January, 1923), 444 f. (Italics are inserted.) The *NS* asked for positive interference against " the White Terror " in Hungary, while it condemned intervention in Russia or assistance in favor of Poland. Cf. *Ibid.,* 1923, *passim.*

[18] Arnold Wolfers, *Britain and France Between Two Wars* (New York: Harcourt, Brace and Company, 1940), p. 247.

Cf. also, *NS,* XXI, p. 288 f, where the absolute necessity for British hegemony of Europe is stated. Also, cf. *ibid.,* p. 489, where dropping the Entente with France and making one with Germany is indicated along with an appeal to the spirit of Palmerston and Salisbury for that the " vital interests of Great Britain are at stake."

that constant British effort was exerted to wean Germany from the Soviet after Rapallo, since any increase in German power benefited Russia; but meanwhile Britain built or sustained German power against France. The Labour Party had to seek a like party in Germany in order to control such a dilemma.

> If . . . Germany was to serve as a check on some power whose political influence and military superiority Britain might have feared, the country could apparently only have been France. It is easy to see why no documentary evidence should be available to prove that this was Britain's thought. . . .[19]

During the Ruhr occupation, Ramsay MacDonald, then leader of the Labour Opposition, echoing the *NS* tone on "hegemony," asked,

> Is it something essential to a demonstration of our amity to France that we are going to turn a blind eye to all the dangers that the development of an enormously powerful European Power [France] is going to offer to us?[20]

Fabianism in all its organs expressed the feeling that the Allied treatment of Germany was unjust: Germany had been misled by the propositions offered before her surrender, which had been repudiated by the Treaty. Fabian spokesmen held that to blockade Germany as the French proposed would be wrong; that although certain reparations should be made to France and Belgium, the British coal industry must not be injured by German coal. Furthermore, Germany should be admitted into the League of Nations; and the League should be made strong enough to express and enforce the common will, not necessarily by an international police force—an expedient not acceptable to Fabians, since no one would contemplate putting the fleet under any save British command.[21]

---

[19] Wolfers, *op. cit.*, p. 247. Under a Labour Government, H.M.'s Stationery Office published *Documents on British Foreign Policy, 1919–1939*, in 1946, but started with Second Series, 1929.

[20] *Ibid.*

[21] L. S. Woolf, "Enforcement of Decrees of the Court," *International Government* (New York: Brentano's, 1916), pp. 406 ff.

On one occasion some concrete effects of German reparations and English debt payment to the United States roused a jovian humor in the editor of the *NS*. When a " realized surplus " of one hundred million pounds sterling was announced for 1922–1923 (Germany had made payment in 1922 of seven hundred and fifty million pounds), the *NS* suggested sending it " in gold " to America.

> It would dismay the American bankers, but unluckily it might also dismay the governors of the Bank of England, who still cherish a sentimental affection for the coins and ingots stored in their vaults. They still seem unable to realize that the credit of Great Britain rests not on the precious metal they so jealously guard, but on the fact that in a year of profound depression British revenue exceeds British expenditure by a hundred million pounds.[22]

The facetiousness reveals an attitude toward America, an economic policy, and an odd patriotism. The implied judgment on the gold standard and this new philosophy of credit will be recalled in the fiscal anguish of 1931. At any rate, the *NS* now based its own bid for leadership upon English financial world hegemony. In January, 1921,[23] the idea of " indemnities " had been scoffed at; the *NS* had then believed an official statement renouncing indemnities would be financially wise and that the proposition would even be politically feasible, because when English politicians mentioned indemnities, " their audience cheers but no one takes them too seriously." But in France it was " unfortunately, otherwise."

Early in 1923, the *NS* began to show some antipathy toward America. Although it criticized Mr. Baldwin for antagonizing American opinion, in an account which any close student of the facts would find shallow and partisan the *NS* said the acceptance of the American debt-funding conditions " annihilate[d] " American " moral pretensions " and imposed on Great Britain a burden which she assumed as " a guarantor," not as a " beneficiary." (That is, she accepted German moneys paid in indemnity and

---

22 *NS*, XXII (April 7, 1923), 761 f.
23 *NS*, XXVI (January 22, 1921), 461.

passed them on to America to discharge the British debt to the
United States.) Yet, "by accepting the American terms *sans
phrase* we have at least re-established our credit, and removed one
of the main obstacles to the creation of a stable measure of international value." [24] This, in spite of having said, "It might have
been better to await a general settlement of international debts
and reparations." Yet to have waited would have been to attempt
the general settlement without first establishing measure of value.
It is not difficult to see why France, where the Socialist labor
front was atomized so that Poincaré ignored it, found no sympathy in the *NS*. France held out, ostensibly, for reparations to
pay war debts, and to finance her rebuilding. As we shall see in
another connection, the Baldwin-Poincaré notes reveal a France
bent, it would seem, on destroying Germany, whence came
England's funds to pay her debts.

An article out of *Figaro* was reproduced in the *NS* in March,
1923. It had borne the three stars suspected of being Poincaré's
mark.[25] Its inclusion in the *NS* demonstrated the fact that much
may be learned from the dismayed utterances of an opponent.
Complaint was made of the refusal of the Allies to help force
Germany to pay for French reconstruction charged by France
against reparations collections. The fact was restated that "Antagonism is inevitable inasmuch as England produces, and seeks to
sell that which France can produce and endeavors to sell." To
Britain was imputed the blame for stiffening German resistance
to French demands: "The degree of resistance of Germany has
been constantly regulated by the attitude of the British Government." The signer of three stars adroitly threatened a Franco-
German alliance. He was realistic:

> While France exhausts herself in vain discussions . . .
> the German capitalists find shelter in the banks of neutral
> countries; they thus escape from our control; they have
> built up vast reserves . . . for [purchase of] raw ma-

---

[24] *NS*, XX (February 3, 1923), 501.
[25] *NS*, XX (April 7, 1923), 767. The article in *Figaro* was undoubtedly
Poincaré's. He said the same substantially in his reply to Curzon's statement
of His Majesty's Government regarding the Ruhr, August, 1923. Cf. Wolfers, *op. cit.*, p. 91.

terials with which Great Britain is ready to furnish [Germany].[26]

The *NS* rejoined [27] with comment that the "elite" in England maintained the opinion that the French adventure in the Ruhr was "not a debatable issue" although popular opinion was less decisive since "its leaders have not yet spoken out." The guidance of popular leaders Fabianism would itself assume. A delegation made up of Labour Party persons had visited the Ruhr and after the reports of its findings, advocating "internationalisation," were published, the *NS* in disagreement suggested the Labour Party should "edit" the pronouncements of any such future delegations.[28] Subsequent comments of the *NS* upon the proposal for internationalising the Ruhr were equally disparaging. Sometimes, however, the expression, "some persons," loyally shielded mistaken Labourites. The Labour Party delegation to France was not so felicitous as the one to Ireland. We find no Fabians boasting of association with the first named delegation, except Ben Tillett who memorialized his own (anti-Fabian) view on internationalising the Ruhr in *Who's Who*.

The foregoing notes represent very briefly the position of the *NS* on the relation of France and Britain where Germany was the point of tension, and Russia that of divergence. As Lloyd George was excoriated for his opportunism, Bonar Law was condemned for his "tranquillity," or "benevolent impotence." "Mr. Bonar Law," it was said, "would loyally support anyone." Hence, if Conservatives would only unite and give him for Ministers, Austen Chamberlain, Lord Birkenhead, and Sir Robert Horne, there would be a "Government which the Opposition could fight" and one which would "say what England thinks"; for "we are not a third-rate Power. Why should we act as if we were?" [29] (Even in its patent belligerence, it did not nominate Churchill for the Cabinet it would like to fight.) Better articulation of British

---

[26] *NS*, XX (April 7, 1923), 767.

[27] *Ibid.*

[28] *NS*, XX (February 24, 1923), 585.

[29] *NS*, XX (April 7, 1923), 765. Let it be recalled the next election took place in December. The Bonar Law-Baldwin Government lasted all through 1922 to the end of 1923.

foreign policy would furnish better rallying points for the Labour Party's internationalism.

So, through 1920–1923, the Fabian organ tried to enlist English opinion by means of its sympathy with the Labour Party and its appeal to a Socialist " elite " in favor of a bellicose attitude toward France. Not so with regard to Russia. The Government of Bonar Law, and Stanley Baldwin's Government, were well aware of Labour's pro-Russian proclivities, even though 1920 seemed long ago. J. R. Clynes witnessed to the following episode from within Labour and Fabian ranks: The threat of civil war in Russia passed; then, in 1920, answering, it was said, Poland's invasion of the Ukraine, " the Cossacks came clattering to the very gates of Warsaw." [30] Following the Pilsudski victory (which was a grave and unexpected disappointment to the *NS*),[31] General Wrangel, his government encouraged " furtively," said Clynes, by Britain and recognized by France, tried to advance in South Russia. Churchill gave orders to concentrate warships in the Baltic, to alert the remaining British troops in Russia and to prepare " floods of propaganda." It was then that

> Arthur Henderson sent telegrams to all local Labour parties, urging that demonstrations should be made against the implication of Britain in a war against Russia.[32]

His suggestions were seconded by the Council of the TUC in conference with the Parliamentary Labour Party (J. R. Clynes, J. H. Thomas, Arthur Henderson) and the Labour Party Executive (Webb, Mary MacArthur, Susan Lawrence) [33] to form a " Council of Action." The threat of war to aid Poland against Russia was removed. This boycott by Labour, led by Fabians, against the Government's implemented policy was " The most formidable challenge ever made to democracy," said the Prime Minister. But, said Clynes,

We knew our own people and the people of Britain and

---

[30] Clynes, *op. cit.*, p. 322.

[31] *NS*, XV (September 25, 1920), 661 and *passim*.

[32] Clynes, *op. cit.*, pp. 322 f. Clynes never questioned his mentors.

[33] *FN*, XXXI (July, 1920). Lansbury was elected in July.

we knew they would not fight a war to set a Romanov
sprig on the throne his father had so vilely misused,[34]

with characteristic confusion as to the issues involved. Somewhat
the same sort of reasoning had stopped the civil war in Russia;
" Whites " were as bad as " Reds " and no one wanted a Romanov.
(This is an early presentation of the pattern so often repeated
down to 1950: British Social-Democrats scold both sides, neglect
to distinguish at the given moment, " Bolshevik " and " Men-
shevik "; also refuse to support the truncated element of
" authority and property.") The differences between Mensheviks
and Bolsheviks were as little understood, outside initiated circles,
as the difference between democracy-and-industrial-pursuits and
the " industrial democracy " of Fabian Socialism. The real
reason for Trade Union interest in Russia was based on what
unionists had been told of the potentialities for trade. This is
not the only juncture in which amazing irresponsibility is to be
remarked. Welcoming the news of a British firm's contract with
the Bolshevik Government to repair locomotives, the *NS* rejoiced
that this would force politicians to stop belaboring the Bolsheviks,
hasten the Trade Agreement then pending, and illustrate " the
reality and urgency of the Labour Party's demand for reopening
trade with Russia as a practical means of lessening unemployment in this country." [35] The editor was not speaking for idealistic Socialism, only to encourage the unions to trust the Labour
Party.

Better reasoning and more trust in what Webb would call " the
nature of things " was found in the observations and conclusions
of Dr. L. Haden Guest, a Fabian who lectured on " Russia Under
the Bolsheviks," July 16, 1920.[36] He described his elaborate
entertainment by the Bolshevik Government; but, since " they
[Guest and his fellow travellers, including Margaret Cole] [37]

---

[34] Clynes, *op. cit.*, p. 323. The *NS*, when the IFTU heard proposals for
similar action during the Genoa Conference in 1922, opposed in agreement
with J. H. Thomas, saying it could only serve "at the head of a national
protest" as, in Thomas' opinion, the Council of Action was in 1920. Cf.
NS, XIX (April 29, 1922), 82 f.

[35] *NS*, XVI (February 5, 1921), 517.

[36] *FN*, XXXI:8 (August, 1920).

[37] *NS*, XV (April 24, 1920), 58. Soviet Russia agreed to receive a delega-

managed to see a good deal for themselves," he told also of terror and militarized labour; of the Soviet village system turning into " praesidiums "—bureaucracies backed by the Army; of laws made by proclamation, and of secret police. This report marks the beginning of a legend which has been uncritically accepted ever since, a two-fold legend. There is no proof that " national patriotism " was anything but repression and there is no evidence that any force remained to counter Bolshevism.

> They [the Bolsheviks] are supported by a strong senti-
> ment of national patriotism due to the fact of the Entente
> Powers attacking Russia. . . . When peace comes, *op-
> position* to the Bolsheviks will arise from the *other
> political parties* and factions. . . . Russia wants help
> and frank criticism. Unless the *Socialists in Germany,
> Russia,* and all other countries can come together and
> take hold of Europe, there is grave danger that a large
> part of European civilization will be destroyed.[38]

This was said at a special meeting for members, associates and subscribers in Essex Hall. If they disapproved of Bolsheviks, they must but wait for the overthrow from within. Russia wanted " frank criticism." Yet this might only rouse patriotism and cement Russia behind their wrong leaders. One point was positively stated: Europe should be Socialist.

Further treatment of the Fabian attitude toward Russia is precluded by the scope of this study; otherwise, the lectures of other Fabians, for example, of Mrs. Snowden and of Julius West, might be discussed at this point; also, those of George Lansbury. All three were visitors to Moscow at one time or another. This suffices to show the position of Fabians in the leadership of Opposition, 1918–1922. It remains but to add that the *NS* attributed to the British blockade the ill-omened success of the Bolsheviks; and, for the sake of " peace " and reconstruction, it hoped the Bolshevik Government—they " have shown that they

---

tion of TUC and Labour Party members after refusing to receive a Commission appointed by the League of Nations. The *NS* promised no " undue tenderness " for Lenin and Trotsky if rumors as to Russia's abandonment of democratic methods and so forth should be confirmed.

[38] *Ibid.* Italics inserted.

can rule "—would be recognized by His Majesty's Government.[39]
Again the inconsistency or illogicality is in the text. In summary,
it can be said that Fabians disapproved of Bolshevik methods;
also of past interventions against them; they hoped for gradual
internal revolution but they would recognize the Soviet State as
presently constituted.

The most vivid account of the culmination of a crisis among
crises at Chanak is found in Winston Churchill's *The World
Crisis: The Aftermath.*[40] It was a story of division: Republican
Greeks against Royalist Greeks; Nationalist Turks against the
Sultan, head of the Moslem cult; British policy against French
policy; French Radical Socialists against Poincaré followers;
British Coalition Cabinet members against other British Coalition
Cabinet members; the Irish issues against the Eastern issues;
the *NS* inspired opinion in England supporting now Socialist
pacifism on Russia, now Labour Party belligerence toward France
or regarding Ireland.

Royalist Greece under King Constantine launched a lone offensive against the Nationalist Turks under Kemal Pasha. France
favored Kemal, who could help her in Cilicia, and Britain favored
the Sultan in Constantinople; and, unofficially, since King Constantine's recall, Britain favored the Greeks as the guardians of
the Mediterranean. French Radical Socialists asked for cooperation of France and England; Poincaré's party made every
step as difficult as possible for Lord Curzon. The Coalition
Cabinet divided between the Churchill group which favored
making peace with the Turks and winning French cooperation in
dealing with Kemal, and the Lloyd George group which was
pro-Greek but was then baffled by the Irish question and misled
by Russia. The Germans at Genoa threw aside caution regard-

---

[39] *NS*, XV (June 5, 1920), 240 ff. There occurred at this time a " trial "
in Russia of a member of the Catholic hierarchy (one case to reach the
press). The *NS* pretended that the case represented the attempt of the
Church to set up a rival system of ecclesiastical courts; it held that the
" priest " should take his chances with any other person accused of pecula-
tions. Then, when after about a year, the prelate was executed, the *NS* raged
in righteous indignation. Cf. *NS*, XXI, p. 12.

[40] Winston Churchill, *The Aftermath: A Sequel to The World Crisis*
(London: The Macmillan Company, 1941).

ing France and openly hoped for a Greek victory while they made a separate settlement with Russia.

At Chanak all these forces converged. Kemal, having established his Capital at Angora, took the road to Constantinople. The Greeks rejected their King again for Venizelos after the disasters in which Kemal's strategic two years of "waiting" eventuated. The British Cabinet now took a stand ostensibly against further Turkish progress in Europe. The sequel to Northcliffe's alarum, "These men mean war!" was tragi-comic. British forces, left unaided by French and Italians and with only the promise of Dominion cooperation, met—with "most formal frowns"—the "unabashed good humor" on the part of the Turks invading the neutral zone at Chanak.[41]

The Cabinet sent a message to its commander in the neutral zone, General Harington, to serve an ultimatum to the Turks, but laid down certain conditions which he was shrewd enough to interpret correctly. As well as Churchill he knew that if Kemal attacked Chanak, it would give the Greeks time to consolidate in Thrace. Kemal did not attack Chanak or quit the neutral zone, nor run into a "death trap in Thrace."[42] "As long as the British fleet held this line of deep salt water [the Straits] the war could not be carried into Thrace."[43] The Pasha agreed with General Harington to confer at Mudania. Here the French represented by M. Franklin-Bouillon deadlocked the Conference by the offer of too great concessions. A British flourish of military might in the Dardanelles released the ensuing deadlock and the way was laid for the Lausanne Treaty to replace that of Sèvres. The English Cabinet, when it united on the eve of "Chanak," had publicly resolved to fall, lose allies, bear the howls of the press, but "force the Turk to a negotiated peace before he set foot in Europe."[44] But, at Lausanne, the Turk was re-established at Constantinople, he regained much of Eastern Thrace, he shed the tutelage of the (French) Capitulations, he regained sovereignty over the Turkish Straits "under the thinnest

---

[41] *Ibid.*, p. 433.
[42] *Ibid.*, p. 435.
[43] *Ibid.*, p. 425.
[44] *Ibid.*, p. 423.

of disguises." Churchill wrote that Curzon made skillful use of prestige gained at Chanak to gain certain concessions, for example, "repatriation" of Greeks numbering a million and a quarter (these Greeks had constituted the backbone of Turkish economic life), and excision of Arab provinces from nationalist Turkey. The *NS*'s reaction is shown in the following comments.

The *NS* said [45] the "war party," "which included the Prime Minister and Mr. Churchill," decided upon "expelling the Turks from the neutral zone by force of arms," (as if the *NS* believed this!). General Harington had angered the war party by his negotiations continued "at his own peril." Only deference for popular opinion had checked a move to censure him. (Churchill writing in 1929 had no anger against Harington to record.) The *NS* admitted the "precise words" of Harington's instructions were not made public. There is no doubt but that the *NS* favored Russia's aspirations toward Santa Sophia and was not prepared to encourage Turkish hegemony on the Straits. It took the usual position: Against its own Government, against the national forces, and in favor of Russia. The old Sultan was a "push over" for Russia.

It was no doubt difficult even then for the uninitiated to ascertain what the *NS*'s objectives were. It opined that the "wrongheaded" policy was "not wholly unintelligible." It would be easy to whip the Turks at Chanak and restore British and Christian prestige, "for it is certainly undesirable that the Turks should remain under the illusion that they can challenge Europe with impunity." But British prestige did not need such measures—only "honesty and commonsense." The Government was expected to argue the Turks out of their position, not fight. "We are not the sentimental people we were ten years ago . . . not inclined to regard dead British soldiers as sufficient justification for any expenditure." [46] Churchill's success in setting up Kemal Pasha to guard the Straits was a hard blow *NS* took the trouble

---

[45] *NS*, XX (October 7, 1922), 1 f.

[46] *NS*, XX (October 7, 1922), 1. It would seem to stand for containing Kemal but not for fighting him. It was against Lloyd George's pro-Greek stand so probably thought of Kemal as a means of curbing Greek aspirations, too. (A weak Greece meant aid and comfort to the Soviets.)

to feign to ignore. The Turk was not a threat to Europe but a road block to Red Russia.

As in several other places, the *NS* writer insinuated that the Coalition was not made up of Englishmen or gentlemen,—" our Welsh-Tory Government." The confusion is only apparent and is part of the psychological technique by which Socialists sought to capitalize on feelings of inferiority induced in those whom they criticized.[47]

Noteworthy, also, from the point of view of method, is the remark that " a few calm lies of the inspired ' Political Correspondent' variety " would have served Downing Street better than " very angry " outbursts of chagrin. (Evidently, the " war-party " was suspected by the *NS* of making a show of chagrin over peace at Chanak.) The *NS* itself used the device of the " correspondent." It seems on this occasion to have been misled by a " Student of Politics " who had served Downing Street as a rager, " inspired " or not, over the Chanak business.[48] We see, however, that the Government concealed its purposes from Bolshevik sympathizers and began to develop a new buffer in Kemal Pasha's Turkey. Kemal knew he could have been ruined at Chanak. Now the Cabinet (Lloyd George had had to relinquish his pro-Greek policy) as well as a Fabian spokesman, for a different reason, favored the Turks. The Fabian would give Turkey under the Sultan " self-determination "—so that it could determine to go freely into the orbit of the Bolshevik Government; instead, the Government mastered Kemal Pasha and so Turkey was built into an " independent " bulwark against a Russia forever yearning toward Holy Sophia on the Bosphorus.

Whether the *NS* knew better or not, it kept up the allegation that the Government was war-mongering. October 14, 1922,[49] " all [was] over in Chanak." Harington had used Nelson's trick of turning a blind eye; " if he had carried out the Cabinet's instructions . . . we should have been plunged into war with Turkey." Lloyd George was claiming the honors of a peace-maker after warlike " ultimatums and manifestos " to the Jugo-

---

[47] *Ibid.*, p. 1 f.
[48] *Ibid.*, p. 2.
[49] *NS*, XX (October 14, 1922), 33 f.

slavs and the Dominions. "But the British public knows Mr. Lloyd George and is waiting to register its opinion" on his "peace-making" and Near East "bungling." "We are never inclined to be prophetic upon any question," so the *NS* could not say if there would be a general election that year or not.

Discussing Lausanne, the *NS* revealed its pro-Russian bent which it did not emphasize, in its attitude toward Turkish "self-determination" before the Chanak denouement. December 16, 1922,[50] the Russians were wrathy. The Government should placate them and recognize the Soviet Government. A week later,[51] the terms of Lausanne were revealed. "Freedom of the Straits" the *NS* termed a hollow, if not mischievous, triumph for asserted British naval power. Fabian C. M. Lloyd contributed "The Danger in the Near East" for the February, 1923, issue.[52] He compared Lausanne and the Ruhr, opined that the Government "amid its wrecked hopes of 'tranquillity' [had no] clear policy." This Fabian friend of Cole blamed the rise of Turkish nationalism on the Treaty of Sèvres and on Lloyd George, who "nourish[ed] the monster" by his pro-Greek policy. Lloyd found fault with Lord Curzon for championing the British Straits plan (sovereignty for Turkey) and rejecting the Russian plan, since to have done so would have made it possible to exert through the Russians "a powerful influence on the Turks." It must be observed that the allegation that the Government had no policy is unwarranted; that it needed Russian aid with the Turks, is factitious. That Turkish nationalism was an unmitigated evil and a mere accident of Lloyd George's policy is not provable. The editorial slant of the *NS* through this period is pronouncedly pro-Russian. Had the *NS* been able to force Lloyd George, Russia would be in Constantinople today. Again the pacifist, if not peace-loving strain: In the question of leaving Mosul (Iraquian protectorate of Britian) to the disposition of the League, Lloyd wrote "the British people do not want to go to war . . . and will rightly refuse to go to war for [Mosul]." [53]

---

[50] *NS*, XX (December 16, 1922), 317.
[51] *NS*, XX (December 23, 1922), 345.
[52] *NS*, XX (February 3, 1923), 506 f.
[53] *NS* writers apparently claimed a certain assurance of competence to

The most effective propaganda weapon which pro-Greeks and anti-Bolsheviks used came from "atrocity stories." The *NS* minimized such accounts with calm reasoning, naming the agitation "Gladstonism"; [54] or it employed the dialectical technique of exposing past injuries inflicted upon the present torturers by prototypes of their present victims. [55] It offered no constructive suggestions regarding Armenians, victims of Turkish ferocity, unless that of Noel-Buxton (Fabian) embodied in a letter to the *NS* from the scene was such.

The conference at Lausanne from November 20, 1922, to July 17, 1923, grew out of the Chanak settlement. Lausanne conferences resulted in the Straits settlement which lasted until Russia's renewed efforts to achieve hegemony for herself at Montreux opened the "great debate" of 1945–1946. Rather unreasonably, "Chanak" lent itself to those internal forces which were shaping up to a well-grounded Party of Opposition in 1922 heading toward capture of the Government by 1923–1924.

In 1920, the threat of war with Russia caused no dissolution. The efficacy of Labour's threat to "down tools" if war were made against Russia had been augmented by the war-weariness of the populace. In 1922, while war-like threats of Fabians against France went unheeded, their criticism of the Government's Turkish policy was seconded in other quarters and resulted in the

---

gauge public opinion. This was a new kind of journalism now permeating bourgeois ranks. It had long been effective in proletariat and doctrinaire milieux. It does not seek to measure public opinion but to create it by polemic. This presuming to speak for "the people" by persons who were not of the people marks the literature of the upper bourgeoisie as unreliable.

[54] In reply to a letter writer, the *NS*'s editor remarked, February 10, 1923, "Post war Democracy" was not "Gladstonism." Cf. *NS*, XX (February 10, 1923), 539. (As of 1950, "dynamic democracy" is *not* democratic republicanism.)

[55] *NS*, XX (October 14, 1922), 33. Cf. also, *idem.* (March 17, 1923), 703, which carried a half-page advertisement of the Society of Friends, pleading for contributions for food for "Pagachev, a district of Russia adjoining Bazuluk" where the peasants were eating grass. The Quakers paid for the advertisement and the *NS* made no comment on conditions in the Socialists' new civilization. Mrs. Webb argued in her last years that climatic conditions had caused the later famine of 1932–33. Cf. Margaret Cole, *Beatrice Webb*, p. 179.

end of Lloyd George's rule. Lord Beaverbrook of the *Daily Express* proclaimed that the situation at Chanak called for resort to the electorate because the leaders in the Coalition Cabinet "meant war!" This was a blow struck upon well-polarized political metal. Already the work for dissolution had been initiated along party lines. In September of 1922, Henderson and Clynes had inserted in the annual report of the Labour Party this conclusion cited by the latter: [56]

> The sooner the record of this Government is submitted to the electorate, and . . . this Parliament is purged, the better for the welfare of the nation.

The Conservatives, having begun in April to re-form their ranks and withdraw from the Coalition, now in October, following the Labour Party's crystallizing pronouncement, recognized that the time was ripe and withdrew from the Coalition, giving for reason their disapproval of the Prime Minister's pro-Greek attitude. Lloyd George on October 19, 1922, resigned the Premiership and Bonar Law consented to head the proposed Conservative Cabinet. The latter shared the conviction, if he was not the servant of Lord Beaverbrook, that the Government was wrong in its ostensibly anti-Turk policy. The latter had visited the area involved and, after the Greeks' collapse in the projected siege of Angora and their retreat into Smyrna, he took a positive stand against the official policy of England. He learned from an interview with the leaders that "these men [Winston Churchill, Lord Birkenhead, and Lloyd George] mean war," knowledge which he communicated to Bonar Law. This statesman then wrote a letter to the press,[57] and the sequel is well known. "Chanak" brought the Tories into power but it disclosed the decided pro-Russian attitude of Labour which now became the Opposition.

The *NS* would have been as little effectual in this as in the matter of France had it not been that Lord Beaverbrook and the *Daily Express* spread similar views on Turks and Tartars to rapidly increasing numbers of subscribers. The *NS*, however,

---

[56] Clynes, *op. cit.*, p. 327.
[57] Cf. Lord Beaverbrook, *Politicians and the Press* (London: Hutchinson and Company, 1925), p. 49.

garnered Labour Party strength as the Conservatives swarmed off from the Coalition, themselves developing a new party spirit. The assumption of an air of chagrin with all the Government's efforts abroad was feelingly expressed, indeed, on December 23, 1922.[58] when " all were expected to be cheerful," and the end of the Coalition was the only approved event in a long list of debacles and grievances ascribed to the Coalition:—" Cannes— Genoa—Anatolia—Chanak—Lausanne—unemployment." Without discrimination as to the causes of failure or measurement of the extent to which Government and Labour had been agreed on political if not on Socialistic objectives, and with the significant omission of the Irish settlement, this sounded the election drums. The *NS* was now clear cut: " We have no love and very little respect for the present British Government [now Bonar Law's]." The downfall of Lloyd George had not been enough. Bonar Law was soon to find his position untenable in his bad state of health and to make way for Stanley Baldwin, May, 1923. The new Prime Minister was Baldwin and not Curzon because of the presence and the attitude of Socialist-Labour. According to Lloyd George's secretary, A. J. Sylvester, it was J. C. C. Davidson, Parliamentary Private Secretary to Bonar Law, who underscored in the mind of Lord Stamfordham, the King's advisor, this attitude of Labour. Davidson had begun to cultivate Baldwin as soon as it became evident Bonar Law's health was precarious. That Webb and Henderson were acquainted with Davidson is a possibility since the latter had served as P.P.S. in Colonies in 1910 and in both the Exchequer and the Leader's Offices in 1916–1920. The perennial interest of Webb in the ministry for colonies since his clerkship there, and the incumbency of Henderson in the war cabinet warrant the inference that Davidson was known to these two Fabians.

The degree of justice to be found in the criticism of the above

---

[58] *NS,* XX, p. 345.

The tensions are reviewed briefly in Churchill's *Gathering Storm,* p. 20. But the part played by Lloyd George in the agreement of December 5, 1921, and the latter's reliance upon Lord Birkenhead are told in A. J. Sylvester, *The Real Lloyd George,* pp. 55–66. " Austen quailed, but F. E. [Lord Birkenhead, who was F. E. Smith] never. He was better even than Churchill in that matter," p. 65.

list of events from Cannes to Lausanne and " unemployment " is
impossible to judge and not part of the present task. The identification of each name must suffice:

At Cannes there met together for the purpose of settling the
amount of reparations the Germans might produce, Lloyd George,
Lord Curzon, Bonar Law, and others, with Briand for France,
Bonomi for Italy, and Rathenau for Germany. Lord Beaverbrook
and L. Guest were observing. Lloyd George had been adamant
with Briand on the eve of the Conference and had sent an ultimatum to the French Minister involving even the breaking up of
the Conference if a certain interview attributed to Briand and
published in a Belgian paper was not repudiated.[59] Repudiation
came in the same night. This evidenced the fact that there was
no soft sentiment in George's friendly attitude toward Briand. A
game of golf in a normal interlude in which the Frenchman and
the Italian caused great amusement by their inexperience, was
used by Briand's opponents in Paris to disparage him as one who
was soft with Britain, and to dissolve his Government. Lost were
the effect of the candor and cooperation of Rathenau, the plans
for mutual agreement between England and France on reparations. Only the project of an International Economic Conference
to include Russia and to meet at Genoa remained. (As Lorwin's
Labor and Internationalism shows, the Labour and Socialist International, as at Berne and Geneva in relation to Versailles, sched-
uled a concomitant meeting in Genoa.) It is hard to find any
reason for Labour Party or Fabian criticism of the Prime Minister's views and policies at Cannes. He aimed to satisfy the
reasonable demands of Socialists without Socialism, so much so
that Churchill accused him of being pro-Bolshevik.[60] On the way
home from ill-fated Cannes, Lloyd George met Poincaré only to
find that the " greedy, suspicious, grasping Frenchman " had to
have everything " in writing " and the pledged word of England
that in the case of threat to French security " everything we have,

---

[59] That the series of disruptive publications of half-truths, if examined and
checked for sources, would make an indictment of Russia is a likely hypothesis. It must be borne in mind that all the Socialist organizations who
spoke through ILO favored the Russian experiment, if not the Russian way
of organizing and the cruelty of Russian methods.

[60] Cf. Churchill, *The Aftermath*, p. 415.

just as we did in the last war " would be used in behalf of France.[61] This was in January, 1922. On February 25, Lloyd George and Poincaré met again. At this time, Conservative criticism in London was repeated to him by his secretary. The Prime Minister then wrote a letter to Austen Chamberlain offering to resign in his favor, since he had a large following of young Conservatives. Chamberlain rejected the suggestion and the Tories were silenced for the time being, according to Sylvester. According to Spender, they were busy with the " Cabin Boy's " revolt. This accounts for the quiet period in the *Fabian News* regarding elections. Conservatives were doing the work and they need only wait, as the *bloc des Gauches* waited in France. Spender [62] credits the Conservatives' youthful organizer, Sir William Young, with preventing an election from being held in 1922 when the Coalition might easily have been returned. Lord Birkenhead dubbed Young the " Cabin Boy " and his movement, the " Cabin Boy's" revolt. Lord Curzon and Lloyd George quarrelled but the irascible Lord stayed on to serve in the Foreign Office. Currently, the honors lists revealed that men of war-gotten wealth were making large contributions to Liberal (Lloyd George branch) Party funds. In any case, Conservatives, at this time, headed off a repetition of the re-election of the Coalition.

So much for " Cannes." As to " Genoa ": In April, 1922, thirty-four nations sent representatives to Genoa, the Conference which was " Lloyd George's Own Child." He was disappointed that Lenin did not come himself. Tchicherin, Litvinoff, and Kassin came, with Rakovsky the official spokesman. The French, headed by Barthou, were unwilling to have Germany and Russia admitted as equals. At this meeting Mr. Garvin and Sir Maurice Hankey were notably present and Lord Birkenhead was at Lloyd George's side, as usual. While a select committee—Sir Sidney Chapman, M. Felcourt, M. Litvinoff, and M. Alphand—was struggling toward agreement, the news arrived from London, sent there by a curious news reporter who had followed a " picnic " to Santa Margherita, that Germany and Russia, through the in-

---

[61] Sylvester, *op. cit.,* pp. 76 f.

[62] J. A. Spender, *Great Britain: Empire and Commonwealth, 1886–1935* (London: Cassell and Company, 1936), p. 634.

strumentality of Rathenau and Tchicherin, with Litvinoff, had arrived at a secret agreement. The basis of the future Treaty of Rapallo, it was officially announced by Rakovsky and Rathenau. Toward the last days of the Genoa Conference, Lloyd George addressed over seven hundred members of the press and called attention to those who " did not want the Conference to succeed. . . . Quarrelsome people who like to keep up hatred and conflict between nations." All present knew he meant the French.[63] But it was also clear that the Russians had been unmanageable. While the *NS* scolded that they should be reasonable about property rights, Sylvester wrote in his diary that they were impossible to convince that the occasion was not one on which to make separate agreements with the several assembled nations. But the most unreasonable intransigence came from the French who feared a resurgent Germany and officially detested Russian Reds. Barthou, never a free negotiator, received up to twenty-two telegrams a day from Poincaré. The latter made a speech at Bar-le-duc which ended all hope for success for the Genoa Conference. In contrast with the tolerance for Germany and Russia and the hope for disarmament entertained by the British Prime Minister, Barthou manifested only harshness " in the extreme." The *London Times* and the *Daily Mail*, Northcliffe papers and Francophile, made the political most of the trouble resulting from the French Premier's confusion of the issue of reparations with the Genoa agenda which was economic and monetary. They even announced that Lloyd George had severed the Anglo-French entente. This was one of those disruptive press releases the printed text of which was disclaimable at its source of origin.[64] Although explanatory letters were read in Parliament, the Genoa Conference ended in bootless efforts of Barthou and Sir Edward Griggs (for Lloyd George) to counteract the allegations. All that was achieved was a document which represented a " breathing space " and the surrender of the problem of world peace to the Hague Conference. Only anti-French sentiment could have moved the *NS* to disapprove this final desperate effort and the weekly could hardly have asked for

---

[63] Lord Birkenhead, in attendance unofficially, was living in his moored yacht, and Lord Riddell usually fronted for Lloyd George with the press.

[64] Cf. Sylvester, *op. cit.*, pp. 96 f.

greater effort against the French. (In January, 1923, Bonar Law faced the same difficulties in Paris with Poincaré. " Only by the utmost tactful handling did Bonar Law avert an open breach.") [65] Commenting on Genoa, the *NS* regretted the Russians sent not Trotsky or Lenin or Radek, who were comparable in skill at international conferences, the *NS* said, to Lloyd George, but the " childishly provocative," " street corner idealist," Tchitcherin— " the Arthur Ponsonby of Russia." [66] This was the only type of criticism the *NS* ever meted out to Russia. After the closing of the Conference in failure, the *NS*, in line with the Tory press, reported the Entente dead and declared no agreement was possible between England and France on Russia, whose representative evinced an " impossibilism " like that of Poincaré. We have seen that the *NS* encouraged the Trade Unions and the Labour Party to agitate for *de jure* recognition in order to foster trade with Russia. Now the *NS* said it was " nonsense " for Russia to ask aid and credit without recognition of the rights of private property.[67] The *NS* seemed let down by the befriended Russians and constrained to placate the property-minded Trade Unionists. That was in spring. By Christmas it threw in " Genoa " for good measure and did not spare the British statesmen criticism for their failure to achieve the impossible, and the Fabian dissatisfaction with the Coalition was saddled upon Bonar Law's Ministry. It is clear that at Cannes and Genoa Lloyd George had the same aims as Labour and his failure was hardly of his own making. He had to uphold the Entente; Fabian adverse opinion of France could be boldly spoken.

As to " Anatolia," as Spender points out, there took place there one of the makeshift efforts to deal with a beaten Turkey and with a lost ally, in revolutionary Russia. In 1919, by the Treaty of Sèvres, the Turkish Straits had been internationalized and " spheres of influence [assigned] to France, Italy, and Greece in the Turkish homelands of Anatolia." [68] The *NS* never approved

---

[65] Sylvester, *op. cit.*, pp. 67–98.

[66] *NS*, XIX (April 15, 1922), 30. Fabians criticize Fabians freely. Lansbury thought Tchicherin was like the Webbs.

[67] *NS*, XIX (May 20, 1922), 169.

[68] A. J. Spender, *op. cit.*, p. 628. Cf. also, *ibid.*, pp. 631–634, for the Chanak crisis.

of Sèvres. "Anatolia" had another significance; it was the scene of terrible massacres and atrocities early in 1922 which provoked the Greeks to active war again.[69] This was really what brought Churchill back to direct England's policy at Chanak where Britain made the stand. It was the reaction to Anatolia which led Churchill to write to Curzon, in April of 1922, his view that Lloyd George was working for Russia at Genoa, which illustrates the view taken here that the Prime Minister had the same aims as Labour: "The great objective of the Prime Minister's policy has been Moscow, to make Great Britain the nation in the closest possible relation with the Bolsheviks."[70] He pointed out the fatuousness of the hope for trade advantages which led to "separating ourselves in our attitude toward Russia from . . . the United States and France." This is strong evidence that Lloyd George was trying again to satisfy the demands of the increasingly vocal Labour element speaking as it did in the *NS*.

This was the period when in September, 1922, Churchill, Austen Chamberlain, Birkenhead and Horne rallied to the support of Lloyd George in what was ostensibly anti-Turk (if not a pro-Greek) policy. It is to be recalled that a little less than two years before Labour had stopped a move to aid Poland against Russia. There was no threat to boycott a war over Chanak. After "Chanak," the Turk was set up to stop Russia at the Dardanelles, a piece of diplomacy far more adroit than the patent attempt to stem Bolshevism in 1920. Fabian spokesmen signalized their sympathy with Russia's drive for hegemony in the Black Sea regions. Socialist organs never referred to their defeat at this point. As Wolfers says, there are no documents to reveal the struggle for hegemony with France; and there are none to expose the use of a new force, nationalist Turkey, against Russia looming over all in the East. The naive support given by the *NS* to the idea of self-determination for Turkey consistently up to Lausanne, would never have made sovereign Turkey the stopper where East and West flow together at the Straits.

We have accounted for the morbid holiday summary, "Cannes, Genoa, Anatolia, Chanak." As to "unemployment"—that drew

---

[69] *NS* refused to be greatly disturbed by the reports of atrocities.
[70] Cf. Churchill, *The Aftermath*, p. 415.

attention to the forces gathering in England proper, creative of
social upheaval.

B. EVIDENCE OF THE GROUND SWELL OF FABIAN-LABOUR

Many persons, including Lord Beaverbrook, believed that the
Chanak crisis was the cause of the Dissolution of 1922.[71] It was
the immediate cause but the underlying cause was less apparent.
The underlying cause was also the reason why the election of
1922 was indecisive and led to that of 1923. The behavior of the
Fabian News is significant. Fabians on the *NS* level kept large
issues before the electorate, while the *Fabian News* like a little tug
working about a freighted merchantman, churned the domestic
waters. Dissolution had been deeply desired, when, in October,
1921, a whole year before the crisis, *Fabian News* called for names
of prospective candidates, not necessarily for publication, " in view
of the approach of a General Election." [72] Then, " many signs and
portents " suggested to members the same idea one month later.
It was announced that forty prospective candidates had been approved and would be helped out of the Fabian Election Fund. This
fund was justified, *Fabian News* stated, from its history. Started
in 1892, it had been efficacious in 1910 and 1918.[73] In December,
1921, reference was made to " the approaching election." Names
had come in and the list was still open; funds were sought.[74] By
January, 1922, Executive approval for the collection of funds had

---

[71] " Lausanne " in the formula of grievance was the first abortive conference; when the second transpired it met little Fabian fault-finding. A glance
at the *NS* for December 2, 9, and 16, 1922, will show the Fabian mouthpiece
expressing encouragement of Russian claims to hegemony of the Black Sea
area (*NS*, XX, pp. 253 f, 285, 317). By February 10 (*ibid.*, p. 533 ff, the
NS was in favor of acceptance of the Curzon settlement; it found France
(which had an eye on Anatolian railways) and not the " Marquess Curzon "
the villain of the piece. The *NS* did not like the situation in the Straits
(Turkish armed sovereignty) nor the settling of the Greeks in Western
Thrace but it was visibly changing over to acceptance of the Draft Treaty
and by March 24, 1923 (*ibid.*, p. 710), still blaming France for recalcitrance
while pointing out her helplessness, the *NS* admitted that respect must be
shown the " tiger " Turk if only for his " inconvenient passion for freedom."
[72] *FN*, XXXII:10 (October, 1921). The Election came about a year later.
[73] *FN*, XXXII:11 (November, 1921).
[74] *FN*, XXXII:12 (December, 1921).

been received and, although *Fabian News* professed to have " no more knowledge than anyone else as to when " the general election might come, it was said that those candidates would receive financial assistance who had Labour Party approval and that of all the trustees of the Fabian campaign fund (all the members of the Fabian Executive).[75] The list of approved candidates had grown by about twenty more names by February. In April, it was remarked that all Labour candidates would need help " in the event " of a general election. Probably the dull tone was indicative of the fact that Fabians were watching the " Cabin Boy " revolt,[76] and that Genoa and Lausanne offered too great a challenge. Their irresponsible pro-Soviet views must have pained themselves as Englishmen. Upon this subject there was nothing more in *Fabian News* until November, 1922, when the campaign was in full swing. Then, the help asked was specified as " personal service " and use of vehicles. Funds received were more abundant than anticipated. There were now fifty-four candidates. Names long familiar to one who has followed Fabian fortunes over the years of their history recurred upon the list. As we have seen above, ten out of the fifty-six Fabians were successful: D. Adams, Clement Attlee, Noel-Buxton, William Graham, Arthur Greenwood, G. Lansbury, H. Snell, J. Stewart, B. Tillett, Sidney Webb. Henderson came in at a by-election. From seventy-six Labour members, the Parliamentary representation of Labour rose to one hundred and forty-two (out of four hundred and fifteen Labour candidates).[77] Other familiar Fabian names figuring in the election and not hitherto mentioned, or seldom remarked, were: Ethel Bentham, G. P. Blizard, Hugh Dalton, J. P. Davies, J. A. Lovatt-Fraser, A. Susan Lawrence, J. J. Mallon, H. T. Muggeridge, Mrs. Marjorie (Wedgwood) Pease, F. W. Pethick-Lawrence, H. W. Samuels (a barrister, authority on labor law; not Viscount H. L. Samuel, who was a close friend of the Webbs), Frank Smith, Ernest Thurtle, T. S. B. Williams.

---

[75] *FN*, XXXII:1 (January, 1922). This set-up was patently such as to insure Fabian control of Labour candidates who had not the immediate backing of union funds.

[76] *Loc. cit.*, p. 202.

[77] *FN*, XXXIII:12 (December, 1922).

Perhaps it was only coincidence that the election of 1923 followed a barrage of books attacking Capitalism. Conservatives were not unaware of the power of such an attack to articulate a party—to draw strength away from Liberals and increase that of Labour. The Webbs' new book, *The Decay of Capitalist Civilization*,[78] had sold out its first edition. With its "theory of the leisure class" it linked itself to Thorstein Veblen's thesis, which the Webbs recommended,[79] and to John M. Keynes' "ringing phrases," for example, "The war has disclosed the possibility of consumption to all and the vanity of abstinence to many." Rejecting Marx's "pretentious blunders in abstract economic theory," it endorsed his "presenting the drama of modern civilisation with the bourgeois as the villain of the piece."[80] While the Webbs apologized for destructive criticism they offered a very positive incentive to the labor-electorate, the picture of a government which could "feed and clothe and house and equip them for peaceful and fruitful production if the same steely incentive [the war effort,—meaning force] were applied." Like resorting to unorganized sabotage, "moral remonstrance and virtuous indignation are useless; if the game is to be one of pull-devil—pull-baker . . . capitalism . . . will die by violence, and civilisation will perish with it from exhaustion." The worker was not to destroy civilisation along with Capitalism. With the ideas went a strategy: First the Party, then the Labour Government; the former produced by an attractive platform and the latter by a compromised program. Then the law must produce a "steely incentive."

The events and current problems of this election year brought to the shelves of the Fabian Bookshop works of famous ex-Fabians: Graham Wallas' *Our Social Heritage*, H. G. Wells' *Washington and the Hope of Peace;* J. A. Hobson added *Incen-*

---

[78] Sidney and Beatrice Webb, *The Decay of Capitalist Civilization* (London: Fabian Society, 1923). They proffered gratitude to "our oldest friend and comrade, Mr. Bernard Shaw, who kindly undertook the revision of the proofs in the midst of a General Election when we were otherwise engaged," p. v. The election was that of 1922.

[79] *Ibid.,* p. 33.

[80] *Ibid.,* pp. 165 f. This is the theme of *Heartbreak House.*

tives in the New Social Order and his *Problems of a New World.*[81]
In regard to these last named books, Hobson was applying to
specific problems his theories which F. W. Galton clarified in
1923; [82]

> Excessive saving operates through deficient demand for
> commodities to slacken the sinews of production and
> produce more capital goods than are able to be put to
> full productive use.

There was, he said, too much saving, and general over-production;
old theories of credit and prices did not account for business
cycles. He sharpened the Keynesian outline.

The books entered into the creation of Party and platform.
Fabian eclecticism found no difficulty in contemplating simultaneously the Hobson and Keynes problem related to excessive
production, and the Webb and Keynes idea of encouraging vast
production by government to care for a total population, as the
government cared for an army in war-time. The Fabian creed of
no-orthodoxy lent itself to selectivity; ideas that were solvents of
the old order and indifferent to the divine origin of Natural Law,
and propositions which urged social stratification in an artificial
economic regimen for which Socialism supplied a cohesive element, met with Fabian agreement. The 1920's were the years of
corrosion of capitalistic institutions. The 1930's were to be the
years of discussion of Planning.

So the arrangement of lists of candidates, funds and constituencies went on, together with the heavy barrage of anti-Capitalist
ideas; and the tiny *Fabian News* discovered these large factors.

Letters, too, served to reveal much: There was talk about
coalescence with Liberals which only pointed up the fact of their
lost identity. The intellectual leadership was divided on the
point of collaboration with Liberals. A. W. Humphreys, a Fabian

---

[81] Cf. also, S. G. Hobson, *Pilgrim to the Left* (New York: Longmans
Green and Company, 1938). S. G. Hobson was a Guild Socialist and left the
Society before World War I. J. A. Hobson was a keener student of psy-
chology than Wallas. These great ex-Fabians continued to be studied by
Fabians.

[82] *FN*, XXXIV:4 (April, 1923). Galton had served his apprenticeship in
Fabianism as secretary for research for Mrs. Webb for many years.

and Labourite of some note,[83] wrote to the editor taking strong exception to the views of the *NS* of the week just past [84] which had found " no division of opinion between Liberal and Labour Parties," as Humphreys quoted, " on all questions of foreign policy and on nearly all questions of domestic policy." He thought the outlook of Asquith and Grey would prove an obstacle to joint effort in the event of such coalescence and he pointed out the impossibility of agreement from Liberals upon the Capital Levy, Unemployment, Nationalisation, and some other items. The important thing about this was the insertion of comment within the published letter by the *NS* editor:

> Can you, Sir, imagine Mr. Asquith, Lord Grey, Lord Cowdray, Lord Crewe, Mr. Runciman, . . . sponsoring such a measure in the House of Commons? [Certainly we can.—Ed., *NS*]. When, where and through whom has the Liberal Party given adhesion to the principle of work or maintenance? [The influential Manchester Liberals have declared for it.—Ed., *NS*]. . . . Do you claim that the Liberal Party stands for nationalisation? [Many Liberals certainly do—probably most—in the lines of the Sankey Report.—Ed., *NS*].[85]

Mr. Humphreys worried: " Whether Labour is to make clear its distinction from Liberalism touches the whole spirit and purpose with which it is going into this election." [86] The standpoint taken by Humphreys was expressed in sterner tones by Walter Scobell, Vice-President of the Frome Divisional Labour Party. He asked space for his letter as " voicing the feelings of a very large proportion of the electorate." He said the proposal of coalescence

---

[83] A. W. Humphreys', *History of Labour Representation* was among the books to be consulted by the Tutorial Classes on Policy and Principles of the Labour Party which were conducted by Sidney Webb " in response to numerous requests " starting in May, 1918.

[84] Reflection upon the speed and dispatch of the rejoinder and comment suggests a bit of collusion: sentimental socialists who abhorred Liberalism and mere Reformism, had to be reassured. Either the Humphrey letter was a plant, so that reassurance should be swift, or the editor showed uncommon dispatch.

[85] *NS*, XX (October 28, 1922), 104 f.

[86] *Ibid.*

with Liberals presented " glaring contrast to the hectic refusals of such a suggestion by the Trade Union and Labour leaders at their respective conferences this year." A truce would be a " moral betrayal since Liberalism was directly opposed to Labour's ultimate goal of the Socialist Commonwealth." Liberals saw in trade a " contest " for " domination " leading to " defense " and military contests. Scobell wrote:

> Your objective is a basis of agreement whereby the legis-
> lative machine can be captured and held for a period of
> years. Our immediate object is the first round of a fight
> [therefore]. . . . Truce and Coalition will only hinder
> the steady progress [toward] our ultimate goal, our
> immediate objective,

which was, while keeping king and anthem along with the Red Flag song, the Socialist Commonwealth. Before the war, " Labour was the child which pushed Liberalism forward," now the " Radical Wing " has been lost forever. Rich Radicals, Scobell wrote, made the sacrifices of going through the needle's eye into the Labour camp. " We have no place for those who will not make the sacrifice." [87] The opinions of Humphreys and Scobell exemplified the injured idealism of socialist-labor, harried by Fabian opportunism. They also served to signal that Fabians remained Socialists while the Party they led must compromise and perhaps live with Liberals a little longer.

A Fabian problem was revealed in this correspondence. Whereas the *NS* offered a strategy, the dissident response contained no programme save to fight on pure principle and with none of the pragmatic compromise which Beatrice Webb mourned. " How Far is Intrigue Permissible? " she asked her diary in 1922, when engaged in retrospect.[88] It is important to note these elements in Labour Party thinking because of their bearing upon future political events. Whether Fabians were confused and ultimately opportunistic, or skilled in finding the lead strings in opposing groups, must be the reader's conclusion. Perhaps they thought Liberalism was dead, never to rise and reclaim the domi-

---

[87] *Ibid.*
[88] Cf. Beatrice Webb, *Our Partnership*, p. vi.

cile which Fabianism had appropriated. Taking cognizance of the *NS*'s warlike attitude toward France and the fighting language of Labourites, brings the reflection that Fabian leadership permitted and waited for every such expression, indulged in fighting talk itself, then came forward with strategic oil for a peaceful surface. In the matter of the letters, the *NS*,[89] in agreement with the left-wing of the Party, replied it would be better if the Labour Party abstained from office for another decade. However, not Party interest but national consideration must guide it and the argument of leaders of Labor proved their inability " to realize the national responsibilities of a Party which ostensibly seeks to express the national will." Fabians spoke to unionists and to Socialists, pure political science, seeking to impose unity on the incongruous elements in the Party.

As was noted above in another connection, under the leadership of Fabians, the Party was in a position to dictate a part of the policy by which it was Stanley Baldwin and not Lord Curzon who succeeded the ailing Bonar Law. Baldwin's vulnerability could not have been unperceived. The last word, " unemployment " in the Scrooge-like Christmas message of 1922 bore divisive implications. There would have to be a showdown on Protection. Churchill thought that Baldwin undertook a preventive attack on the problem to cut off a resurgence of Lloyd George's prestige. Churchill was to write that Baldwin was a more perfect Socialist than MacDonald.[90] This opinion merely serves here to show why Fabians would support Baldwin and not the admirable but stubborn Curzon. Sylvester points to Bonar Law's Parliamentary Private Secretary, J. C. C. Davidson, as the agent of the Baldwin cause to Lord Stamfordham. Davidson's personal ambition found its reward in both the 1923 and 1925 Baldwin Cabinets. He would not have to be an intimate acquaintance of MacDonald, Webb, or Henderson or the other Fabians, his colleagues in Parliament, to know that it was shrewd politics to run with the current and that its force was real. Ronaldshay depicts the part played by Labour in the defeat of Curzon:

It was Lord Stamfordham's unpalatable task to convey

---

[89] *NS*, XX (October 28, 1922), 94.
[90] Cf. Churchill, *Gathering Storm*, p. 21.

to Lord Curzon the decision of the King that, since the
Labour Party constituted the official Opposition in the
House of Commons and were unrepresented in the
House of Lords, the objections to a Prime Minister in
the Upper Chamber were insuperable.[91]

Curzon himself had expressed this principle in 1917. The *NS*
said that nobody wanted Curzon because his manners were so bad.
It is remarkable how Labour spokesmen covered their tracks, at
this moment of greatest importance when the class forming the
Socialist-led Labour Party settled with finality a constitutional
question regarding the class of the Premier—a question left
dangling since the days of Salisbury. In any case, it could not be
expected that a proud and sensitive character such as Curzon's
should be discriminatingly evaluated by Fabian publicists. Lord
Curzon himself wrote: " the Opposition party in the House of
Commons being in the majority a Labour party, the King thought
that the Head of the Government must be there to answer
them." [92] Blanche Dugdale's [93] narrative supports this exposition,
adding only that Lord Balfour confirmed the King's views from
his own experience as leader in Salisbury's day, and noting that
four of the Ministers were peers. In fact, politicians of the
bourgeois mentality who were well able to gauge the ground-swell,
Mr. Amery, First Lord of the Admiralty, and Mr. Bridgeman,
Home Secretary, had expressed to Lord Salisbury their hope that
Baldwin would succeed Bonar Law. The " root of unrest " was
pushing against the edifice of the constitution.

[91] Ronaldshay, *op. cit.,* pp. 352 and 367.
[92] *Ibid.*
[93] Blanche Dugdale, *op. cit.,* pp. 360 f.

CHAPTER VI

THE USES OF "PROTECTION." PART I: SIGNALING THE CONTINENT

A. Fabian Leaders as Proponents of Internationalism and " Free Trade "

In the autumn of 1923, after a short term of Tory Government, Mr. Baldwin, who had replaced Bonar Law in May, made a speech at Plymouth in which he declared that England must have a protective tariff and since his Government was pledged not to enact tariffs, they must have a mandate from the electorate. No one wanted an election so soon again. But one ensued and brought Labour into office, if not into power. The mystery of the cause of the unwelcome election can be explained partially by the exigencies of European affairs. To all appearances, the Government was constrained to break its strong opponent in order to free itself to deal with Europe. Labour in Opposition had made the Government's position on foreign policy unbearable.[1] In any case, Tory policy in dealing with Europe required that Conservatives provide an educative experience for the voters in order to make a radical change in fiscal practices; amorphous public opinion had to be articulated and that section which bespoke Labour reorientated.

When the election of 1923 was declared by Labour Party leaders to have for cause the effort of Tories to unseat Labour, the spokesmen maintained that the issue of Protection was farcical. Actually, on both sides the word " Protection " indicated a view on how to deal with industry in foreign relations. Tories stood for trade under Capitalism, with tariffs; Labour stood for trade under Socialism, with planning or " cooperation." The opinion that the Conservatives intended to try to break the power of Labour was

---

[1] Cf. e.g., Churchill, *The Aftermath,* p. 269. Also, J. A. Spender, *Great Britain, Empire and Commonwealth, 1886–1935* (London: Cassell and Company, 1936), pp. 638–647.

asserted by MacDonald and Henderson, and by the editor of the *NS*. But a Fabian, Henderson, was as responsible for the incidence of the election as any Tory, and his reason was rooted as much in the international problem as was Baldwin's. If Henderson had stated, in response to the Plymouth speech, that he and his Party also believed in a certain amount of protection, he would have been stating the truth and the Government might have gone forward with a well-criticized programme of tariffs, expanding a bit on the already operative " McKenna tariffs."

In order to see how the Labour differed from the Tory attitude it is necessary to see how Fabianism was a creed of internationalism and how the Fabian mentors of Labour cut large figures in the Continental International.

Henderson, out of his long experience with Tory thinking, and never unmindful of the episodes in Petrograd, in Stockholm, in Berne, where he demonstrated a desire to work with Socialists, even those who were national enemies, had seen instantaneously the opportunity and the challenge in Baldwin's Plymouth speech asking for a mandate on Protection, and he had " pushed him off the bank " [2]—that is, he had forced an election, as Mrs. Hamilton relates. " We'll get an election out of this," meant Labour would get a chance to propagandize at home and abroad. Henderson could count on thousands of young men for whom Socialism was a religion,[3] on the increased numbers of unionized non-manual workers among whom the women's vote had, in October, 1923, doubled its count to 868,000.[4] He had ordered the Party staff to arrange a public luncheon at which he hymned Free Trade and asserted the Party's answer to the challenge of Baldwin's " Plymouth plunge." His real objective could have been to increase the power of Opposition by releasing it from the Liberal Party so as to be in a position to dictate foreign policy. Labour under MacDonald was currently taking much responsibility in handling domestic matters.[5] Again, every demonstration of

[2] Hamilton, *op. cit.*, p. 233.
[3] " London Diary," *NS*, XXII (November 10, 1923), 139.
[4] *NS*, XXII (October 27, 1923), 67.
[5] *NS*, XXI (April 21, 1923) 34, refers to the Ministry's surrendering power to the Opposition, for instance, in the case of a strike of agricultural workers.

political action must needs hearten, edify, educate the elements of political Socialism abroad. " Free Trade " consoled the German workman. The McKenna safeguards, aimed against France, were not called tariffs.

If Prime Minister Baldwin placed reliance on the known facts that " Labour had its own views on trade policy: views about bulk purchase, public corporations, and even, in some cases, infant-industry, tariffs," [6] he did not count heavily enough upon what Mrs. Hamilton termed Labour's unanimous opposition to " any super-imposition of tariffs on inefficient Capitalist industry." The reader must guess what Mrs. Hamilton meant. Socialists thought Capitalist business " inefficient " if it did not produce for " need." Their concept of need was far more extensive than the visible market. Withstanding " super-imposition " could suppose that *imposition* of tariffs was allowable. " Industry," efficient or " inefficient," provided jobs. Upon an equivocal attitude the Party built a Free Trade fort from which Fabians bombarded Baldwin's " safeguarding of industry " platform. The fact was that Labour held to a half-and-half view as much as Conservatives. The difference seemed to lie in a policy to work either with Business or with Parties. As Mrs. Hamilton states,

> . . . interest was definitely focused on the Party, so was hope, from those, above all, who looked across the Channel to the great problem of international peace. Henderson had got the organisation behind the idea into such shape that he was not in the least afraid of a strain in the second election.[7]

It is noticeable that tariff and international peace are linked together in Mrs. Hamilton's thought. If she used the words correctly she admitted that " inefficient " Capitalist industry was fitter for nationalization than if it gained efficiency proportionate to that which " infant industry " would gain by protection, and it is tenable that by " inefficient Capitalist industry " was not meant domestic industry alone. Fabian readers of the *NS* were fully

---

MacDonald was becoming a national success. Tory policy makers were using him on the domestic front already, and the *NS* noted it.

[6] Hamilton, *op. cit.*, p. 233.

[7] *Ibid.*, p. 233.

aware of the rise of a newly rich industrialist class in Germany currently typified by Hugo Stinnes. If there was anywhere an industry thriving, it must be warped into the international Socialist system of "democratic" control. The slogan "Free Trade" held out a hope to German workers. Meanwhile, Fabian publicists were demanding that business relations of British private companies with the Soviet Government be encouraged.[8] The Party concentrated its attention upon all those elements of private industry, especially raw materials, involving tariffs and labor supply, which were likely to be brought under State direction with a view to forwarding the economic partnership of Britain and Germany; and it asked private industry in England to work with the Party-Government in Russia—all to a given end, the capture of trade and commerce by Socialism, as Shaw said, "at the consular level."

B. The Fabian View of Germany: Two Rivals in the Field

Fabians saw two great pillars of force in Germany, namely, the Centre and Social Democracy. It might be better to say they saw the tower of the Centre disintegrating (as they believed) and envisioned Socialism replacing it. Affinity for the latter was natural; it was entirely secular. British Socialists unspokenly sought to replace the "tower of the Centre" with an amalgamation of the secular Socialistic forces under a "Labour" order— like the Centre "tower" but more like the shadow of a tower lying aslant the nation, because it was an ideal construct and not a real order. The criterion by which Fabians judged the German problem patterned their judgment of Bolshevik Russia. They could not keep a correspondent in Russia but in Germany there were three: Robert Dell, formerly on the Fabian Executive, and Massingham, who had returned to the Fabian fold by way of the *NS*, after being dismissed from *The Nation's* staff; and there was Levin J. Schücking, son of a prominent German family.

In the Russian case, they assumed that an indigenous movement based upon the zemstrovs and soviets had been captured

---

[8] *NS*, XXII (December 15, 1923), 289. The Marshall and the Becos Companies were estimated to be ready to engage in a business involving £40,000,000.

by a unifying if ruthless force in the form of a partisan committee under a sort of Robin Hood called Lenin, a Marxist "cruel" indeed but "clement," a social democrat. The established one-party rule, Fabians believed up to the time of Lenin's death,[9] could be overthrown by the forces of democracy after the benefits of its dynamism had been appropriated, in organization. Fabian Julius West had not lived to revoke the myth to which he had given currency and which Fabians Haden Guest and Mrs. Snowden enlarged.[10]

In the case of Germany, Fabians had learned before the war from Fabian W. S. Sanders, in a pamphlet published in 1913 [11] that Social Democrats in Germany were imitators of English Socialists and like Fabians were trying to build up and maintain Trade Unionism as well as social democracy. To be noticed was the *separated* growth of the social and the political elements in

---

[9] When Lenin died in 1923, the *NS* carried articles on his character and work. For example, in C. M. Lloyd's "Lenin's Legacy," *NS*, XXII (January 26, 1924), 442, we read this typical piece of philosophy: Lenin's weakness was his intolerance; his firmness in purpose was his strength. He was implacable, a fanatic, yet he made a "masterful experiment," the only European Socialist who did. He was Marxian with a touch of Bakunin and averse to Kautsky. He was "cruel" yet, during the terror, upon appeal was even too "clement." To preserve his achievement and continue his work, England followed by France, to be followed by Italy and the Czechs, must extend credits; for Lenin, far from making any "sordid bargain" contrary to Bolshevism, arranged for credits from private companies. Again, for G. D. H. Cole, "The Socialism of Nikolai Lenin," *ibid.*, 473, Lenin's use of Capitalism was to infuse *power* in the *workers* toward a workers' State. George Bernard Shaw, in a letter to the writer, said NEP was pure Fabianism, and that Stalin "among a million others" spoke for Fabianism today. There might be some connection between this statement and the fact that all *NS* articles on Lenin's demise pleaded that Britain help keep steady the Russian State until control would be established by Lenin's successor and not by some visionary or sentimental groups.

[10] Julius West, *The Russian Revolution and British Democracy, Fabian Tract No. 184* (London: Fabian Society, 1917). Cf. also, Mrs. Snowden's lecture reported in *FN*, XXXII:2 (February, 1921). The ideals of independence, peasant proprietorship, proportional representation, committees on wages, disputes and insurance, and federation with neighbor states were active in 1921, according to Mrs. Snowden.

[11] W. Stephen Sanders, *The Socialist Movement in Germany, Fabian Tract No. 169* (London: Fabian Society) 1913.

Germany which was unlike the Fabian-fostered united or joint growth of these elements in Britain. Like the British Socialists, Sanders said, the German Socialists were proud of their descent in the words of Engels " not only from Saint-Simon, Fourier, and Owen [concerned with social ordering] but also from Kant, Fichte, and Hegel [concerned with political ordering]." [12] The two sets of names of philosophers are indicative, by the fact that Social Democrats trace their lineage to both groups, of the politicizing of social ways of life, and the warping of economics out of the private juridic order into the public order—the State.[13] Like the English—even more so—German Socialism aspired " to bear art, philosophy and science to the masses." (This would mean to cover or overshadow with the political—the Party—all the social orders, estates, industries, associations, and in so doing, to preempt the centre.) Like Fabians, the German Socialists organized women and young people. Sanders stated that, unlike their British counterpart, the German movement had had to go underground: they had been called " Reds," and local religious societies had organized committees to protect youth from their doctrines. Sanders indicated that there was some rapport between Socialist societies and Trade Unions, for organized workers had subscribed funds and erected office buildings for the Social Democrats to use jointly with themselves. But there was no political synthesis of Trade Unions and Socialist societies as yet, in Germany.[14]

The German Social Democrats, according to Sanders, had out-

---

[12] The vital difference between these two elements became clear and its fissionable nature evident to editors and readers of the *NS* when the Wheatley Housing Bill came up under the Labour Government. The Trade Unions were as intransigent on the subject of " dilutees " as the Capitalists on price of materials. The matter recurs weekly in the *NS*, XXIII—(April 19, 1924), 33, for example.

[13] This displacement of Economics was condemned by Pope Pius XII when he addressed the International Union of Catholic Employers Associations. Cf. full text in the *United States News and World Report* (June 17, 1949), 32 f. This address, later described as the *magna carta* of economic freedom, outlines the means of release from Statism in subsidiarity.

[14] Labour's effort to assume equal rights in management could only succeed by national legislation which would destroy free enterprise faster than " nationalisation."

grown their naive belief in "the early Marxian myth of a final collapse of capitalism" and they never used the plea "that nothing but socialism is of any use"—Sanders added significantly— "in order to shirk the task of grappling with immediate problems." This is a fine distinction, it shows a difference between Fabians and pure Socialists while emphasizing the similarity of methods of German Socialists and British Fabians before World War I. Idealistically, the Fabian ethic was, briefly: Never use the "excuse" that only Socialism will work, to cover a disinclination to serve politically.[15] It is strange, unless one reads the phrase discriminatingly, to find the divorcement from a "nothing but" attitude praised. Sidney Webb's stand in speaking to managers in 1919[16] was surely one of "nothing but Socialism will do." In any case, the German Socialists' constant struggle was, according to Sanders, bringing about the replacement of theory with experience so that a "self-respecting, self-confident and purposeful democracy which when it does attain political power, will have learned to use it soberly and with judgment in the tremendous task of *changing the German Empire into a German cooperative commonwealth.*" Here was the telic objective of international Socialism stated at the point of greatest realizability, before World War I.[17] Even during the war, Henderson, with all that his personality connoted, sought collaboration with the Socialist element in Germany.[18] Few took

---

[15] As of 1950, the reading public learned that the Labour Party in Conference rejected the invitation to Britain to confer with foreign Ministers on the Schumann (French) Plan to pool the Ruhr resources. The Party distinctly said it would not cooperate except under Socialism. The Parliamentary Party and the Cabinet has seemed embarrassed but Mr. Laski, whose posthumously published "A Program to Prevent World War III" appeared in the *United Nations World, IV* (June, 1950), pp. 18–21, said Mr. Strachey should be expelled from the Party for taking (as spokesman, no doubt) this anti-Schumann-Plan stand. A single radio newscast, not published afterward, told of Strachey's public apology and reprimand by Attlee in Commons. Laski's article had insinuated, however, that Britain's stand would enable her to be mediator between the United States and U.S.S.R. The truth is that the Party does want "only Socialism" but it is not expedient to demand it now, as it was not in the 1920's.

[16] *Loc. cit.*, p. 54.

[17] W. Stephen Sanders, *op. cit.*, pp. 2 and 23.

[18] Cf. Snowden, *Autobiography*, p. 478.

note of the ending in 1920 of the conflict between "confessional" and "interconfessional" Trade Unions in Germany after the Bishops, meeting at Fulda, had asked for amalgamation or joint conventions of the Catholic Workers Association and the Christian Trade Unions.   This led to a joint platform seeking collaboration of Capital and Labour at the Works Council level, and pressing for some public controls, for shareholding by workers, for solidarity of all trades and classes, and against the " socialist footing of the class war," against socialization, against worker possession of factories or workers' direct influence in industrial affairs in general.[19]

The Fabian Society found two rivals in the field they sought to preempt, convinced that the synthetic jewel of political socialism lay buried in it.   Late in 1920, the position of the British ILP (it must be recalled that it belonged to the " two-and-a-half " international) was discovered in the melee of postwar German Socialism, and the impossibility of the survival of its ideals especially in Germany hinted by adroit reporting.[20]   The *NS* commented on the union of German Independent Socialists of the "left wing " with the German Communist Party and the possibility of this union's absorbing the Syndicalist Communist Labour Party— a drawing together of far-left forces.   It noted that the attempt to find common ground between Communism and the policy of the " right wing " in order to cover that ground with a political party which would also foster a Fourth International, absorbed the energies of the residual Socialists.   This marked out the area left free for Social Democracy.   But the Socialists were divided, left and right, and, most significantly, it was said

> The British ILP, whose Administrative Council has just recommended to the branches for adoption a new programme which is largely Guild Socialism, is in *close touch* with the *minority of the German Independents.*[21]

---

[19] Cf. *ILO Studies and Reports,* Series A, No. 21 (Geneva, 1920).

[20] *NS,* XVI (November 6, 1920), 123.

[21] *Ibid.* Italics are inserted.   Also, after World War II there is obvious association of the British Labour Party with Social Democrats.   Recently, Victor Gollancz received glowing tribute for social democratic action from Clemens Munster, " Das Portrat: Victor Gollancz," *Frankfurter Hefte* (2 Jahrgang, June 1947, Heft 6), 593–596.   Many Social-Democrat biographies date 1945–1950.

It becomes clear upon reflection that ILP was invading the ground which Fabian Socialism should, true to its principles, have pre-empted. Reports from Germany in the *NS* provided surveys and suggestions. If ILP took the middle area, from which it was to be extruded, Fabians were encouraged to consider reaching across it and far into the Left, even into Communist preserves for leverage to create a Labour front. But ILP was not the same kind of rival as the indigenous and dynamic order known as " the Centre."

After the War and the Revolution, Fabians learned if they had not known before, of this other force, the " Centre " which had been " the strongest party in Germany during the last thirty years." [22] In the face of persecution Catholics had developed a movement of far-reaching importance on the people's level, that is, in library associations, music societies, motivated travel—pilgrim-ages. This centre fostered also a People's Association [23] which

---

Carolus, " Botch on the Rhine," *The Nation,* Vol. 168 (May 14, 1949), 549–551, gives a succinct account of old occurrences: Pictured is Scheidmann, opponent of Ebert the future Socialist president who favored the monarchy, proclaiming a free democratic German Republic from the window of a res-taurant wherein he and his fellow Social Democrats had been seated arguing whether the Kaiser's grandson should be enthroned or a republic created when news came that Liebknecht, the Sparticist, had proclaimed a German Soviet Republic. The article is critical of both the Christian Democratic Party and the S.D.P. but British Labour's present-day collaboration with S.D.P. is demonstrated. The " friends " of S.D.P., " the British Labour Party . . . informed " the S.D.P. of the forthcoming instructions adopted in a Washington conference of Bevin, Schumann, and Acheson which yielded to S.D.P. centralizing demands.

[22] Levin J. Schücking, " The Decay of the Centre," *NS,* XVI (March 5, 1921), 637 ff.

[23] The words, " the centre " and " Centre Party " indicate two concepts; the former embraces the latter which serves as the political expression of a social force generated in hierarchical ranks of like-minded persons. When social, i.e. democratic units are politicized, they can be induced to subsume political governance, whether of republics or of monarchies—recalling Italy. The German social centre, which was essentially Christian, was made up of persons united often in free associations or private societies of many kinds which may well have typified that democratic order which Pius XI advised should not be politicized, in *QA, loc. cit.,* p. 30 where subsidiarity is praised; also when he restated Leo XIII's advice against " political democracy." Cf. Leo XIII, *Christian Democracy* (New York: Paulist Press, 1941), pp. 6 f.

found out the most remote voters; it made deliberate appeal to the intellectuals and, again, interested itself in reform movements so that its support was needed to pass labor legislation. According to Levin Schücking, the German *NS* correspondent in 1923, the " Tower of the Centre "[24] was composed of "members of all sorts of social strata from the plain man to the grandee." Schücking's article shows that Socialists in thus delineating or articulating the social areas encompassed by a religious body, made the culture thus created to appear not to be autochthonous, and hence the area became proper spoil, to be invested by Socialism by way of secular "social democracy" toward "industrial democracy."[25] Schücking's report revealed fissures in the "tower" that had been the Centre and this enabled Socialists in Britain to see the possibilities of procuring a social democratic foothold in the cultural area seemingly about to be vacated in the Reich. The tower was cracking because the unique dynamic creative of Centre unity, according to this correspondent, had been "persecution" and this had been stopped by the Republic. In Schücking's view, the imperialistic, even chauvinistic, attitudes of the "clerical" party were changing into acceptance of outright separatism; on the school question, the Centre seemed willing to sacrifice the "throne" for the "altar." This *NS* correspondent did not comprehend as "persecution" the situation he reported wherein, for example, the liberal Republic demanded all pupils' attendance at non-denominational schools. This was a "demand" of the old German Social Democracy[26] and by 1921 it had changed the Centre into "a peerless political adversary." The Rhineland and

---

[24] Schücking, *op. cit.*, pp. 637 f.

[25] This term included in the long run *all working* society, even farming. Agriculture as an industry, far removed from subsistence farming, but bridged into the democratic industrial scheme by cooperatives and State planning of production, was included in "industrial democracy." Cf. S. L. B. (Bensusan), "Bribes for Farmers," *NS*, XXII (December 1, 1923), 237, where this authority on Socialism for farmers complains the Government has no plan for *cultivation control,* no funds for under-standard farmers, no Wage Board, only the machinery for fair wage enforcement. A special study of the agricultural feature of Fabian activity would be most enlightening.

[26] Cf. Sanders, *op. cit.*, p. 24, where the Social Democrat "demands" (not by-laws nor bases) are listed. Fabians advised TUC to formulate "demands" and eschew political statements.

Westphalia had by proclaiming their threat to seek annexation to France or Holland, respectively, won a victory on the school question. When Schücking wrote, moneyed members were deserting the Centre Party, working members were pulling apart in a move against "big Capital," university students were disaffected and moving "left," while upper classes and bureaucrats were moving "right." [27] The Centre Party, he wrote, was not positive whether to endorse monarchism or not.[28] (But, for that matter, even Social Democrats had not been *republican* before the war.)

It was difficult to politicize social theory in Germany. In an analysis of the Socialists' opposition, Schücking said, in "The Difficulties of Democracy in Germany," that in creating the constitution of the Weimar Republic Socialists had been the only insistent republicans. Then, "Democrats" were created out of old National-Liberals and Conservatives who had cloaked themselves in democratic sounding titles like *Volkespartei* in order to participate in the making of the Republic. Schücking did not credit this force with the relative civil order which developed out of the then-reigning chaos of "workmen and soldier councils" bent on proceeding farther with the Revolution, nor with the defeat of Sparticism.[29] But he admitted "the idea of social justice and true democracy had a marvelous growth" after the war, pointed up by these conversions to political democracy. Nevertheless, the movement toward nationalization of mines [30] and for "free schools"

----

[27] By 1923, "the Centre Party" included persons of such diverse character as Erzberger who was assassinated because he signed the Versailles Treaty, and Wirth, the one-time Chancellor; like W. Marx who was a delegate with Stresemann to the London Dawes Report Conference, and Chancellor Brüning. The head of the party was the prelate, Kaas.

[28] Schücking, *op. cit.,* pp. 637 f.

[29] Cf. Carolus, "Botch on the Rhine," *loc. cit.,* p. 228.

[30] J. L. C., "Our Book-Shelf," *FN* (November, 1922), reviewing Alfons Horten, *Sozialisierung von Kohle und Stahl* (Berlin: Verlag Neues Vaterland, W. 62), revealed a nascent Fabian society in the Fatherland:

"It is interesting to learn that the League of the New Fatherland has adopted Socialism as one of its objects. Scientific research and propaganda are to be undertaken on the lines of the Fabian Society (*etwa in Sinne der Londoner Gesellschaft der Fabier*). The Committee's introduction to a valuable study by Alfons Horten on the 'Nationalisation of Coal and Iron' gives also a list of its prominent supporters, of whom the best known in this

for all, was lost, the correspondent said. Furthermore, republicanism was not secure. Because of poverty, school texts full of monarchism had had to be kept in use generally.[31] Indeed, the typical wealthy speculator-industrialist, Hugo Stinnes,[32] and certain groups of Rightists and the press which he could command, advocated return to monarchy. (A tendency on the part of leftist sympathizers to exaggerate incipient rightist movement in order to furnish an excuse for a drive further left must be taken into account in reading reports from Germany.) Another reaction-producing element, anti-Semitism was rising, " the socialism of non-socialists . . . its wire-pullers . . . made much more than an ingenious means of diverting the popular antipathy against capitalism and capitalists " from its proper object. Neurotic as it was, " Anti-Semitism has at present become the supreme way of discrediting democracy all round." [33] This was a study of the forces opposing social democracy. Since September 1922 a reformed Social Democratic Party had existed.

It can be said that the sentiments of British Socialists, quite congruously, chimed with the Social Democrats by reason of their republicanism—something which was not, indeed, an anti-State republicanism, and could be used to foster State-capitalism—their secularism,[34] and the material objectives inherent in " democratic "

country is Professor Dr. Franz Oppenheimer, the economist, who is interested in various schemes of productive cooperation.

". . . The reason for publishing the first pamphlet on the subject of the Nationalisation of Coal and Iron is due to the clear realisation that in a very real sense these commodities constitute key industries in a modern economy. Once they are nationalised it will be a comparatively easy matter to Nationalise or control other industries."

[31] As here reported, *loc. cit.*, p. 204, note 22, textbook changes were made in Thuringia and suppressed by the Reich. Dell's reporting was as lopsided as this argument about texts and monarchical trends shows. However, Socialists of Dell's stamp sought an opportunity to rewrite school texts.

[32] Dell later, in the *NS*, XXII (December 8, 1923), 260 f, blamed Stinnes' class for prevalent luxury spending amid starvation; and he also blamed the Socialists in the Cabinet because, he said, they could have stabilized the currency and would not do so.

[33] Schücking, " The Difficulties of Democracy in Germany," *NS*, XVI (April 2, 1921), 750 f.

[34] As opposed to the Centre. In two articles, " Political Confusion " by Robert Dell, who had been on the Fabian Executive before the war, and

" The Struggle in Europe" by C. M. Lloyd, cognizance was taken of two hypothetical plans taking shape for Europe embodying the Socialism of industrial democracy and the sociality of two ways of life, one agricultural and the other industrial—labor-capital collaboration. Cf. *NS*, XXII (November 17, 1923), 171 ff, and *ibid*. (December 8, 1923), 260 f. Neither hypothecation can be said to have been objectively criticized: Dell stood too far Left in his style of interpretation and Lloyd's attitude was wholly Fabian. Dell overlooked the Church's early grasp of the nature of Communism and Lloyd excluded from his criteria the fundamental Christian societary philosophy informing Belloc's thought. Both Lloyd and Dell outlined mere hypotheses in the manner in which Marx suggested that the wars of the eighteenth century were wars of Protestantism *vs* Catholicism, in his *The Secret Diplomacy of the Eighteenth Century*. However nebulous, the outline of each revealed the misconceptions of Fabians and social democrats concerning the Church. Dell interpreted the suppression of the Munich Putsch as "the defeat of the Pan-Germans by Separatists . . . the Vatican needs a substitute for the late Austrian Empire." He averred that a Ludendorf-Hitler-Kahr Protestant Empire under Bavarian hegemony, a Wittelsbach reigning, was opposed by a Catholic proposal for a *bloc* of nations from Poland to Italy under Austrian hegemony. This meant war because France would form a counter-bloc with Slavonic States including Russia and excluding Poland. All this Dell envisioned as he reported that republicans in Berlin were rejoicing that the Republic had been saved, "Ludendorf and Hitler were really beaten by the Bavarian clericals . . . in particular Cardinal Faulhaber." With more inconsistency, Dell opined that Stresemann should have used the emergency powers to prevent the return of the crown prince. It will appear in another connection that he excoriated Stresemann for using emergency powers against the so-called Labour government in Saxony. Now he advocated outright intervention of the Allies against Munich: It would not be the same thing as the "disastrous intervention in Russia"; it would not be dangerous—the "Fascists" would not fight and the Reichswehr was doubtful; non-interventionists were making to Poincaré a "present of the Rhineland"; "It would probably be enough to send a few aeroplanes over Munich and inform the Bavarian Government that they would bomb the town if it did not capitulate within twenty-four hours."

Since Fabians injected the religious issue, it may be observed that Sidney Webb boasted that British Labour was not secularist nor anti-religious: "The British Labour Party is the only Labour or Socialist Party in Europe that is not secularist and anti-religious." Mrs. Hamilton quotes Webb in her *Sidney and Beatrice Webb*, p. 31. We know that the Labour Party is not a Socialist Party but one devised by and infiltrated with Socialists determined to capture the labor movement. Not to be secularist is a double negative. Some Fabians like Doctor John Clifford tried to be Christians and Socialists. It was said in Clifford's obituary, *NS*, XXII (November 24, 1925), 208,

industrialism. The poverty under attack was not the kind which currently the Quakers were trying desperately to relieve in Germany and Russia [35] but the sort which made for the retention of antiquated textbooks—something Schücking worried about.

Mr. C. M. Lloyd cited Belloc from the *Saint Martin's Review* where the latter, according to Lloyd, argued for a French hegemony and for an agricultural and Catholic " bloc " in Europe opposing the industrial-financial " bloc " dominated by Berlin. Mr. Lloyd's criticism indicated his Fabian way of thinking and exemplified the guidance usually given to *NS* readers on selected topics. " What is Italy doing in this galley [with France, Spain, Poland, Rhine Valley, Upper Danube and parts of the Balkans] ? " Apparently he thought of Italy as an anti-clerical State and one unrelated to Southwest Europe, regardless of the social complexion of its masses. Again: " the domination of this ' agricultural, traditional culture ' bloc or the attempt to put it into operation would not give us peace, but war." He did not state why he should write that this agricultural incentive, bound naturally to reduce the rate of increase of the number of the proletariat, should mean war; but, as Dell had said that the realization of the " Vatican " dream involving Austrian hegemony would mean war, Lloyd said that the favoring of an agricultural civilization and French hegemony meant war.[36] Belloc, of course, had adduced no concept of

---

that he was " gentle " albeit a " fierce writer and speaker." The " wicked " to him were " Episcopalians and Romans." Cf. Clifford, *Socialism and the Teaching of Christ,* Fabian Tract No. 78 (London, 1913). It was first printed in 1897. It is not the purpose to discuss it here nor to trace changes in Webb's thought. The religious attitudes of Wells, Wallas, and Bertrand Russell are well known. C. E. M. Joad who propounds " Common Sense Theology " is head of the Department of Philosophy of Birkbeck College, University of London, since 1930. He is one of the " northern Fabians " according to Mrs. Cole. In general the Fabian attitude toward religion is characterized by a positive indifference which is like the " anti-theism " of Auguste Comte.

[35] Cf. Advertising pages in the *NS,* XXII, *passim.* Relief was begged for (White) Russian adults and German children.

[36] On the score of secularism, incongruous as it may seem to be in a discussion of internationalism, it should be noticed that in October of 1923, a pleasant correspondence took place between two Fabians, Mr. Ratcliffe and Mr. Standring, and the editor of the *NS* concerning their preferences for " funerals without theology," and C. T. Gorham advised the latter, who

industrialized agriculture. To Belloc, agriculture was a way of life, not business. Lloyd said Germany was an "entity" and one particularly at enmity with France. The Belloc ideal which he scorned offered the hope of eliminating Franco-German enmity. In the face of contemporaneous separatism, Mr. Lloyd impugned Belloc's knowledge of Germany psychology. It must be observed that it is doubtful Belloc meant to advocate absolute political separation when he advocated liberating agricultural civilizations from industrial domination. Disregarding the peasant culture which loomed so large in Belloc's mind, Lloyd stated that France was not an "agricultural civilisation" and that she aimed to develop her own and Germany's industrialism. He again made a misrepresentation of the Belloc ideal with his overdrawn picture of "France leading the Catholic peasants of Europe against the Protestant Captains of Industry and Finance in Berlin." Lloyd showed himself incapable of metaphysical thought. His criticism overlooked the main features of Belloc's reasoning—the Benedictine ideal which once created a culture in barbarian Europe by making a fusion of liturgical life with living on and by the land. As we shall see in discussing the Fraser group, young Fabians were seeking to do for modern society what the Church once did for Europe. Concluding, Lloyd wrote, "Neither do we accept the proposition that either France or Germany must dominate Europe," and the rest of the paragraph insinuated that Belloc and France wanted civil war in Germany; it ended saying, "Everyone knows how vital to us is the recovery of German markets. . . ." Lloyd continued, saying Belloc "blandly" asked for recognition of French machinations in the Little Entente and Poland. Turning to the League of Nations, he admitted the League's weakness and suggested strengthening it by the admission of Germany and Russia. He summarized:

> The antithesis between an agricultural traditional France and an industrial and financial Prussia is a false one.

had to improvise on occasion, that there were available at the Rationalist Press Association two suitable manuals. See *NS*, XXII (October 29, 1923), 44. Fabian secularism was patent and concrete. The Tories could not take a position or find a weapon against this monism save in a "red scare." It was with this brand of non-religion that English Socialists eyed the Centre.

> The alternatives are the rule of force and the rule of international law and international common sense.[37] [Toward this end] this country must pursue its struggle with France.[38]

To be as lacking in subtlety as Lloyd, it might be said he advocated war on France so England could run a synthesized or synchronized France and Germany. It is patent that Belloc's ideal of peace in an arrangement favorable to a traditional societary order was not acceptable to the Fabian Socialist who would politicize all social orders, industrialize agriculture, and permeate the political organization of Europe to bend it in favor of a Labour axis. The picture of Fabianism taking a position in Germany which blamed France for Germany's troubles and overlooked the machinations of Communists so far as to encourage the fusion of Socialists and Communists under Moscow leadership, which detested the non-political Socialism of ILP and was inimical to the Centre (something both democratic and hierarchical) does not exonerate the British Social Democrats from blame for Germany's plight. But they were among the first to see America coming in, and a new note crept into Dell's writing. He began to sound an alarm that the German Republic was endangered [39]—he who had advocated " saving " Germany by letting Communists run the Socialists, misguided by his confusion of " medieval " with " fascist." [40]

It may be asked how great was the influence of Schücking and Dell. The answer is found in the fact that they were the only and the constant correspondents employed by the *New Statesman* which was widely read in all liberal circles. Reader reaction was quick on any given issue. There was no reader reaction against the reporting of the German scene save in an almost solitary instance—from Germany.

---

[37] Whatever "international commonsense" may mean, it belongs in a dictionary of terms like soviet equity, and sovereign equality.

[38] *NS*, XXIII (November 17, 1923), pp. 171 f. Compare *ibid.* (December 8, 1923) 260 f.

[39] Cf. R. Dell, "Anglo-German Relations, "*NS*, XXI (October 6, 1923), 731 f.

[40] Cf. Dell's letter of May 10, 1924, in *NS*, XXII, p. 125.

C. Design for " Partnership " by Massingham : Wooing the Left by Dell

Between the times when Labour came into Opposition and when it formed a Ministry, capitalist America, which sought a debt settlement with the France which made large loans to the Little Entente and Poland but was too poor to pay her debts to America, was entering into the effort to bring order into Central Europe. Readers of the *NS* were made aware of the object of a Lloyd George errand to America.[41] It was to " press to an issue the plan of an impartial fact-finding commission on German Reparations that was first proposed in America last December " (1922). Lloyd George had treated Mr. Hughes' New Haven speech embodying the proposal for international investigation as " a positive American policy." Then, French occupation of the Ruhr had thrust into abeyance any concrete action. President Coolidge however, had encouraged the view unemphasized by his late pred-

---

[41] *NS,* XXII (October 13, 1923), 2. Only on December 1, did the *NS*'s Political Correspondent divulge that the Cabinet of Baldwin had coalesced on a " Protection " issue to forestall Lloyd George. Lord Amery had disclosed that a " transatlantic bird " had divulged what was to be Lloyd George's new " thunder " which Tories started by the Plymouth plunge. But Senator LaFollette had toured Europe that summer and by October a chain of events began which led to Locarno. Colonel House announced America would come into a plan to set up a committee of experts on reparations settlement if all parties would consent. Cf. *NS,* XXII (October 27, 1923), 66. This nod to Poincaré meant a face-saving device for France. England reversed itself and asked Germany not to ask to come into the League and to cease resistance in the Ruhr. See, *NS,* XXI (October 6, 1923), 731 f. MacDonald had hitherto (cf. *ibid.*) expressed a complete understanding with Baldwin's Government on the first stand, *i.e.*, urging German resistance. Lord D'Albernon dropped his own activities in which he had been using a committee of experts of his own. German sentiment congealed about the Republic and against England but with some confidence in Labour. The stage was set. It is hard to conceive how MacDonald, who understood Baldwin when his note to France encouraged German resistance, could fail to understand when the exigencies of America's entering the picture changed all. Labour would have to go into power; France and Germany to go a little left. The Dawes Plan, the Commercial Treaty; then Locarno would follow. Locarno was early outlined by the *NS,* XXII (November 24, 1923), 201. Shaw claims to have outlined it in his *The League of Nations, Fabian Tract 226,* (London) 1929.

ecessor. There would be no world economic conference immediately but American adherence to the Hughes' proposal was
positive although it did not connote the assumption of initiative
by the United States. It is impossible to understand the Fabian-
Socialist opposition to the activities of Lloyd George and his kind
unless one sees the shaping up of two forces struggling for the
capture of power. It is not well expressed to say this was the
struggle of Communism *versus* Fascism. These were twin ideologies conceived of Socialism by materialism in Europe, disputing
primogeniture. The struggle which British Fabians, calling themselves Socialists, envisioned was one of Business against Labour.
Capital would soon be coming in from American sources and
German capital would be put to work, the best principles of
industrial democracy must prevent the sinking back of labor to
the level of a commodity. But Fabians held that only as a politicized order could those who worked by brain and hand gain the
potency to dictate the development or evolution of industry in
their own interests. This presupposed a servile or welfare state
but not immediately a monolithic state. Fabian Socialism, except
perhaps in the thought of Shaw and Cole, did not foresee the
State's withering away among free associations, nor envision a
syndicalist utopia in the " orders " of Guildsmen.[42] All the Fabian
literature bears out this description. Statism is the core of Fabianism. Deviations within its margins of techniques, and its tenden-
tious philosophy remain subjects of study and dispute. It can be
seen working in the attitudes of the *NS* on the apparent Baldwin-
Poincaré stalemate, the running commentary on Germany's plight
and France's mischief, and in the hopes expressed for the outcome
in Germany. That the means to ends to many of which no right
thinking reader can dissent were properly chosen, may not always
be assumed. Nor can the acceptance of their monism by one who
assents to their ethos be presumed.

Although the correspondents who kept the *NS* readers informed

---

[42] The Communists did not differ on "industrial democracy" but on the
tempo of the becoming of the servile and totalitarian state, itself a stepping-
stone to anarchy—the statelessness of pristine innocence. They looked no
further than " the Revolution "—the acceleration of the State's becoming all-
administrative, and disappearing. The question of the Party's abdication in
favor of the syndicalistic and stateless society was not discussed.

as to German developments, Massingham [43] and Dell, differed in style, both interpreted events in the light of America's imminence and the "tendency" toward international Socialism in the *NS*. Both are important because they reveal the criteria of the Party attitude on tariffs and the meaning of "Protection." Together they represent the Fabian character on two positions, the social area which they disputed with ILP and the social area to left of that. "Wayfarer" saw in the new Stresemann Government a sort of Oliver Cromwell "cum-Parliament" [44] autocracy in which "Stinnes has played fair." With reparations rendered impossible and security gone (hatred of France "aglow"), the Government which replaced Dr. Cuno had gained one advantage; it served to "ward off a Communist revolution." There was beginning to be a feeling that the Stresemann Government might be the one to get Germany on her feet. The President, Ebert, was a Socialist and Socialists served in the Cabinet. The autocracy which had moneyed backing, and Parliament, could possibly render Germany amenable to England's economic partnership—one in which both Labour and Tories sought to break the grip of France. Massingham, from whom we get the best statement on Labour's idea of tariffs, seemed more devoted to the English and German national interests than Dell, but he viewed possible separatism in Germany with some equanimity while blaming France for subsidizing revolt in the Palatinate and Ruhr and in the Balkans. [45] He revealed the fact that the Government was troubled by knowledge of a *surplus*

---

[43] Wayfarer saw in the Stresemann Government a bourgeois settlement and expected no "man ʌunt" for "socialists." Cf. *NS*, XXII (November 17, 1923), 176. Wayfarer and Dell differed in viewpoint. Pease seemed to find a middle course between them. For example, he reviewed Henry Strobel (Finance Minister in the Prussian Revolutionary Government of 1918), *Socialisation in Theory and Practice,* in *FN*, XXXIII:11 (November, 1922). Strobel condemned Communist methods of socializing industry in Russia and Hungary, and Pease, the Fabian historian (always nearer centre than left or right of it), remarked: "We may query the opinions of English touring parties [Massingham?] and doubt the accuracy of press correspondents [Dell?, Schücking?] but we can hardly question the statements of a German statesman writing for the German public."

But the editor of the *NS* followed Dell for the most part.

[44] *NS*, XXII (October 20, 1923), 43 f.

[45] *NS*, XXII (October 27, 1923), 75.

of steel which Germans might dump on England and for this problem's solution he offered the Fabian proposition: Since Trade was not a "scrap of cut-throats" but "a mutual or cooperative enterprise," Germany's general production should be *increased* to absorb the steel surplus, as it could if developed. Russia, palpably reviving, needed Western *credit* and goods. *German production restored* would absorb more steel than the surplus left after French consumption and it was to "British interest" to enter into "economic partnership" with Germany. It was plain that the *credit* to Russia would come from English bankers and the *goods* from German and English surpluses,[46] created by planning, a word not yet in ordinary parlance but connoted by "economic partnership." To summarize, Massingham pointed out a Germany with which England might work in a free-trade axis, with a view to employment, by increased production made possible by "partnership" which should not be burdened by commitments to the Dominions. England would be senior partner, of course. Agricultural questions were entirely subservient to industrialism. Yet the ILP was agitating the agricultural question. But to speak of agriculture was to involve the politicians in Empire Preference schemes and warning had to be given that the truth of England's (MacDonald-Baldwin) attitude toward Preference and Protection, which impinged upon self-interest and was contingent upon the "partnership" of Germany, must not be told lest it weaken the Imperial bond. So Labour must sloganize "Free Trade."[47]

---

[46] *NS*, XXII (October 29, 1923), 43 f. Nowhere is the system of production for profit and scarcity for price-raising better contrasted with the tenets held by Socialists than here. "Capitalism" was indicted, deservedly. But Socialism, in arraigning Capitalism, presumed to usurp all political factors and even the cultural character of a social unit. By working on masses ideologically and not on individuals ethically, it arrogated all human areas to itself and necessarily failed to be the religion it sought to replace. Its criticism produced a puritanical conscience which manifested a feeling of guilt in regard to possession of property.

[47] Cf. "A London Diary," *NS*, XXII (October 20, 1923), 43 f. Fabians did not in fact argue for Empire preference after this time. J. H. Thomas in his *My Story* (London: Hutchinson and Company, 1937), p. 205, expresses his view based on his Trade Union policy and backed by the brilliant Fabian economist, William Graham, that tariffs should be favored. He narrates the story of the advantage taken by Tories to embarrass Labour on this moot

" We are all imperialists because the Empire has disappeared." was the *NS* answer to Australia and New Zealand and "the maniacs" who asked revision of Bonar Law's pledge of no fiscal reform in this Parliament (1923).[48] Only the fact that Labour held office at the time accounts for later *NS* lip service to agriculture in reporting the ILP conference concerning which the *NS* emphasized "control of importation" and "world regulation." [49] We can see that the Socialist plan to work with Capital *by credit* rather than by tariffs represented the clearest cleavage between the Tories and themselves in the response each side made to hopes aroused by American interest. American interest involved acceptance of the Dawes Plan and this Plan could be pressed upon Germany by a government which could garner some support of " the left." The left would cooperate, however grudgingly, with a government amenable to the ideal of production " for need "— not for profit, which involved tariffs. Massingham's formula on steel exemplified this. It is fairly clear that if Baldwin's political machine wanted the Dawes Plan only a Labour Government could get it for them.

But if Massingham laid down the line on tariffs, Dell laid it down on politics. He was the Socialist " idealist " playing for support of a real Socialist regime—not a mere *modus vivendi* with " autocracy " howsoever Cromwellian, or with Tory pacification schemes, or with the Centre.

In the same week that Lloyd George's departure was interpreted, Robert Dell[50] distinguished between " Socialists and Fascists."

---

point, especially where Labour's official policy and the Dominions' demand clashed. Cf. *ibid.*, pp. 208 f.

[48] Cf. *NS*, XXI, 725 f and 728 f.

[49] Cf. *NS*, XXIII (April 26, 1924), 54. MacDonald and Trevelyan (for Education) had made speeches at the ILP Conference. The ILP was still a power.

[50] Dell was correspondent for the *Manchester Guardian* also, and well known in Geneva. Cf. his *The Geneva Racket* (London: Robert Hale, Ltd., 1941). He greatly favored the Labour viewpoint and the Russian cause. This book was published posthumously by American crypto-Socialists. Dell died in 1940. He had been President of the International Association of Journalists accredited to the League of Nations. Also, he had been expelled from France for disclosing peace negotiations between France and Austria in 1917 and had earlier been charged with treason for proposing to write a

Now, along with the excoriation of Socialists by Communists in Germany came the false identification in opprobrium, of "fascists" and industrialists by Moscow-led Marxists. As if to increase the urgency for greater power for "Labour" in Britain, Dell reported the resurrection, after three days fall, of Stresemann's Government which he considered as a breathing spell which could not last. Hitherto four, now three Socialists were included in the Stresemann Cabinet. He believed there was opposition to the Stresemann Cabinet from Herr Stinnes (Massingham said Stinnes "played fair" (through the *Volkespartei* (Conservatives, according to Dell, who had put on a democratic cloak after the war). Dell was disgusted with what he considered the weakness of the Socialists in Germany. He especially deplored the fact that the parliamentary Socialists had little contact with the Socialist Party throughout the country, while the Socialists in Parliament refused support to Socialists in the Cabinet. He wrote that he saw some probability that Communists by means of the changed policy "under wise Russian influence" would form a united front with the Socialists; and he expressed satisfaction and the hope that since Labour *could not get into power by constitutional methods* there would be "no senseless outcry in England" when "Labour" became strong enough to act. To "conquer power" against the Trusts and deal with Reparations,[51] a government of the "Left" was best for Germany and that should be formed by the Communist-Socialist front which Dell named "Labour." Otherwise a government of "reaction" was "inevitable." This was Dell's message, borne out in all he wrote home for Fabians. Exception was never taken to any of his opinions by editors, contributors or letter-writers save by an occasional German letter-writer.

The correspondent from Germany contributed a great deal to

---

book charging France with having started the World War. Cf. *The Sunday Star,* July 21, 1940, p. A-10, Washington, D. C. Earlier, he had been an ardent Francophile. To compare his reporting in the *NS* with that in the *Manchester Guardian* would be valuable but not for present purposes. He also wrote for *The Nation* in New York.

[51] *NS*, XXII (October 12, 1923), 6 f. On May 10, 1924, he confused "medieval" and fascist while defining "reaction."

the situation in which a subsequent British Labour Government could evoke some confidence in Left, even far-Left, circles.

It is not the writer's intention to precipitate a ready-made opinion as to the attitude which the Fabians' informant assumed; but it may appear to the reader that the Fabians were getting (from the *NS*) and giving out the opinion of one of their own who stood in a special position in Germany. Dell saw rising from the field where the tower of the Centre had fallen, as he believed, three wraiths: Fascism, Socialism, and the ghost of the old Centre. He detested Fascism with its anti-Semitism and militarism but he sometimes confused with it rightist elements which feared and detested Fascism as much as he did. He threw the weight of his opinion to the Left asking for a Socialist-Communist synthesis. Only after the Dawes Plan was about to be accepted when Labour wanted it, did Dell speak well of the Centre.[52] Then he showed the Centre as dignified, consistent, working only on its own terms with the Nationalists who were even then, Dell said, aiming to destroy confidence abroad so that no loan to Germany would be forthcoming. Dell turned even more bitterly upon the *Volkespartei* accusing it of vacillation. If, as some publicists would have us believe, the Communist Party of Germany was then being used by Moscow to further Hitler's rise, Dell could not have known this since even the rank and file KPD did not.[53]

By October 20, Dell reported with scorn that *Vorwärts* and the Socialists in Parliament had "awakened" to the fact that the German Republic was "in great danger."[54] He interpreted statements made in *Vorwärts* to fit in with his own conviction that

---

[52] Cf. *NS*, XXIII (June 7, 1924), 246 f.

[53] Cf. Ossip K. Flechtheim, *Die KPD in der Weimarer Republic* (Offenbach: Bollwerk-Verlag K. Drott, 1948). It seems indisputable that (1) Communists were blind and stubborn in their attitude toward Socialists and in their failure to understand Germany; (2) some evidence supports the thesis that a Moscow-led action defeated the aims of the rest of the KPD; (3) a radical element favored the rise of a die-hard regime on purpose to glean the fruits of revolt against "reaction" for their radical ends; (4) certainly the manner of acting of the KPD, as Professor Ehrmann says, served "at least objectively" to foment the rise of Hitler. Cf. review by H. W. Ehrmann in *The American Political Science Review*, XLIII (April, 1949), 374 f.

[54] Dell's diction smacks of KPD semantics, *e.g.*, "army of reaction."

a "military dictatorship existed." It was "exercised by Doctor Gessler, Democrat and friend of Ehrhardt." As Ehrhardt was the leader of a rabble band of "condottieri," Dell seemed to seek to discredit Gessler by association and weaken Stresemann by stressing sentiments which the latter deemed it inappropriate to express at the time. Dell interpreted the situation by over-emphasizing what *Vorwärts* stated as warning or fear: The Socialists in the Reichstag had gone along with Stresemann and Gessler. (Those in the Government were helpless to prevent those outside it from joining with Communists, as had been done in Saxony.) Gessler was head of the Reichswehr, "the army of reaction." [55] Socialist cooperation had been given, said Dell, with the understanding that the Government would subsequently use its powers against the "military dictatorship" in Bavaria (where, in Dell's judgment, Munich was the ripest place for a Socialist-Communist coalescence). Dell designated Chancellor Stresemann as the partner of Stinnes, one popularly believed to have profiteered out of the inflation, and both thought to be in sympathy with the Monarchist Party—monarchist and militarist, for General von Seeckt was "hand in glove with Doctor von Kahr," the Bavarian "dictator."—"The Fascist organizations know where to go for their arms when the Day arrives," Dell wrote in October 1923. He was quite unfair to Stresemann and Stinnes. He opined, in self-contradiction, that Stresemann played the counterpart of Bonar Law in the stand he took on the Ruhr question. Upon what objective basis opinion formed from data which Dell supplied could be grounded, it is hard to see. His "Labour front" was nebulous. He stated that the Reich was partial to (the now re-

---

[55] Actually Gessler was trying to keep this army from direct reaction. Cf. Robert Dell, "The Reactionary Offensive in Germany," *NS*, XXII (October 20, 1923), 39 f. He casts angry aspersion on *Vorwärts* and the parliamentary Socialists. He favored the Saxony "Labour-and-Socialist" government which he knew was Moscow-led and he was wrathy with the Reich for countenancing the military government set up in Bavaria. This investigator has the permission of Professor David Baumgardt, formerly Professor of Ethics, University of Berlin, to relate that at that time Gessler sought his advice or the ethics of his peculiar position. Gessler was trying to keep things fluid and to keep his hand in to prevent the Reichswehr from going Nazi.

actionary) Bavaria and was supporting " White Terror " [56] in Saxony which, he said, was more loyal than the Reich, to the republic, and where a Communist-Socialist coalescence had set up a " Labour " government. He wrote that cooperation of Socialists in the Reich Cabinet was proving " one of the greatest obstacles to a general united front." In Saxony, for example, Socialists and Communists united might choose secession; so workmen in Bavaria and the Reich must save the Republic. There existed in the Reich, Dell thought, a " veiled " Kapp putsch. The " Fascists " had arms; the workmen none. Reichswehr officers were " re-actionary " and counted, accurately, on the loyalty of their men. Expecting the army to make a union with the Fascist organiza-tions, Dell quoted a Saxon Government statement, " German Capitalism had begun an offensive against the workmen." He,

---

[56] This notion of " White Terror," a term reminiscent of France after the Restoration as well as of Ukranian ferocity aroused by the Red Terror in Russia, was applied by *NS* writers to the civil controls inaugurated by leaders who had to cope with countries once under Communist domination—a prob-lem which is usually not presented to imagination. Fabian feeling came out in a review of Oscar Jaszi's *Revolution and Counter-Revolution in Hungary,* which was graced by an introduction of R. W. Seton-Watson. Cf. *NS,* XXIII (June 7, 1924), 262. The Fabian reviewer said Bela Kun's mistake had been that *he did not handle the peasants as Lenin did.* There was no encouragement for Horthy's civil order, termed " old, narrow, class-rule [d] "; basing itself on ignorance and *servitude of peasants,* hence, na-tionalistic, chauvinistic, corrupt. The Fabian reviewer averred that atrocities listed by Jaszi were undocumented. He concluded that if the Reds had been *cruel* and *ignorant,* the Whites had been *cold* and *refined,* masquerading as " Gentlemen." The writer urged that loans be *not* withheld but that nothing be done by any government to " thwart the efforts of the Hungarian demo-crats as they have thwarted them in the past." The *NS* explicitly advised editorially against the Government's making a loan to the Roumanian King and Queen (they had come to England to plead for one), lest it be used to support reaction and postpone the rising of " democratic " forces. The *NS* took the same attitude toward giving arms to prevent occupation of Bessarabia, saying it did not believe Trotsky had said Bessarabia was the first step to Constantinople. (*NS,* XIII, pp. 219 and 242.)—In the same way in 1950, " progressives " of ADA conviction advise against the United States' supporting " decadent governments " (like Syngman Rhee's republic) and advocate a United States Titoism (formerly Trotskyism) to put on a program in the rescued countries of " dynamic democracy " which means politicized democratic units—Socialism, of course. Cf. speech of Senator Wayne Morse in the *Congressional Record* of July 10, 1950, pp. 9936 f.

himself, said he believed there was an inexplicable lockout in progress; and he insinuated that some explanation might be found in the fact that inflation made some manufacturers wealthy. There had been a sudden and to Dell a mysterious rise of gold prices which seemed " part of the manoeuvre." He suggested that such procedures were calculated deliberately to goad Labour into revolt in order to crush it. It is clear from this reporter's methods that he was not informed of the government's real nature or purpose, and that he hoped to obtain better knowledge of its financial resources by public guessing. He was in touch, no doubt, with some one in Communist leadership. He was positively one of the Labour-minded persons willing to take common action, if not to hold common ideas with Communists. Whether Fabians realized it or not, while their correspondent pressed for a Labour front, even one Communist-created, in Germany, the KPD, while officially breathing slaughter upon Socialists and the " Social Fascists," at the national level, either on account of blindness or because of the secret intent of leaders who would know how to use revolt against " reaction," was serving to propel the rise of Hitler.[57]

The communistic configurations in Dell's thought are silhouetted plainly in the light of his wrath with the " Ebert-Stresemann-Gessler Triumvirate," their " coup d'etat " in Saxony (it was legal), the " cowardice, self-seeking and corruption " of the drifting rank and file of the Socialists, who, he said, were deserting and betray-

---

[57] Guenther Rheinhardt, " Hitler's Prewar Red Allies," in *Plain Talk,* IV (February, 1950), 48 ff, goes much further than Ehrmann, to say that Flechtheim's documentation proves that Moscow used KPD to foment Hitler's rise. H. Remmele declared " when the Fascists will be in power the United front of the proletariat will come into existence and will sweep away everything." (Dell, and those he might persuade would be ready in the " united front.") Reinhardt says Flechtheim shows that Moscow used the immoral Thaelmann in despite of the KPD's Central (national) Committee, to carry out orders inimical to the interests of KPD: 1) the Swastika burgeoned beside the Sickle and Hammer; 2) riots, in 1921 and 1923, ordered by Moscow, weakened the KPD and strengthened Hitler. These were the days of Ruth (Eisler) Fischer's disillusionment. She is still a Social Democrat.

A national cabal has been known to garner resources for patriot ends from financial " corrpution " created by subversives.)

ing the workingmen, as he interpreted the fact that Socialists in
the government had obtained cooperation of Socialists in the
Saxon Landtag to repress the "Labour" government. Dell was
mystified by the apparent acquiescence of the Allied Military Control with illegal rearming, particularly in Munich. This was only
one year after Mussolini's "March on Rome" and already in
Communist parlance the term Fascist bore a stigma. Dell had
adopted the custom of dubbing every anti-Communist group as
Fascist [58] while in the Communist manner he reviled Socialists in
the Government, dividing them from Socialists in the country.
Reasoning such as Dell expressed could only contribute to the rise
of Hitler by weakening the rational support at home and abroad
of the Stresemann Government which had to lean upon Gessler's
help in the hope of avoiding collapse. The attrition caused by
Socialist-Communist coups, for which Dell sought approval was a
constant threat to stability.[59] He called for outright allied inter-

---

[58] The graph of the Fabian readers' growth in knowledge about Mussolini
is traceable in the pages of the *NS* for 1922 and 1923, *passim:* He was an
old Socialist, but Socialist no longer. Italian Socialism was a spent force.
He should control the hoodlums among the Fascists (the *NS* got the idea
of "banding together" out of *fasces* but not the historical concept of
authority and order by law which the *fasces* represented to *Il Duce*).
Respect was due the Italy he had recreated. He had obliterated Trade
Union lines (they were anti-Socialist but also "anti-political and syndicalist") and he had politicized the cooperatives. Cf. *NS*, XXI (August
11, 1923), 510. His proportional representation plan worked all too well
toward personal dictatorship for the head of the Party. But J. M. H.,
reviewing the Labour Publishing Company's publication of Odin Por,
Fascism, told *NS* readers the Turin Constitution was the "work of a radical
idealist" (D'Annunzio); that nationalism was inherently revolutionary in
Italy, that the Social-Communists' mistake when they seized the factories
in 1923 consisted *in not beginning on the agricultural, cooperative-Soviet
level;* and they offered "no alternative State," while Fascists "seized the
State." The reviewer told Fabians that Por was over-optimistic in finding
that the character of Fascism outlined in A. E.'s *The National Being* was
"economic democracy" based on "work, production and the cooperation of
the classes as well as on national feeling"; but J. M. H. did not say why he
thought A. E. was wrong. Cf. "Recent Italian History," *NS,* XXI (Septem-
1, 1923), 598.

[59] Fabian Robert Dell's anger with the Reich and "its socialist president,"
Ebert, for putting down the "Socialist-Communist" governments in Thuringia, for example, was boundless. He saw the objectives of the Reich

vention on legalistic grounds, that is, to punish violation of the Treaty.[60]   He believed—and he was an authority on French

Government only as being for "the Interests" and wrote that the Thuringian and other possible Socialist governments, Saxony, for example, asked an incoming Labour Government in England to "make it a condition of any help to Germany" that *equality* be accorded *Socialist* governments.   Cf. Robert Dell, "In Occupied Thuringia," *NS*, XXII (January 5, 1924), 359 f. [It was unfortunate indeed that certain genuine reforms such as Loeb's State Bank in Thuringia (developing the State by loans, and importing gold) and the Greil school text reforms should have to perish in the expunging of Communism by the Reich; and that a condition of inequitable taxation resulted in the social contrasts of spending orgies in cafés with hunger in workingmen's homes.] Dell believed at this time that Germans were betrayed by their own leaders and industrialists.   Cf. *ibid.,* p. 389.   In his "The Father of the Schieber," *NS*, XXII (February 23, 1924), 564, Dell called Herr Haverstein, President of the Reichbank, the "Father of the Schieber." He snarled, "make the harpies [government subsidized industrialists who offered passive resistance in the Ruhr] disgorge!"   Dell advocated "gold value" for money and taxes.   He admired Loeb in Thuringia and excoriated Haverstein.   Both were bankers aiding their governments; but Loeb's was "Labour" and Haverstein's was the Reich.   The expedient, Communist-guided separatism had his approval.   In other words, he bespoke Fabian support for a Socialist, Labour and Communist-aided front against the party of republican authority, weighting his argument with the recitation of the financial sins of that authority's supporters.   This undermining of authority by the technique of disclosing sins of government officials in order to be in a position to come forward with a program for "social democracy" is one of the penalties of having a political system in which the basis of political authority is ill-defined.   An attitude such as Dell fostered in *NS* readers contributed something in the not-too-long run to the collapse of the Weimar Republic.   It is safe to say, if one will read the biographies of Snowden and Henderson, that Labour's support of the Stresemann, as later the Brüning Ministry, was half-hearted and limited to what would conduce to converting Germany into a "social democracy."   Fabians were against anti-State republicanism save as transition.   No voice was raised to show the quandary of the Reich: the French in the Ruhr, the Socialist educational demands encouraging separatism in the Palatinate, the Communist-led "Labour" governments in Thuringia and Saxony, the Hitler element germinating in Bavaria and the demand for "reparations" which, coupled with the incubus in the Ruhr which must be purged by drastic measures, inspired the device of inflation by printing press money.   (*Supra,* note 57.)

[60] Dell, "Political Confusion," *NS*, XXII (November 17, 1923), 171 ff. He was producing much confusion in *NS* readers.   Later, after an article by the Fabian, Thomson, appeared in the New York *Nation,* the German "Labour" idealists conceived the idea that a Labour-governed England

affairs [61]—that the French Government wished " to come to terms with the German capitalists," so there was scant possibility that the ultimatum he proposed demanding the immediate disarmament of Bavaria and the restoration of Parliamentary Government in Saxony would be accepted. The Saxon Government had been " called upon to resign " by the Reich Cabinet but, as Dell chose to interpret it, the Cabinet was " turned out by force " and, " I understand," [62] he said, " Dr. Stresemann's first idea was to order . . . arrest [of the Saxon Cabinet] . . . for high treason . . . [and] Ebert was quite willing." This " I understand " indicates readers were offered not news but rumor. The more " reactionary " Stresemann might be made to appear, the sharper the revolt in sentiment against him, and the larger the recruitment for Social Democracy.

We have studied the picture of Germany's political plight in some detail in order to know what Fabians were learning as they guided the Labour Party in Britain toward power. Under the slogan of " Protection " *versus* " Free Trade," they looked for means to produce a Russo-German trade axis with an English fulcrum. They made no objection to Dell's correspondence, editorially or by letters. This kind of discussion of the German problem signalled sympathy to the Left, at home and abroad. The fact is that at that time Stresemann and D'Abernon were working out the plans which led to the Dawes Plan, the Commercial Treaty, and Locarno. While Stresemann was pictured as far Right, he actually was gathering the forces of the Left to his assistance, as Lord D'Abernon revealed in his diaries. This is discussed and documented in the section, " Broad Diplomacy." Dell's manifest sympathy

---

would ship them arms. A letter from one Robert Eisler of Feldafing, Bavaria, to the *NS*, XXII (February 16, 1924), 540, indicates this belief but the editor replied that Thomson's article had been misunderstood; there was no suggestion among British Socialists of a Franco-German war with England on Germany's side. The freedom to purchase arms did not mean the Labour government would send arms. One recalls, however, that the *NS* opinion on airplane armament was that enough should be maintained to bargain with France.

[61] Dell, *My Second Country (France)* (London: John Lane Company, 1920).

[62] This " I understand " was characteristic of non-factual or non-documental reporting.

with Socialist-Communist or "Labour-front" Saxony and Thuringia was not consonant with the ostensible objection to "separatism" of which France was the abettor in the Rhineland and Palatinate,[63] although it was consonant with the labour-left-toward-Communist thinking, because the "re-achieving" of unity would come under their "Socialism." Even though Stresemann had the collaboration of the Centre, the support of the army, and the confidence of the Socialists in the Government, he was not to be allowed to forget that International Socialism had a special plan for a German commonwealth. "A new and greater Bismarck will, when the time comes, re-achieve [sic] the unity of the German people without one-tenth of the difficulties which the Iron Chancellor had to face." [64]

Clifford Sharp submitted "The Crusade of Suicide" in the same issue.[65] Useless except as a piece of destructive criticism, it nevertheless indicated the preparation of minds to support a *bloc des gauches*. Sharp associated himself with General Smuts in listing the seven sins of France: Assuming the hegemony of Europe, substituting her own plan for Versailles, subverting the authority and influence of Britain, rousing the vengeance motive in Germany, making the neutral and Anglo-Saxon world pro-German. There would be no war; no one wanted to fight. France had destroyed any possibility of Reparations; France would not pay her debt, so Britain could not pay America.

Just as the editorial policy of the *NS* adopted Dell's view on Germany, but spoke in a less emotional tone, so it followed Clifford Sharp's views on France, especially the opinion that she subsidized militarism in Germany. Later the editor contributed the information that America, like a sleeping dog, had begun to growl.[66] There might be some pressure upon M. Poincaré—in order, it seemed, to collect the debt. C. M. Lloyd wrote "The World, the Franc and the Devil" in November, 1923,[67] urging that the nation

---

[63] *NS*, XXII (October 27, 1923), 65.

[64] *Ibid.*

[65] Clifford Sharp, "The Crusade of Suicide," *NS*, XXII (October 27, 1923), 68.

[66] *Ibid.*

[67] C. M. Lloyd, "The World, the Franc and the Devil," *NS*, XXII (November 3, 1923), 100.

take control of gold in order to control France and speaking hope-
fully of the possibility that America might put pressure upon the
French electorate and so curb Poincaré's mischief. When Lloyd
wrote this the franc had been falling for fifteen months. This
gave French goods a price edge over English exports. Anglo-
French economic relations gave pause, no doubt, to the English
political Socialists whose plan involved selling steel made in Germany to France. For this the triumph of the Left was needed,
and toward that the fall of the franc was contributory. Without
rebuttal, the proposal of outright intervention, or at least of acceptance of a Communist-Socialist coup in Germany, was allowed to
stand as stated. Freedom of expression of the Dell opinion and
the absence of outcry against it was at least a comfort to the Left
which, upon Labour's accession to power in Britain, lent itself
guardedly to the Stresemann Government long enough to push
through the Dawes Plan, which thawed the congealed economic
current of Europe.

D. AMERICA COMING IN: FRANCE TO BE CURBED: " CREDIT "

Henceforth political configurations would be shaped by fiscal
policy. The election challenge, " Protection," was quickly understood: France must be curbed and a Conservative Baldwin could
not do it. Without credit to the Foreign Office, *NS* informed its
readers that Belgium was coming over under London leadership
asserting some independence of France. Italy, too, in all disputes,
was to be counted upon to throw in its weight with Britain. It
had been reported previously [68] that Lloyd George in Chicago had
informed Americans that Germany had made some substantial
payments, that Americans must save Germany and carry out the
Hughes proposal. It is fairly evident from the sequel that Mr.
Lloyd George had learned some of the Republicans' views on protection while in America and was preparing to repeat one of his
great political feats of carrying both issues in his tentative mandate: that is, he was prepared to fight for a " free trade " slogan
and adjust the electorate to some protection in the face of the

---

[68] *NS*, XXII (October 27, 1923), 65 f.

problem of the international debt.[69] The Liberal Party might thus have embodied in itself the best in Tory and in Labour principles. Yet the differences were not only those of party; for Socialists in the Labour Party the " spirit " was different. It was a creed. The " spirit," for Fabian Socialists meant a socio-economic drive beyond the definition of politics, and it was freighted with what has been called the " destructionism " of Progressives.[70]

Economic discussions in the *NS* indicate that Fabians followed Reginald McKenna and John Maynard Keynes, and for the time being, the Federation of British Industries. The Fabian-Labour politicians had evolved but few fiscal ideas of their own. " Deflation," they held, had been " overdone." [71] " Securing stability by intelligent *control* of *credit*" was better, the *NS* thought, than cutting costs of production (wages) and trying to undersell rivals. Governmental order abroad would help create demand.[72] Bank credit must be accompanied by an increased volume of production [70] otherwise it was something mischievous and anti-social. This was said in agreement with Sir Eric Geddes, Keynes, McKenna, and Sir Francis Goodenough, President of the Gas Light and Coke Company of London. But these men meant it to apply on the domestic front and the Fabians applied it to their German-Russian axis. Readers were taught that " the Bank of England has in its power to expand or contract credit at will." An economic *authority* commanded the " weapon " of deflation, the Bank Rate. The *NS* disagreed with the view of Sir Felix Schuster that the gold value of the pound should be raised to its prewar parity with the dollar. It preferred a suggestion to reduce the Bank Rate.

---

[69] Wayfarer, "London Diary," *NS*, XXII (October 20, 1923), 43.

[70] Cf. Ludwig von Mises, " Benjamin M. Anderson Challenges the Philosophy of the Pseudo-Progressives," in *Plain Talk*, IV (February, 1950), 51–58. Professor Mises links the Keynesians with the Marxists as destructionists and says of Anderson's work, "What is needed is a frontal attack upon the whole web of Marxian, Veblenian, and Keynesian fallacies. As long as the syllogisms of these pseudo-philosophies retain their undeserved prestige, the average intellectual will go on blaming capitalism for all the disastrous effects of anti-capitalist schemes and devices," p. 55.

[71] *NS*, XXII (November 3, 1923), 102.

[72] *NS*, XXII (October 27, 1923), 66.

[73] *NS*, XXII (November 3, 1923), 102.

This would bring a quick and ugly deflation; but once this spasm had passed, gold would flow in and trade revive. But, it was conceded, gradual deflation seemed to be the country's official policy. Although far less space was given to fiscal problems than to foreign political problems, it is clear enough that Fabians asked for inflation to raise prices. The new economics of the Royal Society was beginning to be publicized.

C. M. H. Lloyd wrote " Stabilizing Stagnation," [74] wherein he endorsed the Keynes-McKenna proposal for expanding credit and disregarding dollar value. He advocated " giving statutory recognition to the present gold value " of currency, and reducing the Bank Rate to two percent. He noted with approval that America had " checked the expansion of credit twenty percent above the lowest level touched in the slump." He concluded that inflation was necessary to relieve unemployment, having said " Tariffs were not in all . . . circumstances a device of the Evil One " and Labour would not stump the country with the " sole equipment of a Free Trade Trombone." [75]

Fabians hardly foresaw that they would be in authority and perhaps in the position to regulate the Bank Rate in the near future. The pressure for credit expansion and some inflation was directed toward banks. A touch of tariff could be tolerated.

> Who cares about Free Trade or Protection? Either we know nothing about these things or else we know that in neither camp can we hope to find salvation from our present discontents. . . . We are in favor of Free Trade because Great Britain happens to be a Free Trade country. If it were a Protectionist country, we should support Protection. . . . Unemployment [the real issue] . . . [is] a natural and *inevitable* feature of the " capitalist " organisation of industry.

So wrote Mr. Clifford Sharp,[76] the Fabian editor of the *NS*, on the eve of election. On the domestic side, Fabians took a popular tack in their sails. In their recommendations for procuring full

---

[74] C. M. Lloyd, " Stabilizing Stagnation," *NS*, XXII (November 3, 1923), 101.

[75] *Ibid.*, p. 98.

[76] *NS*, XXII (November 10, 1923), 132 f.

employment, not in their attitude on tariffs, lay the reason for their internationalist attitudes.

Credit for English business, credit for Russia and *de jure* recognition, was the *NS*'s plea; although there was little said of German credit and no such close analysis of Russian affairs as of the German. Let the City as well as the Bank of England give the necessary credit to Russia which was now socially normal, and was maintaining, it was said, a healthy currency.[77] " Free Trade " where a Labour Government could manage both British and German production, curbing France, was best for the Russian-British-German trade axis. A modicum of protection should have to be allowed to manage France. There was no indication in the *NS* that it suspected that the Government had taken its official position on protection swayed by the opinion that protection would save British industry from French competition, competition which the *NS* writers habitually deplored. The latter surmised that Lloyd George had acquired a notion of tariff reform but they made no prognostication of what the Tory long view might be. Eventual defeat of Labour and Fabian internationalism was to bring about a steady policy of protective tariffs following the Republican policy in America, designed to reduce the power of France on the Continent in favor of British supremacy. It is strange that at this time the *NS* believed that " isolation," in effect, was disappearing in America. It was observed that the West was making itself felt. Coolidge in the White House [78] was endorsing Hughes' New Haven speech and La Follette was being converted from isolationism; but Reed Smoot of Utah was becoming vocal, and California's Johnson and Borah were pressing for payment of debts by France. Interpretation shows that English and American tariffs had the disciplining of France for objective, an objective the Fabians shared.

" Coolidge, Congress, and Monroe " appeared over the signature of Fabian S. K. Ratcliffe.[79] " Western Progressives " or " radicals " had " invaded Congress " in force " against Eastern party

---

[77] *NS*, XXII (November 24, 1923), 198.

[78] *NS*, XXII (October 27, 1923), 65 f.

[79] S. K. Ratcliffe, " Coolidge, Congress, and Monroe," *NS*, XXII (December 8, 1923), 261. Ratcliffe was a frequent visitor to America.

machine bosses and Wall Street." They were not isolationists, would recognize Russia and would favor government *credit* to support shipping of grains. "America is coming in," but only economically, Ratcliffe inferred. The United States was opposed to alliances (Ratcliffe attributed this to the Monroe Doctrine) and American power was not to be committed to unknown contingencies. Mr. Hughes' words were interpreted by Ratcliffe, differing unemphatically with the editor, to mean "isolation" was to continue. The question was how far America would go toward social democracy in Germany and whether or not she would move solely toward debt settlement. In any case, there had to be a government having authority in Germany. The "dial tone," to use an anachronism, of the "voice of socialism in Germany" changed its pitch.

Meantime, A. E. Davies, Fabian writer of "The City" in the *NS*, was reporting with a noticeable new verve his visit to Los Angeles, where "Southern California exudes oil," and where the Shell Royal-Dutch combine had successfully invaded, he rejoiced to report, the Standard Oil country. He caught the optimism of the outrageous land boom and said he believed the population increase would absorb the inflation created by excessive credit. Los Angeles bankers told him the Balfour settlement of the United States-British debt was "a shocking error": It should have been tied in with France's debt—something which must now be brought to a head. The suggestion that the Western Croesus was the hope of the "unhappy Continent" of Europe was not difficult to detect in Davies' correspondence.[80] Again, "credit" not "protection *versus* free trade" was the Fabian answer to the fiscal problem. "Credit" could be government-controlled in the long view. "Protection" favored industrialists' independence.

Non-revolutionary or gradualist, penetrative or revisionist, as these British Socialists may be called, they nevertheless contributed to the evolving of "the new order," by intellectual agitation— "education." No surcease from turmoil of ideas was allowed. Nevertheless, although they were not "violent revolutionists," they counted upon the natural attritions due to constant criticism

---

[80] A. E. Davies, "The City," *NS*, XXII (December 8, 1923), 284.

to begin to wear down a civilization, in the interest of their professed Socialism.   Waters wearing away the soil irrigate, for a time, the riparian fields.

We see, therefore, that on the points of fiscal policy and internationalism the Labour Party was given or endowed with an ideological formation profoundly different from the Conservatives in objectives and from the Liberals in definitions.   Capitalistic nomenclature underwent re-defining.   Principles of " tariff " and " foreign relations," which Tories honored, became obsolete, " British interest " lost its isolation and " credit " and " cooperation " replaced *raisons-d'etat*.   On one side, British hegemony was directly sought as the fulcrum of an axis for trade, because of British Labour's interest in a " new order "; Industrial Democracy, for all the world, at last.   Beowulf would again reduce the miasma; this time, of " decadent " Capitalism.[81]

The election took place December 6, 1923.   England was not sure then what sort of a Government was in.   No party had a clear majority.   Only the Fabians were sure and ready.   As a result of the election, on the domestic side a " Socialist Government " was said to have been elected by people who voted for a Labour Party which, spearheaded by Fabianism, had forsworn its prime Socialist characteristics, leaving these characteristics sequestered in the Annual Labour Conference Report.   Many men, and more women voted Labour, to find they had elected Socialism.   They had chosen from a program offering tariffs or no tariffs, and they found they had elected an international mandate.

Webb credited MacDonald with having been the first to recog-

---

[81] To follow Mr. John Parker, M.P., and president of the Fabian Society in 1948–1949 when he writes in his *Labour on the March* (Penguin Books, Harmsworth, Middlesex, England and 245 Fifth Avenue, New York, 1947), that " The Old Fabian Society which had been particularly active in the field of ideas in the period immediately before 1914 did not recover its intellectual leadership after the first World War," p. 24, is to be misled. Mr. Parker was quite young in the 1920's and no doubt takes his history of the Society from the founder, E. R. Pease, who ends his account with 1914 and makes some addenda in the 1924 edition.   The Society was in a period of very active maturity in the 1920's.   No study of Fabianism in the fourth decade of the twentieth century will be understood without the story of how the pattern was laid in 1923–1924.

nize the results of the election.[82]   Labour would be obliged to
assume the burden of Government, leaning upon Liberal support;
or, as Webb wrote to the editor of the *NS*,[83] subside into im-
potent criticism.   The Tories indeed had won a postponed victory;
for already threats of a new dissolution were heard; the suggestion was abroad that should Baldwin ask for a dissolution, the
King might refuse and—it was now said—send for a favorite.

The early plan for Labour Party procedure was Fabian inspired.   MacDonald, whose Fabian amanuensis was Herbert
Morrison,[84] invited to Mr. Webb's Grosvenor Street house those
who together mapped out the policy of the Party according to
which the Party would not refuse to take office but would procure
a vote of nonconfidence after the Speech from the Throne, thus
avoiding the necessity of inaugurating the new Government with
an out-and-out Socialist statement, as advocated by the ILP.
Webb was joined in this meeting by Fabians and sometime associates Snowden, Clynes,[85] Henderson, and Thomas, and the non-

---

[82] Hamilton, *op. cit.,* p. 235.   She does not say how she learned this.

[83] Letter to the editor from Sidney Webb, *NS,* XXII (December 15,
1923), 301.

[84] Hamilton, *op. cit.,* p. 200.   Fabian Herbert Morrison worked very
closely with MacDonald 1) when the latter, at Will Crooks' behest, sought
the old Labour politician's seat in 1921, and 2) when MacDonald, knowing
the Continental situation, drew ILP away from its "sentimental" (Mrs.
Hamilton's word) attraction toward "the Soviets."   (To write "Soviet"
today would have a different meaning.)   Kirkwood, *op. cit.,* p. 224, and
other places, shows how little the present-day "soviet" notion was effective
in Clydeside.   Mrs. Hamilton's opinion that the ILP of Clydeside was committed "to a policy aggressive in its emphasis on the class struggle and
contemptuous indifference to international issues, except where Soviet Russia
was concerned" (Hamilton, *op. cit.,* p. 231) reveals the devoted Henderson
follower's viewpoint but is contradicted by everything in Kirkwood's *My
Life of Revolt,* as well as by the review of Cole's writings discussed *infra*
in another connection.   The principal localism and professionalism im-
bedded in Guild Socialism to be found in this group constituted an obstacle
to a world-wide movement to bring Labour into power.   It appeared to
Fabians as the nearest thing to the recalcitrant and splintered Socialist
groupings of the Continent which British Socialists had to contend with in
international conferences in pursuit of their designs to evolve from international Labour Socialism, political power.   They vilified and disparaged it.

[85] Cf. His Lecture of November 3, 1922, Mrs. Webb, chairman, *FN,*
1921–1924, Appendix.

Fabian MacDonald,[86] whose daughter, Ishbel, was a Fabian, soon to be the first lady of No. 10 Downing Street.

It was characteristic Fabian strategy that on creating the Ministry they decided to maintain the usual panoply and customary uniforms. Henderson would have preferred not thus to demonstrate "continuity" with the past but he had a more important fight on his hands, the ILP demand for a Labour Government's King's Speech, emphatically Socialist. The less to alarm the Tory feeling of England, the more Fabians must discipline the Scottish left. Those who stood on their principles and hoped that the advent of Socialism was to be marked by a breach with the past were disappointed. Their disappointed attitude was termed "sentimentalism." [87] So, with the usual British pageantry, the Socialist Government merely shifted into office on a vote of nonconfidence in a Tory Speech from the Throne. They were destined to be remarkable for "constitutionalism."

A certain amount of concern for the national interest can be credited to both sides. To Tory interest in the general good might be attributed the tranquillity with which the Government changed hands; for Baldwin might have resigned immediately and saved himself humiliation but to have done so would have caused confusion, or "Chamberlinite inanities." [88] Labour's gradualness and

[86] Fabian mistrust of MacDonald probably stemmed from the knowledge that he was capable of making peace with a reaction farther on the Right than Webb. Again, MacDonald was currently incurring the enmity of Wheatley. Wheatley's friendship was cultivated by the Fabian Society. He died in 1930, unattached, detested by Mrs. Hamilton the biographer of the Webbs, Henderson, and MacDonald. On November 19, 1924 (cf. *FN,* XXXVI, January, 1925), he had lectured to them, for example on "The Difficulties of Capitalism," when Mrs. Webb presided. He was a leader of the Clydesiders whose interest in revision and repudiation of reparations and debts, sprang from a particular reason in Clydeside industry. Mrs. Webb introduced him as an "administrative Socialist," no longer to be thought a "Red Revolutionary." But in his ensuing lecture, he said he was "more of a revolutionary than ever" but despaired of achieving economic welfare through the masses: Only through persuading capitalists to support nationalization should the revolution be brought about.

[87] Hamilton, *op. cit.,* p. 236. It is interesting, and not unimportant, that to adhere to a principle in the face for a demand for an utilitarian practice in expediency is by Marxists called "sentimental."

[88] Wayfarer, "London Diary," *NS,* XXII (December 15, 1923), 300. The

indefiniteness prevented a ("Red") Socialist scare from materializing in a great flight of capital from the country.[89] It is important to emphasize a matter easily overlooked but very important in the interpretation which this study puts upon the data: There was an accord between the Conservative and the Labour Parties. As late as November 10, 1923, Massingham used the exact words, "unspoken entente with Opposition."[90] and again the editor on December 1, 1923, exposed the fact that Conservatives needed better spokesmen for "Protection" than they had, that Labour had no objection to Mr. Baldwin who could do far better than Lloyd George with Poincaré; but Baldwin's only fault was, he could not make Europe pay attention.[91] Mr. Davies' weekly column, "The City," reported a slight break in the stock market, and an early rally. But to the self-interest or patriotism of neither Party is the quietness of the transition attributable. The United States of America was about to accept responsibility for the guidance of economic recovery in Europe.[92] Furthermore, no one was

NS's Political Correspondent believed Chamberlain wrote the Baldwin Plymouth Speech. See, *NS*, XXII (November 3, 1923), 100.

[89] In the debacle of 1931, the flight of gold was a tragic contributing factor. Cf. Sidney Webb, *What Happened in 1931: A Record, Fabian Tract No. 237* (London: Fabian Society, 1932).

[90] Wayfarer, "London Diary," *NS*, XXII (November 10, 1923), 139.

[91] "Post Election Prospects," *NS*, XXII (December 1, 1923), 232 f.

[92] C. M. Lloyd, writing "The World, the Franc and the Devil," *NS*, XXII (October 27, 1923), 65, describes Lloyd George's activities in America. Cf. *Ibid.* (November 3, 1923), 100 ff, wherein Lloyd sought gold control to control France and pointed out possibilities of American pressures upon the French electorate curbing Poincaré's mischief. The franc had begun to fall eighteen months before. Cf. *Ibid.* (February 23, 1924), 557. It continued falling in February, 1924, up to Poincaré's replacement by Herriot (to drop again soon afterward and continue to fall until Poincaré's return in 1925). This gave the French an economic edge over British manufacturers and made "pre-war parity" impracticable. Cf. Spender, *Great Britain, Empire and Commonwealth*, pp. 624 ff. The undermined value of the franc, having reached the equivalent of 100 to the £ some time before the "fall" in February, 1923, had been reported by Davies who now, with "smug satisfaction," recalled having in December of 1921 advised Englishmen holding francs or investments payable only in francs "to turn them into sterling while the pound can be purchased for less than frs. 52." Cf. *NS*, XXII (February 23, 1924). The *NS*'s view was one of gratification. France would come out of the Ruhr unbought, pay her debts to the United

sure what were the terms of the Baldwin-Poincaré meeting. The *NS*, although otherwise taking the view that Baldwin would do as well as anyone, had fallen little short of recalling Cannes and an awkward game of golf when mentioning Baldwin's "vacation" and meeting with Poincaré. In any case, both Parties held that Germany should not be Balkanized. Tory experience with Europe led Baldwin's party to expect nothing but non-cooperation from Socialists unless they could deal with Socialists. Both Tories and Fabians hoped that an aroused America might bring France into a conference. Fabian leadership, disgusted with the splinter parties and the Socialist "ineptitude" in Europe, hoped to create a Labour front and a trade axis abroad and at home. Theoretically, they hoped the commission of experts would provide the data by which the Stinnes type industrialist might be controlled by social democracy. Concretely, MacDonald's Government pressed for and achieved the Dawes Plan. In order to understand their behaviour, we must learn their concepts of what were the conditions and proposed solutions on the international scene. The world-view of British Socialism was not so easily discoverable in 1923 as it would later become.[93] We have seen in another connection Harold Laski's subtle disclosure that the British attitude regarding the Ruhr and the Schumann Plan was one which might put England in the position of mediator between the United States and the U.S.S.R.

E. The Fabians Deploy: One Eye on the World

Henderson,[94] Webb, and MacDonald exemplified the Fabian

States and Great Britain and oust Poincaré. The international significance, and a chance to replace Poincaré by someone having the support of the *Bloc des Gauches,* outweighed the price-war and its ill effects on British employees, in the *NS*'s judgment.

[93] Cf. Elaine Windrich's (Stanford University) review of Francis Williams' *Socialist Britain* in the *Political Science Review,* XLIII (April, 1949), 374 f.

[94] Brand, *op. cit.,* p. 226, shows Henderson presided at the London Conference of the Labour and Socialist International in June, 1922; he was president of the Second International. Cf. *ibid.,* p. 199. He had reconstructed it in 1919 at Berne. *Ibid.,* pp. 192 ff.

MacDonald was inseparable from him and Webb in all the international

international spirit.[95]   Webb was the moulder of plans and policy, an ideological welder of a unity pragmatically based on "industrial democracy," and world trade.   Henderson, the typical politicizing Trade Unionist, was ideologically at one with Webb on international order.   His organizing talent made him capable of creating a party embracing every estate and of gleaning votes from any sympathetic issues, while guiding the Trade Unions which were committed to the Second International and engaged in warding off the efforts of the Third to capture them.[96]   MacDonald, no longer a member of the Fabian Society but closely associated with Mr. Webb and Mr. Henderson, was the typical "politician" whose own concepts of ILP standards and Labour-front ideology mattered not, because his demeanor was perfect to serve as the human masthead of the Party machine, and his capacity for international achievement was such as to prove a credit to the perspicacity of Henderson and the tolerance or management of Webb.   Mac-Donald was of all these leaders the most international in feeling and experience.   He had obtained from Lord Kitchener a

---

scenes.   In fact, it was he who had entree to the chambers of State in Europe and acquaintance with the leaders like Vandervelde, Jaurés, and Camille Huysmans, and who introduced the others.   It was he who, next to Henderson, did most to keep the Communists "fractional." Cf. *ibid.,* p. 199.   Snowden, *op. cit.,* p. 475, says MacDonald and Henderson each believed he was "keeping an eye on the other."

Webb's influence at Geneva in 1920 is described by Brand, *op. cit.,* p. 214. Again, it was evinced at Hamburg in 1923, where he reported the resolution on the workings of the Versailles Treaty.   Fabians and close associates with Fabians at this international meeting were, besides Webb, F. Jowett, Ethel Bentham, Susan Lawrence (Labour Party delegates); Arthur Henderson, J. R. MacDonald, J. H. Thomas (Executive); H. N. Brailsford, C. R. Buxton, Clifford Allen, J. H. Hudson and John Scurr (ILP); while Mrs. Webb respresented the Fabian Society.   Cf. *ibid.,* p. 228.   Thomas reported on the eight-hour law and Brailsford on "working class action to oppose reaction." See *ibid.,* p. 230.   Stuart-Bunning, another Fabian, was prominent in International Reconstruction.   *Ibid.,* p. 202.   Cf. also, *Studies and Reports* of the International Labour Office at Geneva, Series A, No. 6, which is Webb's report on the Labour and Socialist International of October, 1920.

[95] Webb often spoke of "spirit."   Students of his methods in the future must account for his old-fashioned *zeitgeist.*   Difference in "spirit" must be taken into account in the scrutiny of the dialectics of each side.   This is part of the new nomenclature—perhaps one should say, the new nominalism.

[96] Cf. the ILO *Studies and Reports,* Series A, Nos. 6, 4, 3, 13.

" ticket " [97] by means of which he had travelled over all Europe
and the battle fronts during the War, while contacting his friends
and fellow idealists, Albert Thomas, Vandervelde, Jaurés, Huysmans. Meeting the Scots of the Hardie tradition at a time when
they were incensed by the Defence of the Realm Act and Conscription, he played upon their sentiments regarding the " brotherhood of man," and enhanced his own popularity greatly by an oratorical apotheosis of Hardie while he took the mind of the crowd
off its own troubles by injecting the note of internationalism:
" One of the last times I saw him, when the freezing finger of
death was quietly touching him, we talked of the International." [98]
Weir reports the saying that the MacDonalds were always on the
far Left—at Culloden. When coming into power MacDonald told
his supporters that everything depended upon the European settlement [99]—meaning that leftist ideals should fall into abeyance for
the time being. Understanding the Scots who belonged to the
International, MacDonald appealed to their keen nationalism; he
inveighed against the obnoxious Act. His eloquence leaped to
Hardie's internationalism from the local " boulder of Whinstone "
and " freshness of the hills. " [100] MacDonald fitted into the Webb
machinery very neatly.

There are several other names of Fabians whose internationalism was leading the Party on a synthesized domestic-international
front and whose names were to be well known as the history of
the League of Nations devolved; Lord Parmoor (Cripps),[101]

---

[97] Cf. Weir, *The Tragedy of Ramsay MacDonald* (London: Secker and
Warburg, 1938), p. 65. Where Mrs. Hamilton credits Henderson with re-
habilitating MacDonald after his " fall " due to charges of pacifism, Weir
shows him reestablishing his own great popularity by this appeal to international brotherhood and the spirit of Kerr Hardie, while making an omission
his hearers overlooked, the question of how best to prosecute the War.
"Before this he had been respected and admired; now he was idolized and
worshipped." Cf. *ibid.*, p. 86.

[98] Cited in *ibid.*, p. 81.

[99] *Ibid.*, p. 134.

[100] *Ibid.*, p. 85.

[101] If not a member of the Society he was closely associated with Mrs.
Webb and her sisters, especially Kate (later Lady) Courtney, who got the
clergyman elected *malgré lui* until he became a peer.

Arthur Creech-Jones, Philip Noel-Baker, Marion Phillips.[102]
These would have, as Massingham disclosed, the collaboration of
Lord Haldane and Lord Acton, Lord Russell and Lord Kimber-
ley.[103] Fabians' internationalism was not merely "politics" to
win power at home, but it had repercussions on the domestic scene
where Fabianism deployed itself on three fronts: The *NS*, which
guided broad Lab-Lib Party sentiments and tactics, supplying
selective information on Socialist activities ignored by other
papers; Webb on the Labour front as Chairman of the Party Conference and in Parliament; Henderson and the whole Party trying
to garner the uncommitted votes to be found outside TUC and
Socialist Societies. Maintaining among readers and followers a
dichotomy of thought and action, they themseves worked separately but to a single end. The ticket was said to be "Labour";
the election was said to have chosen a "Socialist Government."
Where Continental Socialism splintered, Fabian leadership, by
separating its leading elements and personalities and allocating
them to separate spheres, kept the unions, the Party, and Socialism
in loose but effective conjunction. The personalities thus deployed
on different fronts were well known names. Here they become
symbols. At this time, Sidney Webb had given up the editorship
of the *NS*. This was the year of his great address, "What Labour

---

[102] Cf. Lord Parmoor (Cripps, Charles Alfred, Baron Parmoor), *A Retrospect* (London: Heinemann, 1936). Also, cf. H. Duncan Hall, a Fabian whose
British Empire and Commonwealth was written at the request of Mrs. Webb
in 1917 and, with the assistance of Mr. Webb, was circulated in the days of
rebuilding the *Basis*. Hall was to become a member of the Carnegie Institute
for International Peace, connected with Harvard University, and to prepare
data for U. N. Trusteeship problems. Cf. his *The League Mandates and the
Problem of Dependencies* (for restricted circulation only) in the Library of
Congress, Washington, D. C., 1945.

[103] Wayfarer, "London Diary," *NS*, XXII:334 (December 2, 1923). The
most concrete reduction of international theory was the success in keeping to
the eight-hour law in Germany, for the sake of British workers.

See, *NS*, XXII (October 13), 2. Concretization of large ideals and deep
theories of internationalism has often taken very humble forms such as the
ILO achievements regarding manufacture of matches and women's working
hours, and the eight-hour law. Regarding ILO, cf. G. I. T. Shotwell
(editor), *The Origins of the International Labour Organisation*, Vol. I,
History (New York: Columbia University Press, 1934); consult Chart following page 497.

Intends." [104] The *NS* in 1923 relegated to temporary oblivion two main points of Webb's Conference and Henderson's Trade Union platforms, namely, the Capital Levy and revision of the Versailles Treaty.[105] This does not mean that there was a rift in Fabian ranks, it merely put Webb, now an M. P., in a position not so illogical. He, as Chairman of the Labour Conference, could stand by the Capital Levy and the *NS* could eschew it, while " Henderson kept the Trade Union sections steady." [106] In April, 1923, the *Morning Post* had referred to the *NS* as " Mr. Sidney Webb's Organ," and disavowal was forthwith made by the Fabian editor, Clifford Sharp (Webb's protégé for many years), who stated Webb had not been editor for more than a year and that his adverse views, for example, on the special (Smillie) Labour delegation's project to internationalize the Ruhr, were his own. The *NS* was " private enterprise " and not the official organ of the Labour Party.[107] So, if the *NS* was free, it is evident that Webb, too, was free to encourage, from the viewpoint of national interest, an international over-view. The stated objective, international co-

---

[104] *Loc. cit.* It was reported in the *NS,* XXI (June 30, 1923), 350. We have seen how it was printed and circulated at a later date.

[105] Clifford Sharp, " The New Statesman, The Labour Party, and The Capital Levy," *NS,* XXII (December 15, 1923), 294. " Nationalisation " had been dropped in favor of unification in the mines' problem. Cf. *NS,* " The Miners' Problem," XXI (June 30, 1923), 354 f. The Poor Law Reform was " not party capital " for either side, so was dropped as an issue but the war-interrupted progress in reform should be resumed; for the Ministry of Health charged with Poor Law administration was an over-taxed office. Cf. *NS,* XXII (October 13, 1923), 3.

The advantage to a Party of having a Socialist Society to vivify its pristine principles, or obscure them on occasion, is remarkable.

Nationalization of Land had a set-back in July, 1923, when the compulsory registration of land transfers was abolished over the Labour-Liberal— Asquith, George, and Chamberlain—objections. The traces of Lloyd George's early connivance with the Fabian land programme, 1909, were thus obliterated. The workings of the Land Valuation Department had been " widely regarded as preparations for a wider change in our land system," *NS,* XXI (July 7, 1923), 378 f.

[106] Hamilton, *Henderson,* p. 231. Cf. also, *ibid.,* p. 218, regarding Henderson's personal interest in the fruitful life work of Mary MacArthur (Mrs. W. C. Anderson), the organizer whose achievement with women's unionization was vital and unsurpassed.

[107] *NS,* XXI (April 21, 1923), 33.

operative industrial democracy—under a Socialist ethos—was never lost sight of, regardless of disputable domestic election issues. It was immensely important for the propagation of world-wide industrial democracy that the working class—union men and women—and Socialist leadership be kept together for political action as a party, regardless of the existence of disparate ideas in the different groups. The outcome of cleavages in some countries and suppressions in others was all too patent. This was most true of Germany, and *NS* readers were kept aware of it by close reporting. The focal point of Fabian interest and the reason for Opposition Gallophobia—Germany—formed the Western end of the optative Labor-front axis which had its Eastern end in Russia with British internal Socialism at the fulcrum. France was, of course, the antagonist and the Treaty of Versailles the foil for both countries.

It was all very convenient: Henderson holding the Trade Union front had to get elected on a revisionist fight; MacDonald, the best loved on the Continent, played his politics close to home; Webb, who had done most effective writing for the International, held the Party to domestic reconstruction; and in general, while running reports over individuals' signatures on Germany especially, the *NS* fought the election on the level of particular domestic politics: fiscal ideas,[108] Trade Union and CWA squab-

---

[108] The proposed fiscal policy was sketched in the *NS*, XXII (October 27, 1923), 66. To develop exports, increase demand and seek not merely to undersell, was the counsel given. In E. M. H. Lloyd's "Stabilising Stagnation," *NS*, XXII (November 3, 1923), p. 102, *NS* readers learned Labour's Free Trade convictions were not deep; Employment, not Protection, the preoccupation. The *NS*, XXI, p. 662, raised the question of tariffs and farm subsidies merely to show the futility of either.

The report of A. E. Davies, on tour in America, could but dull consciences on the matter of British debt to the United States. Davies did not approve the American policy of exempting from taxation United States Bonds and Municipal bonds. He was more than customarily excited about the current inflation and the huge building program in progress; but the heady air must be called to account for the statement that with British payments the United States was erecting its public schools! Long a member of the Fabian apostolate to America, Mr. Davies is listed also among the vice-presidents of the Public Ownership League of America, headed by Carl Thompson. It includes among its well wishers E. Keating, editor of *Labor,*

bles,[109] the Poplar imbroglio,[110] the maladroitness of the Minis-

Washington, D. C., a paper which highly approves British Labour Government; also, Mr. Harold Ickes; and other provocative American names appear: Elmer Benson, former Governor of Minnesota, now a CIO chairman, J. M. Coffee, Jerry Voorhis, former M.C., W. Patman, M.C., William Lemke, M.C., Glenn Taylor, and A. Capper, former U. S. Senators. Prominent is Stuart Chase, who tried to establish a Fabian Society in America, in the 1920's in Boston and in the 1930's in Chicago, according to his letter to the writer in reply to a query; and Upton Sinclair, author of EPIC, the "End-Poverty-in-California" plan. The latter two belong also to the League for Industrial Democracy headed by H. Laidler, at the 40th anniversary celebration of which Mr. Creech-Jones (a British Fabian long active in the ILO) made an address on the British Labour Movement. Mrs. Roosevelt is an active member. Cf. a pamphlet, *Forty Years of Education* (New York: League for Industrial Democracy, June, 1945) and the pamphlet, *Thirty-Three Years in the Public Service* (Chicago: The Public Ownership League of America, 1946). Under "Provincial Societies" from 1925 to 1930, for example, FSAR reported the League for Industrial Democracy "of New York." LID has many branches. Mr. Harry Laidler and a party of travelers were entertained by Mrs. Webb, F, L, Dodd, Harold Laski and F. W. Galton in the Fabian Common Room, July 8, 1930, when the Americans were en route to Russia.

[109]Trade Union and CWA disputes were recurrent: A strike of Trade Unionists against their CWA employers, (*NS,* XXI, 67), brought out the Fabian attitude, which it was recommended the organized workers should assume, precisely, that a Committee of the Trade Union General Council should prevent a strike, or once it had begun, settle it. See, *NS,* XXI, 351. The TUC should have "plainly" told the Dockers their strike was futile, (*NS,* XXI, 534), and it should have settled the NUR strike (*ibid.,* 535). In these last two items the personal leadership of Bevin and of Thomas was challenged. Fabian leadership would desire to direct through the TUC. Cf. John Parker, M.P., *Labour Marches On* (Middlesex, England: Peguin Harmonsworth, 1947), p. 24.

The newspapers had been trying to emphasize the division between Trade Union people and the Labour Party and the November 24, 1923, *NS* took cognizance of it and stated the Party worked for ideas and not for a class, *ibid.,* XXII, 199. Later, the *NS* recognized and sought to heal the breach, saying that TU members and Labour Party elite represented the fusion of "hand and brain" workers and of "rational" and "constructive" appeals. Cf. G. D. H. Cole, "The Labour Voter," *NS,* XXI, 234 f. But TUC should keep its own corner and let the Party lead it politically and "end bickerings" for "poorly led, it constituted a national danger," (*ibid.,* XXI, 639, 726, 727).

[110]Concerning Poplar: G. D. H. Cole, "The Poplar Imbroglio," *NS* XXII, 71, for example, recounted a revolt of local residents against the way the Poor Law worked, bringing out the principle that "national economy"

try [111] and Party alignments, and the constitutional [112] question

should govern the relief of poverty. The *NS* assumed the old Fabians' stand against local Guardians. Before the imbroglio was settled, the *NS* (November 3, 1923), 131, had fully decided that the Ratepayers Strike was illegal. To have clung to the "national economy" policy which would throw local relief into the hands of the Minister of Health (Sir Joynson-Hicks) would have been to lend its assent to the Churchill-Chamberlain reform whereby funds gathered by national taxes should be appropriated locally on the basis of "equality." Cf. George Lansbury, *My Life*, pp. 129–169.

[111] Criticizing the Ministry, for example, it was said: Not "we" but "they" (the Government) brought war with France near. C. M. Lloyd writing "Pax Gallica" in the *NS*, XXII (October 20, 1923), 36, at the same time expressed dissatisfaction with Stresemann and Stinnes in Germany. As a contingency of the Election, the editor once considered the feasibility of using Lloyd George in the Foreign Office as a foil for Poincaré (*ibid.*, December 1, 232) but by December 15, the *NS* had taken the line that MacDonald should assume the Foreign Office, *ibid.*, 289. (After 1931 he was always accused of personal ambition in this matter.)

Through the early summer of 1923, Lord Curzon's diplomacy ("Malevolent Impotence," *NS*, XXI [May 12, 1931], 133) was under constant criticism on the point of Russian trade and *de jure* recognition. Cf. *NS*, XXI (May 26, 1923), *passim*, but particularly page 185 where his stern attitude on the settlement of certain points of international law was compared with von Bechthold's ultimatum to Serbia. The Russians were commiserated for having to endure his bad manners and they were congratulated (*ibid.* [June 9, 1923], 254, 285) on their commonsense, even if pride had suffered. Trade Agreement had been saved; *de jure* recognition should be the next step. The *NS* ridiculed the fears of its opponents with such expressions as "the naughty Bolshevik representatives" and "nasty thing" and "Great Red Beast," *ibid.*, 284.

The *NS* advocated, in opposition to the Ministry, the abandonment of Singapore for the Japanese were filling the mainland opposite that British naval station; but the *NS* assented to keeping enough air power to have a bargaining position against France in future conferences. Cf. Massingham in the *NS* (October 20, 1923), 44.

Although this seems to be unrelated, it has importance not contemporaneously overlooked in the world plans under Fabian consideration. Cf. H. M. Tomlinson (of *The Nation and Athenaeum* staff, later with *The Clarion*), "Singapore and the Earthquake," *NS*, XXII (November 3, 1923), 105 f, and *ibid.*, XXI, 129 f. The Labour principle sought to decrease the power of the Navy.

[112] A constitutional issue arose in the unusual circumstances of a three-party Parliament. Asquith made a qualified claim that the King was not bound to grant a dissolution, and that a Minister in a permanent minority could not demand a dissolution. Massingham took the view that Anson,

arising from premonitions. Since he could leave the responsibility
for domestic arguments to the *NS*, Webb did not need to evade
the Capital Levy or revision of the Versailles Treaty or internationalism with a *trade* basis—large issues which kept his un-
homogeneous Labour Party front smooth. Although no longer
editor of the *NS*, he was not without a mouthpiece. The *Labour
Magazine,* advertised as the organ of TUC and the Labour Party,
listed some contributors, three out of five of whom were Fabians:
Mr. Webb, Major Thomson, who had written on European problems,[113] and Noel-Buxton.[114] The last named was something of an
expert in both Eastern affairs and agrarian problems.

---

following Lord Aberdeen's advice to Queen Victoria and also to Gladstone,
had settled that a dissolution was not invariably granted and no rebuff to
the Sovereign was involved should the Minister be defeated at the polls.
Cf. Wayfarer, " London Diary," *NS* (December 22, 1923), 333 f. The editor
of the *NS* assumed a typically Fabian attitude: MacDonald disagreed with
Asquith but his article in the *New Leader* had hinted that renouncing personal
whim and considering the fact of being " within a short time of election," a
Prime Minister would not without good reason put the country to the
trouble; so, MacDonald was not " revolving crude projects for dishing his
opponents." To those who said he could not procure a new election, Fabians
answered for MacDonald that he should not. See, *NS*, XXII (January 5,
1924), 353. Massingham referred to a rising effort to revive the prerogative
and recorded at the same time that Baldwin had been granted his dissolution
against the better advice of the King who had asked that his objections be
minuted; and now, against Hearn, he cited Bagehot that the reigning
sovereign had the right only to be consulted, to encourage, and to warn.
See, Wayfarer, " London Diary," *NS*, XXII (January 5, 1924), 364. The
fact of the King's right to send for a favorite and form a government did
not emerge clearly until 1931. In 1924, no Fabian allowed it to be stated
articulately.

[113] It was Noel-Buxton, no doubt, signing N.B., who reviewed C. B.
Thomson's *Old Europe's Suicide* in *FN*, XXXII (January, 1921). The
Brigadier-General had held staff and state positions in many countries, since
the Agadir crisis. He was said by Buxton to have " sacrificed a career " to
write and work with the Socialist movement. The underlying criticism
Thomson made scored the Entente failure to carry on " self-determination "
in the Balkans. Buxton compared the book favorably, with Keynes' work
and subtly raised the question outlined in Thomson's thought: Will the
Socialist solution require force? It is a question of *morals* at bottom;
" how far [will] the schemes of reform be supported by the necessary
majority of men . . . occupied in the main with other things than reform."
—To interpret: The few convinced reformers will have need of some sort of

MacDonald, because of his talent for foreign affairs, properly headed the Party. Although neither Webb nor Henderson trusted him, as of 1924 the *NS* backed him stoutly. MacDonald would advocate working with the Treaty and the League, even though Henderson, having neglected his own election, to win a seat later at a by-election as in 1922, made a plain issue of revision of the Versailles Treaty. Concerning this, the Labour Prime Minister's silence baffled some Fabians.[115] Nowhere is there more typical Fabianism than in these three sets of facts: Henderson's loyalty to MacDonald as a Party leader and his candid stand against him on the revision issue;[116] and Webb's behind-the-scene legerdemain,[117] his left hand guiding the constituent parts of the Labour Party front with the carrot of the Capital Levy and Nationalisation, and his right hand creating the policy of the political branch as the effects of the election became evident; Mr. MacDonald's fronting for all issues until he was scarcely recognizable as ILP; or distinguishable from a Tory.

We have seen the deployment of forces and made a survey of concepts generated by the mere mention of " Protection."

---

force to achieve their reforms; " force must be the secondary weapon of politics." (The secular religion had need of a " secular arm "—the military.)

[114] *NS,* XXI, 177.

[115] Mrs. Hamilton, *Henderson,* p. 240, can find no reason for MacDonald's evasive stand on revision. It should be recalled that Webb was advising the Party, intimately, and that Webb was the official reporter of the Treaty problems at the Hamburg International, 1923. The incident is a significant sample of the Fabian technique. In the campaign of 1923 with the Dawes Plan on the horizon, it was no time to harp on " revision," although Henderson was about to get himself elected on a revision platform despite the Prime Minister's objections.

[116] *Ibid.,* pp. 238 f.

[117] Cf. Beatrice Webb, *Our Partnership,* pp. 6 f. *" Son Eminence Grise "* was Camille Huysmans' nickname for Mr. Webb. His principles of these years, 1922–1923, are all set forth in *What Labour Intends: The Capital Levy,* as noted above. Webb's speech to the Annual Labour Conference was favorably reported in the *NS,* XXII, 382.

CHAPTER VII

USES OF "PROTECTION," PART 2: COMING INTO POWER

A. An Overview

The Conservative Party, attempting to take the measure of Labour, could see that while Fabians gave currency to a view friendly to Communists regarding Germany, the Labour Party could be relied upon to work with Stresemann; and on the domestic scene, while Labour encompassed the socializers and the impudent left-wingers, in general it could be expected to perform like another political party. While the scene in the present chapter lies in the field of domestic politics—an area never unaffected by decisions regarding the Dominions and colonies, and one impossible to isolate from continental policy—the principal study herein is the peculiar nature of the Party which Fabians built as a robot to express themselves. Although in this chapter data used above reappears, its relation to the whole is different. The accent here is on small items the significance of which would be lost unless the reader were provided with the larger perspective of the preceding treatment. Again the dates run from points back of the point of arrival at power, to find the underlying rapport between Labour and Conservative forces, and the part played by Fabians in this rapport.

In the ensuing discussion of Fabian Socialism in a three-Party field, the following points will come to notice: The effect upon the political parties of having a national "three party" experience in which one Party, only nominally political, was led by pragmatic Socialists who based their premises upon secular sociology, defined their Socialism as a "purpose underlying a tendency," and evinced a philosophy becoming totalitarian. That the third Party was much like a secular religion was the result of politicizing the economic ordering of society. Traditional political thought was baffled by the new ethos, a quasi-religious fervor animating a

245

social centre and invading politics. The experience of political campaigns produced two effects: Clearer articulation of " Labour " which was the precipitate resulting from the compounding of socio-economic ferment and politics, and a new form of Toryism showing the influence of this climate of socio-political opinion. Liberalism went into eclipse. It lost its identity as methodological opposition to Conservatism and kept only the potentially mischievous position where it supported either side at will.[1] Outside of their unreconcilable philosophies, Toryism and Labour became so alike that in the future one must absorb the other or the tensions purposely created to maintain differences would create a civil war. Of course, at the philosophical level, Socialism was revolt; " Labour " was anomaly. Here the preparation is made for 1926 and 1931. The third Party forecast the One-Party. The One-Party is a chimera but the results in a civilization of development in face of a chimera are alien cultural products.

The election was projected on the part of Conservatives to break Labour leadership of Opposition and to garner the liberal or " reform " voting strength, thus freed, for a newly-wise Conservative Party. Fabian leadership of Labour under attack assumed a " tranquillity " of its own and acknowledged that the Baldwin policy was the same as its own, that only the " spirit " was different in the opposing forces. This assumed tranquillity had for its reason the possibility of agreement with Russia (looking toward recognition) and the containment of France. Occasional eruptions of " wild " Labour feeling had to be disciplined by the intellectual leadership. Meantime, the " ruling class " (the Churchill-Birkenhead type) evinced a forthright way of dealing with " Reds " and " Bolsheviks " without such delicate distinctions as Fabians made.

---

[1] Cf. Sir Harry Slesser, *A History of the Liberal Party* (London: Hutchinson and Company, 1944), pp. 164 f. He concludes: " if it be false [that Liberalism has converted the other two Parties] the failure of Liberalism may prove to be an unqualified disaster." He had also said, " a resurrection of Liberalism . . . may depend upon the possibility of the recapture of the vision of the basic invaluable quality of personality," and he indicated the surrender of juridical determination in civic functions to the administrative bureaucracy, inevitable when both other Parties should agree on the surveillance and education of the individual and his welfare.

With the rising possibility of achieving greater power [2] in Opposition (and with the hope not to have to lead H. M.'s Government so soon), Fabian editorial policy brushed aside the Churchillian reaction as being too obvious. The Tory conversion to a " Collectivism " which embodied the concepts of the shareholder government along with Imperial preference, was for Socialists a greater menace than the Churchill reaction which now could but divide the Liberals the more; and it became imperative for Fabians to place a stumbling block for Conservative prestige. They must induce Tories to fall into some form of reactionary blundering: Conservatives might revive the veto power of Lords, or legislate the reduction of political power of Trade Unions. Eventually, the only " reactionary " thing in which the Tories remained vulnerable was the question of tariffs, one on which Fabians were also divided and vulnerable. Long before the Cabinet themselves tentatively raised the question, the Fabian press worried " Protection " out of news and gossip; but when " Protection " was finally offered as a challenge, there arose a possibility that that part of Labour which found tariffs a not unmitigated evil might follow the Baldwin thesis toward a solution of Unemployment. To all appearances, " Protection " was a term of doubtful meaning but as a challenge it was productive of an election obviously designed to reduce Labour's new strength. It put in power a Labour Government which stood long enough to turn the tide in Europe before being sent to Coventry if not into the wilderness for five years. But before that happened, the experience of 1923 had taught Conservatives (minus their die-hards) and Labourites (minus their scene-makers) that they had much in common—always with that difference which a philosophy of Socialism made in men of politics.

Fabian Henderson forced the challenge and clinched the half determination of Mr. Baldwin. Fabian writers produced the slogan: " Protection *versus* Labour." Yet both sides knew that tariffs were a weapon against France, the Fabians' *bête-noir;* and

---

[2] It has appeared that Labour in Opposition had great power. This was already true when Lloyd George formed the Coalition. Then he feared their Opposition and so sought to bring them into the Government. Cf. Thomas, *op. cit.,* p. 43.

that Protection would boomerang against English farmers. (Fabians acknowledged neglecting the farm problem.)[3] Both sides were informed by an ulterior motivation: The Tory for " imperial " exchange under Capitalism; Labour for such Dominion cooperation as looked toward a world order and Socialistic internationalism.[4] On one side was the slogan " free competition " under tariffs—the Government being a shareholder; on the other, " free trade," a shibboleth—controls being sought in an international trade axis through State Capitalism.

Knowing that the discussion of " empire preference " would by its revelations create poor inter-Dominion harmony, the Fabian leadership of Opposition headed by J. R. Clynes used " Unemployment " as the reason for urging an October meeting of Parliament simultaneously with the Imperial Conference, no doubt to be in a position to propagandize the Labour tenets.[5] " Credit " rather than " Preference " was becoming the underlying principle of the Fabian fiscal policy.

So we see the technique of this Socialist Society demonstrated in trying to find the Conservatives guilty of class-minded blunders, while chiding its own " left-wing " for developing class-configurations. We see the *NS* dropping the Capital Levy as not an election issue, and bringing forward an industrial programme as set forth by the in-and-out Fabian whose Guild-Socialist views it rejected, G. D. H. Cole. We see that Labour had for tactics boundless eloquence flowing from convinced economic determinism and a crusading enthusiasm which elicited services and goods in place of funds.

The factors of Party unity were published for the *NS* readers: Voting statistics, the manipulation of class-differentials, the programme and a philosophy. In the face of some examples of mass-

---

[3] Reported in the *U. S. News and World Report* (June 11, 1949) is Labour's tentative plan to nationalize farms.

[4] J. H. Thomas almost single-handed clung to the effort to achieve Dominion cooperation. Cf. the account in Snowden, *op. cit.,* II, pp. 774 f, and Thomas, *op. cit.,* pp. 205 ff.

[5] The repercussions in Africa, India, and Canada were notable. Cf. *NS, passim,* 1923 and 1924. Cf. especially Lord Olivier's letter to the leader of the Swarajists in Madras, against " communal representation "'and endorsing the policies of Morley and Montague. *NS,* XXIII, 209 f.

manipulated and near-riotous polling, the promise of great smooth-
ness in government was, not unreasonably, made. The Asquith
story is illustrative. The techniques of social control were maturing:—A synthetic riot is a piece of very skilled control.

There were to emerge from the Election two forces: Political
Conservatism and Socialist-Labour. The latter absorbed the
position if not the substance of that "Centre" which Lloyd
George and Churchill cerebrated. Labour moved in a quasi-
religious mood. Fabians wrote of "England," the "constitutional" way, the typical Prime Minister, the "race," the "nation."
Readers at home should fear no change. Abroad, however, some
as far away as India looked for a new order.[6] Too soon; but in
Europe the dynamism of the Left was captured for the nonce.
Anyone going through the materials of this story can see why the
Fabian Government was characterized by unstable equilibrium and
easily overthrown a year later. The Party tried to be "constitutional" and patriotic. It was in reality a secular religion, and out
of place " in politics." [7] So far, in a manner, we have presented
hypotheses. The documentation for this survey follows. First,
however, we should see the position of the "third party" in the
political field. The "third party," Socialist-Labour, was one of
equivocal nature and often it manifested dual attitudes.

B. The Third Party: Its Equivocal Nature

It has been thought that the Baldwin Ministry committed
"suicide" at the end of 1923. Close study of the Fabian organ
which led the Labour Party intellectually does not clear up the

---

[6] The expectations of India, for example, are voiced in the Fabian organ,
NS, XXIII, *passim*, but cannot be discussed here. The gold-and-credit
standard under which the ruling classes of India, in competent understanding
of the English ruling class, debased India's silver after 1924, was the
standard of Fabians as well as Tories. Under such a standard the masses
were controlled. While the struggle went on between India and England
for political power, a Socialist-labour ethos was rising all the while under
the guidance of those represented by Annie Besant, now again a Fabian. In
1931, silver was again rejected in favor of credit, by Fabians for TUC.
Cf. *LYB* (1931), 105–109.

[7] Cf. again Richard V. Burke, "A Conception of Ideology for Historians,"
The Journal of the History of Ideas, X:2 (April, 1949), 183–198, note 38.

problem entirely but it reveals that the action of the Baldwin Ministry was not party suicide, and that the issue was not so much Protection as Unemployment involving far-reaching external implications and internal contradictions. From the internal contradictions an unbearable situation arose.

The conflict lay between those who in the past—Tory or Liberal—had guided Britain in the world of trade and diplomacy, and the new Labour ethos forming a "third" Party. (It is quite in keeping to speak on the one hand of an ethos and on the other, of persons.) At the time, the Cabinet divided on new lines—Tory *versus* Die-hard—a struggle ultimately seated in agricultural *versus* urban Toryism. This normal dispute Labour's publicists saw and exploited; but it was not the underlying fissure in the philosophical basis of British political life.

On the surface it might seem that the Opposition which was powered by a new young movement shared all the ideal objectives of both old parties; but socialists remained unsatisfied with the order in which all found themselves. Labour "intellectuals" were capable of making subtle distinctions between method and means, so that Labourite and Tory seemed to be at loggerheads while actively pursuing the same societary ends. The activity in each case arose from a philosophy. The pursuit was inspired by reasons which must be productive of cultural effects quite diverse.

Conservatives (and old school Liberals) conceived of politics and of the political arts as the habiliments of the State. Their ancestral pattern, taken from Hooker's *Ecclesiastical Polity*, retained the imperative, "Render to Caesar!" so accepted the State and political virtue objectively as an organism and a technique fitted for the service of society and the embodiment of divine Authority and order. The philosophy of Socialist-Labour was an end-product of rationalist-liberalism: It did not view the State objectively; so it could not use political science as anything but a means to power for social control. It did not articulate the State as an entity separate from society, nor respect political science as the servant of the inviolable State. Actually, the philosophies of the Conservative and of the Labour Parties were antithetical; but in 1923, only a vague fear of "revolution!" measured the difference between them. Dispute, *e.g.*, on "Protection" conjured up instead a false alike-ness capable of fatally deceiving the nation. Theretofore, the Conservative reaction had tried to pin down the wrestling force; but each time the giant with the middle-class brain struck the earth, contrary to Conservative expectations, he arose with new strength. In 1923, he was put in harness for Tory good purposes, but briefly.

The atmosphere of 1923 was very different from the matutinal freshness of the rise of Socialism in 1919 when the Capital Levy and the profiteers stood forth to do battle. Now Socialism in party politics was "larnin' to be a twoad" in the political pond—to straddle issues and live amphibiously, on tariffs or no tariffs. Calling itself "Left," the Labour Party was by nature a socio-economic "centre." It too harnessed its own "left," the sentimental Socialists, to its own good purposes.

On the domestic front party activity produced exact articulation; and out of the inchoate party materials came three clear forces: Socialism-with-Labour, Liberalism with its memories, Conservatism with new life and power. Out of the inter-action of these parties came the power which ruled England until World War II, the Baldwin-MacDonald unspoken understanding. We have seen the ambiguous Labour Party exercising itself in questions regarding Russia, France, Germany, also the entrance of America upon the scene, which was closely related to domestic politics. And outside that periphery, never overlooked but not brought under immediate interpretation, lay Ireland, Egypt, India, and Singapore,[8]

---

[8] There was some discussion about South Africa. Smuts in his international actions was a hero to the Fabians and trusted by them to bring about the order they desired without their surrendering to the demands of "imperialism" as the majority of Fabians did in 1902. The Fabian Colonial Bureau was extremely active. East and Central Africa came in for deep study. South Africa was a political problem complicated by Socialist anti-racism and Fabian affection for Smuts. Cf. *NS*, XXII (November 17, 1923), 166. Cf. also, *NS*, XXIII (April-October, 1924). Again cf. Lord Olivier, *Imperial Trusteeship*, Fabian Tract No. 230 (London: Fabian Society, 1929); also R. C. Hawkins, *Central Africa and The League of Nations*, Fabian Tract No. 186 (London: Fabian Society, 1918). Smuts' African Monroe Doctrine was endorsed. Yet when he was overthrown in 1924, the editor did not repine but advised encouragement for a Labour Government in South Africa. Cf. *NS*, XXIII (April-October, 1924).

Through 1923 and 1924 the Labour-guiding *NS* was adamant against the fortification of and maintaining of an effective fleet at Singapore. It con-

where the inconsistencies of Fabian practice with Fabian thought were glaring.

We here propose to sift the materials in the first two categories only—domestic and dominion affairs—to show how the Fabians worked and what social forces were put into action. The parallels between 1919–1931 and 1939–1949 are striking. If history were merely repeating itself it would be wasted effort to write of the first date span; but, more than mere parallelism, there is definite continuity. That the continuity was not broken by the unparalleled catastrophes which befell the Labour Party in 1924 and 1931, as the student of the later time-span will find, Labour owes thanks to the Fabian Society. By the end of 1923, when power was thrust upon the Labour Party, the character of Fabian-led Socialism stood fully revealed. This character was evinced by the attitudes assumed in reporting domestic affairs and in the techniques demonstrated in the use of foreign affairs to produce the tools of domestic control. On the part of Labour the purpose of gaining domestic control or using Fabianism's inherent forces internally had the concomitant objective to create an external front, a Labour front in nations proximately related to England on an economic basis.

Why was there another General Election in the winter of 1923? It must be said that Labour rank and file seemed not to know why but was made very strongly suspicious that the reason was to take preventive action against Labour by *NS* reporting. By their daring to raise " Protection " as a challenge, Conservatives disclosed the fact that they were aware of their own strength, seeing Liberals divided into Asquithians and Lloyd Georgians, and seeing Labour but thinly covering its own weak seams where Scottish ILP members shied away from the English Trade Union dominance, while in Parliament they but uncomfortably mingled with the "intellectual" Socialists who were Fabians. Aware of the potential divisiveness of the question of tariffs among Labour Party members themselves, the Conservatives knew, too, that Labour had no

---

ceded the Japanese paramount interest and noted their infiltration. It advocated keeping only enough air power to " bargain " with France. Cf. *NS*, XXII (October 20, 1923), 44, and *ibid*. (November 3, 1923), 105 f; also, see *NS*, XXI (May 12, 1923), 129, and *NS* (June 30, 1923), 349. In *NS*, XXII, 688, the editor advocated leaving the Japanese question in the Pacific to the United States and letting Australia defend itself.

Party funds. The Tories had stolen enough thunder from reform movements to entertain the hope of replacing Liberals in the coalescence which Labour must make with one group or the other. This way, they might garner popular support, or better, draw Lib-Lab membership to their side, away from Socialist and Trade Union leadership. Any politician could gauge by the momentum the fact that Labour was heading toward a climax. Webb said it would triumph in 1926. If Tories intended to break Labour, they did not reckon acutely enough upon the flexibility of Fabian leadership which was able to keep Labour ranks intact by synthesizing all antithetical theses and unifying the diverse parts of the Labour Movement.

The awareness of political possibilities on the part of the *NS* kept Labour Party members of the " worker by brain " type in touch with Cabinet news, some of it quite intimate. The *NS* picked Baldwin to replace Bonar Law before the country was fully aware of the imminence of the latter's resignation. Baldwin's commonplace talent was preferred by the *NS* to Curzon's " purring felinities." [9] Curzon would have brooked no dictation from Fabians. *NS* divulged mysterious overtures to Chamberlainites on the part of the ailing Prime Minister. Of course, to approach the Chamberlains was to sidle up to tariff restoration. The *NS* noted the swarming off of Lloyd George's party, and its rupture with Labour—to fight the " red peril "—leaving only a remnant of Liberals to coalesce with Labour.[10] Nowhere did the *NS* reveal the part played by the Opposition in the King's rejection of Curzon for Prime Minister. The definitive biography of Sidney Webb may tell the story. The biographer of Curzon is sure Labour was accountable for Curzon's disappointment. At first sight, the fact that Salisbury in the House of Lords was backing Baldwin against Curzon would seem to have no special significance. But Salisbury had been Lord Privy Seal, 1903–1905, when the Liberals to whom was addressed Sidney Webb's " Intercepted Letter " routed the Tories. While the *NS* exposed the fact that already Baldwin was running the political machine along with Neville Chamberlain and Sir Douglas Hogg, it remarked that Curzon, save for his

---

[9] *NS*, XXI (April 28, 1923), 68.
[10] *NS*, XXI (May 5, 1923), 100.

" howdah " [11] manner, might even then have been heading, as Prime Minister, toward a " combustible climax " had he been in Commons.[12]

The policy of Labour early in 1923 seemed to be to try to get along for a while. There were uses for tranquillity. When Baldwin officially replaced Bonar Law, the *NS* noted that here was a businessman who might cope with realities in the Ruhr question although it was aware that the French believed him friendly. Yet at this early date *NS* raised the question as to whether he was " Die-Hard " or Protectionist. And within one week after accepting Baldwin the *NS* was criticizing the Government concerning minutiae: Insisting upon punctilios of procedure, the *NS* pointed out that there was no precedent for the use to which Baldwin put parliamentary recesses [13] and it prophesied his would be the last Conservative Government for a long time—reckoning, of course, upon a normal life-span for the Government. Fabians were probing the political situation for something by which to discomfit the Baldwin regime, but gently, lest responsibility come too soon.

The current financial boom in America gave all industry a fillip and employment as a subject for agitation dropped from view, but only temporarily.[14] Then, Baldwin was seen to be veering toward some cooperation with Labour. Curzon in the Foreign Office, succeeded in getting a Russian trade agreement and the Opposition, with an eye to recognition of Russia *de jure*,[15] scored a point in getting Baldwin to promise that Parliament would resume in October. Labour power was growing, especially in handling trade disputes. A noticeable movement " back to the unions " took place.[16] Stronger unions meant all the more reason for a trade outlet; so Curzon might be useful; but the *NS* pitied the Russians for having to put up with him. The *NS* did not seem lacking in objectivity when it reported that the Salisbury group was jealous of Curzon, hence were backing Baldwin; and asked if the " veiled

---

[11] *NS*, XXI (May 26, 1923), 189.
[12] *NS*, XXI (May 12, 1923), 132.
[13] *NS*, XXI (May 26, 1923), 186–189.
[14] *NS*, XXI (June 2, 1923), 223.
[15] *NS*, XXI (June 9, 1923), 254, and ibid. (June 16, 1923), 285.
[16] *NS*, XXI (June 2, 1923), 223.

history " of the Bonar Law Government was to be repeated.[17] Since this indicated a pursuit of " tranquillity," the *NS* contented itself with the Ministry's " second class brains " and accepted a policy of tranquillity as better than a rush of defensive reaction. This restraint distinguished British Socialists from Continental agitators; yet it was easy to be restrained when the effort brought so desired a result as recognition of Russia. The *NS* thought Lord Birkenhead had captured the Younger (" Cabin Boy ") anti-Labour movement.[18] Birkenhead was marked for defeat; and at this time, " Bob " Smillie stood successfully for Parliament at Morpeth on an ILP Socialist platform running counter to the influence of Birkenhead. All the argument of the Snowden-Mond[19] debate (Reform without Socialism *versus* Reform for Socialism) was rehearsed again—a cloud of fear of Socialism on the tranquil horizon. Smillie was elected on a programme for land re-distribution and veterans' assistance. The *NS* could not ask total tranquillity, and it backed Smillie, fairly, although he was an old-fashioned Socialist of the most " sentimental " stamp. Tranquillity was relative, as was the *NS*'s policy regarding " Labour " candidates. And tranquil reassurances were given.

The *NS* advised that Liberals should not unite with Conserva-

---

[17] *NS*, XXI (June 9, 1923), 256. That meant either that Salisbury would stand in the political equation to Baldwin as Beaverbrook to Bonar Law or as Baldwin to Bonar Law. The *NS* did not know whether die-hards or reformed Tories should rule Baldwin's Cabinet. (Curzon's was not a " second-class " brain, although he commanded little loyalty.)

[18] *NS*, XXI (June 23, 1923), 316. This was to result in his defeat, along with Chamberlain and Churchill, by " wild men " in December, 1923, just when Liberals were entering " coalescence " with Labour. Cf. *NS*, XXII (December 1, 1923), 232.

[19] Cf. Philip Viscount Snowden, *An Autobiography*, II, 1919–1934 (London: Ivor Nicholson and Watson, 1934), pp. 581–588. The Snowden-Mond Parliamentary debate hinged on the relative merits of Socialism as opposed to " measures of social redress [which] by removing the evil effects of monopoly and waste, will conduce to the well-being of the people." The future Viscount concludes: " Socialism had now become the big issue in British politics." This episode represented an early example of dropping the disguise of Labour politics to disclose the unmitigated Socialism of " Labour " leaders. Susan Lawrence memorializing Ellen Wilkinson (*FQ*:53 March 1941, p. 10) says " she shared Socialist [not " Labour Party "] power for a few brief months."

tives. This advice was given, ostensibly, because the latter Party tended to dogmatize concerning what had always been viable. Flexibility marked Liberal assent to Socialism which itself was a " tendency " and not a dogma.[20] The value of keeping things fluid was understood. The Liberal Party had a strong foothold in certain densely populated areas and it was more to Labour's advantage to keep Liberals amenable to the shifting expedients of Labour than to allow them to adopt the political orthodoxy of the Tories.

Massingham had lately rejoined the fold of Fabianism by way of journalism. There were already rumors his *Nation* was to be taken over by the *NS*. His column, signed " Wayfarer," was, in any case, incorporated into the *NS*. Weekly, as we know, he contributed a " Diary " from London or Berlin. Now he announced that Baldwin's foreign policy was something with which he and his readers could agree. Nevertheless the sequel will show that the *NS* continued to seem baffled as to what Baldwin's policy was; [21] it seemed to be making an effort to find a basis for cooperation. With shrewd skill, Labour leadership, especially by means of the Fabian-educated press, controlled its own " sentimentalists " and acquiesced in the Tory policy without approving it. They were sparring for time.

On July 7, 1923, Liberals might easily have perceived a distant-voiced threat of Labour's coming into power. A contributor [22] wrote that there had transpired during the week two paradoxical events: 1) Some Labour members in Parliament had behaved riotously and had been suspended [23]—Wheatley, Maxton, John

---

[20] *NS*, XXI (June 23, 1923), 317 f.

[21] *Ibid.*, 323.

[22] Volume XX has no table of contents. In the other volumes a contributor can be identified by finding the page, then the title opposite the name of the writer selected by guess. Political-industrial articles will usually be Cole's; political economic, Sharp's; foreign (far-East), Buxton's or C. M. Lloyd's. " A Political Correspondent Writes " was James Drysdale; *NS*, XXIII, 11. Never signed, the column was highly literate, and characterized by figures drawn from the theatre and historical data out of an immediate rather than a renaissance past. His death in 1924 was lamented; he was said to be " nearly infallible" and " irreplaceable." He, like R. Dell, also wrote for the *Manchester Guardian*.

[23] *NS*, XXI (July 7, 1923), 380.

Muir, and others. (The *NS* at that time hoped they would soon outgrow their "minority infantilism.") 2) The Labour Party Annual Conference had taken place and had been marked by " dullness not of lethargy but of sobriety and self-restraint." (It is very significant of Fabian control that only a " faint and quickly smothered echo " had reached the Conference from the " scenes " in Parliament.) On the occasion of this Conference Sidney Webb had made the presidential address studied above.[24] The commentary, using a device by which " party line " is set forth as consensus, pointed out as being the "clear meaning of the Conference" a method and an objective: Gradualism, meaning frictionless change " at each stage only with full public consent"; and Socialism as the *Party objective* which was *accepted from Mr. Webb* without debate or dissent.

> Socialism as a policy admits, indeed, of many and inconsistent interpretations; but Socialism as a general objective remains full enough of meaning to serve as a powerful *force for unification.*[25]

Readers learned that Socialism was not accepted *" sans phrase "*; it was " not a body of doctrine but a constant purpose underlying an active tendency of political practice." The writer warned scenemakers and impatient Labour members to bear in mind that their actions could be "linked up with the usual talk about Bolshevism and class-warfare." But—and this was set far enough away from the last expression to avoid being linked up with it—

> The Labour Party is Constitutionalist to the backbone; indeed, we are tempted to say that it shows *too great a respect* for the established ways of procedure—a respect it will be *driven to modify,* at least a little, when it will

[24] Printed as *The Labour Party on the Threshold.* Reported as " Labour Confers," *NS,* XXI (July 7, 1923), 382 f.

[25] It must be observed that even though a baffled metaphysician must ask if this dialectic demonstrates " clear meaning," it is a clear demonstration of the leadership's straddling of theses and an exact statement of Fabians' two platforms (dialectic): 1) A pragmatic adjustment to measures regardless of doctrine; 2) a drive to collect the coefficients of reformism into their movement, deliberately called Socialism when perhaps another name would describe it.

have to face the real difficulties of exercise of power for the purposes it has in view.[26]

These statements might placate some Liberals but Birkenhead, Churchill, and Lloyd George refused to accept the distinction which Fabians made between Labour Socialism with its half-acquiescence in force (what else can the words " driven to modify [constitution- alism] " mean?) and Bolshevism with its open drive for power by civil war or by revolt induced against " reaction." The corrosion of gradualism was too subtle for the electorate to grasp; and so these practical politicians spoke of " Reds " and " force " and " revolution." Echoes of trenchant warnings from the above- named Liberals are discernible in the *NS*'s admonitions to scene- makers against incurring such terms of reproach as " Bolsheviks " or " Reds." The Socialist leadership was cautious and admonished to gentleness. The two strongest Parties in England approached more closely to each other acquiring likeness in practical politics if not in the " spirit " of their " tendency."

Fabian-Labour kept its equilibrium when confronted with Con- servatives in possession of all its reform thunder. The new Tory liberalism, counter to its nominal die-hardism, embraced most of the reforms which formed the basis of Labour agitation. Viscount Milner published in 1923 his *Questions of the Hour*. Largely re- printed from the *Observer*, it had had some currency. The *NS* ran an unsigned review entitled, " Tory Collectivism." [27] Here Milner's views were accepted with approval as being something more than those of a Tory converted both from Gladstonism and from the " idols of retrenchment and *laissez-faire*." Nevertheless, he might believe, as he did, in governmental participation as a " Deferred Shareholder " in industrial organizations to control trusts and collusive price-fixing; he might advocate Whitley Councils and a National Industrial Parliament of employers and employed; he might endorse experimental public ownership of certain industries, for example, the collieries; but he did not say that *only* Socialism could achieve these things—he was still a Tory.

---

[26] *NS*, XXI (July 7, 1923), 382 f. Italics are inserted. This was a view thoroughly consonant with Laski's *Crisis and The Constitution* of 1932, that only revolt or civil war could bridge the chasm from King to Socialism.

[27] *NS*, XXI (July 7, 1923), 398.

His book performed, it was acknowledged, three services for Labour Party members: 1) It criticized Labour's indifference to the decay of agriculture; 2) it pointed out the welcome fact that " Socialist doctrine " did not include essentially " free trade " or " free imports "; 3) it evoked, by criticizing the tactics of the Opposition regarding Empire administration, emigration, and economic cooperation, the enlightening statement that

> Constructive thinkers in the Labour Party are beginning to realize that a policy of economic cooperation in the British Commonwealth is not incompatible with the " cosmopolitan " ideal, and may even prove a valuable stepping-stone to the international solution of world problems.[28]

So, there were uses for " Preference." In the course of the discussion the difference between Labour as a Party and the One-Party was disclosed. The clever reviewer said—and a divisive distinction between Labour and Socialism is patent—that though the Labour Party might quarrel with Milner on Imperial problems, Socialists could have no reason to object to his views—Labour, once in a position of responsibility, would come around to the Socialist view on emigration and the " humane administration of our tropical dependencies." [29] Thus it was also disclosed that socialistic " Anti-imperialism " and the acknowledged need for control of raw materials would, Fabians guiding, find synthesis eventually, under Socialism if, under a Labour Government, politicians should produce nothing more than definitions of the problem. Admirably astute as this example of Fabianism is, it encompasses a proposition which any awkwardness would render deadly to itself. Enlightened Toryism had equipped itself with leaves taken out of the Labour book. A Fabian thanked the plagiarist for the assistance his writings afforded toward the in-

---

[28] *Ibid.* The conversion of " cosmopolitanism " into " true internationalism " was the object of study in Webb's Tutorial Classes, it will be recalled.

[29] Mandated places were to be " humanely " allowed to continue to be " native," in custom, costume, and law. Cf. Rita Hinden, " The Imperial Aspect " in *FQ*:58 Summer 1948, pp. 15–19. The native system is retained by Lever Brothers. (Cf. T. C. B. Watson, " Margarine " in *FQ*:25 Spring 1940 pp. 16 f.) But Margaret Cole relates that Ellen Wilkinson " snapped " that she preferred seeing little natives scrubbed and going to Sunday School.

doctrination and correction of Labour. The *NS* also accepted the noble Lord's service to itself in propagating its broad tariff principles, while it announced that it believed only Socialism, a " different spirit," could effectively vivify either collectivist Tories or particularist Labourites on the ultimate peaks of internationalism. The important thing for us at this point is to see that Labour as a Party, itself was under tutelage to Socialism;[30] also to learn of the new-born convictions which the Tory mentality absorbed from the atmosphere of Labour propaganda.[31] Two ingredients make up the substance of this propaganda: Information for the initiated and a pabulum for the naive.

The *NS* review of Lord Milner's book also revealed a political weather eye for large blocks of votes. While attesting willingness to learn about agricultural problems, it bespoke State protection for the consumer as well as the producer. The shepherding of the agricultural workers offered small contentment to farmers themselves; for, of course, organized workers could be induced to vote with urban workers.[32] The *NS* tempered its pleasure in the Milner adaption of Socialist protectionism with the long view that Protection was a " temporary phenomenon, bound up with the present system of individualist trading, which is destined to give

---

[30] The views on "economic cooperation" and "tropical" administration and the position of the Empire in a world order all reappear in the United Nations' Charter. Cf. writings of H. Duncan Hall, *e.g., The British Commonwealth of Nations,* edition of 1920. Mr. Hall was on the League secretariate and is now working for the Carnegie Endowment for International Peace. Cf. also, A. L. Lowell, President of Harvard, and H. Duncan Hall, Professor of International Relationships of Syracuse University, *The British Commonwealth of Nations* in World Peace Foundation Pamphlets, X, No. 6 (Boston, 1927), pp. 573–691.

[31] Cf. Keith Hutchinson, *The Decline and Fall of British Capitalism* (New York: Scribners, 1950), *passim.* He shows how Tories enacted most of the laws by which he believes Capitalism fell.

[32] Fabian interest in farming marked by the creation of Labour committees, notices of books, *e.g.,* Fabian F. E. Green's study, is traceable in *Fabian News.* A study of this angle of Fabian activity would be rewarding but could lead to no other conclusion than is found here. There is, clearly, no indication that Fabian Socialism intended to foster an agricultural system essentially individualist. " Industrial democracy," by extension, would turn agriculture into Business; as such it would come under State Planning and price control.

place more and more to cooperative and collective enterprise."
(Of course, this spells Fascism.) Socialism and Imperialism
could not be joined but Labour under Socialist guidance might find
a formula for world cooperation through Empire administration.
With these nice distinctions, vital ones, indeed, the Socialist intellectuals baffled and bedeviled the politicians of the old parties.
It would seem there was something esoteric in " the spirit."
Labour did not con it exactly and Toryism could not learn it. At
least the vocal Churchill-Birkenhead-Lloyd George group were
determined to defeat it as " Red."

The Liberal Sir John Simon had tried to use " gradualism " too
in his campaign. The *NS* found his definitions faulty. Gradualism such as Sir John Simon professed was not satisfactory. He
was fated to be " negative." [33]

It was discovered that a Grey and Curzon " duet " in the House
of Lords under the leadership of Haldane (Labour's " gramophone," perhaps) seemed to cant of new found harmonies between
the Tory tenor and the Labour counterpoint.[34] A columnist made
readers aware of a new break in old " Coalie " party unity: Baldwin, Grey, and Curzon were aligned against Lloyd George,
Churchill, and sometimes, Birkenhead. The latter group planned
a " centre party." The writer pretended not to be too sure of
Haldane's position. This centre-party was never more than an
adumbration, projected by a brilliant idea to realign Conservatives
who had learned the reform programme with Labour men who
disliked outright Socialism along with Liberals of the Churchill
stamp. This made an outline of the heart of England even as the
Centre in Germany once delineated a central German culture; but
the Centre Party of Germany represented an activity external to
" the Centre." The Fabians saw it taking shape, with distaste.

---

[33] *NS*, XXI (July 21, 1923), 434.

[34] Haldane's *Problem of Nationalisation* had been reviewed in *FN*, 1921,
by J. H. Macrae-Gibson. Even with the introduction by R. H. Tawney
and H. J. Laski, the reviewer, an authority on Whitley Councils, warned
Fabian readers that there was a certain naivety in Haldane's viewpoints on
the army and the civil service (he did not say " fascistic ") which should
give democratic Socialists pause when choosing candidates for office. This
Fabian's judgment did not prevent Haldane from occupying a ministerial post
a little later. He was a Webb associate. *NS*, XXI (July 21, 1923), 436.

They prevented its growth; it was never more than an idea. The Haldane-Baldwin " gramophone " indicated that the socio-economic centre politicized by Fabians claimed the forces which the Churchill-Birkenhead scheme needed. It was too late.

By July 28, the suspended ILP members were reinstated.[35] The *NS* thought the affair had had " factitious importance," that " one of the greatest barriers between the classes is their inability to appreciate each other's form of humor." Now, Fabians could not have been ignorant of the fighting reaction caused inevitably by reference to " the classes." They professed not to endorse class warfare. It would be hard to find a more adroit handling of such a problem as the obstreperous back-benchers presented: The paternal, half-sympathetic warning to these earnest men that they were making a " class " of themselves. The incident, however, enabled Mr. Baldwin to face down his " die-hards " and assert his leadership, although the effect was not constructive. On August 4, the Political Correspondent, becoming extremely clairvoyant, noted the effect of such " facing down ":

> The impatience recently manifested by the Conservatives at the *negative domestic policy* of the leaders may be expected to become acute, probably finding expression during the recess in demands for a plunge into Preference and Protection, anti-Trade Union legislation, Second Chamber restoration and other forms of party suicide.[36]

Fabians could keep their path of tranquillity while the " wild men " from Glasgow induced a reaction destined, in full strength, to be lethal in the subject. The prophecy was imperfect: " In what may be their last Parliament," Conservatism could not conceivably allow " its reactionary instincts to be immobilized " for another session. The new " collectivism of Conservatism " was expected to produce reactivation of inherent " reactionary instincts." [37] If Tories might thus be induced to endorse tariffs, tighter trades dispute laws, and a revived veto in Lords, these blunders would ruin them. Nevertheless, the full length of " suicidal " reaction was never run.

---

[35] *NS*, XXI (August 4, 1923), 486.

[36] *Ibid.* Italics inserted.

[37] *NS*, XXI (August 4, 1923), 488.

Tories heeded the warning and became more and more like their antagonists.

Divisions in the Cabinet were revealed again to the *NS* readers when, on August 11, it was divulged that Baldwin was supported by Curzon, Lord Robert Cecil, and Mr. Neville Chamberlain against the very politicians who had championed Baldwin for Prime Minister rather than Curzon—Lord Salisbury, Mr. Amery, Mr. Bridgeman, Sir W. Joynson-Hicks, all die-hards, and "domestic tyrants," who might be expected to bolt. It seemed to be the Ruhr question which made the cleavage now, although the tariff question set harder lines of division. Eventually, the Tories eliminated all the "reactions" except tariff, and split on this old fiscal argument alone,[38] so Baldwin went to the people. In doing so he dished his die-hard reactionaries and arrived at a *modus vivendi,* if not an understanding, with Labour. How deep was the rapport between the two parties was to be demonstrated after the climax and dénouement of Labour politics in 1924.

The historical minded columnist appealed to Baldwin to revert

---

[38] Tariffs would have been quite possible along with a "reconstruction" program involving Government participation, or even with the lend-spend program (Keynesian) advocated later. The issues of the day, "retrenchment" *versus* welfare-spending, were never differentiated from the issue of "Protection" *versus* Free Trade. Welfare spending could have been had along with tariffs. Ostensibly, Labour stood for Empire Preference and Free Trade; Tories stood for Preference and Protection. The more independent the member states of the Empire became, the more pressure for Protection. Socialist Labour tolerated Preference as "economic cooperation." The Tory view was that protected industries meant fewer unemployed laborers to "dump" on the Empire, less relief in "doles," possession of an economic weapon against France. Actually, "Free Trade" was, as an Opposition slogan, mere "politics," a doctrine held in disbelief by Fabian-Socialist leaders themselves. When the *NS* Correspondent called the campaign a throw-back to 1840 he was not stating a fact which he must have recognized, that only persistence of a style of thinking forced any "liberal" to profess a free-trade credo. The new Labour style would have another fetish, "true internationalism." Internationalism for Labor-*qua*-Labor connotes uniform standards of working conditions and pay, elimination of "coolie" labor, together with a flow of raw materials unhampered by a profit-from-scarcity policy. Socialist internationalism, accepting all of these proposals, eschews, "naiveté," and aims at political control of commerce by Socialists—in other words, Power.

to precedent and to seek the arbitrament of the House of Commons (where, indeed, Opposition by asserting itself on either side of the tariff question would gather more power). Asquith, he recalled, had timidly done so in the matter of the reluctantly formed Coalition he had headed. The correspondent had heard that Austen Chamberlain was about to be invited to leave his party. (Knowing the Chamberlain preoccupation with tariff, one might then have suspected the Cabinet breach was even fraternal.) And the correspondent stated for what it was worth the facts of the case of Mr. McKenna. Baldwin had proposed making him Chancellor of the Exchequer overlooking, it was alleged, the fact that the nominee should have a seat in Commons. It was well known that Mr. McKenna was a " free-trader," although he was the author of the Protection of Industries Act and at the same time he was heralded as the man possessed of the genius needed to save Europe. He was not elected.

> The convert [McKenna] was expected to swallow everything, and it is rather straining credulity to suggest that it was some belated scruple about Free Trade that stood in the way of the experiment.[39]

The hint to appeal to Commons could only have been a dare. There was enough concrete protectionism in Labour to have respected Chamberlain and enough free trade Millism to have rejoiced at McKenna's accession to the Cabinet *malgré*-Chamberlain. Yet neither Chamberlain nor McKenna should have any real support from Labour-in-Opposition. The Fabian-minded publication was but prodding the tariff question into the open, at the time.

It is very evident that the spokesman and columnist did not desire a dissolution. In fact, only the week before, he had said that the Opposition had done no better than the Asquithians. Now he said he believed Baldwin could have the support of both Houses if he would show " a restrained but not too dejected version of the spirited John Bullish tradition of his political ancestors." He meant that Baldwin should assert British hegemony over France in Europe; a thing the P.M. could not do without some tool—war or tariffs.

---

[39] *NS*, XXI (August 11, 1923), 512.

On August 25, 1923, the prediction regarding Austen Chamberlain was invalidated. The latter resumed the leadership of the Conservative Party. The Correspondent presented a puzzled air about the "francophile" and "gallophobe" alignments in the Cabinet; but he was clear about the "protectionists of the Midlands pulling in one direction and the Free Traders of Lancashire in the other." He wondered if "mischief" were not the Chamberlain "game." [40] The connection of tariff questions with French policy was becoming apparent. The Fabian had nothing to gain from allowing union men and "workers by hand" to learn, from any interpretation he might make, of the beginnings of an effort of the Government to deal with France by tariffs.

It was Neville Chamberlain, the Postmaster General, the onetime Minister of Health under Bonar Law and Baldwin, who became Chancellor of the Exchequer, in place of McKenna. Chamberlain observed that McKenna's defeat revealed his party's weakness. Although Neville Chamberlain noted in his diary his efforts to ingratiate himself with the Labour people (somewhat like the action of a Roman Senator making it up with the Goths) he recorded that Stanley Baldwin had to remind him of his manners, because it was his custom to treat them like "dirt." (Yet we see him persuading MacDonald to stay in office in 1931.) The awkwardness of his position resulted from his reformist attitude and his sympathy with the Labour leadership in its struggle with the left-wingers. Chamberlain, it was well known, was a francophile. A change was developing in the attitude of Labour toward France.

On September 1, 1923, a sense of *bonheur* was detectable in an *NS* article, "Politics," describing amorphous party masses, blurred party lines, "tranquillity" in a word: 1) Curzon's was the opinion of all England,

> [2)] . . . a Labour Prime Minister would act very much as Mr. Baldwin is acting, [3)] . . . the Labour Party is in almost complete agreement with that most "Conservative" of non-party organisations, the Federation of British Industries [FBI], on unemployment.

The balance was precarious, however:

---

[40] *NS*, XXI (August 25, 1923), 560.

> Mr. Asquith may not quarrel with Mr. Baldwin, but
> Mr. MacDonald sooner or later certainly will. . . . The
> Federation of British Industries is for the moment *at one*
> on the most urgent of domestic problems, with the Trades
> Union Congress; but it is, we may be sure, but a transient
> alliance.[41]

When division should develop in this alliance, the Liberal Party
would have to decide to move left or right. The writer hoped that
in two or three years there would emerge but two major parties;
he was indifferent as to whether it was the name Liberal or Conservative which was to disappear. He hoped for an early return
of party spirit.[42] This sequence shows that party lines were falling
along lines of worker and owner demarcations and that this
stratification did not produce well-articulated political parties,
naturally, *i.e.,* unartificially. Here was a Fabian blind spot. They
were incapable of forming the concept that economic division could
only unnaturally be politicized.

Massingham led out with the shock designed to produce differentiation when, on September 22, he reported what he considered Baldwin's failure in the matter of the French-Ruhr problem.[43]
" These things virtually destroy the Baldwin legend, which many
of us have tried to sustain so long as there was the shadow of
ground for believing it." This was euphemistic in the extreme.
Now, he believed, there would be Opposition with two-thirds of
the political sense of the nation behind it.[44] In the same strain, the
Political Correspondent pondered, at the end of September,

---

[41] Baldwin had served as financial secretary to the Treasurer of FBI and
had headed the Board of Trade. *Who's Who* lists only his educational and
political activities.

[42] *NS,* XXI (September 1, 1923), 584 f.

[43] The Curzon Note protesting occupation was sent August 11. Stresemann took office August 12, and suggested a Rhine Pact on September 2.
On September 27, the German passive resistance ended. Cf. Wolfers, *op.
cit.,* p. 394. Dell said later (*NS,* XXII, 171) that the English Government
was believed to have advised the Germans to end it. But in October (*ibid.,*
33) the German action was a mystery to the *NS.* Mrs. Hamilton, *op. cit.,*
lets it be known that Madame Stresemann was a person particularly well
liked by Arthur Henderson. Of course, this could not be a point emphasized
at the time we are concerned with.

[44] Wayfarer, " London Diary," *NS,* XXI (September 22, 1923), 672 f.

whether Mr. Baldwin were a "whole-hogger" or a mere "mug-wump," whether he were loath to break with his "praetorians," whether he would yield to "a new Protectionist push," whether he were looking to the Imperial Conference to boil up the fiscal issue and leave it to cool in the "multifarious Dominion Parliaments." The writer had lost his assurance that an appeal to Commons could rid Baldwin of his die-hard encumbrance.[45] It is allowable surely to question whether or not it was the Tory Party which developed the "Protection" issue originally. The Fabian organ was working on it in early Fall, and creating the link-up of fiscal policy with foreign affairs and Dominion policy.

The Imperial Conference met on October 6, and the *NS* was unhappy that it met behind closed doors. The British public was understanding, the *NS* said, but it should rightly learn what went on, *especially* in the *economic sessions*. About this time, J. R. Clynes, as chairman of the Labour Party's special committee on unemployment, in correspondence with the Minister of Labour, had ascertained that nothing concrete was proposed concerning Unemployment at Cabinet meetings during the recess. The Labour Party therefore demanded the reconvening of Parliament, and the *NS* suggested that Party members and the Trade Unions work up such a campaign that the matter of Unemployment would be first on the agenda of Parliament. Nevertheless Labour offered no concrete propositions, not a road to repair nor a schoolhouse to build nor a leaf to rake. With the removal from the political foreground of nationalization and the capital levy, it would be reasonable to expect at least a makeshift program to be offered. The connection between the agitation for open conferences on the Empire level and for the reassembling of Parliament is patent enough. It afforded propaganda to the "labour" constituency of each delegation to a conference doomed to failure.

In connection with the Imperial Conference, the ideological leadership of Labour exposed some Socialist accommodations: 1) They were all imperialists now because the Empire had disappeared—but the author of the article, "The British Commonwealth of Nations," assumed a critical attitude toward Australia and New Zealand and the "maniacs" in England who held out against tariff

---

[45] *NS*, XXI (September 29, 1923), 696.

reform; he said, " We are not ourselves fanatical Free Traders."
2) Now, " inter-Imperial " trade was desirable and, with General
Smuts, the writer hoped that the Dominions would help " swing
the influence of the British Empire into world politics." 3) Desirable also, was the creation of an instrument for " keeping effective
touch between London and the Dominion Capitals," *viz.*, some kind
of assembly.[46] No doubt a means of penetrating such a council
would be found by Fabians.[47] The Fabian Colonial Bureau was
ready with a Colonial programme deeply concerned with cooperative handling of raw materials.[48] As it sought to do in England
the Fabian organ sought to direct the attention of the Dominions
to policies outside the domestic periphery, in order to develop, in
the international political hinterlands, labour-Socialist sentiment.
Such a direction had ideologically unifying effects, internally,
similar to those obtained by an attack from outside. Two following points show the effect of thus loosely defining Fabian tariff
policy.

The presage of things to come, made on October 6, 1923, proved
correct. Having learned it " with surprise," the correspondent
retailed the story of a split in the Cabinet on fiscal principles and
a move for dissolution; also of a campaign of " education " for
" Protection " in the North, and he admitted

> . . . so favorable a moment for recapturing the industrial
> vote from Labour and at the same time catching the
> country in a tariffist mood, is not likely to recur.[49]

The Imperial Conference had precipitated the Protection problem.
With perfect consistency, an article, " Protection for Wool," in
the same issue, *i.e.*, October 6, set forth the Fabian concept of

---

[46] *NS,* XXI (October 6, 1923), 728 f.

[47] Fabian Ernest Davies, M.P., son of A. E. Davies, LCC, the saviour
of Fabian Society in the late '30's, is presently Parliamentary secretary to
Mr. Hector McNeill, one-time British representative in the United Nations
at Lake Success. Mr. McNeill is listed in the Fabian Socialist Propaganda
Committee in *FN,* 52:11 (December, 1941).

[48] Its work, especially in connection with India and Africa, and its contribution to the Trusteeship System and the Chapter thereon in the United
Nations' Charter, would make an edifying and rewarding study. Cf.
especially the writings of Fabians Rita Hinden and Arthur Creech-Jones.

[49] *NS,* XXI (October 6, 1923), 728.

tariff and at the same time provided a picture of the way Fabian Socialism would work in the world of trade; Bradford, England, through its Chamber of Commerce, had demanded protection for its wool industry on the eve of the Imperial Economic Conference. The Fabian writer gave Bradford short shrift, and revealed both the secret of its timing and the connection with the fact that French producers at the time had a differential advantage. He "pressed" for the admission that "a depreciated exchange in itself does nothing to facilitate the sale of goods, unless the internal level of prices fails to readjust itself to the changed external conditions." So, even if France was profiting temporarily, there was no reason to safeguard Bradford, especially since she had done so well during the post-war boom. "Practical considerations of expediency" were the only ones governing the question of

> . . . Free Trade *versus* some form of discrimination . . .
> We do not bow down before the Free Trade idol, or hold
> that what Manchester thought yesterday England is
> bound to go on thinking evermore.[50]

But, according to the *NS* writer, this case of Bradford was an example of the work of "powerful vested interests"; the municipality had been able to persuade the Trade Unions to go only so far with them as to endorse an inquiry, the unions, to the editor's relief, having stated in advance that they did not believe in protection and that not only specific industries should be studied but all those protected under the Safeguarding of Industries Act. Even this dutiful recitation of Fabian preachments got small meed of praise. In the editor's opinion the return of big business was the Trade Unions' fault. They had been "too slow" after the war when the "scientific" methods used during the war were discarded. These methods had consisted in bulk buying and the elimination of middlemen from commercial transactions; "We showed how the costs could be lowered and the world trade organ-

---

[50] Here Manchesterism is dropped from the Fabian eclectic liberalism as, during the same year, were Ricardianism and Cobdenism. *NS*, XXII (October 20, 1923), 36. Ricardianism was now a reproach to sentimentalists; and Cobdenism to Free-trade Labourites (or to unionists who made "mistakes"). But who would not say of Labour, as Marx said of Cobden, that their heart and calico were in Moscow? Cf. *infra*, Chapter IX, note 11.

ized scientifically from top to bottom." An elucidation of principles ended the article:

> We want to see the Empire bound closely together into an economic confederation; we do not want to see it take the wrong turning towards a Customs Union. This is not because we have a strong theoretical dislike for Customs duties, but because we are concerned, not so much with imposing handicaps on the foreign producer as with improving the efficiency of our own methods of production —in which we include those of the whole Empire—and with squeezing out the water—in the form of unproductive capital and labour—now employed in redundant speculative and trading processes. . . . A tariff is too often a cloak for inefficiency or speculation; we want an adaptation to present and future conditions of the scientific methods which were applied to the solution of the wartime problems.[51]

That "scientific organisation of the whole course of production from the primary producer to the seller of the finished goods" might not exclude protection was not denied. Presented here, it must be observed, was a blueprint of a section of the corporative state; the entrepreneur is not eliminated but the state assumes the planning function, meeting with other corporatively formed States in the Empire Assembly whose design is indicated above.[52] The British Fabian Socialist industrial method was indefinite in 1923. It had "scientific" appeal and seemed to advocate a system of international control. There was an obvious tendency toward a one-world policy—the word is anachronistic.[53] Proponents of that Protection which international political-economic planning

---

[51] *NS*, XXI (October 6, 1923), 729 f.

[52] In fascistic ordinance, the whole order would be politicized. In an ideal communistic ordinance, the state would be removed after the entrepreneur, and all orders would be run by committees elected by the worker-owners. It is conceivable that more than one party could exist in a fascist ordination because the state survives and supersedes its corporative parts. The socialist-communist ordination replaces the state with the One-Party.

[53] E. H. Carr, *The Soviet Impact on the Western World* (London: Macmillan and Company, 1946), pp. 23 f. As E. H. Carr writes in 1946, "Nothing substantial had been added to Marx's vague notion of a self-organisation of the workers into communes or communities of producers." He cites Lenin's words of 1918 in corroboration, and shows that Britain learned the

would require had no concern for Bradfords which were particularistic, dominated by "interests," subversive of the vacillating unions.

Apparently still hoping to avoid the election, the Correspondent wrote more guesses about Neville Chamberlain's protectionism and Baldwin's effort to have McKenna, a free trader, in the Exchequer. He said Baldwin was a Jekyll-Hyde personality; but the appearance of inconsistency was equally characteristic of *NS*. Wayfarer Massingham pointed out the preference-protection dilemma of Labour and the fact that the *Herald* was a free trade paper. He added significantly that the women's votes were shattering to any tenderness toward the Dominions—higher prices of tinned fruits mattered greatly to them.[54] Ambiguity on Preference was perfectly explicable pending an election, the women's vote was larger than the farmers'. Even after the Plymouth "plunge," when Baldwin plumped for Protection publicly for the first time, the Fabian writer implied that Baldwin's motive was political, directed toward particular constituencies. He would have readers believe the Bonar Law pledge not to touch tariffs in the current Parliament was insincere. A Labour-Protectionist blend was proposed, he had heard, with Lloyd George and another Coalition Cabinet. He imagined the "palaver" about Protection was intended to try the sentiments of Yeovil, Warick, and Rutland. If by-elections in these places went against him, Baldwin would at last be free to get down to "a run of brilliant government successes" unmarred by Protectionism which woud otherwise only defeat him. The wily writer suggested indirectly that Protection might be forgotten if the seemingly "forbidden" topics, Trade Union election funds and Second Chamber reconstruction were introduced:—If there must be an election, *NS* hoped the Tories would make class-minded blunders.

But after the death of Bonar Law and the end of the briefest Prime Ministership and the most turbulent Parliament (also the least effective), as reported November 3, Baldwin went "wholehog" for Protection in speeches at Swansea. He seemed to be

---

benefits of State overall planning and the inadequacy of the profit-motive alone, not from Socialist thought but from the war effort.

[54] *NS*, XXII (October 20, 1923), 43 f.

openly expecting Labour support. (We have seen above, how Henderson got an election out of this, instead.) The Fabian spokesman suggested he "bring his universals down to particulars," to obtain this support. This "glacial theme" had recalled the tariff problem of 1906. It was asked if the challenge had been made to the Opposition or to Conservative die-hards; if Protection were the issue, even. It was certain Neville Chamberlain had monitored the Plymouth speech. Was it not equally certain that he had outbluffed his chief? Perhaps an election could be avoided. It was said that Salisbury, while backing Baldwin to worst Curzon, whom *NS* considered one of the "dangerous" men in the Cabinet, would not permit a dissolution until the veto of the House of Lords was restored.[55] It seems that if Tories could not be brought to publish a reactionary programme, they would find one could be made for them by propaganda. This sort of writing helped Baldwin to divorce the die-hards.

But by November 10, an election was in the offing and the *NS*, tongue in cheek one suspects, asked, "Who on earth can have devised it?" The prospect offered nothing for agriculture and little for industry. Then the editor endorsed the theory that the overthrow of Labour was the intention. Conservatives had the most money to spend; Labour had nothing save human assets— which it were unwise to overlook.[56] The gauntlet had been thrown down; and *NS* publicists articulated the issues. Picking up Lord Cecil's remarks, which dismissed both Protection and the Labour proposals as "quack remedies," the correspondent proclaimed them the alternatives of the election,[57] thereby devising the campaign slogan. Meantime, Clifford Sharp, writing "The General Election," admitted that the Labour Party's Free Trade convictions were not deep; if Protection won, it could get along with Labour; but Labour did "mean business" by its unemployment programme, the real hope of the nation,[58] according to the Fabian editor.

As to the exact nature of the schemes, the readers had need of

---

[55] *NS*, XXII (November 3, 1923), 107 f. Salisbury was still trying to do this in 1933 (cf. Feiling, *op. cit.*, p. 237). It was a "reactionary" move Fabians could have made capital of and invites deeper study.

[56] *NS*, XXII (November 10, 1923), 129.

[57] *Ibid.*, 132.

[58] *NS*, XXII (November 10, 1923), 132 f.

other sources of information. Writers seemed to be idling, waiting for a chance to come to grips with a project. Nationalisation and the Capital Levy were not mentioned now save in the inner circles of Fabianism. A platform endorsing " Production for need and not for profit " seems to have been as far as Sharp would go. Averse to subsidy for farmers, the Fabian spokesman had nothing to say of subsidy for industry. Viewing election prospects he noted that Labour was

> in a mood of enthusiasm in which material difficulties vanish. To thousands of young men, Labour policy is a religion. . . .[59]

Another columnist fairly shouted that at last a " catastrophe," and one that was " irremediable " for Conservatives, had been produced. The new Conservative policy of Protection would be a blow to Agriculture, to Labor—" which after all is a national interest "—and to the import trade. Meanwhile, Massingham, seeking, it seemed, to allay worries as to national safety, wrote of the " unspoken entente with the Opposition " of Baldwin's Government, on foreign policy, especially. In the opinion of this writer, this is a very significant admission. At the time, it went unchallenged and unrepeated.

Editorials, always more lucid than Wayfarer's or the Political Correspondent's columns, stuck to immediate propositions and were outspoken. If foreign policy generated the underlying disagreement, this was not hinted where it was said, " To be led by a Baldwin and a Bridgeman, an Amery and a McNeill, with Lord Derby as Nestor, must be a discouraging and a depressing experience." This was to say that their Tory spirit was obnoxious to the new spirit. But " What a tangle to explain to the electorate! " Baldwin had made terms with Free Trader Derby and refused to do so with Austen Chamberlain. At any rate, Labour had the best

---

[59] *NS*, XXII (November 10, 1923), 139. The arrangement of either Wayfarer's ideas or those of " A Political Correspondent " does not reveal the writers' thesis. Interpreting their remarks was a task suited to the " intellectual " rather than the workingman. It was characteristic of Fabians to be making the Government's foreign policy a constant target for criticism and at the same time to lay claim to having the same objectives—and it was not mendacious. The spirit of the opponents was different.

rhetorical talent and the clearer course. The handicap of the
Capital Levy was to be dropped as utopian, though the editor
hoped the House of Commons "will keep it in the forefront of
their programme." The editor advertised for free cars and for
money, voluntary help and unpaid work.[60] Wayfarer too, advised
dropping the Capital Levy, and re-echoed the editor's ideas, adding
only that he suspected the Lords and Dukes were withdrawing
from the Cabinet or demanding Balfour's return. (Arthur James
Balfour's international success was well known. Thus to recall
his name exposed the Tory effort to deal with the international side
of the struggle,[61] and to call upon the talents of the "ruling
class.") "Honest Mr. Baldwin," said C. M. Lloyd, was protesting
inconsistently that there would be no tariff on wheat or meat no
matter what other tariffs were raised. That the question was
linked to external policy, Lloyd showed by comparing viewpoints:
While the Tories sought to save Europe from Socialisation at
the hands of Mr. MacDonald, Labour planned Empire cooperation
for full employment. The Fabian had a clear grasp of the implications of "wheat and meat" for the Empire but he only
pointed out that Protection which did not cover agricultural
products was not "honest." Thus Mr. Lloyd expressed the general line taken by Fabian leadership: They professed "free trade"
and advocated some tariffs in order that Trade Union mentality
might be satisfied and Labour Party unity secured. Fabian
propositions could wait.[62] Baldwin should have no credit for his
concern for the tables of the poor, however.[63] The Socialist

---

[60] *NS*, XXII (November 17, 1923), 165.

[61] *Ibid.*, 175. Having articulated "Protection" the Labour intellectuals
rejoiced in the fact that the Tories could not explain their position to the
electorate. The latter were not to be upset by the Capital Levy.

[62] *NS*, XXII (November 17, 1923), 168.

[63] Great international planning, Imperial or Socialist, was prone to overlook immediate things and local human needs. The old line politicians had
at least a care for these problems. Guild Socialism was immediately concerned with them; but the overlooked principles of "free association" and
"subsidiarity" would have taken care of them. Cf. G. D. H. Cole, *Guild
Socialism, Fabian Tract No. 192* (London: The Fabian Society, 1920), p. 3:
The "control of industry by the workers" is what Guild Socialism means.
The old Socialists' idea had been a "conception of democracy as an organisation of consumers." On page 5, Cole says, obliquely criticizing Fabian

offered no solution for the problem which " free trade " posed for agriculture : Protection for meat and wheat would bring more land under cultivation and hire more agricultural workers. On the other hand, "agreements " at the international level primarily concerned the industrial workers and encouraged governmental planning of agricultural production in disregard of rural life save as a means of success for industrialism :—The Kulak in England was to liquidate himself ; scant Socialist concern was evinced for him.

Fabian Cole caused some embarrassment when, fortuitously, no doubt, three of his books came out coincidently with the " off the bank " election. The review of these three books of 1923, *Trade Unions in Munitions, Workshop Organisation, Labour in the Coal Industry,* marked the distressing differences between Fabian Trade Union expedients and the strong Scottish ILP principles. Cole's work, it was said, was " Utopian." His notions about industry-wide organization were based upon the example of the " unofficial " steward of the Clydeside. (One recalls Kirkwood.) Clydeside demonstrated, it was unfairly stated, " a destructive revolutionary movement " which constituted a threat to Trade Union Organization as well as a threat to Capital, even though it represented for Cole the struggle for " democratic control of industry " to take place after depression should be ended. In this way, the Fabian weekly impressed upon Trade Unions its own leadership of worker opinion toward Labour Party voting. Whether the delineation of the ILP-Clyde situation was correct or not, is irrelevant. As the Correspondent realistically pointed out a bit later, if Baldwin won on a Protection policy, he would be out of office in no time, because Bonar Law's Glasgow, even if ship building were accelerated, as it currently was, would not tolerate tariffs. It is evident that that portion of Fabian-Socialist thought which was uncommitted to free trade would have its own troubles in Glasgow. It cannot be too clearly stated that Fabian gradualness involved setting aside Socialist principles and substituting a " tendency " when the occasion demanded the surrender. Little by little the differen-

---

tactics, " You want the various democracies, the various proletariats, to be organising in such a way that they can effectively cooperate, not organising all the world over in accordance with some hard and fast mechanical system which ignores national differences." But Cole re-embraced Fabianism.

tiating characteristics of a movement like Glasgow's were altered in favor of conformity, by Fabian technique. It produced a synthesis finally by grappling itself upon one principle possessed in common by London and Glasgow socialist-labor; that was political labor organization. As stated elsewhere, relativism governed the choice of Fabian expedients.[64]

The practice had its reaction upon the character of Fabian Socialism. A new body of thought, British, practical, utilitarian, humanitarian and pacifist, was growing out of the rejection both of continental doctrinairism and of particularism of any kind. Demonstration from the criticism of Cole's work and the Fabian attitude toward Bradford must suffice for the time being.

In addition, it should be said the student cannot avoid formulating conceptual patterns which might be named "the two plans" of Socialism: Anarchy and totalitarianism. These plans had in common "democracy in industry," whether in a stateless society or under state Capitalism; in both, the Party furnished the dynamism—planning, control, motivation. Fabianism in 1924 was capable of making an adjustment of "tendency" under mere regulated free enterprise. To all appearances Fabians simply intended to establish a few controls like Government Corporations—transition, this was, and not a plan. Like a construct in physics, the kinetics of Fabianism are demonstrable; its potentials bear watching; what it was doing was not all its "spirit" made it capable of doing. In 1923 the Fabian Society, as a body, had arrived at no agreement on either "plan."

> Nothing is more significant in the world today than the collapse of Socialistic [ILP] doctrines . . . [The "virtue which has passed out of Socialism"] has diffused itself through men of many different groups. . . . It will group men anew—to their surprise often and mortification at their strange new companionships.[65]

This was said while dismissing forever the ILP. It was written

---

[64] Cf. Viscount Haldane, *Human Experience* (New York: E. P. Dutton and Company, 1926).

[65] Cf. Cole, "English Socialism in 1924," *NS*, XXIII (September 6, 1924), 613 f. He terms Socialism an old faith whose "virtue" has not gone into Communism. The article destroys the *raison d'être* of the ILP and and silently lights their path into Fabianism.

by Cole who in September, 1924, was getting over a bout with
Communists in the FRD and was in transition himself, en route
back to the Fabian Society which he rejoined formally in 1929.
He was beginning to see the worker-controlled world beyond the
monolithic State which is a platonic shadow of a State. The ethos
of Socialism led to a vision of self-determination at the industry
level, to "freedom" from economic stress and social tension
whereby producers worked for themselves, the consumers. That
"savings" in consumers' or in producers' hands and in the hands
of owner-employers contributed to "national assets" was never
accepted or affirmed. The sleeping partner, Government, became
the Planning State. The Planning State subsuming all economic
processes must become the withered-away State because it destroys
the national assets of its individualities, its own matrix. Cole
shared this ideal concept with Marx.[66] Political ordering and
private law would disappear or be subsumed in a paternalistic
central committee. Courts would then be guided only by equity
which, in the absence of absolute ethical standards, must devolve
upon Party policy. The Webbs and Shaw and those who understood them in the Society realized that their very benevolence
would make it impossible for the deceived Socialists to comprehend
that they were all being led into the one-plan, One-Party, commune
("commune" means a not-state) ruled by the elite.[67] Only
Beatrice worried about the "intrigue" she found herself involved
in, yet she was the most outspoken on the idea of rule by an elite.
Statements made after the election show a capacity for synthesizing both "plans," in favor of "more public ownership" and "less
state interference." This implied lessening the number of legal

---

[66] Some liberals argue that the Marx-Cole apparatus allows so many
socio-economic elements to escape "planning" as either to defeat the evils
inherent in their conclusions or permit toleration of dual systems; Marxist
cum non-Marxist existing together. However, we are presently concerned
with the effects produced from trial use of the pattern. Chesterton said that
Christianity had never been tried. We rejoin, the pattern alone has produced
marked effects on society. So must it be with Marxism.

[67] Cole is still beaconing toward the utopia of freedom which he feels lies
beyond the transitional condition of State Capitalism. Cf. his criticism of
the Party's Programme of 1950. And Shaw maintained to the end what he
said in 1931: "We are either Communists or MacDonald-Snowdens, whatever
that is." These points are noted elsewhere in this study.

roadblocks in the path of functionalism. Balfour, Lloyd George, Asquith, most of the old statesmen, were baffled and the politicians of " second-class brains " bewildered by this thing called a third party. It was a party preoccupied by ballots and administrative enactments, but one whose members seldom worried about the " rule of law," or the judicial system.

C. Class and Style

On November 17 a letter signed by Ramsay MacDonald and Arthur Henderson was printed in the *NS*. It declared that there was no doubt that the election had been precipitated by the Conservatives of set purpose to break the power of Labour, a party without funds but with vote-getting appeal and a somewhat positive outlook on foreign policy. These Labour Party leaders—Henderson acting in a dual role—made a plea for contributions to a Labour Special Election Fund. The office was not at the Fabian headquarters. It will be recalled that the Fabian Society maintained a fund to support Fabian candidates who were endorsed by the Labour Party.[68] As he surveyed opposing Parties, the Fabian editor saw other factors of the campaign: 1) The voting strength, 2) the appeals to inverted middle-class snobbery, 3) the programme and philosophy. The Conservatives had taken a risk, indeed. Bonar Law had gleaned *five* million votes; *eight million* votes had created the Lab-Lib Opposition then in existence.[69] Furthermore, the very greatness of the statesmen now united in the Liberal ranks, Lloyd George, Churchill, Birkenhead, on account of the style of thinking created by prevalent Labour Party mentality, was not an asset to themselves. The editor sensed that it was becoming the style to disparage those born to prominence or gifted beyond standardized norms. Votes would follow the style. The *NS* did not speak very plainly: " Lloyd George is taboo and Mr. Churchill is anathema . . . in many constituencies. The Tory candidate would not accept the help of Lord Birkenhead at any price." It would seem that on the level of popular psychology

---

[68] *NS*, XXII (November 17, 1923), 176.

[69] *Ibid*. From these statistics it would seem that Baldwin's Party did not even take a calculated risk but intended to ground the lightning of Socialist-Labour.

some had acquired a "ruling-class" stigma. Actually, however, these three above-named liberals were "red-baiters" and the Tories who shunned Birkenhead's aid seemed to seek two ends: Their own party's well-defined articulation, and to put the Lab-Lib-Socialist fusion to good use on the level of foreign policy.

At the end of November, the editor of the *NS* answered the "song" of the Press which currently proclaimed that the Labour Party was running so many middle-class candidates that it was not a workingman's party, and unworthy of Trade Union support.[70] He answered that he approved the "broadened basis," of brain and hand workers because the Party needed middle-class men in Parliament and the workingman liked a national party without any "exclusive appeal to a particular class." This was significant; a National-Unionist effort was being exerted to alienate Trade Unions from Labour, and swiftly the Fabian glossed over the trace of discord.[71] The new "Socialist snob" was appearing. It was generally understood that Fabians believed the union leaders were overworked and tired and that brain workers should replace them in Parliament. But the editor came back to the main issue. Again, he asked, "who in the world" believed Baldwin would get a mandate? Protection was a bogus issue. "Protection is a phantasm; Free Trade is the *status quo.*" Labour alone, while

---

[70] *NS*, XXII (November 24, 1923), 199. Elizabeth Brandeis, "Memories of a Socialist Snob," reviewing Beatrice Webb's *Our Partnership* in *The Progressive*, Vol. 12 (August, 1948), 31 f., points up the "essentially anti-democratic character of her [Beatrice Webb's] Socialist beliefs," her "faith in efficient public administration, in government by a high-minded elite . . . ," her advocacy of "a substantial measure of compulsion of the individual in the interest of the community."

[71] The truth was that union leaders liked "class" and its accoutrements and preened themselves a good deal on their association with Royalty and nobility. It even softened Kirkwood to the point of apologizing for his harsh speech, that he yielded to Lady Astor's invitation to meet the Prince of Wales at her home in order to get some action on completing the Queen Mary. Beatrice Webb would not take the title, Lady Passfield, and accepted exclusion from the peeresses gallery in the House of Lords but she let it be known she had visited there to hear Lord Passfield speak in that historic assembly. Margaret Cole has no pretensions to nobility and needs none. She can boast of her friendship on the literary level with Chesterton and her association with Naomi Haldane Mitchison and the Countess of Warwick.

fighting for its life as were the others, had a programme for unemployment:—The programme was not immediately forthcoming.

At last, but two weeks before election, a concrete industrial platform took shape for the *NS*'s readers, and that its author was G. D. H. Cole should not surprise students accustomed to Fabian criticism of Fabians.[72] The Fabian spokesman for the Glasgow style of thinking became the spokesman for the united Party. " One thing needful," he wrote, was a remedy for unemployment: To increase the *volume of work* not of doles, to develop or encourage *plans* which now were blocked by the *timidity of capital* or the retrenchment policy of old-fashioned economics. A coal conservation scheme allied to electrical development had been frittered away after the war by the " interests." Transport development connected with improvements in the canal systems had been wrecked by the " Luddism " of the railway owners, likewise the proposal to exploit small ports. To build roads, expedite drainage and afforestation, expand plants, only Labour (by Fabian spokesmen) urged. Town and regional housing projects and technical education had been resisted by the rest with the result in the last case of throwing more young people upon the labor market.

It is in nothing inconsistent that Cole should delineate the most concrete of plans while unable to attain full approval of his Guildman's doctrine. Perhaps the best synthesis of the " two plans " appeared in the criticism, " Mr. Bertrand Russell's Socialism," in the same issue.[73] Russell's work met with more approval than Cole's. At the time Cole was nationally but Russell internationally famous. The latter's group-guild ideas and his ideal of non-central government were accepted in the light of his internationalism and his anti-war viewpoint. But where his philosophy fitted the current pragmatic scheme best was seen in his notion of world unification and pacification based upon he knew not which of three possibilities: American hegemony, a Western European bloc, or Russian dominance. The Fabians expected their expedient acceptance of empire preferences to lead to a world order or at least to the discovery of a principle upon which to build a cooperative world. That is why Russell's work was more acceptable than

---

[72] *NS*, XXII (November 24, 1923), 220.
[73] *Ibid.*, 220.

Cole's particularistic ideals. It was an adaptable philosophy. But it was Cole's programme which was the Labour Party's boast of uniqueness.

It took tremendous effort to keep the non-miscible elements of labor and socialism together. Cole's programme appealed to workers and presented expedient proposals.

No press supported any Labour candidate,[74] but Labour strength increased in Manchester among other industrial centers. (Manchester had been a Liberal stronghold where the *Manchester Guardian* shared the talents of correspondents like Robert Dell and James Drysdale with the *NS*—not to speak of Asquith irenics, Keynesian economics and what Webb called the "tendency of political practice"). Significant indeed was Mr. Churchill's candidacy not for "Tory and Labour Lancashire" but for Leicester where "an attack on a Labour seat [was] considered better tactics than a challenge to Conservatism." [75] This was indicative of growth in Labour Party sentiment independent of Trade Union sentiment. But Trade Unions too took on new growth. Apathy was waning and a wave of strikes, temporarily subsided, threatened to recur unless the new demands being formulated in current industrial conferences should be met after Election.

> So in the world of Labour [the editor of the *NS* wrote] political and industrial activity are working together, with only this difference, that the better the Labour Party fares in the Election the *less likely are the extreme counsels to prevail,* or to be needed, in the *industrial organisations.* The indications are that, more than at any previous time, the Labour forces are achieving a balanced development of industrial and political activity.[76]

The *NS* was aware of a unique balance in Britain as it surveyed Russia, Italy, and Germany, where with rising dictatorship the

---

[74] *NS*, XXI (September 1, 1923), 591. The *Daily Herald* was about to collapse but was rescued, principally by TUC money. The Cooperatives refused to assist. Cf. *NS*, XXI (September 15, 1923), 638; also *NS*, XXI (June 2, 1923), 230.

[75] *NS*, XXII (November 24, 1923), 200.

[76] *NS*, XXII (December 1, 1923), 231. Italics are inserted.

Trade Unions were disappearing.[77] The third party had not only a hold in the hustings and unions; it fastened upon outright class-consciousness. Fabians knew that the balance of trade unionism and political socialism in the Party was precarious.

The above reassurances against " extreme counsels " were written in the same week that the *NS* Correspondent speculated upon the returns from Paisley. He recalled that in a triangular fight, the first time Asquith had won by 2,000 votes; the second time, in a straight fight with Labour (Asquith had actually two Labour opponents), by only 200 votes.[78] The commentator half guessed that the Conservative vote would elect Asquith;[79] and in fact the election of 1923 saw Asquith re-elected by 790 votes. But the effect of this reaction against Labour candidates, however slight, was increased class-mindedness. The most ironic circumstance of the third party tangle was that the anti-Asquith Labour Party

---

[77] For example, in reference to Italy, cf. *NS*, XXI (August 11, 1923), 510. In reference to Russia: Lenin controlled the trade unions by a capitalistic plan, the NEP, by which the industrial worker was given all political power by representation. (We have noted elsewhere the document which shows how the unions recovered from their "mistakes," in grasping the real meaning of Bolshevism.) Under a dictatorship and a one-party system, this placed all power *over* the unions in the Party, and therefore, in the Secretary's hands. Cf. *NS*, XXII (February 2, 1924), 472 f, where Cole contributes "The Socialism of Nikolai Stalin." C. M. Lloyd had hailed the NEP as a policy which took the "hands" of Moscow off the peasants' "necks." *NS*, XX (March 3, 1923), 621 f. He was pleading for concessions to Russia, like giving her a free hand in the Straits, in order to get her trade, ahead of the French. " Soviet " had once meant power in people's (peasant's) hands. "The Soviet" power was transferred to the industrial level exclusively and Lloyd's reported liberation of the peasant was special pleading.

[78] Cf. Spender and Asquith, *Life of Lord Oxford and Asquith,* pp. 347 f. Spender gives a 300 vote majority.

[79] To the observer, the Paisley situation reveals an eddy in the Labour Party stream of force which was beyond Fabian control. A counter-invasion of Paisley came from Glasgow. At Paisley, a man whose career represented the apotheosis of Liberalism, finally met defeat at the hands of bloc-voting democracy. Mrs. Violet B. Carter (née Asquith) describes the experience. Cited in Spender and Asquith, *op. cit.,* pp. 347 f. On December 1, 1923 (*NS*, XXII, 233 f), Cole said that if Asquith became Foreign Minister he would have Labour support and if Clynes became Foreign Minister he would have Liberal support.

set forces in motion in 1920, when the combined efforts of J. H. Thomas, Ramsay MacDonald, Lord Haldane, Charles Trevelyan, and Arthur Ponsonby, ably countered by University men from Glasgow, failed to defeat him,—forces which matured simultaneously with an overwhelming Tory reaction, nation-wide in 1924.[80]   The 1923 Election was the last time Conservatives would save a Liberal in Paisley.   The next time, "controlled" Labour forces would take command and harness the forces from Glasgow to the bandwagon of Rosslyn Mitchell.   But in 1923 Tory votes brought the Asquith success which led to Labour's accession to power.   Otherwise, he would have been defeated in 1923 by the group which beat him in 1924.   The fact that Asquith was responsible for the Labour Government and for its instability and final overthrow explains the raid.   But the story is less illustrative of the way Labour was garnering its constituencies, than of the way Fabian leadership was approaching a Conservative position.   The exigencies of politics prevented society from dividing into two classes, the *majores* and the *minores*.   Nevertheless, the big names were gone, and Fabians intended that through themselves the *minores* should rule.   At the cost of running ahead of the story the new forces operating in Paisley must be studied in order to discover their nature; they were beginning to function in other constituencies less well recorded.   The great Liberal who had stood in 1920 for most of the things Fabians advocated, such as revision of the Versailles Treaty, liberation of Ireland, Free Trade, and German reconstruction, was defeated by

> . . . the jungle tactics of Glasgow . . . cold-blooded, organised obstruction and rowdyism, drilled yells and catcalls and the howling of uninspired and unspontaneour insults . . . argument and appeal . . . [played] no part whatsoever . . . [for] a new generation of young men who had ripened into voters, almost it seemed since the last election, were determined to give a solid class-vote to Labour no matter what we (or their own leaders either . . .) said or did . . . an enregimented [sic] class army against which ideas and reasoning were quite powerless.[81]

---

[80] Spender and Asquith, *op. cit.,* pp. 330 and 344 f.

[81] *Ibid.,* pp. 348 f.   This was Labour, ILP, at work in the hustings.

The fact that Glasgow's Rosslyn Mitchell had wept over Asquith's defeat in his favor[82] is indicative, even symbolical, of the effects these politicians found in forces they could and did unleash. Asquith was the victim of the Liberal dilemma whether to become an out-and-out anti-Socialist Party or remain the Party of "ordered progress," and a make-weight with Labour. He fell between two schools of progress—Socialist gradualists and Socialists in a hurry. In spite of Labour opposition in his constituency, to a certain extent, he had collaborated with the Fabian inspired Party in Parliament, refusing to take an outright anti-Socialist position. His biographer says he hoped to prevent a bourgeois *versus* working-class division[83] in English society. Ironically enough, the year that marked the first great defeat of the new Party was marked by his own defeat by a *well-articulated class vote*. Revenge for what Labour spokesmen chose to consider his calculated wrecking machinations called forth something like a class "*putsch*" in Paisley. It is not certain whether or not the leadership of Labour could unleash or check at will, these class-line forces; but Mrs. Carter listed "organized obstruction" and "drilled yells." So far it would seem that Socialism in Britain was motivated by pragmatic reasons of Party and chose not to act solely for the shock and thrill of manipulating the mass mind. If Asquith strove to prevent a bourgeois *versus* worker cleavage, the Fabians also eschewed "class-warfare"; but a weapon of class warfare, the "class army" did Labour's vengeance upon Asquith to elect a Fabian—from Glasgow. The techniques make memorable historical data. It is doubtful if as yet politicians realized that the collaborator-liberal faced an unenviable fate which no claims of gratitude could ward off.

Nevertheless, Rosslyn Mitchell is listed on all Fabian candidate rosters in the 1920's. Cf. *e.g.*, *FN*, 35:11 (November, 1924). Because the Labour candidate was Mitchell the rowdyism was favorable to Fabian purposes. Intriguing is the situation wherein English Labour intellectuals fought "university men" from Glasgow who supported Asquith in 1920, and then joined in "jungle tactics" with Glasgow men against Asquith in 1924.

[82] *Ibid.*, p. 350.

[83] *Ibid.*, p. 343. Asquith evinced the wisdom of the old-school patriot-politician who knew that in the two-party system the political life of a people moves not in the horizontal but the vertical interaction of civil groups.

D. Tariffs: A Basis of Understanding *Vis-a-Vis* Authoritarian Europe

To resume the domestic story of the Election of 1923, Mr. Drysdale, the Political Correspondent,[84] tattled that it was suspected that the Protection issue had been *raised to forestall Lloyd George* who was returning from America, there having let it be known he meditated upon tariff reform. He had perceived the developments of the future far in advance of either Tory or Labour Parties. His electioneering genius was feared and respected. Moreover, his Party was reuniting. When Mr. Amery had boasted of "forestalling the forestaller," it had seemed a bit of whistling in the dark. While neither the wraith of a reunion of Liberals [85] nor the ghost of a constructive Center Party, designed to capture half-free-trade Liberals, part-protectionist Tories, and workingmen ill at ease with Socialism, can explain the unwanted Election, some explanation as to why Tories risked it and Labour precipitated it lies with both these spectres. The return of Lloyd George from America is symbolic—if nothing more—for, upon the welter of foreign financial problems, simultaneously, the long shadow of America approaching had fallen. "Protection" had some connection with the industrial program which was proposed by and among those who were afraid that the Socialist's "new social order" would prevail in a world order. Fabian criticism of the foreign policy of the Baldwin Government showed that the new order was imminent to a degree. On the other hand, the Tory Party had not broken from the Coalition in 1922, bootlessly; it now had an opportunity equal with the Labour Party to increase its breadth and power. In this student's opinion an hypothesis that there existed an understanding between Labour and Tory leaders is supported by certain intangibles in the

---

[84] It was not then known who this Correspondent was. He was recognized as the trusted correspondent of the *Manchester Guardian* in the galleries of Parliament. It is an interesting point that both Drysdale and Robert Dell wrote for both the *NS* and the *Manchester Guardian*. Thomson wrote in *The Nation* of New York and Rebecca West in the *New Republic*. Ernest Thurtle was the British agent for *The Nation* (of New York).

[85] ". . . admitted [by pooling their funds] to a foretaste of the advantages of a Capital Levy," as the facetious correspondent wrote.

data: 1) There was the Henderson-MacDonald access to the Socialist councils of Europe now desperately cornered by the Communists. 2) There was some intuition that Stresemann would be able to get left-wing support for his policies if he could work with some one not officially connected with the Entente, and some few persons knew of Henderson's friendly rapport with Madame Stresemann (something which recalls that he had managed the ardent Mary MacArthur and had preserved her confidence in him even when his measures—as sometimes it happened—defeated her Trade Union purposes). There was also the all-too-sudden pouncing of Henderson upon the " Plymouth plunge " speech, (which purported to be merely a feeler and not " whole hog " as at Chelsea) wherein Baldwin gave the signal " Protection " and Henderson leaped to the response, " We'll get an election out of this! " at a time when nobody wanted an election and so much in the *NS* statements, as we have seen above, supported the view that Conservatives and Labour could agree on most points.

Labour was learning much from the discussion of tariffs, and trying as hard as ever Lloyd George did to carry water on both shoulders—some tariffs and no tariffs; and the Party in general hoped not to have to take full ministerial responsibility so soon as 1924. One last effort on the part of the *NS* and Fabians to shift the burden of looming responsibility upon other shoulders showed in the article, " Post Election Prospects," written by Clifford Sharp, December 1, 1923.[86] Baldwin was no longer master, he noted, but the Liberals had money and talent; even though Birkenhead and Austen Chamberlain had been ousted by " wild men," [87] there was still Lloyd George who stood in satisfactory opposition to Poincaré. It made no difference whether Liberals or Labourites led; the Capital Levy was out and Nationalisation could wait. Labour would have to sacrifice prestige, however, if it were to enter Coalition. Under Labour leadership there might be a possibility of having Asquith and Lloyd George in the Cabinet, in Foreign and Colonial Offices respectively. Let it be Asquith or

---

[86] *NS,* XXII (December 1, 1923), 232. Cf. also, Hamilton, *Henderson,* 596.

[87] This is not a counterpart of the Asquith story. It is a play, contrived to imply there were " wild men " on both sides.

Clynes, Simon or Henderson, even MacDonald—it was all one. Baldwin's only fault was *his inability to make Europe pay attention:* [88] A choice between setting up a government of all talents able to cope with France [89] and a straight Labour government, which could be undermined and sunk, was made in favor of the latter possibility by the Liberals who, in readiness to connive in any contrivance of the Conservatives to shatter the Labour Party early in its life, entered into coalescence with Labour to create a government.

By December 15, it seemed MacDonald would become the next Prime Minister; and it was learned he planned to head the Foreign Office, also. Fabians Webb, Clynes, Snowden, were to run Parliament.[90] Now, at last, there would come recognition of Russian Government *de jure.* Two businesses, the Marshall and the Becos Companies, were ready to open trade with Russia to the extent of about £40,000,000.[91] To the query why this sudden quiet on

---

[88] At this very moment the decision had already been made in Mr. Webb's house that Labour would not refuse to serve, nor would it enter a Coalition, nor make the Speech from the Throne a Socialist declaration. Cf. Hamilton, *op. cit.,* p. 235.

[89] There was an understanding no doubt which the *NS* could not pry out by its carping at the Baldwin "vacation" in France. Cf. *NS,* XXI (September 22, 1923), 661; also, *ibid.* (September 29, 1923), 171. In spite of Dell's report that gossip had it H. M.'s Government told Germany to surrender, an *NS* contributor said Poincaré forced Germany to surrender.

[90] *NS,* XXII (December 15, 1923), 289. It came out that NUR, J. H. Thomas' organization, had contributed to the Labour Party ten thousand pounds for the election. Thomas' inclusion in the Cabinet was repugnant to some Fabians. Cf. Mrs. Hamilton, *op. cit.,* p. 236. The *NS* attitude toward his actions was generally critical, as it was toward Clynes. Thomas was "not admirable" (*NS,* XXII, 438 f); Clynes, "inept" (*NS,* XXIII, 2). Both of these political labor leaders, always under Fabian tutelage, took vengeance in their memoirs by giving the Fabian Socialists little credit for the force of the Labour Movement, by fairly ignoring them. In their persons Fabians notified labor unions that political leadership was better left to "the Party," *i.e.,* the intelligentsia. Actually, political acumen was not the gift of either section of the Movement, unioneers or "experts." The Party constituted the political machine in every constituency, made the programme, dictated the vote. They needed but one politician and they had two, Henderson and—a better politician—MacDonald.

[91] *NS,* XXI (September 8, 1923), 605. Also, cf. *NS,* XXI (September 15, 1923), 634.

Labour's part, and this reluctance, the answer is to be found in the picture of Europe where elements which Socialists call the forces of reaction were taking a hand, while a new hope blew from the West. Authoritarianism was rising in Europe coincidently with the re-entry of America upon the scene of economic chaos. This study cannot include the story of the rise of Mussolini. The *NS* reporting his methods and successes,[92] early expressed disagreement with his system of proportional representation,[93] which some Liberals advocated.[94] Concerning P. R., Fabian Professor Herman Finer examined the question and settled it for the Fabians in the negative. He referred to the extant devotion to J. S. Mill's political synthesis, and, characteristically British and Fabian, Dr. Finer concluded:

> Institutional change is not less a matter of experience than of logic. Proportional representation, where it has been tried, has not notably improved the quality of legislative assemblies. It does not, on analysis, seem endowed with the remedial virtues inherent in its aesthetic appearance. Our Electoral System suffers from temporary rather than permanent error. What it needs is to be built upon the foundation of voters educated to a judgment made with full minds. It is in a change of social principles rather than of voting expedients that we shall find the results we require.[95]

The opinion that Mussolini and Lenin were the exceptional statesmen [96] in Europe and the acknowledgement of Il Duce's diplomatic

---

[92] *NS*, XXII (June 16, 1923), 286.

[93] It is to the everlasting credit of the Fabians that they rejected Proportional Representation. Cf. Herman Finer, *The Case Against Proportional Representation, Fabian Tract No. 211* (London: Fabian Society, May, 1924). ". . . men and organisation which look to making the world safe and happy for democracy might better turn their attention to examining the conditions of research and policy-making within the Parties, rather than occupy their time in preserving [Millism] an ancient and sterile faith," p. 13. Graham Wallas was a teacher of Herman Finer.

[94] *NS*, XXIII, p. 124. Nevertheless, P. R. was distinctly adopted as a principle in *Labour and the New Social Order*, Webb's basis for the Labour Constitution.

[95] Finer, *The Case Against Proportional Representation*, p. 14.

[96] *NS*, XXII (October 13, 1923), 1.

prowess by the hint that Italy had swayed British diplomacy in the
matter of the Corfu incident showed a certain respect for the
master of Italy.[97]   Although there was present in all accounts a
note deploring his rowdy methods, Mussolini was not held accountable for the barbarities of Fascism, as Lenin was excused for
the atrocities of the Cheka.[98]   The editor of the *NS* as late as
February 9, 1924, found Mussolini " pernikity " but " not so bad
as his speeches." [99]

The rise of " reaction " and one mode of its expression in the
form of Fascism increased the expediency, for any English Government, of encouraging the .Left in Europe, as a matter of
policy.[100]   Dictators unhampered by palpable popular antipathy
would be hard to deal with.   In the upshot, Labour, despite Fabian
hankering for the cool shades of Opposition, was called to
fulfill a mission in Europe by an electorate fundamentally conservative, awaiting the American solution for economic chaos on
the Continent.

To see the kind of information which *NS* provided and to
know that Webb and his associates could interpret the data, if the
rank and file could not, improves the chances of understanding
what it was Sidney Webb [101] undertook to do by his letter to the

---

[97] *NS,* XXI (October 6, 1923), 732.

[98] *NS,* XXIII, p. 3.

[99] *NS,* XXII, p. 498.

[100] *NS,* XXI (September 22, 1923), 662.   Margaret Cole shows that she
detested the Dolfuss government more than the Hitler or Mussolini dictatorship.   (Cf.   *Growing Up.* 171.)   Fabians " rescued " Austrian Socialist
" comrades " who fled from " Red Vienna " (of which Mrs. Cole speaks with
predilection).   She indicates that, for her, Hitler was preferable to a
Catholic " reaction."   Her information came from Hugh Gaitskell and
social democrats who supported the communist version of the story of the
firing on the Karl Marx Hof, " killing my Viennese comrades . . . this was
two years before Guernica, remember."   She links the two incidents; " Guernica made up my mind [that her socialism was communism albeit unblemished
by Stalinism and that she abhorred what she conceived to be Catholic
reaction]."   In speaking of these matters Mrs. Cole descends from the level
of " secondary passions." (Cf. Lord Olivier, " Moral " in *Fabian Essays*.)

[101] *NS,* XXII (December 15, 1923), 301.   Webb, Massingham said, had
revised his Liberal figures downward and Conservative and Labour predic-
tions upward, as of December 1.   (*NS,* XXII, 266.)   Did Labour-ites have
better means of forecasting the vote than " the rest "?   Mrs. Carter, on the

editor: "Why All This Doubt?" the erstwhile editor asked.[102] Then he outlined the resolution of the doubt quite simply: When its leader should be called by the King, upon the vote of non-confidence after the defeat of amendments to the Address, Opposition must accept responsibility. By alternative, it must commit itself to silence or bootless criticism. Responsibility, by the law of life and growth, must be undertaken alone; the matter of "difference in spirit" made Coalition impossible.—The Fabian vatican had spoken: The inclusion of Lloyd George and Asquith in a Cabinet with MacDonald was impossible. The Labour Party must act alone, and fall, wiser for the experience of responsibility.

Opinion and action taken with regard to the French and German situation exemplified the attitude of Fabian Socialists toward the European question enough to demonstrate it for our purposes, as has been done in the previous chapter. It would be most rewarding to study Fabian opinions on Hungary where the Horthy Regency displeased them and their respect for Bela Kun paralleled that for Lenin.[103] It would repay the time given to it to measure

---

eve of Asquith's defeat, in 1924, felt sure he would be elected by a 1000 vote majority.

[102] *Ibid.*, 294. Webb had resigned "more than a year ago," having differed with Clifford Sharp, the current editor. There was no real breach. Webb was Chairman of the Labour Conference which adhered to the Capital Levy; Sharp dropped the Capital Levy from the campaign platform. Although Glasgow insisted on retaining it, it was not good "politics" and so was shelved by *NS*. The Fabian left and right hands were not unaware, actually, each of the other's doings.

[103] *NS*, XIV (January 17, 1920), 426, was tolerant of Bela Kun, unsympathetic with Count Apponyi, ridiculed Churchill and others who "smell Bolshevism" everywhere in Europe and revealed England's hand in trade connections in Buda-Pest. Difference "in spirit" is shown in this attitude on trade in Buda-Pest and trade with Russia. Cf. *NS*, XV (April 10, 1920), 2, where it spoke out against the anti-Communist reaction, naming it "White Terror" and saw no excuse for curbing labor organizations, even though infested, as they must have been, with Communists. That the Proletariat saw no middle way between reaction and Socialism was an observation well taken. The *NS* regretted "Red Terror" and "White Terror" indiscriminately and the *reaction* which set in, as well. On February 15, 1920, the *NS* printed a letter from Alexander Broz (Czechoslovak Press Bureau in London) quoting the Minister, General Friedrich. It described conditions being reenacted everywhere in Europe: Failure of the promises of the Entente, and of Coalition; deception by "pacifism, socialism, communism";

the not unlimited Fabian satisfaction with the eventual Christian Social republic of Austria where a " Fabian " was the first president of the Austrian Federation [104] and to assay the effect of the publication and comment by C. M. Lloyd of Hilaire Belloc's suggestion of a Catholic-bloc and Austrian hegemony which would be as " authoritarian," [105] as it was imagined the Vatican desired.[106] Suffice it to say that as authoritarianism, from which Fabians failed to distinguish the forces of conservation or of mere Right, was about to be welcomed in Europe, a reluctant Labour Party, Socialist led, was about to cast itself from the pinnacle of an English temple.

E. Fabians Stood Where " Protection " Divided England

As antagonist in the struggle for a Labour front in Germany and the assertion of hegemony over France,[107] the *NS* had Lord Rothermere's *Daily Mail* of Paris with its pro-French policy and its criticism of British policy. The *NS* found the alliance of Lord

---

the rise of Catholic and monarchic forces, standing alone with their last rifles. The *NS* reported such "reaction" with disapproval. Cf. *NS*, XIV (February 14, 1920), 552.

[104] *FN*, XXXII (February, 1921). Dr. Michael Hainisch seems to have represented the type of Christian who believed up to the pronouncement of *QA* (*op. cit.*, p. 43) that Socialism purged of objectionable features might be embraced by Christians. In an interview with A. Emil Davies which had been denied when requested as by a London County Alderman and accorded when A. E. D. presented a letter from the Fabian Society, Hainisch spoke of his book on private property in a Socialist State and of his belief that Socialism which "represents a sense of duty rather than rights," would *arrive* " rather through extensions of the co-operative movement in all its branches than by direct State action." A. E. D. later met on the train an Austrian who had attended Fabian Society meetings in Vienna where Hainisch and Count Metternich, the former Austrian Ambassador in London, and founded a branch of the Society.

[105] *NS*, XXII (December 8, 1923), 260.

[106] *NS*, XXII (November 17, 1923), 171. Fabians were better prepared than Catholic commentators to see that the creative idea in *QA* was a demand for organization. The Church offered principles on which to construct a social-economic apparatus productive of Social Justice; the Socialists constructed their apparatus with a different " spirit."

[107] *NS*, XXI (June 16, 1923), 288 f.

Birkenhead with Lord Rothermere a " conscienceless paradox " [108] not easy to contend with; but it soon after dropped its own francophobia. The *NS* thought of a *zollverein* of Fabians' own defining—not the usual notion of customs union—between England and Germany based upon " free trade." It observed that protectionists were *nationalists* and their objectives rather political than economic,[109] and it predicted a struggle between nationalists and Communists in Germany.[110] In England and in Germany Fabians intended to occupy the middle ground. Fabians were half-protectionists and *not* nationalists. They spoke of " free trade " only to keep the middle ground in Germany. They hoped to use tariffs to rein France. The *NS* assumed it expressed the general feeling of the country when it noted that Baldwin's majority at by-elections at Leeds and Portsmouth had been reduced due to resentment of his francophilism.[111] There was a division in English national life between an upper class, pro-French mind and a labor-class, anti-French mentality which the Ruhr question tended to emphasize regardless of the triple party divisions. Without the Ruhr and tariffs, Labour might have been isolated by the upper-class sections of the other Parties. As it was, the two questions evoked consensus of the rank-and-file Conservatives with " intellectual " Labour. When Lloyd George's Party plumped honestly for some tariffs it made it possible for upper-class Liberal and Conservative Parties to fuse against the third Party; but by refusing to coalesce, the Tories retained the three-Party set-up.[112]

---

[108] *NS*, XXI (August 18, 1923), 536.

[109] *NS*, XXI (July 28, 1923), 463.

[110] *NS*, XXI (August 4, 1923), 485.

[111] *NS*, XXI (August 18, 1923), 536.

[112] When this happened in 1931, it was fatal to the Labour Party. The question of tariffs, however tentative in 1923, kept them from fusing then. When they fused in 1931, Labour had dropped its gallophobia. In 1922 Tories and Liberals saw the Labour Party as a threat; many Socialists saw it as an instrument of propaganda only. A non-Fabian Socialist, L. MacNeill Weir, *The Tragedy of Ramsay MacDonald, A Political Biography* (London: Secker and Warburg, 1938), p. 99 says Austen Chamberlain and Bonar Law (p. 101) saw the great political danger of " Labour Against the Rest," or a rising popular notion that Labour was " the alternative government" as their greatest problem in 1922. At the time of the Chanak crisis the danger headed up to the Constitution *vs* Socialism. Cf. also *ibid.*, p. 113.

The Rothermere press, advising the support of a Liberal here and a Conservative there, was especially futile. Fabianism knew better how to invest the middle ground.

Another technique contributed to Labour solidarity. The Labour Party was not permitted by its mentors to indulge in particularism of a patriotic, much less a local nature.[113] As it was in the matter of Bradford wool, and as in the Poplar affair regarding the Poor Law administration, national or local self-interest was deliberately overlooked in the matter of coal. The British coal industries were beginning to benefit from the situation in the Ruhr. No credit was given the Government which had withstood the French suggestion to blockade a strip of German coast and had thus favored the English coal industry.[114] No sustained objection (there is some criticism, however) to current British or allied occupation of the Rhineland was noticeable in the *NS*. Nor is there such adverse criticism of the handling of the Saar as of the Ruhr problem. Yet Kantorowicz [115] was ready to

---

Weir finds MacDonald a Fabian still at heart (p. 40) but Weir does not account for Fabian action in his exposition of the mystery, to him, of how a party, not *per se* Socialist yet committed to " the Capital Levy and Socialism by an Act of Parliament " came in committed to constitutionalism. He condemns MacDonald for accepting the Premiership yet makes no reflection upon the fact that Fabian H. N. Brailsford's *New Leader* urged the acceptance of responsibility, as did Webb. Weir cites Mrs. Hamilton and relates the surprise of the "propagandists" to learn MacDonald had decided to take and hold office rather than go out on a Socialist Speech from the Throne (*ibid.,* p. 133).

[113] *NS*, XXII (December 8, 1923), 257. Cole, in 1922 had said " sectionalism requires to be superseded by a wider loyalty." Cf. *NS*, XIX (April 22, 1922), 58 f. Guild or corporative idealism embraces subsidiarity and local management.

[114] *NS*, XXI (August 18, 1923), 538. The rejected idea of a blockade is noted in *NS*, XXII (November 24, 1923), 208.

[115] Hermann Kantorowicz, *Germany and the League of Nations, Fabian Tract No. 212* (London: Fabian Society, 1924). Kantorowicz, like Dell, believed the British Government advised Germany to cease passive resistance, even though Baldwin's last note to France had intentionally stiffened German resistance. Kantorowicz also believed the British Government had advised Germany to join the League, then postponed the action. This was doubtless caused by America's coming into the picture and seeking to induce a reasonable attitude in France. (Kantorowicz was later a visiting professor in Columbia.)

tell Fabians that Saar policy alone kept Germany out of the League. It was April, 1924, before they learned this, however. The Ruhr—the French occupation of the valley, illegally, was the main argument of British Socialists by which they kept the Labour Party a "third party" and free from a coalescence of both other parties against it. Some tariffs to punish or control France, having been accepted by "free-trade" Labour, could be used equally effectively to control Germany.

F. FABIAN "CONSTITUTIONALISM"

In the winter of 1923, English domestic politics signalled hope to the German left-of-center, by Labour's rising; while Tories had to take the blame for curbing German resistance in the Ruhr and checking German aspirations at Geneva.

A succinct summary of the quality of British Constitutionalism, appropriated after the election by Labour's publicists, was contributed by the diarist, Massingham, and the cosmopolitan, S. K. Ratcliffe, in the issue of December 15, 1923. In telling the story of what happened after the general election of December 6, Wayfarer [116] pointed out that by not immediately resigning, Mr. Baldwin had given Labour a chance to organize, allowed the Liberals to take their proper share in the "fairly happy issue," and "*stopped the special inanity of a Chamberlain administration.*" [117] Undergone, the Tory disadvantage and Baldwin humiliation had resulted in avoidance of confusion, and had prevented further advantage to the Rothermere-Beaverbrook press. As far back as August, the *Times,* for its "good feeling and good sense," and the *Observer,* for its knowledge of governing personalities and "insight into the tradition of English government," had been praised in contrast to that "unspeakable combine" [118] which had "surpassed its bad

---

[116] Wayfarer, "London Diary," *NS,* XXII (December 15, 1923), 300.

[117] Our italics point out an overlooked element in the usual discussion concerning this period. It is reasonable to hold that a quite different contour would have been given historical lines, had Chamberlain headed a Government in 1924. This shows that Baldwin rejected an alternative *in order* to put Labour into Government. Chamberlain was loyal and selfless and never understood Baldwin's way of withholding approval. Cf. Feiling, *op. cit.,* p. 269.

[118] Lord Rothermere's *Daily Mail* of Paris which Lord Birkenhead joined

record in anti-patriotism" (by being pro-French).[119]   Now in
December, Labour marked the demise of its partner-party with
less heartlessness than Conservatives showed.   Liberalism had
rendered "service to the State in a critical hour" by "straight-
forward constitutional tactics" so as not to "end its career in the
servitude of a beaten and discredited Tory Party."   The Labour
Party, which the Liberals now served in Coalescence, not Coalition, was "a constitutional organisation under sober and experienced leadership."   With justice, Massingham claimed historical legitimacy; politically, the Labour Party was the child "not
of Karl Marx, but of English Radicalism and English self-government."[120]   In place of reaction as in 1921 and 1922, Labour
would take over "in the cause of social peace," the device of
Lloyd George, namely "Constructive social reform."   Although
"*the*" problem of the National Debt was to be studied, it should
not make trouble.   The City was "reassured" that the Capital
Levy was not to be rushed.   But

> . . . the workman will feel that he is getting back some-
> thing of his own.   In return he will be asked to do his
> honest best to make his friends' Government a success.
> *If Capital* assists this *fair deal,* it will in no way be penal-
> ized.   [No crying "Socialism in our time"; this was a
> Capitalist-dependent Government still.][121]

---

in "conscienceless paradox," was meant.   Cf. *NS,* XXI (August 18, 1923),
536.

[119] *Ibid.*

[120] But in these days Laski's *Karl Marx* and the Webbs' *Decay of Civilization* sold steadily in the Fabian Bookshop.   Cf. every *FSAR,* 1924–1930.
The rate of turnover was only slightly more than that of Shaw's *Common
Sense of Municipal Trading* and Wells' *This Misery of Boots.*   The leadership was not looking backward to English origins.   As to Wells, indeed he
was out of the Society but his obituary in *FN,* 57:8 (September, 1945),
written by Cole, acknowledged the Society's debt to him and his "twin ideas
of human unity and world planning."   His ideas, Cole said, were not wrong;
there were "temperamental differences" between him and the "Old Gang."

[121] Wayfarer, "London Diary," *NS,* XXII (December 15, 1923), 300.
The added italicizing of "fair deal" is self-indicative.   Other italics also
are inserted.   After President Truman's Speech on the State of the Nation,
1949, "fair shares" long in Fabian usage, came into parlance in the United
States.   "Equality of sacrifice" appeared first in *Tract 188.*

One might ask why it needed saying then that

> Labour is no outlaw from the Commonwealth. It is a
> national party—even the greatest of national parties—
> and every crisis with which I am acquainted has shown
> that the *British quality* goes right through the *race,* and
> infuses workmen quite as much as dukes, if not a great
> deal more so.[122]

Mr. Massingham had just previously described Mr. MacDonald
in terms of the oldest tradition: " For all the philistinism of our
time," MacDonald's air of distinction was esteemed. Less eloquent than Jaurès, not so supple as Briand, he ranked high in the
" Parliamentary movement of the Left." An unspoiled intellectual, he had kept his *style* in spite of the demands made by popular
leadership; his character was as " stainless as that of Burke or
Gladstone." His friendship with the late John Morley and his
being well-travelled were marked assets.

To this description of the orthodox head of England's Government if we add the national pride exhibited in a letter to the editor
by Fabian S. K. Ratcliffe wherein, citing Burke, Pitt, and Disraeli,
he inveighed against the contemporary habit of saying " this country " and not " England," we can learn something about election
psychology and Fabian national interest. The letter carried a
snide reference to the Scotsmen and Welshmen in politics. It took
its lead from a statement in the press criticizing the expression
" USSR " as one which dropped the great name of Russia. Ratcliffe, himself an East Anglian, out-heroded the *Morning Post,*
taking it to task for playing on " its favorite theme," " The
Socialist Peril," without itself saying plainly, " England! " The
incident recalls the words of David Kirkwood of the Clydeside.
Quoting, in characteristic fashion, the Bard's lines ending, " This
blessed spot, this earth, this realm, this England," the Scotsman
wrote, after the launching of the Queen Mary, " But I wish
William Shakespeare had said, ' this Britain '! " Such data are
highly indicative of the mentality of the Socialists of Britannia,
ruler of waves. If the patriotic outburst came as part of the
initial effort to establish a Government by the new Party, it was

---

[122] *Ibid.*

nonetheless quite genuine. And it portrayed more integrity than did Tory squeamishness which avoided breaking the tension between old-fashioned patriotism and the new-style indifference to it. It is something not to be forgotten in the study of international Socialism as exemplified by Fabianism. And it is highly significant that it was, in a Philistine decade, the Fabians who rediscovered the virtue and the culture found in patriotism. The Fabians were clever electioneers pragmatic to a fault, schooled in expediency and hiding their principles as a matter of strategy; but they were not unconscionable hypocrites; their equivocation in capturing unions for Socialism and Socialism for the Party and the Party for power was sublimely motivated. It is not uninteresting to note that *race* and *patriotism*—not to say nationalism—were so emphasized in England in the year that saw the Munich Putsch and the anniversary of Mussolini's so-called March on Rome. Yet it cannot be said that tranquillity ruled for beneath the surface Fabians saw a threat. Taking cognizance of Asquith's expressed opinion that a Government which was *forced* out had no right to a dissolution and Mr. MacDonald's opinion that the King must send for the leader of the next largest Party but that he need not always grant a dissolution, the author of " Labour in the New Year " [123] said another election would only add " spice and anger " to the Labour sentiment and create a " menacing movement." The possibility was mentioned that a " favorite " might form a government. By 1931 resort to this constitutional expedient was more welcome to the public than it would have been in 1924.

G. Fabians and the Unstable Equilibrium of the Party of " Labour "

The new Labour Government, calling itself Socialist, lacked a sense of security. Of undetermined fiscal and even monetary principles, of divided political force in the Movement, and of divisive objectives among the unions, Fabians were aware. They attempted a form of tutelage of Labour leaders and even of the Cooperative Wholesale Society. Nevertheless, a very stable element in the Movement was contributed by Fabian Women.

---

[123] *NS,* XXII (January 5, 1924), 358 f.

Publicists urged a more concrete catalyst than " sentiment " or " rationalisation " in a more direct connection of labor organizations with Parliament. Unconsciously following the ancient practice of unstable tyrants, yet fortunately provided with a genuine challenge, the Labour Party was led to look abroad for political activity upon which to focus a common national interest. Some elucidation of these seven items follows.

There fell on the scene a new light on currency which the Fabian reviewer regretted came too late for election.[124] It marked, said the reviewer of Keynes' new *Tract on Monetary Reform,* the end of the gold standard and the substitution of a " dollar standard "; Keynes was " sceptical " of the Genoa plan for American cooperation. The *NS* reviewer asked why if gold value could be regulated like a bank rate by government monopoly, could not the value of wheat, coal and so forth? The reviewer found that Mr. Keynes' thought, however weakened by respect for his banker readers, was a " contribution to collectivist thought."

The editor of the *NS*[125] remarked upon the " triumph " at election time of the " propagandists," the " non-commissioned " workers in the " ranks of the Labour army." With characteristic Fabian discrimination, he remarked that MacDonald's speech to the celebrating Party (he attended the celebration this time, feeling more one of the real leaders than an ILP idol) was meant half for the outsiders who must be reassured because they were fearful, and half for insiders who must be restrained because they were impatient. The Party drew its strength, he said, from " active membership in the constituency organisations " rather than from the Trade Unions which financed it.

This was tantamount to self-congratulation for innumerable were the occasions when the *NS* had counselled, somewhat peremptorily, that the unions leave politics to the Labour Party and that local party organization be strengthened; also it had tried to cudgel the trades organizations into leaving their disputes in the hands of a committee of the General Council of the TUC (something quite different from submitting disputes to the tribunal of

---

[124] " J. M. Keynes, *Tract on Monetary Reform,"* NS, XXII (January 5, 1923), 372.

[125] *NS,* XXII (January 12, 1924), 382.

an Industry Council). Trade Unions which left politics to the Party and disputes to the Council would be leaving their fate, generally, to Fabians. (Fabian Margaret Bondfield became chairman of the Trade Unions Council early in 1924.) During the period from April to October 1923, some of the following examples of quasi-directives came from the intellectual leadership of labor. For example, the *NS* [126] stated flatly that a joint committee of the TUC and CWS, headed by the General Council, should have *prevented* the strike of certain unions against a unit of CWS.

Again,[127] a dockers' strike, which was "futile" should have been avoided by TUC's having "told them so." In this strike, Mr. Bevin was *opposed* by the stevedores. There may have been some connection between this fact and that reported earlier,[128] that henceforth, individual Communists might represent constituent groups in the Party conclaves, although the Communist Party itself could not be a constituent of the Labour Party. However, the problem which agitators developed was the very real one of "casual" labor on the docks.[129] In another instance, the *NS* [130] urged that the TUC should "plainly tell" bickering unions within the National Union of Railwaymen that TUC would settle their quarrel. This would be to go over Mr. Thomas' head. Fabians faced a rival Socialist society in the Labour College which, by the autumn of 1923, was fully Marxist and antagonistic to WEA; and then TUC complicated the pattern by endorsing both schools.[131] Several pages further on,[132] the editor said the Trade Union movement was a "national danger" if ill-led and badly —our italics—"*co-ordinated.*" TUC, he conceded, was an improvement but the work of the Labour Party "overcast" the

---

[126] *NS*, XXI, 351.

[127] *Ibid.*, 534.

[128] *Ibid.*, p. 350.

[129] As to Mr. Bevin's Fabianism: He was a party to the re-formation of the Society in 1939. He always had *NS* support. He was a bit more "radical" in his early period. Belonging to "Zip" in the 1920's, he joined the Socialist League with Stafford Cripps (against the "intellectuals") in 1931. Cf. Mrs. Cole, *Growing Up*, pp. 145 and 150.

[130] *NS*, XXI, 535.

[131] *NS*, XXI (September 15, 1923), 635.

[132] *Ibid.*, 726.

industrial side of the organization within the movement. Again,[133] TUC was ordered back in its own corner, as it were, *to leave politics* to the *Party,* when the editor learned some TU members had argued for *Protection.* Those bickering Trade Unions *must* leave the influencing of this worst possible of Governments (1922–1923) to the Party. (That tariffs constituted an economic question rather than a political one, and that Fabians admittedly used Free Trade only as a political slogan, will not confuse but only clarify the techniques of Fabian leadership.)

Upon occasion the *NS* was understanding and benevolent as when it explained away the Boilermakers' strike which had been undertaken against TUGC counsels. The prolonged strike in the shipyards and that of the bricklayers who had a peculiar " dilution " problem showed the *NS* on the side of the unions rather than concerned with the care of those numerous ones who were the " dilutees," as, among the dockers, were the " casuals." [134] " The flow of labour to the docks must be regulated," the *NS* said. " Regulated " was a strong word to use on the eve of Labour's coming into power.[135]

Although failures in cooperation must come as one contributor wrote from the fact that TU leaders did not feel " at home " with " the elite " in the movement,[136] nevertheless at the time when Labour M.P.'s created " scenes " in Parliament and were suspended, the *NS* reconciled, if only in print, the most divergent characters, Webb and Wheatley. Between the person we have learned to think of as the " grey eminence " and one of the " wild men " from the Clyde [137] the *NS* said there was no fundamental

---

[133] *Ibid.,* 728.

[134] *NS,* XXII (November 3, 1923), 99.

[135] *NS,* XXII (January 26, 1924), 439. The dilution problem came in for more ample discussion in connection with the story of the Wheatley Housing Bill and the Labour Government's view on education.

[136] *NS,* XXII (December 1, 1923), 234 f.

[137] Wheatley was a greatly loved leader who could quell an angry Irish crowd with a smile. Cf. Kirkwood, *op. cit.,* p. 85. " It was John Wheatley who prepared the Dilution of Labour Scheme which became the basis for the whole of Great Britain, and worked perfectly until the end of the war." *Ibid.,* p. 115. Kirkwood's part is shown on page 117. On these pages of Kirkwood the names of John Wheatley, Rosslyn Mitchell, and James Stewart appear in the light which makes it easy to see why Fabians cultivated them.

difference in thought. Both were revolutionaries. Both were " constitutional." Both were " evolutionary." Although " scenes " were useful, they were inexpedient for a Party which, unlike that of Parnell who used the technique to good effect, was headed for responsibility and power.[138]

Coal miners and their leaders were usually not scolded by the *NS*. One recalls that Webb from 1922 represented a coal mining district and that he had been on the Sankey Committee in 1919. Once the *NS*[139] editor evinced a hope the miners could settle a current dispute *without Government intervention*. It must be remarked that this evinced a radically " associational," even " syndicalist," viewpoint; but H. M.'s Government was Labour then and had to be impartial. And this was but shortly after the *NS* had criticized NUR splinter unions and had said that Mr. Thomas was not " admirable " in his struggle with Mr. Bramley " who was not strong in tact " while even Fabian T. C. Cramp's manifestoes were not " allaying bitterness "[140]—TUC should work to make the Railway workers one union. When the new general charter of TUC was adopted and a new secretary named, the *NS* did not supply the names of officers but noted that the separation of politics and Trade Union activities was consummated and advised that " demands " rather than " resolutions " be the expression of such activities.[141] The distinction between " demands " and " resolutions " marks the difference between representatives and those represented, of course; constituents make demands, legislators and political policy makers pass resolutions. Whether union men resented such directives or not, their mounting power to demand was to be dissipated by the reaction to the brief episode of a " Labour " Government. But in 1923 they were under tutelage.

The names of Mitchell and Stewart appear in all the lists of Fabian candidates in the elections from 1922 onward. One must distinguish Labour candidates and Fabians who were Labour candidates. There existed a Labour Election Fund and a Fabian Parliamentary Election Fund. Presumably a Fabian might receive help from both. The Fund was not usually totally expended. Cf. any *FSAR* from 1924 to 1930.

[138] *NS*, XXI (July 7, 1923), 379 and 385 f.

[139] *NS*, XXII (March 1, 1924), 590.

[140] *NS*, XXII (January 26, 1924), 438 f. Bramley was on Fabian lists by 1919.

[141] *Ibid.*, 655.

The Cooperative Party, now a constituent of the Labour Party, refused to become part owner with the Trade Unions and the Labour Party of the *Daily Herald*.[142] The editor of the *NS* regretted the failure thus to get " new blood " in the paper. The polite tone indicated respect for the Cooperators' acumen, but the known financial plight of the newspaper suggests a different interpretation. The Cooperative movement was growing. The same page of the *NS* carried an item which served as a special signal to a marked group: A. V. Alexander,[143] Cooperative Member of Parliament and head of the Cooperative Congress —once, as had one time been true of unionism, a " stronghold of Liberalism "—had become Parliamentary Secretary to the President of the Board of Trade. This time the *NS* did not name his grey eminence, who was, of course, Sidney Webb; the intention was to draw attention of Cooperators to the prominence they had achieved.

Two prominent women of the Labour Party and of the Fabian women's group took their seats in Parliament in January, 1924, with the congratulations of the *NS*, Margaret Bondfield and Susan Lawrence. For the third woman of the Labour trio, Dorothy Jewson (ILP), the *NS* rather grudgingly added felicitations, remarking she had " done good work in NFWW." All three had worked in unionizing women workers and in bringing the National Federation of Women Workers into the General Workers' Union.[144] This was concrete, but two more subtle elements were noted: " sentiment " and " rationalisation." A glance at the *Fabian News* reveals the prominence, at this time, of women in the ranks of Socialist-Labour, especially in Fabian activities. Indeed a large part was played by women in the constituencies in spreading the " sentiment " which a *NS* contributor believed, even before the Election, was a greater force than that created by mere numbers of Trade Unionists and Cooperators. These latter, even though their organizations were *ipso facto* constituents of the Labour Party, might conceivably vote Liberal or Conservative, but

---

[142] *NS*, XXIII (June 14, 1924), 274 f.
[143] As of 1949, Defense Minister in H.M.'s Government.
[144] *NS*, XXII (December 15, 1923), 290 f.

the " sentiment " among persons outside organized labor or CWS would overbalance this loss.[145]

The extent to which this " sentiment " had contributed to the growth of Labour numbers in Parliament can be measured by some data concerning Fabian Women and women whose candidature was supported by Fabians: In by-elections of 1921, out of six Labour candidates, four were women.[146] Of five candidates put up by the Birmingham Fabian Society, three were women; and twenty-four women stood for Labour for Royal Halloway College Fabian Society. In that year, seven out of twenty members of the Fabian Executive were women.[147] In 1922, out of fifty-four candidates in the general election, four were women.[148] In a by-election list in December, 1922, four out of five were women. Although in December, 1923,[149] only four women out of sixty Fabians ran in the general election, a by-election list was fifty per cent women's names. Even though in September, 1923, only two out of twenty-two Fabian candidates were women, in the preceding July a by-election list had showed one third of the candidates to be women. In November, 1924, where a year before four were women out of fifty-four who ran, eight out of eighty Fabian candidates were women. Again, in a by-election list half were women's names. The women's contribution to Labour " sentiment " is patent.[150]

In an article in the *NS*, " The Labour Voter " discussed above, there is given a succinct characterization of the process of " Rationalisation " which, if we may borrow an Emersonian phrase, was the " tuning down " of Nationalisation. We have seen

---

[145] " The Labour Vote," *NS*, XXII (December 1, 1923), 234 f.

[146] *FN*, XXXII:2 (February, 1921).

[147] *Ibid.*

[148] *FN*, XXXIII:11 (November, 1922).

[149] *FN*, XXXIII:12 (December, 1923).

[150] Beginning in 1942, local Fabian Society news was listed in *FN*. Women's names were few during the war years. In 1946, however, there were thirty-four leading women's names in seventy-four items concerning locals. Locals up to 1942 were few—five or six at most. Yet the local labor organizations were very active, and women were prominent in them. Great growth in local Fabian Societies came after the re-formation in 1939. It would seem that the revived Fabian ethos rejuvenated the Party out in the provinces after the quiescence of 1931–1939.

how this tuning down, or rationalisation was applied to the coal mines by " unification," to the Capital Levy by abeyance, and even to Socialism itself by declaring it a purpose underlying a " tendency."

" Sentiment " and " Rationalisation " were not enough. A more concrete political connection between the Parliamentary Labour Party and the Trade Unions was sought. For example, Frank Hodges, leader of the Coal Miners and a man well thought of in Fabian circles, was elected to Parliament and, by the rules of the Miners' Federation of Great Britain, must resign his secretaryship of that body—but not of the International Federation which he headed. The *NS* [151] argued for a modification of the rule to allow so favorable a connection to be kept, although it also suggested relieving the incumbent of some of the work. The miners' unions, however, maintained their rule. Those who had allowed " twicers " had been ill-served, as the editor acknowledged.

So much for the survey of the political scene somewhat from the social level as Labour assumed Government in 1924. The new tranquillity had its foundation in reason. The news came as no surprise to *NS* readers that at the Pilgrim Dinner, reported by Wayfarer on February 9, 1924,[152] Mr. Kellogg placed the United States within the orbit of the " Super-State," as the *NS* termed the jurisdiction of the World Court, which had been constituted at the Hague. Kellogg had suggested an arbitration treaty, " compulsory in character and forming a model," for arbitral and judicial settlement of disputes between America and Britain. At the same time, making the reason for the " model " obvious, he revealed the American resolution to press France for the settlement of her war debt. As we turn to a review of the accomplishments of the Fabian Government, we see why its best work was within the field of foreign relations. And its successes there were to be credited to the leader whom ILP demanded in 1922, now in 1924, the Prime Minister, Ramsay MacDonald.

To summarize briefly we list those items which demonstrated the equivocal nature of the Labour Party and its dual attitudes: its character—political party or secular religion, 2) its use of do-

---

[151] *NS*, XXII (December 8, 1923), 258.
[152] *NS*, XXII (February 9, 1924), 507.

mestic when it sought foreign objectives, 3) its proclamation that conservatives forced the election while it precipitated the election itself, 4) its uses of " tranquillity " and quarrel with Curzon, 5) its dual attitude toward its own " sentimental " socialists, 7) its " constitutionalism " and destructionism, 8) its " cosmopolitanism " and unitary internationalism, 9) its double meanings for " reform " for " class " for " collectivism," 10) its ambiguity on " free trade," on tariffs, on imperialism, 11) its pretended tension between Cole-ism and Webb-ism—between No-State and All-State, 12) its seeking law to remove the rule of law. These twelve points of meditation the one word " protection " evoked.

Because the consideration of them advances the study of Fabianism in the political life of Britain, several of these points were given separate treatment : the electioneering use of class and style, the use of tariffs as a basis of inter-party understanding— England *vis-a-vis* authoritarian Europe—and the almost self-sacrificing acceptance of the role of wrecking French ascendency by Fabianism. MacDonald was the instrument of Fabianism despite his equivocal position in the Society. So was the Party. Men and Party might collapse ; Fabianism was less destructible.

H.   MacDonald and the " Sentimental Socialists "

There was a voice that cried in the wilderness for years. L. MacNeill Weir, the author of the only biography of MacDonald to which Mrs. Cole referred in her *Beatrice Webb*,[153] virulently blames MacDonald's character for the compromises which the Labour Party made during the election period, and after. Weir, although he declares that the Labour Prime Minister was still a Fabian at heart,[154] evidently cannot see that it was the presence and action of Fabianism which ghosted these compromises. It is a fact that Henderson, Thomas, and Snowden, rivals in internationalism, union leadership, and Socialism, although they were Fabians, voted against MacDonald and for Clynes for Party Leader. *Sidney Webb backed MacDonald,* whose name had been proposed

---

[153] Margaret Cole, *Beatrice Webb*, p. 162. By ignoring the works of M. A. Hamilton and Lord Elton, Mrs. Cole evinced bias.

[154] Weir, *op. cit.*, p. 40.

by Emanuel Shinwell.[155]   All the compromises MacDonald made
were those dictated by the *NS* and by Webb.   All the aspirations
he betrayed were those of the " sentimental " Socialists, like Weir:
When he decided to assume the Government, to maintain tradition
in the matter of costume, not to make a Socialist Speech from the
Throne, to muzzle the Clydesiders by warning the Tories that
" scenes " in Parliament would not be tolerated, to hold the Capital
Levy and Treaty Revision in abeyance—these were all Fabian
compromises.   Fabian Webb and the *NS* writers knew Mac-
Donald's weaknesses of character.   He had struggled for the
leadership among them, as he struggled against the ascendency of
Henderson and Snowden [156]—the former representative of Party
preference for English Trade Unionism against Clydeside shop-
stewardism; the latter, of undiluted ILP-ism against Trade Unionism.   MacDonald was immensely popular among those followers
of Keir Hardie who reverenced the great name long after losing
the non-political principles he tried to give them.   MacDonald was
always the acclaimed orator at Labour Conferences.[157]   The new
Prime Minister possessed aplomb and had entree to European
circles.   Undoubtedly, he was also the best dialectician on his feet
of all this breed of dialecticians.   He was indispensable to the
Fabians who were not noted for charm so much as for intellect.

Weir reproaches MacDonald bitterly for the treatment accorded
Henderson in the matter of Cabinet appointments.   He does not
comprehend that Fabian Major Thomson, a long-time associate
of Webb, served much more as amanuensis than merely as a golfing partner domiciled at Lossiemouth with the future Prime Minister at the time when the latter was making his Cabinet selections.
Weir cannot trace the source of the shrewdness which, he cynically
acknowledges, was manifested in the selection of names highly
representative of every constituent element of the Labour Movement, a selection which placed Fabians in vital positions in the
Ministry: Arthur Henderson became Home Secretary because he

---

[155] *Ibid.,* p. 108.   Shinwell later defeated MacDonald at Seaham in 1935.
Cf. *ibid.,* p. 527.   Seaham was Webb's bailiwick.

[156] *Ibid.,* pp. 219–221.

[157] Writing even in 1938, Mrs. Hamilton, *Henderson,* p. 370, noted that in
July of 1931, in Berlin, the " British Prime Minister made a great speech."

would not accept the original plan that he remain in self-effacement out in the constituencies in order to maintain Party machinery; Lord Olivier, Secretary for India; Lord Thomson, Secretary for Air; the Rt. Hon. Sidney Webb, President of the Board of Trade; Major Attlee, Under-Secretary for War;[158] Rt. Hon. P. Noel-Buxton, President of the Board of Agriculture; William Graham, Financial Secretary of the Treasury; Arthur Greenwood, Parliamentary Secretary to the Ministry of Health; James Stewart, Parliamentary Under-Secretary for Health for Scotland.[159] William Adamson, a Scot, was Minister of Labour. Wheatley, the Clyde leader whom Fabians tried to cultivate, was Minister for Health—a "sop," said Weir, to the Left.[160] It was to reassure the people that there should be no fear of revolution that Lord Chelmsford was made head of the Admiralty; and Lord Macmillan, Lord Advocate for Scotland. These adjustments were characteristic of Fabian tactics rather than of MacDonald's association with Liberals, for which Weir criticizes him.[161] Shaw had pointed out the uses to Fabian purposes of the leader's talents, when he had written that MacDonald had turned from a " fron-

---

[158] It was not so anomalous a thing as Weir finds it that this post was offered to Henderson, who was then seeking election, and was a pacifist. He had been in the War Cabinet and had prosecuted Kirkwood under the Defense of the Realm Act. A Fabian move most truly, had he accepted, it would have conduced to the furtherance of Labour Navy reduction plans; but Henderson declined and was elected on a revisionist platform embarrassing to the Prime Minister, to Webb, and perhaps to Mr. Shaw, who was about to settle the League of Nations, as he said himself, "I . . . proposed the arrangements effected later at Locarno." George Bernard Shaw, "Fabian Failures and Successes," *FQ,* 41 (April, 1944), Diamond Jubilee Number, page 4.

[159] *FSAR* (1924), 16. As stated above, in a move to "permeate" the Cooperatives, A. V. Alexander, Cooperative M.P., was Parliamentary Secretary to the President of the Board of Trade, Sidney Webb. The pairing of H. Morrison and MacDonald, of Thomson and MacDonald, and of Greenwood with Wheatley, also, of William Graham (Fabian) with the more ILP-minded Fabian Snowden in the Exchequer and at the Hague, are comparable examples of "permeation."

[160] Weir, *op. cit.,* p. 146.

[161] *Ibid.,* p. 51. Fabian association with Liberals is well known. In 1929–1931 a prime objective on the part of Fabians writing in *The Clarion* was divorcement from Liberals.

deur " to a " parliamentarian." The point was lost on Weir even when he cited the words from Shaw.[162]

Weir cannot grasp the sheer Fabianism which he thought was mere confusion in MacDonald's first speech as Prime Minister, January 21, 1924, in which he made a dichotomy of " nature " and " mind " in the Labour Party. He does not appreciate the effort to straddle Labour and Socialism, nor the fact that Mac-Donald was signaling to the Socialist-Labourites that Socialism was still in their " nature " and but temporarily out of " mind "; even as Fabians removed the Capital Levy from the campaigns but hoped it would be kept in the forefront in Parliament. Mac-Donald tried to allay fears of the destruction of the nation, flight of capital, and wild excitement expected by persons aware of the Socialist nature of the Party so he calmly said they did not have any socialistic behaviour " in mind." With this interpretation, let us look at the passage Weir cites in drawing the inference that MacDonald was already a traitor. The wooliness is characteristic of Fabian straddling and not of the later confusion in Mac-Donald's words due to his broken health around 1935.

> This country sooner or later has to become acquainted with the *driving hand* of Labour. . . . Stories [such] as those told by Sir Robert Horne . . . statements . . . regarding, not what is in our mind, but what is in our nature—a somewhat different thing—regarding, not what we would deliberately set out to do, but what we were bound to do by the laws of God himself—being Labour, to destroy the nation, destroy its credit . . . —the sooner that sort of thing is proved to be sheer rubbish the better it will be for everyone concerned. [With a view to the Clydesiders.] I hope that the experience which the country and the Empire are to have of a Labour Government will make it absolutely impossible for any such statements to be made or any such ideas to be held. [The Left must be quiet.] [163]

It can be taken that Sir Robert had looked into the *nature* of the Labour Movement and erroneously ascribed it to what was in the *mind* of the leaders of the Party for present action. Horne

---

[162] *Ibid.*, p. 31.
[163] *Ibid.*, p. 155. Italics are inserted.

misinterpreted their nature and overlooked their mind, and that
" mind " of Socialist leaders was one in which Trade Unions were
to be nationalized (in Shaw's strong diction) and Clydesiders were
to be controlled. " The Fabian Society exists not to furnish the
Labor [sic] Party . . . with another squad of Yesmen, but to
head off the bolts of the Labor Movement in the wrong direction,
and keep it to its vital points," Shaw wrote, looking back on this
episode of taking office.[164] Horne whose fears MacDonald would
assuage was only one of the bewildered politicians who believed
he knew the nature of Socialism. He confused the composite
mind of Labour-led-by-Socialism with the direct-actionist mind
of Trade Unionism and missed the part Fabianism played in heading off the bolts of either. The " nature " of " being Labour "
seems to have confused even MacDonald—unless one concludes
that he was revealing the exact Fabian truth: the nature of Socialism was destructive; workers had no destruction in mind. The
Continent was listening, too.

It io time to recall, ending this chapter dealing with the effect of
a spirit of internationalism imbuing the leadership of a politicized
social centre called a Third Party, that the Webb idea was an
Order, whether the Weirs, the Snowdens, the Hamiltons or the
MacDonalds knew it or not. This socio-political anomalism, half
Party, half Order, furnished the Baldwin Conservatives with a
much needed arm on the Continent in 1924. The Poincaré
Cabinet fell in May; then Herriot and MacDonald sent a joint
letter to the Marx-Stresemann Government. Opposition of the
German Nationalists to the Dawes Plan was broken.

A glance at the *NS* from April to October 1924, shows an
ascending line of success in surmounting the continental impasse,
a holding of the line in Egypt, India, Ireland; then a sickening
descent to small particulars when the Campbell case loomed like a
scarecrow on the horizon. The line of agreement ran deep.

---

[164] George Bernard Shaw, "Fabian Failures and Successes," *FQ*, 41
(April, 1944), 1–5. Shaw spells it " Labor " in 1944.

CHAPTER VIII

THE FIRST "SOCIALIST" GOVERNMENT

A. Some Effects of Politics on Socialism

The few historians who have written of the period find not much to relate. Labour, having to rely upon Liberal support, could do little to implement a programme.[1] Asquith, implored by "men, women and lunatics" to save the country from "Socialism and confiscation," kept the "two upper-class" parties from uniting and preserved the balance in the House; and, far more important, he kept the Liberals from becoming an adjunct or wing of any party, for the time at least. To Tories-for-Protection or to Labour-for-the-Capital Levy—he could deny support at any time. But he complained that the leaders of Labour expected Liberals to be hewers and drawers only; that Labourites feared fraternization —a sectarian attitude—and did not understand their minority position.[2]

Furthermore there was scant agreement among the Labour Party's constituent parts; there was only "spirit." The inherent weaknesses of a politicized socio-economic centre began to show in the antagonisms of Trade Unionists and "intellectuals"; even within these groups there existed a division between Clydesiders and English workers, between Fabian gradualists and "sentimental" Socialists inside or outside the Fabian Society.

Outside of the usual Parliamentary Party organization, the Labour Government devised a Consultative Committee[3] as liaison

---

[1] Spender and Asquith, *op. cit.*, pp. 342 f.

[2] *Ibid.*, p. 544.

[3] Mr. Henderson devised this Committee. In the 1929–1931 government its function is more notable than here. Cf. *e.g.*, Snowden, *op. cit.*, II, p. 983: "I resented deeply their [the Cabinet's] weak surrender to the dictation of the Trade Union Congress. By this action they had shown that they were not a national Party but the servants of an outside caucus." We shall see that *The Clarion* Fabians considered the Committee a device for breaking the dictatorship of the Cabinet and reasserting the initiative of Parliament.

between the Parliamentary Labour Party and the Cabinet; further-more, this Committee, or a representative from the Party in Com-mons, met with a TUC Committee at need: " In the end [Asquith] found himself powerless against the growing resentment of the House of Commons at the appearance which Ministers presented of being at the mercy of an outside and irresponsible body cor-recting and revising their decisions." [4]   The chagrin of Parliament was one thing but the effect upon democratic processes was an-other.   The more committee organization was devised, the less had rank and file persons to say; leadership in several committees might be identical, in persons or in ideas.   And when an extra-legal foregathering occurred the action could be blamed on " back-benchers."   This is what happened in the Russian Treaty and Loan Case.

Spender says the Wheatley Housing Act alone represents the Labour Government's contribution to national progress. " Poplar," [5] symbol of dilemma, showed how easily the Liberal leadership could unhorse Labour in any Parliamentary tilt—its only signifi-cance except for the demonstration it provided of vacillation between principle and practice, and the momentum given Poor Law reform which culminated only in 1927 under a Tory regime. When the time was ripe, the Campbell Case afforded the moment for Dissolution and the ensuing election was assertedly lost by

---

[4] Spender and Asquith, *op. cit.,* p. 345.

[5] Snowden, *op. cit.,* p. 630. G. Lansbury's Poplar, we have seen, marked an about face in *NS* thinking. At one time, *NS* favored national assumption of some of the onus of poor relief; now (*NS,* XXII, 529) it asked if " local democracies were to be submitted to a certain bureaucracy? " Wheatley had rescinded his cancellation of the Mond (his predecessor's) order which had passed on sur-pay to the state. Now surcharges were ac-cumulating against the Poplar Board of Guardians who were supported by the local vote in their revolt against Poor Law charges. Most of the rates, the *NS* said now for the first time, were paid by non-voters, absentee owners. Asquith had threatened to move a vote of Censure had not the Mond pro-cedure been restored. In any case, the Labour Government was protected by its earlier pronouncement that it would not resign on a " snap vote " nor vote upon a vital issue without due notice.

Lansbury's humane endeavors, raising the dole, improving work-house clothing, food, type of work and house-regulations, make a moving story. The burghers could not support in the 1920's the charges assumed in c. 1901. Cf. Lansbury, *op. cit.,* pp. 138 f.

Labour because of the Zinoviev letter and the Red Scare raised by its publication.

The story would be brief if this were all of it. But Fabians claimed to have inaugurated " administrative and financial reforms," [6] as well as to have improved relations with foreign countries. It can be conceded they made patterns and performed a rehearsal of a Labour, if not of a Socialist, Government. The improvement in foreign relations is undeniable—whether, in Asquith's phrase, due to luck or skill is disputable. Indeed, Tory politicians, if they were sure they would never need the pattern again, might boast that they used Labour to mature Conservative aims in Europe. In the effort to identify some of the " reforms " and to find the effect of attempting social welfare by political action on the part of economically conditioned groups, we examine briefly a few items in the area of domestic politics which interested Fabians.

The Wheatley Housing Bill demanded exercise of the best Labour tactics. It drew a line of tension between Fabian norms (dilution) and Trade Union monopoly (anti-diluteeism) because of the need to watch the *votes* of Labour. The Clydesider, Wheatley, a wise, experienced and popular Irishman, was given this one effective measure to handle; and the *NS* advised him weekly on procedure. According to their plans, the Local Authority, true to the principle of " decentralisation," was to handle the housing units, once built. To finance a unit the State contributed nine pounds and the Local Authority about one-half that amount in addition. The rents were to be kept at pre-war levels plus the amount necessary to keep the annual subsidy down to a little more than thirteen pounds.[7] The problem was not found in these matters but in the efforts of Mr. Wheatley to get contractors and workers to agree and the workingmen to supply enough labor by permitting " dilution," or the " open shop." The *NS* was never very positive in support of dilution despite the fact that the Webbs had written in *Industrial Democracy* in the introduction to the 1902 edition [8] that it was the " great merit " of British Trade Unionism that it had rejected the " Device of Restriction "

---

[6] *FSAR* (1924), 1.

[7] *NS,* XXIII, 146 f.

[8] Passfield, *Industrial Democracy* (London: Longmans Green and Company, 1902), liii.

and followed the "Device of the Common Rule" which was
consonant, they said, with economic science. Now, however, the
encouragement of dilution was but half-hearted.[9] At the risk of
appearing cynical, it must be observed that union men with jobs
and dwellings had votes.[10] At another time, the *NS* said [11]
Wheatley could simply go ahead and build under the old Act of
1919 and on his official authority. It would take fifteen years as
the program now stood, whereas, with more dilution of labor, the
Conservative measure would take three years. This was meant to
be a warning, no doubt, to Trade Unionists, to encourage some
compromise. The bill passed and went into effect, only to be
altered by the succeeding Tory Government. The one successful
measure was a Clydesider's triumph.[12] From the story certain
facts stand out: Trade-unionists were less benevolent, less concerned with the houseless than politicians; a labor-party is an
anomaly; "intellectual" or quasi-spiritual leadership if committed
to a Party cannot balance the demands of opposing interests without negating one or other of its principles. Fabians, as stated
above, never won Wheatley's adherence.[13]

----

[9] *NS,* XXII, 467.

[10] At this time, the *NS,* despite protestations to the contrary, was supply·
ing the need of a Party organ. It disclaims being a Fabian Society organ
but a letter from Lord Davies and statements made by Shaw in Pease's
History (Pease, *op. cit.,* p. 227) show that it was, at least in the 1920's, the
mouthpiece of leading Fabians if not the *organ* of the Society; if not a
Labour Party organ, the voice of Fabians advising the Party; if never a
Trade Unionists magazine, the bulletin of Fabian political opinion for the
Party to which unionists belonged. Davies certainly considered it a Fabian
"organ." A letter in reply from a Secretary in the *NS* editorial office stated
that the *NS* was never and is not now the organ of the Fabian Society.
This would have been true if the words Labour Party stood in place of
Fabian Society. Also, it is true of "Society" but not of "Fabians." It
made its own way financially but Fabians received it at a discount and it
printed Fabian documents and supplements.

[11] *NS,* XXIII, 242. Wheatley was also faced with "the Rings," *i.e.,*
builders' trusts. A Builders' Guild was created and died, unwept by Fabians.
It was dismissed as a good lesson for Cole. The Webbs encouraged only
consumers', not producers', cooperatives. Cf. *NS,* XXII, 498.

[12] He was not included in the next Labour Government. Cf. Snowden,
op. cit., p. 700. MacDonald detested him.

[13] The *NS* linked Wheatley's name with Webb's even while it scolded ILP
northerners for their "scene" making. Cf. *NS,* XXI (July 7, 1923), 379

The general question of housing rents drifted, then died,[14] illustrating Labour's helplessness when Liberals held a Tory view; but of greater significance is the demonstrable helplessness of Labour leaders forced to try to carry out particular union demands which were politically inexpedient: the renting and the *rentier* classes existed and voted still, although the ideological leaders spoke of liquidating them. On the other hand, there was carelessness on all sides for that class which cannot get a job— the never-employed carpenter, like the " casual " docker and the misplaced urbanized proletarian. In still another connection will be shown the inadequacy of politicized industrial democracy to compass all welfare, its perennial need to find caretakers for an unemployed segment of industrialized society, or else merely to ignore the voteless. " Rents " and " casual labour " suffered neglect because of politics, that is, because the agency to agitate reform was the agent of reform and subject to political rather than cultural social motivation. (A Culture, found in its products, results from the community's pursuit of that which it loves.)

The Home Office commenced writing a new factory bill. Henderson brought it in. Long and involved, it came too late to pass in 1924.[15] Mr. Tom Shaw, Minister for Labour, having revived the Trade Boards,[16] and having abolished the " gap " of three weeks without payment of unemployed benefits to insured persons who had already collected benefits twelve weeks longer than their contributions warranted, drafted a new Unemployment Insurance Bill.[17] This became law, raising the existing rate of benefit.[18]

The term " Unemployed workers " included those who had never worked, and the bill, when it came up, was found to have an educational clause which aimed at giving to young persons now leaving school at fourteen, in-service training instead of taking them out of the labor market by raising the school-leaving age.

---

and 382 f. This represented on the part of the Fabian publicists a direct bid to the back-benchers for cooperation.

[14] *NS,* XXII, 745, and *NS,* XXII, 146.

[15] *NS,* XXIII, 275.

[16] *NS,* XXXII, 534.

[17] *NS,* XXIII, 147.

[18] Cf. Snowden, *op. cit.,* p. 699.

The London Diarist wondered how Haldane and Trevelyan (advocates of state aid to public education) could possibly accept it,[19] representing as it did "obsolescent trade unionism."[20] Tom Shaw was not primarily interested in education. He withdrew the offending clause.[21] Not because it represents the confusion of thought on youth and unemployment, but because the leadership's growing impatience with Trade Unionism comes to the fore, is this item important. Massingham opposed with literary violence Shaw's ideas of "in-service" training—the intellectual and the union leader clashed. This Government, the former said, "was not put in to rule England in the spirit of the least enlightened Trade Unionism." It was responsible to a "progressive England" in dealing with "the children of the people."[22] Fabian thought was tutoring the Trade Unionist. Too pragmatic even for utilitarians, the Trade Unions were apparently unaware of the educational plans of Fabians.[23]

A bill of Snowden's modified the Means Limit in old age pensions, so as not to discourage savings so much as by the

---

[19] *NS,* XXIII, 218.

[20] Cf. Passfield, *Industrial Democracy,* p. 770. A corroborative section, the passage however shows the Webbs urging the policy of raising the school-leaving age and increasing technical education *in schools.* But Tom Shaw was standing on ground correctly described as "trade-unionism."

[21] *NS,* XXIII, 211.

[22] *NS,* XXIII, 188.

[23] Public education, and secularism therein, was their objective, as we shall see in another connection. Another fissure in the Party was prevented from appearing until 1929. To push their viewpoint now would jeopardize their Government as it did later; but later the cry, "Resign, Resign," could be heard and unashamedly disregarded, signifying the progress made in techniques of control.

The aims of altruism and humanitarianism are equated and identified with "Christian" in quotation marks, by Mrs. Cole in her *Education for Democracy* (London: Allen and Unwin and the Fabian Society, 1942). Social values, according to Mrs. Cole, have no relation to any "religious instruction"—again, her quotation marks—"All other roads lead to Fascism . . . decent social values can only be taught with real effectiveness in a Socialist community," p. 68. Readers should regard the semantics of "Fascism" and "medieval" with attention. The "medieval" church is now "fascist" in Fabian parlance. In 1950, it is identified with "decadent" forms of government (republics).

former method whereby an income of ten shillings a week, from whatsoever source, disqualified the aged from the full pension. The political branch was valiantly trying to cope with a societary problem, the industrially unemployed. Its every effort repeated the formulae of the " industrialised " society. Snowden's masterful analysis of the economic problem, simple as it was, proved tragically correct ten years afterward. Half the million unemployed were abnormally conditioned by the depression in three staple industries—shipbuilding, engineering, cotton—all dependent upon foreign trade, wherein exports stood at a price level ninety percent above pre-war levels and imports at only a fifty percent higher level. To sell more cheaply, costs must be lowered; but the Labour Government's effort to lower *production* costs was aimed only at *transport* costs,[24] not wages.

Labour had for agriculture only more industrial formulae. Mr. C. R. Buxton's short and efficient Agriculture Act established—of all things—County Wage Boards.[25] If friendly, these could connive with farmers to evade the law; if unfriendly, they could ruin them—something surprising only when the crude expression, " the liquidation of the kulak," is forgotten.

There were many indications of the antagonistic nature of the relationship of Fabianism to Trade Unionism. Unions left the marks of their initiative upon the Party. Of old, Snowden had thought and recorded later: " I never considered the Trade Union basis of the Labour Party as ideal." Money, they could provide, indeed, but Trade Union officials were not, he said, politicians. Of course, this was the usual Fabian attitude often stated by the *NS*;[26] but in 1924 it was personified in the Chancellor of the Exchequer and his conduct toward the TUC Members of Parliament. (Snowden seemed to disregard most Fabians save Webb, Graham, and Henderson, whom he evaluated as politicians only.) Again, Snowden thought that the Trade Union movement was too often defiant of authority. Yet others thought that trade

[24] Snowden, *op. cit.*, p. 702. The real historical mystery is that a country which controlled India, vast new provinces in Africa, Singapore, and Hong Kong generated no dynamic ideas in the face of its " surplus " shipbuilding, engineering, cotton industries.

[25] *Ibid.*, pp. 701 f.

[26] Cf. Snowden, *Autobiography,* I, pp. 224 f.

unions were too easily led:—Litvinoff had written to Tchitcherin
that they must support the *Daily Herald* which "acts as if it were
our organ," or else "it will go 'Right,' Trade Unionist." [27] In
the matter of Party discipline, the Trade Unions themselves had
once insisted that a Labour member who dissented from the majority must resign. As early as 1906, this rule was rescinded and
the "conscience clause" adopted. Snowden says the Trade
Unions then "wanted protection against being required to support
extreme socialist proposals." [28] Fabians could not have it all one
way.

Likewise indicating the tension between leaders and led, J. H.
Thomas in *My Story* [29] speaks of one of the Clydesiders, George
Buchanan, who knew the Unemployment Insurance Act most
intimately and "hated Labour's official Gang." Thomas writes
again, "in a struggle between the ordinary trade unions and the
Intellectuals, who, by the way, have become much more vocal in
recent years in proclaiming Labour's policy, Ernest Bevin can be
relied upon to let it be clearly known who pays the piper." [30] And
yet Thomas feared Bevin as a would-be dictator and tells how Ben
Tillett, Fabian and Trade Union politician, discovered Bevin and
promoted his leadership in order to have surcease from fighting
ex-Fabians Mann and Burns. Bevin, although he belonged to
"Zip", was not recorded a Fabian until 1931 when G. D. H. Cole
lists him as a founder of the New Fabian Research Bureau along
with Attlee, Cripps, Dalton, Pritt, and Henderson, "a good mixed
bag." [31] Bevin, in the 1920's the champion of unions as the Party's
subsidizers, was by 1931 one of "the Intellectuals," himself.

Weir tells in his *Tragedy* that MacDonald called the Trade

---

[27] *Ibid.*, p. 538.

[28] *Ibid.*, p. 134. The "conscience clause" served the Party in the birth
control question (*supra*) and the school question (below).

[29] Thomas, *My Story*, p. 253.

[30] *Ibid.*, pp. 277–278.

[31] Cf. Cole, *The Fabian Society Past and Present, Fabian Tract No. 258*
(London: Fabian Society, 1942), p. 13. *The Clarion's* Reporter, as it will
be seen below, tells how Bevin learned his economics on the MacMillan
Commission, 1930, and he learned at the same time not to be "apologetic"
about Socialism. D. N. Pritt was brought over to the U. S. to defend the
appeal of the eleven Communists before the Supreme Court, 1950.

Unionists " Poor Law Socialists." [32] The *NS*, which was sympathetic with the MacDonald views in most matters in 1924, also stated [33] that aims of the TUC were, the ending of the Poor Law, Unemployment Insurance, and reduced hours of labor. The last item, the *NS* said, was " impossible " as it presupposed a " new order." The inference to be taken was that the TUC must wait for Socialism to remake its world for it. Over and over again the sphere of their activity was delimited for the Trade Unions, by publicists directing that they omit political in favor of social objectives. Their money and their votes would repay the advice and direction on political questions which they received.[34]

Henderson was preparing a Franchise Bill but no particulars were vouchsafed in advance. Proportional representation was suggested as, doubtless, one of the items critics would be glad to have in advance. The *NS* said the connection was " silly." [35] But a Socialist element, of the kind that throve independent of Fabianism, was known to favor P.R., as did the Liberal Party. It would have given the latter some advantage; [36] they polled such large numbers in few constituencies that their representation in Parliament did not show their numerical strength. We have seen that Fabians rejected P.R. under the direction of Herman Finer's study. Here was a minor point of difference between sentimental Socialists, and gradualists, who were willing to work with the old political machinery.

B. FABIANS IN THE MINISTRIES

So much for the " Labour " front and the impact of political exigencies on Fabian norms in the field of reform. There is scant substantiation for the *FSAR* claims that " administrative and financial reforms " were made by the Labour Government. Nevertheless, behind the façade of " Labour " was a strong Fabian supporting structure. Although the Labour Government's efforts

---

[32] Weir, *op. cit.,* p. 396. By 1929 MacDonald was so poor a Socialist himself that he had remaining to him only the support of the unionists in the Conference.

[33] *NS*, XXII, 499.

[34] Cf. Passfield, *Industrial Democracy,* p. 839.

[35] *NS*, XXIII, 179.

[36] *NS*, XXIII, 124.

failed, the patterns for a Fabian regime were laid out. The *NS*
spoke of harmonious relationships in identifying persons charged
with the Ministries, and said nothing of their Fabianism. The
Fabian Society Annual Report of March, 1924, did not identify
the Fabians in office, save as five in the Cabinet and " as many " in
minor Ministries. Occasionally, *Fabian News* took notice of
Fabians in office under " Personal Notes." Twenty-two Fabians
were elected to Parliament.[37] *Fabian News* announced a testimonial. dinner for the elected Fabians, the expectation that R. H.
Tawney would be Chairman, and that the five members of the
Society who were Cabinet Ministers would attend; but with
studied disregard for an axiom of chronicle writing, it omitted
their names, which were Olivier, Thomson, Webb, Henderson
and Snowden.[38] In the *Fabian News* it was stated under " Per-
sonal Notes " that Dr. Somerville Hastings and Miss Susan
Lawrence had become Parliamentary Private Secretaries to the
Minister of Education (Mr. Charles P. Trevelyan, not named).[39]
Fabian Margaret Bondfield was Under-Secretary of State for
Labour, Fabian Colonel T. S. B. Williams became Parliamentary
Private Secretary to the Board of Trade, whose head was Mr.
Webb. At this time, a link which became a permanent association
was formed between a Cooperator and Fabian-Labour when A. V.
Alexander, who was head of the Cooperative Party, became also
Parliamentary Private Secretary to Mr. Webb; likewise, Fabians
Dr. L. Haden Guest and Arthur Greenwood, to the Minister of
Health, Clydeside leader John Wheatley; and Fabian Ernest
Thurtle, who was married to one of George Lansbury's daughters,

---

[37] A Fabian, Pethick-Lawrence, obtained the seat for Leicester previously
held by another Labourite. *FN* did not gloat over the fact that the second
of the defeated candidates was Winston Churchill. Cf. *FN*, XXV:1
(January, 1924).

[38] Evening dress was optional and vegetarians were to state their require-
ment on their application. There is so much ado about these matters that
one interpreting their spirit must notice such minutiae, as indicative of a
meticulous kindness characteristic of this secular " religious order."

[39] Close to Mrs. Webb but not often listed as an active Fabian, as far as
can be ascertained, he was more radical and austere than most Fabians.
Cf. Samuel, *Grooves of Change,* p. 346 f, where Beatrice writes of their
travels together and Trevelyan's " living philosophy of Soviet Communism,"
and his austerity.

to the Minister of Pensions, Mr. F. O. Roberts.[40] The Clydesider, John Muir, was Fabian Thurtles' colleague in Roberts' office. Here were three offices where non-Fabians, however amenable to Fabian guidance, were further offset by Fabians. Two Fabians to help Mrs. Webb's protégé, Trevelyan; Williams to balance Alexander in Webb's domain; Fabians Guest and Greenwood to assist Wheatley and doubly Fabian Thurtle to balance the more radical Muir in the kindly Roberts' office. Another source reveals that Fabian Noel-Baker was Parliamentary Private Secretary to Lord Parmoor.[41] Fabian William Graham, Financial Secretary of the Treasury was at Snowden's side in Parliament. Discreet, infallible on figures, he was indispenable to his chief.[42] Fabian Josiah Wedgwood was Chancellor of the Duchy of Lancaster, a sinecure.

A little more information in the way of some names without their official connection, came with the chronicle of the dinner in *Fabian News,* Tawney presiding.[43] Over two hundred members had heard Miss Lawrence toast the Government; Henderson, the Party Whip,[44] and Lord Olivier, Secretary of State for India, replied. Lord Thomson, Minister for Air, replied to St. John Ervine's toast to the evening's guests, one of whom having been received with musical honors, Sidney Webb (Board of Trade), responded to W. S. Sander's toast to the Fabian Society, as also did Edward Pease, founder and historian.[45] Major C. R. Attlee,

---

[40] Alexander and Roberts appear on Fabians' lists after this date.

[41] Parmoor (Lord, Charles Alfred Cripps), *A Retrospect* (London: William Heinemann, 1936), p. 196.

[42] Snowden, *op. cit.,* II, Index; fifteen entries under Graham, all laudatory, p. 1089.

[43] He had lectured in January in the King's Hall (Fabian) Series on the need for an international authority, a redefining of the State in terms connoting the end of State sovereignty. Then Mr. Mosley had presided. See, *FN,* XXXV:1 (January, 1924). The Series was on "Civilization" which Mr. Webb then defined as "society with a surplus productivity" (*Ibid.*). The attack on "Sovereignty" was launched simultaneously with assertions everywhere of a stronger Statism and a merely functional definition of human life.

[44] Although temporarily out of Parliament, he had for lieutenant in Parliament as Assistant Whip, Fabian Ben Spoor, a Protestant minister.

[45] His son, also a Fabian, was married to Marjorie Wedgwood, daughter of Fabian Colonel Josiah Wedgwood.

a Parliamentary Secretary to the Prime Minister (offsetting Weir), proposed the Chairman. Noted for unavoidable absence were C. R. Buxton, Minister for Agriculture, Arthur Greenwood, Parliamentary Secretary to the Minister for Health, and James Stewart, the one Fabian Clydesider.[46]

Evidently, the Chancellor of the Exchequer, whom Pease listed before 1914, was not in good standing. His lameness may have precluded social activities. Mrs. Snowden was an active campaigner for Socialism and a Fabian of prominence. The future Lord Snowden was more ILP than Fabian. About one-third the total ILP membership was not Fabian,[47] but the Snowdens had met at a Fabian Society meeting. Snowden was to resign from the ILP in 1927 since it was then drifting, he said, from " evolutionary Socialism into revolutionary Socialism." [48]

Snowden speaks of the Trade Unionists' dissatisfaction with the fact that out of twenty Cabinet members, thirteen belonged to the non-Trade Union section of the Party; only seven were Trade Unionists. He does not name them but they were: J. R. Clynes,

---

[46] Nowhere can a list be had directly stating Fabian membership or offices. The Society cannot supply a list. Mrs. Cole suggested the writer might be supplied with old *Annual Reports* from Dartmouth 11, SW, London, but these are to be found in the. Library of Congress. The writer has made one from election lists, and " personal notes " published in *FN* and obituary notices in *FSAR*. Two letters, one from Mrs. Cole, another from a secretary, Eve Saville, indicate that even the Society has not complete files or rosters, and Miss Saville expressed surprise to find certain names *not* in their files, *e.g.*, that of Aneurin Bevan and Alfred Spender.

[47] Cf. Pease, *op. cit.*, who gives this proportion of ILP to Fabian.

[48] Snowden, *Autobiography* II, p. 746. His objection to the ILP drift puts him on the side of Fabians in principle. His autobiography shows deep appreciation of Webb and friendship with both Sidney and Beatrice who were first to propose Snowden's going into Lords in 1931. Cf. Snowden, *op. cit.*, p. 927. His closest associate in these days was to be William Graham, a prominent Fabian and economist who was at his side in the Exchequer and at Geneva. Mr. Graham was unstintingly praised by Snowden, (*ibid.*, pp. 654, 924) until 1931 (*ibid.*, p. 974). Mr. Graham figures prominently in the story of the period as told by Mr. J. H. Thomas as well as by Viscount Snowden. Incidentally, Mr. Graham's election manager, Fabian Mr. Job Gill, was a prominent Freemason, Oddfellow, and Quaker, up to his death in 1923. Fabian Clifford Allen (later Lord Allen) married Mr. Gill's daughter.

Hon. President of the National Union of General and Municipal Workers, formerly a " piecer "; J. H. Thomas, a president of the I.F.T.U., formerly an engine driver, now head of NUR; Tom Shaw, Secretary of the International Federation of Textile Workers, once a weaver; William Adamson, General Secretary of three divisions of Scottish Miners' Associations, formerly Chairman of the Parliamentary Labor Party, 1919–1921; John Wheatley, an organizer and laborer in Clydeside foundries, Stephen Walsh, a Clyde workman, ranking leader with Clynes in 1918–1922; Vernon Hartshorn.[49] The last named was one who was greatly respected in labor circles. It must be recalled he was President of the South Wales Miners' Federation and Sidney Webb, who represented Seaham in Durham County, a coal-mining constituency, was the author of the *Story of Coal* (1924),[50] and had served for the coal miners on the Royal Commission which issued the Sankey Report. Hartshorn became a member of the Privy Council in 1924 and was Postmaster General that year. Undoubtedly he was a Webb " find." He was very popular and guided the miners away from radicalism. Along with Hodge of the steel mills (he was not in the Cabinet—probably steel workers were too capitalistic), Thomas, the socially popular railway engineer, and Clynes, the diminutive former mill piecer, had all been with Henderson as far back as 1903 in LRC.[51] They now continued to head their organizations, outside of their Parliamentary work. They were associated with Fabians, through Henderson, who in 1924 gave over the Secretaryship of the Party to Fabian James Middleton, and through Webb, who in 1923 was Chairman of the Labour Conference. Both Webb and Henderson knew the political acumen of the leaders and the strength of the demand for recognition of their followers. The TU segment of the Cabinet was more a Henderson construct than a Webb one. Where Snowden, the ardent Socialist, disagreed with Fabian Henderson's " we must take the Trade Union movement with us," [52] Webb simply

---

[49] Snowden, *op. cit.,* p. 606.

[50] *NS*, XXII, p. 771.

[51] Hamilton, *op. cit.,* p. 40. Snowden said Frank Hodges' " great ability was wasted " by his appointment as Civil Head of the Admiralty.

[52] Snowden, *op. cit.,* p. 958.

warped Labour into the Socialist Movement without philosophical quibble. The policy took toll in 1931. The rest of the Cabinet and some names of lower rank show Webb's influence the more powerful.

The surprise reported in the *NS* concerning the appointment of Lord Olivier could not have been shared by those who knew the history of the Fabian Society.[53] He was one of the original Essayists. He was no " dark horse" but obviously the right person for the India Office by reason of his experience in colonial affairs. A literateur in his own right, he collaborated with Webb in a book, *Socialism and the Individual.* Shaw credited Olivier with being a lone exception to the general Philistinism of Fabians.

Lord Chelmsford was a former Viceroy of India. Snowden[54] believed he was not even then a member of the Party. His religious connections may have associated him with Parmoor. He was among other such things a Knight of Justice of St. John, Jerusalem-in-England. He had been on the London School Board, 1900–1904, during the Webb controversy with Wallas over subsidizing non-provided schools and he had been a London County Councillor, 1904–1905, and Alderman in 1913. Service in Queensland and in New South Wales preceded his India service. Webb was formerly a clerk in the Colonial Office, it will be recalled; Webb also had long experience in the London County Council. The reason for this *Unionist Party* liberal finding his place as First Lord of the Admiralty is easily perceived. It is a little more difficult to find a reason for the assignment of Fabian Frank Hodges of the Steelworkers to the Admiralty—save for the question of the few cruisers abuilding—because the Fabian Government " sank the Navy."

Snowden[55] is confused also as to Haldane's nomination. Miss Naomi Haldane (later Mrs. Mitchison) was prominent in the

---

[53] *NS*, XXII, 438.

[54] Snowden, *op. cit.,* p. 607; and Francis Williams, *Fifty Years' March,* p. 304, where he blames MacDonald's poor choice on his " congenital lack of faith in the ability of his political colleagues." But Williams did not know, it seems, that the Fabian Brigadier General Thomson was MacDonald's " golfing partner " when he made the Cabinet list.

[55] Snowden, *op. cit.,* p. 607.

Fabian Women's Group and Lord Haldane, her father, was a close personal friend of the Webbs. Snowden does not know that Haldane became a member of the Labour Party in 1920 convinced about " Nationalisation " by war-time experience. Haldane, upon his death, was said in the *Fabian News* to have been for a long time a member of the Society.[56] His sympathies with the best in German thought and culture were well known. He was a perfect complement for Parmoor whom he had sponsored earlier for a peerage, in order to procure Parmoor's talent for the Judicial Committee of the Privy Council.

Snowden thinks Brigadier General Thomson came into the Socialist Movement through the War. He seems not to know the place of the Brigadier General in Fabian history,[57] nor his close association with MacDonald during the Cabinet-making days at Lossiemouth. The loyal Fabian had been defeated for Parliament but was made a peer. At it were, *per saltum,* Olivier, Thomson and Arnold, all Fabians, the latter Under-secretary of State for Colonies, were elevated to the Cabinet. Having never held elective office, they attained their Cabinet status by way of being given peerages.

Snowden accounts Parmoor a recent recruit to Labour. Parmoor says it was the Labour Party's stand on Revision and the like international principles which claimed his adherence.[58] He was also one of those who believed as MacDonald did—or preached—that Christianity led to Socialism, one the outcome of the other.[59] Parmoor's first wife, the mother of five children the oldest of whom was Stafford Cripps, was a sister of Beatrice Webb. Another sister, Lady Kate Courtney, campaigned actively for the then Mr. Cripps (*père*) for Parliament. At Lady Court-

---

[56] *FN,* XXXIX (September 9, 1928).

[57] Cf. Pease, *op. cit.,* p. 266.

[58] Parmoor, *op. cit.,* pp. 188 f.

[59] Cf. *ibid.,* p. 195, citing MacDonald's speech at Brighton Free Church in March, 1924. Cf. also, Lord (Henry) Snell, *Men, Movements and Myself* (London: J. M. Dent and Sons, 1936), pp. 111–120, where this secularist writes: " I has been my privilege to see the ecclesiastical mind [Church of England—not non-conformist] change from unconcealed horror of what they thought the word Socialism involved, to an understanding tolerance, if not approval of Socialist principles."

ney's Cheyne Walk house, he met the MacDonalds [60] and the Hendersons.[61]   He had been associated with the Webbs and Mrs. C. R. Buxton along with Dr. G. P. Gooch and C. P. Scott of the *Manchester Guardian* in the cause of a just peace in 1919.[62]   The Parmoor estate became the rendezvous for many of the great names in "the Movement" and for visitors such as the German delegation to the London Conference [63] to discuss, for one example, Germany's joining the League.   Haldane, as Chancellor, in Asquith's Premiership in 1913, pressed Parmoor's acceptance of a peerage.   Parmoor possessed talent and connections and idealisms like Haldane's; and, temperamentally, he was well-suited to the House of Lords.   And then, for the Potter ladies, especially Kate Courtney, it would have been a task at every election to get him elected.   Snowden in surprise at Parmoor's inclusion says he was "a high Tory and a devoted Churchman—the last man in the world one would expect to ever become identified with the Socialist Movement."   To this, rejoinder is found in Parmoor's *Retrospect:* Upon his Bishop's advice, he contributed his support to Labour and not to Socialism and he eschewed the principle of "delegacy," *i.e.,* Parmoor, like Slesser, considered his vote his own and not to be cast by dictation from the Party caucus or TUC conference.[64] He had been a Liberal-Unionist but had changed his views regarding Ireland to conform with the Fabian persuasion; and in doing so, cited St. Thomas More for a precedent on changing one's mind.   He was so scrupulous as to consult his Bishop on Socialism and was reassured that while the Socialist view on property was heretical, he might collaborate in the Government in order to do good especially in the judicial and international fields.[65] The Bishop said that hitherto society's leaders had not had faith, had not believed in the eternal principle which makes "what is

---

[60] Parmoor, *op. cit.,* p. 187.

[61] *Ibid.,* p. 226.   The Potter girls' cousin was Mary Macauley, wife of Charles Booth.

[62] *Ibid.,* p. 142.   The elder (Sydney) Buxton had collaborated with Cardinal Manning to effect the successful outcome of the Dock Strike led by Ben Tillett.   Cf. Snell, *op. cit.,* p. 107.

[63] Parmoor, *op. cit.,* pp. 201 and 206.

[64] *Ibid.,* pp. 193 f.   John Scurr was disciplined for exercising such self-will.

[65] Snowden, *op. cit.,* p. 193.

expedient also right," [*sic!*]. Parmoor was given for his guide, Philip Noel-Baker,[66] a Fabian who had had some experience at Geneva in the League of Nations Secretariat. Parmoor, as Lord President, was charged with League of Nations' affairs and given a " special room " in Sir Eyre Crowe's office and Noel-Baker " was allotted on the first floor of the Foreign Office."

Snowden makes no mention of the fact that Fabian Lord Ponsonby was named Under-Secretary of State for Foreign Affairs, a position in which he was to do notable if unsuccessful work on the Russian question. His *Now is The Time* [67] appeared in 1925. In writing it, Ponsonby was assisted by Mrs. Swanwich, a prominent Fabian woman associated with Henderson and Parmoor at Geneva [68] and Clifford Allen (later Lord Allen, after 1931 when he followed MacDonald) who was once (1912) a member of the Fabian Executive. A journalist (*Daily Citizen* and *New Leader*) and a Conscientious Objector, Allen was associated with Mr. Webb, Henderson and Tom Shaw among others in creating the new International in 1923.[69] Therefore, the collective opinion of Fabians Ponsonby, Swanwich and Allen would be as it read in 1925 :

> The doctrines of Socialism, which are going forward, should always be shown to be indissolubly linked with Internationalism, disarmament and peace; and conversely, it must be shown that none of these latter can be permanently established except on the basis of a Socialist society.[70]

This was the same viewpoint Webb expressed on the domestic side : Only Socialism will do. Ponsonby's thesis was : Authority, in a Great Conspiracy, " popularizes war." Socialism must assume authority and make war unpopular and impossible. This was the man and these his ideas and associates standing nearest Mac-Donald in the Foreign Office. Not to be forgotten, however, was

---

[66] Parmoor, *op. cit.,* p. 196. Among his publications, Noel-Baker lists *The Geneva Protocol,* 1925.

[67] Ponsonby, *Now is The Time* (London: Leonard Parsons, 1925).

[68] Parmoor, *op. cit.,* p. 233, and Hamilton, *op. cit.,* p. 250.

[69] Brand, *op. cit.,* p. 229.

[70] Ponsonby, *op. cit.,* p. 187.

the civil servant, Sir Eyre Crowe. Weir thought Sir Eyre agreed
with MacDonald; Snowden and Parmoor said he did not.

Four or five other names are significant. Snowden did not
know why Lansbury was left out. The ex-mayor (1919–1920)
was the present M.P. for Poplar. Snowden later noted that Lansbury was stigmatized by " Poplarism " at the time (1924).[71] That
Emanuel Shinwell, National Organizer and Parliamentary Agent
of the Amalgamated Marine Workers' Union—he had never been
a laboring " marine worker "—was now Parliamentary Secretary
to the Department of Mines is overlooked by Mr. Snowden.[72]
This was the time that " Labour's latest and not least promising
recruit " joined the Party and the Fabian Society, only to become
a protégé of MacDonald and a thorn in the side of Thomas.
Oswald Mosley's appearance with John Strachey as his ghost
caused an historical repetition of the Wellsian episode and likewise left its mark on the Society. This rich man who came into
the Movement and tried to change it disgusted Snowden. On
April 5, 1924, he was hailed in the *NS* as a " sane idealist." [73]

Sir Patrick Hastings will be found the Attorney General in the
Campbell case. The *Fabian News* in December, 1923, listed him
K.C., M.P., as a Chairman of one of the King's Hall (Fabian)
Lectures.[74] Henry H. Slesser, who had drafted the early Poor
Law measure at the time of Beatrice's " crusade," was a legal
authority indispensable to the Party but was *persona non grata* to
MacDonald. He should have outranked Hastings but the latter's
amenability was such that it might be construed as complacency

---

[71] Snowden, *op. cit.*, p. 760.

[72] *NS*, XXIII, 54. He was destined much later to defeat MacDonald in
Sidney Webb's constituency, Seaham in South Durham. The *NS* advised
the " reorganisation of the whole system of coal supply " in reporting the
questionnaire sent out by Mr. Shinwell; it advocated (*NS*, XXIII, 87)
" unification " in the matter of the mining industry which would end in
nationlisation. It advised Fabian Shinwell " nothing in the coal industry
corresponds to the economic views of the agricultural producer " (*NS*,
XXIII, 87). (It would be well if Fabianism exempted agriculture from the
industrial producers' apparatus, as it exempts coal from economics based
upon " marginal values.")

[73] *NS*, XXII, 74 and 756.

[74] *FN*, XXXIV :12 (December 12, 1923).

with the Fabian views.[75] It was undoubtedly Webb who, in spite of MacDonald, arranged for Slesser's appointment as Solicitor. This former Fabian had an enviable record as a labor lawyer and an authority on Trade Union law. Slesser wrote that " it had become [1919] a matter almost of instinct to frame any proposal whatever for the reformation of earth or heaven in Parliamentary language." [76]

In choosing an ambassador, theory clashed with utility. The *NS* was reluctant to agree to Sir James O'Grady's being appointed,[77] as it was supposed he would be, to Russia as the first English ambassador. Weir was chagrined that O'Grady was not appointed. O'Grady was the choice of the " sentimental " Socialist, not the Fabian type.[78] So, again we see the enthusiasts under tutelage to a pragmatic and controlling intellectualism. O'Grady became Governor of Tasmania. Ex-Fabian Slesser,

---

[75] Hastings did not serve in 1929. Slesser then went " on the bench " into the rare judicial atmosphere above politics to replace Lord Sankey in 1929. Webb was still loyal to a good labor lawyer.

[76] Cf. Sir Henry Slesser, *Judgment Reserved* (London : Hutchinson and Company, 1941), p. 69.

[77] *NS*, XXII, 497. The *NS* pleaded inconsistently against spoils-system appointments. O'Grady figures in the narratives of various pilgrims to Moscow, serving as it were " the Finland Station " literally and figuratively.

[78] In this connection, the name of ex-Fabian Herman Slesser usually cropped up as an alternative. After he became Solicitor General he was seldom conversant with MacDonald's thought. Cf. Slesser, *op. cit.,* p. 108. The future was to find him a Catholic convert, and a critic of Fabian Socialism. Slesser narrates in his *Judgment Reserved* that because O'Grady, his friend, was sent to Tasmania (Weir makes bitter reflections on this lowly assignment) he, Slesser, was enabled to obtain a seat in Parliament for O'Grady's constituency. Slesser was enlightened by Sidney Webb as to the reason why he had been asked to take silk at an unusual time. He had been baffled and so consulted Webb only to learn it was the necessary step toward nomination as H.M.'s Solicitor General. Slesser records that many persons like O'Grady seem to have been promised positions in the Government and found themselves excluded or shunted about like the latter. Evidently, Webb had some trouble managing everything with MacDonald. The latter surely never appreciated Slesser, but Webb knew his value as a successful solicitor and Trade Union lawyer regardless of the fact that Slesser had quit the Fabians in 1915—one of the few who withdrew because of disagreement upon the philosophical basis of Fabianism.

Webb's friend, obtained O'Grady's seat in Parliament and became Solicitor General.

Harry Gosling, who boasts in *Who's Who* of his apprenticeship (under father and grandfather) as waterman and lighterman, was named Minister of Transport and Paymaster General in Mac-Donald's Government. That he was President of the Transport and General Workers' Union could explain his selection, but not so interestingly as the fact that he had been on the London County Council from 1898 to 1919 for one division and until 1925 for another. This indicates early and long association with Webb, Tawney, Susan Lawrence, and A. E. Davies. He was to reorganize London Transportation even though he entered upon his term of office faced with a long hard bus strike. He prepared and got passed his London Traffic Bill, acting with his customary " sweet reasonableness " and with " complete knowledge " of London's problem, as Snowden narrates.[79]

Fabian Hamilton Fyfe, novelist, playwright, and propagandist, now became editor by special request of the *Daily Herald,* the TUC and Labour Daily organ. A Lecturer on Spain and on the Russian Revolution of 1917, in 1917, 1918, and 1922, Fyfe traveled all over Britain talking on the topic, " The Meaning of the World Revolution of 1919." His name is found in sympathetic association with Fabians in the *Fabian News.* His sympathies were entirely Socialist, although he was the biographer of Lord Northcliffe.

At this time, a change not easily detectable took place in the *NS* attitude toward France. Sisley Huddleston, having long experience as a correspondent in France for the *Times,* joined the *NS* staff. He was the author of *The Labour Who's Who;* [80] and he wrote for American periodicals among which were *The New Republic* and *The Atlantic Monthly.* He was the biographer of Poincaré. It was not widely known that Robert Dell had been expelled from France for publishing the story of the Austrian Emperor's peace offer in 1918, of which President Wilson had not been apprised. It would seem that enlisting Huddleston as a weekly contributor was an indication on the part of the *NS* of a

---

[79] Cf. Snowden, *op. cit.,* p. 705.
[80] *NS,* XXII, 449 and *Ibid.,* 459.

changing attitude toward France. Huddleston wrote sympathetically of *le beau pays*.

It is no wonder that Sidney Webb, alone of all the Fabian members of the Government, was received with musical honors at the Fabian testimonial dinner. Only Fabians could know how truly the Government was a Webb construct. The seams and splices of the Party needed constant care if not repair, notwithstanding. Symbolic of the problem: No Fabian organ publicized the fact that Arthur J. Balfour in 1924 accepted Webb's invitation to head his Committee on British Trade and Industry. TUGC boycotted it and so rendered nugatory its belated report in 1929.[81] But for Webb this was not a problem but a demonstration. Fabianism must reduce the liberals, the industries and the unions.

The *NS*, fully subservient to the spirit of expediency and gradualism, counseled self-control to ILP members, and to Pacifists; "every sensible Socialist is an opportunist." This reads like Webb's own formula, "every instructed person." A debate on "the delicate problem of socialism" under the Chairmanship of Fabian Clifford Sharp[82] was reported as "MacDonald and the ILP" in April, 1924.[83] Fabian F. W. Jowett, Minister of Works, against the pacifists' contention that now was the time to put on the full Socialist program, said that at the time total disarmament, for example, would destroy the Government and produce a militarist reaction. Agreeing, the *NS* added that the Government, as a minority Government, had no right to impose a Socialist program now; MacDonald's "bookish association" with Socialists left him still with a preference for the term "Labour"; paramount were the "national" issues, not Party issues.[84] Their problem, the editor said, was France and Germany, and it was no good "whistling in a graveyard." But this was exactly what the

---

[81] Hamilton, *Sidney and Beatrice Webb*, pp. 269 f. Balfour's political "philosophical doubt" accounts for his becoming a symbol of the development of Socialism out of Liberalism. Cf. Dugdale, *op. cit.*, II, p. 316 to end.

[82] Clifford Sharp died in 1935, having served on *NS* since 1913. Kingsley Martin succeeded him as editor.

[83] *NS*, XXIII, 56.

[84] This was a point which the bitter Weir missed in his tracing of the word "national" in MacDonald's semantics.

NS was doing when it said that ILP had no desire to thwart MacDonald. Earlier, in apparent tongue-in-cheek flattery offered to Trade Unionists, the *NS* had boasted [85] of MacDonald's " intercourse with representative men " and asked, rhetorically, who might know more about England than Mr. Webb, Mr. Hartshorn, Mr. [Tom] Shaw, Mr. Clynes, Mr. Hodges, a group whom even non-Laborites considered " interesting and of high political value," men who had spent most of their lives in " social administration." Thus, the *NS* coined a new term for the function of trade union officials—" social administration." The names selected were Labour Conference names, skimmed off TU Congress lists, wherein Webb bestrode like a colossus the two elements, Fabianism and Trade Unionism. " Pure " Socialism was not represented in this *NS* list.[86] Palpable persuasion as this *NS* listing was, it dissembled the " intellectual " structure of the Government, revealing only the Trade Unionist front, which the Prime Minister, it was said, supplied in " psychological things," with a " superior psychological insight." [87]

C. " PROGRESS " AND CONTRADICTIONS

There were two reports of progress,[88] one after three weeks, and the other after three months: " Three Weeks Work " listed 1) the " Geddes Ax " of economy and job-insecurity lifted from the necks of Civil Servants, 2) Trades Boards revived, 3) the eight-hour day established by the Washington Convention through Margaret Bondfield's efforts (not adopted), 4) Mr. Wheatley's success in settling the Poplar problem so that the way was open to " effective welfare services by local authorities with the aid and sympathy of the Central Government," [89] 5) in time housing-building would start; consultation of " master builders and operators " had begun, 6) Mr. F. O. Roberts in the Pensions Ministry

---

[85] *NS*, XXII, 507.

[86] *NS*, XXII, 534.

[87] *NS*, XXII, 533. Weir *passim* is severely critical of the claim for superior insight made for MacDonald.

[88] *NS*, XXII, 534, and *NS*, XXIII, 56.

[89] This was a promise only. The Poor Law was destined to be changed by a succeeding Tory regime. Cf. Feiling, *Neville Chamberlain*, pp. 126–148.

was to be counted upon to have humanity and common sense. It was not reported that his trade was printing and his status that of Honorary Life Vice-President of the Northampton Labour Party and that his Undersecretary was John Muir, the former editor of the Clyde Workers' news organ.[90] Muir's being placed in the Pensions Office was a tactical move as he represented not the intelligentsia nor the Trade Unionist, but the Guild and shop-steward mentality of the Clyde. Men like Kirkwood and Stewart had demonstrated effective charity and justice in their stormy defense of the workless and evicted in Glasgow. Muir, like Wheatley, had no great love for British Trade Unionism. A sentence in Kirkwood's *Life of Revolt*, " the out-and-out Trade Unionists attacked him [Wheatley] for having agreed to dilution [Wheatley's scheme]," [91] indicates the fissure in Party construction which had to be covered if not filled in. Public commentary showed only the smooth side. But the Party policy makers had been embarrassed already by ILP forthrightness. Shortly after the Government was formed,[92] Churchill had been gored to bovine vocality against the Red Flag Song and the Internationale when the heroic John Muir had made a speech in Commons against private ownership. The Webb-MacDonald problem, keeping enthusiastic Socialists under control from political necessity, is understandable and the sixth item was meant to be reassuring to the readers of *NS* that Roberts would be efficient in the pensions office even if Muir caused trouble. It was hard, however, to keep the Labour front intact, even though the *NS* reassured the public that 7) France, Cologne, India and the City were beneficiaries of the new stabilizing of politics and economics. This, of course, was ephemeral, one of those " psychological things " commanded by MacDonald's " psychological insight " and managed by the *NS*. It was true enough that the European situation was bettering. The ensuing chapter attempts to assay the contribution of

---

[90] Wheatley, Kirkwood, and Rosslyn Mitchell knew who wrote the article for which John Muir, along with Bell and Gallacher, went to prison during the war, when Henderson, striving to anglicize the unionism of the Clyde, was working close beside Lloyd George.

[91] Kirkwood, *op. cit.,* p. 118.

[92] *NS*, XXII, 720. Clynes naively believed they had to get out Whitaker's *Almanac* to learn what posts to fill. Ever since 1924, Whitaker's carries a notice that offices of the Royal Household are left to the King's choice.

Labour to that amelioration. In the precipitation of certain measurable results which crystallized in amorphous European politics,
Fabian gradualism served as a catalyst; but the claims made by
this first report were supported by prophecy and hope rather
than fact.

The second report, on the eve of Snowden's Budget message,
was more heartening still to those whose aim was the destruction
of the old order: 1) They had achieved peace with Russia—*de
jure* recognition; 2) the "atmosphere" in Europe was better;
3) the "white elephant" of Singapore had been abandoned;
4) the military services had been wisely dealt with, that is, cut
back ruthlessly. In this connection, some characteristic inconsistencies must be remarked: Admiral Beatty, whom they would
have allowed to resign over the Singapore and the cruiser questions, said to Mr. Thomas, "You know, Jim, you politicians are
going to land us in a hole before long, and we shall pay dearly for
your milk and water policy!" Thomas' answer had the Fabian
ring; munitions are costly, money were better spent in social
services.[93] It was also usual for Fabian thinking to disparage
the armed services as mere social ornaments.[94] Five cruisers were
abuilding, however, justified by need for employment and the
threat that a projected Franco-Italian alliance would close the
Mediterranean and sever the Greeks. To answer the charge that
Russia was building up a navy, it was said this was but for her
own security. The fifth and sixth points again were ephemeral:
Progress was reported on unemployment, housing, agriculture and
education.[95] It was said new services create new markets; so
plans were afoot for electrical development under national or
regional control—not in private hands—for railroad expansion,[96]
for school buildings, roads and bridges (municipally regulated
under a uniform law). The Poor Law was to be replaced by
amending the Unemployment Insurance Act. (This Neville
Chamberlain achieved in 1928.)

Each item, above named, posed an insuperable problem caused

---

[93] Cf. Thomas, *op. cit.*, p. 221, and *NS*, XXII, 616.

[94] *NS*, XXII, 558.

[95] Trevelyan and Ellen Wilkinson were sternly bent on closing inefficient
non-provided schools. There were too few of any kind.

[96] Clynes, *op. cit.*, II, p. 43.

in each case by the uniform solution which Socialists attempted, that is, industrialization: 1) In the question of employment, the residuum of potential " dilutees " or casual laborers (as in the current Dock strikes) ;[97] 2) in housing, the relation of Central to Local Authority, like the problem of " Poplarism "; 3) in agriculture, the threat from the middleman or from government planning, which made " big business " out of agriculture, hitherto a way of life. The *NS* was " sick of waiting for the farmer to make it possible for the government to help him." [98] There is more to be said on these last ephemeral gains, agricultural and educational.

Noel-Buxton brought in an Agricultural Wages Bill upon which the *NS* commented, presuming as usual that its readers were aware of the proposed legislation and of most of its provisions— which again indicates the level of literacy assumed of its readers by the *NS*. It appears from the remarks of the editor that farmers, owners as well as renters, were practicing *laissez-faire* and not cultivating all the arable land possible, governing themselves by the rule of price based on scarcity and surrendering themselves to the tyranny of Covent Garden and United Dairies (middlemen). The reformers suggested a County Control Board and a Wages Board to administer respectively state subsidies for cultivation and minimum wages for workers.[99] The private good of the farmer was not listed as an objective, nor was the development of agriculture as a way of life projected. In the background of Fabian criticism runs an unspoken hint to farmers to collectivize, voluntarily. The *NS* editor disapproved a suggested tax on imported barley which was meant to encourage planting; likewise, the proposal to subsidize increased cultivation. He hoped Buxton would be firm against encouraging County rather than National

---

[97] The editor of the *NS* supported Bevin who had a jurisdictional strike on his hands at the Docks. Cf. *NS*, XXII, 558. *NS* proposed " blue-ticketing " to control casual labour; appealing to the authority of Mr. William Beveridge, it was urged that all casual labor be abolished in all industries. Cf. *NS*, XXII, 590. No dilution here. " Decasualisation " was urged—and one big union. Cf. *NS*, XXII, 439.—Industrialized democracy was perennially faced with the problem of the urbanized unemployed.

[98] *NS*, XXII, 244.

[99] *NS*, XXIII, 244.

control, because individuals, he said, could not "stand up" to a local board. It is notable that this is the opposite principle from the Housing Act procedures and contrary to the usual encouragement of local control. The *NS* supported the proposition of a Wages Board (this could break a farmer, of course, if he didn't "do something" about a money crop); and it advocated the organizing of Cooperatives.[100] That Cooperatives would be guided by national directives, and politicized,[101] goes without saying.

In regard to policy in the field of education it has been shown that Trade Unionists and Fabian thinkers differed; but the industrial labor market dictated the methods of both sides. Propaganda for industrial democracy should enrich the curriculum envisioned by the latter, while in-service training to delay new workers from reaching the labor market would satisfy the former. Outside of the educational sphere, the *NS* approved of Trade Union policy; for, discussing industrial revival, it stressed not "relief" but training-in-service of the *never employed*. It was admitted this constituted dilution; but that was necessary, especially in the Housing program.[102]

A strike wave set in but in no case was the anomaly of "Labour" governing more patent than when the Vienna State Opera Company visited England only to find that the musician's

---

[100] *NS*, XXIII, 211.

[101] *Agriculture and The Labour Party, Fabian Tract No. 228*, by G. T. Garratt, a Fabian, appeared in 1929. The ideas had crystallized then into a proposal to nationalize the land (not farmers) and to control Dominion meat and wheat prices by nationalizing the trusts as well as milk and meat. In 1924 these ideas were only embryonic. To compare the ideas of Bensusan, *NS* authority on agriculture, and Fabian Garratt would be a rewarding study. The hypothesis suggests itself that a more "agriculturalist" viewpoint in the writings of Fabian Bensusan in *NS* was slowly warped toward an industrialist viewpoint in the Fabian Tract of Garratt. The politicized socio-economic order which excluded agriculture as a way of life and treated agronomy as a cog in the industrial wheel was creating a *social* vacuum which was bound to cause a reaction as such. (The results of an *economic* vacuum created by the war-guilt-Reparation thesis became patent in the economy of every nation by 1931.) Hesitancy in dealing with agricultural questions postponed the politicizing of farm organization, while an economic safety valve, the Cooperative, assumed sizable if still inadequate proportions.

[102] *NS*, XXII, 443 f. The "gains" were wishful and immaterial so far. The constant publishing of aims had educative value, however.

union, with the backing of the Royal College of Music, was picketing. Mr. Tom Shaw (Trade Unionist) would have liked to extend to the Viennese the Government's welcome; but it was politically not feasible. Then it was stated that " Labour" men, once elected, became H.M.'s Government and were no longer Trade Unionists. The *NS* view was not that of the unions, but of their instructor: Union " Labour," once elected to public office, could no longer be partial to trade union objectives but must represent the public. In the ensuing months the unions tested the Labour Government severely and often a strike had to be settled on sentiment or personal " pull " rather than on its merits as when Thomas and Clynes found it necessary to plead for patriotism and to portray the King's " despair," in order to get strikers to go back and finish the work on the Wembley British Empire Exposition. The Exposition itself was planned with the purpose to stimulate trade and " re-knit " some " loosened " Empire ties,[103] said the harried Clynes.

Some of the leadership's policies made the lot of unionists reciprocally harder. The Fabian leadership was tolerant of Communists. Publicists of the Party consistently maintained that as Communists had no labor following they were not dangerous. The *NS* advocated cooperation on the part of Trade Unions with the Unemployed Workers' Committee, admittedly Communistic.[104] We have seen that the *NS* advocated coordination of Trade Unions and the Trades Councils, local organizations not then affiliated with the TUC, which were then Communist controlled. The *NS* asked that these two groups meet in a joint advisory council linking them to the TUGC, since " local labour formed an element in the Conference of the Labour Party "—a matter of votes and an effort at penetration. This was done May 10, 1924.[105] It was politically expedient and brought into the TUC and the Labour Party persons not classifiable as workingmen so much as craftsmen. Again, on questions pending abroad, editorializing on the ITUC meeting in Vienna in 1924, the *NS* said the IFTU had invited back the Russian Trade Unions; it believed they existed

---

[103] Clynes, *op. cit.*, II, p. 54.
[104] *NS*, XXIII, 147.
[105] *NS*, XXIII, 115.

independently of the Soviet Government. That the "Red" International Labour Unions "caused revolts and supported minority movements in other countries" *NS* was aware, but it simultaneously accused Mr. J. A. Thomas of "folly" in his attitude toward the current unofficial strike of NUR, led, it acknowledged, by Communists. Thomas meantime acted on the belief that this strike was so inspired. While the *NS* asked public support of disciplinary measures, it alleged that the railway men had real grievances.[106] To emphasize grievances, to disparage the leader, to disregard ill-starred inspiration, represented *NS* method of proffering Fabian guidance. Mr. Thomas was a president of the IFTU and he records taking a stand in a public letter against revolution, class-warfare and class-prejudice; a position which IFTU, in an official letter, repudiated.[107] Mr. Thomas was the object of special Communist odium [108] because he had collected a fine for libel from them in 1921. (It was told above; the money was forthcoming only after a mysterious handing over of a box of chocolates filled with jewels. It was common knowledge in these days, as pages in the *NS* evince, that many things Russian were so financed.) Thomas always maintained that those who advocate "class conflict" "traduced" him, and not his fellows for whom he devoted every Sunday for years to building the NUR from a group of downtrodden men to a self-reliant union. Mr. Thomas recorded that Communists resented his not having "the railwaymen dragged in to support every tin-pot dispute." He judged it a "mistake not realizing the tremendous work in an underground way, they [communists] perform"[109] and he

---

[106] *NS*, XXIII, 274.

[107] Cf. Thomas, *op. cit.*, pp. 88 f. "Comrade Thomas" was requested to withdraw his statement rejecting class-war. He refused.

[108] *Ibid.*, p. 196. NUR, as of 1950, endorsed the Soviet inspired "Stockholm Appeal" regarding "peace" and the use of the atom bomb. The left-wingers seem to have won out in Thomas' old and much-loved NUR.

[109] *Ibid.*, p. 280. Mr. Thomas, when Colonial Secretary, had for Parliamentary Private Secretary, George Isaacs, the head, he says, of an important Trade Union, a person willing to do any, the most servile, work. Cf. Clynes, *op. cit.*, p. 92. Isaacs' union was a newspaper printers' union affiliated with the Trades Councils. It is to be recalled that when, in 1926, Thomas was working fervently to prevent the General Strike which he knew would destroy his life work, the NUR, a strike (cf. Thomas, *op. cit.*, p. 14),

described their capitalizing on Trade Union apathy and their exploiting of grievances. Their aim, he said, was chaos in industry. He related how Litvinoff, expecting Labour to form a regime in England, had called at Unity House and asked to interview the Labour Executive Committee; to be "promptly refused" with "annoyance." Litvinoff believed that foreign affairs were henceforth to be controlled by Trade Union officials, not in embassies.[110] The Fabians let the Communists roam abroad letting Trade Unionists resist as best they might.[111] The Communists, it was said, should be ignored because they had no labor following; but propaganda-wise the Reds provided whole cloth from which Fabian socialists cut segments to suit their gradualist patterns. Furthermore, a very unusual picture of Russian social conditions was run without editorial dissent by Massingham in the *NS*. Russia, he said, wanted to sell her own goods to her own peasants, not German or English goods, and political pressure was being

---

unauthorized and quickly repudiated (cf. Thomas, *op. cit.*, p. 126), occurred in the *Daily Mail* press rooms and furnished the reason for Baldwin's refusal to negotiate further to avert the threatening General Strike. Cf. Thomas, *op. cit.*, p. 273. The *Daily Mail* answered a request for information regarding the printers' union which precipitated the strike in 1926, and concerning the affiliations of this union, by stating they had no information which would be of interest to the inquirer. Further clarification is outside the scope of this study. It is noted here only to take cognizance of a possible result of the "pairing" technique of those who made the Cabinet and Government set-up. The "rightist" Trade Union Thomas was "paired" with the head of a difficult-to-handle union. Fyfe, in his *Behind the Scenes in the General Strike,* says that Isaacs was secretary of the Machine Men, the National Society of Operative Printers. "He wanted the *Mail* to appear." Also, the editorial staff of the *Daily Mail* was pro-labor. We cannot learn who authored the article which caused the strike and precipitated the General Strike by ending negotiations.

[110] Thomas, *op. cit.*, p. 274. It would seem that Litvinoff was under the same impression as the "mistaken" Russian Trade Unions who "did not understand" the New Economic Policy.

[111] There is admirable shrewdness in such practice: Fabianism is made to seem the alternative to communism and a refuge, since Socialism will have been made to seem inevitable. *NS*, XXII (November 24, 1923), p. 219, ran an advertisement of Allen and Unwin (Fabian) of the Labour Sevens' *Aims of Labour*. The publishers capitalized on the fact that Baldwin had dealt at length with this book in his Swansea speech. Fabians let the opponents work for Fabianism.

exerted by workmen in the State factories for the protection of home industries. The Peasant, said the Diarist, pays and pays until he "flies" to the "vote and the Parliament." No present-day reader finds anything which rings true in this picture of Lenin's, now Stalin's Russia. Only C. Delisle Burns' *Short History* supplies a similar socio-economic picture of Russia under the NEP, but a little later. But this explains the otherwise enigmatic toleration of Communism by British Socialists. Regardless of the political imperialism and diplomatic mendaciousness which D'Abernon pilloried, the social changes in Russia were depicted as holding out a budding promise which the British Socialists feared to injure lest a trade treaty fail to materialize. If G. B. Shaw and Lansbury later thought and stated that NEP was pure Fabianism, the editor of the *NS* had in 1923 stated that NEP was capitalistic but advancing toward the workers' state, the State to control or own all capital.[112] It is possible, and appears evident from *NS* policy, that Fabians saw an obverse picture of themselves in Russia, *i.e.*, an explosive, fervid, action on the margins of a hard core of "industrial democracy": Let Litvinoff and Tchitcherin and Radek fuss, let classes and persons disappear or suffer, let a reputation for malicious intent to deceive surround the Soviets in diplomatic circles as Lord D'Abernon remarked;[113] beneath all this the NEP prospered. In fact, Wayfarer saw or was led by some interested person to see a conspiracy on the part of Zinoviev and Radek to destroy a rising representative movement in Russia in favor of their peculiar imperialism and to *discredit moderate Socialism* before it was proven a "force of social construction."[114] However, the editor found Tchitcherin and Krassin not "reasonable or business-like" and warned that despite "recognition," Russia could not get credit by decree.

Favorable Fabian opinion of Russia and the policy of tolerating the infiltrating subversive elements could only give the Trade

---

[112] *NS*, XXII, 473. (*Vs* Zinoviev, Stalin decreed the "Eastern Detour.")

[113] Lord D'Abernon, *The Diary of an Ambassador* (New York: Doubleday, Doran and Company, 1930), III, p. 28.

[114] *NS*, XXII, 540. This information throws light on the future fate of these old Bolsheviks, who perished in the 1936 "trials." Massingham's source of information was a disciple of the new school of Soviet thought, the throw-back to gradualism, and the eventual recapture of czarist power.

Union official cause for grief. Henderson at the Home Office ordered the policing of Communist meetings. This met with the scornful criticism of the *NS* [115] and insistence that Communists were harmless because they had no great number of followers. But minding one's manners toward Communists was not the only lesson the *NS* taught.

At the same time, the *NS* criticized Labour members for incivility toward Liberals.[116] Clifford Sharp made a plea early in 1924, for support to Mr. Lloyd George's campaign to rehabilitate Liberalism and prevent its disappearance despite the complaints of Socialists like Weir who, as Parliamentary Private Secretary in the Premier's office, complained of MacDonald's association with Liberals.[117] The Diarist, indeed, had dubbed the Liberals "vulgar" when he had scolded them for quarrelling [118] with Labourites. On the other hand, a letter from one J. H. Harris to the editor of the *NS* complained that Labour forced the cooperation of Liberals in Parliament and then embarassed them in the constituencies by "obtrusively" giving "fair play" to Tories and "no quarter" to the Liberals.[119] Editorially the *NS* said that Labour was under the superior tutelage of a Liberal "Governess" [sic] (Sir John Simon) and of Mr. Pringle. It smoothed the surface for readers by showing how the "Communist-pacifist" ILP voted *with* MacDonald on building some cruisers and how the Minister of Health (Wheatley) combined with MacDonald to win through by retracting a rescinding order on the Poplar question (they had to go back to Mond's order to keep Asquith from censuring the Government); and finally, how it was impossible that a wedge could be driven between the Liberals and Labour as only the former would suffer thereby. Reassuringly, it was stated that the effort of the Press, which aimed "to detach the Government from the Party" (Weir found such words prophetic) would come to nought.[120] So, "Civility" was ordered toward Communists, and toward Liberals—without showing this juxtaposition,

---

[115] *NS*, XXIII, 30.
[116] *NS*, XXIII, 30.
[117] *NS*, XXIII, 145.
[118] *NS*, XXIII, 10 f.
[119] *NS*, XXII, 758.
[120] *NS*, XXII, 477.

indeed. It was a characteristic Fabian position but it did not assist workingmen to avoid the machinations of their enemies.

Snowden's budget was awaited with bated breath and received with applause on all sides. The *NS* [121] said it was " not socialism but points toward socialism." The Capital Levy, of course, was debarred from consideration but the Liberals endorsed Snowden's ideas on taxing land values, on super-taxes and higher death duties. The editor termed " nonsensical " the idea evidently current that Socialists " nourished a secret love for Protection," but he thought they could have been spared the repeal of the McKenna duties on cars, pianos, clocks, films. This attitude, positive and negative on Protection, surely justified the above mentioned " nonsensical " suspicion. The synthesis, " Free trade and low tariffs," will reappear on the German scene. The editor recalled the principle of *taxation for reform,* to obviate economic and social inequalities [122] and remarked that the programme was set forth in the platform of the 1919 Labour Conference—Webb's work, one recalls. Strangely enough, Mr Snowden had the close cooperation and deeply appreciated assistance of a Fabian, Mr. William Graham, who figures here and at the Hague and at Geneva as a very able economist. Mr. Thomas, a convinced Trade Union protectionist who stood for imperial preference,[123] with whom Graham was also closely associated in later years, remarks that Graham was not " riveted " to free trade. In fact, Thomas and Graham held that *to force the issue would break up the Movement.* The issue was straddled very adroitly by the Socialist Chancellor of the Exchequer who so delighted the City, and the Fabian economist. We find Mr. Snowden [124] also promising a Mothers' Pension if Labour stayed in office and Mr. Graham withdrawing a Pension Bill in order to bring in a more liberal one obviating the

---

[121] *NS,* XXIII, 456.

[122] Cf. R. H. Tawney, *Equality* (which is dedicated to Beatrice Webb) (New York: Harcourt Brace and Company, 1929), pp. 218 f. and 265, where Tawney deals with restraint of liberty and " stagnation " which precedes " confusion "—on the road to Socialism and equality. He concludes that if things purchasable by wealth are provided by the State, the desirability of wealth and the roots of wealth-creating inequality will be removed (p. 272).

[123] Cf. Thomas, *op. cit.,* p. 205.

[124] *NS,* XXII, 558.

Means Test.[125] These proffers were made for political reasons although they embodied Fabian Women's projects of long standing. The political uses of the Budget were as patent as the serious-minded Snowden could countenance.

Two trends developed which were to stultify the next Labour Government. These were destined to fructify in the " national " Government of 1931 : First, the Tory espousal of agitated reforms, a process named by Fabians themselves " Tory collectivism," and, second, the tendency on the part of Fabian intellectuals to draw back, to compromise their radical principle when acting as an element of the Party and yet, from this very experience in Party, to grow more radical as they moved toward creating an Order in imitation of the myth of the Jesuits. The incidence of a Wallas, a Wells, a Mosley, a G. B. Shaw (in his later years boasting of being a Communist), a Trevelyan and the Webbs, all moving ideologically into a concept of *control* by some kind of force not necessarily bloody, indicates the relentless logic of the dialectic of materialism.[126]

D. Tories, Trade Unions and Truce with France

In 1922 Labour Opposition had been confronted with Clyde-siders who made it clear they expected Labour to carry out its pledges on Socialism. In 1924 the back benches were again populated by the forthright men from Glasgow but H.M.'s Government found certain sympathies among members of its Tory Opposition. The typical Trade Unionist, Thomas, saw much to praise in the old-party members : Alfred Mond (Lord Melchett) who believed " bad labour conditions do not pay " and who stood high in Trade Union confidence; [127] Sir Ben Turner who contributed more than others on the labor side in a certain conference with TUC members, called by Mond; [128] Baldwin whom Thomas thought not

---

[125] *NS*, XXIII, 179.

[126] Sir Stafford Cripps lectured often on " Control " after 1931. Cf. e. g., *FN*, XLIII (December, 1932). Mrs. Webb's predilection for an Order something like the Jesuits or like the Russian Communist Party, or like the Japanese Samurai, is set forth by Mrs. Cole in her *Beatrice Webb*, p. 158.

[127] Thomas, *op. cit.*, p. 255.

[128] *Ibid.*, p. 255.

" indifferent to the lot of the common people or opposed to organised labour ";[129] Birkenhead who later wrote the acceptable formula for ending the General Strike and who defended Thomas openly;[130] Neville Chamberlain always " anxious to improve the lot of the workers "; Lord Hirst who " worked like a Trojan to bring capital and labour together "; Sir Herbert Samuel, whom Thomas convinced he should return to collaborate in ending the Strike by working with those meeting secretly in Sir Abe Bailey's house to reach a strike settlement, in 1926.[131] It is interesting to speculate what would have been the picture of England had these men replaced the Fabians with Trade Unions, had they galvanized workmen into a Party as the Fabians did. They could not have offered " nationalisation "; they could have developed " free associations." Socialists who like Maxton were determined " never to make any barber a capitalist "[132] criticized, even as Weir criticized MacDonald, Thomas' association with these Liberals and Tories. Thomas knew from personal experience the men and matters whereof he spoke, personal experience which withdrawn Socialists denied themselves. At the same time, Socialist Snowden, a man who despised the Trade Unionist mentality but appreciated Thomas, praised unstintingly Norman Montague, the Governor of the Bank of England. To oversimplify, not without substantiation: Tories verged on collectivism as political collectivists became more like Tories. The most patent indication of this change in Socialists-in-office was the new outlook in France to which attention will be directed further on.

Further to illustrate the Tory " reform ": An editor of the *NS* wrote " *Virginibus Puerisque*," a sarcastic account of Mr. Baldwin's speech to a youth-gathering in which he had touched upon the Home Office's preparing new factory legislation, the Board of Trade's investigation of profiteering, the Ministry of Health's housing propositions, had praised Whitley Councils and, re-

---

[129] *Ibid.*, p. 229.

[130] *Ibid.*, p. 231. Slesser narrates that Birkenhead connived with bench and Government to set the nearest precedent for the Campbell case, the precedent of Government interference for reasons of policy in a prosecution. This happened during the war, in 1918. Cf. Slesser, *op. cit.*, pp. 64 f.

[131] *Ibid.*, p. 106.

[132] Thomas, *op. cit.*, p. 253.

echoing Kirkwood, had said that understanding business was not the workingman's part, but " responsibility " was " their share of control." The disparaging editor had Mr. Baldwin on the hip, however; he noted that the boasted example of support of Trade Unionism by Disraeli was followed by the effort to legislate against Trade Unions by the successors of Disraeli in the Conservative Party.[133]   This was an early presage of 1926–1927; Fabians had good reason to feel such a prophecy stirring.   They too must find a means of control of the labor element.   The reformed Tory mentality modified its anti-labor trend but sought political control of a Socialist-guided force that was feared; and the evolutionary Socialists, Labour Party guides, arrived at a point where control of the Trade Unions, *i.e.*, of the socio-political force generated by organized labor, seemed an objective which if undesired was unavoidable—if Socialism and not Trade Union Capitalism was to emerge victorious.   The political action of Fabian leadership oscillated between a Trade Union and a Tory mentality while itself remaining free; but crystallizing within itself was a hard core called " control."   This it was which was going to make necessary a long apology for Freedom after the debacle of October, 1924.   It was going to bring Mrs. Webb to see the perfection she dreamed of in Russia and " with a grand gesture [throw] Gradualism over board at a Fabian gathering in the early spring of 1932." [134]   (It must have been that she saw Fabianism revivified by the Coles as that which would produce the Order when she returned to the Society in 1939.)

In the mind of a Fabian founder, an idea, not to be expressed until after the defeat of Fascism, then rising, was beginning to take shape.   As usual, far in advance of his contemporaries, G. B. Shaw was to say in 1944, reviewing Fabian history on the Diamond Jubilee of the Society: " We shall have to defend [after the War] as best we can their [Nazi-Fascist] nationalisation of Trade Unions." [135]   In this article Shaw recalled that he had long

---

[133] *NS,* XXIII, 116 f.   The article showed there were two reasons for " reforms ": 1) the conquest of Power; 2) response to the demand of the electorate for ameliorative measures: 1) Socialism; 2) will of the community.

[134] Hamilton, *Sidney and Beatrice Webb,* p. 291.

[135] *FQ,* 41 (April, 1944), 4 f.

ago questioned Edward Pease, who had triumphantly announced they had "roped in the Miners' Federation" and "the money difficulty no longer existed": "What then becomes of Socialism?"[136] What indeed: It had to develop a technique of control of Trade Unionism and it had to find a *modus vivendi* in Europe. The first half of the decade of the 1920's saw the deaths of Wallas and Wells and the rise of Mosley; and Shaw, who in 1924 approved their spirit, recorded that these years marked his enlightenment on Foreign Affairs when he "proposed the arrangements effected later at Locarno [Locarno was a hardened form of the fluid idealism in the Geneva Protocol] when the war had been adjourned after four years fighting."[137] Shavian Mosleyism promised control of union sentiment now to be shifted in favor of France. The road to Locarno lay through France.

The "atmosphere" regarding France was at least twice reported to be better[138] when France was still spoken of as the "only serious and dangerous enemy we have in the whole world,"

---

[136] *Ibid.*, p. 2.

[137] *Ibid.*, p. 4. The hardening of fluid concepts into notions of control, even an "iron curtain" concept, is demonstrated in the ensuing discussion of Locarno. It represented the meeting of minds, at an international level. Because he was *looking backward* as he judged the contemporary scene in 1944, it will assist in interpretation of the 1920's to note Shaw's reaction in 1944. "At this moment . . . newspapers and Parties claiming to represent the extreme left are scheming for the utter eradication . . . of Fascism, which means simply the Geddes Ax taken out of the Tory toolchest and applied to Military Communism as after 1918, and . . . are . . . demanding the reimprisonment of Oswald Mosley. . . . Professed socialist papers are more reactionary . . . than the *Times,* the *Observer,* and the *Economist* [and] Mosley is none the worse for their ravings; but Herbert Morrison and Ellen Wilkinson, whose prestige is part of our own political stock in trade, are considerably embarrassed by them. From such idiotic truckling to what Ellen rightly calls mob hysteria the Fabians must do all they can to head the Labour Party off." *Ibid.*, p. 4. Apropos of what has been written here of Fabian collaboration with Liberals, Tories, Fascists, and Communists, Shaw said: "The true Fabian is not and never can be a Party man or woman . . . All Fabians have their price, which is always the adoption of Fabian measures no matter by what Party." He added, "The Beveridge Report is quite as likely to be implemented by an Eden Cabinet as by a Stafford Cripps one. . . . Mr. Eden must have our support even if our own converts on the left denounce the Fabian Society. . . ."

[138] *NS*, XXII, 590.

and when MacDonald's good style was credited with the improvement in Franco-British relations.[139] After the winter of 1923, the Labour Government and the editorial policy of the *NS* turned toward the *Entente.* The change commenced when the *NS* admitted that the fall of the franc which unseated Poincaré had been manipulated: " We were forced to seek the salvation of Europe in the temporary ruin of France "; it was " an abominable thing " but there was " no alternative." The long watchful waiting for the *bloc des gauches* to win through was over. Baldwin, Asquith and Lloyd George supported the Labour Prime Minister who pressed France and urged Germany to accept the Dawes Report " *sans phrase.*" [140] With France going left, Reparations would come " down from the Moon "; Henderson's campaign programme took on added significance since a moratorium and an agency of international supervision for reparations was being worked out.[141] Webb said a " change of spirit " would be Revision enough, after the French election.[142] Then, the " Europe of science and rational feeling and humane endeavor to which nationalism is the chief obstacle " would emerge. The *Entente* must remain.[143] Naive persons and those out of touch with the *NS* failed to perceive the new trend toward sympathy for " rationalist "—not nationalist— France. Mrs. Hamilton refers to " ILP post-war hostility to France " as having a surprising recrudescence in Snowden, whom she criticizes in 1929 as " ignorant " and a " nationalist " and not a Trade Unionist.[144] Nationalist and militarist France was to be replaced by the France of " Civilisation and humanity." [145]

---

[139] *NS*, XXII, 696. After Whitsuntide in 1923, Lord Balfour and Lord D'Abernon vacationed together at a golfing resort. Dugdale, *op. cit.*, II, p. 359.

[140] *NS*, XXIII, 148 f.

[141] *NS*, XXII, 468.

[142] *NS*, XXII, 592 f.

[143] *NS*, XXII, 468 f. In the *NS*, " Nationalist " was a recurrent omnibus term used often to designate all who were not internationalists; sometimes, merely the Right.

[144] Hamilton, *op. cit.*, p. 316.

[145] *NS*, XXIII, 219. Cf. also, *NS*, XXIII, 242, for indications of the spirit of political Socialism:—There is no hesitancy to weaken the barriers against Russia. In the summer of 1924, the Roumanian rulers sought a loan from England to help them in their struggle to hold Bessarabia against

To complete the picture of the domestic background against which a few brilliant strokes of diplomacy were laid, let it be said by way of summary:

In searching out the attempted reforms and studying the secret of Cabinet-and-Ministry-making of the Labour Party, we find that certain problems took their rise in the fact that the intellectual leadership was a peculiar Socialism, Fabianism. The Party programme was stymied by dependence on Liberals, by the sectarianism of some Labourites, by antagonism of union men against the leadership and by the check which Conservatives, otherwise in agreement on policy, exerted upon Labour where it was subservient to " outside " influences. Antagonism of the Fabian mentality against the Trade Union mentality, reciprocated the Trade Unionists antipathy for the political leadership. Even among Socialists themselves some stood for such things as P.R., the Capital Levy, absolute Revision, further Poor Law reform, which Fabians now rejected or held in abeyance. Fabians and certain elements of the Party possessed a reliable common bond made up of hatred for France, interest in Germany and loyalty to Russia. Vote-consciousness handicapped rent control; the voteless were in danger of being ignored. Some proposed bills snagged themselves on such questions as whether factory reform should be effected before Socialism should be established or only afterward. On questions such as using education to control the labor market, lowering only transportation costs to balance imports and exports without touching wages, setting up county wage boards with or without government subsidy for agriculture, and controlling middlemen or trusts, Fabianism interposed gradualism between the Party's demands and the public.

An appearance of harmony was given by the construction of the Cabinet and the Ministries. Fabians were distributed on a plus-

---

Russia. The *NS* at every juncture argued against the loan and denied that Trotsky ever said Bessarabia was the first step to Constantinople; the *NS* was seeking an " honest and democratic government in Roumania." Very non-Tory in this viewpoint, the *NS* was quite traditional in regard to Egypt. Cf. *ibid.,* 219. The *NS* insisted on retaining the condominium in the Soudan; since her frontiers were tangent with French and Italian sections, Egypt came under the European State system. No imperialism: " keep Imperialist objects out of it "; the difference, a " liberal spirit."

and-minus system to counter-balance non-Fabians in office and govern Trade Unionists and Clydesiders. The Trade Union segment of the Government was a Henderson-and-Webb construct. The remaining segments, Fabian or Fabian-associate, were Webb constructs.

Socialism posed a " delicate problem " of which Fabian gradualism assumed the solution. Two reports of progress showed wishful thinking or merely ephemeral gains but underlined the problem raised by the attempt to apply industrialism as a social panacea. When organized labor reverted to direct action, Fabianism won through by an appeal to sentiment. A principle re-stated that government must be for all and not for a single class jarred the complacency of those who believed " labor " had acquired a monopoly on social and economic gains.

Fabian toleration of Communists made control hard for Trade Union leaders, on the domestic front; on the side of foreign affairs, there appeared a tendency to seek trade and overlook ideas. Readers are prepared to understand the complication of the trade treaty problem and the Red Scare, which caused Labour's failure to be reelected.

Fabians taught manners toward Liberals and toward Communists. That Snowden-Graham construct, the Budget, made a synthesis of " free trade and low tariffs," even as ideals and pensions went together to make good politics, on the domestic side. The Party itself was so divided on " Protection " that only Fabian equivocation saved the Movement.

Two trends developed in Fabianism: A toward-Tory mind and an elite-control mentality. The first took both political sides toward an " understanding " with France. Both parties for different reasons—to appearances only—aimed at control of Trade Union forces. And both for not so different reasons, moved toward Locarno. France swung a little left while in Germany the ministry garnered some support from the left and in England, Labour swung a little right; so the Dawes Plan went into effect. The strange understanding between Fabian and Tory mentalities produced an interesting effect to be seen in the section which follows on " Broad Diplomacy."

E. Broad Diplomacy

Two baffling arguments in which neither antagonist ever spoke definitely—Protection and the Entente—swirled over the area of political life but an understanding on the part of the electorate and the parties, however inarticulate, was disclosed in the general satisfaction found in the culmination—Locarno. When certain men—Lord D'Abernon, Balfour, Asquith, Churchill, Geoffrey Dawson of the *Times,* and " several newspaper magnates " fore-gathered at Sir Abe Bailey's London house to celebrate a " Belshazzar's feast of a refined order " honoring " my [Lord D'Abernon's] part in Locarno." [146] it marked the culmination of a long series of important moves made by the British Ambassador to Berlin, and the concretizing of what was shown in the last chapter to be the policy of that Fabian leadership which had the closest touch with political realities. In this case the political leadership did not run counter to the ends urged by British Socialists: " Revision " was now the Dawes Plan. Webb had said, when MacDonald was embarrassed by Henderson's carrying Revision to the hustings in 1924, that if reparations were scaled down, that would be " revision." The Protocol was now the Pact of Mutual Guarantee; but more important still, the notion of " economic co-operation " was now the Commercial Treaty of England with Germany. In 1922, Lord D'Abernon, having often consulted Schacht and Ritscher, Berlin bankers, had arranged to get expert study and advice on currency for a German Government whose leaders professed to him to have no knowledge of such matters. He called upon his friends, J. M. Keynes, Professor Cassell of Stockholm, and R. H. Brand, with some others. Cassell and Keynes, but especially the former, were doubtful about the prin-

---

[146] Edgar Vincent D'Abernon, *Dawes to Locarno, 1924–1926* (New York: Doubleday, Doran and Company, 1931), p. 212. Sir Abe Bailey called himself in *Who's Who, 1931,* " one of the principal Transvaal mine owners " and boasted of his being " sentenced two years " for reformist activities. The close association of Balfour and D'Abernon has been noted: likewise Balfour's being chosen by Webb to head the " Balfour Commission " on British Trade and Industry. Set up to find a way to defeat the majority against curbs on competition it numbered Lord Sankey among its members. Hamilton, *Sidney and Beatrice Webb,* pp. 269 f.

ciple of a fixed gold basis; argued that more fluidity would bring more rapid circulation. (That reasoning explains perhaps why the Dawes Report led to the Young Plan.) Inflation was not caused by the unmitigated Machiavellianism which some attributed to the German leaders of 1920–1923; D'Abernon, on November 14, 1924, " take[s] leave to doubt the truth of this supposition " which he had recorded November 4, as hearsay opinion.[147] But D'Abernon's experts had stepped aside for the " Dawes " experts whose Report was adopted after Herriot had visited at Chequers and MacDonald had gone to France and both had written directly to the Reich to plead for agreement (Left support for Stresemann).

To the " fluidity " of League idealism, of Protocol metaphysics and of printing press Inflation, the concreteness of gold and " iron-curtains " were welcome antinomies. D'Abernon had managed to forward his friends' findings to Paris but only after the demise of three persons: of Reichsbank President Haverstein, " a public danger," of the elder Stinnes, a " great supporter of his views," and of Helfferich, " arch-priest of inflation," [148] followed by the more complete ascendency of Stresemann. Then the recommendations of the above-mentioned experts gained attention. D'Abernon's private study prepared the Germans for the reception of the Dawes Plan.

The plan outlined in the Dawes Report was the creation of Schacht and Owen Young under the Honorable Charles Dawes' signature, devised with the encouragement of Hughes, D'Abernon, and Kellogg, and supported by the influence of Keynes in Webb-MacDonald-Henderson-Parmoor circles. Schacht was the mainstay of D'Abernon in German financial reorganization. The reforms he made—goldbacking of the currency and the end of the inflation—paved the way for the success of the Dawes Plan. After the Pact of London based upon the Report was signed on August 16, 1924, the Labour Government completing what Conservatives had inaugurated, Lord D'Abernon forthwith proposed the Commercial Treaty. This was the first public proposal, September 22, 1924; it was proposed again October 28, 1924, when Conferences were already under way. On November 14, the new

---

[147] *Ibid.*, pp. 114 f.
[148] *Ibid.*, p. 110.

Tory Government, but ten days after Election, signaled its assent
to continuing negotiation which had begun October 21, 1924.
Since the Versailles Treaty prohibited any ally from making a
commercial treaty with Germany for five years, January, 1925,
was the earliest date publicly possible; and the Treaty was already
in order by that date—ready for initialing.   It was ratified in
Berlin August 15, 1925, and in London October 18.   Meantime,
Locarno was initialled October 16, 1925, to be ratified in December.   The sequence of dates shows the intermeshing of Lord
D'Abernon's activities over which the episode of a "Socialist"
Government in England passed, like one of the whirlwinds one
sees on the placid surface of a broad Western plain, apart—
wrapped in its own activities.

From January, 1924, until October, Labour had been H. M.'s
"luckiest" Government.   In October they went out, driven by a
"Red Scare."   *FSAR* indicated that Fabians were "confident
that this set-back is only temporary and that at the next opportunity the verdict of 1924 will be reversed."   (The next opportunity did not come until 1929.)   When Labour fell, the
Dawes Plan had begun successfully to function and a leftist
French Government was acting reasonably.   The way was set and
the road open to Locarno.   Providence, planning, or plain luck
had produced the coalescence of a German Government centered
about Stresemann and under a Sociaist president, which had accepted the Dawes Plan.   Planning is the only hypothesis within
our province, slender as the present evidence is.   Stresemann was
quasi-nationalist, an uneasy member of the *Volkespartei,* and an
unconvinced anti-monarchist.   D'Abernon admired and appreciated him.[149]   The Ambassador had worked for several years

---

[149] *Ibid.,* p. 16.   This, in spite of the misinformation coming home from
Dell who, detesting the Socialists in office (not those collaborating with
Bolsheviks in the provinces), called Stresemann a monarchist and reported
all "nationalists" (confusing Right, Centre, and Fascist) as being against
accepting the Report, while he dubbed the Centre an "absurdity" and wanted
the three parties to get together with the Trade Unions as in England—
forsooth—and form a Government. Cf. *NS,* XXII (December 1, 1923), 237.
By June, 1924, Dell sang a new tune.   He had begun to see that reluctance
of groups to accept the Report was part of their bargaining technique.   He
had come to the conclusion that the *German* Communist Party was "quite

toward the consummation brought about by Stresemann who successfully manipulated the splintered Socialists and the hardening nationalists into acceptance, first of currency reform, then of the Dawes Report. The latter group, the nationalists, had desired to adopt the Dawes Plan but dared not endorse it on an election platform. The news about the difficult position of rightist elements in Germany, as it appeared in the spring issues of the *NS*, was calculated to create antipathy toward them as " reactionary "; and only after the acceptance of the Report was credit given to the Centre, which had pulled left (mild Socialists) and the right (nationalists) together " on its own terms." From Dell's reporting, it would have been hard for the uninitiated to divine in April, 1924, how far " fascist " extended into the reporter's meaning of " nationalist." At this time the KPD dubbed all Socialists and those they collaborated with, " Social Fascists."

No Tory and never a Liberal has risen up to claim " we planned it that way " but the effect of confidence inspired in " Labour " circles in Germany by the rise of British Labour to power was not unnoticed by Lord D'Abernon. He was capable of laying claim to the special virtue of " insular instinct " to which he credited the recoil from the Protocol of Geneva, where there was, he said, too much Latin and Catholic influence. In the Diary which he was keeping, masterful in understatement, it is clear that he was fully aware of the usefulness of the dynamics of " the left," even the splintered left. He found himself *persona grata* [150] to the MacDonald Government, upon his visit home early in MacDonald's term. (Of course, the plan was discussed.) And like the editors of the *NS*, he was fully aware of the threat to England of French hegemony—against which only Labour had been outspoken. Furthermore, although no one can say exactly why an

---

incapable " of leading Trade Unions into a Labour Party. He thought Trade Unions should " *alone* create a new party of Labour" emancipated " from the tutelage of the Socialist Party and the interference of politicians of all sorts." It will be recalled he once endorsed the idea that the Labour-front should be Moscow-led. *NS*, XXIII (June 21, 1924), 306 f.

[150] The *NS*, wily and ostensibly righteous, said early in 1924 there ought to be no spoils system. The " no spoils " principle left D'Abernon in office or explained why his resignation was not accepted. Cf. *NS*, XXII (January 26, 1924) and *ibid*. (February 9, 1924), 437 f and 498.

election was precipitated in the Fall of 1923, its sequel made available forces which had been withheld in the checkmate in Europe. The Commercial Treaty when it came from its Tory adopters embodied " Free Trade and low tariffs "—a consummate Fabian synthesis. There can be no doubt that the psychological effect of Labour's rise to power in England hastened, as much as the fall of the franc, the rise of the Left to power in France. Only five months later, Tory skill capitalized upon the resultant amenability.

Locarno was not, however, a Socialists' ideal consummation. That would have been rather the Protocol which in its compulsory arbitration features showed a tendency to crystallize a disputed metaphysic and so fill the gaps in the League Covenant. In defining an aggressor and making explicit the finding of force to carry out measures against an aggressor, it was designed to strengthen the League. " Insular instinct," Tory, Liberal, and Labour, defeated it: Socialism might one day take the aggressive. The Locarno understanding, ignoring the Dominions as the Protocol did not, accepted England as a Continental power and crystallized Lord D'Abernon's conception of an " iron curtain "—" a barrier between France and Germany." [151] It seemed like old orthodoxy.

Long before the Pact of London the Germanophile British Ambassador, confiding in Herr Karl von Schubert, Secretary of State, had opened his mind concerning the Pact of Reciprocal Guarantee,—" *Das Kind*," [152] his brain child. He confided to his record the result.

> October 16, 1925.—Pact of Mutual Security initialed at Locarno. Formal signature is to take place in London on December 1. All is well.[153]

The Pact bound England and Italy, in the event of any future Franco-German conflict, to take the side of the non-aggressor:— England became arbiter of Europe again and the balance of power

---

[151] D'Abernon, *op. cit.*, p. 211.

[152] *Ibid.*, pp. 151 f and 210. He had inveigled Stresemann, the voluble, into having his portrait painted by Augustus John. During the sittings D'Abernon, in his halting German, indoctrinated the helpless sitter with his scheme, " *Das Kind*."

[153] *Ibid.*, pp. 111 and 199.

was restored. The Ruhr had been evacuated by France on a pre-date; the "sanctions" cities likewise. But the Allies were still in Cologne. The *NS* editor revealed a year before that Baldwin had lost the advantage the British held in Cologne, their "Gibraltar on the Rhine," and that MacDonald would "change all that." [154] So it was. Lord D'Abernon summarized the effect of the dynamism released by the British election of 1923:

> It is certainly an anomaly that both the Commercial Treaty with England [155] and the Pact of Mutual Security will be carried by a Government nominally of the Right, on the real foundation of support from the Left." [156]

The Pact of Mutual Security, crowning point in the Ambassador's system of pacts, had started in Stresemann-D'Abernon correspondence, was relayed to France and England, kept prudently secret and allowed but slowly to filter into French and English consciousness by Herriot who had earlier knowledge from London (January 20, 1925) and, after the Election, by Neville Chamberlain. There was some fear that the Right extremists would kill the negotiations or, perhaps, the negotiators.[157] Lord Crewe, abetted in the inner sanctum by Sir Eyre Crowe, had handled the Foreign Office in collaboration with D'Abernon espe-

---

[154] *NS,* XXII (January 12, 1924), 381.

[155] D'Abernon, *op. cit.,* p. 185.

[156] *Ibid.,* p. 184. Schubert and D'Abernon rejoiced that Herriot for some unrevealed reason kept the German-initiated suggestion secret. D'Abernon leaves the matter to the day when the secret history of France during these years is written, and thanks Providence—while advising delay in enquiring. Cf. *ibid.,* p. 8. Some of the forces at work are indicated by the fact that when Chamberlain forthrightly proposed a bilateral pact with France (cf. *ibid.,* p. 155), Balfour, Birkenhead, Curzon, and Churchill opposed him, giving as their reason the fear that the fluid relations between Germany and Russia might thus be solidified. (Rapallo was still on the books.) When delay, and the return to Tory Government, to all appearances cooled Germany's ardour for her own proposal, Chamberlain began to fight for it and to build public opinion for the Pact of Mutual Security and Reciprocal Guarantee, beginning with a speech at Geneva explaining the rejection of the Protocol. In D'Abernon's record it was noted that MacDonald, leader of the Opposition, on this occasion had "also spoken wisely." Cf. *ibid.,* p. 157.

[157] *Ibid.,* p. 140.

cially in the negotiations for a Military Commission of Control.[158]

The episode of Labour Government left untouched the Tory foreign policy and even served it by the creation of amenability in France and Germany. That there was masterful timing and manipulation of social forces by the talented " ruling class," called in the *NS* " second-class brains," in allowing Labour to come to power only for so long as it should take to precipitate governments in France and Germany capable of utilizing the force of leftist sentiment, cannot be claimed for the Conservatives with material substantiation. It cannot be denied on the other hand that the election which was designed either to put Labour in office or to annihilate it as a political force was necessitated by the stalemate encountered by Tories in France and Germany.

The Dawes Plan was a Keynes and Schacht construct which had American backing. It was made feasible by Reichsbank President Schacht's and Chancellor Luther's [159] currency reforms on the principle of gold-backing and by loans from English financiers backed by the Bank of England.[160] As early as January 31, 1924, " astonishingly rigid " reform was remarked by D'Abernon. This was, no doubt, the explanation for the movement on the gold market which Dell had ascribed to Reich maneuvers having a rightist turn which Dell detested. D'Abernon took the measure of Hughes and Young and Dawes according to his estimate of the correlation of American idealism with American business sense, as he disclosed in his Diary. There can be no question that the man who inveigled Stresemann into having his picture painted by Augustus John [161] in order to create for himself the opportunity of talking about " *Das Kind* " and its prenatal care,[162] even though he spoke faulty German to the quick-thinking Minister whose rapid oratory was thus perforce silenced, did not let Americans who came to encourage Schacht or to " observe " the experts, leave without seeing his dream.[163] At home, the Fabian leadership and the Labour Chancellor, assured of the collaboration of Norman

[158] *Ibid.*, p. 208.
[159] *Ibid.*, p. 126.
[160] *Ibid.*, pp. 109 ff.
[161] *Ibid.*, p. 16.
[162] *Ibid.*, p. 121.
[163] *Ibid.*, p. 49.

Montague, Governor of the Bank of England, all endorsed the Dawes Plan openly, and the Labour Government put to use the sympathy it stimulated abroad to insist as no Tory Government might dare insist on the adoption of the Plan " *sans phrase.*" [164] The Labour Government achieved a Tory objective; then, a Tory Government capitalized on the Trade Treaty which Labour initiated. Both were ultimate goals of the British Ambassador, and steps to Locarno and the Pact of Mutual Security.

Inaugurated December 2, 1924, the Commercial Treaty embodied the meeting of minds as it marked the confluence of political energies and it bore the imprint of the struggle over " Protection " and/or " Free Trade." [165] " Her Free Trade and her low tariffs " adducing " the widest possible interpretation of the most favored nation " clause constituted the " advantage offered by England." The Ambassador gloried that for the first time [166] " reciprocity " was written into a trade treaty. This meant that Germany, while protecting her industry and dealing on a free trade basis with England, gave reciprocal treatment to British-made goods, as England treated Germany's. France had hoped to effect such a treaty and had, along with Belgium, begun to " strengthen the commercial elements of their diplomatic staffs in Berlin." [167] The Ruhr position had been expected to afford France leverage. France and Belgium had tried to begin negotia-

---

[164] *Ibid.*, p. 65.

[165] Speculation might be made upon several contrasting points: 1) The willingness of Chamberlain to encourage the negotiations begun by the " free trade" Labour Government tending toward the disadvantage of France; 2) his pretensions in delaying assent to the German-initiated Pact of Mutual Guarantee until he should be assured the French anxieties regarding security should be allayed; 3) his need to be converted from devotion to a bilateral pact with France. Was it necessary to placate the Right in Herriot's France, to make a show of *Entente Cordiale* now that the program of the Left was proceeding and France was all but mortally wounded by the Commercial Treaty? It offers no contrast with Fabian forward thinking: Chequers marked the end of angry utterance against France on the part of Fabian thinkers; the Commercial Treaty gave quietus to fears of French hegemony on the Continent, and henceforth only the ILP retained " a dangerous measure . . . of post-war hostility to France." Cf. Hamilton, *op. cit.*, p. 316.

[166] D'Abernon, *op. cit.*, p. 114.

[167] *Ibid.*, p. 106.

tions in London at the preliminary meetings leading up to the Pact of London, but they were already too late. The currency reforms and the Expert's Report had had from their incipiency this economic end. This is clear in the triumphant words of D'Abernon. MacDonald's Government had achieved the synthesis " free trade and low tariffs "; it was a thoroughly Fabian formula. The Conservatives had but to take over the project and sequester their Protection policy.

D'Abernon offered to resign after the London Pact was negotiated but MacDonald, who had doubtless learned about *" Das Kind "* when the Ambassador visited London shortly after the Labour Government took office, kept him at the Berlin post.[168] The prevenient Ambassador had the generosity to attribute the success of the London Conference to MacDonald, calling it his great contribution.[169]

However, a hasty review shows Labour-Liberal energies converging with Conservative national self-interest. The French were precluded from getting the commercial treaty they sought with Germany because Labour achieved the Dawes Plan's acceptance. But Labour had been provided with a ready-made success which it surrendered back to the makers of the Pact of Mutual Security. *" Das Kind "* had been discussed around December 8, 1924, by D'Abernon with Schubert. This was two days after the official Trade Pact discussion started; January, 1925, was the earliest date a commercial treaty could legally be made. But the understanding on that date was already so clear that the text of the sequential pact, that of Reciprocal Guarantee, was forwarded (in secret) on the date the Commercial Pact might first be openly discussed. Schubert had recalled, when asked for his recollections by D'Abernon that he had talked of the gestating pact " during the last three years—once I remember in 1923." The Commercial Treaty accelerated the momentum toward Locarno. On January 21, 1925, the Diary reads: " Surprise would be even greater [than the surprise found in the moderate and progressive tone adopted

---

[168] It was not in the least impossible that a foreign officer might be asked to resign. Henderson to the fury of the Opposition dispensed with the services of the British representative in Egypt in 1929, Lord Lloyd.

[169] *Ibid.*, pp. 31 f.

by Luther and Stresemann] did the public know the contents of the memorandum Pact of Mutual Security [supposed to be German-inspired; and kept secret by Herriot] which I forwarded to Londan last night." [170] The important point is that this Pact would have been impossible even to suggest without the Commercial Treaty; and this Treaty could only follow on the gains flowing from the London Pact (Dawes) ; and neither the Dawes Plan nor the Commercial Treaty might have materialized without the " new atmosphere " in Europe which enabled Rightist movements to glean support from Leftist sentiment encouraged by the rise of Labour, fronted by intelligent idealists, to power in England. The election of 1923, falling midway in the dynamic creative of the three pacts, did not interrupt but implemented the force of that dynamic. The main-stream of Socialist philosophy veered away from the Geneva Protocol and flowed back into the old English current. When the Protocol died aborning, the opinion prepared for its reception strengthened the acceptability of Locarno. No one claims to have planned it that way. The fortunate D'Abernon believed in " insular instinct."

F. Narrow Diplomacy: " Biscuits," Campbell, and the Red Letter

Russia was extended recognition *de jure* forthwith upon Labour's coming into office. The City and some companies already set up for the purpose began economic transactions for the success of which *de facto* settlements were needed. In August, Lord Ponsonby for the Foreign Office engaged in negotiations with Russian emissaries in a Conference to settle the claims of British investors who had been despoiled by Bolshevik confiscations of British properties in Russia. No figures on these evidently substantial claims were ever known to the Labourite writers; but upon settlement of them hinged the possibility of a loan to Russia, for trade purposes, to be guaranteed by the Government. The Russians countered with claims against England for interference in the civil war following the Revolution. Ponsonby and those of the same mind, Weir, Hamilton, Clynes, Snell,

---

[170] *Ibid.*, p. 123.

and even Slesser, urged the negotiation of treaties—there were three drafted to cover the problems separately. MacDonald was somewhat reluctant; and the Conservative press spoke against ratification. The proposal of these treaties really impaired the stability of the Government as constituted; *NS* tried to inspire a movement to set them aside. They came before Parliament under the agreement that the House was free—no Party line. They were ratified on the day after Parliament recessed for the September holidays. In the ratified form another date for settlement of the claims was set and any subsequent loan was made contingent upon that settlement. Nevertheless, the country was aroused; Conservatives and Liberals drew together. This might be considered the real cause of Labour's fall, if no other factors were discoverable. But the intervention of Russian emissaries along the lines of TUC and Parliamentary Party connections became known and met with disapproval. It clarified nothing to recall that in June the Parliamentary Party had been thought to have said there were no negotiations afoot and in August a treaty was introduced, even then but one day after it had been stated that negotiations had broken down. There was a reasonable fear that such confusion was the result of "intervention." Even so, the good atmosphere created by the Pact of London was spoilt by the breaking into the news of the Campbell Case rather than by the treaties. The September recess found the treaties going into effect and the Campbell Case under advisement—the ILP was angry about it. A way out was being sought. MacDonald's "luck," as Curzon called his Continental success, was running out. So much for external appearances. In an ensuing section, we look a bit deeper for explanations.

As if to show that "Red"; machinations would not be tolerated, the Government had arrested for a seditious manifesto published in late July, one J. R. Campbell,[171] a wounded veteran, who was

---

[171] Campbell, acting editor of the *Workers' Weekly,* published a plea to soldiers and sailors to refuse to use their arms against their own class in labor disputes. He was indicted, by orders of the new recruit to Labour and the Fabian Society, Sir Patrick Hastings, Attorney General. John Maxton, "most picturesque figure" of the Clydesiders of whom Wheatley was "boss" (cf. Mrs. Hamilton, *op. cit.,* p. 231), told Hastings that Campbell, a war hero, was only the acting editor of the *Weekly;* and Hastings

acting editor of the *Workers' Weekly*. Campbell's act was " part of a characteristic campaign by the Communist Party to try to present the Labour Government to the workers as the tool of reaction and oppression," [172] according to Francis Williams, M.P. Conservatives in the House " asked questions " and the Director of Public Prosecutions advised prosecution. Perhaps Sir Patrick Hastings was naive; he authorized the Prosecutor to institute proceedings. This was early in August. The angry questions of John Scurr (Catholic, Fabian, ILP-er) brought forth the story of raid and arrest. Back-benchers Maxton, Lansbury, and others ardent for the Russian treaty which they knew was shaping up, imagined they saw in the arrest the effort of the Prime Minister to use scare tactics to prevent Ponsonby's treaties from being acted upon favorably. They also professed to see an attempt to muzzle the left-wing by the threat so to deal with them because of the manner and content of their harangues. Tom Dickson shouted amidst the " general uproar," " They will probably lose half their party ! " And it indicated the real reason why the case was withdrawn.[173] Further, the whole business was a case of stumbling into a well-laid Communist trap, with the circumstance that any defense attorney (the Communists threatened to employ Sir John Simon) would exploit for sympathy the wounds and the record of the acting editor. The treaty question and the Campbell Case thus are seen to run parallel. Upon Parliament's reconvening in October, Lloyd George and the Conservatives, seeking to defeat the Government on account of the treaties, moved a vote of Censure alleging that the Campbell case had been withdrawn for political

---

withdrew the case. Conservatives moved a vote of censure for the Government's having done so although at worst they had only used " policy " in selecting a case for prosecution. Asquith helped defeat this, then moved a select committee to investigate. For this he had Tory support. MacDonald, rather than assent to the select committee's investigation, decided to resign. It is pretty clear from most accounts that he was only looking for a chance to resign. The most legalistic discussion of the Campbell Case is in Slesser, *op. cit.*, pp. 65 and 146, and the most cynical in Weir, *op. cit.*, pp. 174–183, 188, 194, and 391. But there are no clearer facts to be found in any other treatments of the case, except perhaps in Francis Williams' *Fifty Years' March*, pp. 309–317.

[172] Cf. Williams, *Fifty Years' March*, p. 309. Williams is a Fabian.
[173] *Ibid.*

reasons. Asquith moved an amendment proposing a select committee to investigate; Patrick Hastings made a clear and frank statement of his part in the case, and everything would have converged to extend the life of the Labour Government but for MacDonald's announcement that if either move passed, " then we go." One historian of the period, the latest, Francis Williams, thinks MacDonald's hurt pride was the reason for his, " then we go," because he had been hurt by criticism for having accepted a car and income to run it in the form of stock in a biscuit corporation from a friend who was at the same time a benefactor of Glasgow University and a recent recipient of a baronetcy. The colossal ambition and the shrinking sensitiveness which his vilifiers ascribe to MacDonald could not exist in such proportions as they adduced in one character. Any one who had campaigned as much as MacDonald, especially under the scourging accusation of " pacifism," would hardly break up the Government embodying (to all appearances) the life ambition of himself and his colleagues to express a pique or from self-pity. Meantime, the *Daily Mail* was holding for publication—it must have been holding it if it was sent September 15—the Zinoviev letter. The Foreign Office got it only on October 10, two days after the Government's defeat in Parliament. The Office sent it to MacDonald on October 16. It is inconceivable that the *Daily Mail,* which had shouted in headlines, " No money for murderers," on the question of the loan, in August, could have held the Zinoviev letter back except to save ammunition for the campaign they must have known to be coming as early as mid-September. The existence of such a letter was far more fearsome than the dismissal by the Government of the Campbell Case, whereby the Government seemed to be yielding to its left-wingers. The " Red Letter " was a rallying summons to the Communist Party of Britain giving directions on how to supersede the Labour Party of MacDonald which it designated as " reactionary " (two months after the Campbell manifesto and probably part of the same scheme). The Foreign Office, which was acting, MacDonald afterward said, to protect him, published, along with the letter, the draft of a note of protest to the Russian Government which the Prime Minister had tentatively initialled, on the day the *Daiy Mail* gave the Letter to the public—three days before the election.

This is all any one knows or divulges about the Letter. It was signed by the ideologue, Zinoviev, and by the Finnish Comintern member along with " MacManus." The last named was a " red " Clydesider the factualness of whose association with the upper councils of the Soviet Party Kirkwood greatly doubted. It is hard to see how Zinoviev's missive could have failed to show that Mac-Donald was *non grata* to the Communists. It certainly revealed, as also did the Campbell Case, that MacDonald's machine was encumbered, hopelessly, by the left-wing Socialists ranging from Fabians, including the " just " John Scurr, the pious Lansbury, and the Tschitcherinesque Ponsonby, to non-Fabians including Gallacher and the lovable and uncontrollable Maxton. The public in any case refused to accept the soporific, " Communists hate Socialists." They sensed the Party's vulnerability because of the common philosophical basis of Communism and Socialism.

The *NS* had revealed a long time before that trade was going on apace with Russia. Evidently not even the Communists really wanted the treaties, since they timed the Campbell publication to coincide with the treaty making. Webb's prophecy that by 1926 Labour would go in with a clear majority was extant. That it paid to shake off, or prune (this word was used again in 1931) or to discipline the left-wingers was proved by the great gains made in the Labour Party vote—five times that of 1923. The large body of votes scared out by the Red Scare was Labour's defeat and Fabian leadership's gain.

" There had been interventions," Asquith wrote. We propose now to study the various interventions occurring within the outline of the above story.

G. " Interventions " and Recoil

The Fabian turtle thrust its head out of its shell, and withdrew it—out, on certain experimental excursions; in, to await a better season for social democracy.

The general recoil from an experiment with Labour Government occurred at the point where the intervention of an " outside " element induced disgust. The Fabian recoil came on the left and right, and even from its TUC center: On the left from its own pure-Socialist element which demonstrated possible amenity to Sovietism; on the right from its own conservatism which found itself amenable to Christianism. While some, especially the Liberal allies, resented the TUC voice at the political level, and others resented the interferences of spokesmen for a foreign power, within the leadership of Labour itself there was a recoil from its own heavy charges of impolitic Socialism and from its impact with another autochthonous force it had felt in Europe. Fabianism recoiled to wait, motivated by something Lord D'Abernon approvingly termed " insular instinct." [174]

When Labour went out of office in October, 1924, Fabians took the reverse philosophically publicly assuming the attitude that the resignation of the Government was unnecessary. The *NS* had pleaded with MacDonald to hold on. Now the *NS* said it had foreseen the outcome all along and it proceeded to try to salvage MacDonald's European gains by suggesting Austen Chamberlain for the Foreign Office and working against Curzon's resuming it. From the outside, if not from the view of the sentimental Socialist, this was the correct attitude. MacDonald and—looking over the list of Fabians in Parliament—Sidney Webb were perhaps the only ones save Asquith who comprehended the unbearableness of the parliamentary situation especially where the misery took its source in the feeling that Labour members and Ministers were under pressures from outside forces.[175] And it is indisputable

---

[174] Cf. " On Reconstruction to Social Order," (*QA*) of Pius XI (Washington, D. C.: NCWC, 1942), p. 40, where is noted the recoil of Socialists from the conclusions their creed must arrive at in Communism. This study shows that social democrats recoil also from their near approach to Christianism; it supports the papal pronouncement: " Whether considered as a doctrine, or as an historical fact, or a movement, Socialism, if it remain true Socialism, even after it has been guided to truth and justice on the points we have mentioned [no longer even censorable on class-warfare and abolition of ownership] cannot be reconciled with the teaching of the Catholic Church *because its concept of society is utterly foreign to Christian truth* [it holds " human association has been instituted for the sake of material advantage alone "]." *Ibid.*, pp. 41 f, italics added.

[175] Cf. Spender, *op. cit.*, p. 659. He describes the committee of twelve (known in 1931 as the Consultative Committee) which acted as a " liaison body " between the Party and the Cabinet. Often it modified or corrected the Cabinet position and its activities seemed even welcome to the Ministers.

that they knew that to remain in office would destroy the Movement. Recoil was imperative.

What some of these "interventions" were can be seen by looking at TUC, for example. The TUC had not yet consolidated all the big unions under its General Council [176] and was being infiltrated by Communists who would have made the future of a Labour Government still more unhappy. How far Communism had infiltrated may be seen from the fact that in 1925 the TUC nearly became anti-political, that is, "direct actionist." It required all the efforts of Fabian T. C. Cramp [177] to smooth out the Labour Conference and muffle leftist invective against MacDonald which had been heard already in 1924. Not only was TUC being drawn away from the political leadership of Fabians, whom MacDonald still personified; ILP-ers expressed sectionalism and self-interest in their criticism, and the Party made itself difficult on the score both of Russia and of Geneva. When in August, 1924, the *NS* [178] said the Communist "Minority Movement" was more political than industrial "*a la Russe*" (as the shop-steward movements during the war had been) and that it would "cut no ice," it was dissembling its fears and assuaging those of its readers

---

Of course, this situation involved the debate whether a member must be only the mouthpiece of his constituency (or of his party) or whether (in accordance with Blackstone) he represents the Commonwealth.

[176] *NS*, XXIII (August 16, 1924), 539.

[177] Cf. Hamilton, *op. cit.*, p. 259. Cf. also, H. Hessell Tiltman, *J. Ramsay MacDonald: Labour's Man of Destiny* (New York: Frederick A. Stokes Company, 1929) (p. 244). In 1925, at the ILP Conference (not to be confused with the Labour Party Conference) in Gloucester a member criticized the Labour Government on eight points: 1) Pensions postponed, 2) Gretna factory, despite TU pressure, unused, 3) Glasgow dockyards left in disrepair, 4) number of inspectors of ships reduced, jeopardizing sailors' lives, 5) unemployed benefits denied thousands one day when the Government was at a royal levee, 6) no care taken of certain police strikers, 7) the failure to settle the Sudan, 8) using troops in industrial strikes. The same year at the Labour Party Conference in Liverpool, Bevin of the Transport Workers moved that never again should Labour take office without a clear majority. At MacDonald's instance, this was rejected (p. 246). Incidentally, *The Observer* (cited, p. 248) praised MacDonald's stand regarding the Sudan. In 1924, as in 1929, Labour and Tory views on the Sudan question were identical in meaning if not in expression.

[178] *NS*, XXIII (August 30, 1924), 587.

with an air of calm.   The interpretation was hardly accurate.
Regardless of how *NS* or Fabians characterized shop-stewardism,
it is certain they looked upon it as "anarchy."   Any association,
communist-inspired, socialist-inspired or of Christian derivation,
which represented the principle of subsidiarity was anathema—but
politely—to Fabians.   In this instance the "minority movement"
was a communist nuisance.   The Campbell Case upon which the
Government dissolved was not half so meaningful as the fact that
during the last stage of negotiations for the Russian Treaty,
Russian Communists addressed members of the Parliamentary
Labour Party on the premises of Parliament.   Not only spokesmen for the Conservatives and the Liberals, who were realistically
fearful of Red machinations, but also MacDonald, who could not
have been alone in his wariness of Bolsheviks, took exception to
such proceedings.[179]   But it was far more adroit—and one is
tempted to mock the *NS* editor's characteristic phrase, "Who in
the world could have advised it?"—to dissolve over a domestic
question, that of the Government's being accused of tampering
with justice, than to brave criticism on the score of countenancing
foreign tampering with diplomacy or to go down on some issue
derived from TUC tampering with Party politics, tampering concerning which the Churchillian Liberals were very vocal.

Cases like the Campbell Case became routine thereafter.   For
example, Slesser as a Liberal and an Anglican argued for days
before a judge and jury that the actions of a large group of
Communists, prosecuted for disseminating literature urging
soldiers to use their arms only against the enemies of their class
and not against their own class in a labor dispute, did not constitute sedition nor incitement to sedition.[180]   (The jury nevertheless
found them guilty.)   Asquith alluded to the effects of intervention, saying,[181] "After the intervention of a group of Labour
Members [that is, in August, just one day after the Prime Minister had said that treaty negotiations he was believed to have denied

---

[179] Ponsonby is shown by Tiltman, *op. cit.*, p. 224, to have used the intervention in order to get the negotiations, which had broken down on a minor
point, resumed.   He stated that *three* treaties were already drafted.   Evidently this was not what Snowden understood.

[180] Cf. Slesser, *op. cit.*, pp. 176.

[181] Spender and Asquith, *op. cit.*, p. 345.

to be afoot in June had broken down on the question of confiscations of British property in Russia]," Ponsonby's treaty was introduced carrying H.M.'s Government's promise to guarantee a loan. Asquith recorded how the House was revolted by the inconsistency of MacDonald and the incongruity of the notion of the Government's guaranteeing private loans to Russia.[182] However, it was the Campbell Case involving Government "intervention" based on policy, and not the Russian treaties, which caused the dissolution. (The two stories run simultaneously and are hard to disentangle.) MacDonald chose to resign if the select committee to investigate the handling of the Campbell Case were adopted. Any "interventions" which a Select Committee might have brought to light remain unknown. Asquith was disgusted and chagrined that the Liberals should be so traduced by the lack of " skill or luck " of the Labour Party. He paid for their ineptitude with his political life as we have seen in reviewing the new electioneering techniques above. Yet, to Lloyd George his enemy in the Liberal Party, and to the latter's ability to reach a *modus vivendi* with those Tories who grasped the meaning of the international situation, is Asquith's powerlessness to preserve the unstable equilibrium in Parliament attributable.[183] The Lloyd George Liberals joined the Tories on a vote of Censure against the Government for having failed to prosecute the Red. The countenancing of seditious utterance and the Ponsonby treaties were the cause of the bad atmosphere but the House had been free on the latter. While " intervention " furnished Fabians a stick to beat the dogs of " undisciplined " Party members, and afforded a reason for dissolution, it is also true that the political leadership had to find a way to stop the experiment; because the interventions were only too real. And it is not at all impossible that MacDonald and Baldwin (backed by Balfour, friend of Asquith) had made an agreement, although it was not so diabolical a treachery as Weir made it out to be.

The Fabian biographer of Henderson and of MacDonald

---

[182] *Ibid.*, p. 345.

[183] Tiltman quotes MacDonald on this point but exchanges Lloyd George's name to read Asquith's in the conspiracy to overthrow Labour. Tiltman is mistaken according to the other Labour Party members' memories. MacDonald was quite clear on the point. Tiltman, *op. cit.*, pp. 230 f.

(1929), Mrs. Hamilton, ignores the Campbell incident. She was elected to Parliament only in 1929. Her account of the dissolution appears made up from hearsay and she confuses the "interventions." The Campbell Case was dismissed not only because of Maxton's plea but also because back-benchers, even John Scurr, threatened to bolt if Campbell were tried for something no more heinous than what they themselves so often perpetrated. The intervention on the Russian Trade Treaty [184] was more important to the Tories and to the electorate. Mrs. Hamilton simply remarks, " There had been an incident—of which a great deal too much was made in the Press—implying too much back-bench pressure to accelerate [treaty] negotiation." [185] In both cases Party policy was reversed, seemingly as a result of " intervention." While in the treaty matter the intervention came from Russian Communists directly upon M.P.'s through Trade Unionists, the " intervention " in the Campbell Case was that of a Clydesider, James Maxton, a friend of the indicted man, called into conference, Williams says, with the Attorney. The treaty intervention revolted the House, the people and the wiser Labour Party politicians, and was palpably objectionable. The significance of the allegations regarding intervention in the Campbell Case was farcical in comparison, taken from a legal standpoint and apart from the general situation, of which it was only a token. MacDonald assumed an air of injured innocence and went down to defeat, following a decision calculated to preserve the appearance of Party unity. It was not unusual for prosecutions to be selected by policy and policy caused this case to be set aside. Apart from the fact that it was inhuman to prosecute Campbell, the leadership elected to save the Party from divisive self-criticism, and to avoid hardening a fluid left wing by giving it a martyr. (The outright Socialists asked in Parliament if they should not be arrested on the morrow for the same offense.)

Fabian writers stood together in defense of the Party. Clynes [186] says Haldane agreed on this procedure; Weir,[187] to

---

[184] Slesser writes there were two treaties and says of them that they represented MacDonald's finest work. Cf. Slesser, *op. cit.,* pp. 107, 109, 110.

[185] Hamilton, *op. cit.,* p. 252.

[186] Clynes, *op. cit.,* II, pp. 61 f. Where Slesser says the Labour Govern-

sustain " our policy," that is, the selection of cases by policy, cites the Lord Chief Justice. It is certain Slesser, the Solicitor General, approved of Sir Patrick Hastings' decision and fairly certain that MacDonald had nothing to do with it, although he repeatedly justified his position by saying his law officers advised him.[188] While Mrs. Hamilton seems to imply that the ILP members were Russophile and blameable for the pressure put on MacDonald and by him upon the Attorney General to withdraw the indictment of Campbell, Slesser believe Hastings acted independently; but Slesser was never in MacDonald's confidence. Indeed he often disregarded his orders. The Campbell Case " intervention " took the steam off the intra-party trouble that was coming to a boil. It afforded the " straw man " or the " whipping boy," self-selected by the Party leadership.

More truth about the intervention in the treaty matter is told by Snowden: [189] The treaty was to come up in a few days and the Government was said to be expecting to be defeated on it; but the Party had safeguarded itself by leaving the House of Commons free on it. There was therefore no cause for resignation in the treaty question, technically. (So, it seems that Mrs. Hamilton's confusion of the two events is inexcusable.) Snowden writes:

> Some of the Soviet delegates [on treaty business] had been in touch with certain of the Labour members and Trade Union officials during the whole Conference [on the treaty]. They had been *telling fairy tales* about the hundreds of millions of Russian orders which were waiting to be given to British industrialists as soon as the treaty was signed. When the announcement was officially made by the Foreign Office that the Conference had broken down, the Soviet delegates got to work with

---

ment used the " Red Scare " to excuse their failures on the domestic front, Clynes says their " enemies " found they were doing " too well."

[187] Weir, *op. cit.,* p. 179.

[188] Slesser, *Judgment Reserved,* p. 105. But the *NS* blamed MacDonald for his confused handling. It seems not to have been well informed during August and September of 1924 as a perusal of the memoirs and a scanning of its pages will indicate. It was wiser for *NS* to assume the air of a liberal, non-partisan observer.

[189] Snowden, *op. cit.,* II, p. 698, italics added. The *NS* had been " telling fairy tales " all along. Cf. *NS* (October 10, 1923), 33 f.

this group of British Labour members and Trade Unionists, and a meeting was held in one of the rooms at the
*House of Commons at which all the Russian delegates
were present.*[190]

The sequel was an appeal by those impressed with Soviet " fairy
tales " to Lord Ponsonby to resume the Conference under a
formula which Snowden, to whom it was submitted, called a
" face-saving " device. He knew the preliminary conditions for a
loan—the one thing the Russians wanted—would not be met, so
he feared nothing. He believed that a token political treaty might
pass, if made contingent upon an economic settlement which was
to be postponed to be dealt with by a commission on terms which,
he knew, would never produce a settlement. In his memoirs, he
admits he made a mistake in permitting this " face-saving " effort.
(Free-trader, life-time Socialist as he was, Snowden's early
naivety on this score is amazing.) He declares it was a mistake
to have allowed these trade-seeking members to place the political
members of the Party in so awkward a position. MacDonald had
said in May, that for a loan to be guaranteed by the British Government was out of the question. In August, the Foreign Office
announced that the treaty negotiations had failed. Suddenly a
treaty of a political nature was presented which left the economic
settlement to the future but secured a guarantee for a loan under
the Export Credit System.[191] Ponsonby's explicit instructions
had been to the effect that there should be no guarantee of a loan
until debts of the Soviet for confiscations were settled; and the
Soviet delegates had pressed for treaty and loan, and no settlement of debts. Indeed, they countered the debt claims with still
greater Russian claims for damages caused by Britons. Ponsonby's effort to get something in the nature of a political treaty
and Snowden's acquiescence in yielding to those whom the Soviet
delegates had persuaded that the English owed the Russians four
thousand million pounds, created MacDonald's predicament. It is
fairly certain he did not care to make the treaties at all. It was

---

[190] *Ibid.,* pp. 682 f. Italics are inserted. Mrs. Hamilton, ILP of Scotland, appears as a Fabian-Labour M.P. in the pages of *The Clarion,* 1929–
1931. After the National Government was formed she followed the
anti-MacDonald party segment.
[191] Tiltman, *op. cit.,* p. 224.

learned that pressures were being exerted and that strange influences penetrated inward from the periphery of "wild men," and sentimentalists and Trade Unionists; and it was alarming.[192]

Mrs. Hamilton praises all Fabian Ponsonby's efforts but does not distinguish the real negotiation from the "face-saving" plan. There can be no doubt that the intrusion of the Soviet delegates, all of a part with Zinoviev's intrusion at Unity House and Tschitcherin's proffered monetary support for the *Daily Herald* furnished rather real data for those who worried about Sovietism's march to power. Fabian C. Delisle Burns, in his *A Short History of the World, 1918–1928*,[193] says that exactly six Labour Members of Commons intervened with Ponsonby for resumption of negotiations, that the treaty signed August 8, one day after Parliament adjourned, represented the first of two tentative treaties, that the question of claims of British citizens, "ambiguously recognized" by Russia, was reserved to be dealt with in the second treaty, together with conditions for a guarantee of credit. Fabian Burns affirms "the activities of the Communists made these obstacles [political and economic] insurmountable." Burns sees the main difficulty of the Government then as the one created by the threat of Sovietism. The methods of the Labour Government's lesser officials like Ponsonby, and of the gullible Trade Unionists, only increased the trouble of the Labour Government by spreading fear of its capture by Sovietism. Such "intervention" prepared the Opposition to react promptly against the Government the next time it seemed to be taking orders from its Russophile left, and this was the Campbell Case. Although it has little to do with the story it may be said that whereas, to all appearances the Communists did not wish a Fabian-led Government in Britain to succeed, already the difference between the ideology of Russia's sentimental Socialists and the "pure-Fabianism" NEP, of Stalin's Government,[194] was being sensed abroad.[195]

---

[192] Mrs. Snowden, an ardent Fabian, was an "authority" on Russia, and frankly Russophile. It is possible she influenced Snowden's assent to the interventionists.

[193] C. Delisle Burns, *A Short History of the World, 1918–1928* (New York: Payson and Clarke, 1928), pp. 186 f.

[194] *Ibid.* Shaw named NEP "pure Fabianism" in 1931; yet in 1931 the change recorded in 1936, commenced. An aspect of "free enterprise"

Yet Fabians were responsible for the credulity of persons whom they had taught. On October 20, 1923, the *NS* observed sarcastically:

> The insidious Mr. Wise has now got his bloody-handed friends from Moscow into the most respectable British circles. Not only has an Anglo-Russian Company for the purchase and shipment of Russian grain been formed, but behind the Company stands the City.[196]

This was put in such a way as to mock all fears and cynically, it went on to urge greater aid to Mr. Wise's competitors from publicists and financial sources; and the editor added " British workmen are unemployed who might be producing [agricultural machinery for Russia]." [197] *NS* advice was plus-and-minus, stop-and-go.

Clynes seems to have been one of those enlightened by the Soviet delegates on the debt owed to Russia by Britain. He was

---

attributable to NEP practice was then condemned in favor of " Socialism in everything." See Chaptre XIII, note 7.

[195] Zinoviev, head of the Politboro, spoke openly in Moscow in disparagement of the British Labour Party and pilloried MacDonald at the Fifth World Congress of the Communist International. (Tiltman, *op. cit.*, p. 222.) Zinoviev was destined to die as a " wrecker," when the Old Bolsheviks perished in the purge of 1936. By that date "NEP-ism" was condemned also. MacDonald, as an old hand in the political game, should not have been hurt by the Zinoviev letter though his critics say he was. The abuse of MacDonald should have shown that the Bolsheviks disapproved of the " reactionary" Labour Party and ought to have boomeranged upon any scheme of the Tory press to show a tie-up with Moscow. MacDonald had a way of appealing to pity and he could have thought its publication would do him no harm and would check the Clydesiders.—Observers who rely on the enmity between Communists and Socialists should consider that sibling jealousy, however violent its manifestation, is usually a superficial characteristic overshadowing, but temporarily, deep and fraternal mutual acceptance.

[196] *NS*, XXII, 33 f. A certain E. F. Wise, C.B., lectured in 1927 on " The New Corn Laws," R. H. Tawney presiding. *FN*, XXXVIII (January, 1927).

[197] The reader can scarcely resist an adverse reflection upon the assumed omniscience of this Fabian voice, if it is recalled that this was the time of the terrible starvation years (1921–1923) in the Ukraine. Where did the grain Russia would ship originate? Cf. Edmund Walsh, *Total Empire*, (Milwaukee: Bruce and Co.) 1951.

in a position to learn of the Soviet attitude since, of course, he acted as leader until MacDonald returned from Geneva. He omits mention of the meeting of Soviet delegates with Members of Parliament and Trade Unionists in a room in the House of Commons; omits also the story of the six Labourites who carried the resolution of this gathering to Ponsonby and Snowden. He shows himself impressed by the data with which Soviet delegates countered the English charges of Czarist debts and demands for compensation to British subjects for confiscations by the Soviet. The Bolsheviks, remembering no doubt the Alabama claims, listed damages caused Russians by English " interference " in their civil wars and by blockades; they computed these, as said above, at four thousand million pounds. Clynes swallowed this because he believed Russia " one of the biggest potential markets in the world for the goods we produce." [198] This was the very line taken hitherto by the *NS* and its correspondents save for the one quotation taken from Massingham cited above.[199] It was also Henderson's view when addressing Trade Unionists, as has been said. It is not surprising that Trade Unionists believed in glowing possibilities of trade with Russia but that the Chancellor of the Exchequer, Snowden, ILP member and old-line Socialist as he was, did not so believe although he abetted the effort to log-roll the treaty. We know Mrs. Hamilton criticized Snowden because he was not a Trade Unionist and always lacked Trade Unionist views. His sympathy with Russia was ideological and juridical; he stood for *de jure* recognition as already granted, no more. Even as a Socialist he was not a " whole-hogger." He was self-

---

[198] Clynes, *op. cit.,* p. 52. He did not specify what sort of goods might be exchanged and his class was careless of the losses industrialists and businessmen or bond holders sustained from Soviet confiscations. The City was involved. Cf. *NS,* XXII (October 20, 1923), 33 f.

[199] As said above, Burns' *Short History* substantiates Massingham's unusual view, but as of 1928 when Stalin's State Capitalism was in control. Lansbury, in 1920, drew a cheerful acknowledgment from Lenin that what was going on in Russia was Fabianism, which was being used as a step toward Communism and was dependent upon the progress of Socialism in other countries for its evolution into true Communism. Cf. Lansbury, *op. cit.,* p. 243. In 1926, he proclaimed (in a tone which protested too much) that he had seen again the same pattern; but now he deplored Stalin's Godlessness and the Communist Party's criticism of " Labour." *Ibid.,* p. 264.

taught to a degree. Nevertheless, the glowing hopes of people who listened to Russian " fairy tales " had first been aroused by the Snowdens, by Clynes, Henderson and other Fabians, and especially writers in *NS*.

The 1924 Election, turning out the Labour Party and giving a very clear Conservative majority, has always since been said to have hinged upon the Zinoviev Letter. The text is in the appendix to Volume II of Snowden's autobiography. He would have been noble to have included the Foreign Office Note to Rakovsky, the Soviet representative in London. The Letter was a directive to the British Communist Party on how to capture the power of Government especially by militarizing the working class areas and defeating " bourgeoise " rearmament. Also, it abused MacDonald. The *Daily Mail*, controlled by the Duke of Northumberland, had a copy ready to come out the day the Foreign Office, under Sir Eyre Crowe (MacDonald being absent, campaigning), published it along with a note to the Russian Ambassador.[200] It really seems as if the Red Letter could have worked either way, for or against the Labour Party. (Actually, the Labour vote was larger than ever before although the Conservatives gained more constituencies.)

Burns writes that it was the Secret Service which supplied a copy of the " Red Letter " to the Foreign Office on October 10. The fact of its publication by the Foreign Office the same day as by the *Daily Mail*, along with MacDonald's note, according to Burns, weakens the contention that a fear of the Government's Red leanings alone, swayed the voters.[201] Sir Henry Slesser, too, in his *Judgment Reserved*,[202] implies that commenting Labourites in recounting the history of the 1924 election take refuge in Red-scare excuses for unsuccessful domestic performance. He thinks the " face-saving " treaty suggestions were " innocuous " and even good. Although he withheld full loyalty to MacDonald generally, he pronounced these treaties to be high points in MacDonald's

---

[200] Mr. Churchill, whose association with the Duke and the Tory-controlled Press was to be demonstrated in the Strike, stated in a reply to this writer's inquiry that he knows no more than is presently publicly known about the Red Letter.

[201] Burns, *op. cit.,* p. 188.

[202] Slesser, *Judgment Reserved,* pp. 96 and 98.

diplomatic achievements. Fabian Burns and ex-Fabian (since 1915) Slesser present the story in what might be termed an adult perspective in contrast with the emotional narratives of Weir, the partisan presentation of Mrs. Hamilton, the baffled accounts of Thomas and Clynes, the studied displeasure of Viscount Snowden, and the sentimental re-telling by Francis Williams, one of the led. Slesser said the people approved the idea of a Treaty with Russia and that to bring out Zinoviev's letter was necessary in order to defeat Labour by arousing fear.[203] Neither Burns nor Slesser believed it a forgery; it had many prototypes. The case would seem to be supported by the evidence of Fabians themselves, that the Labour Party, whether the Red Scare had anything to do with it or not, had certainly been obliged to ask for a dissolution because it could not carry out its program and would have lost its following had it continued in office. So, it retired to the more comfortable haunt of Opposition unburdened by the need to rely upon a Liberal segment for support, and unhampered by those it led who kept demanding " Socialism now."

MacDonald and the Cabinet—*there was no struggle*—used the threatened Censure vote and the compromise creation of the select committee in connection with the Campbell Case " to ride for a fall," according to Snowden,[204] Mrs. Hamilton,[205] and Weir.[206] Weir is specific and charges that there arose a Tory intrigue to overthrow the Labour Government, an intrigue revealed to have been known to the Cabinet as evidenced by Thomas' " withering contempt" when he turned his reply to Asquith into " the first [speech] of the Election Campaign." [207] From the viewpoint of this study, the names Weir gives are significant. They were the names of men who had an eye to the international scene, rather more than the Asquithian Liberals: Lloyd George conspired, says Weir, with Conservatives Austen Chamberlain, Lord Birkenhead, and Sir Samuel Hoare [208] to dish the Asquithians without whom

---

203 *Ibid.,* p. 110.

204 Snowden, *op. cit.,* p. 696.

205 Hamilton, *Henderson,* p. 253.

206 Weir, *op. cit.,* p. 183.

207 *Ibid.,* p. 183.

208 *Ibid.* These men 'had experienced Communist obstructionism at Genoa, for example. Lloyd George's Secretary, Sylvester, reveals it between the

H.M.'s Government must dissolve, and so to create a working Tory Government which, on international problems, would have Labour-in-Opposition's support. Weir also insinuates that there was a deal made by which the Government escaped the vote of Censure and agreed that when Tories and Liberals united on the select committee to investigate, they would resign and go to the country. Weir's theory is not acceptable. Had they incurred a vote of Censure there might have been no dissolution; the King would have sent for Mr. Baldwin; but then, Baldwin's Tory Government would have had the Asquith Liberals to contend with or to placate. As it was, the election "dished" the Liberals, and broke the Asquithians. The *NS* noted that this consummation was part of the "Long View"[209] and was MacDonald's view as well as that of the Socialists who were against cooperation with Liberals. If MacDonald, "for whom the old gang could never go far enough," as Shaw once said, was trying to use Baldwin while Baldwin used MacDonald, the evidence is a well-kept secret so far. In the long view, the forces set in motion by Socialist agitation and the Tory-Labour rapprochement must move in the "inevitability of gradualness" toward the decline, then the fall, of British Capitalism.[210] There are scant available data on how or where stood Sidney Webb in 1924. For 1931 we have his *What Happened*. Whatever the degree of disgust with MacDonald, he could not dispense with him yet.[211]

---

lines in which he deals with French impossibilism. Cf. Sylvester, *op. cit.*, p. 91.

[209] *NS*, XXIII (October 18, 1924), 36.

[210] Cf. Keith Hutchinson, *The Decline and Fall of British Capitalism,* in which he carries out the thesis of the "Long View." Tory Governments did the work of Socialist destructionism.

[211] Cf. Beatrice Webb, *Our Partnership,* pp. 471, 476; also, Hamilton, *Sidney and Beatrice Webb,* p. 271. This writer has a strong suspicion Webb had taught Clifford Sharp the meaning of the "Long View." Sharp was to express the idea more patently still in 1931. Clifford Sharp had been the only hope of the Society when in 1911 Beatrice mourned that there were no young men save Sharp to carry on, should the Old Gang take George Bernard Shaw's example or follow his advice and resign. There existed among Fabians patent antipathy toward the old gang and an anti-Beatrice "cave." Webb was returned by Seaham although he insisted he had come to Parliament too late. Mrs. Cole thinks the Webbs had doubts about the wisdom of creating a "Labour" Party. In 1926, they packed off to

It is clear in Hamilton's *Henderson,* and in the Asquith and the Snowden accounts, that the Labour Government unhorsed itself.[212] It chose a domestic issue on which to fall, hoping, it would seem, thus to avoid the dispute on the eastern international problems. These the Tories nevertheless managed to conjure up by means of the Zinoviev Letter.[213] The western international problem was shaping up politically into manageable form as the result of homeland changes. It was better in any case to keep Russian matters fluid. France now going Left, it seemed, still retained her grip (economically based) upon the Little Entente.

Although the writers we have cited and also Fabian Brailsford, editor of the ILP *New Leader,* and Lady Snowden, then lecturing in Canada, blamed MacDonald for the debacle, Henderson refused adamantly to displace MacDonald in the leadership; [214] and Sidney Webb kept his peace. MacDonald was a tool by which British Fabianism captured the International, and his Government was the means of England's regaining the hegemony of Europe.

So much for "interventions." They were not more important in shaping the course of Fabianism in the political life of Britain than those things from which Fabianism recoiled.

There was another power whose influence was still more to be evaded, that Church which had enunciated clear and defining condemnation of 1) Socialism, however disguised or reformed, 2)

Passfield Corners—Crown lands "inalienably safe," says Mrs. Hamilton. The Fabian Society stayed in London but Fabianism had its citadel in Passfield Corners whither many liberals who were not Fabians came "on pilgrimages "—long past the April of English Socialism.

[212] To survey the Party affiliation of the majority of holders of bonds in German municipal and State enterprises—all very successful—is beyond the scope of this study but if Tories invested as they did, Labourites approved the enterprises. Money to expand home industries or renovate, for example, the Railways as Thomas urged, was not to be had in sufficient supply.

[213] Weir makes a great deal of MacDonald's slow action and hesitant reaction to the news of the publication of the Zinoviev Letter, as if to insinuate MacDonald wanted its effects to transpire. That he had an agreement with Baldwin to turn the tide in Europe and then retire, or, that he saw Labour must be defeated because of its non-homogeneous condition, needs none of Weir's animosity to stimulate imagining.

[214] Cf. Hamilton, *op. cit.,* p. 256.

Communism, and 3) the monolithic state.[215] We have noted the Fabian attitude of preference for social democracy on the Continent. Christian Democrats and Christian Trade Unions were disregarded and the Centre disparaged. Slesser, before he became a Catholic, pointed out the religious ignorance of the Society generally. Mrs. Webb thought of her own Socialism as a religion and desired the Party to become a religion governed by an Order like the Jesuits. She assumed some erroneous viewpoints which would be insignificant if they did not measure religious literacy. She imagined that religion denied legitimate reliefs such as smoking or an extra cup of coffee (she was sleepless at night with her scruples on this score) ; [216] that the Christian religion condemned all profit-taking; that all capitalists worked only for profit unaware of any social obligations and incapable of being made aware of them or of acting morally so long as they worked for profit.[217] She appears as a badly instructed person and possessed of a puritanical or jansenist " blue law " conscience. Another leading publicist, Mrs. Hamilton, like Lansbury, Clynes, Snell and most of the autobiographers except Slesser who points out the real difference between materialistic good-doing and acting from supernatural Faith, talked of Socialism as " faith " in a religious sense.[218] Mrs. Cole manifests animosity toward what she imagines to be political Catholicism in her *Growing Up Into Revolution;* likewise her own " faith " is a self-made religion

---

[215] Henderson was a Wesleyan minister. His tolerance was never so great as to give the impression he might be pro-Catholic. When it was suggested the Government might be represented at the Vatican, his reply was that such a move was improbable because the Prime Minister was a Unitarian and he was a Wesleyan! Although in the case of Russia, he insisted one distinguish between the Party and the Government, he let his own religion dictate his nation's policy toward the Vatican state. Later, in 1941, it became apparent that Fabians thought of the Catholic Church as " fascist." Cf. *FQ,* 20 (Summer, 1941), pp. 5 f, and *ibid,* 29 (Spring, 1941), 32.

[216] Cf. *Our Partnership,* p. 471. Mrs. Cole thinks Beatrice would have been happy to learn she was to be buried in Christian Westminster and that Sidney would have agreed for her sake.

[217] *Ibid.,* p. 482.

[218] Hamilton, *op. cit.,* p. 59. The correct meaning of religion is " to bind together again "—God and man.

based on an unscholarly, if not ill-tutored, attitude toward the Bible. Incongruous as it may at first appear, the reader is asked to consider the fact that at Geneva, in ILO, and in the forces gathering to produce the Protocol, Catholic thought and the more refined norms of Socialism approached agreement. However, at the point where it should have become Christian societary doctrine, Fabianism recoiled. All the evidence points not to ill-will but to ignorance and fear of ecclesiastical influence. To try to state more succinctly the awkward fact that the mentors of the Socialist Labour Party were persons of religious illiteracy who made bold to treat with criticism and contempt the religious forces found at work in the international sphere would be less than objective. From the kind of "intervention" generated by such forces recoil was swift.

There are two considerations which we are about to examine which, understood separately and in juxtaposition, help to explain why the Socialist Government resigned at the time it did, at the point when one of their greatest achievements was taking shape, the Geneva Protocol; for even as an unratified measure it stands as an achievement. In itself it was worth the struggle to continue in office. Some data taken from a domestic situation throw light on attitudes otherwise inexplicable in foreign affairs.

First: When MacDonald, because the general situation was not manageable and not because a select committee was something to fear,[219] after consulting the Cabinet, resigned, it brought bewilder-

---

[219] The *NS* assumed an air of innocent surprise. What was so to be feared about a select committee? The *NS* supported MacDonald all through the episode of Government until he induced the dissolution. The *NS* tried to head off another election by pointing out the half-finished business in education, afforestation, Trade Boards, and the Webb surveys in the Board of Trade. It failed to note, these surveys under the chairmanship of Balfour were boycotted by TUGC. (Mrs. Hamilton, *Sidney and Beatrice Webb*, pp. 269 f.) Cf. *NS*, XXIII (August 9, 1924), 514. Then it was happy that it had been decided to drop the Campbell Case. An "adult democracy" needed no protection against "sedition." *Ibid.*, p. 534. A week later it was furious against "the Russian treaty." It said "no loan" and "no compensation":—Let the Russians float a loan and "satisfy the City." Indicating the ultimate source of the "Crisis," as the *NS* termed the dissolution of 1924, the *NS* pointed out that the all too naive explanation of the Daimler car and the Biscuit Shares would bring criticism *from the Party*. In

ment to his Parliamentary Secretary, L. MacNeill Weir, to whom we are indebted [220] for a clue to another possible reason. Weir tells the story of a peculiar bias Mr. MacDonald possessed which was demonstrated in a later (1929) division in the ranks of the Parliamentary Labour Party. Quietly, inexorably and unashamedly, MacDonald made it necessary (according to Weir)

October, early, the *NS* warned that in a possible election (*NS,* XXIII [September 29, 1924], 662) Labour could not win. *Ibid.,* p. 722. " No loans and no resignation," it pleaded: MacDonald had got into the predicament but he was clever enough to extricate himself and Party. (*Ibid.,* p. 724.) Again the Party division was indicated (*NS,* XXIV [October 11, 1924], 2) when it was said the Dawes Report was not popular with a segment of the Party (the miners had been fairly persuaded to accept it). The *NS* tried to keep calm after the Crisis came. At the Party Conference, the Communists had had to be defeated but the *NS* said that it was " nonsense " to try to exclude them from the unions on account of their " politics." Well, the Protocol was not going to go through anyway. (England was not ready for so great a commitment.) The *NS* made a very revelatory observation: " but for the Crisis " the Foreign Minister of the Labour Government would have been given " rough handling " at the annual Conference. (*Ibid.,* 2 f.)

But a few pages further on, Clifford Sharp under " This Absurd Crisis " took the characteristic Fabian viewpoint: This best of Foreign Ministers had done an " unintelligible " thing. True, he had " that high horse of his " and his vanity and could " lose his head." He had treated the Liberals and Asquith, the greatest living statesman, very badly. (*Ibid.,* 4.) A week later, Sharp had learned something which made the Crisis less unintelligible. There was " The Long View and the Short View." MacDonald's was the long view: Break the Liberals sooner and sooner will come a Labour Government with a clear majority. Sharp took the short view: Garner the present gains, keep alive the three Parties. Cf. *NS* (October 18, 1924), 36. By the next week, the *NS* was more explicit. (*Ibid.,* 65 f.) Anti-Socialists were making a two-party situation based on class lines. The *NS* disapproved, but did not recall that Sharp had warned against the anti-Liberal Labourites doing the same thing.

In connection with this matter, it is pertinent to recall that Beatrice Webb, as far back as 1911, had written: " We did not assert, or even imply in our propaganda that the proposed enforcement of a national minimum of life for all inhabitants, all the time, was impracticable under profit-making Capitalism. Rightly or wrongly, we believed in ' the inevitability of gradualness.' " They were content to leave the future to take care of itself " though we ourselves were convinced Socialists." Cf. Beatrice Webb, *Our Partnership,* p. 482.

[220] Weir, *op. cit.,* pp. 257 ff.

that Trevelyan bring in an education bill which provided no state assistance to " non-provided " [Catholic] schools, while it required building and curricular expansion in order to raise the school age.[221] Then he allowed his Government to be defeated on the subsequent amendment which all knew must be introduced as it was by a Fabian and a Catholic,[222] John Scurr. The " conscience clause " sent too many Labourites into the Tory lobby that day. Weir, whose thesis is that MacDonald betrayed his Party, is sure Mac-Donald was swayed by his anti-Catholic feeling in permitting matters to come to such a pass. Postponed again was the triumph of Graham Wallas—complete secular education—which Sidney Webb had balked since 1902. John Scurr, head of the Parliamentary Consultative Committee, as we have said, a Fabian and a Catholic, introduced the opposing amendment to the bill. Catholic Labourites voted with the Tories. It meant a decisive defeat for the Labour Government of 1929, but MacDonald unblushingly refused to heed the cry which went up: " Resign! Resign! " The risk was calculated, no doubt, and the incident emphasized the secularism of the intellectuals while measuring the strength of Catholics in the Movement—a " stress measurement " which showed lessening rather than increasing power in the Movement. Weir [223] is corroborated upon the point of Mr. MacDonald's anti-Catholic feeling by ex-Fabian Lord Slesser who mentions it explicitly.[224] Slesser in his " Through Anglicanism to the Church " in *The London Tablet* [225] says that the liberty he exercised in

[221] It is doubtful if Trevelyan had any tenderness for " non-provided " schools although he had agreed to a compromise with religious leaders on 50–75% help. Cf. Weir, *op. cit.*, p. 252 and p. 254, which reveals Trevelyan's attitude and belies Weir.

[222] This is a rare combination. Margaret Cole wrote that C. Delisle Burns did not outgrow his " Jesuit " training altogether. It seems he was Anglican. Cf. James Oldmeadow, *Cardinal Bourne* (London: Burns Oats), 1948, p 236.

[223] Weir, *op. cit.*, p. 258.

[224] His anti-Catholicism was, in this student's judgment, not bigotry in MacDonald but a cultural vestigial emotion like those attributed by Kingsley Martin to hereditary coal mine owners loath to surrender traditionally claimed properties to social controls. Cf. Kingsley Martin, *The British Public and the General Strike* (London: Leonard and Virginia Woolf, Hogarth Press, 1926), p. 125.

[225] Slesser, " Through Anglicanism to the Church," *The Tablet,* CXCII (November 20, 1948), 326 f.

approaching economic and social problems from a Catholic stand-point (when he was not yet a Catholic) was justly derived from his having been elected upon a platform compiled from *Rerum Novarum* and St. Thomas, and that the exercise of this liberty earned him " the distrust of my *very anti-Catholic leader, Ramsay MacDonald.*" [226]

The second consideration is as follows: An international pattern was forming upon the periphery of action where Socialist idealism and Catholic principles meet. Socialistic internationalism indicated the desirability of a League of Nations, and more especially of its appendage, the ILO, and for this end eschewed much ideological particularism. Catholic nations saw in the League a lack of executive implementation, beyond mere utopian ideals. In the act of producing the Draft of the Protocol of Geneva was a meeting of minds. (Parmoor offers the document.) To confront aggression with " solidarity," to reduce armaments, to induce compulsory arbitration before the Permanent Court, were the aims of the signatories. But a certain kind of particularism reasserted itself when an order came to the British delegates not to sign it, upon the eve of their doing so. It was only when Henderson returned to London that he learned the Government was about to resign. There would have been time to sign and ratify the Protocol. A remark of Lord D'Abernon's throws light upon the question: He found too much Catholic influence at Geneva. By taking these exhibitions of attitudes from two fields and from both periods of Labour Government, the story of the recoil at Geneva becomes more intelligible.

Suddenly, before the dissolution, when the British delegates were about to sign the Draft of the Protocol after learning that, almost unbelievably, Briand would sign for France, the order came from MacDonald to desist. Everyone concerned, especially Henderson and Parmoor, says the imminency of dissolution dictated it. But Parliament did not dissolve. It had to stay in session through October to get the Ulster Boundary Bill through the House of Lords.[227] Weir and Mrs. Hamilton, idealist concerning the Socialist International, bewail the incident and berate MacDonald.

---

[226] *Ibid.* Italics are inserted.
[227] Cf. Spender, *op. cit.*, p. 658.

Yet the resigned attitudes of Henderson and Parmoor are too nobly sustained to raise any questions as to their comprehension of the Prime Minister's attitude. The *NS* expected the Protocol would fail of ratification and but for the crisis cause embarrassment to the Prime Minister at Party Conference time. The Fleet, so blithely scaled down in the early days of this "Socialist" Government, became the darling symbol of Socialist isolationism.

The Protocol embodied the principles Lord Parmoor had laid down when accepting office: "The three problems of disarmament, arbitration, and security should be approached as an indivisible whole." [228] The proposed document set a date for a disarmament conference upon which all the rest of the settlement hung, made arbitration compulsory for all nations, and gave a world-wide authority to the Court (through the Optional Clause). It defined an aggressor and determined how and when an international police force might be called upon.[229] The British delegation, of whom Sir Cecil Hurst and Sir H. S. Smith are the only names not found in some well-known association with outstanding Fabians, had held important positions and taken prominent part in the Protocol's development: Fabians Henderson and Mrs. Swanwich had labored for its adoption. Anglican, and Fabian-familiar, Parmoor had striven to create it as the embodiment of his ideals for strengthening the League. Parmoor, Liberal Lord Hurst,[230] Hen-

---

[228] Parmoor, *op. cit.*, p. 224. D'Abernon (*op. cit.*, III, *passim*), meantime, having put Security first had later deferred security to Currency Control. He had achieved his aims in the Dawes Plan, accounting it Labour's triumph and was currently engaged in getting his Commercial Treaty, out-maneuvering France.

[229] This raised a hue and cry about the Fleet's being put at the disposal of an outside authority.

[230] Hurst, whose willing cooperation Parmoor achknowledges (*op. cit.*, p. 197), was serving in his capacity of legal advisor to the Foreign Office in which he had served as assistant or head since 1902. He became a judge on the International Court and England's member at the Hague in 1929. Sir Hubert Smith had been associated with Labour on the Liberal side since his lectureship on Political Economy to students under the Oxford University Extension and Toynbee Trust (1888), and his commissionership for Labour in the Labour Department of the Board of Trade (1893) and during his permanent secretaryship to the Board of Trade (1919) and tenure as Chief Economic Advisor to H.M.'s Government from 1919 on (ending in 1929). The reader by now must be aware of the measurement for usefulness to the cause provided Mr. Webb by their mutual associations.

derson, and C. R. Buxton had worked on the committee on reduction of armaments. Henderson took the leading part for England
on the subcommittee to prepare a Draft Proposal. It is significant
that Parmoor and Viscount Cecil, in whose office Noel-Baker had
served as secretary, wanted the draft, as adopted, to be rewritten;
and Parmoor proposed that Sir Cecil Hurst do the revision for
England, but the Labour Government rejected this proposal.

It was generally conceded that the League lacked sanctions.
Parmoor championed sanctions in the Protocol and endorsed the
change which was made from the wording of the Covenant:
"recommend" was concretized to "call upon" in the case of
nations asked to provide means to enforce sanctions.[231] Fabian
Mrs. Swanwich was the only woman who addressed the Assembly.
She publicized the demand of women for peace. Liberal Lord
Hurst was credited by Parmoor with couching the Protocol in
terms which won unanimous consent in the Assembly. Professor
Gilbert Murray, whose name is found associated with Fabians as
a lecturer of great authority, ever since the days of Beatrice's
"Destitution" Committee and the Minority Report, had served
as third delegate at Geneva upon the Prime Minister's departure.
Later he told Parmoor that the Protocol was, in his opinion, rejected because "people allow considerations of party advantage to
outweigh realities."[232] This allowed the inference that the

---

[231] Attempting to define an "aggressor" in the face of Japan's fear she
would incur this epithet by "protecting" her nationalists in a foreign country
and Australia's fear the Council would impinge upon "domestic jurisdiction," Parmoor and Hurst procured the ruling that the fact of having made
previous appeal to the Council should preclude a nation's being defined as an
aggressor, and they made concessions on "domestic jurisdiction" which were
as weakening as "self defense" would prove in the future Kellogg Pact.
(The way was cleared for Japanese intervention to protect nationals in
Manchuria.)

[232] Parmoor, *op. cit.,* p. 227. The professor was not unaware that Poland
and Hungary, by 1924, would have given a forthright answer if asked to
name the aggressor whom Pilsudski and Horthy had conquered. In 1925,
Gilbert Murray contributed the introduction to *Social Insurance,* the "report
of a Conference arranged by The League of Nations Union and held at The
London School of Economics, November 23rd-26th, 1925, on the subject of
'Social Insurance in its National and International Aspects and in Relation
to the Work of the International Labour Organisation of the League of
Nations.'" The speakers included Sir Kingsley Wood, M.P., Miss Ellen

Labour Party Conference would have divided against the Prime Minister if he had allowed the Protocol to be endorsed; or perhaps Professor Murray meant to blame the Tories insofar as MacDonald's order not to sign it was apparently moved by a Tory conviction. (He could have allowed it to be signed and let the Conservatives bear the onus of rejecting it.) That it was Tory mentality which rejected the Protocol seemed to be confirmed by Austen Chamberlain's speech at Geneva (1925) soon afterward. MacDonald's concession to the Tory view had a Tory reason: " English good sense." It was not patently the work of Fabians that the Protocol failed of ratification, but of " the Party " which enveloped their activity, with their assent.

Lord D'Abernon, the British Ambassador to Berlin, looking back to this disappointment, had something very provocative to contribute. Upon the later occasion of the rejection of Germany's request for a place on the Council as a condition of joining the League of Nations, Lord D'Abernon, who had then favored Germany, remarked that the rejection of the Protocol was necessary and good because there were already too great French and Catholic influences at Geneva; the " dilution of the Council by adding Spain and Poland [demanded as a condition for admitting Germany] was rejected by English good sense." And he traced back the course taken by " English good sense ": " It was strangely right when refusing the Protocol "—it " remained for *insular instinct* to pull them [the delegates] back." [233] The character of Fabianism cannot be understood without a grasp of the significance of this recoil.

Lord D'Abernon was English Ambassador to Germany from 1919 to 1926, that is, through the term of Labour's First Government without break. No final conclusion can be made from these scant data; neither can they be ignored. In showing that MacDonald's Government was arriving at a Tory mentality while the Labour Party was reassuming ideologically the shape of its constituent social parts, it may be recalled that the fashion of the Conservative mentality was to reject those international products of

---

Wilkinson, M.P., The Rt. Hon. Sir Alfred Mond, Bart., M.P., Mr. H. N. Brailsford, *et al.*

[233] Cf. Lord D'Abernon, *Diaries*, Vol. III, *Dawes to Locarno* (New York: Doubleday, Doran and Company, 1931), p. 226. Italics are inserted.

idealistic thought which by their nature satisfied standards which
transcended simple international idealism and were measurable by
Catholic propositions. For instance, the Baldwin Government, in
the *NS*'s words, had treated the draft conventions of the ILO " as
if they were products of the evil one." [234] Thus, too, had the
Washington Hours Convention remained unratified.

In the Foreign Office, headed by MacDonald, the permanent
head was, as noted above, Sir Eyre Crowe. He was a believer in
the Entente and a loyal adherent to the policy of King Edward
VII toward France, but in regard to the Protocol his judgment
was set against submitting to the Permanent Court of International
Justice any British question or allowing British armed forces to
be called upon by an international police. It is implied in all the
accounts, except Weir's, that Sir Eyre did not favor MacDonald,
and that he warped the Prime Minister's policy toward the Right
whenever he could. It would seem rather that MacDonald and Sir
Eyre learned to understand each other and that they were agreed
on the Russian situation; but on the Protocol, MacDonald probably did act not only in consideration of his Party's non-conformist views, but in deference to the " spirit " in the Socialist
world which had considered the overthrow of Bela Kun an undesirable " reaction." Lord Parmoor's account of the situation
in the Foreign Office is acutely objective. [235] He speaks of the

---

[234] *NS*, XXI (May 12, 1923), 130. Also, cf. *Catholic Review* (Washington, D. C., weekly), October 2, 1949, first page, wherein the fact of the
embodiment of papal principles in ILO is recorded, as it was in other
sections of the Catholic press the week of October 2, 1949. It is remarkable
that Socialism met Catholicism on the international labor front with far
greater mutual comprehension than on a domestic or particularist front.
Marx's writing for Internationals was toned down to general and universally
acceptable principles, as we have seen, citing Lorwin, above. This is merely
a phenomenon of the relationship of natural and supernatural religion; at
some points they are identical. There remains the fact that British Socialism
and the *NS* fought the Belloc proposition for consideration of the existence
and exigencies of agricultural southern Europe, culturally Catholic. They
criticized it as being a Vatican cerebration and countered by proposing
universal Industrialism under Socialism, non-agrarian. Tory negation im-
pacted both Socialistic and Catholic thought on the juridic level, feeling no
doubt it could afford to ignore their mutual criticism on the lower levels.

[235] Parmoor, *op. cit.*, p. 195. Sir Eyre Crowe was a typical Conservative
as all his utterances show. Cf. Spender, *op. cit.*, index. His influence on

conditions which he made with MacDonald on joining the Government:

> Lord Haldane and myself should work together arranging the general business of the House of Lords when I was out of England at Geneva, but all questions relating to foreign policy or the League of Nations were to be answered in the House of Lords by myself as Lord President of the Council, from information directly derived from the Foreign Secretary and the Foreign Office.[236]

There came a time when Lord Parmoor learned he was not getting such information. He had been given an office room in the Foreign Office and he had noted the early relief manifested by the personnel when MacDonald's advent removed the haughty personality of Lord Curzon; but the charitable one-time Vicar-General is very clear to state that soon the attitude of the permanent staff became most hostile to the Labour politicians in the Foreign Office.

When MacDonald, seeing perforce eye-to-eye with Sir Eyre, stopped the signing of the Protocol, there was outcry only from Socialists like the idealistic Mrs. Hamilton and the bitter Weir. Yet a sizable segment of the Party would have handled the Prime Minister roughly had he endorsed it. The reason seems evident: Socialists were pacifists but organization for peace should be made to inhere in Socialism. MacDonald understood this better than the idealists did. Parmoor, and Henderson even more so, acted resignedly and patiently, thus signifying that most leading Party feeling was ready for Locarno. In the person of Fabian Philip Noel-Baker who was Parmoor's secretary, the attitude of Fabianism in regard to order in Europe is symbolized. He had had experience as secretary to Lord Robert Cecil, who had created the Draft Treaty of Mutual Assistance at the League's fourth Assembly in 1923 which was rejected by the Labour Party because it set up " regional " Pacts and, *NS* alleged, reaffirmed " balance of

---

MacDonald, if Weir is any judge, was strong and MacDonald trusted him—much as Snowden trusted and liked Norman Montague of the Bank of England.

[236] Parmoor, *op. cit.*, p. 197.

power."[237] That he could serve both sides in pact-making is symbolic of the meeting of minds on a hardening policy, in the drift between "iron curtain" propositions and covenant theory. On one side, the Draft Treaty of Mutual Assistance was too "hard" for Labour; on the other, the Geneva Protocol, too idealistic for Conservatives. The first set up too much armed aid for pacifists' acceptance, the second set up too much moral pressure, where the Catholic populaces of Europe might one day voice the indictment of an aggressor, and call upon the United Kingdom to participate in repressing an injurious act. Because the Protocol favored a "medieval" (The Fabians' usual word for Catholic)[238] European feeling, it could be foregone and the exigencies of domestic politics might take full sway. As to the position of Webb and Henderson: Webb's protégé, Clifford Sharp, was anti-Vatican and he himself positively secularist. From 1922 to 1932, despite his activity for Labour, Webb was growing toward sympathy with Soviet ideals.[239] He did not break with MacDonald until 1931. Mrs. Hamilton[240] reports Henderson's loyalty to MacDonald and says that "anyone who addressed Henderson on any other assumption [by proposals to oust MacDonald, which would "play the Conservatives' game"] got a dressing down such as did not encourage repetition." Mary Agnes Hamilton is sometimes naive.

The Party had had enough of unhappy relations with M.P.'s who resented the "outside" influences affecting the Labour Party, and enough of dependence on Liberals to get through a few reforms. Either they must get a clear majority or hand over power to Conservatives, whom they now termed "collective." In the latter contingency the upward dynamic on European settlement had been given a fresh impulse, and the way was set for some reforms, such as that of the Poor Law; Labour in Opposition

---

[237] *Ibid.*, pp. 221 ff.

[238] Cf., for instance, the picture opposite page 168 in Slesser, *op. cit.*, captioned "Medievalism Under Difficulties." Slesser is questioned as to whether he meant St. Thomas Aquinas or "Jimmy" St. Thomas. Slesser is pictured with the *Summa* under his arm. "The medieval church" was the term used for the Catholic Church up to the time when things Catholic began to be called "fascist," in Fabian circles.

[239] Hamilton, *Sidney and Beatrice Webb*, p. 291.

[240] Hamilton, *Henderson*, p. 257.

would be more powerful than in office and would obtain release from the pressure of its own impatient utopians. To stay longer in office would be to wreck the Movement. The Trade Treaty with Germany, and the treaty looking toward security and mutual aid against oppression, at Locarno, set up the mechanics for a rise in living standards. The stage was well set for the next five years.

H. SUMMARY

The political element in the " Labour " Movement had been embarrassed by dreamers; the ideological ones and the trade-minded. Some of these tried not to worry about Communists, others like Fabian C. Delisle Burns and Trade Unionist Thomas did worry. There were differences of opinion as to the reality of the promised trade but the political element had to keep alive the hope of raising production figures for the sake of the unemployed. The Government chose to resign and the agreement to do so, while some Socialists screamed " betrayal," was rather unanimous among Labour Party politicians. Nothing else explains the loyalty of Henderson, Webb, Clynes, Snowden, Haldane, and Parmoor to MacDonald as leader. In 1924 they kept together as a Party and preserved the Movement by choosing not to go on demonstrating broken promises. Sadly, they let their highest achievement die aborning because the Geneva Protocol went beyond the description of that which secular Socialism could control; they chose to render concrete in Locarno, by a Tory compromise, what had been fluid and capable of a Christian synthesis at Geneva. The meeting of minds, Tory and Labour, was to be designated " insular instinct." Only those who loved Henderson and hated to see him fail in anything [241] or those who detested MacDonald out of disappointment that as a Labour politician he " betrayed " pure Socialism, even though his " Long View " was identical with theirs, or who, like Snowden, believed MacDonald would do almost anything to destroy Henderson's work out of jealousy, criticized the administration on the score of the Protocol. It represented a recoil on the Right, as the debacle of the Russian treaties represented

---

[241] Mrs. Hamilton emphasizes the Optional Clause, also, as a Labour device.

recoil on the Left. If Sir Eyre Crowe and D'Abernon [242] now called the turns, the gradualists saw the gain and could wait. Much is symbolical in the Draft Treaty of Mutual Assistance and the Geneva Protocol; Locarno was the best compromise possible at the time. " The City " would remain London.

After 1924, Henderson and MacDonald worked together in transactions to amalgamate the Two-and-a-Half with the Second International and to capitalize on the now revealed " gulf between Communism on the Russian model and democratic Socialism," in Mrs. Hamilton's words. " MacDonald had some magnificent sparring matches with the giants of the Third: Radek and Bukharin; the long and slow business of reaching terms with the ' Two-and-a-Half ' [Adler's] was mainly Henderson's task." The reconstructed Socialist International resulted. Adler and Tom Shaw resigned and Henderson became President of the re-aligned Second.[243] No doubt there was some deep and unspoken understanding in " the Long View." [244] Stalin bridged the "gulf."

---

[242] Symbolic too was the refined Belshazzar's feast in Sir Abe Bailey's London house. If D'Abernon, whose triumph it celebrated, remembered that there had been handwriting on the wall, he failed to record it.

[243] Cf. Mrs. Hamilton, *op. cit.,* pp. 277 f. Bukharin was working to sovietize Europe; and Borodin, China (Stalin's Asia Detour).

[244] To borrow the light of the 1930's brings clarity to the "Long View": Henderson was a real " saint " of the social gospel. He used his Wesleyan pulpit for the development of the Movement and the Party. (Cf. Hamilton, *Henderson,* 601). After the Crisis of 1931, he was heard to mutter, " I was ready to play second fiddle all my life, but he [MacDonald] wouldn't have it." Cf. Hamilton, *op. cit.,* p. 401. Yet they were together at Geneva when Henderson presided over the Disarmament Conference and MacDonald represented a Baldwin Government. Mrs. Hamilton describes but does not evaluate the data found in the sad picture of Brüning's pleading and Nadolny's sickened anger placated and managed by Henderson, so humanly and sympathetically, while every measure to give to Germany equality and prestige which would have bolstered Brüning's government against rising Hitlerism, and bring peace to Europe, was defeated by messages from Baldwin to MacDonald. Henderson wanted peace but he was willing to wait and work for a Socialist world to have it in.

CHAPTER IX

FREEDOM *VERSUS* LIBERTY

A. REACTION TO CRITICISM FROM WITHOUT

Having served its purposes, the Labour Government went out and its Fabian mentors took stock of the criticism evoked by the election of 1924. The criticism was double-barrelled: Labour could not cope with Russia and it lent itself to infiltration of Communist-Socialism. The Red "Scare" represented an over-simplification of the menace of Socialism. The MacDonald Government might have successfully avoided the stigma of Bolshevism by choosing as it did, a domestic issue upon which to fall,[1] but for the Tories' exploiting the well-known sympathy of Labour with Russia by producing the Zinoviev Letter. The scandal of the Campbell Case was *not* that interference from back-benchers was used to preserve a Red miscreant from the course of the Law, but that interference on the part of members of the Government estopped the Attorney General.[2] As a Government, Labour lost prestige. The Government by making the creation of the select committee concerned with the Campbell Case its reason for resigning made an issue of its pride rather than its Red sympathies. Even though the *NS* sloganized "no loan and no resignation," making it appear that the effort to make the Treaties with Russia was the cause of going to the people, this was not the case. The Treaties were submitted in Parliament for a free vote with the understanding that the Government would not resign if they were not accepted. Because there was no good reason for resigning

---

[1] Cf. Clynes, "Did We Tamper With the Law," *op. cit.,* pp. 62 f. By his preoccupation with this point of picayune significance, Clynes reveals the naïvety of his character and the improbability of his ever discovering the real nature of the Socialism he professed.

[2] Hastings was quite amenable to the leadership but he decided not to prosecute before seeing MacDonald, on Maxton's pleading; Slesser, the ex-Fabian Solicitor, was scarcely aware of the proceedings. Cf. Slesser, *op. cit.,* pp. 104 f.

which could be made public, and because it carried a message to the investor class, the *NS* took the attitude that the reason for going to the people was really the Treaties. By coincidence, the Zinoviev Letter argued forthwith that the "bourgeois" treaties should be the signal for seizure of Britain by the Communist Party. Commercial interests dissatisfied with MacDonald lent themselves to exploiting this bogey. Slesser gives the impression that the idea of the commercial treaty with Russia was gaining ground popularly, a thing which made the Zinoviev Letter "necessary."[3] Fabian C. Delisle Burns says also that political obstacles stood in the way of a policy based upon economic considerations and he blames the Communists for the difficulties they caused Labour by their open criticism in Moscow of the Labour Government. So both these sure-footed writers show the Red question was real and affected two classes of critics. Neither Burns nor Slesser consider the Zinoviev Letter a forgery. A forgery could easily have been made because so many such letters were about in Norway, the United States, and in Germany. For the same reason, it could have been genuine.[4] Burns says the Secret Service supplied a copy of the document they held.[5] It directed

---

[3] *Ibid.*, p. 110. The *NS* conceded the Election *lost from the first* but did its part in the campaign as if it did not comprehend the "Long View" of MacDonald and Henderson.

[4] Cf. Williams, *op. cit.*, p. 314. None of the memoirs hitherto cited ventures a guess as to how the Foreign Office and the *Daily Mail* got their copy. Official investigation found it genuine. Francis Williams' demand that the original be published [sic] is naive.

[5] Weir, *op. cit.*, pp. 189–194, says it had been held since early October. He also says Sir Eyre Crowe and MacDonald were in perfect agreement but he offers no documentation. If MacDonald sought to let it be used, it was 1) to discipline his followers, or 2) with fear they *might* be otherwise elected. If this were true, his reasons for not wishing to be elected were: 1) A gentleman's agreement with Tory leadership, 2) his knowledge that the Movement would be ruined by a political crystallization—a term of office doing standard politics and never to reach Socialism. The "Long View" revealed another fissure in the idea of a "Labour Party." The ideal of non-political social *movement* had been captured to form a Party using the carrot of "Socialism." A choice had to be made in 1924. Webb, in 1924, as in 1931, considered the pruning or shock which resulted would do the Party good. Cf. Hamilton, *Sidney and Beatrice Webb*, p. 290.

the British Communists to " Corrupt the Allegiance of the armed forces."[6] Burns' account is the most evenly considered:

> . . . the letter, together with Mr. MacDonald's very vigorous criticism of it forwarded by the Foreign Office to the Russian representative in London, was published by the Foreign Office on the same day as that on which the *Daily Mail* published it; and in the general atmosphere of suspicion in regard to Russia and the Communists generally, it was impossible to say that any single event influenced the electors.[7]

The " general atmosphere of suspicion" is better described as " insular instinct" sensing a threat to English liberties.

No one can form an opinion without consideration of the fact that although Sir Eyre Crowe, the civil service head of the department, is thought to have worked at cross purposes with his Chief at times, a Parliamentary Secretary thought the agreement betwen Sir Eyre and MacDonald was perfect. The latter says he saw a tentative draft and that the Office sent it out to protect him. Parmoor believed that the attribution to MacDonald of the Note to Rakovsky discredited Labour in the eyes of those who favored a Russian trade treaty. This is a telling point: There were persons who desired the trade treaty and lost confidence in the Labour Government's ability to treat with Russia—commercially.[8] Parmoor says he never heard of the Zinoviev Letter before it was published and implies it was Sir Eyre Crowe's management which militated against the Government.[9] Neither Ponsonby, at 10 Downing Street at this time, nor Haldane, was told about the letter.[10]

The electorate made it abundantly clear that they would have none of Sovietism, while the vote of the core of Labour showed it did not equate " Socialism" and Sovietism and others, successors of Cobden and Bright, evidently prefered Curzon's method

---

[6] Cf. Burns, *A Short History of the World, 1918–1928,* pp. 188 f.

[7] *Ibid.,* p. 188.

[8] Parmoor, *op. cit.,* pp. 211 f. Weir, *op. cit.,* p. 194, thought MacDonald used the appearance of clumsy handling to ingratiate himself with the Tories.

[9] *Ibid.,* pp. 196 f.

[10] Weir, *op. cit.,* p. 189.

to MacDonald's.[11] Fabians made a great deal of the fact that the Labour poll was a million votes heavier than in 1923; but then the general vote was larger than ever due to the scare and it divided on Tory *versus* Labour lines. Two groups or interests, those who thought Labour could not manage Russia and those who feared Bolshevism, defeated Labour. With the Scare which arose from the threat to liberty inherent in both Socialism and Communism we are presently concerned.

Much had been said throughout the campaign about the relation of Socialism to Liberty. Fabians defended Socialism and its definition of " Freedom "—not Liberty. And they intelligently sought a spiritual basis for " Freedom."

George Bernard Shaw had refused office in the late Government.[12] While Pease wrote " Victory in Sight," Shaw disclosed a point of view different from the historian's in a chapter which the latter incorporated in his *History of the Fabian Society.*[13] In 1924, Shaw looked further back than upon that day's triumph and his retrospect cast light upon the future: He said that, long before the tide had turned, albeit with the " same water," at the time when his deductive economics (Ricardo on rent and Jevons on

---

[11] Cf. again Carl Marx, *The Eastern Question* (London: Sonnenschein and Company, 1897), pp. 232–236. Marx judged Cobden's interest in the cloth trade with Moscow the key to his absorption with " free trade " and ascribed to this interest ascendancy over patriotic, religious, or cultural drives in British statesmen's attitudes toward Russia.

[12] Cf. Clynes, *op. cit.,* p. 46. This is the only account which mentions the fact. The union leader was nonplussed by the intellectual's refusal to serve in Commons or " waste his time in the House of Lords " as " our spokesman." Clynes speaks erroneously of Shaw's " invaluable work as a propagandist of Labour's thought." Clynes lacks a real grasp of the fact that Shaw was a propagandist of Socialist thought which was repelled by the inclusion of the Trade Unions in the movement.

[13] Pease, the Fabian without guile, is the type generally accepted in superficial opinion formed upon the idea that Fabians are good Christians or trying to do the work good Christians leave undone. A letter to this writer from Neville Braybrooke, son of Fabian Patrick Braybrooke and editor of the literary *Wind and Rain* (London), expresses this view. Such opinion accepts the tenets of social democracy uncritically. Shaw, wily, guileful, profoundly penetrating, was one Fabian who, along with Margaret Cole who has no charity for him, admitted being a Communist, and had from the beginning pointed out the ultimate conclusions of their logic.

value) had been supplanted by the Webbs' " historical concrete economics " in their *Trade Unionism* and *Industrial Democracy*,[14] Graham Wallas who, though out of the Society, was still Fabian at heart, had showed up the " staleness " of their movement by his studies of Chartism and his life of Francis Place;[15] that while it was averred that one might be a Christian and a Socialist, the actuality was the opposite and in the atmosphere of the Society, spiritual persons " starved." [16]

Shaw was too intelligent not to know this meant more than that they, being always " Philistines," failed to appreciate Ruskin and Wagner, as he complained they did. Here was a succinct description of the " spirit " of Fabianism as of 1924: Concretized economics (down from the moon of theory—to unions) ; activation of ideology (away from the staleness of Mill's and Owen's socio-economic constructs—to political action). This very concretization and activation precluded flights of artistic enthusiasm or excursions into spiritual bournes (not to speak of the human good derived from sociality—mutual and equity associations capable of flourishing under the dynamism of Charity). In the conflict between social movement and political action the latter had won the ascendency.

Yet Shaw himself contributed to the " starving " atmosphere. He had, by 1924, arrived at positive conclusions on the economic objectives of Socialism which he expressed as " equal distribution " and as the

> . . . only solution that will realize the ideals of Socialism. . . . This is not fully accepted as yet in the movement, in which there is still . . . the old craving for an easy-going system, which, beginning with " the socialisation of the means of production, distribution, and exchange " will then work out automatically without interference with the citizens' private affairs.[17]

Shaw took support from Plato's idea of " qualified rulers," adding that " without qualified rulers a Socialist State is impossible," as

[14] Pease, *op. cit.*, p. 277.
[15] *Ibid.*, p. 278.
[16] *Ibid.*, pp. 279 f.
[17] *Ibid.*, p. 283.

impossible as achieving it without " interference with the citizen's private affairs."

This only marked out a great change, one which had already transpired. The old republican ideal of people from all walks of life choosing one of their number to speak for them on common political interests, one who represented all, including or regardless of his own way of life, is to be discarded in favor of choosing a " trained ruler," an expert, who may lack personal experience in the business, political, professional, or religious life of a community. We noted how Laski found the need for using politicians to render the experts' political inexpertness bearable to people.[18] His treatise on this point served to illustrate a trend rather than to produce a constructive return to republicanism.

Shaw reduced political instrumentation, as he had reduced economic objective, to a concrete form. His words were redundant and ephemeral-sounding: " Democratisation of Democracy." He thought of this as creative of a " positive organising force." Some meditation upon this theme will disclose the meaning that with multiple committee-forming, the problem confronting all planners, fixed in the individuality of voters in municipalities or in factories is removed. The small committee, the factory unit, the neighborhood gathering, makes for facility in carrying a majority; these lilliputian political organisms are easily carried by the one informed member and in this way a *monopoly opinion* can be produced.[19] In this way, the tension found in an uneasy majority procured in the face of one or more active oppositions and bound to respect the best thought in the *minority*—the old way of republican government—is resolved. Unanimity, emerging from the assent or consent, however critical, of the minority to designated authority, is transformed under " democratised democracy ";

---

[18] *Supra,* p. 171. Students of comparative government will recall that Fascist Mussolini, whose State was constructed of politicized social orders, was, before the commencement of World War II, building a " brain trust " of political scientists to develop the political arts as well as the other arts in The Academy.

[19] In this way, the virtue of non-stratification, the social adhesion produced by the fact of persons joining groups having diverse objectives is lost, and a party line established which defeats all ends save its own. Cf. Arthur M. Schlesinger, " Biography of a Nation of Joiners." *American Historical Review,* vol. L (October, 1944), 1–26.

it is no longer unanimity but only acquiescence, forced or flaccid (and it is possibly the subversion of the real majority). The result defines itself as One-Party rule, the product and producer of monopoly-opinion. Shaw said " a positive organising force " was the fruit of democratising democracy; thus he implied democracy was to be henceforth an unchecked Force, not merely, as of old, " a check on tyranny." If one could read Shaw, it was hardly necessary to have a Zinoviev letter.

Up to 1924, some of the old anarchies of Guild Socialism remained to plague the Fabians. Shaw wiped out the " imaginary issue "; for now, said he, both groups had arrived at the idea of " pooled products "—for equal distribution.

He had said, back in 1919,[20] that the Society would have done better to have taken on Wells' ideas outright and let the " Old Gang " go, to get along as they would, " somewhere, somehow "; and now in 1924, he writes, " Here [in the economic and political objectives above stated] are two large jobs already in sight to occupy future Fabians. Whether they will call themselves Fabians and begin by joining the Society is a question which will not be settled by the generation to which I belong." [21]

---

[20] Cf. F. E. Lowenstein, " The Shaw-Wells Controversy," *FQ*, 41 (April, 1944), 15–20.

[21] One cannot help the feeling that the old lion of St. Pancras Vestry is bidding for the sympathy of the offspring to whom he pathetically says adieu. It could account for the Cornelia-like devotedness of Margaret Cole to the members of the " Old Gang," (except Shaw) whom she idolizes dutifully, while she criticizes. Cf. her *Beatrice Webb* and her preface to *Our Partnership*. A generation later, the newly formed Society was in the forefront of the Labour Party and had chosen the road of " control." They had nationalized all the promised items, even " labour," and, beginning to survey effects, were hesitant to find the coal miners still unhappy. Cf. the review of Margaret Cole's report, " Miners and the Board," *FN*, 60:5 (May, 1949), 74. One reads " the Group argues with conviction [having provided " no statistical sample," however] that there are remedies for the miners' disappointment about many matters, and that unless action is taken true disillusion may set in." The change from nationalization to Socialism was under study. Yet in 1947 (cf. *FN*, 58:5 [June, 1947]) the Executive seemed trying to recall the Society to its old vocation, that of the Old Gang and not of the Wells-Shaw development. It is so significant as to need full quotation:

" This Annual General Meeting endorses the following statement of the aims of the Society:

" The principal aim of the Fabian society should be to influence, stimulate,

Writing while Labour lived its brief day of power, his was no note of triumph but only of warning: Between bending every effort to create a politicized centre and forming cadres to transform the circuit of popular power in a democratised democracy led by trained rulers, lay the choice of the future. Shaw thought it did not matter really what choice was made. A new synthesis was taking shape: Out of decentralized social ordering would come the monopoly opinion to inform the monolithic state itself—that robot which must result from politicized economic and social units. Shaw offered no synthesis, only a choice. There is no indication that British Socialism made the choice so offered; few understood Shaw. Within another decade, however, the " Old Gang " had swarmed off. But when Wells died it was said his spirit had always been one with the Society. We refer in another place to his idea of the " priesthood " of social responsibility.

The shape of " The Order " is perceivable in the words now coming into use: Cor rol, force, elite leadership, equal distribution. But for the immediate future Fabians were still calling themselves Fabians and looking to the next Election by defending

---

and instruct the vanguard of the Socialist movement rather than to engage directly in mass activities. For this purpose the role of the Society is primarily to conduct research, to assemble and interpret significant facts, to serve as a forum of discussion at a relatively advanced level, to maintain a continuous intellectual initiative in the formation of constructive policies, and generally to act as a radiating centre for new ideas. The development of cadres in the Labour movement is an important aspect of this objective. The dissemination of ideas emerging from the parent Society's work among a wider public can be carried out to a considerable extent through the provincial Fabian Societies.

" While the Society can usefully devote a limited amount of attention to writing memoranda for Labour Ministers and Members of Parliament, it should take care not to become absorbed with current affairs of immediate practical importance to the detriment of questions of future importance. The Society should resist the tendency to disperse its resources by attempting to cover too wide a field, and should concentrate on problems of major significance. The Society should welcome financial aid for its work from outside bodies or persons, but its work is unlikely to reach a high standard unless the subjects of investigation are chosen primarily with a view to the interests of the members taking part in them."

" Buffet Tea will be available at about 4.30 p.m. ANDREW FILSON, General Secretary."

Freedom. The " Labour " Movement had had political experience and had contributed to the historical dynamic the peculiar force which was its own. Fabian Socialists had learned empirically the effect of political action directed toward economic ends through social magnitudes. And they had learned that a fear of losing Freedom [22] could move the electorate.

Thus it came about that Professor Harold Laski (of whom Shaw said in his interlinear reply to this writer's letter, which was thus returned, that he was a fairly representative Fabian) took upon himself the task of explaining the nature of Freedom in the Socialists' conception, since the electorate had exhibited a fear more instinctive than rational in October, 1924. The Society published and sold Laski's *Fabian Tract No. 216, Socialism and Freedom,* which came out in July, 1925. He wished to appease the fears found current. He enumerated the feared threats to freedom: 1) " Bureaucracy," 2) Platonic Utopia, 3) the threat to the family, 4) the peril to artists and thinkers, 5) the " absence of a leisure class," 6) the loss of the apprentice' dream of becoming the Boss, 7) the loss of color and variety in an era of planning, 8) the loss of " chance and vividness " when " no man remains . . . eager and able to be master of the event . . . mediocrity . . . uniformity." By antithesis, he remarked that an " idyllic picture " which lacks " the single merit of accuracy " was presented by those who sought amelioration without Socialism. He listed these admitted gains: 1) The increase in real wages, 2) social insurance, 3) increased educational opportunity, 4) an awakening national conscience regarding slums, infant mortality, preventable accidents in industry, inequality before the law, a harsh penal system, 5) charity more widespread, 6) growing unity of classes, 7) the " spirit of progress " keynoted by concern for the right of the individual. This list contributed by ameliorists did not, he said, " possess the single merit of accuracy." The reader seeks in vain for the assuagement of the listed fears; the rest of the article is an elaboration of his antithesis.

---

[22] The semantics of " Freedom " as opposed to " Liberty " are very significant: Freedom is something bestowed on dependents; Liberty is an inherent quality, sometimes resisted or denied but irremovable. Fabians spoke of Freedom.

Laski's "Freedom" is very difficult to define, even in fourteen pages full of materialism [23] wherein "fellowship" is the preserver of the commonwealth "whether [men] will or no," a discovery to be made by

> . . . experiment with the best in themselves. But, so to experiment we need to be members of a *State* to which the allegiance of men is given with a *passion* at once *vivid and intelligent,* and, to that end, it must be a State conceived in justice. For justice is the twin-sister of freedom and each lives in the victory of the other.[24]

Indeed, Laski's thesis on "Freedom" is identical with Shaw's

---

[23] Cf. H. J. Laski, *Socialism and Freedom* (London: Fabian Society, 1924). ". . . in the appreciation of [art; for artists are the *true* leaders of civilization] lies the most joyous experience *life can offer,"* p. 12. Italics are inserted. Laski was a professed atheist. Cf. Mrs. Hamilton, *op. cit.,* p. 399.

[24] Italics are inserted. Mr. Laski's psychology presupposes a high perfection in men, utopian if not unique—*passion* and *intelligent* action; in another place he says "the discipline ordained *can be made instinct* with justice." Again, on page 13, "we build our philosophy on hopes not on fears," as if a successful dichotomy of these emotions could be made. Again, on page 6, "from wonder is born indignation, and from indignation thought." Slesser, also, comments upon the belief in human perfectibility which once he and his colleagues cherished. But, after years of Thomistic study, Slesser argues that law and property (and liberty therein) are part of fallen human nature's need, and he calls for "the application of vocational fraternity" to abolish invidious distinction between employer and employed by uniting both in one common operative entity. (This is the understanding of vocational group or *ordines* held by Wilfred Parsons, S. J., whereas, William Smith, S.J., of the New York Labor School, finds the *ordines* in Industrial Councils. In the English translation, "Vocational Group," has doubtful meaning in *Quadragesimo Anno*). Slesser finds that vocational cooperation is "but partly represented in the trade union, for trade unions, both of employers and employed, represent respectively, but a moiety of the industrial process." Slesser feared the *vastness* both of syndicalism and of the Labour Party which unduly subordinated the individual. "It is therefore rather to the smaller form of industrial guild than to vast and mechanical structures that the Labour Party, if it be persuaded to base itself on medieval tradition, will be forced to look." Cf. Slesser, *op. cit.,* p. 141. (He had hitherto, in a complimentary sense, found all their true tenets "medieval," *e.g.,* their stand against *absolute* property, *unjust* price, *usurious* interest, the *plutocratic* state.)

"concrete economics"; it lies in "equal distribution" and "pooled products." He too insists on the training of rulers. With what sounds like Cistercian idealism, he writes, "It is only by freeing ourselves from the tyranny of things that we can enter into our heritage." But the parallel with Citeaux ends too soon: "Freedom is impossible as long as the *division of property* is not referable to principles of justice." [25] Laski seems to equate the artist with the man of freedom and the libertarian. And he says "true Socialism is a libertarian, and not an authoritarian, Socialism." But, while he has averred that in the Socialist order artists' "perception and insight will be their own," he shifts sights in the next paragraph to Socialists in general and continues: "Rules made must be rules to which the *average man* has consented . . . discipline ordained can be made instinct with justice . . . [and can] win the . . . allegiance of erect-minded men." Laski's Socialists do not suggest that freedom and conformity are synonymous; but they do insist there can be "*no freedom* until those things about which *conformity is demanded* have been established only with the common assent of the com-

---

[25] Since we have made the reference to Christian Communism a telling distinction may be added by pressing the analogy further. Mr. Laski's State embraces *all* men as Socialists, immured in a system where the souls of men are regarded as of too great worth to be degraded by a "mean struggle for bread." No, his monks are all artists, leisured by equal distribution; but if they jump over the wall as we learn an occasional Cistercian sometimes does, falling back into that society we call, with wider connotation than "State," the nation, Mr. Laski's monks have no place to go. This Citeaux of materialism has enveloped the nation. Their State has bounded all things in Socialism. But compare Thomas Merton, *The Waters of Siloe* (New York: Harcourt Brace and Company, 1949), wherein Christian Communism fully adopted offers in radical form the solution to modern over-emphasis on industrialization, in the form of a radical agricultural and liturgical way of life, wherein property is held in community and distribution based on Charity (not "charitarianism")—"to each according to his need; from each according to his ability."

Incidentally, Shaw speaks of the heads of the ILO, Mr. Albert Thomas and his staff, as neo-Carthusians in his *Tract No. 226, The League of Nations* (London: Fabian Society, January, 1929). The Fabians, to date, appear to believe the "medieval" Church and its orders have disappeared leaving only myths for them to appropriate. If that is how it is in England, America is something else to reckon with.

munity." [26] It is clear to us then that the artists' perception and insight will be formed upon the media of an order wrought by the demanded conformity with the average and the common.

Mr. Laski is in full agreement with Mr. Webb that reform as society may, the only real re-formation is that accomplished under Socialism. Also, in this essay at least, he is a gradualist, saying that where Socialism " has been overemphatic as in Hungary and Italy, it has suffered appropriate penalty." [27] Like Webb, he considers " religious toleration " a mark of freedom's progress and to this he equates " toleration " of Socialism or growth in " faith in Socialism." He counts with this freedom before the courts of law, as one mark of progress although he believes the courts are partial to the wealthy and thus divide the rich and poor still more. He takes *one class,* as Webb does not—the miners, their health problems and educational limitations, and their insecurity, as his basis for Socialists' " scepticism of the freedom effected by the present order." He counts as slaves—in a breathtaking transition those who in homes devoid of beauty, live a life of unending routine, obeying their masters " from dumb inertia "; for, although they have political power, they are spectators in politics and " forced " to remain private persons. Whereas, " at the base of society their main desire is to be let alone," " at the summit "— this is Mr. Laski's transition—they mainly desire notice by the keyhole-listening fourth estate, to be at the right first night or to be painted by the right artist; and the same as to clothes, books, travel. [28] Laski's " slaves " equate " private persons "—those either shrinking from view or those craving flashbulb notoriety. He does not say how Socialism can keep the base and summit dwellers from exchanging places when the laborer has gained control of the condition of his work, and has achieved a " share in making the orders under which he lives," when the laborer has attained an " opportunity for creative leisure," and the *education to judge* that conditions he assists in making are as " intelligible " as the orders of a " medical man or a sanitary engineer " and are

---

[26] Laski, *Socialism and Freedom,* p. 12, italics added.

[27] *Ibid.,* p. 6. Clearly, in *The Crisis and the Constitution,* Laski submits that the boundary line between not-socialism and socialism cannot be crossed by gradualism—only by political cataclysm.

[28] *Ibid.,* p. 5.

" referable . . . to principle which can be established as rational by scientific investigation." [29] Mr. Laski contends that *only* Socialism can produce the last-described desirable state of workers. It is not a unique assumption. The Socialist, he says, does not " dogmatise" as to the forms social ownership should take; he merely " insists" that effective administration for community interest can come solely from community possession. But some industries will " still be left in private hands" although the owners' *motive* can no longer predominantly be " profit." Still, a man is free; free to marry, to beget children (but they will by the State " be trained to an understanding of the meaning of life "), free in " religious belief," free not ever to be unemployed, free to help make rules, and to " get elected." Under Socialism there will be no nepotism, no caprice, no danger of anyone advancing by taking advantage of his fellows.[30] He does not say what moral force will make men so perfect under Socialism. There is no evidence that the laborer or the artist shall be free not to be a Socialist, or not to entertain an intelligent " passion" for his State.

Laski had not the forthrightness nor the penetration to ultimates, nor the honesty of Shaw, but both taught the same doctrine. Nevertheless, Laski's vision embodied more anarchism (rulerlessness) than Shaw and less design to develop a special class to rule than W. A. Robson whose *Standardisation* is to be reviewed.[31]

In October, 1926, William A. Robson, a member of the New Fabian Group, but long a Fabian, wrote for publication and sale by the Fabian Society, *Socialism and the Standardised Life.* He attributed to fear of the Standardised Life on the part of large numbers of persons otherwise full of " sympathy for the under-

---

[29] *Ibid.*, p. 8.

[30] *Ibid.*, p. 9.

[31] W. A. Robson, *Socialism and the Standardised Life* (London: Fabian Society, 1926). Ex-Fabian Slesser, *op. cit.*, p. 151, and Fabian Sir Josiah Wedgwood, when in Parliament, established a practice of safeguarding the liberty of individuals, or human liberty, by a vigilance which kept them in their places in Parliament when undebated measures were being passed, exercising a power which was theirs in Government or in Opposition to say, " Object." Together they prevented many obnoxious measures of both Tories and Labour from being passed.

dog," all the impervious resistance to "irrefragible economic reasoning," statistics, and even "dramatic horrors" by Socialist writers. But he said these sympathetic persons were all wrong; for Capitalism, it was, which produced dread uniformity. Like Laski and Shaw, he too adduced the example of craftsmen and artists: Where an artisan is forced in conformity with custom "to provide an ugly funeral for his wife," yielding to silent pressure of public opinion, the artist poses as a Bohemian with "elaborate disregard for standardised conventions" in inverted homage to class conduct; each case represents a perversion produced by Capitalism. Robson believed biological standardization would be changed by Socialism's removing economic unequalities and the resultant "dysgenic" organisation of society, using Shaw's phrase. At the risk of begging the question, Robson expatiated upon the desirable standardizations produced by large Capitalistic enterprises and sought by Trade Unionists particularly in ILO objectives. But fortified by the opinions of Professor Taussig, of Graham Wallas, and of W. H. Hudson, Mr. Robson warned that the danger of encrustation of civilization by standardized customs is real and not to be dismissed lightmindedly. He, too, like Shaw and Laski, believed equality of income would enable men to resist the tyranny of standardized conventions.[32] Robson expressed greater respect than Laski evinced for the whole system of government administration which relied on "an equality of treatment being meted out and a potential equality of service being rendered . . . to all [at least] falling within the ambit of a particular class,"[33] and he cited the wisdom of Sidney Webb to sustain his view that in democracy's "catering essentially for minorities" it is the similarity of the individuals which is insisted upon rather than their differences.

If the Socialists wish to establish a society in which life shall be tolerable, they will have to pay more attention to

---

[32] His assumption confuses the psychological with the socio-economic. Because a man had only the amount to spend which any other has does not preclude the possibility of his spending it without regard for the opinions of his neighbors. Robson's psychology, like Laski's, assumes the perfectibility of human nature in the way exemplified by Rousseau's *Emile*.

[33] *Ibid.*, p. 7.

the differences between human beings than to the similarities among them.[34]

With great wisdom he warned [35] that Socialist doctrine should be kept within narrow limits to be wide enough to "embrace those who want a full and deep and diverse life"; nor should it become so comprehensive as to establish a dogma on every important question. While he admitted Socialists are right who believe that the Socialist outlook on Property should be accompanied by general justice in all fields, he said no such thing as demanding this was advocated; for a man could be a sinner and a Socialist. But if Socialists were to be sinners, life would be intolerable and Socialism would be proved a failure. The virtue of "seeing life as a whole" must be left to development in individual minds, never projected in institutions and group organizations, else in fields where freedom and diversity are of the first importance coercion would be introduced.

Professor Robson was self-contradictory. He worked himself into the trap of total social control which Shaw and Laski devised. Socialism for him was the "apotheosis of the Many" *led by the Few who cannot by nature be standardised:* Socialism, aware of the importance of the Few, eschews the educational experience of the United States where even though the barriers of wealth and kinship are broken down in the educational system, standardization has nourished the average and starved the exceptional child.[36] So, with characteristic positivism, he advocated the special training of a new elite to *exemplify diversity* alongside the uniformity of the masses. As for Laski so for Robson, the only sin was to aim low. His Socialists should aim to produce great pictures and great inventions, to achieve the formulation of great scientific laws and not leave them to chance, far less should their aim be merely to "level up" the bottom strata. It is for the Socialist Commonwealth to produce desirable environment. "Socialism alone," offers such "enrichment of human existence." [37]

---

[34] *Ibid.*, p. 15.

[35] *Ibid.*

[36] He overlooks the great diversity discoverable in the adaptation which American people have made from the fairly uniform education offered.

[37] All these Fabians are favorable to Russia. Robson, even though he

Common to all three writers are these several notes: 1) They are confronted with the people's fears of forced standardization; 2) they assume the artist class to be leaders of civilization though not of the ruling group, *i.e.*, likely to be the most horrible examples of rebellion against standardization and capable, if properly treated—not to say trained—of providing the spiritual pabulum of *the masses;* 3) they argue that the Few or the elite are to be trained for political leadership and to provide diversity (for the artists' contemplation and dissemination, no doubt, since they say masses tend to standardize whatever they receive regardless of Socialism or Capitalism); 4) they equate the State with all societary magnitudes within the nation and the economic order; 5) they treat reforms of men as persons, reforms of systems of business, and forms of Trade Union practice, as extraneous to themselves and their system; and they do so with tutelary contempt because they hold to the slogan that only Socialism will do. Only Robson pointed out some things to be avoided by sincere Socialists.

This was in 1926 and the wave of the future was rising in Labour Party gains even though by October, 1926, the Trade Unions had been broken on the wheel of the General Strike and the Act of Parliament controlling contracting in and the use of funds of Trade Unions was taking shape. (It was amended but not repealed by the Labour Government of 1929–1931.) The Fabian Society, although nothing in *Fabian News* indicates it, and only the uniformity in membership, constant book sales, and obituary notes would suggest it in *FSAR*, was drifting. The most impressive indication of activity is the formation of the New

---

disapproved of Russia's criminal code which ruled that certain books be removed from libraries, compared the United States unfavorably with Russia, as nations equally standardized, to prove his contention that there is no connection between the Standardised Life and either Capitalism or Socialism. However, Robson's judgment on America is made upon the data of the Scopes trial (concerning Darwinism) in Tennessee, the Higgins Patriotic Text-Book Bill in New York, and the "standardising regulations" enforced upon Freshmen (known in the United States as "hazing") in American Universities. Like Shaw and the *NS* generally, Robson believed the Ku Klux Klan coerced "*huge masses* of American citizens to conform to certain *standard* sentiments and customs." Cf. *ibid.,* p. 13. Italics are inserted.

Fabian Group "to revive the glories of the old," as Professor Laski said in introducing Robert Fraser's *A Social Philosophy for Fabians,* like Robson's, published and sold by the parent Fabian Society, in 1930. Although it came out when the Party was in office, it appears from internal evidence to have been in preparation some time. The impression is given that Professor Laski trained the youngsters who wrote it as a symposium which Robert Fraser edited, to doubt the old Mill and Jevons solutions, to assume an outlook more "complex," because they had shaped their background from T. H. Green, Leonard Hobhouse and Professor Tawney and had formed their minds under the impact of Mr. and Mrs. Hammonds' "classic books." They had acquired political skepticism, according to Laski's preface, from Wallas.[38] Now free from the "dogmatic confidence" of the old Society they are dubious of their power to cope with the problems they see; they assume Mr. Fraser's cautious hypothesis in "fascinating contrast" to "Mrs. Besant's certitudes." That is, Mr. Laski finds them so. We find that, as there was a statement of aims by seven members of the Labour Party striving in 1923 to preserve cold Socialism in the melting heats of political activity, now, on the eve of another political experience when the "Old Gang" appears too weary to give more than an order for printing, new, young

---

[38] Cf. Graham Wallas, *Human Nature in Politics* (London: Constable and Company, 1948). Wallas (page 169) proposed assaying the "new tendencies," *i.e.,* the finding of contrivances for measuring press influences, class instincts, saloon conversations, as potentials in controlling political forces. He states as his hypothetical objective: "Some day the conception of a harmony of thought and passion may take the place, in the deepest regions of our moral consciousness, of our present day confusion and barren conflicts. If that day comes much in politics which is now impossible will become possible [the "sense of the State," "remembering Athens"]. The politician will be able not only to control and direct in himself the impulses of whose nature he is more fully aware, but to assume in his hearers an understanding of his aim [expressed] in that grave simplicity of speech which in the best Japanese State Papers rings so strangely in our ears [Science with them had allied and indeed identified itself with that idea of natural law which had, Wallas said, always underlain their various religions], and citizens may learn to look to their representatives, as the Japanese army looked to their generals, for that unbought effort of the mind by which alone man becomes at once servant and the master of nature." *Ibid.,* p. 198.

thinkers struggle with the old dogmas armed with skepticism and " the right amplitude of mind." [39]

The pamphlet is a childish mimistic thing, repeating the orthodoxy of non-orthodox Fabianism with a reassertion of what its authors believed to be Aristotle's union of the " sociality of man with politics." They make the uncritical assumption that the " early Christian Church " saw socio-economics as irrelevant to the " unseen " world; and they produce the quite usual confusion of " State " with nation. There is also a confusion of nineteenth century *laissez-faire* with the supposed " automatic beneficence " of " Progress." Like their elders, they hold the State as the All of social well-being; they equate not political freedom with economic power, nor economic freedom with political power, but freedom with equal distribution.[40] They speak of " equality " as equal distribution (and admit of allowable exceptions to uniformity). They owe their notions of equality to Shaw, their concept of social directive force to Wells, their grammar of politics to Laski, their business concepts to Webb's slogans, "expertise "

---

[39] Cf. Harold Laski, "Introductory Note" to *Tract No. 234,* which is Robert Fraser, *A Social Philosophy for Fabians* (London: Fabian Society, 1930). It is analyzed throughout using a few words in quotations for semantic reasons.

A parallel action takes place in the United States today. Students for Democratic Action (SDA), the junior affiliate of Americans for Democratic Action (ADA), echo their elders on resisting "reaction from the right or the left." "Expanding for academic freedom, student rights, and non-discrimination," Columbia University SDA sponsored "educational meetings on the German situation [pro-Social Democrats], United States' atomic policy [re the circulating Stockholm Petition, Soviet-inspired, against the use of A-bombs] . . . ran a drive against any aid to the Franco regime in Spain, worked in the Lehman [ADA] campaign for Senator. . . ." Cf. "Extension of Remarks of Hon. F. D. Roosevelt, Jr.," *Congressional Record,* Tuesday, August 1, 1950, p. A5857. Cf. David Williams (Fabian, Rhodes Scholar, CIO-AFL, director of London Bureau of ADA) "Labour Britain and American Progressives" in *FQ*:53 March 1947, pp. 7–10. Cf. especially p. 10 where intercommunication of "Labour" and ADA is shown: a twice-monthly "London Letter," sent to "opinion formers," a "trades union press agency covering over 100 American labour journals," touring lecturers, etc.

[40] Actually, "Political Economy," in the original synthesis, bore reference to the socio-economic well-being within the civil framework—both the support and the concern of the political order but distinguished from it as family from State.

and "measurement and publicity," their institutional inventions to Beatrice Webb. They too, without the "horrid" word "intellectuals" or even "elite," profess that the "group" directs society by spreading the fruit of its research "downward"; also, "the Party" is defined as the "instrument of legislation." There is no room for the Party's educative experience from contact with other Parties, mutually respected. The slight changes in ideological coloration noticeable in the New Fabians cannot be explained without reference to the fact that in the immediate environs, on platforms and in Conferences, two new spirits Herbert Morrison and Oswald Mosley raised their banners; and two pathways lay open before these youngsters, too: 1) The way of "the Party" and "the group" and 2) the way of decentralized social order [41] (both ways neglect the definition of citizenship in terms of relation to the State as informed by political science), wherein "decisions were taken by those who have a major interest in the results" and the individual registered his will "at the source of social decision." Anyone could see that the easier path to take was the first. To these young joiners Fabianism, although the Fabian Society consists of Socialists, is not Socialism: It is a "doctrine" and a "method" and Socialism is no longer the only means of social salvation. The political empiric has changed that.[42] Democracy, the absolute sovereignty of the people, is the New Fabian doctrinal objective. This is not so new as they imagine; it is inherent in Shaw's "democratised democracy." But the "method" is defined now as to "persuade the influential" (not to appeal to the people); to give order to the "administrative aspects of philosophical tenets," and this by *a*

---

[41] Decentralized social ordering is subject to socialistic manipulation, whereas decentralized civil ordering is a desirable preventive of "too much government." The Fraser group did not make this distinction.

[42] This is not the only place where it is stated in Fabian circles that Fabianism is *not* Socialism. It heralded, faintly and far away, the new "dynamic democracy," an expression which is becoming current in 1950 in antithesis with "decadent governments" (republics). "Dynamic democracy" is still social democracy, i.e., politicized social configurations dynamized by the One-Party. Cf. "Contest for the Minds of Men," a speech of Senator Wayne Morse of Oregon in the *Congressional Record,* July 10, 1950, pp. 9936 f, especially the editorial used for text.

group (the Fabians) "temperamentally" unsuited to street corners, whose publications carry the Socialist preachment "latent under the facts."

This is the atmosphere of the 1920's and still there is talk of Democracy. The 1930's will see the word recalled with doubt of its potency. Now, however, the arranging of "administrative aspects of philosophical tenets" is calculated to achieve the effect of a One-Party and monopoly-opinion program. Where decision is taken "at the source of social decision," "Democracy" is to function through the persuaded influential ones. Let a political situation be as heterogeneous as the twenty-two Soviet Republics, the *administrative aspects* of philosophical tenets work out according to the opinion of the persuaded and the influential working at "the source of social decision." Democratised democracy meant decentralisation for centralisation.

A whole dissertation might be written on this pamphlet, the product of the Fabian "*Pueri Virginesque,*" (recalling *NS* sardonic comment on Baldwin's appeal to youth) by taking cognizance of the history of the Society, to which allusion is made, and the impact of rising Fascism as of 1929, or by merely engaging in criticizing the philosophy. Here we have only to note how the children of the Fabians were indoctrinated and sent into political action dogmatic in their anti-dogmatisms, equipped with philosophical assumptions not altogether indisputable. To list a few of the assumptions: With youthful dogmatism they say, "Experience and modern psychology combine to *insist*" and "the view we take is concise" that "the good life is impossible except in a good society." (They probably mean a State which subsumes all economic life of the nation.) This would be quite Thomistic if it meant that the State is a perfect society because it *can* provide for or protect for the families (a family is an imperfect society) which constitute the nation whatever is needed for their perfection, civilly, economically, juridically, even religiously. But by "good society" these young Fabians mean a society of a certain kind, one assuming all societary good as its own to create and dispense, the State which assumes the contours of the Nation.[43] As to "good life" they mean a life of freedom from

---

[43] In our concept the State is inherent in civic coefficients belonging to the

economic inequalities and provided with the material elements of
living, even of psychological *materia* for the arts.[44] Their State
is not something which provides the means to complete the family's
perfection to enable the family or the familially ordered group to
complete its contribution to society [45] and to develop its individuals'
personalities.[46] Their State exists for the individual and his
" rights," immediately, and for them " equal rights " depend on
equal freedom, *i.e.,* freedom of economic opportunity. They allow
that the law of equality may admit of dispensations ; inequality may
be tolerated for special need and even be demanded by the social

---

societary units which constitute the Nation and retain to themselves elements
not proper to the civil construct, the State.

[44] In 1949, at the Blackpool Labour Conference, atheistic Harold J. Laski
was chairman of the Labour Party Executive Committee. Cf. Michael
Straight, " British Labour Takes Stock, A Report from Blackpool," *The
New Republic,* 120 (June 27, 1949). " The older laborites demanded a
return to a pioneering faith. But the leadership was strangely silent in
response, knowing at heart that the problem is, instead, to liberate the people
from outworn formulas in search of a new synthesis. Herbert Morrison
declared, ' Our new economy needs a new social driving force; we must set
ourselves more than materialistic aims. . . .'

" Richard Acland, former head of the Commonwealth Movement, carried
this doctrine to an appeal for the introduction of religion into public life.
Aneurin Bevan, the agnostic, matched Acland's spirit with another kind of
religious fervour . . . the delegates, roaring with laughter and shouting
assent, [when he said] ' suspect those who speak of religion in abstract terms.
Never in the history of mankind have the best of religious ideas found
greater expression than in the program we have carried out.' ' Suffer little
children ' [he quoted and added] ' What is national planning but the insistence
that human beings make ethical choices on a national scale? The language
of priorities is the religion of Socialism . . . Our programs are but the
prosaic instruments of a great design.' "

[45] The doctrine of the Mystical Body is precluded. The State should leave
to " free initiative of citizens . . . the cultural areas," says Pius XII in an
address to the Eighth International Congress of Administrative Sciences,
August 5, 1950. (*The Catholic Mind,* July, 1951.)

[46] The idea of divine vocation is completely removed. The Address cited
(n. 45) states that the State is a " moral organism," a living entity: The
" last word " does not belong to " mere organizational technicians." Government is exercised " in the name of the State, not of man immediately . . . of
the country in such a way that individuals never find themselves submerged
under the weight of State Administration." (*The Catholic Mind,* July, 1951,
pp. 460 f.)

quality of the work performed. Here the young thinkers arrived at a very old concept arising from the hierarchy found in the "nature of things." (The *NS* in 1924 had argued that ministers of government and Members of Parliament should for efficiency's sake ride first-class in trains from London to their country homes and back, and it opined that the Prime Minister should have a car for his use, better provided by the State.[47]) But in general equality must be "imposed" by "social control," that is, control of production and distribution. The Fraser group concluded that Benthamism failed by "leaving untouched" the question of social and economic denials of a good life. For these young thinkers the good life depends on education for political policy; it is evaded by war so politicians who make wars must be rejected. Already rejected are *laissez-faire* and the Christian Religion, specifically. These writers are "collectivists," they say, because "profit" as a motive is not morally or practically efficient to achieve the "deliberate and instructed will of society." As to "bureaucracy" which they disclaim, they say Fabianism does not imply the "superiority of the decisions of a centralized bureaucracy over the decision of the people" but since bureaucracy, an element of modern government, is an "inevitable element," it should be of "high quality." They do not underscore their two not altogether incompatible ideas: 1) The decentralization of authority and 2) the invention of central committees or councils to work in connection with elements in Parliament—nothing more or less than a political subsuming of the "lobby."

All this committee-making serves the uniform or monopoly opinion and the one-party system. It is safe to say the Fraser group did not see so far as Laski or Shaw. They thought bravely of a government which would "consult" and they *invented* means to speed up the lagging institution of Parliament, a "circle of advisory committees around the legislature." They think it is admirable (although it was not *invented*) that the Cabinet developed to embody responsibility after a hundred-year search for an institution adequate to democracy; yet, in the "mild peroration" (self-styled) they say democracy has never yet existed.

Their philosophical assumptions on "Property" are a "fas-

---

[47] *NS*, XXIII (September 20, 1924), 662.

cinating contrast" to older certitudes, certainly: Property if unequal gives unequal *power* and perverts the State by means of the Press and the Universities as in America.[48] Democracy has "no respect" for such general welfare as a legislative or executive branch made up of moneyed men might envision; such welfare could only be for their own ends and a subterfuge.[49] One must conclude that hedonism and materialism in the training of these young thinkers leave no doubts with them that men can be other than beings determined by their economic self-interest. Terribly old-fashioned, even in the late 1920's, was this working assumption that *homo economicus* really existed. Property to them is *economically* harmful in proportion as it seeks profit and not social gain; they assume that profits and gains to society may be physically separated completely. That a legitimate profit contributes to savings which in turn builds national assets was unthinkable. The rich have no place in their society.[50] Fraser's group continue:

Property is *spiritually* harmful; men of *no property* have to *take orders,* and do not control the conditions of their work.[51] As

---

[48] Shaw might be thought far too intelligent to join Laski, Robson, and the group which dictated Robert Fraser's pamphlet, if one did not know that exactly like Robson, he mistook the Ku Klux Klan for a vital movement and like *NS* and *FN,* in which his lectures dealing with the Klan were announced (*FN,* appendix to 1924), he considers it the new world "fascismo."

[49] Feiling's *Life of Neville Chamberlain, passim,* surely negates this view.

[50] *Rerum Novarum* insists throughout on 1) right to land ownership, 2) benefit to society from right use of riches, 3) immorality of taxation which drains away private wealth. Cf. especially page 29.

[51] Pius XII insists that not all private enterprise comes within the sphere of public right; that the proprietor always remains master in economic decision; that the latter is "obliged to contribute to the increase of national assets by savings." "Proprietor" may be an "individual, or an association or a foundation of workers." Cf. full text of address to Delegates of International Union of Catholic Employers Associations. *U. S. News,* June 17, 1949, 32 f.

Outside Socialist circles the aim in striving for "Control of conditions" is not to avoid obeying just laws but to procure economic justice, and assist in creating the conditions for social justice. "Economics [are] the living product of the free enterprise of individuals and of groups of individuals freely constituted. Enterprise . . . is amenable to the private juridical order of economic life." Pius XII, *ibid.,* p. 33.

to "wealth," it is "the reward of sterile leisure." As to class, "Lambeth and Rhondda Valley" is the metonyme used—coal miners to typify or symbolize all workers.[52]

---

[52] With academic exactitude, a critical bibliography is appended to this eleven page Fraser pamphlet. There are thirty books and nine Fabian tracts. The authors are exactly fifty percent Fabians including Ernest Barker whose account of English Hegelianism and of the "influence of German idealism in English State Socialism" is remarked. To Harold Laski's *Grammar of Politics* is owed "more than can be expressed in words" but was fairly stated in eleven pages. Robson taught them the defense of delegation of judicial powers as a necessary result of the development of the social service State, *i.e.*, boards and bureaus to replace courts; Tawney, the functionlessness of our society. The Webbs in the "only book" of theirs that "has nothing whatever to do with Socialism" probably inspired their confidence in Fabianism above Socialism by *The Decay of Capitalism*. Herman Finer provided the knowledge of the Civil Service for purposes of politicizing; and Pease, the history of the Society from which again they picked the Poor Law Minority Report as one of their past glories, and the birth control studies made among Fabians and early universalized, as a glorious use of statistical data. Kingsley Martin's story of the General Strike seems to have whetted enthusiasm without inspiring respect for history. (It is a disillusioned ideological account.) Graham Wallas' "best analysis of the psychology of politics," has not left so clear a mark as Lippmann's *Public Opinion,* about which they have this to say:

"We live in a pseudo-environment created by the Press, which corresponds exactly with our actual environment . . . catastrophes . . . inevitably occur since our actions are prompted by the one environment, and yet have their effect in the other."

Of course, they thought Cole "vigorous and dogmatic" on unemployment, currency, education and agriculture, but not prophetic in his *The Next Ten Years,* etc. They thought C. Delisle Burns' *A Short History of the World, 1918–1928* a good "introduction" to Toynbee's annual volumes published by the Institute of International Affairs. To nine Fabian tracts on kindred problems they added Woolf's *Imperialism.*

They read some non-Fabians; indeed the leakage of distilled Socialism from its new bottles is traceable to the atmosphere of books like H. N. Carver's *Distribution of Wealth,* called the "core of economics." "Damaging to orthodox Socialist theory," this study makes it "implicitly clear" that interference "with the unit returns of capital and labour" is dangerous and that "reduction of inequality lies through redistribution of property, and not by raising wages at the expense of profits." (This is far removed from the abolition of Capitalism advocated by the Fabian Socialist critics of Fabianism in politics.) And then, the "development of the idea of semi-autonomous industry" as an idea with a future was found in *The End of*

As we are about to consider the General Strike of 1926 we conclude the selected list of philosophical assumptions made by the Fraser group with this gem: " The General Strike was the answer that *men* gave to a State that seemed to them faithless to its own purpose." They listed Kingsley Martin [53] as their source on the strike but the Fabian, the future editor of the *NS* (beginning 1931), does not offer full warrant for such a statement. True, Martin saw class-struggle as inevitable, saw the " two nations " of Marx and Disraeli, said that " democratic conventions give way " in a struggle for self-preservation or mere justice: [54] It is true he saw a " revolutionary future for England." In Martin's view—pure-Socialist rather than Fabian—any future Labour Government must risk " dismissal upon a piece of constructive Socialist legislature " or lose the faith of the wage earners (not " people ") as they surely must by " playing the party game." The " democratic faith " of " constitutionalists " will but doubtfully stand the test if Labour " finds the money for internal reorganisation by a policy of disarmament." [55] This did not only mean that the Party with the money to spend on welfare would not be opposed by voters worried over lost liberties; it meant that, given a political majority, the Labour Party must find the money to become State Capitalist to the end that private Capitalism be obliterated. Martin also endorsed hereby the " Long View "—the

---

Laissez-Faire by J. M. Keynes. *Imperialism, the Last Phase of Capitalism* (now so worn a theory), which was then " the best modern statement of the Marxian theory of Imperialism as the internal Contradiction in Capitalism," and *The State and Revolution,* " more advanced and esoteric " than Laski's *Communism,* were listed, the works of V. I. V. Lenin.

These young thinkers produced a creative idea in the concept of autonomous associations *versus* the State, which they only half grasped. Communist mentors used the same idea to break up society into " soviets " for purposes of assuming control by monopoly opinion in the One-Party. The Fraser group are more Laski-ite than Martin-ite. They do not follow through to the envisioning of a Public Statute or Constitution, which might be developed as a subsidiary and free agency for social-economic peace in the Industry Council system. It was glimpsed, then lost to view by Martin.

[53] Kingsley Martin, *The British Public and the General Strike* (London: Hogarth Press, 1926).

[54] *Ibid.,* pp. 112 f.

[55] *Ibid.,* pp. 121 f.

standpoint that Socialists ought to go out or stay out of political office in order to preserve the Movement.

Martin's every word shows the impossibility under which the politicized section must labor. His history is better than the average determinist's but moves in a dreary circle nevertheless. He shows Protestantism and nationalism moving toward "democracy," its inherent *tyranny,* twinned with "religious toleration," which grew from the loss of the "living force of social faith." He wrote that nationalism moved toward imperialism and the Leviathan State, fostered then consumed by economic and political prosperity; that the idea of private property (which once meant land "mixed" with a man's labor) was now, after its fixation in the seventeenth and eighteenth centuries, connotative of the absentee owner and the shareholder. Since no peasantry remains, civilization moves the more rapidly toward destruction; men do not prefer peace, but love the joy of battle. Come full circle, Communist and Capitalist strive for domination of one class over another, and so the revolt against tyranny must begin all over again. Martin's cyclic history, for all its monotony, divulged a great secret: [56] The TUC was not revolutionary but might become so, for by being so labelled it was liable to be induced to extend its demands into fields of which it was ignorant, or which lay beyond its competence. It represented association *versus* the State, a conflict of sovereignties. If Parliament represented consumers, TUC represented producers and those who would avoid disaster should accord TUC respect. Martin is not sure but he suggests that had the Industry Council system of 1919 not been dropped, TUC, "accepted as an authoritative body representing the wage earners," would have become a powerful agency for peace, exemplifying the "professional conservatism" of which "Liberals" would "soon be complaining." [57] This throws great light on the reason for the opposition of the Webbs to Whitley Councils endorsed by other Fabians like Macrae-Gibson. Martin sees that a "constitution" developed out of definitions by the Courts and

---

[56] *Ibid.,* pp. 107 f.

[57] *Ibid.,* p. 109. Let those who favor a Labour Party in America recall that Fabian-Socialism destroyed the Whitley Council, or Industry Council System in Britain, by the doctrine of "non-alliance."

based upon labor law might have resulted from retaining Whitley Councils. (This is the "Public Statute" envisioned in papal principles.) This is a point in Fabian Martin's message which the young Fabians missed.[58] It opens a great void, a chasm of hopeless fear over which Slesser had found a bridge when he wrote in 1941 "Who Goes Home." [59]

The last statement cited from the Fraser group is indicative of the uses to which history was put by the new Fabians. It overlooks the meaning of Martin's historical discussion and does not do credit to the Hammonds. Opinion on both sides agreed the General Strike was a terrible mistake and a failure which created a mechanical reaction. Every genuine labor leader [60] deplored [61] it except the head of the miners. Every real liberal worked to avert and then to settle it fairly. The *NS* excoriated the inept handling which brought it on, and some Labourites hinted [62]

---

[58] *Ibid.,* pp. 124 to 128. Martin, too, relies on Laski's *Grammar of Politics* and on Keynes' *End of Laissez-Faire.* Martin deplores the dropping of the Industrial Council System as begun in 1919. Cf. Martin, *op. cit.,* p. 109. The "victory" in dropping the Councils was a Webb-over-other-Fabians victory. Said Martin, the Industry Council system of 1919 was "the one policy which might save the Constitution, *if that is what Constitutionalists really desire.*" (Italics supplied.)

[59] Slesser, *op. cit.,* pp. 232–250.

[60] Cf. Clynes, *op. cit.,* pp. 75 and 81. "We of the Trade Unions *bought national peace* in 1926 at a terrible price. The cost to my Union alone was over £20,000." The King, Clynes relates, expected "all this" [His Royal surroundings] to "vanish" if the Strike came. Clynes says the Trade Unions saw to it that it did not "come to the worst." *Ibid.,* p. 82.

[61] Cf. Thomas, *op. cit.,* pp. 106 f, where he tells of urging Samuel to come, when Baldwin rejected the offer of aid from this former head of the Royal Commission on Coal of whose Report acceptance was pending. Thomas arranged meetings in Sir Abe Bailey's house between TUC negotiators, the miners' leaders, and Samuel who was in touch with his former Commissioners. Thomas was always severely criticized by Socialist editors. Cf., *e.g., The Clarion,* 1930, *passim,* when the editors were all Fabians.

[62] Weir, *op. cit.,* p. 207, says, "It is now known that the aim of the Government was to compel the Trade Unions to call a general strike." Weir gives no other documentation than Clynes whom he cites (Clynes, *op. cit.,* p. 73) as noting "jubilation" of "hot-headed Tories" at the prospect of smashing Trade Union power—in 1925. Snowden excoriates Trade Unions for precipitating it, and MacDonald for "treachery and betrayal" in ending it. There was no unity at headquarters. Snowden says the TUC was in the

none too delicately that Baldwin provoked it, unable to control his "wild men," *e.g.,* Churchill. Two sections only were well served: the first, the very radical wing which detested labor leadership and needed the muddy waters of social upheaval in which to fish for control of the Movement, taking advantage from the splintering of Trade Unions, as Martin shows;[63] and the second, the extreme Tories who aimed to curb Trade Unionism, either because Unions were becoming powerful to demand higher stipends or because they provided the moneys which sustained the Movement which in the eyes of conservatives was fearsomely Socialistic. The TUC, whose leadership threatened the Strike in bluff, was afraid of a drive to lower wages generally. The propaganda of Tories never touched Fabianism, but always blamed the Unions for the Socialism which actually emanated from the Society and from the ILP but was not thoroughly absorbed by the Unions. No one on either Conservative or Labour side was well aware of the capture by Communists of effective salients of TUC in 1925. Martin notes their aims[64] and the *NS* constantly urged ignoring them[65] even while it prodded the too independent and too democratic unions into affiliating under TUCGC.[66] Mrs. Cole, whose husband was close to sources at the time, wrote that this capture was

---

dark while Fyfe of the Labour newsmen's corps says they had their spies and knew every move. The Trade Unions never realized the forces against them, *e.g.,* the non-union workers. The Council made "a serious mistake in making arrangements for the General Strike while negotiations with the Government were still going on." Cf. Snowden, *op. cit.,* p. 730. Snowden was "not sorry the experiment had been tried," the Trade Unions "needed a lesson of the futility and foolishness of such a trial of strength." Cf. *ibid.,* p. 731. Snowden read the minutes of all the conferences and finds no one, until Lord Birkenhead focused the issues, ever "came to grips with the problem." Cf. *ibid.,* p. 732. In another connection we see the ideological indefiniteness, really the "Long View," of Martin, *op. cit.,* and the concrete action, in getting out a journal, of Hamilton Fyfe. Cf. Fyfe, *Behind the Scenes of the Great Strike* (London: The Labour Publishing Company, 1926). Neither fulfills the purposes of the title of his book; Martin does not touch *public* opinion and Fyfe gives only one scene "behind the scenes." They typify Fabianism. (Publishers, unconnected with Party, soon liquidated.)

[63] Martin, *op. cit.,* p. 116.
[64] *Ibid.*
[65] *NS,* XXIII (August 30, 1924), 587.
[66] *NS,* XXIII (August 16, 1924), 539.

made.[67] The Fabians treated the Strike with as scientific objectivity as they had treated the Boer War, the Dock Strike, and World War I: To demand a radical adhesion to principle, would cleave the Society lengthwise or to demand outright repudiation of " direct action " would alienate the Unions and sever the Labour Party head from trunk.[68] Ellen Wilkinson's poor novel, *Clash,* which had stirring reviews and advertisements in the *NS,* described a typical Fabian's participation and depicted devoted personal enthusiasm for workers' causes in a manner which established prestige and earned worker confidence for the Society.

So much for the General Strike. During this interim, 1924–1929, Slesser, the expert on labor law, was noting his criticisms of Fabian-Socialism. He fought the reaction which produced the Trade Unions Bill of 1927, but he criticized the philosophy which had produced the demand for reaction. Slesser, who attributes his mental formation to Fabianism which he espoused at R. C. K. Ensor's direction,[69] was " awakened " by Wells' writings, and like Shaw, is inclined to think Wells was more right than the Webbs, whose predominance in the Society ended Wells' adherence. Slesser's criticism of Fabianism [70] coincides with Shaw's but is

---

[67] Cole, *Beatrice Webb,* p. 157.

[68] When, after the settlement, the editor of the *NS* wrote, " Should We Hang Mr. Churchill or Not," *NS,* XXVII :682 (May 22, 1926), he opined that the Strike had taught everyone something very valuable. No General Strike *without violence* could win. The left wing would have a hard time converting Trade Unions to revolutionary ideas. Hang the " blood-letter " to be safe, however. The humor is not to be lost sight of. Ben Turner, an old Fabian who went with his local group into ILP, says that he suspects Churchill had something to do with the situation at the *Daily Mail* which gave the Government the excuse to cut off negotiations. Cf. Ben Turner, *About Myself* (London: Humphrey Toulmin, 1930), p. 295.

It was said that Fabians felt that a long step had been taken toward Socialism. Yet Fabians recoiled from their own conclusions; actually a long step was taken in reaction, and Fabians manifested no great efficacy either in Opposition or in the 1929 Government toward getting the Trade Disputes Act of 1927 repealed. It curbed the Trade Union movement. The hands of the moderate Socialists, the gradualist parliamentarian group, were strengthened.

[69] Slesser worked up through the Fabian Nursery and was proudly elected by the Nursery to the Executive. Slesser, *op. cit.,* p. 19.

[70] For current confusion of fascism and Christianism cf n. 70 below.

based on Thomism: 1) Fabians were agnostics (except for a few like Stewart Headlam), 2) they were ignorant of all the Reformation had robbed them of (excited about the hypothetical descent of man from simians, they " cared and knew nothing " of the " more ascertainable views of their less remote ancestors of the Middle Ages "),[71] 3) the " spiritual character of the civil material with which they hoped to build Utopia was never illumined by a Fabian tract as it was in Wallas' *Human Nature in Politics*," 4) " the Fabians ignored history [this is not to say they did not use history], so they overlooked traditional human insufficiencies "—" of Sin and Fall we reckoned nothing," [72] 5) missing the great overtones in Wells, his " vague proleptic designs," they kept the " timorous middle class " engrossed in administrative proposals; but fundamentally Wells and his opponents were agreed: They were all Progressives, Spencerians who ignored the Huxley question about evolution's being possibly dysgenic. Shaw alone doubted the intrinsic necessity of Progress and was nearest to Wells who was Nominalist, Pragmatist, and Pantheist, and thought of himself as " part or partner " with a " Striving Deity." Then, Slesser says,

> the time had still to come when the Vitalists, following Butler, Bergson and Sorel, possibly Schopenhauer and Nietzsche, would succeed in over-emphasizing will and emotion by decrying the cautious processes of reason, so as to produce our present [1941] disorders.

He was speaking of 1906 and overlooking 1926. Long before, Slesser himself had advanced an organistic (Holoism) view of man as " but a unit in a higher organism—the State " when he was fighting Belloc. Then he was on the side of MacDonald, if not of Vitalist Shaw: but before 1931, Slesser was convinced that Belloc had been far in advance of his age when he warned of the

---

[71] Slesser, *op. cit.*, p. 18. Fabians are Social Democrats and not in any sense Christian Socialists although the contrary was asserted in a recent BIS pamphlet. Many non-Catholic Christians are Fabians, but Fabianism is not Christian Socialism. *Vis-a-vis* Europe, Fabians collaborate with Social Democrats. It is clearer to write " Christian Social party" than " Christian Socialists," words Leo XIII considered a contradiction in terms.

[72] Cf. F. Neumann's review of *Aus Beispeil Osterreichs* by Joseph Buttinger (*Als Manuskript Geduct,* 1951), in *P.S.Q.*, LXVII:I (March, 1952) 138–140.

menace of the Tyrant State which, while it complained of plutocracy's destroying men's freedom, inconsistently sought " not to restore their freedom but permanently to curtail it by harnessing men in their productive aspect, to the irresistible chariot of the State."

Slesser says the Society and the Party " though urging drastic change " had no coherent outlook at all; a condition of mind which Mr. Pease in his history of the Fabian Society finds to be very English and very admirable. We must credit Slesser with having set forth most clearly the fact that in the amorphousness of the thought patterns of Fabianism was an internally developing metaphysic of Tyranny.

We have seen the efforts· to reassure the electorate, to define Freedom in Socialism. From 1924 to 1929, as the Party strength improved, the nature of the philosophy siphoned into it by Fabianism from the pure-Socialist stream must fail to convince anyone that Liberty, as distinguished from Freedom, was not jeopardized. In 1929, the electorate took a chance on the reliability of Fabian-Socialism to remain " very English " and returned the Labour Party to power.

B. Coping with Criticism from Within

The fissure between the leadership and the Party segments was ignored by the Labour campaigners of 1929. In an ensuing section, we compare the clear statement of what some Fabians expected the leaders of the Party (also Fabians) to produce, and the platform of 1929. The Capital Levy, ardently advocated in 1923, in 1929 yielded to a simple project to despoil the *rentier* class. Criticism within the Party seems to have effected this change.

A little book had come out in 1923,[73] when Labour, on the

---

[73] Seven Members of the Labour Party, *The Labour Party's Aim* (London, Allen and Unwin), 1923. The publishers, Allen and Unwin, used some diligence to assist this investigator to discover the names of the writers. They were able to suggest two names which are very likely ones of Fabians of the highest calibre: one, a woman prominent in the Socialist International and the party organization; the other, a professional historian whose widow could supply no information. Since the Labour Party headquarters were obviously reluctant to confirm these two names or supply others, they are not being revealed here. The writer is certain that two writers were Fabians,

threshold of power, was exhibiting a tendency to act like any other political party and " larnin' to be a twoad,"—at least in the eyes of pure-Socialists, " sentimental " Socialists and idealistic Fabians not in office. Against the straddling of issues and compromising of principles of the political leadership which was Fabianism, a group of seven Socialists, calling themselves " members of the Labour Party " but otherwise anonymous, had written this book full of rather subtle distinctions in Socialistic thought. Baldwin had used it as campaign material in 1923, according to an Allen and Unwin advertisement carried in the *NS,* November 24, 1923.[74] Certainly the book was not the work of Trade Unionists but of members of the intelligentsia. It was also not harmonious with the ostensible Webb-gradualist mentality, nor yet with the aggressive Socialism of ILP. It was not far from being of the Wells-Shaw school. It is suspiciously like *The Clarion,*[75]

---

and contributors to *The Clarion.* That they called themselves members of the Labour Party and not of the Society gave their anonymity greater safety; but their insistence that they were Socialists unsatisfied with the Snowden exposition as too negative, and their invoking the agreement of colleagues in the labor world in " the great movement of right," makes it doubtful that they came into the Labour Party save by way of intellectualism. They intended to formulate anew Socialism for the Labour Party.

[74] *NS,* XXII, 219. The writer does not consider this a mark of undying hostility to Socialism on Baldwin's part.

[75] *The Clarion,* as was disclosed in January, 1932, when it became the *New Clarion,* was edited by Ernest Davies, the son of A. E. Davies, almost single-handed. It printed Fabian lectures and had as contributors Fabians C. Delisle Burns, Marion Phillips, Mary A. Hamilton, Harold Laski, G. D. H. Cole, George Lansbury, Hugh Dalton, Herbert Morrison, Josiah Wedgwood, Norman Angell, A. E. Davies, Mrs. Webb.

It is strange that this list, up to the name of Dalton, is very like one which could be made from the old F.R.D. given by Margaret Postgate Cole. From Webb back to Dalton, it represents the " moderates " and those whom earlier the radical young persons of F.R.D. dubbed " the Great." But as of 1929, *The Clarion* represented the amalgamation of the groups and the victory of the long-suffering Mrs. Webb in winning back Cole. (She once invited him to dinner and asked Mrs. Cole to come in for coffee!) A difference had formerly existed over the question of " worker control " which Beatrice called " pernicious nonsense." Now with Shaw's " democratising democracy " the synthesis had been achieved: Mrs. Webb had acknowledged that Guild Socialism had contributed the " bridge " to her industrial democracy (under State-aided Capitalism). But Cole, in 1950, still looks beyond

after Ernest Davies and F. L. Stevens revived it in 1928, making it more Fabian-Socialist than the *NS*. *Clarion* now listed many Fabian contributors, and named the more active M.P.'s in connection with Parliamentary situations, who were invariably Fabians. The *Aim* was the work of Fabians—" the others," not the " Old Gang " and not the new Mosley type. The only two authors' names discoverable were those of Fabian contributors to *The Clarion*. They remained anonymous to avoid the charge of being " sectional or schismatic."

The Seven of 1923 stated their disagreements: (1) with Lenin and Communists for describing only the past and for expecting world revolution, mistaking both the character of the State and the

---

the triumph of the Webb-Shaw-Wells system to a re-birth of associational freedom under the Party. Cf. M. Cole, *Growing Up Into Revolution,* pp. 61–79.

Henderson also did his part in gathering the young intellectuals into the Movement, especially Harold Laski, to whom he stooped in surprising humility in order to win him over. Cf. Hamilton, *op. cit.,* p. 272.

Slesser, for one, doubted up to 1941 the reality of the Socialism of the Labour Party. To become a member one joined a federated cooperative society or Trade Union, or one joined the Party and supported the immediate programme. Slesser found the only requisite for membership " condemnation of the acquisitive assumptions of the modern commercial and industrial world—Plutocracy." " Euturists " who believe " exemption from the imperium of mammon " is discoverable and " regressivists " who, like Slesser, believe that " a sane human society was in the process of being achieved in medieval times . . . [a] development . . . [which was] distorted by a false philosophy . . ." make likely members. This is the view that has prevented Fabianism from being condemned as Socialism is condemned, *nominatim.* The proportion of such thought as Slesser's to the opposite thought can be judged by the reader. Writings would indicate that Slesser's simple anti-plutocracy was almost solitary; but probably a large segment of the Labour Party membership inarticulately felt as Slesser did and ignored the ideological sound and fury. Individual workmen did not join the Party as persons, however, but as part of a bloc.

Slesser has become a Catholic since writing his *Judgment Reserved.* He feels that (Slesser, *op. cit.,* p. 248) his Parliamentary life was a failure. He had tried to affirm an avowed Christian policy—" the alternative to Christian politics is Tyranny black or red." Socialist MacDonald " did not desire his assistance in his new Government " (1929) and gave him a place on the Court of Appeal. The contrast in spirit between Slesser's philosophy and that of " the seven " ought to impress those who think Fabians are Christians.

proper methods of transformation; [76] (2) with Marx, because, belonging to the intelligentsia not to the proletariat, he had not foreseen the power of Trade Unionsm; [77] (3) with the Webbs for overlooking international issues [78] and for elaborating details of government schemes that were " too conventional "; [79] 4) with the ILP for not stating principles, only urging practices; 5) with Mac-Donald and Snowden for never being "comprehensible"; [80] 6) with Guild Socialists for being obsessed with " one idea "; [81] 7) with the

---

[76] The F.R.D. split up into Socialists and Communists on the point of the Russian Revolution, once deemed glorious by all. Mrs. Cole herself visited Russia as a member of the New Fabian Research Bureau. She furnishes data all of which she notes with disapproval but she drops the data, after giving the impression of objectivity, to generalize in favor of the U.S.S.R. Cf. Cole, *Growing Up Into Revolution*, p. 23.

[77] Cole, *Growing Up Into Revolution*, p. 63. The F.R.D. did not in 1918 recognize the divisional nature of Trade Unionism: the leaders, the (apathetic) membership, and the rank and file. Mrs. Cole thinks they of the movement learned too late.

[78] This is simply impatience. The Webbs were " internationalistic " enough but understood the interplay of domestic and international issues better than others.

[79] *The Clarion* editor seemed to entertain an attitude of amused and filial disrespect toward the Webbs and a puritan-Socialist attitude toward Fabians. For example, he speaks of Mrs. Webb's " complete charm" which brought a crowd to Admiralty House (Alexander's dwelling) for a reception and describes Lord Passfield as " trotting" from salon to cloakroom worried over the congestion as if lacking confidence in the "inevitability of gradualism." See *The Clarion*, II:4 (April, 1930), 99. Again: Fabians are criticized for going to Lord Londonderry's reception for Naval Delegates, held especially for visiting Americans, rather than to their own reception given the same night for Fabian M.P.'s and Ministers. See *The Clarion*, II:2 (March, 1930), 67. The F.R.D. had been founded by Beatrice but members were currently pacifists as well as Guild Socialists; they were sure they were more enlightened than their elders especially on " functionalism " and internationalism.

[80] The young "cuckoos" in F.R.D. were especially impolite to Snowden. Cole, *Growing Up*, p. 70.

[81] Cole, *Growing Up Into Revolution*, pp. 66 f. Her group, F.R.D., called itself " The Movement," and it was all Guild Socialist. So the Coles and William Mellor, a former evangelical minister and a close associate, were not in on this document. Nevertheless among this group must be found the Seven. To read *The Clarion*, 1929–1931, is to find these seven criticisms consonant with its policy. It is probable that the approach toward apprecia-

French, Italian, and German Socialists for offering no restatements, just "controversial commentary upon the work of dead socialists."

On the positive side they believed British Labour (Socialist) was the hope of the world; that the "socialist conquerors of Trade Unionism" had intermarried with their "subjects" to produce offspring which had the qualities of both.[82] It was all very well, they said, to be Parliamentarian and palliative but palliatives should not hamper the march to the "abolition of Capitalism and the establishment of the Socialist Commonwealth." "Reformism" meant merely to harden Capitalism, not abolish it; it made of Labour only a political party—"in," then "out." Despite the boasts of Fabianism that they had influenced Conservatives in the reforms they adopted, the Seven wanted "bedrock" Socialist organization, not "progress weighted with reactionary criticism and reaction mitigated by progressive criticism."[83]

The Seven pressed toward "the world we seek to create": The Capital Levy was *bad* if it only delayed the end of Capitalism. Guild Socialism was better than such bureaucracy as was demonstrated by the nationalization practiced during the War. The "worn out garments of a past ideology," *i.e.,* slogans about Rights, Freedom, Equality, Service, Conscience, minorities—all needed rehabilitation. The Seven were sick of "workers of the world unite"—that was meant for the workers of the little indus-

---

tion of Mrs. Webb evinced in its pages as in Margaret Cole's personal story, coincided with the graduation of Cole out of his Guild ideas, approaching the Webbs and returning to the Society. The spirit of the Seven found itself a new dwelling in *The Clarion* after 1928.

[82] We have seen the domestic tensions of the so-married and to identify the offspring we get no assistance from "the Seven." Shaw saw the need to subjugate unions and seven years later Cole made an enlightening synthesis in *The Clarion*. Cf. Cole, "Trade Unions and the Government," *The Clarion,* II:2 (February, 1930), 41.

[83] This, of course, is the product of two parties such as exist in the United States where such activity is mutual self-criticism, elections are made unanimous, and majority makes a measure the law of the land for all; not where one party dominates and opposition stratifies into constant conflict, or the minority goes into revolt. The Seven did not see that what they demanded was stratification. In this they came close to the Webb-Shaw-Wells construct—functional *blocs* controlled by an élite.

trial countries of small western Europe and was now overblown; and " self-determination "—what did it mean? The ideals of the Seven embraced internationalism which did not allow patriotism, but permitted exercise of self-interest to sovereign states on such matters as a choice *of form* or *of policy* of their government. There was another old garment, " Peace "—" a social situation." They asked for something positive, an organized system for developing resources. Wars to them were " national enterprises " not peculiar to Capitalism or religion, but due to a political tendency. If social order be only for the proletariat, it is crude; if referable to religion, culture, nationality, it is childish. However, *only those who work* are eligible for political or social status in international affairs. A care for " interests of neighbors " no nation has the right to neglect, yet national considerations are not powerful enough to override the " distinct interest of a group which has a characteristic tradition and ideal of life." Non-interference and Free Trade are childish slogans to the Seven: The abolition of sovereignty means only that no state in regard to another will be final arbiter of its own rights. The Governments of Sovereign States, controlled by peoples governed *must have their relations* (inter-State relations) *politically organized.*[84]

As to " Property," the Seven could concede [85] that over the food a man was about to eat he might have absolute property

---

[84] Cf. Mrs. H. Swanwich, *Labour's Foreign Policy,* and G. B. Shaw's *The League of Nations,* 1929. Shaw's writing is ideological: Why should " two estates " be at Geneva? Only the ILO should be there. Albert Thomas is " the ' Pope' of this ' Catholic' " [sic] ordering. Mrs. Swanwich excoriates the Tories for their weakening of the League by secret diplomacy, *e.g.,* their working with France, Spain, Poland—encouraging the aspirations of these nations to be admitted to the Council, a policy which kept Germany out of the League—and with Italy regarding spheres of influence in Abyssinia. The " self-defense" clause in the Kellogg Pact, the " understanding " with France in the disarmament conferences, the delay to ratify the eight-hour convention, the failure to adopt the Optional Clause and the principle of "All-in-Arbitration," the refusal to surrender sovereignty, even Sir Austen Chamberlain's *hesitancy to encroach* on the *sovereignty* of *minorities* under the Mandate system—these are all criticized. (This attitude of " doing for " minorities and impatience with respect for liberty is characteristic. The latter respect for liberty is predominant in the Liberal Party's platform of 1929 as shall be shown further on.)

[85] Like the catechism of the vows on Religious Poverty.

rights. That was as far as their concept of private property would let them go. As to Capital, " irritating the Capitalist and placating the workers " were not Socialism's true methods. Present day taxation (Snowden's) and wage demands (Trade Unionism) only tended to destroy the usefulness of the Capitalist. Socialism must be positive in pursuit of two objectives, communal enterprise and the abolition of Capitalism. The old Socialist " nationalisation of means of production, distribution and exchange " was obsolete. Gone with it should be the Webbs' notion of two parliaments, one political, one social; for this was impossible in the face of international economic interrelations— just *one* Parliament for all would do. From Russia deliberately the Seven took " no representation without service " upon which to base the franchise, that is, the determination of voting rights by occupation rather than by residence. They wanted a strong executive overseeing a " coherent policy in all departments," and subsidiary Councils to obviate the dictatorship of the Cabinet.[86] Concerning " individuals," the Seven " laugh out of Court " the idea that Socialism favors atheism and free love or that experts will ride roughshod over " regimented individuals." Indeed, said they, " A social philosophy which sees a restriction of liberty in social regulations should by this time be out of date even in the Universities! "[87] Socialism was not religion, it offered no theory of morals but it affected and intended to affect education and social standards. Education should produce a person who was a " vigorous associate of other men " and make the individual " subordinate to new and better society." The " freer world " is is the " better regulated " one. Law " creates the area for the exercise of powers which is freedom." *Some kinds* of art and religion, of dubious genuineness or value, may *not* be able to

---

[86] The reader will have to puzzle with the writer the meaning of " strong executive " in juxtaposition with the plan of checkmating the Cabinet. In 1930, desperate in the face of clogged Parliamentary machinery and international stalemate from rising nationalisms, *The Clarion* ran Mrs. Webb's " My Parliament " (II [December, 1930], 347 f). She considered the Cabinet a dictatorship. She advocated removing domestic and social measures from Parliament and giving them to her new Assembly.

[87] *Ibid.*, p. 92.

exist even in the areas of freedom which are not defined by law.[88]
The Seven offered no ideas about education of "the elite"; for
them, whatever education is to be had should be for all. And the
usual negating reservation follows—allowing only for difference
of intellectual ability—youths could stay in school or go to work.[89]

As to marriage: The Seven stood for the abolition of "economic subordination of women," in property, alimony, or career.
They professed holding no philosophy of sexual morality. Only if a
pair have children should society be concerned. The Seven conceded
"the State or the industrial community" is not the sole guardian
of children; there is something to be said for the thing called
"relations of the generation"; the only "good interference," as
in the best families, is some "small scale and variable organisation." (This probably means something like Scouts.) But "*no
socialist community could exist* in which there was reckless and
unthinking procreation of children." No Malthusianism, however: Socialists must educate parents to improve the quality of
children and eradicate the "superstition" of the "excellence of
numbers." (This is their contradiction, as stated by them.)

The Seven, insisting they themselves are not sectional or schismatic, add that there will always be various kinds of Socialism
because men of different creeds and cultures adopt Socialism's
economic and political ideals.[90] The Seven close their restatement
with the prospect that Socialism is to do the "service" which *the
Church* "in the early middle ages" did among "warring and
ignorant tribes."

So much for Fabian criticisms of Fabians, recalling on the eve

---

[88] This is a distinct threat to religious liberty. Tiresome as the reitera-
tions are, it must be observed that these non-schismatic, non-sectarian critics
of Fabianism agreed on the nature of Freedom with the professedly Fabian
members whom we have cited above. It was freedom found in regulation.

[89] A constant source of wonderment is this pompous arrival at solemn
definitions of what every one knows. It has the effect of making hearers
and readers doubtful of things long taken for granted. When they have
taken their mental picture apart and put it together again, it has acquired
an exponent of Socialism. The practice doubtless played no small part in the
persuading of voters and candidates to concede superiority to and bestow
confidence on the Fabian intellectuals or those things which they supported.

[90] This does not seem logical; but the reader must hitherto have noted
certain inconsistencies in Fabian thinking.

of election the fact that " The Fabian Society consists of Socialists " when the leadership, seeking to garner the votes of " workers
by brain and hand " (unions and cooperatives), and the *NS*,
founded by Shaw and Webb, now run by Fabian Clifford Sharp,
were trying to defeat Conservatives by negative criticism; and
all were in danger of forgetting Socialism while Labour seemed
to be becoming just another political party. After 1924, and all
through the regime of 1929–1931, *The Clarion* warned against
this danger; and, by its criticism, it pointed up the distinction
between the Party and the Government. Looking back on this
manifesto, after the Labour Government dissolved, we are able to
see that among the Socialists even in the ranks of Fabianism there
was a divided will: One section wanted gradualism to mean penetration of Labour and slow, sure capture of the Movement for
Socialism (the Blatchford ideal: To have Socialism we must make
Socialists); the other wanted Socialism to weld hinges of easy
relationships for the non-homogeneous parts of the Labour Movement and so, in a Party, to capture political power.[91]

With this, the voice of intimate family warning sounding in
their ears, Fabian political leaders had essayed a Government.
When it failed, Socialism was found to have created a two-
headed monstrosity, a Janus, if not of War, of Power: A Labour
front with a leadership looking both ways to " votes " for power
and to Socialism for paradise; and a Movement animated by a
materialistic philosophy of welfare which many Britons feared
would destroy all they cherished of Liberty.

It is a patent illustration of the best Fabian method, that pure-
Socialists were allowed to establish the collateral of Socialist
doctrine upon which the trimmers banked when Socialism was re-

---

[91] Cf. Tiltman, *op. cit.,* p. 31, where he explains how Socialists at a Trade
Union Congress in Glasgow, 1892, conspired to capture the Trade Unions for
Socialism; and again, *ibid.,* p. 32, where the Maxton-Cook Manifesto in
1928 (ILP) had for objective the retention of Socialist power and stood for
a bolder programme than the Labour Party so formed could put forward.
The Clarion claims the ILP was born in its office in 1892 and boasts its
" contribution to the cause of Socialism greater than any other journal."
Cf. " G. B. S., You and Us," *The Clarion,* II :3 (March, 1930), where G. B.
S. is noted as about the oldest subscriber who then wrote, " at last *The
Clarion* [1930] has a twentieth century air about it," to the editor's delight.

quired as backing, or concerning which they could deprecate the sentimentality as occasion demanded.

C. Comparison of Platforms

The threat to liberty was the keynote of the criticism of Labour politics from 1924 to 1929. If it allayed the fears of the electorate, the answer to the criticism changed nothing in the Fabian spirit. To contrast the Liberal Party's platform and that of Labour shows this to be true. To examine *Can Lloyd George Do It?* by J. M. Keynes and H. D. Henderson (both of *The Nation and Athenaeum*) in contrast with Fabian Pethick-Lawrence's *National Finance* [92] and Fabian R. H. Tawney's draft of policy and programme entitled *Labour and the Nation,* adopted at Birmingham in October, 1928, is to find the difference in spirit and to lay the groundwork for criticism of the financial policy of Fabians in 1931. The " Foreword," written by MacDonald for *Labour and the Nation* referred again to transforming Capitalism into Socialism. Interposed between " transformation " and the means to achieving it (*i.e.,* " every parliamentary opportunity ") lay a formidable list of evils to be coped with by gaining command of industrial and political power. Both kinds of power were attainable through and with Trade Unionists, said MacDonald.

The remnant of the Liberal Party created a " pledge " for Lloyd George and published *The Yellow Book* of 1928 embodying " Britain's Industrial Future." [93] Briefly, " The Pledge Examined " had four characteristics: It outlined a programme of works, a financial system of Credit, a truly English attitude of mind and a certain deference for liberty (especially regarding private ownership of railways and banks). Works like roadbuilding were devised to care for the worker-transfer problem without increased taxation but by loans to industry,[94] with the design to attract workers to new scenes of endeavor (Miners, " permanently redundant," [95] depressed their own labor market

[92] Fabian Tract No. 229 (1929).

[93] This book was not to be ignored by anyone who thought " straight," said the *NS,* as quoted in the flyleaf of *Can Lloyd George Do It?*

[94] The Hoover-created RFC had its pattern herein.

[95] All the reforms of 1925–1928 were overlooked in Labour Party

by refusing to venture forth from ancestral once-green valleys).[96]
Keynes explained that this credit system would not cause "inflation " *so long as loans outside the country were halted* (Conservatives as individuals and Labour as a matter of principle encouraged
loans and made them to German municipalities, states, and industries).[97] The "flight of gold" would only follow upon loans
made abroad. There were certain fields where population increase, decentralization of industry, and the need to develop
parks, or roads, called for *public* development. Rural preserva-
tion had hitherto been owed to private munificence. These
Liberals spoke as Englishmen of downs, moors, and lakes, of
Surrey Commons, South Downs, Salisbury Plains, Dartmoor,
Exmoor, Peak and Lake Districts. They had once seen Shelley
plain where the Fabians had seen only his father-in-law. Liberals
did not, like the Fabians, intend to discriminate in credit or loan-
making so as to develop some and repress other industries; they
would bring out the measures now pigeonholed by economy-
minded Tories, measures which were the "children of the most
active and progressive brains." There stood on the statute books
the Trade Facilities Act which would enable extensions of service
to be developed—telephones, electricity, drainage. The Tories
had cut the subsidy for Housing; they would, by building a million
houses in ten years, not merely replace and barely provide housing, but clear the slums. Railways, semi-privately owned, would
be encouraged to borrow money and rationalize their equipment.
The Bank with its admittedly dangerous power over the rate would
be counted upon to second rational plans.[98]

---

propaganda. Cf. *The Clarion*, n.s., 21 (January, 1929), 1. The miners'
plight was exploited to create a demand to reduce the financial power of
the wealthy. The *rentier* and Trade Union classes were enjoying a rising
standard of living, as Keith Feiling points out, alongside of the continued
decay of a proletariat of over a million in spite of huge Government spending in benefits. Cf. Feiling, *op. cit.,* p. 128.

[96] The rest of the New Deal Public Works program is outlined—traceable,
not to Socialism, but to Keynesian Liberalism. The Liberals had great
generalship and no soldiers. What if they had retained the members of
Trade Unions and Cooperatives on their rosters?

[97] Cf. Davies, *Public Ownership, Points From Prospectuses* (London:
Fabian Society, 1928).

[98] Recently, with savings going out of the country so fast, the Bank had

The Liberals' economics were as concrete as Keynes' ideas could be and free from any ideological bent such as using taxation to raise or lower a class of people, or to diminish or increase populations in specified classes: They hoped to transfer the " permanently redundant " workers by *attracting* them to industries which would be revived by loans.[99] The plan counted on the reality of resultant *indirect employment* (never publicly considered by the other parties) and on increased purchasing power from wages to make savings in insurance payments. If the programs cost three hundred million pounds with no return to the Budget (not to speak of national income or well-being) it would cost the Budget eighteen million a year, which was two and one-half per cent of the national revenue. This was not formidable. Only five per cent increase in employed population would raise tax-yield one and one-half per cent, and the rest of the bill could be met by reducing armaments seven and one-half per cent.[100] The Liberal programme could be relied upon, however, to cost even less. If certain revenues and " betterment " funds were assigned for the Road Fund, it would cost the Budget nothing. Instead of building one hundred thousand houses, they could build two hundred thousand houses. In three years, for subsidies and charges on rates the Budget would pay out five million four hundred thousand pounds, but there would be an appreciable return from rents and one hundred and fifty thousand men would be employed. Telephones and Trade Facilities loans would pay for themselves. With the gain to the Unemployment Fund of twenty-five million pounds yearly, a quarter of the capital cost of each year's programme would be balanced within that year; and an eighth would be recovered through gain in revenue from increased national

---

raised the rate to keep back the gold. *The Clarion,* n.s., 21 (February, 1929), 2, inveighed against it, shortsightedly. And Fabian Sir Josiah Wedgwood in his " Fantastic ' Cures ' for Unemployment," *The Clarion,* n.s., 21 (January, 1929), 6, argued for a lower rate enforced by law.

[99] A pamphlet of the British Information Service, BIS, *Contemporary Britain* (New York: 1950), pp. 14–15, boasts of achievements along these lines—produced in the 1930's, *i.e.,* by the Baldwin Government. Incidentally, this propaganda, issued by a Labour Government, dissembles altogether the Socialistic nature of H.M.'s Government.

[100] This item they had in common with Labour.

income; thus "nearly half the capital cost would be recovered *at the time.*" All was contingent upon the plan to embargo foreign issues. The programme was understated in all respects, according to the authors of *The Pledge Examined.* They were encouraged by Pigou's *Industrial Fluctuations,* the public statements of Sir Josiah Stamp, and McKenna's *Post-War Banking Policy* to proclaim that to increase the volume investable—at home—was not inflation. Consumption going up, imports would increase; it could not, they wrote, decrease exports. The Treasury's preoccupation with "conversion" (*i.e.,* of the Debt) to loans at lowered rates of interest, was, Keynes and Henderson said, dogmatic, blundering and premature. "Wait for an ideal conjuncture of conditions [when world rates are low] and "pull off something big." The rate would fall because of abundant savings—that was to the national interest, but if outlets should then deliberately be curtailed and investments in home industries be stopped, it would be disastrous. Act positively, they urged—"using" enriches the country. The Tory treasury had instead been "choking off" whenever possible, only to create "the worst of all worlds" by using backward equipment, and getting low profits; income tax was high in rate and low in yield so that no relief to taxpayers and no social reforms were possible; unemployment was rampant; the rate of saving was off: so interest rates, defying any effort to lower them, remained high.

Keynes and Henderson pointed out one difference between themselves and Socialists. Socialism would take from private enterprise the financial means for social services; the Liberals offered national assistance to further those ventures which no private enterprise would attempt, and they would make loans to private enterprise, thereby to increase employment. One hundred million pounds in surplus saving were lent abroad yearly under the Tory regime.[101] Keynes' proposition depended upon creating

---

[101] Cf. Davies, *Public Ownership,* p. 10, for example, where in *Berlin Beats London* the author tells that Baring, Rothschild and Schroder issued in London, July, 1927, £3,500,000 of City of Berlin six per cent bonds for overhead Tubes. The City of Berlin owned every service from its trainways to its slaughter houses. The wily Fabian listed only one such bond issue in London but followed it with arguments for the prosperity of Municipal Corporations such as "VIAG," a German Government company dealing in nitrates, aluminum, electricity, mines and banks, and numerous subsidiaries.

credit for home investment and making sure the Bank did not deflate the currency. There was every indication the Bank would welcome the opportunity to cooperate since in 1927 it produced the effect of an embargo upon foreign issues in national (and self-) defense. A source of savings for home investment should be found in reduced lending. English loans were financing overseas Governments and municipalities.

Where Liberals sought to deflect the policy of the bond market toward home issues, the Fabian financial experts directed their quest for financial power against the *rentier* class.[102]

It is instructive to contrast with the reasonings of Keynes and Henderson the Fabians' *National Finance*. The Fabian Socialists selected a class to prosecute, directly. The *rentier* class had prospered during the years after the war; incomes of 1920 were worth double value in 1929.[103] Fabians boldly assumed that the active producing element in Society lost what the *rentier* class gained.

This company's six per cent bonds were quoted in New York. It held, because of its diversity of interests, an "advantageous position with respect to the acquisition of *foreign exchange* for the service of the bonds" (Page 14). Bavaria's State-owned Banks, Mines, Forests, Vineyards, Brewery, Spas, Opera Houses, and Theatres, had profited from a $15,000,000 six and one-half percent loan in New York in 1925. Davies selected fewer London loans than he might have. Fabians approved of the policy of foreign loans. Tories engaged in making them. (Davies instanced as a prosperous municipal project, Los Angeles' Power and Light, city-owned.)

[102] Slesser wrote in 1944, "Whether . . . a resurrection of Liberalism is probable may depend upon the possibility of the recapture of the vision of the basic invaluable quality of personality." [Otherwise, "planning by competent authority must be the prime concern of governments and society" which have adopted the view that sociology "has exploded the vision of the free autonomous individual."] "The decay of party government may assist the progress of benevolent surveillance . . . when all are agreed how to organise and educate the citizenry his prospects of independence are poor. . . . If it is correct [that Liberalism has converted both other parties; its fall] is but an incident in the general acceptance of libertarian ideals; if it be false, the failure of Liberalism may prove to be an unqualified disaster." Cf. Slesser, *A History of the Liberal Party* (London: Hutchinson and Company, 1944), pp. 163 f.

[103] That this economically healthy segment of society and its source of income was not affected by non-production was seen by Keynes, no doubt, but he applied the financial remedy to the ailing segment while Fabians, seeing all society "as one," would penalize the healthy for the sick.

Made for a different reason, Pethick-Lawrence's list of Church-ill's "economies" and "cuts" corresponded with Keynes'. In Labour's more positive view, the Party had for tasks: 1) expanded social services, 2) control of Banking and Credit, 3) cutting the armed services. For the social services (some one hundred and thirteen million saved from the military establishment would not suffice) there must be direct taxes and these should be, of set purpose, discriminatory: Surtaxes from income investment which would be "graduated," steeper inheritance taxes, and (assuming as the writer did that an owner does no service to the community by maintaining a building where the community enriches it) high taxes on urban ground value. Strangely, Pethick-Lawrence sug-gested at another point, that they might be so successful as not to need to increase taxes. (The principle of discrimination, it must be remarked, would thus yield to expediency.) In Labour's scheme no liberty to act rationally was to be left to the Bank of England; it was to be reconstructed into a public corporation, its Board to be made up of members both of the Treasury and of the Board of Trade, together with representatives of Industry, Labour, and—without subtlety—Cooperatives. Simplifying all financial problems, Fabians in politics used this equation: Falling prices caused exports to drop, and hence unemployment. They rejected the remedies offered in the name of inflation and deflation as being mutually irrelevant, like scalding and freezing, since one was not a remedy for the other. "Stabilisation of price level" they, like the Liberals, took from Sir Josiah Stamp. "National Develop-ment" meant housing, road-making, bridge-building, as it did for the Liberals; but not as things which reimbursed the Budget by indirect employment and consumer activation, rather as things to be paid for out of funds extracted from the *rentiers*. Socialist "Labour" advocated Municipal Banks. They made no mention of foreign lending, and understandably so; they took a vital interest in the German municipalized industries. Credit which the Bank must create was to them of two kinds: Quantitative, which, do-mestically used, could be expanded without inflation or going off the gold standard or producing unstable exchanges; [104] and qualita-

---

[104] Keynes thought this could not be done without an embargo on foreign loans to stop the flow of gold.

tive credit, designed to discriminate among industries selected for death or survival. The next Chancellor would have a chance, said the Fabian exemplifier of the Birmingham programme of 1928, to do "memorable" service, provided he possessed good judgment, the support of the Party, and the will. For judgment upon that "memorable service" there will be Webb's *What Happened in 1931*.

Labour was elected in 1929 and forthwith, Snowden, whose Socialism was like a Sunday religion having little effect upon his Monday economics, became Chancellor of the Exchequer again. If the Labour Party had intended, really, to do the works of Socialism and keep the pledges made to all Socialists of whatever stripe whom it lashed to its mast, it should never have chosen Snowden for its Budget maker.[105]

In the intervening term, 1925–1929, three important events took place. A "General Strike" occurred in 1926 and in 1927 the Baldwin Government passed Neville Chamberlain's National Health Insurance Act which ended the old Poor Law.[106] In April 1928, it became known that in America, publication of trade-news revealing "trade disturbance and unemployment" had resulted in dismay to which "nothing in recent history . . . [was] comparable." [107]

---

[105] The old F.R.D. (1917), which reformed into S.S.I.P. (Zip in 1929) and later (1932) into the New Fabian Research Bureau, certainly never approved of Snowden. Cf. M. Cole, *Growing Up Into Revolution*, p. 70: "We were pretty rude to him although we would always cooperate temporarily with pacifists against Labour leaders"; also, cf. pp. 112 and 152 f, where she excoriates Snowden for alienating French public opinion at the Hague.

[106] Cf. Keith Feiling, *op. cit.*, pp. 140–143.

[107] *NS*, XXX (April 7, 1928), 814. The financial history of these years involving Norman Montagne's visit to U. S., the behaviour of the Federal Reserve and restricted diaries in L. C., is not beyond average understanding and should be written.

CHAPTER X

BETWEEN 1925 AND 1928

A. FABIANS AND THE STRIKE

Fabians took varying positions but all on the left, in regard to the Strike of 1926. In regard to its countermove, the Trades Union Act of 1927, Fabianism was more of one attitude which nevertheless differed somewhat from that of the unions.

To abbreviate a story which all Labourite writers tell in exquisite detail: The miners were warned, upon the subsidy's expiring, that wages would drop and hours be lengthened. Every student of the economics of the situation agrees that the wage scale in general was too rigid. The miners, however, were the victims of being the "marginal" value makers, like the "worst land" in the land-based theory of value. They responded with the slogan, "Not a penny off the pay; not a minute on the day." There ensued a general lockout. Meanwhile, the TUC had signified it would under such circumstances, anticipated since 1925 when the Government started the subsidy, support the miners by *pressuring Parliament to coerce the owners*—to do what, is a little unclear in their statements. They did not sloganize "rationalisation" or "nationalisation" nor even "unification." Not to lower wages, and to shorten the day to seven hours, were aims vaguely hoped for. To stop the fall of wages was the real problem. Ostensibly the TUC intended to stand by the miners in their struggle with the owners; but their attack was made upon Parliament to force it to deal with owners by laws.

Lord Birkenhead had produced a formula involving wage readjustments, which the TUC representative *had accepted*, when at midnight of the deadline date the machine men of the *Daily Mail* struck because of an editorial they were to set up which, they asserted, impugned the patriotism of the working class. Hearing of this, the Baldwin Cabinet served a twofold ultimatum: The TUC was to repudiate the machine men and withdraw strike

notices. Promptly, TUC repudiated the *Daily Mail* strikers.[1]
Nothing was said of the notices by TUGC. These notices were
out and the date to begin the Strike set.[2] This fact and the fact
that it was distinctly stated that the strikers' aim was to coerce
the Government, renders doubtful the TUC position and the
legality of the Strike under the Trade Union Act of 1906. This
Act upheld the right to strike and had been interpreted to exempt
from trial for breach of contract individuals acting upon strike
orders, or unions on strike; but it did not legalize a General Strike,
or one against the Government, nor a " sympathy " strike. When
the Cabinet broke off negotiations (union negotiators reporting
back on the repudiation found the rooms darkened and deserted),
the strike notices, as they knew, would automatically go into effect.
Forthwith Sir John Simon and Astbury J. in an *obiter dicta*
called the General Strike illegal while Sir Harry Slesser upheld
the legality of it. Some publicists like Fabian Kingsley Martin[3]
said it was not a General Strike; others like Churchill said it was,
and as such, Revolutionary. Fabian Burns said it was against
the Government and not against the owners and that it *was* Revolutionary, although the leaders were not revolutionaries. It was
broken when Sir Herbert Samuel's proposal took shape in Lord
Birkenhead's formula and was adopted by TUC, without the
miners. The Government had finally (four days late) published
the Archbishop of Canterbury's appeal against a " finish fight."
It was deplored that Cardinal Bourne arraigned himself on the
side against the constitutionality of the Strike. His Eminence was
publicly upbraided by Catholic M.P.'s,[4] led by Fabian John Scurr.

---

[1] Recall this was George Isaacs' organization. He was in 1924 Parliamentary Private Secretary to J. H. Thomas.

[2] The unions prepared to see to continuous service for hospitals and the
like and for food distribution. The Government had prepared well in
advance an emergency system which worked with fanfare and military
show a little on the ridiculous side.

[3] We studied Martin's *British Public and the General Strike* in connection
with the Fraser Group. Its best use was to inform the young Socialists
with a ready made " public opinion." As such, it contributed to young
voters' support of the Party in 1929.

[4] Cf. Roger H. Saltau (of the London School of Economics and Political
Science), " The British Political Scene Since the General Election," *The
American Political Science Review*, XXIII (November, 1929), 892–907.

The Cardinal's position would not have been so difficult to comprehend if at any time the undermining Statism then endemic in British Socialism had ever been subjected to ecclesiastical criticism, officially. On the other hand, also, distinctions had not been made in the public mind and Socialism had been lumped with Communism, so that those who advocated Statism and what is now called " destructionism " of the permeating type escaped the correction meted out to catastrophic Socialism. This resulted in a general acceptance of penetrating gradualist Socialism as mere reformism.[5] In its polite, welfare-bent, tolerant and studious if thoroughly secular spirit, it had moved the parts of the Movement into position without Church help but with great assistance from Evangelical ministers like William Mellor, Ben Spoor, Canon Donaldson, and five others in Parliament. The quality of outright ILP Socialism was more easily reprehensible as being more patently comprehensible; ILP if it advocated slower political action asked for more " direct action " to win the Movement for Socialism.[6] Therefore, the political spearhead of the Labour Movement escaped close scrutiny of its Socialistic tendencies or of its definition of Socialism.

Also " sentimental "[7] Socialists did not compass in their ra-

---

Saltau, while showing how non-conformist chapels had contributed to forming the Labour Party, remarks "the existence of the Socialist Roman Catholics—a combination which would be unthinkable on the Continent," p. 898. Cf. Oldmeadow, *Cardinal Bourne,* pp. 141 f, which counters this.

[5] *Ibid.* Saltau shows how the real meaning of the election of 1929 was a new Liberalism and not Socialism and that this was understood by Labour and accounts for MacDonald's retaining the leadership—those outside the Socialists preferred him to Baldwin. He shows how the threat to his position came from his own Party (Maxtonites) and how the " alternative vote " would have articulated the real strength of Liberalism. But Saltau, while accounting for the Right Liberals and the Left Socialists, omits the real Socialist center of the Labour Party, the intellectual leadership not too accurately marked down as " moderates."

[6] After the Strike, MacDonald, and, a little later, Snowden left the ILP; both preferred political action to more thoroughgoing Socialism.

[7] By " sentiment " is not meant the oratorical " pity and love " Socialism of MacDonald. His speeches and writings cited in Tiltman, *op. cit.,* show his Socialism to be ·a natural religion and respectful of the justice of private property. " Sentimental " Socialists make Socialism a religion and offend those who compromise it for political ends as they are offended by

tionale any connivance with Capitalism. They were more loudly vocal than Fabianism and more devoted to direct action. Their manners and those of the colorful group once comprised in FRD put the General Strike idea beyond the sympathies of Cardinal Bourne, also, the fact that the terminology linked " General Strike" with the syndicalism of George Sorel. This vocal Socialism was nearly as frightening to the electorate—quite properly—as Moscow-directed Communism.[8]

But Fabians appeared in so many desirable liberal connections that they could hardly be believed to be subversive of private property or of liberty. Webb wrote for the *Economic Journal,* founded and edited by Keynes, as did Fabians W. H. Macrosty, R. H. Tawney, Viscount Haldane, Hugh Dalton, Barbara Wootton, D. W. Robertson, and others. The London School of Economics founded by Webb but left to its own devices in pursuit of truth was after all no Socialist camp of sedition but a highly respected school becoming world-renowned. Everybody liked the *NS*, if only for its literary articles and good style. The John Scurro and other Roman Catholic Socialists had no fears. That the Seven spoke like pure-Socialists, that Laski, Shaw, the Fraser group, the Mosleys,[9] and Mrs. Webb envisioned an Order govern-

---

those who do not bend every political means to the end—the eradication of private ownership, or worker-control.

[8] *The Clarion,* founded by Robert Blatchford and nicknamed " the old Expirer," was devoting itself to Socialism of a Fabian sort but was emphatic that the objective of the Labour Party was to achieve Socialism and not merely a Socialistic Labour Government. To abolish Capitalism was its constant preachment and its preachers were all Fabians.

[9] Mrs. Cole, who writes that she would have become a Communist in 1926, like R. Arnot and F. Horrabin and Ellen Wilkinson, had it not been for their having to take orders from Moscow, impugns MacDonald's Socialism because he liked the company of the great; specifically, *e.g.,* he was " thick" with the Mosleys (Lady Cynthia Mosley was the daughter of Lord Curzon) ; but Mrs. Cole tells of her own pleasure in the households of Frances, Duchess of Warwick (converted to Socialism by Blatchford's criticism of her debut— a strong point in our data on the use of psychology especially in abusing personages), and that of the Mitchisons (Mrs. Mitchison was Naomi Haldane) in the ducal luxury of Craignish Castle in Argyl, and in the Italian villa of Doctor Stella Churchill, a Fabian. Cf. her *Growing Up Into Revolution,* pp. 139–142, and p. 97 where she states, "I never became a Communist although I was far from being opposed to them."

ing " industrial democracy " and creative of the monopoly-opinion of One-Party, that Webb in 1923 had said, " only Socialism will do "; could hardly be known far from Tothill Street and was not taken very seriously at Transport House. That the straddling of issues and pragmatic compromise of Socialist principle on the part of the political leaders were rousing criticism from within; that the unions were committed to Socialism by Fabian leadership as well as their ILP mentors were facts hardly understood. So Cardinal Bourne, among the few who saw the meaning of the thesis of the Webb-Moderates and the harm which would come to unionism from reaction created by an irresponsible leadership, had cause for alarm seeing the syndicalist implication of the term " General Strike." In a sense, when Fabians used this term, " General Strike," it was to humour that section of the Movement which believed it would never be mature until it experienced one. The action of ILP in repudiating [10] the former Labour Prime Minister and the fact that as Tiltman says, corroborated by others, there was a Labour element which had wanted to " try " a General Strike since 1912 [11] would have been enough to arouse Cardinal Bourne. That the Strike was not a " General Strike " is the opinion of Fabian Kingsley Martin, who describes the Fabian rather than the public climate of opinion without drawing conclusions; and of ex-Fabian Slesser who argued in Parliament (without MacDonald's sanction) against the opinion of Sir John Simon, which was that the Strike, as a sympathy strike, was illegal and so rendered the unions and individuals liable to ruinous fines and the like. That it was intended to coerce Parliament and the Cabinet was never denied, but that it was therefore Revolution, as the Cabinet held, was always denied by Fyfe, Martin, Slesser, and general Fabian opinion. The *NS* held and taught that a successful General Strike without violence was an impossibility. The Cardinal's position was one such as would be formed upon the facts that ILP-ism and Fabian self-critics clearly aimed at obliterating Capitalism, and that the Strike was admittedly aimed at coercing the Government. The Cardinal was more on the side of the workers than they knew. They were being led into the shambles of Reaction.[12]

---

[10] Tiltman, *op. cit.*, pp. 266–268.

[11] *Ibid.*, p. 252.

[12] A strike is considered lawful in Catholic thinking only as a last resort

There is no commentator who adjudges TUC action all through the Strike agitation, better than stupid or tragic—Thomas, Clynes, Henderson, MacDonald, and Mrs. Cole, and Snowden.[13] Mrs. Hamilton all but ignores it because Henderson played so small a part, merely sitting on the platform with MacDonald when the Strike vote was taken and " going along " because regardless of strategy the wage scale was " the thing." [14]

The General Strike came from conditions which were maturing before the Conservative Government was formed in October, 1924. The general economic condition of England was one productive of Trade Union apprehension of a universal attack on wage scales, something which with its unstable equilibrium, the Labour Government could not have survived without fission in the Movement.[15] Mrs. Cole in *Growing Up Into Revolution* says, " Labour, which had declared so loudly that it would cure unem-

---

—like war. The attempt to call this Strike " General " made a general statement incumbent upon the Cardinal. There is no more moving passage in any of the Labourites' memoirs than that in Ben Tillett's *Memories and Reflections* (London: John Long, 1931), pp. 147–156, where the work of Cardinal Manning, whom Bourne succeeded, is recorded in connection with the Dockers' Strike. Bourne countered Statism by encouraging familial societies.

[13] But no Labour commentator deals with the real problem of TUC, that of keeping in line men whose ranks were impregnated with Communists who fomented the " direct action." When one finds a bull in a china shop, one should be very calm and quiet oneself.

[14] The wage scale was the crux of the matter in the struggle between Labour and the rest from 1926–1931. The standard of living was high for those receiving wages except miners, considerably higher than the price scale warranted. Where Labour advocated world cooperation, more production, wider markets, the Tory mentality in every nation moved steadily toward national self-sufficiency. In England " The Unemployed " served as pawns for both sides while employers argued that labor was an item in cost of production and labor spokesmen merely countered with their power to hold the wage line. Later, after the 1929 Crash, the low price scale came into the argument. It is interesting to speculate what the result might have been if the wage and standard of living scales had been allowed by labor to correlate in 1926–1929 under an impulsion of simple nationalism.

[15] The attempt to correlate high wage-scales, low living costs and the dole was postponed until reduction of the unemployed benefits became the point of issue, and of fission, in 1931. Labour votes and victories in the constituencies increased steadily from 1926 to 1929.

ployment, had not the slightest idea how to do so"; therefore she and her friends formed the S.S.I.P., "to form a group of intelligent workers for Socialism." [16]   The goal they set themselves was a Socialist Government in 1929.

The Tories may or may not have provoked the Strike. Trade Union and sentimental (Weir-type) Socialist opinion is positive that Baldwin aimed to bring on the Strike once it threatened, or that Baldwin's Cabinet insisted on the strategy despite a possibly more statesman-like attitude on the part of the Prime Minister. A legitimate question arises as to whether Fabian leadership could have prevented this Strike which had been postponed since 1921. Fabian leadership of the Party of the Movement knew that labor had nothing to gain from a General Strike; yet no one in the leadership did anything to prevent it from shaping up, although they called it senseless once it had begun.

The crux of the argument falls at the point where peace was at hand and the machine men at the *Daily Mail* [17] walked out. One writer said George Isaacs pleaded in vain against this action. It is possible that the walk-out represented the effort of left-wingers in the Trades Councils under Communist leadership to precipitate the Strike when it was learned TUC was for avoiding it. Every Labourite memoir blames the Government for refusing to continue negotiations but only now are we learning, and that from connections so remote as to appear unrelated, that large segments of the Movement had been destroyed by Communism. In 1923–1924,

---

[16] M. Cole, *Growing Up Into Revolution,* 139.

[17] *The Daily Mail* of today appears to have no record or information to offer on the subject. Inquiry was made as to what larger authority, Trade Council or TUGC, these men were responsible, but no reply was forthcoming on this point. If any conspiracy to provoke the strike was suspected, were it of communist or Trade Council influence, the paper would not hesitate, one should surmise, to state it. On the other hand, if peace were desired, why should the Duke of Northumberland's mouthpiece have given an inflammatory editorial to the machine men to set up? It was known that the editorial staff was pro-Labour. It is possible that 1) Tories wanted the Strike to eventuate in order to crush the Movement, and 2) that Communists infiltrated the editorial staff to produce the provoking editorial in order to precipitate the Strike. These latter gave signs of organizational activity in the East End, especially where they tried to carry out the Moscow directives to militarize the poor (and defeat the "bourgeois" attempts to "rearm.")

directives for sovietizing came from Moscow transmitted and executed by the half-breed East Indian-Scandinavian, the skilled dialectician, Ryani Palme Dutt. (He had been associated with the Coles in FRD, now LRD, up to 1923 and was an editor of the *Labour Monthly,* newly founded and announced in the *FN.*) " The Communists played their part in the death of the National Guilds League and the Guild Socialist movement . . . [when] the new othodoxy of the Left split its intellectual protagonist." [18] The Trades Councils, small Labour Parties, and small Trade Union branches had, by 1925, been captured by the Communist Party, which was part of the Third International and Moscow-directed. They took tight control because they were ordered to, according to Mrs. Cole who continued to work for LRD (the former FRD) up to 1926, although Douglas had resigned in anger in 1924. LRD had been won for Communism " by a deliberate campaign." The Coles had removed to Oxford, and, during the General Strike, they devoted themselves to liaison work. This consisted in delivering the *Workers Gazette,* which Mellor and Fyfe, Fabians " going along " with TUC, got out. They did this in order to keep undergraduate Socialists (Hugh Gaitskell and John Dugdale, among them) from " driving buses and trains for the Government out of sheer boredom." [19] When it is recalled that in 1923–1925 the *NS* and most Webb-Shaw-Davies Fabians kept saying Communism should be ignored because it had no labour following, the question arises as to whether the uses of Communism to destroy what Fabians could not always otherwise control were not understood. Mrs. Cole and Douglas and their radical Oxonian students thought of Guild Socialism as " the Movement." Certainly the Webbs and Henderson, the *FN* and the *NS* did not.

The Strike lasted nine days, then the TUGC announced that a satisfactory basis of settlement in the mining industry could be formulated. Reaction set in immediately: Lockouts, failure to rehire, recriminations, followed by the Trade Union Act of 1927.[20]

---

[18] Margaret Cole, *Growing Up Into Revolution,* p. 101.

[19] *Ibid.,* pp. 102 and 122 f.

[20] Cf. Slesser, *op. cit.,* pp. 205–231, where his full analysis of the Act and his adverse opinion of it are set forth at length. On page 231, the " juniors " who were outstanding in this fight are mentioned. Slesser had little help

When Tawney wrote in *Labour and the Nation*,[21] in 1928: " The dangerous revolutionaries are not those who seek power to initiate reforms which are long overdue, but the reactionaries who dam the stream till it bursts its bank in a raging torrent," he omitted a concluding step in reasoning. While blaming the Liberal Party for its having sacrificed itself to elect a Conservative Government after having endorsed labor-agitated reforms, Tawney and his colleagues failed to note that communists and those who induced a Strike which was illicit intended to put " reaction " to use. Reactionary measures were calculated to drive the unions to desperate direct action. Instead the Fabian leadership of labor in the Party found to hand the advantage that TUC, restrained and curbed by law, must trust in the Labour Party to extricate it from its bonds. Only Fabianism gained anything from the Strike.

When it came to passing the Trades Union Act, Slesser fought against it, " the greatest conflict in [his] life," for the reason principally, that he feared the loss of liberty to individual workingmen more than the loss of union strength. He knew he was the " chief expert in England " on labor law. Nevertheless, he had been relegated to the charge of " a minute subsidiary provision " in the memorandum which the Party made out to apportion the parts to be taken by Labour Members of Parliament in the fight on the Act.

> For the rights of men to cease to work when the Union
> had told them to continue they [Labourites] had in the
> past shown little sympathy. I was determined that the
> fight should be, at least in part, upon a deep principle and
> not be obscured by an over-insistence on trade union
> rights as such. In the event I was successful.[22]

save from " Mr. Rossyln Mitchell, one of the alertest men in Glasgow, and the most immaculate Socialist member of the House." Mitchell was a Fabian.

[21] R. H. Tawney, *Labour and the Nation* (London: The Labour Party) 1928, p. 14.

[22] Slesser, *op. cit.*, pp. 202 ff. The contrasting treatment by Webb and by MacDonald of the former Fabian and historian-to-be of the Liberal Party is indicative of the way Webb tried to use and save all the talent possible for the Movement while a narrower sectarianism governed others. There is a strong parallel between MacDonald's attitude toward John Wheatley which was maintained against the better advice of Snowden, and his attitude

Expecting the Labour Opposition to end " in vague declamation "
and not believing that " this was the desire of the back benches,"
Slesser rose, though he was not on the Speaker's list, and made
" the most important speech I ever made in Parliament " : The Bill
prevented free termination of contract, and limited freedom to
refuse to accept employment, or freedom to collect funds for relief
as " furthering a dispute " ; the Act held workmen liable for
coercion produced by action on the part of leaders, thus confusing
" instrument " and " agent." The Act also confused " General
Strike," and " genuine trades dispute " with a sympathy strike.
The Government " forgot " to include legislation against " general
or wide lockouts." In the end, as Slesser predicted, " the Act in
practice proved useless " and " the defeat of the Government in
1929 was largely due to this legislation." [23] No defense of liberty
and the Common Law, such as Slesser made, was forthcoming from
active Fabians or on the part of the Party. In the light of what
has previously been pointed out concerning the need to control the
unions on the part of Order-minded Fabians whose politics came
so near being " tory," it is small wonder that none of the accounts portrays the glories of a campaign to repeal the Act nor
depicts the defeated ranks of the Socialist-led labor movement
going down, heads bloody but unbent. The Act stayed on the
books until 1945. The political-Socialist leadership was apathetic.
Macrae-Gibson,[24] a Fabian and an authority on the Whitley Councils, disclosed that the Act was designed to prevent unionized civil
servants from committing their organisation to a Party " with

---

toward Slesser, against the better advice of Webb. John Wheatley was a
Catholic and Harry Slesser quite near becoming a Catholic at the time. The
difference was culturally basic.

[23] It was not useless as a campaign promise in 1929. Cf. Tawney, *Labour
and the Nation,* pp. 7 and 16. Strangely, the Labour Government of 1929–
1931 failed to repeal the Act. Even in wartime the TUC continued to
demand its repeal (cf. Slesser, *op. cit.,* p. 225). *The Clarion* kept urging
amendment through 1930; it was finally repealed *en masse* in 1945. Mrs.
Cole says this was the Labour Government's *only class legislation,* an amazing statement.

[24] Cf. J. H. Macrae-Gibson, " Notes on Administration," *The American
Political Science Review,* XXIII (November, 1929), 922–929, edited by L. D.
White of Chicago and subtitled, " The British Civil Service and the Trade
Unions Act of 1927."

the particular aim of removing all danger that in any event such as the general strike of 1926 Government employees might be called out on strike," and also " to prevent representation of direct civil service interests in the House of Commons." It was recalled that the Union of Postal Workers and Civil Service Clerical Association had on an occasion, selected a constituency for one of their members (full-time employees), and had run him for Parliament as a Labour candidate. Macrae-Gibson showed in November, 1929, that the prohibition against affiliating such a union with a Party was indeed resented, but that to repeal Clause V which was concerned with this problem, would result in " reaction against political commitments, though not in any reduction of the political activities of the service organisation." This very Fabian document evinced no Fabian determination to repeal the Act only a concern to placate the Trade Unions to whom the Party, as Macrae-Gibson said, was deeply committed.

Of a certainty, the intellectuals publicly deplored the bungling of TUC leadership which stumbled into the Strike of 1926. It is also certain that " direct-action " sentiment was stirred up against leaders both of the intelligentsia and of the Party because they curbed the Strike. MacDonald was read out of the ILP and had to be chosen by the Moray and Nairn Divisional Labour Party to be a delegate to the Conference, because, as Tiltman [25] says, " Only delegates nominated by the constituent bodies forming the Labour Party are entitled to vote or to be appointed to any office on the Party Executive." (This disfranchises a mere Labour Party sympathizer and joiner, and obliges him to follow the Conference programme in the creation of which he had no part.) There was no going back to the Fabians with MacDonald but his speech before the General Strike was perfectly Fabian: " No greater calamity could come over the country "; [26] *all* should, however, stand by the miners; but the " biggest union " with which to win through, said MacDonald, was " public opinion and reason."

When it was over, Fabian Mrs. Hamilton wrote:

> The failure of the whole strike movement shifted emphasis back to the political side . . . Direct action had

[25] Tiltman, *op. cit.*, p. 268.
[26] *Ibid.*, p. 251.

been tried. The general strike idea had been got out of the system.

This was the typical Fabian statement [27] and it reveals the reason why the Fabians did not prevent the Strike.

Some incidental features of the Strike are to be remarked: Fabian Hamilton Fyfe, in setting up the *Workers' Gazette,* encountered difficulty with Trade Unionists whom he must employ. They incurred his wrath by insisting on union rules and wages even in the emergency. He was assisted in getting out the *Workers' Gazette* by Fabian William Mellor,[28] night editor of the *Daily Herald,* who did yeoman service. Fabians also assisted officially in continuing to administer a Miners' Relief Fund long after the Strike ended. Listed in August [29] and in November, [30] for instance, were Sarah Simpson, A. R. Green, I. Aingren, A. H. May, Miss A. Sloan and P. G. White. These were names of typical persons unknown to fame among the faithful two thousand Fabians. It is significant that the Fabian Society by charitable works kept the sympathies of strikers even while they gave only lip service to the whole project, as in the Dock Strike long before.

B. The Programme of 1928

Fabian leadership had realigned the Party after 1925. Henderson, surprised and disappointed in the Dissolution, as Mrs. Hamilton believes, took means to reshape the " rattled " Party. He displaced Ben Spoor, the inept Fabian and disillusioned Wesleyan minister, as Chief Whip; then he ignored the left-swing toward direct action on the part of TUC and, going against MacDonald, who detested a " programme," produced [31] a programme to " compel [the Conference] to face responsibilities," a programme " designed to throw up the major lines of Party policy . . . for

---

[27] *Ibid.,* p. 275.

[28] He is identified as the FRD member and associate of the Coles during the War. He was then a radical Guild Socialist; but he had trained for the Evangelical Ministry. Cf. Margaret Cole, *Growing Up Into Revolution,* p. 60.

[29] *FN,* 37:8 (August, 1926).

[30] *FN,* 37:11 (November, 1926).

[31] Cf. Mrs. Hamilton, *op. cit.,* pp. 259 ff.

delegates . . . and for the public." A Fabian, T. C. Cramp, who was president of the Conference in 1925, defended the leaders (principally MacDonald) who were then under attack. The floor work at this Conference was admirable. Before Bevin could move his resolution never again to give sanction to " any future minority Government," MacDonald had been put forward with a " series of powerful speeches on constructive issues." Bevin's resolution was lost by two and one-half million to one-half million votes. (Mrs. Hamilton's logarithms.) [32] MacDonald had been converted to Henderson's " view about programme " which was that an authoritative programme, if it could not prevent the Press from talking nonsense, would protect the candidates and the Party; and it would prevent Labour spokesmen from " talking nonsense." When Harry Pollitt asked for " Socialism in every sentence of it," Henderson recalled his own vote of thirty-five years ago for Socialisation of means of production, distribution, and so forth, and added: " We want to get on . . . the use of phrases, now that the Party has reached its present stage, is not going to help us." Thus Henderson placated the far left and implied possible difference in doctrine between his Socialism and Pollitt's. The banner of Socialism of thirty-five years ago was not to be refurbished, just taken for granted. To read this Programme, written 1925–1928, is to find that scorn was cast upon those who feared " Socialism " and to find Professor Tawney setting forth his own brand of nationalization or " municipal Socialism " which is identical with what he observed of public ownership in America in 1924.[33]

---

[32] These votes were given en bloc. It is unfair to count individuals in this instance. One of the greatest reforms of ILO was that carried on by one Monsignor Nolens, Netherland Government delegate, 1928, to reassert individual responsibility by individual voting; he " attacked what he called group discipline." Offering consultation instead of hard and fast attitudes, he spoke against secret meetings, abstentions, agreements of minorities to vote with majorities, etc. Cf. (Anonymous), *The International Labour Organisation: The First Decade* (London: Allen and Unwin, 1931), p. 237.

[33] Tawney told in another document of his amazement over what he saw in America in 1924: Federal " controlled " railways, running through State or National Parks to towns where the gas and water were city-owned (he omitted bills paid through banks) ; county schools, part of a State education system where texts were supplied free and where he heard professors from

The drafting of the Programme fell to MacDonald, Lansbury, F. O. Roberts, T. C. Cramp, Herbert Morrison, Ellen Wilkinson (she was a Communist in 1929, according to Mrs. Cole—but still a Fabian), Oswald Mosley, C. Trevelyan, and Henderson. Six at least were Fabians. " The Mosley star was very much in the ascendant "[34] and he and the charming Lady Cynthia (née Curzon) were " on close terms of intimacy with the MacDonalds." Mrs. Hamilton thinks Snowden's main differences with Mosley were traceable to the latter's " authoritarian position." The Programme was published as *Labour and the Nation,* drafted " mainly " by R. H. Tawney.[35] According to Henderson's biographer, the debates of that year, 1926, brought into focus two new stars, " not Maxton, not Mosley, but Herbert Morrison and Hugh Dalton "; both of these new stars were Fabians in the entourage of " the Great " at the time when the young FDR was making a pest of itself in the place that was Mr. Pease's boarding-house.[36] In this nest of young cuckoos, to use Mrs. Cole's comparison, there was division too.

A word about the philosophy of the Programme: It was built upon the old " worker by hand and brain " idea and upon " doctrineless Socialism."[37] Socialism was a creed by which the strati-

---

State universities praise free enterprise. Cf. Tawney, *The British Labor Movement* (Williamstown, Mass.: The Institute of Politics, Williams College, 1924), p. 172. He overlooks the point that all these glories were attained under a liberal not a Socialist " spirit " which his esteemed colleague said in 1923 was the only spirit capable of producing them.

[34] Mrs. Hamilton, *op. cit.,* p. 262. In the ensuing Thomas-Mosley altercation, MacDonald stood by Thomas, as will appear below.

[35] Tiltman credits MacDonald with more work on it than Mrs. Hamilton does although she was the author of two biographies of MacDonald. (If Henderson proposed using MacDonald's power, Mrs. Hamilton agreed.) The document was defended against Maxton and Wheatley by MacDonald. Fabian Mosley was " with them on programme though against them on leadership," according to Mrs. Hamilton, *op. cit.,* p. 262. Mrs. Cole had a poor opinion of the document. Its " ammunition [was] largely provided by Lloyd George's Liberal research department." Cf. *Growing Up Into Revolution,* p. 125. (This student finds that Mrs. Cole knew little about Fabians until she grew out of revolution into the NFRB and went on to the reconstruction of the Fabian Society of 1939.)

[36] Cf. Mrs. Cole, *Growing Up Into Revolution,* pp. 60 f.

[37] Cf. *Labour and the Nation,* p. 6. By seeing men as one class, labor, it

fied society was to be striated, as it were. The morality of the creed was " the familiar commonplace that morality is in the nature of things." The Labour Party was,

> . . . the political organ created to express the needs and voice the aspirations of all who share in the labour which is the lot of mankind . . . the force which sustains society is not passive property but creative effort . . . [and] the Labour Party *since it holds that creed is a Socialist Party* . . . [it aims] without violence . . . [by] scientific knowledge . . . [at the] deliberate establishment . . . of a social order . . . to secure . . . the largest possible measure of economic welfare and personal freedom.[38]

The Programme, which did not envision in " welfare " and " freedom " freedom for " Economics," or personal liberty, became Henderson's " book of words," says his Fabian biographer. This is understandable especially since a relic of the Geneva Protocol, the Optional Clause, Disarmament, and Recognition of Russia were also embodied in this, Fabian Tawney's articulation of Labour's aims. It expressed no regret about the Geneva Protocol, only that its contingent Disarmament Conference did not transpire in 1925.[39] Mrs. Hamilton terms the objective of the Party the " union of labour and learning." She points out that MacDonald, like Henderson, " believed in Socialism," but unlike Henderson did not think it would work. Yet Henderson, who affirmed if he did not confirm his Socialism, believed still more in the Party, and was " a marvelous stage-manager." A chief problem had been the Press which had played up two ideas: 1) Trade Union's General Conference had swung far left toward Direct Action in 1925; [40]

---

fell short of the principle of *vocation* which Slesser found in St. Thomas and sought in vain in "industrial democracy." It made men to be horizontally ordered as workers by hand, by brain, by initiative, by experiment, on farm, mine, or factory. It did not conceive of a perpendicular ordering wherein, creating the Product, for the Common Good, men follow a *vocation* grouped in a family-ordered way ranged from the Capitalist to the greasemonkey in united effort toward getting out a product for the good of all and to make a contribution to society. Cf. Oldmeadow, *op. cit., passim.*

[38] Cf. *Labour and the Nation,* pp. 5 f., italics supplied.

[39] *Ibid.,* p. 44.

[40] Cf. Mrs. Hamilton, *op. cit.,* p. 259. It is a great pity that the noble

and 2) "MacDonald must go," which was also a part of the ostensible Communist line. It was Fabianism which realigned all in order to gradualness. It retained and confirmed Trade Unionism again under a Programme nominally Socialistic. It retained the leader, whom ILP had repudiated because he favored political over socialistic action, because the liberal core of England believed he could do better than Baldwin in handling the European situation.[41]

Labour and the Nation chided Russia for intervening in the internal problems of other nations but demanded full trade with U.S.S.R.; it also asked aid for "the Chinese people and the world" not for "financial groups belonging to imperialist foreign Powers," to prevent the revolt of Asia against the West. The name calling can be but subterfuge. "People" and "world" have to find implementation which any displeased group may denigrate with terminology. These are the times when Albert Thomas was journeying in the interest of the International Labour Office (but

---

qualities of *Labour and the Nation* cannot be delineated here. It is a greater pity that some group which had no objectionable philosophies such as that this was an age "clamant" for a "secularist way of life," did not adopt so dynamic a policy toward the very real need for education free from unfair class distinctions from "Nursery to University," (*Ibid.*, p. 37); or strike out boldly for efficient production (not merely for price), (p. 49). Perhaps it would be fairer to say it was a pity that this dynamic group which assumed responsibility for their brothers' welfare was a group historically deprived of religious literacy.

[41] In internationalism, Mrs. Hamilton believed, must lie the cure for England's ills. She credited Stresemann with the conception of the Locarno Treaties and D'Albernon with "help," censured Austen Chamberlain for the return of Poincaré, and the Government for dwindling trade with Russia following the Arcos raid, the abrogation of the treaty (of 1924), and the increasing acerbity of Franco-German relations induced by Anglo-French conversations. She never mentioned the Anglo-German Trade Treaty, the floating in London and New York of loans, and selling of bonds of German States and municipalities which owned the German coal fields, nor investment by Englishmen of every party in these bonds. So long as this crux was not embraced, any debate about solving miners' unemployment was sure to be only a bid for power. Mrs. Hamilton is the typical Fabian following the Party line unreasoningly. As late at 1938, she should surely be responsible for the perusal of D'Abernon's *Diaries* which came out in 1929–1931. She does not cite them; perhaps she misinterprets D'Abernon's role out of partisanship.

also in the interest of the Labour and Socialist International) into China, to learn that China, while not Capitalistic, was not in favor of the Third International. Where a warlord of South China imputed to the Second International the blame for the non-integration of Europe and China, Thomas was explaining to him the " democratisation" of Capitalist industrial life in Europe.[42]

Part of the reinforcement of Labour's prestige from 1926 to 1929 was due to the reconstruction of the Second International. When Russian dictatorship drove out of the " Two-and-a-Half " Adler, Longuet and their followers, Henderson collected this added strength for the Second, but not without MacDonald's " magnificent sparring matches with the giants of the Third," Radek and Bukharin. Fabian C. R. Buxton also accompanied Henderson " on international journeyings." Fabian Susan Lawrence witnessed his " ovation " one day in the Conference in Brussels in 1928, a day when Henderson, after a purple-spotted harangue by Vandervelde, holding a " wad of typescript," read a speech in his " usual one-tone, level, sonorous voice." [43] International political aspects kept the Labour Party united and interested while interest in the other Parties lagged because they took a great deal for granted from 1925 to 1929. " From the Shetlands . . . to Lands End, . . . the country [was] covered by a network of Labour Party Organisations." These were flattered no doubt by being consulted if not merely indoctrinated on international attitudes. International considerations resulted in Henderson's becoming head of the Foreign Office in 1929.

Mrs. Hamilton takes her subject out of the country for the Baldwin interval. If Fabian reactions to the passing of the Trade Unions Act of 1927 and to the Poor Law Reforms of 1928 were all but apathetic, their negative position was more marked and bore clearer markings on certain socio-religious issues. There took place a fight over Catholic relief and on the Prayer Book,

---

[42] Cf. Edward J. Phelan, *Albert Thomas et la Creation du B.I.T.* (Paris: Bernard Grasset, 1936), pp. 290 f. It shows the catholicity of Socialism. Thomas did not walk alone. His path often crossed that of Borodin in China. In 1929 Stalin had 1500 " agrarian" Chinese boys being educated at the expense of U.S.S.R. in the Far East University in Moscow.

[43] Mrs. Hamilton, *op. cit.*, p. 279. " This was John Bull! " Mrs. Hamilton interprets the ovation.

matters which served to bring out Fabian indifferentism and materialism. As described by Slesser,[44] the secularism, *i.e.*, absolute religious indifference of Socialist and Fabian thought is marked, especially on the Prayer Book question and on Birth Control. Slesser was an Anglo-Catholic at the time and failed, as did Protestant Rosslyn Mitchell, to cut through the mists of confusion in this argument. Mitchell, cited verbatim by Slesser,[45] said that

> [reservation of consecrated Wafer and wearing of vestments to signify] was transubstantiation, and that was the dividing principle between the two churches. If the Church of England wanted that, then let her have it . . . but if she did not want it, then she could not pass this Book. In one generation, with the Deposited Book, they could swing over all the children of England from the Protestant Reformed Faith to the Roman Catholic Faith.

Of the Labour M.P.'s, Slesser says,

> Their Roman Catholic associates they tolerated, regretfully, as persons otherwise supporting Labour, but possessed of exotic unintelligible views which had received the toleration of time and Act of Parliament.[46]

The Party leadership by means " minatory and appellant " tried to keep Slesser from debating at all.

Fabian Henderson was more of a Party man than a Fabian. The women in the Movement, whom often he had to placate—or submit to their revilings as he cheerfully did at times—were probably more Fabian than Party minded. In 1927, their demand to have Birth Control instruction sponsored by the Ministry of Health, was defeated by Henderson's reasoning that " those sacred issues that came into direct conflict with the religious convictions of multitudes of our members " had always been kept outside. However, the ladies always won their point when he was absent. One of his greatest platform achievements was getting a reversal of what had carried in his absence on the Birth Control issue.

---

[44] Slesser, *op. cit.*, pp. 205 ff.
[45] *Ibid.*, pp. 132 f.
[46] *Ibid.*, p. 134.

Henderson argued effectively against injecting religious and domestic matters into a political party platform. He knew of course that it would not do to alienate the Catholics in the Party. Slesser describes their attitude in Parliament [47] where their " expression " of the Catholic viewpoint was " allowed " by the Party. (An effort was made to disallow Slesser's voicing identical views because he was not a Catholic.) This was another of the points where, by compromise, the majority consensus was not allowed to offend supporters and the unity of the Party was protected, by Fabian skill.[48]

We must turn to Keith Feiling to learn of the constructive reforms carried out by Neville Chamberlain in the Ministry of Health, and to the *NS* or *The Clarion* to find out what was its Fabian reaction, seeing the subjects they had long agitated carried through by others. The Poor Law was altered to cope with the " new " poor and to defeat Popularism. Popularism, in Fabian Lansbury's way of thinking, was the correct way of dealing with the poor, *i.e.*, by not merely providing relief—" outdoor relief "— but by subsidizing a life such as the Lord intended them to have, as he said. Even more shocking than the conditions at Poplar where Lansbury's system brought it about that " marriages were made and children maintained, on the dole," Neville Chamberlain found " sovietized " sections in Chester-le-Street in Durham

> where the large Labour majority had used their power
> to subsidize wages, [ignoring family collective earnings]
> to favour trade unionists . . . [At the time of the General Strike] they constituted themselves an emergency
> committee, distributed relief to almost the whole mining
> population . . . regardless of private means, and suspended officers who refused to break the law. It looked

---

[47] Slesser, *op. cit.*, p. 151.

[48] Susan Lawrence wrote a novel, *Clash*, to tell the inner story of the Strike. She describes the environs of the Hall where the Strike vote was to be taken and she includes among the persons milling about, the " inevitable " women peddling birth control literature. In 1949 the Labour Government had to repel the notion that contraceptive vending machines were favored by the Health Ministry. Fabians Tillett, Lansbury, and Turner deplored the complication of political Socialism with the free-thinking domestic sociology of some socialists.

as if a trade union masquerading as guardians, were
financing an industrial dispute out of public funds.[49]

The reorganization of poor relief on lines of Local Government
with the abolition of Boards of Guardians was the fruit of long
pressure coming from W. A. Robson's Local Government Bureau
of the Fabian Society, and from the ever-increasing circulation
of *Local Government News,* his organ;[50] and it meant for the
Webbs the end of three decades of agitation for the control of
destitution. They appraised it in an Epilogue to their *English
Local Government* in 1928. But in doing so, they left unanswered
their own question. Should the unemployable be treated with a
disciplinary attitude or supported for poltical reasons? This was
the old unanswerable riddle of industrial democracy. The Webbs
raised the question with the greatest acuity and realism and without the slightest allusion to the possibility that an answer lay in
agriculture. They ignored even the projects Lansbury had developed successfully. Untroubled, they left the question unanswered. But the concept of " the masses " had been crystallized
in England's garden-variety socialism.

---

[49] Cf. Feiling, *op. cit.,* pp. 139 f.

[50] Cf. *F.S.A.R.,* 1924–1931, where this is reiterated with classical formulation not to speak of the history of the Poor Law agitation by the Webbs who
thanked the Baldwin Government for the Act outlawing " outdoor relief "
at last, in the *English Local Government* of 1928, p. 985.

The Webbs and Ellen Wilkinson (famed in Poplar history) approved
Neville Chamberlain's system of audit and control. Cf. Feiling, *op. cit.,*
p. 141.

CHAPTER XI

THE GOVERNMENT OF 1929–1931

A. Its Fabian Content

This chapter deals with the composition of the Government of 1929 and the Fabian reaction to its failures of which the angriest expression was Harold Laski's. It surveys, also, the general attitude of *The Clarion* which portrayed the state of mind of Fabians to the point of facsimile and so provides silent, sardonic commentary upon the wrathy expression of Sidney Webb as he " dished " MacDonald without lament for the fall of H.M.'s Labour Government.[1]

There were certain parallels with the Government of 1924 to be found in that of 1929–1931. In the relative position of the Capital Levy stood the idea of " family allowances." [2] It was said that this idea stood in the place of the historical agitation of land for the peasants. Like the Capital Levy, it stood aside because as was the case with the Government of 1924, the Party had no majority; and the " right to work " replaced the member of the equation named " community ownership." [3] Unlike 1924, this time dissent of sentimental Socialists like Maxton and Bevin against taking office without a majority was resolved by Conference majority vote rather than by a letter from Webb after election;[4] unlike 1924, this time there would be no doubling. Again the Party had grown from the influx of individual members; seven hundred thousand new women voters had joined the Labour Party.[5] Trade Unions listed fewer members but tradesmen were

---

[1] Mrs. Cole wrote, " We were so profoundly relieved to be rid of Mac-Donald at last," in her *Growing Up Into Revolution*, p. 155.

[2] Cf. *The Labour Year Book of 1931*, published by the General Council of the Trade Union Congress and the National Executive of the Labour Party (London: Labour Publications Department, Transport House, 1931), p. 7. (Hereinafter, *LYB*.)

[3] Cf. Snowden, *op. cit.*, II, p. 179.

[4] Cf. Hamilton, *Henderson*, p. 281.

[5] Cf. Snowden, *op. cit.*, II, p. 756.

impelled by the reaction to the Trades Dispute Law [6] to favor Labour. " Contracting in " had scant effect on the volume of the vote. Again recourse was had to political action; as in 1923 after a wave of strikes, so in 1929, after the spasm of the General Strike. Again the Labour Party had a " Programme," *Labour and the Nation,* in place of *Labour and the New Social Order.* The former, couched in Tawney's phrases was evolved by Fabians from a " mandate " of the Party Executive: George Lansbury, F. O. Roberts, T. C. Cramp, Herbert Morrison, Ellen Wilkinson, Oswald Mosley, Charles Trevelyan (not on any Fabian list but a friend of the Webbs), and Arthur Henderson along with MacDonald.[7] Again the Big Five met to decide policy: [8] MacDonald, Snowden, Clynes, Henderson, Thomas. Webb was not in evidence. Henderson's biographer believes he might have opposed MacDonald's leadership—presumably, had he followed his inclination— but he remained " loyal." The fact is that the Labour Party Conference where the real weight of labor was a force, favored MacDonald who, with one of his " big speeches " [9] had won rejection of the resolution (Wheatley's),[10] supported by Maxton, like Bevin's in 1925, not to accept the Ministry without a majority in Parliament. MacDonald had been very close to the work of drafting *Labour and the Nation* which was to be Henderson's " book of words." [11] Whereas in 1923–1924 the ILP had demanded MacDonald's leadership, now it was the Trade Unionists of the second and third class (in Mrs. Cole's classification) plus the liberal core of England against Baldwin, which favored MacDonald. The Con-

---

[6] *LYB,* p. 11.

[7] Cf. Hamilton, *op. cit.,* p. 262.

[8] Cf. Snowden, *op. cit.,* II, p. 755.

[9] Hamilton, *op. cit.,* p. 260. Working to promote MacDonald's leadership was the Fabian Quaker, Walter Newbold. His objective was disarmament. Cf. Snowden, *op. cit.,* II, p. 249, and Weir, *op. cit.,* p. 432. The use of Fabians in " behind the scene " places as in 1924 is a repeated pattern. Newbold had been a Fabian since 1908 and by 1924 was an ex-Communist. He had been on the Labour Research Department, 1922–1926. L. M. Weir, a former Academy Head, was Parliamentary Private Secretary to MacDonald until replaced by another Fabian from the London School of Economics, S. F. Markham, a Mosleyite at the time.

[10] Cf. Snowden, *op. cit.,* II, p. 760.

[11] Hamilton, *Henderson,* pp. 262 f.

ference had repudiated the proffered leadership of the Wheatleys, the Maxtons, and the Mosleys. Young Fabians in *The Clarion* were keeping an eye on Ernest Bevin and his four million union men. There was no personality in 1924 comparable with Ernest Bevin now becoming a politico who could be counted upon to keep Trade Unionists out of splinter movements like Mosley's, and to remind the politicians " who pays the piper." [12] Again there were a half-hundred Liberals representing a disproportionately larger electoral segment than their numbers signified but no Asquith to hold the balance. The suggestion was made that Labour coalesce with Conservatives, but Snowden with his " free trade " sentiment, Henderson who had made " free trade " part of the bone-structure of the Party, and Thomas whose railway men could get along now with or without " free trade," steered the Party away from coalition or coalescence with Tories on the basis of this ancient antagonism.[13] The veteran Lloyd George became the arbiter of Parliamentary policy. But, like the realism of 1924, the realism of 1930 drew the Labour leaders far over into the " right " orbit of Tory thinking before the denouement.[14] In 1929, in place of Asquith, a still form and a silent power stood in the background. Once, and then with such elaborate protestations of confidence in the absolute constitutionality of its actions that he contradicted himself, Lord Passfield alluded to it; again, the closest scrutinizer of the actions of the Minister who headed the Foreign Office alluded to it with studied objectivity: [15] the form and the power of the King of England.

The proportion of men of Trade Union mentality to the intelligentsia was thirteen out of twenty in the Cabinet of 1924; in

---

[12] Thomas, *op. cit.*, p. 278.

[13] Cf. Snowden, *op. cit.*, II, p. 758.

[14] Cf. Weir, *op. cit.*, p. 451, where he tells of Neville Chamberlain's collaboration in the composition of Snowden's speech on the crisis. Also, *ibid.*, p. 316, where Weir speaks of Baldwin and MacDonald having mutual friends. Weir describes a scene wherein the Prime Minister sent for Baldwin in a very agitated mood; and he insinuates that then it was that Baldwin took the measure of the P.M., and dictated the Cabinet's formation. Cf. Weir, *op. cit.*, pp. 310 f. Weir ascribes the financial plight of the time to Tory and City machinations devised to get Labour " in a corner " by " financial jugglery." *Ibid.*, p. 397.

[15] Cf. Hamilton, *Henderson*, p. 312.

1929, most of the Cabinet were Fabians, or their associates, as were twenty-one out of fifty-four in the Parliamentary Party. As to local parties and TUC, Fabians predominated in both camps. Almost as if Socialism was a religion which stood in danger of its being forgotten and required to be preached in season and out, the admonition to bring it in everywhere is given, gratuitously, in a discussion of " rationalisation " in the TUGC's *Yearbook*.[16] The state of tutelage of Trade Unionism was more abject in 1929 than in 1924 even though Trade Unionism, *per se,* was more clearly articulated. The *Yearbook* of 1931 shows definitely indigenous leadership but the usual permeation of Fabians in the upper groups and in advisory capacities, where about three-fourths were Fabians. Those most easily identified were: In Defense, Basil Hall; Finance, A. E. Davies and Commander J. M. Kenworthy; Education, R. H. Tawney and Barbara Drake; Home, Barbara Ayrton Gould; International, C. R. Buxton and L. Woolf; Land, Josiah Wedgwood; Legal, Arthur Henderson, Jr.; Local Government, Herbert Morrison; Health, Somerville Hastings and G. P. Blizard; Science, G. W. Thomson; Transport, C. T. Cramp.[17]

As in 1923–1924, Henderson came into the Government of 1929 with fresh laurels gleaned from internationalism. M. A. Hamilton, now a member of Parliament, gloried in the international assiduities in 1924–1929 of the new head of the Foreign Office.[18] Two new Clubs, the National Labour Club headed by MacDonald and Henderson, having a roster of officials about fifty percent Fabian, and the National Trade Union Club, having a Fabian Chairman and about a third of its officers Fabians, had come into existence in 1924 and 1930 respectively. Among other purposes, one was to give hospitality to foreign visitors and to provide a place comparable to the hospices had by " our comrades on the continent." [19]

---

[16] *LYB* (1931), p. 9.

[17] *Ibid.,* p. 16. *FN* boasted that seven Fabians were elected to the Labour Party Executive at the Brighton Conference, 1929: Ethel Bentham, Barbara Gould, George Dallas, Hugh Dalton, George Lathan, George Lansbury, Herbert Morrison.

[18] Cf. Hamilton, *Henderson,* pp. 277 f.

[19] *LYB* (1931), pp. 24 and 26.

Once more the problems of India,[20] Egypt, and Singapore, harassed the Foreign Office. Again the Government inherited a half-formulated reparations plan; for, at the Kellogg Pact Conference in Paris in 1928, suggestions had been put in motion for what turned out to be the Young Plan of 1929. The Labour Party leaders were now openly francophile in contrast to the gallophobia of 1922–1924.[21] Empire Preference had been rejected by the Labour Government of 1924 [22] but the Commonwealth was slowly taking shape. Australia, for example, was able to assert her interest in decisions affecting herself by insisting upon the agreement to protect Singapore. The Labour Government which had stopped fortification in 1924 now agreed to resume such—in five years.[23] Churchill's difference with Baldwin

---

[20] Six out of sixteen British Round Table Conferees were Fabians: Oliver Stanley, Earl Russell, Lees-Smith, W. A. Jowitt, Henderson, Wedgwood Benn, besides MacDonald, Sankey, and Thomas.

[21] Cf. Weir, *op. cit.,* p. 347. Weir's inculpation of MacDonald reveals some matters he was not concerned with but was in a position to be informed upon: Henderson revealed that France was willing to earmark *credits* for rediscount to Britain to the amount of £20,000,000 (Weir, *op. cit.,* p. 405) but Garvin had disclosed that France, seeking Germany's ruin, did not wish to lend *gold* which might be re-loaned to Germany (Weir, *op. cit.,* p. 403). Weir says that Harrison of the United States Federal Reserve Bank did not know England needed a loan. He implies that the Prime Minister used the urgent need of a loan and the "condition of the borrowing," *i.e.,* cuts in extravagant or anomalous doles, to induce a state of affairs wherein the Cabinet would resign.

Two points of extreme interest came to light: The Fabians had become positively francophile and they now exhibited the scantest concern for Brüning's plight in Germany; Balfour judged that they considered Hitler's movement to be fairly acceptable Socialism. Weir tells a sad story of the occasion when Snowden, at a seven-power monetary conference (July, 1931), was making a sympathetic plea for the German case (Brüning was present) and MacDonald scribbled a note to Stimson indicating non-support of Snowden, who, at that table, was sarcastically referred to as "the member for Germany." (Weir, *op. cit.,* pp. 449 f.) The antagonism of Fabian Socialists (from whom Snowden was eccentric) and of Ramsay MacDonald toward the Centre in Germany, and their known anti-Catholicism cannot be overlooked. As to later evidence of their attitude toward Brüning cf. Hamilton, *op. cit.,* pp. 413, 416, and 417.

[22] Cf. Blanche E. C. Dugdale, *Arthur James Balfour* (London: Hutchinson & Co.), 1936, p. 375.

[23] Cf. *LYB* (1931), p. 493.

over India parallels his position on "Chanak" in 1923. Again the Beaverbrook and Rothermere press stoc⌐ with Churchill against his Party and drove the Tory leadership toward Labour on foreign issues.[24] A parallel dynamism is seen in which the energy of Socialist-Labour contributed its peculiar impulsion to the fructifying of the Young Plan (paralleling Dawes'), the India Round Table Conference (paralleling the Commercial Treaty plans), and the post-crisis Commonwealth (paralleling Locarno). The description of this parallel dynamism lies outside the scope of this study by reason of its time-span.

The denouement came when MacDonald, in the crisis of 1931, formed what was really a Tory Government. Both Parties had succumbed to the orthodoxies of western European finance. For a moment a new idea vital with challenge had lighted the gloomy horizon; then it was gone and the "West" fell back on "gold and credit." The allegation of L. MacNeill Weir, who was MacDonald's Parliamentary Private Secretary, that MacDonald and Snowden failed to heed the suggestion of Garvin in *The Observer* that the war debt be converted and an unnecessary sinking fund retired, while instead they sought economies in "cuts" in "the dole" in order to force the Cabinet to resign may be considered spiteful, but it uncovers some pertinent facts. The fact that Fabian publicists offered no other solution to the fiscal problems than the old one leaves them without a position from which legitimately to inculpate their Prime Minister.[25]

It was the Fabian economist who wrote the report of "The Depression" in the *LYB*,[26] who diverted the stream, as it were; and the dynamic of Western trade flowed back over its old channels, having been dammed up with "overproduction." The stricture of gold glutted goods in England and Germany, and clotted gold in America and France. For a brief moment, the plight of the East, deprived of purchasing power by the loss of monetary status of silver, the medium of exchange of the millions, received consideration. The expressions of J. A. Hobson, J. F. Darling, and witnesses before an American Congressional Com-

---

[24] Cf. Weir, *op. cit.*, p. 292.
[25] *Ibid.*, pp. 416 and 427.
[26] *LYB* (1931), pp. 93–109.

mittee on Banking and Currency regarding the revival of trade with the East, and the need for goods in India and China, for example, were approved and the remonetization of silver—plentiful and too cheap only when treated as a mere commodity—almost fastened upon the Trade Union mind as the means to lift the floodgates of exchange:—Suppose the silver of India became money again and the Indian people could buy English goods and—there are political possibilities—should call their enslaved souls their own when the gold-based power of native potentates should be reduced. The workingmen seemed on the point of demanding remonetization of silver. Then some one (probably Cole, who had published his ideas on credit) proposed that " credit," that is, paper money based on controlled gold (nationalized), would serve to give currency the needed elasticity. *None* of the arguments for this latter method *adverted to the East.* The switch was almost imperceptible. By devaluation the West reestablished circulation in the old knotted tangle of its economy. There was no further discussion of currency for India and China. The high adventurers of " Labour " had shrunk before a challenge too daring.[27] After all, there were forces becoming articulate in India and China which any Party in power in England would need to control.[28]

Having seen the historical setting into which they stepped and the block of stumbling upon which they fell, it seems almost to mock them to review the names of the men put forward by the brave Movement. The Cabinet was so much made up of Fabians

---

[27] Cf. " The Causes of the Depression," *LYB* (1931), p. 93.

[28] It is running ahead of our story to recall here that the Economic Conference of 1931 proved abortive because the United States President was taught shortly after it opened that the only result could be the tying in of America with the " sterling bloc." The idea of the remonetization of silver was, with its Eastern implications, present in the conference. It was *not* this idea which was rejected by the United States but the *English adaptation* of it: 1) nationalize-gold-and-credit, 2) allow the pound sterling thus devalued to seek its own level. (After dropping, it regained a steadily rising value.) At this conference, Senator Key Pittman of Nevada, whose only interest in silver was political and economic (he was a miner), allowed himself to be led into the " triumph " for silver which, although it cost the banking industry and the United States Treasury large sums, did not remonetize silver. Cf. B. M. Anderson, *op. cit.,* p. 359. Silver was remonetized, then " nationalized " after 1936, in the United States.

that the report of the Society in the *LYB* ignored the percentage in the Ministry and stressed the percentage of Fabians in the Parliamentary Labour Party.

The Prime Minister, repudiated by the ILP and endorsed by the Labour Party Conference, counted on Herbert Morrison, the foe of Maxton and Wheatley,[29] on Mrs. Hamilton, the writer, on William Leach, a Trade Unionist, and Walter Newbold, Fabian Pacifist,[30] to support him. Three out of four here named were Fabians. Indeed, the lady M.P. from Scotland defended him well in *The Clarion,* and persistently pointed out to the back-benchers that the Party was " weakest in the technique of support." [31] Yet when he sent his Parliamentary Private Secretary, L. MacNeill Weir, to three of the above-mentioned persons to sound them out upon the question of following him into the National Cabinet, they declined. This may have been due to the way the matter was represented by Weir.

MacDonald had wanted Thomas to be head of the Foreign Office. Their mutual " Socialism " had now a rightist basis, Trade Unionist for the most part.[32] But Henderson demanded and got the Foreign Office. Again Snowden was Chancellor of the Exchequer, with Fabian Pethick-Lawrence for Financial Secretary.[33] Fabian Hugh Dalton, along with Susan Lawrence of kindred experience in internationalism,[34] came in as Parliamentary Private Secretaries. Henderson came to the Foreign Office pledged to recognize and establish trade with Russia.[35] He had the assistance

---

[29] Snowden, *op. cit.,* p. 760.

[30] Weir, *op. cit.,* p. 435.

[31] Cf. *The Clarion,* II :8 (August, 1930), 227.

[32] Cf. Godfrey Elton (Baron), *Life of James Ramsay MacDonald, 1866–1919* (London: Collins, 1939). This author, like Clifford Allen, now Lord Allen, followed MacDonald in 1931. The Epilogue in Elton's *Life* is an encomium of MacDonald's peace efforts and successes on the Continent, not unmerited. Cf. Godfrey Elton, " No Alternative—Socialism or Radicalism," *The Clarion,* II :2 (February, 1931), 45 f.

[33] Snowden, *op. cit.,* p. 760.

[34] Fabians in international activities included A. Fenner Brockway on the executive of the International (*LYB* [1931], 414), C. R. Buxton on the Committee for Minorities (*ibid.,* 415), and on the International Advisory Committee of Socialist Women, Barbara Ayrton Gould. The ILP representation in this sphere was the larger.

[35] Hamilton, *Henderson,* pp. 311 f and 309.

also of Fabian Drummond Shiels (at Geneva) and of Charles Buxton who was adept at managing " the fussers." [36] Lord Ponsonby became Undersecretary of State for the Dominions. Ten out of twenty-one Undersecretaries of State were Fabians like C. G. Ammon for the Admiralty under A. V. Alexander, now a Fabian, and Ben Turner for Mines. The sinecure of Lord Privy Seal was given to J. H. Thomas [37] with the understanding he was in charge of the works and production programs. Thomas was capable of the most understanding attitude toward men like Birkenhead, Baldwin and Neville Chamberlain.[38] He acquired the dubious assistance of another sinecure holder, the Chancellor for Lancaster, Oswald Mosley, whom Henderson dubbed " the rich young man " and who had for determined follower the literary light, John Strachey. On condition that he might be Secretary of State for Colonies, Sidney Webb became Lord Passfield and entered the House of Lords. He would be followed by Fabian Harry Snell, as Lord Snell. He joined Beatrice's one-time brother-in-law, Parmoor, president of the Council and leader of the House, also Lord Arnold, Earl Russell, Lord De La Warr, Lord Ponsonby, Lord Marley, and later, Lord Noel-Buxton. Ten at least out of the seventeen Labour Lords were Fabians. One was henceforth to belong to the Consultative Committee. This was Lord Snell, who also assisted Webb (Passfield) in the Colonial Office. An innovation designed to procure party discipline, attendance records were kept to insure interest on the part of the Labour Lords in the fortnightly meetings of the Parliamentary Labour Party.[39]

---

[36] *Ibid.*, p. 278.

[37] Snowden, *op. cit.*, II, pp. 765 and 776, is favorable to Thomas.

[38] Thomas, *op. cit.*, pp. 229, 231, and 235.

[39] Cf. *LYB* (1931), p. 216. The other Labour Lords were Kinnoul (George Harley Hay), a student of seventeenth century social agitation; Kirkley, created in 1930 (William Joseph Noble) of the Chamber of Shipping of the United Kingdom and of the Baltic and International Maritime Conference; Marks (Percy D'Evelyn Marks) of military precedents and now Paymaster Commander; Sanderson (Henry Sanderson Furniss), professor of economics of Ruskin College and member of the Central Executive of the WEA, the author of a Memoir of C. S. Buxton and contributor to the *Economic Journal;* Kimberly (John Wodehouse) who seemed to take delight in his inconsistency by writing in *Who's Who,* as his sole claim to impor-

To resume consideration of the Cabinet of 1929: Parmoor had for Parliamentary Private Secretary Fabian Arnold Forster; Lord Sankey was Chancellor. The legal team was completed by W. A. Jowitt, a Fabian, as Attorney General, treasurer of the ILP [40] and representative of the Socialist cooperatives and professional societies in the Labour Party Executive; [41] and J. B. Melville, the Fabian member from Gateshead who was Solicitor. The Home Secretary was J. R. Clynes whose Trade Unionist mentality seemed to hold Socialism as a sort of Sabbath religion. He had not been distinguished of late by chairing Fabian lectures. His necessary presence in the Royal household on stated occasions was not calculated to frighten his hosts. A Fabian of several years' standing now was Secretary of State for India, Sir Wedgwood Benn. This appointment appeared to be exceptional for he was a newcomer to Labour, as Snowden believed; [42] but he had been associated with Fabians long before he joined the Labour Party. Tom Shaw was identified in the first Labour Cabinet. Like Clynes, he must needs be in the Ministry but it would seem his greatest effectiveness was the reassurance which his position as Minister for War might give to European Socialists. Fabian Lord Thomson, already a disillusioned observer of European politics in 1919, was Minister of Air. The Commissioner of Works was Fabian George Lansbury. Thomas [43] thought he was only a good propagandist but *The Clarion* always praised him for administrative work; for example, in his having Buckingham Palace cleaned up and procuring radios and central heating for the inmates of poor houses. A Fabian was Minister for Health, Arthur Greenwood. Henderson advanced the appointment of Fabian Margaret Bondfield as Minister for Labour. [44]

---

tance, "owns about 11,200 acres." The newly created Lord Marley noted down his Fabian membership. He belonged to the Council of Magistrates Association and was treasurer of the Union of Democratic Control.

[40] *LYB* (1931), p. 21. W. A. Jowitt (now Chancellor) became a Fabian in 1929. Cf. *FN*, XLI:1 (January, 1930), where he expresses his joy at presiding at a meeting instead of remaining "an admiring member of the audience" as before.

[41] *Ibid.*, p. 13.

[42] Snowden, *op. cit.*, p. 765.

[43] Thomas, *op. cit.*, pp. 247 f.

[44] Snowden, *op. cit.*, p. 759.

Fabian Noel-Buxton, destined for the House of Lords, had for Parliamentary Private Secretary, Fabian Lord De La Warr in the Ministry of Agriculture. The radical Socialist and Webb intimate, Charles Trevelyan, was Minister for Education.[45] The Board of Trade was under Fabian William Graham. A. V. Alexander, the only link with Cooperators, now a Fabian, became First Lord of the Admiralty. Lees-Smith, a Fabian, had wanted this place [46] but, through the influence of Snowden, he was given instead the Postmaster Generalship.[47] Lord Arnold, MacDonald's friend and the Paymaster General, also favored Lees-Smith. As a young radical he had adhered to " Labour " in 1919 after breaking with his army precedents and going through Ruskin College. Snowden had characterized William Adamson as "an inept miner," when the latter had been Parliamentary Party leader. Now he was Secretary of State for Scotland; the Undersecretary was Fabian Tom Johnston, founder and editor of *Forward,* who had long been a Trade Union leader as well as a professional publicist. F. O. Roberts who had been Minister for Pensions in 1924 held the same post in 1929. His position in the Movement was notable; he was Chairman of the National Labour Club [48] and a member of the Executive of the Trade Union Club— honorary and social positions duly accorded a member of the Trade Union Section of the Executive of the Labour Party [49] who was an advisor for Defense in the special advisory section of the Party. The Minister of Transport was Herbert Morrison, one of the brilliant young group whose principles were still fluid and who troubled the calm of general gatherings with their unanswerable questions. Morrison had backed MacDonald when Bevin had demanded that the Conference go on record against taking office if able to command only a minority in Parliament.[50]

[45] Cf. Hamilton, *op. cit.,* p. 419, where he turned Moscow-ward after 1931. Cf. also, Beatrice Webb, *Our Partnership,* p. 128, for his devotion to the Fabian "junta." Trevelyan followed the Webbs into the conceptual "new civilization," which they discovered in Russia. Cf. Samuel, *op. cit.,* p. 346.

[46] Snowden, *op. cit.,* p. 765.

[47] *Ibid.*

[48] *LYB* (1931), p. 24.

[49] *Ibid.,* p. 13. One finds an embryonic organizational apparatus in Party and in TUC set up parallel with governmental apparatus in a State.

[50] Hamilton, *op. cit.,* p. 260.

He was also Henderson's man.[51]   The great recruit of 1924, Haldane, was dead, but in the House of Commons Doctor Christopher Addison, newly converted to Labour, was rising in prestige under the guidance of Mary Hamilton and her good pen. He was among the four Ministers who, all Fabians, addressed the Conference presided over by Susan Lawrence at Llandudno in 1930.   The Webbs had tried to take in John Wheatley in 1924; now the MacDonald-Henderson-Morrison influence resulted in the mistake of relegating " Boss " Wheatley to the obstreperous back-benches where, with Kirkwood, now on the National Administrative Council of ILP,[52] and with Jenny Lee, a Fifeshire miner's daughter (LL.D. from Edinburgh), together with a sharp young Welshman, Aneurin Bevan, as Snowden related, he persistently " insulted " the Government.[53]   The doomed John Scurr was Chairman of the Standing Committee of Housing—Arthur Greenwood's charge.   Fabians L'Estrange Malone, Ernest Thurtle, and Chuter Ede, the Surrey school teacher and organizer of educators, were singled out for notice by Mrs. Hamilton;[54] and, impartially, she mentioned Tom Dickson, former editor of *Forward,* as one of the best speakers; also, pointedly, W. B. Taylor, of Wayland Smallholders Association, an agriculturalist.   Before the term of office ended, readers noticed the names of Stafford Cripps, linked with land valuation bills,[55] and Clement Attlee

---

[51] *Ibid.,* p. 266.

[52] Along with the veterans, R. C. Wallhead and J. W. Moor, on this Council, there was the Fabian Fenner Brockway. Cf. *LYB* (1931), p. 21.

[53] Snowden, *op. cit.,* p. 759. Jenny Lee and Aneurin Bevan are now man and wife. *Re* Scurr, cf. Oldmeadow, *op. cit.,* p. 236.

[54] *The Clarion,* II :8 (August, 1930), 227.

[55] Snowden, *op. cit.,* p. 907. Snowden was amazed when Cripps became an "unconstitutional and revolutionary Socialist." When on October 27, 1932, Sir Stafford Cripps spoke on " Political Institutions," *FN,* XLIII :12 (December, 1932), and the " Transition to Socialism " (this series had been on " Transition "), he asked, " Can the forms of constitutional democracy be altered in time to be efficient instruments of the change [to a Socialism not "without tears "] or must there be violence and disorder? " Parliamentary tradition once based upon smooth continuity of policy must now proceed by a series of " jerks." Delegating authority to the judiciary by Orders in Council and Statutory Orders was not a proper expedient, said lawyer Cripps. Administrative congestion from the growth of social services, for example, even a guillotine could not cope with. (This was after the crisis of 1931.)

rising to prominence. When Hartshorn died and Mosley resigned, Attlee became Chancellor for the Duchy of Lancaster.

It was almost an omen that the TUC man and Fabian, Ben Tillett, was the first Labour Party person elected in 1929. The Government's accomplishments were listed in the *LYB* of 1931.[56]

Sir Stafford disapproved of the slow process of legislation and the "gorgeous excrescence" of the House of Lords which "under other administration [than Toryism] was an active enemy." Socialism was "essentially unicameral." He advocated instead of the old "constitutional" methods of creating new peers or asking for dissolution and a new election, further development of the new system recently discovered in the flexible constitution exemplified in the creation of the Tariff Commission. "Why not proceed further, on the same lines, by appointing an external body of Socialist experts, to suggest and deal with emergency measures?" The new arrangement which he suggested was designed to "overhaul and speed up" parliamentary machinery: Annual Financing and Planning Acts passed after only two Parliamentary "stages" rather than the old-fashioned four, to be worked out in detail by "Special Permanent Committees" utilizing the otherwise wasted abilities of private Members of Parliament. The transition might take years (working under this speed-up plan!), Parliament meantime becoming an organ for expression of opinion, criticism of the administration, control of the executive and—this is very significant—arbitration between producer and consumer. We see the tendency toward administrative statism and away from a rule of law. There is similarity of view with Cole and Laski who demand the rule of "experts." There is to be found in the reports of Sidney Webb's visit to Soviet Russia a like notion of the movement forward toward Socialism by "jerks." Gradualism was by now actually subject of debate, between A. E. Davies and E. F. Wise. (Cf. *FN*, XLIV:6 [June, 1933]; Wise had had experience in Soviet bulk purchasing.) It hinged upon the gradualism of stiffly graded taxes and the revolutionary seizing of eight basic industries without compensation as advocated by the more ardent Socialists and contemporary pamphleteers. Snowden should not have been amazed.

McAlister Coleman, "Portrait of a Successful Sourpuss," *The Progressive VII* (March, 1948), errs in saying Cripps was a Fabian only in the early days "when that remarkable conglomeration of high pressure brain power was permeating the British middle-classes with reformistic, Socialist ideas," pp. 11 f. Cripps is still a Fabian. Cf. almost any *FN* or *Fabian Quarterly* or *Fabian Annual Report*.

[56] *LYB* (1931), pp. 198 f. Currently *Day to Day Pamphlets,* a series printed by Hogarth Press and the Fabian Society was circulating nine pamphlets four of which dealt with Russia and had for authors Maurice Dobb, Aneurin Bevan, M.P., E. J. Strachey, M.P., George Strauss, Parliamentary Private Secretary to Morrison, Minister of Transport, and C. M.

It was a characteristic list interlarded with Socialist propaganda phrases, but it indicated the tendency of the Labour Party to endeavour to carry out election promises, especially those made to ᵗade Unions: " Anomalies " of the 1925 Pensions Act were removᵉd; Russia was recognized despite continuous questioning regarding Soviet propaganda; despite objection in the House of Lords, proof in cases not genuinely seeking work—" n.g.s.w."— was left to the Labour Exchanges and allowances were raised while unemployment insurance was extended to fifteen-year-olds; a coal bill carrying the " district levy " and the " spread-over " was adopted making the operation of these principles hinge upon agreement between the coal- owner Association and the Miners' Federation; the Naval Conference was held; unemployment—the ᶠault, it was reiterated, of Capitalism—had been attacked by the Development Act, which created a Roads program and allowed unemployment grants whereby a hundred thousand pounds had been expended in gas, electric and dock works—a fine program checked by the depression , educational measures taken to curtail the juvenile labor market " owing its cause to Capitalistic conditions of industry " had not yet taken effect; the Economic Advisory Council, a means toward " public control and strengthening consumer power " had been devised; a Public Works Facilities bill had been passed; a Roads Traffic bill granted authority to municipalities to undertake developments without seeking special permission of Parliament each time, regulated not speed limits but penalties for careless driving and made compulsory insurance covering third parties; a land drainage plan which had originated in the House of Lords was credited to the Government; housing measures now were concerned not with building houses to let, save for small places for aged workers, but with slum clearance; in the armed services the death penalty for offences was restricted to two categories; the India Round Table Conference had been held. Stymied still were school bills, the Washington Convention (eight-hour law), a bill to create a Consumer Council and the Agricultural program. The interlarding of

Lloyd. Cf. H. J. Laski, *The Crisis and the Constitution* (London: The Hogarth Press and the Fabian Society, 1932), flyleaf. Bevan's is the only name not easily identifiable as a Fabian. Like Citrine, he lectured at least once under Fabian auspices.

anti-Capitalistic sentiments in the account would seem protesting too much. Reforms like the above named ones could be attained by some great enthusiasm, some channelized proper indignation, some common impulsion fusing aroused public conscience. Many good people of England named this impulsion Socialism, and the spokesmen for Socialism called the enemy " Capitalism "—indiscriminately; yet they meant by State-aided Capitalism to rule England. The Anglo-Christian mentality lent itself to Social Democracy as a restatement of its Protestantism; Fabian Socialism captured the force so lent to Socialism, to turn a social gospel into State-less Socialism, eventually. These heavy implications lie in the list of reforms attempted by a Labour Government compiled by Fabians for the workmen's *Labour Year Book.*

B. FABIAN REACTION TO THE GOVERNMENT'S FALL

The collapse, when it came, served to clear the ideological air. In sections of the socialist world disappointment early in 1931 started a rebound toward independence and away from political action. " Back to Robert Owen " and away from the Party, a movement which had been inculcated in 1917, was urged even in 1930 by a Fabian, W. Henry Browne.[57] Cooperatives, he said, were the proper means by which to " transmogrify the common life of all classes." This was also a reaction to the recurrent despairing suggestion of dictatorship. G. E. C. Catlin contributed to *The Clarion* " Mr. Wells Sees It Through," [58] in which he reiterated the appeal to " social control " and endorsed Wells' notion of the " priestly psychological attitude." When Clifford Sharp wrote " Parliament Vindicated " *after the Crisis,* he indicated the resolution of tension. In a sense, he spoke—and with a Fabian voice—the mind of the electorate. The National Government had been given " a free hand, a blank cheque and a Socialist at its head "; indeed. a mandate had been given by an electorate never so well educated. The best democracy on earth had given Mussolini and Stalin a " long farewell." The Bolsheviks were shut up; the Fascists, dead. The " flappers " had voted with credit to them-

---

[57] *The Clarion,* II :9 (September, 1930), 257.

[58] *The Clarion,* IV :3 (March, 1931), 58. Catlin was then attached to Cornell University.

selves. English prestige was mounting; the debt to the United States, reduced. Parliament could start all over again; the whips were meeting rebellion to party-line rule and that was a good sign. Between the anarchy of Owen and the dictatorship of Wells, Fabian Sharp pointed out a *mesa*. Even his colleagues suspected a mirage.

This Fabian editor of the *NS*, writing in *The Clarion,* reveals the line of thought by which, it is fair to say, Ramsay MacDonald might have expected to swing his old Party into line behind him. It carried Margaret Bondfield, Tom Johnston, Lord Sankey, J. H. Thomas, Clifford Allen and about ten others—never named; *The Clarion* indicated it were better not to name them, and to wait. The revealed thoughts of Henderson, Webb, Laski and L. Woolf, whom he cites, show that the Fabians decided upon the strategy of leaving him alone, party-less, as the " King's favorite." Their action in leaving him party-less put him in a position of inability to ask for a dissolution. That, as was established in 1923, was a Royal prerogative and would not be exercised while the large Government majority existed.[59] And they had brought themselves face to face with a situation which enraged them, one in which the balance of power turned upon the will of the King, a Tory dictatorship—and, after the election, one with a huge majority in Parliament.

In a further chapter we remark the gap in the line of thought noticeable in *The Clarion* when it changed over from praise and excuse to blame of MacDonald. Mrs. Hamilton was slow to change although Weir had warned her, Morrison, and Leech, before the rest. The personal hostility of Webb was allowed to appear in his *What Happened in 1931.* At this point however it is appropriate to examine the expression of the leading ideologue, the mentor of *The Clarion's* editor, Professor Harold Laski, in *The Crisis and The Constitution.*

---

[59] Cf. Laski, *Crisis and The Constitution* (London: Hogarth Press and Fabian Society, 1932), p. 36. Laski's analysis served to precipitate the constitutional question which, had it been more clearly grasped at the time the Party made its decision to expel MacDonald and his associates, might have changed their course. The course was set by Henderson and Webb, to save *the Movement*. Otherwise, the centrifugal elements would have flown off—out of the Party.

The hint that it was the King who had " dished " the Socialists is not too faint to be perceptible as the cause of the professor's pique. The part played by the King had, he said, been " brilliantly concealed." Two elements stand out in Laski's acute analysis : 1) Socialism presupposes that people or parties do differ " about the foundation of society " and are not " fundamentally at one." In other words, Socialists assume an inherent inability of " the investing class " to act under any other impulsion than the profit motive. That their savings might contribute to national assets is, on Laski's part, inconceivable ; Laski assumed absolutely that no motive of national interest could balance the profit motive in the Tory Party bound together by property interest alone. He silently equated Capitalism with Nationalism when he endorsed that global anomy whereby the " sovereign State . . . would necessarily disappear." Such a disappearance would be " obvious commonsense ". even though it would " demand an interference with the motive of private profit so vast as to be incompatible with the survival of a Capitalist society." [60] 2) For " Labour " to achieve Socialism means, Laski said, civil war ultimately, because, until a " new metaphysic " is developed regarding the function of the King, his prerogative will always provide for conservatism an escape from that Socialism which aims to eliminate the " investing class."

Laski adduced some data from which he concluded that the "constitutionality " of Party rule was demonstrably an accretion of custom of comparatively recent origin. He alluded to Lord Bute and the Younger Pitt as historical " favorites " and found it necessary to re-examine Coke's phrase which termed the King a " dignified hieroglyphic." Civil war, then, is the only resort of

---

[60] *Ibid.*, p. 41. The King, of course, symbolizes that fundamental agreement about the foundation of society which Professor Laski denies. The present writer's definition of " sovereignty " is consonant with that of Pius XII Christmas Allocution 1944 and embraces that " autonomy," independence " and " interdependence " which Maritain would substitute for " sovereignty." Exaggerated " sovereignty " results from loss of the Natural Law basis of society. " The natural law is more than a negative norm, more than a frontier closed to the infiltration of positive legislation, and more than a simple technical adjustment to contingencies . . . [it is] the soul of positive legislation . . . gives it its form, its meaning, its life." Cf. Pius XII Address, *loc. cit.*, saying who shall have " the last word " for the State and speak for the Country in *Catholic Mind* (July 1951) p. 460f.

" Labour " which may have won a " mandate " which the Monarch negates. Laski used the words of Leonard Woolf to confirm the finding that this " precedent might be developed so that the Crown could be used to break down the democratic system of Party Government, and to introduce . . . a system not materially different from a dictatorship." [61]

Professor Laski's comments confirm the deductions made so far by this study: 1) Trade Unionists are not primarily interested in politics. Yet the fact that their former " distinctive monopoly " of hiring halls and mutual insurance have been usurped by the social service state, make it necessary they should be political and should develop " institutions " to assist the Party toward the realization of Socialism. Unions exhibit a deplorable lack of a Socialist mentality, according to Laski. 2) Socialism involves acceptance of the Balfour-Bagehot proposition that basic conflict

---

[61] Laski, *The Crisis and The Constitution*, p. 35. Professor Laski responded to a query from this student, which had been based upon a review in *FN*, one which had compared Laski's idea of " revolution " with that of Berdyaev, that the comparison was odious; that Berdyaev was a poor Marxist and a mystic while Laski was a neo-Marxist and no mystic (he was an atheist); that he " believed in revolution " if by that was meant, 1776, 1789, 1848, and 1917. (This writer protests the inclusion of 1776 in this list.)

Laski had approved the general trend in 1929: Parliament was no longer an organ of authority, but " an organ of registration of the Cabinet." His own criticism of the House of Lords had not advanced beyond that of Bentham and Bagehot. He would allow it to fall into desuetude while increasing the function of Commons to include two formulas, a formula for international cooperation replacing state sovereignty, and a formula for swift readjustment toward decentralization in domestic politics. He would begin increasing the respectability of private members by giving them powers to hold " Hearings "—" the system which had worked so well in Massachusetts." The " good," he said, in politics is " the satisfaction of the maximum demands of the people " and toward this he advocated " the German plan." The system of checks and balances must be eliminated, said the professor.

One fears the safeguards of democracy, long treasured, yield to " unity." It is surely unnecessary to point out why the expressions of the years under study are said to be marked by the attack on Democracy.

As to the " German plan," cf. *FN*, XL:12 (December, 1929). One recalls Ben Turner's experience at a Socialist international meeting in Germany where soldiery sat glowering from the platform and heated discussion between Lancashire and Yorkshire men caused the Conference to be peremptorily closed. Cf. Turner, *op. cit.,* p. 155.

between two Parties which differ about the nature of the foundations of society is necessarily revolutionary. Tempted to affirm his revolutionary Marxism, Laski twice put aside the thought but ended by advising Labour that without the " new metaphysic " regarding the King's function, and without acceptance of Socialism by all of society, they had best prepare themselves for the necessary struggle to ensue upon their winning a majority Government—civil war if the King made use of the precedent of 1931; revolution if the Tories resorted to economic sabotage, or both. He recalled, as in his letter to this student, 1789, 1848, 1917—omitting, in this connection, 1776.

Three conclusions observed in many other aspects of this investigation again confront the reader of this highly representative Fabian: 1) The Fabian-fronted Party calling itself Labour was not sure it wanted Socialism; 2) the third Party had destroyed the element best suited to the expression of democracy—a two-Party system where fundamentals are accepted by all and methods or character-coloring form the area of debate; 3) the politicizing of social elements had usurped the place in ethics and conscience, of religion. This had created a secular religion. The objectives of this " third Party " were unattainable unless religious fervor evoked the " courage at all costs " to carry it beyond the " mere conquest of a majority."

Keith Feiling [62] reveals the part Neville Chamberlain played in the formation of the National Government. The Conservatives and Liberals who rejected MacDonald's Cabinet's last proposals convinced the Prime Minister it was his duty to avoid the imminent financial crash. MacDonald was also convinced he must split the Labour Party and go on with the Labour Moderates (suppose Webb and Laski and Henderson had agreed to do so). When Chamberlain suggested a National Government MacDonald had proffered help but had refused to join and " I intervened," wrote Chamberlain; " had he considered, that though not commanding many votes in the House, he might command support in the country . . . had he considered the effect on foreign opinion? "

Again, Chamberlain wrote in his diary,

Truly the Conservative Party is a wonderful embodiment

---

[62] Feiling, *op. cit.,* pp. 192 f.

of good sense, patriotism, and honesty. What would have been the astonishment of the Socialist executive, if it could have overheard the Conservative executive agreeing to allow the man who had all his life opposed them, now to have the credit of carrying out their own policy just when the whole country has come round to it.

His point of vantage is at least as good as Laski's. It is certain that though a segment of the Parliamentary Labour Party entertained a devotion to the national interest like that of the Tories as here described, it was not a segment of workable size, as MacDonald discovered.[63] No one would have been able to discover the real reason for MacDonald's dilemma except for the existence of a periodical which reflected very faithfully the destructive criticism of the Government by Socialists, some of whom demanded " Socialism in our time," many of whom were doubtful of the advisability of the Labour Party's assuming Government, all of whom felt the Movement was more important than the Party, none of whom had any fiscal principles beyond destructionism.

C. *The Clarion* POSITION AND THE WEBB ANALYSIS

A Socialist organ, *The Clarion*,[64] nicknamed from its history

---

[63] As early as December, 1930 (*The Clarion*, II :12, p. 352), Barbara Shaw, much macarized cartoonist, depicted " A Christmas Party at the House." Baldwin as " Gandhi " pats the head of Simon, Snowden reads Churchill's *Life* with the author, and Lloyd George dances with Thomas (wearing ermine), a bald Jewish character embraces an owlish-looking Webb (waving " the White Paper "). In the center, MacDonald woos a shy, long-haired figure labelled ILP. The college professor's mortarboard appears in the left background (Trevelyan). In the right background, a woman's figure (Mrs. Bondfield) wields a broom and kettle. It was prophetic: Nearly a year before the denouement, the National Government solution was so imminent that a cartoonist projected it.

[64] The investigator is the recipient of a very kind and informative letter from Mr. Ernest Davies, M.P., dated January 21, 1950. It was from him the information about Mr. Stevens came. In general, the column, " Our Point of View," was attributable to Mr. Stevens or to both the editors, and " Our Reporter's Note Book " was always written by Mr. Davies. It is most interesting to learn that Mr. Davies, now an M.P., resigned from the Fabian Executive in 1940 to enter the BBC and that Mr. Stevens is now Press Officer for the Federation of British Industries. A Fabian still, he is, as Mr. Davies writes, politically inactive. As has been stated, Alderman

" The Old Expirer," in its prime had bugled " Boots! Spurs! " and sent its fellowship far afield on bicycles. These " Clarionettes " carried propaganda and met at stated times on picnics. " Merrie England " seemed their motto and seasoned their methods. Founded by Robert Blatchford, *The Clarion* had stood for the ILP kind of Socialism, exclusive of the Clydesider element. It might have been omitted entirely from mention in this study except for the fact that from 1929 to 1931 it was the voice of Fabian-Socialist criticism of the Government. It was edited, with the assistance of Fabian Tom Groom, by Ernest Davies, the son of the arch-Fabian Alderman A. E. Davies, and by the former's friend Mr. F. L. Stevens, a Fabian too. Over fifty percent of the aggregate of its contributors and all its staff were active Fabians. Individual issues show a higher percentage of Fabian contributors. Mac-Donald's name always headed the list thereof up to August, 1931; but nothing from his pen appeared from 1929 to 1931. Lord Passfield was reported to be happy in the Colonial Office.[65] No writing of his appeared but Mrs. Webb's plan for Parliamentary reconstitution was printed in *The Clarion*. The Parliamentary situation was reported by Mrs. Mary Agnes Hamilton; the international situation by C. Delisle Burns; and other Fabians— Marion Phillips, Lord Ponsonby, George Lansbury, J. D. Beresford, Bertrand Russell, Cole, Shaw, the Davies, father and son, Josiah Wedgwood, Mrs. Webb, Hamilton Fyfe, Norman Angell, Harold Laski, H. W. Nevinson, Lord Snell, Arthur Greenwood, Vera Brittain, Maurice Dobb, J. M. Kenworthy (an officer in

---

A. E. Davies, L.C.C., in a very kind letter to this investigator, said the *NS* could be considered a Fabian organ. Since the *NS* (cf. Pease, *op. cit.*, p. 227) developed a character of its own, it need not be exhaustively nor exclusively used as a source especially after 1924. It was not a Fabian organ but an organ of political Fabianism. It was in no way an organ of the Labour Party. Professedly, that was the *Daily Herald*, which was also the organ of political Trade Unionism. *The Clarion* supplies much Fabian source material for the period 1929–1931.

[65] Mrs. Cole in her *Beatrice Webb* draws attention to the fact that he was very unhappy about the Palestine imbroglio which he was obliged to handle. Webb's years in the House of Lords, according to Shaw, were the only years Sidney Webb ever wasted. Cf. Sidney and Beatrice Webb, *The Truth About Soviet Russia,* with a preface on the Webbs by Bernard Shaw (London: Longmans, Green and Company, 1942), p. 13.

H. M.'s Navy), Oliver Baldwin (Stanley Baldwin's son), H. C. Laycock, Norman Tiptaft, G. E. G. Catlin (then of Cornell University), Virginia Woolf, Ed Carpenter, Wickam Steed, Fenner Brockway,[66] Chuter Ede, Fitzwater Wray (Kuklos) and J. B. Priestley—were frequent contributors. There were no Fabians, as far as can be known, in the list of the " Old Fellowship " recalled in an account of a " Clarion Reunion." [67] That occasion was the fortieth anniversary of Blatchford's foundation of *The Clarion*. Mr. Davies and Mr. Stevens rescued the publication from expiring in 1929 and made a Fabian voice of it from 1929–1931, although it kept the ILP feeling and the merry spirit given it by Blatchford.

In May of 1931,[68] " Our Proletarian Contributors," under " Our Reporter's Note Book," made a very feeble attempt to override the objection some persons had made that there were too many of the intelligentsia writing for *The Clarion*. He boasted that he himself was a " proletarian " because he had once worked in Woolworth's and swept snow in New York. Then he listed four names, P. Gibbs, H. Fyfe (the only Fabian), L. Britton (who had an article in the current *Clarion* on " ragamuffins " and was once a ragamuffin himself), T. Horsley (who had once, Davies said, been a tramp). Then the reporter praised the ILP back-bencher, Maxton, an anti-Fabian Socialist, said he made a good chairman, had a quick mind.[69] The names of Gibbs, Britton, and Horsley were not featured again in connection with contributions to *The Clarion*, however. Later, Maxton is reported to have lectured to the

---

[66] *The Clarion,* I :7, n.s. (July, 1929), listed women in the Parliamentary Labour Party: Ethel Bentham, M.D., Marion Phillips, D.Sc. Margaret Bonfield, Susan Lawrence, Mary A. Hamilton, Mrs. Picton-Turberville, Cynthia Mosley, Jenny Lee, Ellen Wilkinson. They were all Fabians except Clydesider Jenny Lee, the youngest and a " revolutionary," who was introduced by Bob Smillie and Jimmy Maxton. *The Clarion,* 23, n.s. (March, 1929), 3.

[67] *The Clarion,* III :9 (September, 1931), 275. Alex Thompson mourned the deaths of two Fabians, the " motherly " Marion Phillips and the " modest, gentle " Graham in *The Clarion,* III :12 (December, 1931), 30. He attributed their deaths to " ministerial responsibility." They were, indeed, estimable characters deeply devoted to a cause they deemed a crusade.

[68] *The Clarion,* III :5 (May, 1931), 131.

[69] *Ibid.*

Fabians though he was apparently not " at home " among the respectable upper middle class who disagreed with his finding £4 10s
a week enough to live on.[70]   There were fewer old Fabian names
thereafter until " The Crisis " followed by the reorganization
under the title, *New Clarion*.   Then they were all back. " Crisis! "
shouted the editor, now Mr. Stevens, in September, 1931 : " Think
it over with the most brilliant and authoritative writers of the day."
There were few names of non-Fabians of any note save Gals-
worthy—and later Fabian lists include him.[71]

Throughout the months one followed in *The Clarion* the activities of leaders in the Labour Party in Parliament everyone a
Fabian: Morrison, Graham, Attlee, Cripps, Bevin, Johnston, Dalton, Shinwell, Mosley, Lansbury.   There was a tendency to slight
MacDonald and make up for it by praising his daughter, Ishbel.
In " Veteran Fabians," the Reporter said the Fabian lecturers
numbered six who were past seventy years of age, that Laski was
but half Shaw's age and Ishbel MacDonald a splendid foil for the
latter's perennial lecture.[72]   There was a tendency also not to give
the emphasis to European politics which marked the *NS*, although
The Clarion never took the focus off Russia, and C. Delisle Burns
contributed a League's-eye view of Europe, monthly.   *The Clarion*
writers tended to find fault with the mere liberalism of Snowden;
and " Uncle Arthur " Henderson, though always praised, was not
idolized, exactly.   They showed perfect respect for Margaret
Bondfield (there was only silence regarding her following Mac-
Donald in 1931) ;[73] also, they evinced an affectionate disrespect

---

[70] *The Clarion,* III :4 (April, 1931), 99.

[71] As to Tom Williams, H. M. Tomlinson, M.P. (formerly of the staff
of the *Nation and Athenaeum*), Alexander Thompson (long a faithful I.L.P.
writer), and Tom Shaw, the writer has not been able to find them listed
among Fabians on election or lecture lists in *FN*.   The only other source is
in obituary notices.   Mr. Ernest Davies wrote that all connected with the
management were Fabians.

[72] *The Clarion,* II :7 (July, 1930), 195.

[73] The Lord Chancellor, Lord Sankey, was chairman when Laski spoke
the week after Cole.   *The Clarion* prophesied in 1931 that Sankey alone of
all those fourteen who followed MacDonald into the National Government
would be readmitted to the Party.   Cf. " Our Reporter's Note Book," *The
Clarion,* III :10 (October, 1931), p. 283.   The rest were to be " excommunicated."

for the " Old Gang," [74] casting aspersion, as we noted, upon the senility of lecturers on Fabian platforms. Nevertheless, every matter of importance regarding the Fabian Society was reported; for example, Cole's return, Mosley's defection,[75] and the organizing of new groups.[76] Fabian lectures were reported also, closely if not verbatim. The editors proposed Fabians, Herbert Morrison, H. B. Lees-Smith, Harry Snell or Tom Johnston to replace Vernon Hartshorn who had died, and to replace the deceased Fabians, Lord Russell and James Stewart, whose deaths it reported in " *Ave Atque Vale.*" [77]

" Fabians to the Rescue," [78] was one caption. It asked for a revival of the Research Bureau because Labourites had been impressed with the Liberal economists' reports given in Liberal-Labour conferences. And it argued against Cole's leaving politics for journalism. It also chided Bertrand Russell for undermining his hearers' faith in Democracy in his Kingsway Hall Lectures. The Reporter complained likewise of Shaw's attack on Democracy but there was never any complaint about Laski's utterances. When comparing " the Don " and " Adonis "—*The Clarion's* comparison—the editorial critic preferred Laski to Cole, finding " a spiritual quality " in the former's " academic mind." Again, in " Fabians Resolve the Crisis," [79] it announced sixty Fabians ready to teach and study in Frensham Heights School in Surrey. This school

---

[74] The " Reporter," Ernest Davies, wrote of seeing Sidney Webb, now Lord Passfield, " trying his hand " at square dancing at a Fabian Summer School, in a paragraph where he complained of Passfield's becoming too dignified now to lead the singing at a meeting. The ILP Socialist spirit demanded a Quaker simplicity in Socialists.

[75] Cf. *The Clarion*, III:4 (April, 1931), 99. E. Davies reported the New Party's debut and how the Trade Unions saved the Labour Party (no credit was given them) by Ernest Bevin's refusal to split his Movement consisting of 4,000,000 Trade Unionists. He prevented their following Mosley.

[76] *The Clarion*, III:7 (July, 1931). The Reporter noted " Zip," the Society for Socialist Inquiry and Propaganda embodying Cole's idea to spread Socialism (a Wellsian echo). It created an implement for " Loyal Grousers," as Francis Meynell termed them. Amongst them (cf. her *Growing Up Into Revolution*, p. 139), was Margaret Cole. (Francis Thompson was sheltered by the Meynell family.)

[77] *The Clarion*, III:4 (April, 1931), 103.

[78] *The Clarion*, II:11 (November, 1930), 311.

[79] *The Clarion*, III:9 (September, 1931), 255.

would present new aspects and would exhibit no monotony since Lord Passfield was lecturing. *Clarion* announced also that the opponents of the National Government would conduct the Kingsway Hall lectures on " Capitalism in Dissolution," listing Barbara Wootton, A. E. Davies, Norman Angell, S. K. Ratcliffe, H. J. Laski, and " of course " G. B. Shaw.[80]

Books written by Fabians were reviewed and given good notices. So few were the reviews each month—three at most—that the selection represented a large measure of editorial responsibility. Samples of these reviews show an almost pedagogical tendency and reveal a quality of thought peculiarly *Clarion*-Socialist, as if using Fabians to develop the ILP mentality. For example: Bruce Ironsides, reviewing Tawney's *Equality*, said that like Wallas' *Acquisitive Society*, it was an indictment. It was time, he said, for a restatement of Socialist aims, " spiritual ends "; and it was " only obstinacy " to urge that all that was required now was " machinery to bring [Equality] about." [81] It may be observed, sympathetically, that the quest of Socialism was for a means of perfecting man to enable him to perfect the machine. They wanted a religion without theology.

W. H. Warburton's *History of Trade Union Organisation in the North Staffordshire Potteries* bore an introduction by Tawney. It was reviewed by Fabian Josiah Wedgwood who hastened to " explain " the slowness of unionization in his inherited business.[82] It was simply a business with a tradition. Its heir seemed to be truckling a bit to Trade Union opinion outside his plant.

The editor spoke of " iconoclasts " in reviewing Fabian Pethick-Lawrence's *This Gold Crisis* in which a condition of low and falling prices, as a monetary not an economic phenomenon, was blamed for the crisis. With too much being produced there was too little gold to move it far enough; so the consequent glut

---

[80] One recalls George Lansbury's remark that Tchitcherin reminded him of " our own " Fabians, the Webbs, Shaw, Wells, and Haldane: " Nobody can ever know as much as they do, be as wise as they look, or at least try to make us believe they are," and a page or two further on he asked Lenin to employ the Webbs at teaching administration. Lansbury, *op. cit.*, pp. 240–243.

[81] *The Clarion*, III :3 (March, 1931).

[82] *The Clarion*, III :4 (April, 1931), 102.

ruined prices. *The Clarion* found Norman Angell's *Can Government Cure Unemployment?*, which was done in collaboration with Harold Wright, valuable for a transition period; but the work was weighed and found wanting for being Liberal and not Socialist. He found little wrong with Lord Melchett's similar *Why the Crisis;* but he recommended reading *Das Kapital* in place of any of these treatments of the economic crisis. It would seem to have been a proper place to urge that "devaluation" which later, after it was successfully employed by the National Government, was claimed as an idea original with the Labour Party.[83]

Again, an editor credited Ben Tillett whose memoirs he reviewed as "Adventures of an Agitator," with making the Labour Party Socialist.[84] The notion that there might have been a Labour Party which was not Socialist was never contemplated by Fabians. To have made the acknowledgment that, whereas "worker-hood" is an attribute of social man, to politicize "labor" is to postulate a total or universal belief and to necessitate the ultimate rule of one Party, was unthinkable.

The resemblance of Cole's *Gold, Credit, and Employment* to the Liberal platform, which advocated keeping gold and credit at home, was not underlined by the editor who reviewed it. Cole did not advocate devaluing the pound, the "external" value of which he found too high, although a year later Fabians Bevin and Citrine[85] did so as leaders of the TUGC. This received no emphasis in *The Clarion* until after the crisis. Cole merely suggested restricting the use of gold to the domestic economy.[86]

---

[83] It was Trade Unionists Bevin and Citrine who were credited with having suggested it.

[84] *The Clarion*, III:11 (November, 1931), 320.

[85] Citrine lectured under Fabian auspices in August, 1933. Cf. *FN*, 44:8. He and Bevin had to belong to a Socialist society in order to take their places on the International. Bevin was one of the reorganizers after 1936, having gone far left after 1931, and turned back. The mentality of the two men is "Trade Unionist" but one cannot state that their philosophy is unspoilt by a Socialism the basis of which they would find more difficult to learn than the economics of which at first they were innocent.

[86] *The Clarion*, II:9 (September, 1930), 263. The Fabian commentator was not averse to remarking in another connection that Cole repeated himself for the hour following his half-hour exposition of his subject. Cf. *The Clarion*, I:11, n.s. (November, 1929), 5. It is traceable to ennui no

Mrs. Webb was allowed by the reviewer, Thompson, to evaluate Fabian Wickham Steed's *Life Under the Soviets* and, by emphasizing the patronage given to opera in Moscow,[87] to increase the illusion as to cultural growth in all Russia.[88] This is notable as

doubt that no one has been found to observe that Cole arrives at the already accepted compromises of " pure " Socialist principle with political or economic realities by the verbose process of higgling over distinctions. Compare his Fabian Tract, *Labour's Second Term,* a comment on the draft " Labour Believes in Britain " (written for the Fabian Society and offered for discussion to the *Labour Movement*), with F. A. Cobb, M. P., *The Art of the Possible* in *FN,* 60:3 (March, 1949). Both agree on the compromises with Capitalism necessary under the circumstances. Cobb defines " Socialism " as democratic socialism dependent upon " the acceptance of the common good motive " and states that we must accept and use the motive of self-interest *until* we generate a new one. Cole defines Socialism as a " way of life," a life of *equality* (admitting inequality of brains and authority, denying only the advantage to be gained from birth or riches). Both aim at controlling the Trade Unions: Cole by a vision of utopia; Cobb by realism, recognizing that a programme which will not " harness to the national effort those forces which are prevalent in this country today [profit motivated] . . . will not work." Both try to placate the sentimental Socialist: Cobb in the Party; Cole in himself. It is interesting that Cole calls Keynesian liberalism and State Planning " bastard socialism," p. 7. His patent motivation is vote getting—— defining theory. A very interesting parallelism exists in the programme-adaptation of 1929, 1945, 1950:—Each time compromise set back the objectives consonant with their higher ideology and set forth for immediate attempt social service aspects and vote-getting measures. The study of these parallels would be rewarding. In any case, Chairman Cole's performance has what Mr. Laski would call " the single merit " of clarifying the Socialism from which deviation is measured.

[87] The British Broadcasting System was approved by P. R. Leslie who wrote a monthly column on it. " Dictation for Demos " was one telling title. Leslie agreed to the appointment of Sir John Keith as " dictator " especially since he would have the cooperation of Mrs. Hamilton and C. Delisle Burns. Cf. *The Clarion,* II:3 (March, 1930), 34. He approved the control and liked Bartok, Stravinsky and Honegger—although he favored less of pseudo-religious atmosphere on Sundays. The underlying reason for the good press for BBC was that Mrs. Snowden headed it until after the National Government came to power. Once in 1931, the Oxford Labour Club asked why the Government had no money to subsidize the Schneider Trophy contest but did subsidize opera, and the Reporter, Davies, wrote that the answer was " Mrs. Snowden." Cf. *The Clarion,* III:4 (April, 1931), 99.

[88] Cf. Margaret Cole, " Beatrice Webb," *Fabian Quarterly,* 38 (July, 1943),

having transpired *before* her visit to Moscow. It is quite possible Beatrice and Sidney saw the duchy of Moscow as an England and the twenty-two Soviet Socialist Republics, if they thought of them at all, as colonies.

Fabian Vera Brittain reviewed *Divorce As I See It,* a symposium in which three Fabians, B. Russell, H. G. Wells, and Rebecca West, collaborated with Fanny Hurst, Warwick Deeping, Leon Feuchtwanger, Andre Maurois and Noel Douglas. The lady reviewer wrote " The Elect Consider Divorce " and deplored that the " injunction " of a " teacher " of " 30 A.D.," an era when women were unprotected in the scheme of civilization, should influence the Catholic Church which " still " forbids divorce.[89]

The editor commented on the Labour Party's *Local Government Handbook* saying that Socialists would only waste their time being town or borough Councillors. Yet Lansbury and the Fabians believed in permeating all councils. Lansbury's life illustrated time and again the efficacy within a committee of one or two Socialists who were well primed as to rules of order.[90] The new

---

1–4, where she expatiates upon the " thrill " that was theirs—the Webbs', the Coles', and Shaw's—at the sight of the new society they saw rising under the one-party system of new civilization in Soviet Russia " after planning began."

[89] *The Clarion,* III :9 (September, 1930), 296. With assent to his advocacy of making open questions " the superiority of exclusiveness in love," or " that it is a good thing for children to be brought up by their parents," " bristles with valuable ideas " was the reviewer's comment upon Russell's frank acceptance of extra-marital freedom and birth-control. Under the newly emergent State seen by Russell, " economic utility of fathers will entirely disappear." ·This was during the years when there was marked advance in the activities of the Women's Group and Mary Agnes Hamilton, M.P., remarked that morality was " breaking away from artificial standards," and sexual relationships were to evolve a " code to be derived from equitable community relationships." She hoped for the emergence of the new community from out of the " unregulated State," and by a new moral standard —whatever that might mean.

" Motherly " Marion Phillips had reviewed it less enthusiastically, with some incertitude in *The Clarion,* II :1 (January, 1930), 22. To the question " Is Bertrand Russell Right? " she answered, no; but her reason for the negative was materialistic : Let there be a morally stronger and less selfish race which has achieved *economic freedom,* before *law* and the barrier of custom be let down. Socialists, we see, insisted upon the perfectibility of man.

[90] *The Clarion,* III :3 (March, 1931). This kind of permeation furnished

view represents the fact that the work of local permeating had been fruitful and was hardly needed now that Fabians held White-hall and Westminster.   Under the caption, " The Struggle in Local Government," A. E. Davies reviewed Robson's *The Development of Local Government:* Whether in developing municipal banks, or the beauty of municipalities or parksides, all England lagged behind Europe.   Every Fabian knew from the constant repetition in the *FN* that since 1923, Robson had headed the Local Government Bureau of the Society and edited *Local Government News* which had steady, if very slowly increasing, sales.   Now the editor drew attention to the fact that for any positive progress to be made by a local government a special Act of Parliament was necessary.   European cities were far in advance with schemes for municipal banks and civic development.   The " Clarionettes " seemed unaware that American cities, or counties, or states build bridges, roads, or banks without national legislation or special act of Congress.

When Laski came to evaluate *Machiavelli* by Ettore Janni he was illuminating: " Socialists have still to make up their minds about the place of moral obligation in politics."   Concerning " the limits of practical statesmanship," Laski wrote, " a brief period of responsibility would make [the idealist who shudders at the pragmatic " Prince "] more tender to Machiavelli's stark realism . . . [being] not . . . [yet] willing to condone . . . he would [not] be so anxious to condemn." [91]   The characteristic balance, of " condone " and " condemn " must leave the disciple's will paralyzed.   Yet Laski remained the accepted mentor of the young editors, Stevens and Davies.

The Clarion therefore appears as much the organ of Fabianism as the appropriated nest of yesteryear appears the natural habitat

---

the pattern for Shaw's " democratising democracy."   Some anti-communists imitate the cell-idea or the cadre system of penetration.   Committee-wise permeation by an elite and permeation of the masses by cadres when this is done by religion and Charity (i.e., the gift of Love of God-and-man and God's presence in souls by Grace) is something vastly different in fact and in effect from such permeation done by a Party.   The Party borrows the trappings of religion.   It must.   Charity is dynamic and creative.   The Party dictates a plan.

[91] *The Clarion,* II :9 (September, 1930), 263.

of that subject of many a motet in once Merrie England, the cuckoo. Editors, contributors, and news-names were all Fabian. The books selected for review bore the Fabian message warped to the ILP masthead: A doubtful position on political morals and princely politics; a very useful criticism of the unprogressive attitude of civic executives; the countenancing of an ignorant viewpoint on marriage, birth control and divorce; the half-instructed feeling toward Russia; the vague shapes of new fiscal principles, partly Keynesian liberalism, partly anti-*rentier,* which groped toward the realism of too little " gold "; the truckling to Trade Union opinion; the arguing as to whether the machinery of Parliamentary procedures and franchise would suffice or whether instead of working on improving the " machine " they should not " restate " their " aims." [92]

The important contribution of *The Clarion* to the history of the period was the unconscious but thorough-going exposition of the conflict among the segments of " the Movement." The Party and the Government, the Trade Unions and the intellectuals, the social-Socialists and the political-Socialists, anarchistic-Socialists and dictator-Socialists, the emergent planning groups and the secret catastrophic connivers, the over-bold theorizers in the economic field and the realistic compromisers. Conflict focused itself in a fiscal problem.

Mr. Webb, now Lord Passfield,[93] told *What Happened in 1931,*

---

[92] " Aims " were well restated in early 1950 by Cobb and Cole. Since their objective to be realized presupposed perfected man and a society convinced of the desirability of seeking the " common good " and organized under the dictates of social justice, both aim-staters lowered their sights to " compromise," awaiting the consummation of human perfection, with Capitalism. They had arrived at something Thomas Aquinas found to be common knowledge and summarized before A.D. 1274. Cf. Cobb, " The Art of the Possible," *FN,* 60:3 (March, 1949). Cobb accepts the profit motive for the time being—men being what they are, whereas Cole in *Labour's Second Term, Tract 273,* 1950, rejects as " bastard socialism " either Reform or Planning.

[93] Cf. Snowden, *op. cit.,* p. 927. Just before the denouement, Lord Passfield and Mrs. Webb called on Snowden to request his cooperation in their new scheme: Snowden to become a peer so Passfield could retire; Parmoor to surrender the leadership of the House of Lords to Snowden. The latter declined.

a review of which is in order that we may understand the data gleaned from *The Clarion* leading up to the Crisis of 1931 and beyond. Webb was fully aware of the conflict of the segments, but he fairly ignores it. Such conflict had a real function in the Long View. By studying what Webb wrote, the reader may be enabled to discover why he wrote it, outside of the aim to " dish " Mac-Donald.

Webb [94] found MacDonald's National Government, elected by sixty-nine percent of the voters, to be a *Party Dictatorship*. (There had been cast six million votes for Labour, electing about nine percent of the Parliament.) We learn from him that the Labour Party, as " blind " as any other, had " special difficulties "; not having a majority it was unable to obtain " closure." The Labour Cabinet had been overworked; the Prime Minister himself lacked time for social intercourse with the members of the Party.[95]

Webb worked off his wrath in *non-sequiturs* about the way a National Government came about. Despite his saying that Mac-Donald " alone " knew the steps in advance, he outlined the history of the rise of the idea of a National Government. It was designed, he said, to absorb the Opposition. The Opposition he characterized as part of that " mystic entity " known as the British Constitution. Passfield gave three sources for the idea of a National Government: 1) Garvin of *The Observer* had suggested a National Government because the Labour-Liberal majority in Parliament would not accept his tariff scheme.[96] 2) In June, 1931, it " was said

---

[94] Cf. *What Happened in 1931: A Report* (London: Fabian Tract 237, 1932).

That Webb thought, or said, that MacDonald alone knew all the development in advance—the formation of the National Government, and the hastily produced Election—and that he promised to answer how this " statesman " managed it, what caused the landslide, what significance it would have *on the world,* is at least naive: Baldwin was the real ruler of England. The blindest spot in Webb's account deals with the King's part.

[95] The Prime Minister, Webb said, came to spend his " scanty leisure " in " less disagreeable " company. Cf. *ibid.,* p. 4. Webb's words of studied politeness grow in potency from apologetic disparagement to personal remarks of the most objectionable sort based on judgment of motive. Cf. *ibid.,* p. 4.

[96] Webb said the rejection of the Tariff in 1923 was " decisive." That the vote on the platforms was " decisive " is highly disputable, in the light of this investigation.

privately" there would be a National Government by September.
3) Empire preference, " food taxes," tariffs against " dumping "
from Russia, the United States, and the Argentine; the demands
of " agriculturalists," produced the secret impulsion toward a
National Government.[97]

The reader should bear in mind that underlying Webb's criticism
of the fiscal basis of the Labour Government's failure in 1931 was
the fact known to him and to the Party intellectuals that when they
were taking over the Government in 1929 without any of the
reluctance shown in 1924, they were inheriting a depression. It
was known in April of 1928 that " trade disturbances and unemployment " in America caused " anxiety " to which " nothing in
recent history [was] comparable." [98]

On page three, the former Minister for the Colonies said taxation was, in 1930–1931, " colossal." On page five, he accuses
Snowden of ineptitude for his not having greatly increased taxation. He said the Budget of 1931 was a " faulty " budget to be
excused by reason of Snowden's illness.[99] Webb admits that it
was no longer necessary to maintain " certain cash balances " with
which Snowden had helped balance outgo, and that the policy of
borrowing to cover the Unemployment Insurance Fund was begun
by the previous Government. Webb said the Hoover Moratorium
cost the Government eleven million pounds; but Mr. Churchill
writes [100] that Germany's payment was never put into the Exchequer but was forwarded directly to America, England thus acting as America's collector.

---

[97] Webb wrote that " dumping " by the Soviet was " no more than the
competition of cheaper commodities." Apparently, he intended by polite
definition to render it more palatable.

[98] *NS*, XXX (April 7, 1928), 814.

[99] *The Clarion* editor said, " Mr. Snowden's Third Budget is not a Socialist budget," III:5 (May, 1931), 130. Webb's revelation was, of course, political assassination; Snowden shortly sent notice to his manager that he would
not run again. Mr. Snowden considered Webb his friend. The Webbs had
asked Snowden to accept a peerage and to replace Webb numerically in the
House of Lords. Snowden refused because he wanted to finish the work
begun on the Budget problems. Passfield offered Snowden Parmoor's position
of leadership. Snowden assented only to a future arrangement to resign
from the Chancellorship and take the Colonial Office (Webb's) without going
into the House of Lords. Cf. Snowden, *op. cit.*, II, p. 927.

[100] Churchill, *The Gathering Storm*, pp. 24 f.

Webb unfairly averred that the existence of the Liberal Party alone prevented MacDonald from "cutting out" of the "body politic" a "large proportion of the electorate," by suddenly cutting certain recipients of aid off the payroll. (A cut of ten percent in a situation where prices were extremely low would not amount to "cutting off the payroll"; but the franchise is still related to income in England.) Also, Webb stated for a fact something which no other source declares, namely, that the May Committee, invented by Liberals with Tory assent, was created for the purpose of finding means to cut public expenditure. But Webb put two things together, the public May Report which caused a clamor in the Press for reduction in taxation, and the private warning by the Bank of England to the Prime Minister and the Chancellor of the Exchequer concerning the alarming drain of gold which created the demand for "cutting" expenditures or the dole. A *few dozen* financial houses were under stringency to render back to foreign governments, bankers and "merchants," accumulated short-term deposits to the estimated amount of four hundred million pounds. Most of these funds had been loaned out to similar businesses in "various continental countries" and it was difficult or impossible to recall them without destroying Austrian and German credit. The London houses were solvent but had to borrow gold from the Bank of England which held it only to back fiduciary notes. The Bank of England borrowed gold from New York and Paris, then in August it advised H.M.'s Government either to borrow gold or to declare a moratorium on gold payments. That this latter proposition if carried out would destroy British credit was a common opinion. New York demanded a restoration of confidence by Britain's balancing the budget with support of Parliament and the Opposition, and by cutting expenditures in Unemployment Insurance. The Cabinet had already decided to do both these things, Webb says, "by additional taxation and by making any prudent economies"; nevertheless it refused to accede to what MacDonald was to term the "condition of the borrowing"—cuts in unemployment insurance.[101] When the Cabinet resigned, everyone expected to find a Baldwin Government on the morrow.

---

[101] Evidently it was due to the publishing of the American demand that the consent to make economies followed Cabinet refusal to do so. MacDonald

The chagrined Lord Passfield alleged that the eventuation was MacDonald's work; alone he had "*staged*" the "drama." Nevertheless, Webb repeated the current saying that the King devised the National Government.[102]   The Parliamentary Labour Party, unlike the Conservative and Liberal Parties, refused endorsement and somewhat gradually adopted the attitude of finding MacDonald's action a betrayal.[103]   That the flight of gold, caused by fear that runs might occur abroad, now persisted is made by Lord Passfield to appear part of MacDonald's treachery.   In four weeks, Britain "went off gold," and business began to improve.   Webb said MacDonald had "threatened" that credit would be ruined if the Government should go off gold.   *The Clarion* did not at first state that it was MacDonald who had "threatened" but the Press; and that by so doing, the Press had put it over on both sides, Tories and Labour.[104]   No one on the Labour side ever urged the gold embargo.   Cole had written a bit about economizing with it but like those of Pethick-Lawrence his writings on this point were not promulgated among the Labour and Socialist faithful.   Webb related the beneficent effects, however: A fillip to exports of textiles and an echoing effect on other export markets.

How Henderson developed an Opposition and so destroyed the reality of a National Government, according to Webb's definition of it, is set forth in *What Happened*.   Despite opposition the "Economies Bill" was passed embodying recommendations of the May Report for cuts in teachers', policemen's, and civil servants' salaries in their respective departments by "orders in council." Webb said that this Government by "ministerial fiat" was a potentiality which "may, one day, be made use of for a much greater revolution ' in due course of law.' "[105]

---

told Weir the whole Cabinet favored cuts until TUC intervened; but Henderson denied this (Weir, *op. cit.*, p. 395).

[102] Snowden, *op. cit.*, II, pp. 879 f, tells of MacDonald's conferences all through 1930 with Liberal leaders to achieve a national (non-Party) policy on unemployment.   Baldwin had refused to attend, but it was sufficient that Chamberlain knew and cooperated.

[103] *The Clarion* failed to register this opinion in September.   It was rising in October and became bitter only after Election in November.

[104] The simple political expedient of using Brer Rabbit's implorations against being cast into the "brier patch" never dawned on the Socialists.

[105] Webb, *op. cit.*, p. 10.   Lord Passfield must have forgotten that Sidney

When Webb intended to upbraid the National Government for holding an Election (as promised) and for the way the Election was conducted, he admitted perforce that their method of coping with " the Crisis " had been a success. " The Crisis had been surmounted," economies effected, the Budget balanced by taxation. He ended by saying this National Government was now a Conservative Government (it could be nothing else since Labour went into Opposition) ; that MacDonald has been embraced by the *rentier* class as part of their " last ditch " defense of themselves. Then Webb made a revealing survey of the wreckage of Labour in politics.

Labour had benefited from a good shock and some pruning. The Labour Party had been " prematurely born into governmental life " ; its M.P.'s had been " injuriously affected " by what were only " accidental successes." They had not the talent to govern and some of them exhibited a habit of mind of being in opposition. The Party should proceed now with education and not commit itself to any save general principles ; keep up a steady stream of propaganda for one project at a time and develop friendly social intercourse among themselves. Webb demanded that officers " consult " with the Party ; yet he proclaimed that the Party had no talents " in this generation of mediocrities."

Having merely remarked the dissension in the Party, Webb betook himself with Beatrice to Russia, but not until after the Scarborough Party Conference. He could not help knowing there was an irremediable reason for the Party's failure to unify its sections. Mrs. Cole tells of the Webbs' disappointment in the Labour Party and their predilection, long since conceived, for an " Order " —the " Jesuit " system, the One-Party, the Samurai (she thinks

---

Webb had advocated advancing the Liberal reforms of 1906 by administrative procedures, by-passing Parliament, also, and that Fabian W. A. Robson envisioned administrative boards which should develop a judicial mentality evolved from administrative regulation.

Dr. Heinrich Brüning wrote, in a letter to this student, dated December 5, 1950, " The present Lord President of the Council, Mr. Morrison, has introduced a motion asking Parliament to authorize legislation by orders-in-council in all matters ' in the interest of the country.' That would have been impossible in Germany [before Hitler's Enabling Act] . . . The confusion in regard to law and administrative orders has become a tragedy, today in England as well as in this country."

Wells must have smiled) which Beatrice [106] especially delighted in finding in Russia. Mrs. Cole does not underscore as she should the fact that they found what they looked for; the pattern lay in outline in their minds. But she intimates as much in expressing mild surprise that Beatrice did not avow her errors regarding Russia as she has done regarding woman suffrage.[107] Distinctly the Webbs decided to dish MacDonald and to chastise the Party, while Henderson, to hold the Party together, led Opposition but remained loyal to MacDonald and worked with him in Geneva on international business, in the ensuing years. His was the only vote against expelling MacDonald from the Party.

We must indict the Webbs for not stating the reason for the unstable equilibrium in the Party. We must indict them as well for MacDonald's ruin in the eyes of the Party. If the Trade Unions had, a generation before, gone on their indicated path toward support of individual Liberal candidates, syphoning "socialistic" or well-rounded reform measures into the Liberal programme, if MacDonald, as the tendency was for Labour leaders to drift into orthodox Liberalism, had been let alone, honestly to be embraced by the old Liberal Party as usually happened, the squabbling heretics of Socialism would not have gained such leverage.[108] MacDonald was a really superior man. Let it be admitted he possessed the faults of his environment; but he would not have had to smash the hopes of thousands of worshipful followers whom he himself had led into the morass of an

---

[106] From the time of his return to Fabianism, G. D. H. Cole urged a system of "Labour Corps" and Shaw abetted him directly.

[107] Margaret Cole, *Beatrice Webb*, p. 158. Cf. also, Mrs. Cole, *Growing Up Into Revolution*, p. 98: "Again and again during the twenties . . . Beatrice told me that what Britain and the world needed was a new Dedicated Order [*sic*] something like the Society of Jesus." Mrs. Cole says those who joined the Communists "felt, as Catholics feel, the need of some human authority [*sic!*] to explain, interpret and guide." Mrs. Cole says Beatrice felt this way and that Socialists who became Communist felt this way—the need for guidance and prodding—yet she excoriates the Labour Party (not mentioning the Fabian publicists thereof) for making the League of Youth "ask Mamma" for guidance on all political issues.

[108] Cf. Churchill, *op. cit.*, p. 19. Baldwin was the real ruler of England from 1922 to 1937; he kept MacDonald on his Tory left and separated from but harnessed to Neville Chamberlain on his liberal right.

Experiment, had he not been taken in by the Webbs and the Fabians, if he had not been captivated by the idea of politicizing the Trade Unions and permeating with Socialism and a One-Party mentality all who *worked* in any way. The Experiment had to fail because its basic ordering was unnatural. To indict is not to judge.

There follows a description of the conflicts indicated so passingly by Lord Passfield. We may place ourselves upon the scene exactly where Webb stood if we avail ourselves of the leverage given by Mrs. Cole's description of it, made available in her *Growing Up Into Revolution*.[109] The Labour Party had succeeded in presenting itself (a) to the Tories and the floating voter as incompetent weaklings in the field of finance, and (b) to the extreme left as tools in the grip of a wicked and anti-social force called " the City " and " Wall Street." (The Webbs, now in the process of conversion to the U.S.S.R., agreed with both opinions, more or less.)

> But we of S.S.I.P. [and also of the N.F.R.B. founded by Cole in 1931 when many Zips went into the Socialist League] did not realize how big the disaster was, we were so profoundly relieved to be rid of MacDonald at last; and we observed that the Parliamentary Party, all save a not particularly distinguished handful [let the reader judge] was holding together under the leadership of Henderson [who was to vote against expelling Mac-Donald] and Lansbury.[110]

" What happened in 1931 " was that the Webb-Shaw team went to Russia and the Henderson-MacDonald machine turned again to Europe. Doubt became certainty about the futility of the inevitability of gradualness. The lightning of crisis had revealed the chasmic difference between Conservatism and Revolution; but those who took the high road to Russia and those who took the low road toward Europe were Socialists in search of Socialism and their paths were destined to re-unite. Shaw was correct: They had to be Communists.

---

[109] Cf. M. Cole, *Growing Up Into Revolution*, p. 155. Mutual friends believe the title should be " Growing Out of Revolution." But the writer is inclined to take it at its face value or else to consider it from a semantic viewpoint, meaningless.

[110] *Ibid.* Interpolation and comment exactly marked according to author's conditions.

CHAPTER XII

CONFLICT OF INCONGRUITIES

A. Internal Conflict

The monism and the inherent materialism of Socialism prevented its fitting into the pattern of the spiritual area it had usurped. To pass over the conflict of those incongruities which had been created by politicizing social units, by lifting all elements of economic life into the public sphere, and by attempting to achieve coherence through an artificial theology called Socialism, would be unfair to the Prime Minister whose task it was to resolve the conflict and who had to lead England in her relations with a world which was turning desperately to nationalism. Fiscal collapse resulting from economic ineptitudes and socio-political conflicts of ideas,[1] faced England in 1931.

The Clarion writers and their readers were warned in 1929 that only for Marxists was there a Socialist interpretation for every-

---

[1] For ten years since Versailles there had been no fixed principle of fiscal policy in any nation save perhaps France where it was " security." Socialists always blamed the unstable conditions upon " Reparations." Usually little account is made of the fact that the dynamic of English and Continental political life was magnetized off its course, as it were, by the conflict of Socialism with the order of things and its inherent conflict with itself. The subject is matter for another study. Too easily have the quasi-Socialist historians of the period placed the cause of Europe's collapse at the door of Versailles. " We had learned Maynard Keynes' lesson all too well," writes M. Cole in *Growing Up Into Revolution*, p. 170. They have never measured the part *reaction* to that Socialism which was imprudently bruited about, played in making Versailles an instrument of three conflicting ideals: The Covenant, the ILO, and Reparations. Cf. Benjamin M. Anderson, *Economics and the Public Welfare* (New York: Van Nostrand, 1949), Part III, " The First Phase of the New Deal, 1924–1932 [sic]," pp. 113–297. Two psychological factors fructified in an attitude of *"sauve qui peut":* the discouragement of the employing class which everywhere heard only unconstructive criticism; and the necessary failure of the self-confident Socialists who though splintered into groups ranging from communist to " christians " capitalized on the political instability which their uncooperative ideologies produced.

thing. The author of *Heartbreak House* (1918) had so concluded, after saying that " No paper should be run as a Socialist paper for there is not a Socialist interpretation for everything." This was the Shaw of 1929, as Davies reported, an " old man," disillusioned and dissatisfied. The younger Fabian seems to have misinterpreted him,[2] or misconstrued his meaning. Earlier the octogenarian Blatchford had written of the ".chastened policy of Labour due to a recognition of political and social realities ";[3] and he had cited J. R. Clynes: " Socialism which might be to the general advantage in a community of Socialists, could not be successfully imposed by a Socialist minority upon a majority of individuals." So Blatchford added,

> If some eager young Socialist believe that the country is ready for Socialism in our time I can only say that I am unable to believe that and I sincerely hope no Labour Government will frame its policy upon that erroneous faith.[4]

Here were two nestors, Shaw of the Fabians and Blatchford of the sentimental Socialists, denying the applicability of Socialism to all things and all times. Their advice was followed by the Government but the Government was given no peace; pure-Socialist ILP back-benchers, and certain political Fabians eager to prove their Socialism or placate the fanatic element continued to agitate for " Socialism now." It was Fabians of the latter kind who kept *The Clarion* from expiring from 1929–1931. This monthly manifested the internal struggle involved even in the effort to define Fabian Socialism.

A young Fabian wrote of a " delightful attack " on Fabians made by the non-repentant Graham Wallas. The editor was mistaken in thinking Wallas had not lectured to Fabians since his resignation from the Society. He had lectured in 1921.[5] Now he

---

[2] *The Clarion,* 1 :10, n.s. (October, 1929), 5.

[3] *The Clarion,* 1 :7, n.s. (July, 1929).

[4] *Ibid.*

[5] *FN,* XXXII :8 (October, 1921). W. A. Robson pointed out Wallas' doubts about liberty under Socialism (*FN,* XXXII :7 [July, 1921]). In October, Wallas lectured on " The Limits of Political Democracy." It is doubtful that many of the Fabians understood him. Robson finds him ex-

accused the Fabians of departing from the original contention that Socialism *rested solely on an economic basis.* He seems to have been unimpressive. The political Socialist of *The Clarion* reported correlatively that Shaw had recently criticized the Fabian adoption of a *constitutional* programme: It would not work—it could not attain Socialism.[6] These two observations went unheeded. But it is important to note that the Fabians who formed the Government were riding roughshod over, not only the mentality of Trade Unionism, but of thorough-going Socialism.

Another Fabian, C. Beresford, an educator, spoke of " Cutting Across the Patterns." As an educator, he detected with distaste the setting of a mould, a patterning of thought for young minds and he grasped at the idea of a restated *individualism of personal responsibility* to combat Communism. He said that although a member of the Fabian Society should not, by encouraging self-expression, encourage the growing " exploiter " that is, the child who is innately Capitalistic, he himself scrupled about imposing a system upon unsuspecting charges. But he found excuse for " education for Fabianism by persuasion " and hoped he might be allowed one personal opinion, that the set pattern could be escaped by " individualism of personal responsibility."[7] Uncertainty on educational as well as on economic and political standpoints is apparent, but the quest for a philosophic basis went on, or at least the effort to make a synthesis without one.

---

traordinarily subtle and compressed. It is evident Wallas' ideas swung between the near-anarchy of free Socialism based solely on an economic principle and such control of the masses as went beyond the limits of republican democracy.

[6] Cf. *The Clarion*, II :12 (December, 1930), 343. The concept of nonpolitical and merely economic Socialism offers interesting speculation on possibilities of free association and community enterprise. Cf. Clement Attlee, *Labour in Perspective and Twelve Years After* (London: Gollancz, 1949). His main thesis is quasi-religious, a Socialism that will bring Trade Unions into perfect collaboration with industry; and he concludes that State Capitalism is designed to produce liberty. One could exchange Attlee's definition of Socialism for a papal statement, if it were given a theological basis—the " if " is significant of impossibility. " Collaboration" may also have the meaning of synthesis. In the Socialist ethic it usually means absorption. Also, " industry," State-owned, can " collaborate " only through the Party.

[7] Charles Beresford *The Clarion*, II :11 (November, 1930), 317.

The Fabian editor signaled, " Demos Defended: Professor Laski to The Rescue: A New Bill of Rights!" when advertising three of Laski's books. He found a new Socialism in *Dangers of Obedience,* but he wondered if Laski were not really worrying about Democracy while reaffirming his belief in it. Laski possessed the "mind of a demagogue" with a " modicum of idealism," as was to be seen in *Liberty and the Modern State.* With *Socialist Tradition in the French Revolution* the editor came to conclude there was nothing really new in Laski's Socialism except "a plea for equality." This was the thesis about *equal* treatment of rich and poor prevalent before the crisis.[8] The Fabian editor, pondering his mentor's words as he vended his wares, had some misgivings: Did not the being allowed to follow conscience result in anarchy? In confusion this former London University student, who boasted of Professor Laski's having made the youth of his day Socialists, now asked, " How will those of whom the Government is not representative maintain their liberty and follow their conscience?" It was characteristic of his school of thought to deem a minority to be unrepresented. (They lacked the philosophical basis which would have led them to find authority,

---

[8] Cf. Sidney and Beatrice Webb, *English Local Government*, Part II (London: Longmans Green and Company, 1929), pp. 826 f., and 829. The *Minority Report* and the *Prevention of Destitution* (1911) did not suggest a "subvention of working-class households": Not wage earners, nor Trade Unionists' Congresses, nor Labour Party Conferences asked for such subvention; but the politicians who sought to avoid "intolerable toil of thought," and the industrialists, worked out the Insurance plans whereby, by 1928, "nearly every working-class family in Great Britain has . . . a continuous ledger account with the National Government . . . for Unemployment, Health, and Old Age Insurance, Pensions [widowhood or orphanage]." So Poor Law Guardians who found cases *not* having such benefits made sure they were provided, in the name of "equality"; whereas the true Communist principle was "To each according to his needs," rather than uniformity or identity in the public services. (Cf. *Ibid.,* pp. 568 and 571.) (Drainage for all and special help to the sick poor, for example, the Webbs term "communism" and a further refinement thereof. This illustrates how hard was the cake of custom formed upon British civilization. We do not think in America that "drainage" signifies any sort of "ism.") The book demonstrates the Webbian premise that the welfare State is not Socialism but a means to it. The Webbs lent themselves to the development of a welfare state knowing that it was a means to the destruction of State-ness.

bound to safeguard the common good, to reside in those whom the majority designated to wield it.) The editor proceeded to take refuge in assent to denials of liberty, such as were expressed in five acts of the Fabian Socialist Government: An Emergency Power Act, the denial of refuge in England to Trotsky, the official Secrets Act,[9] censorship of news about India.[10]

Confused direction was all that Fabians running a Socialist organ could offer. A year before it had been said that the Labour Party aimed at "conversion of the electorate to a belief in Socialism" and not merely the obtaining of votes;[11] and, "Socialism is not a philosophy of government; it is a philosophy of life."[12] Then, "Dangle" or Alexander Thompson boasted that *"The Clarion* made Socialists before the Labour Party was born."[13] So now we see that the Fabian writers in a Socialist organ proclaimed Socialism as the objective of their collaboration with Labour. The non-Socialist world which read the more literary but less entertaining *NS* believed that the light of Socialism was being kept under a bushel—perhaps was to be snuffed out.[14] *The Clarion* was more

[9] This made it a crime to divulge facts intended to be kept a secret by the Government.

[10] *The Clarion,* II:6 (June, 1930), 175.

[11] *The Clarion,* 23, n.s. (March, 1929), 17.

[12] *The Clarion,* 24 n.s. (April, 1929), 1.

[13] *The Clarion,* III:8 (August, 1931), 241.

[14] John Chamberlain, writing "Smothered Without Debate" under "Bookman's Horizon" in *Plain Talk,* IV:4 (January, 1950), 48–51, says "without ever mentioning a 'Socialist' program, the Fabians have achieved their object"—the "Harold Laski type of socialism is the English reality." Readers of this study so far will not be able to agree with Mr. Chamberlain about Fabian secrecy. John Chamberlain reviewed *The Road Ahead* by Mr. John T. Flynn, whose documentation upon Fabianism would bear amplifying. Cf. Flynn, *The Road Ahead* (New York: Adair, 1949).

But Mr. Flynn's correlation of Fabian and ADA characteristics is not far wrong. This writer has a letter from Mr. Jolley who says quite simply that Fabians may be found associated with ADA. There is the added evidence that SDA consider England under the Labour Party Government the mecca of their travels. They, ADA and SDA, proclaim the same objective, "social democracy." Cf. *The Progressive,* 25 (September, 1949), p. 14. And there is the exhibit of direct collaboration by Mrs. Cole with a Labour "educationist" in the Ladies' Garment Workers' Union and New York Liberal Party, Mark Starr, noted above, page 65. Besides the connections indicated by David Williams in *FQ* there is that typified by the recent publication by

forthright. Until the day when they would " see humanity as of two kinds—Labour, and what is damnably otherwise " when a Tory would be as " obsolete as the Beatitudes " [15] as H. M. Tomlinson wrote under " Signs of Change," the Labour Party, which alone of all others believed " in its ultimate success and the fulfillment of its ideals " must unfortunately " rationalise " its position, play for time, try to get its viewpoint to the electorate—according to the writer of " Our Point of View." [16] This appeared at the time when *The Clarion* celebrated its most successful year as a monthly with articles by Beatrice Webb, Harold Laski, and, as usual, M. A. Hamilton and C. Delisle Burns.[17] Mrs. Webb looked ahead to changing Parliament; Mr. Laski criticized " Democracy "; Mrs. Hamilton upheld the Labour Government; and Mr. Burns contributed a synthesized view on several foreign countries, friendly or hostile.

Fabians had begun their political course in intermingled action with the Liberals. Now there are Fabian Socialists and mere Socialists using together the old ILP mouthpiece to detach the last Liberal connections. " Dangle," on the very eve of the Government's downfall, clarioned " There's a Good Time Coming ! " He had some data upon the increased relief of poverty (rather than an upturn in the depression) and he recalled that the ILP had endowed the Party (Manchester, 1893) with the " fourth Clause " which had freed it from " servile dependence on Liberal plutocrats." However, he reproached the Party now for steps that had failed in the fields of Mines and Transport (the State's competing with railways was a failure even as a step toward Socialism) and he attributed their failure to Liberalism: Socialists were ready, he said, with boots and spurs, but the blood was freezing in the veins of those loyal to the Party,[18] because the Party was chained to the Liberal Parliamentary Party.

In the meantime, no one indicted for liberalism Fabian Herbert

---

the League for Industrial Democracy: Harry Laidler, *British Labor's Rise to Power* (1945).

[15] Cf. *The Clarion*, III :8 (August, 1931), 229.

[16] *The Clarion*, II :11 (November, 1930), 310.

[17] Students of the " movement " must dispute with Mr. Churchill the application of his aphorism that never did England owe so much to so few.

[18] *The Clarion*, III :8 (August, 1931), 241.

Morrison,[19] Minister of Transport, soon to be elevated to Cabinet rank, when he advocated England's imitating American development of roads, parks, entrances.[20] He urged his hearers to see Rye Beach in Long Island, and to relinquish their ancient allegiance to the age and beauty of the Tudor countryside in favor of modernization. Tomlinson may have had Morrison in mind when he said it was "time John Ball did a little more dreaming" and pleaded against loss of the Tudor relics in a machine age. He then argued that they might as well have Stalin or Mussolini if their Socialism involved loss of their antique treasures.[21] This was the article wherein Tomlinson saw in the future humanity of two kinds—"Labour, and what is damnably otherwise." Morrison, the typical Fabian, more than Tomlinson, the sentimental Socialist, might imitate liberalistic America and the Roman modernizer and not fear either dictatorship or liberalistic pollution. So we see Fabians could not agree even upon the advisability of modernizing the countryside. They divided on the choice either of developing facilities of different sorts or of preserving the England of John Ball.

In a far different field, American creativeness was imitated. Socialists heard of President Hoover's RFC [22] from the exposition made at a luncheon at which the Prime Minister and a number of financiers learned of America's plan to expend 2,000 million pounds in modernizing equipment, in building public works, and the like, by means of borrowing. There would be no extraneous or non-democratic bodies to execute the plan.[23] The Fabian editor approved but hastened to reassure readers that if proposed for England, this scheme should be based on Socialism and the onus for its rejection thrust upon the Tories. In other words, this

---

[19] *The Clarion,* I :10 (October, 1929), 5.

[20] *The Clarion,* I :10 (October, 1929), 5.

[21] *The Clarion,* III : 8 (August, 1931), 229.

[22] An Economic Advisory Council was set up following lines laid down in *Labour and the Nation.* Mrs. Hamilton said it was "vital to economic reorganization in the *national interest* and on *socialist* lines." The world had yet to learn that these two italicized elements were antithetical and that their attempted synthesis would mean National Socialism. Mrs. Hamilton remarked that this council was modelled upon the well-known Hoover Commissions. Cf. *The Clarion,* II :3 (March, 1930), 69.

[23] *The Clarion,* I :12, n.s. (December, 1929), 3.

liberal program if adopted should be made so Socialistic that the Tories, though constrained to vote for it, would have to countenance such Socialism as would enable the Party to act as if with a mandate for Socialism.[24] Meantime, readers learned that the standard of living of Englishmen was higher in 1929, than that in any other country of Europe; that Thomas was pressing for increased production for export; that the national handicaps lay in foreign trade and creation of work. Mr. Thomas was then, although it was not yet generally known, engaged in persuading the Bank of England to back his projects. He was to win the Bank's assent on condition he should also persuade the industries to reorganize.[25] But his Fabian critic plumped for increased social services lest his readers recall that the Keynesian Liberal programme made for Lloyd George's campaign in 1929 had stressed a plan much like that involved in RFC seeking to increase production by loans to modernize industry and transport, thereby creating work and shifting by attraction the perennially unemployed to new fields of labor.[26] He warned, without exemplification, that democracy was endangered, yet he wrote these surprising lines: " As to improving trade, international agreements, the strengthening of and the participation in, existing cartels for limiting markets and rationing production are necessary." [27] Often, one must observe, there was conflict within the mind of individual Fabians. The alternative to such a conclusion as the above must be that the benefits of cartelization were preferable to those from natural growth derived from creative work and production for export: A large social segment then remained dependent upon " social services."

---

[24] The alternative to this interpretation, irritating as it may be, is that these particular Socialists (all Fabians) did not wish the plan, resembling RFC as it did, to be adopted because collapse which it would prevent favored their objectives. Yet similar schemes were already in use in Britain, namely, Export Credit schemes, Trade Facilities Acts, and the like. Cf. Webb, *English Local Government,* pp. 696 f.

[25] " Thomas' scoop " was somewhat unsympathetically reported. Cf. *The Clarion,* II :1 (January, 1930), 3. It is certain that *The Clarion* never wanted Thomas to succeed. As to the need for " rationalization " and a Sherman anti-trust law, cf. Anderson, *op. cit.,* p. 162 f.

[26] The machinery for this scheme already existed. Cf. Webb, *English Local Government,* p. 685.

[27] *The Clarion,* I :12, n.s. (December, 1929), 3. Some innocent fascism.

The handicap of collaboration with Liberals took odd forms. The Government's Coal Bill was a weak one measured by the programme for coal set forth in *Labour and the Nation*. Now the Liberals in the persons of Lloyd George and Mr. Samuel urged that since the Sankey report suggested it, they should all stand for *compulsory* amalgamation of the coal mining businesses. In the end, the Liberals abstained from voting in order not to defeat the Government. This was January 1930, and no Party wanted to precipitate an Election. The Fabian reporter took comfort in the feeling that the high level of the debate on the Coal Bill restored confidence in Parliament.[28] The fact was it had demonstrated the mastery which Liberals had over the Labour Party Government and its Programme.[29] They must choose a Socialist measure to go down on, in any case, was *The Clarion's* advice looking toward one of two possible results: a mandate for Socialism if an election transpired, or the more effectual position of being in a strong Opposition.[30]

Another Liberal Idea growing out of a Tory adaptation of Keynes' proposal to keep gold and credit at home, was repudiated by Fabians of *The Clarion;* this was the "Empire Crusade" of Lord Beaverbrook which advocated a correlative use of sterling in the Empire orbit. The Fabian horizon was colonial—whereon to exercise barter-based "cooperative" purchase and marketing.[31] Meantime poor Mr. Thomas was, they gloated, "burked" by the Bank of England which employed Henry Clay, a Fabian economist, to investigate Thomas' propositions. It was thought the

---

[28] The traditional parliamentary procedures were under constant attack by Socialists and Fabians.

[29] *The Clarion*, II :1 (January, 1930), 26.

[30] *Ibid.*, p. 4.

[31] *The Clarion*, II :2 (February, 1930). A "colonial" world is a smaller world than "Empire." Socialism was conceived in a small world; "workers of the world" meant workers of industrial Europe. Colonies form the kitchen gardens of the "industrial democracy" system. These socialistic Englishmen would set India free but undertake a huge Governmental-plus-Monopoly ground-nut project in Africa and refuse, out of respect for tribal cultures and land-tenure customs and laws, to allow development toward modernizing methods among the native coconut growers, in their African Trusteeships. Cf. Olive Holmes, "People, Politics, and Peanuts in East Africa," *Foreign Policy Reports*, XXVI :14 (December 1, 1950) 154–164; also, "Unilever's Africa," *Fortune*, XXXVII :1 (January, 1948), pp. 57 f.

Bank people intended to prevent Thomas or Labour from having the political credit for the economic gains promised by the expansion of plant, through loans.[32]

So we find the Party encompassing a conflict of ideas: Fabian Socialists against Liberals, Socialists against Fabians who collaborate with Liberals in fiscal policy or in domestic work-creating policy and in Parliament. Fabians afield criticized Fabians in Government for "rationalising" Socialist tenets. Fabian questioned Fabian on liberty under Socialism, on doubts about democracy — whether force or freedom should prevail; on the political basis—whether constitutional methods or methods economically catastrophic should succeed in attaining Socialism; on the desirability of using an economic basis, alone; on whether Socialism was a total creed or whether it was desirable to have it now, or not.

B.   PARTY *versus* GOVERNMENT ON THE FISCAL PROBLEM

There were still other areas of conflict. Fabians, as Socialists, criticized the Labour Government and spoke of *the Party* as against the *Government*.

W. Arthur Peacock in July of 1929 reviewed "A German's View of Labour" as he called Egan Werthheimer's *A Portrait of the Labour Party*. The "varsity dons," as Peacock called them—Cole, Laski, Lloyd, and Tawney—were rated by the German author as having non-political but very "real influence," more than a dozen Parliamentarians, and Peacock, although he believed their influence was exaggerated, said it was an error to rate them more effective than Hugh Dalton, Harold Lees-Smith, Philip Noel-Baker (who were Parliamentarians). On either side the reader will recognize all as Fabians. Peacock thought Werthheimer gave too much prominence to Fabians in the Labour Party. The tendency of ILP-minded persons to belittle Fabian influence is noticeable here. It occurs even in a fellow Fabian.[33] Credit for creating the Party was claimed by the ILP and not disputed by the Fabians who rather chose inconspicuousness.

At this time, the Labour Party was patently critical of the

---

[32] *The Clarion,* II:2 (February, 1930).
[33] *The Clarion,* I:7, n.s. (July, 1929), 4.

Labour Government, and the condition worsened as August, 1931, came nearer. In February, 1930, the editors insisted that the Consultative Committee should demand to know what the Prime Minister expected to get passed and, it appears, force the passage of this modicum against Opposition obstructionism or Liberal reluctance. The "political reality" of that of which they often complained, Cabinet dictatorship, had not come home to them.[34] Since a legislative programme could not be formulated without Liberal assent, the proposal seems to have been intended to force the Labour Government to resign. By April, 1930, the Labour M.P.'s were reported to be "despondent" over the Government's scant achievement.[35] There was, it was said, dissension in the Cabinet.[36] Mr. Thomas "unfortunately" agreed with certain gloom-ridden economists (so did *The Clarion*). Yet there existed some men whom the editor called City optimists—they were all Fabians—Mosley, Lansbury, T. Johnston. A memorandum issued by them revealed the divisive opinions on fiscal matters which were splitting the Cabinet. One side, "the City" side, favored the principles found in the survey made by Henry Clay for the Bank of England, the other side favored the position taken by the Economic Advisory Council. This Council had been set up (in imitation of one of President Hoover's Commissions) by the Labour Government for Mr. Graham's guidance. It had for secretary the Liberal, H. D. Henderson, who had collaborated with J. M. Keynes on the Liberal Programme of 1929. These represented the two schools of thought on fiscal policy between which the Labour Movement foundered. While Labour M.P.'s despaired some Fabians raised high hope by commencing an extensive works program. This involved the Thomas *versus* Mosley struggle.

---

[34] *The Clarion,* II:2 (February, 1930), 35. After the National Government was formed the *NS* editor wrote in *The Clarion* that at last Parliament could reassert its independence of the Cabinet. Cf. Clifford Sharp, "Parliament Vindicated," *The Clarion,* IV:3 (March, 1932), 53 f.

[35] *The Clarion,* II:4 (April, 1930), 99.

[36] Davies (*fils*) boasted in another place that he had a source of information directly from Cabinet circles. Cf. *The Clarion,* III:10 (October, 1931), 283. In another connection, he had remarked, upon finding Oliver Baldwin smoking a pipe, that he had been assured Baldwin was not smoking his father's tobacco.

Mr. Mosley after disputing every step of the works program with Thomas resigned from the Cabinet and disappeared temporarily from the immediate scene—to return briefly the leader of a Fascist movement. Meantime, Labour opinion also rejected Cole's scheme to form "labour corps" for slum clearance, a scheme endorsed by Shaw—one suspects, in a mischievous exposition of the necessary conclusions which those who laid the premises disliked to draw.

The fiscal policy and the works program were not the only points of division in Fabians' own ranks. Lansbury and Greenwood lambasted the chief executive of the Poor Law without naming Miss Bondfield. The old order in the workhouse—the compulsory bath, the dreadful clothing, the diet of bread and cheese, and rock-breaking for occupation, remained unchanged, and Fabians of the social persuasion criticized Fabians in political office, unmercifully.[37]

The Cabinet had been divided as far back as May, 1930, and the Party as represented by the Consultative Committee was dissident with the Government. Said the Reporter, "I am backing *the Party* to force the hand of *the Government.*"[38] He placated his ILP readers with the assertion that there would be *no pact* with Liberals although he reported there was *an agreement* not to turn Labour out until an Electoral Reform Bill which the Liberals favored should be enacted. The Liberals had begun to advocate "the Alternative Vote" in place of "Proportional Representation." The Labour Party was not sure of how much good it would do Labour but the Liberals were trying for any method which would give them a showing in Parliament in larger proportion to the electoral strength they possessed in some geographic areas. They polled heavily in certain large constituencies. Labour's promise to consider "A.V." procured some otherwise unwarrantable cooperation from Liberals.

The Davies-Stevens column of August, 1930, a whole year before the breakup, outlined the position taken by those who would use constitutional measures to achieve the social revolution. The assumption of the writer seemed to be that the only other position possible was one against the "social revolution" taking place at

[37] *Ibid.*, p. 100. *Clarion* also ran a series advocating abolishment of capital punishment.

[38] *The Clarion*, II:5 (May, 1930), 131.

all. The Government, in theory responsible for the weal of all, was deemed to lack courage, to have a too moderate " get through " policy, to have so far " accomplished far less than was expected of it." Although three points, consisting of reforms at home and abroad, protection against the " worst features " of Capitalism, and unceasing propaganda for Socialism, were announced as the " constitutional " standpoints, the Government was reminded that the " attainment of socialism is the be-all and end-all of the Labour Movement." [39] The observer looks for a definition of Socialism in vain, and falls back upon " doctrineless socialism " of the Programme. At this time economists were advising that the worst of the depression, " the economic blizzard," was over; so Labour people were warned that Tories would want to take credit for the improvement which would be notable in a few months; therefore an election could be expected within eight months. There would be no Lib-Lab cooperation even then. " Party discipline " would count. But another hiatus between the Party and its members showed up: " The Labour *Party* must be more tolerant of its *members'* socialist opinions and less tolerant of traditional and ancient forms which hold up progress." " Traditional and ancient forms " referred less to the social forms and amenities than to the Parliamentary techniques by which a Cabinet ruled and managed Parliament. " The Party " spoke to " the Government " by means of the Consultative Committee—in vain. Members reiterated their creed of Socialism to remind the Party in Government—equally in vain. Cabinet control of Parliamentary techniques had been evolved from the need to contain centrifugal forces of non-conformism, long ago. Here was the Fabian asking for Party discipline and admonishing the Government [40] to heed the *Party's directives* coming through the Consultative Committee. When the " discipline " broke down and whips found themselves facing rebellion soon after the election in 1931, Fabian Clifford Sharp rejoiced in the recovery of democracy [41]—to all appearances.

The fiscal problem increased in scope and intricacy when in October, 1930, the undersecretary of the British treasury and the

---

[39] *The Clarion,* II :8 (August, 1930), 222.
[40] *The Clarion,* II :8 (August, 1930), 223.
[41] Cf. Sharp, *supra,* note 34.

former deputy secretary to the Cabinet, Sir William Fraser and Sir Tom Jones, were sent to Washington to explore, the writer guessed, the possibilities of Debt cancellation. The Fabian writer exposed the unannounced move of his Government. Even though he knew cancellation of the War Debt, if achieved, would keep Labour in power a long time, he said the mission acted by " stealth." There had been a conference of representatives of the Bank of England, the Federal Reserve, and the Reichsbank, in New York. Although most writers blamed the French for the failure of the recent Naval Conference, now it was said it was *secrecy* which crippled it at birth; and it was implied that secrecy would cripple this improvised monetary conference also. The Government had no organ whereby to plead for cooperation. On the other hand, it had no means to prevent the divulgence of Cabinet " leaks." [42]

Concurrently, there existed great anxiety about India. The Government refused to use force against Gandhi's civil disobedience and passive resistance but they received no encouragement from editorial remarks. MacDonald was as involved with India as Henderson was with Egypt; both were arriving at a Liberal-Tory solution. Mrs. Besant, having taken her theosophy from India, had bestowed her Fabianism upon the newly resurgent political forces in India. It would involve a special study to trace this dynamic. Egypt was the object of no such solicitude from Fabians as was India.

Meantime, MacDonald was consistently praised by his biographer, Fabian Mary Agnes Hamilton, in her monthly contribution to *The Clarion*. In answer to her " Nothing to Grouse About," Davies wrote, " Much to Grouse About " in May, 1931, when France had wrecked the Naval Conference and made a successful disarmament conference impossible. He groused about Snowden's " Liberal " budget and said " the Party " was wondering when the Government would face the electorate on a Socialist issue and cease that " grovelling " toward the Liberals which showed that Lloyd George was now the dictator of the Labour Party. He prophesied that Cabinet reconstruction was coming; younger men were to be elevated and others transferred to Lords. For the first

---

[42] *The Clarion*, II :10 (October, 1930), 279.

time in this organ, readers learned of the menace of overproduction.[43] It was not mentioned again until after the collapse in August, 1931. The editorial of the same date decried the omission of " progressive taxation " in Snowden's third Budget; the editor was dissatisfied because it postponed a reckoning by banking on economy and the prognosticated return of prosperity,[44] and he advocated increasing taxation to build up revenue to meet the progressive expenditures of another year's Labour Government. If there were no such funds, there would be, he said, no votes at the end.[45]

So we see some Fabians whose sentiments were nearly akin to the ILP feeling, expressing themselves as the voice of " the Party " against the Government, disapproving its " Liberal " Budget, revealing its secret move to correct the imbalance of international finance, mocking its failure to achieve " the revolution," goading its reluctance to submit to guidance from a parliamentary committee.

The Party's spokesmen exposed the division in the Cabinet and revealed that the cause lay in the field of opinion on fiscal policy.

Material on the two fiscal opinions which were dividing the Cabinet was scant. In fact, ideas upon how to handle the employment problem were few and these not constructive. Mr. Thomas with his ideas for industrial modernization, wore out his energies trying to get increased production of certain British specialties like handbags, and succeeded in many ways in raising exports and employment. He received almost no encouragement from Fabians of either *The Clarion* or the *NS* circles. Shaw always encouraged Cole's idea of a labour corps and *The Clarion* watched Mosley, then Thomas' antagonist, with an ironic patience, noting the conclaves with Cole and others in week-end parties at Easton Lodge [46]

---

[43] *The Clarion,* III :5 (May, 1931), 131.

[44] Anderson, *op. cit.,* pp. 244–255, believes that prosperity was really just around the corner and was demolished by England's going off the gold standard.

[45] *The Clarion,* III :5 (May, 1931), 130.

[46] Easton Lodge was the estate of the Countess of Warwick. Cf. her *Life's Ebb and Flow* (New York: Morrow and Company, 1929). Lady Frances (Maynard Greville) had laid plans to turn Easton Lodge over to the Labour Unions for a Labour College. She says, " the Coal Strike of

with the satisfied assurance that no harm should come to the Movement since Mr. Ernest Bevin was in attendance too.[47]   But the
reader looks in vain for a concise plan or creative idea as to how to
handle the fiscal problem.   The best direction from their greatest
expert was a burst of exasperation: Webb wrote in 1928:

> It is hard to say which policy would do the greater harm
> [" cutting down on Health and Education estimates, re-
> ducing the Government establishments, stopping any
> extension of Training Centres, and postponing the neces-
> sary perfecting of the insurance and pension systems "
> (all *Tory* measures); or making " imprudent extensions
> of Unemployment Insurance Benefits . . . in Uncondi-
> tional Outdoor Relief and all the rest of the relaxations
> of 1920–1928 "]. . . . In this brainless rivalry it may be
> doubted whether Parliamentary institutions and Political
> Democracy would survive.   Which of two political
> Parties would be *driven to set up a dictatorship* might
> depend only upon an accident![48]

It was admitted in 1931 that 1928 and 1929 had been prosperous
years but in the same breath it was reiterated, only the Cooperative
Commonwealth could cope with unemployment.[49]   The Webbs,
however, had written in 1928:

> We claim no expert knowledge for these suggestions of
> how to prevent unemployment and how to treat the Un-
> employed for whom provision has to be made . . . the
> world will discover the appropriate remedy only by
> actually attempting to do the job . . . trial and error.[50]

Their bafflement was thus expressed in their masterful appraisal of

---

1927 so depleted the resources of the Unions that there was nothing left
over for education."   *Ibid.,* p. 330.   Her philosophy is shown in two
sentences: 1) " Capitalism is not the only enemy of progress.   Ignorance
and prejudice are tougher foes [in union circles] "; 2) " There seems to be
an acknowledged but secretly conscious recognition that the only solution of
life's problems lies in the Gospel of Love."   She was spared seeing the hard
core of the Liberal-Socialist-Communist formula, the " *non-serviam.*"

[47] *The Clarion,* III:1 (January, 1931), 3.
[48] Sidney and Beatrice Webb, *English Local Government,* p. 1007.   Italics
are inserted.
[49] *The Clarion,* III:1 (January, 1931).
[50] Sidney and Beatrice Webb, *English Local Government,* p. 1013.

the new Local Government Law which they appended to their constructive analysis of the old Poor Law and in which they thanked Mr. Baldwin's Cabinet for the abolition of the old Board of Guardians. The Webbs, throughout this great work, show that they consider " Outdoor Relief " or the dole, a politician's panacea demanded by those who will collect what the unemployed spend— the electorate. Their most constructive suggestion is the " Framework of Prevention of Destitution." They do not try to settle whether " Equality " is the goal or equal opportunity even, saying that equals applied to unequals result in unequals; but they demand as the foundation of any kind of community the prevention of destitution.[51] It is easily seen at this point why the Webbs left the Society, as they did. (Beatrice returned in 1939.)

In 1930, Cole wrote *Gold Credit and Unemployment*. A brief notice of it appeared in *The Clarion* without expository review to indoctrinate their readers. Cole did not advocate devaluing the pound, but he complained that the external value of gold was too high so that exports were off. His ideas ran obliquely in disagreement with the Keynes-Henderson thesis that gold should be kept at home for expansion of domestic credit, by advocating the discontinuance of the use of gold on the domestic front.[52] In August, Fabian C. Delisle Burns wrote, " Why Fence Off the Empire? " He rejected the Beaverbrook thesis which would, in a manner, expand the Keynes' gold theory to the whole Empire; that is, increase the scope of the term domestic to include the Commonwealth and give sterling the corresponding position of gold. Burns was between two fires. The Trade Unions were currently advocating a "closed Empire" and the International Federation of Trade Unions

---

[51] *Ibid.*, p. 985. The Webbs' thesis diminishes to a single point and so negates the broad basal Augustinian (Anglo-Christian) thesis concerning the nature of civic community, to wit, that a true republic involves the pursuit of Justice and since pagans (not atheists) cannot pursue that Justice which is rooted in the one true God, they may form a community productive of a republic by pursuit of something they love in common. In the writer's opinion, this is the touchstone of disagreement between Catholic concepts concerning the nature of the State (involving the right to revolt if this basis is threatened) and the philosophy of Social Democracy. Cf. St. Augustine, *City of God*, Bk. XIX.

[52] *The Clarion* II:9 (September, 1930), 263.

(IFTU) with Citrine (ex-officio, an officer), were repudiating tariffs. Burns, the Fabian historian, was of the opinion there should be a measure of tariff protection.[53] Burns' thought was clearer by December, 1930, but the international aspect of fiscal matters still absorbed him. There should be, he said, international cooperation—with those countries which were not preparing for war. Thus he blinked the well-known German situation.[54] The Government should arrange for the *" economical use "* of the gold supply. Finally, it should prevent deterioration of the standard of life by what means he did not say except that he defined wages as purchasing power, not as production cost, and he insisted that *control* of the standard of living is quite possible since the problem has none of the uncontrollability of an earthquake, for example.[55] Only one Fabian commentator, Pethick-Lawrence, attacked the problem of low prices. In Burns' thought, smoothly as it reads, the instigation of dictatorship is insinuated.

Clever writing could not produce constructive criticism or creative ideas. Fabians seemed to desire to stay in office only to propagandize. When the National Government materialized there was no great alternative which stood rejected, except an adamant attitude against reducing the dole. The dole uncut and benefits unmitigated seemed the sole objective of Fabians who expressed themselves within the Socialist *milieu*. But it will be recalled Pethick-Lawrence was currently attempting to shift attention from wages to prices which were unsoundly low at the time. When Margaret Bondfield sought to raise the borrowing power of the Unemployment Insurance Fund to two hundred and fifteen million pounds (twenty-five million more than the legal limit), and to obtain a six-month extension of the legal time for borrowing, small account was made of the strain upon the Treasury.[56] Sharply, the

---

[53] *The Clarion*, II :8 (August, 1930).

[54] As to fiscal reasons for the poor Franco-German relations, cf. Anderson, *op. cit.*, pp. 234–240.

[55] *The Clarion*, III :12 (December, 1930), 35.

[56] A normal transaction was involved, the loan of funds from a " consolidated fund " which included Postal Savings. Such a loan brought interest into the Treasury. The " scare " aroused by Snowden during the ensuing campaign, regarding the danger to Postal Savings, was not altogether mendacious. Cf. Weir, *op. cit.*, p. 441, who blames Runciman for starting the " scare."

Tories who opposed were pilloried for cruelty: They insisted on
" full stamps " for " full benefits " and " strict justice." It was
generally recognized that there was a widespread abuse of the law.
To curtail this abuse, an " Anomalies Bill " had been introduced.
Its framers followed lines laid down by the Trade Unions General
Council to curb unnecessary benefits. There existed a large class
of " spongers." [57] It is notable that the only effort to cut down on
" Poplarizing " expenditures came from the Trade Unions. The
Anomalies Bill was the creation of TUGC.[58]

Herbert Morrison from 1929 to 1931 struggled to create a public
corporation to handle and reform the London Transportation system. This idea of a public corporation was old in western United
States. It was hailed among Socialists as an origination and the
best means of laying a foundation for Socialism. In June, 1931,
Morrison came in for severe criticism of the way he handled the
expropriation of the London underground transport facilities. A
letter to the editor (Mr. Davies or Mr. Stevens) spoke of " Collectivism at 9% (signed " Judas ") and was captioned by the
editors, " Morrison Butters the Shareholders." [59] In this issue,
Ernest Davies as " Reporter " captioned his comments, " Herbert
Morrison Derailed." Morrison had agreed to give the owners of
the London underground 7 and ¾%, increasing to 9% in two
years.[60] This was said to " reprieve " the Capitalists and it was
suggested he had been " bullying " his colleagues into " reaction."
In the August issue, the Reporter's father rectified the errant

---

[57] *The Clarion,* III :7 (July, 1931), 198.

[58] Tom Williamson, M.P., contributed " Bursting the Tory Bubble," *The
Clarion,* III :8 (August, 1931), 235 f. He described the machinery set up to
advise Parliament concerning " anomalies " of Poor Law administration and
Unemployment Insurance. These had been pointed out in the Webbs' *English
Local Government, op. cit.,* p. 1005, in their famous " Epilogue " of 1928
upon the Local Government Act of 1928. " The Act of 1929 does little more
than pass over to the Councils the powers that the Board of Guardians have
possessed since 1834." These found no third way to save themselves from
the alternative of " unconditional Outdoor Relief " and the " Workhouse
System," and all were concerned with the " worst of social diseases, . . .
voluntary and *intentional* pauperism." (Italics supplied.)

A world without any agricultural way of life was hopelessly morassed
in its own industrialism.

[59] *The Clarion,* III :6 (June, 1931), 177.

[60] *Ibid.,* 163.

thinking of both letter writer and editor. This financial expert explained that the reported gain to the underground shareholders of 2% up to 9% was exaggerated, that Lord Ashfield had persuaded the reluctant owners to accept the low valuation of shares as assessed *before* talk of nationalization ran up their value. All was well.[61]

This conflict of financial ideas was very significant. There were few in the Movement, outside the Trade Unions, who held publicly such capitalistic tenets as Alderman A. E. Davies, L.C.C.[62] His son was the rescuer of *The Clarion* and he was to be the one link of Fabianism with its past through the 1930's. Among the pages of Volume II of *The Clarion* a pamphlet was found by this student, probably one of the sort which was mailed out with *The Clarion*, often. Entitled "How to Invest Safely," it was written by Alderman A. E. Davies, L.C.C., whose name headed the list of trustees of three Cooperative Investment Trusts. With Sir D. Drummond Fraser, and F. W. Crittenden, the elder Davies, who was perennially a member of the Fabian Executive, solicited investors. The Trusts were designed, he wrote, for small investors. Their reliability was attested by the fact that they were backed by Midlands', Lloyd's, National City, National Bank and Trust Company of New York, the Royal Bank of Canada, the Bank of Montreal, the Deutsche Bank and others. Prospective investors were told that wealthy men learned long ago to hand over their money to experts to invest for them in order to benefit from the pool thus formed, wherein only dividends were distributed and profits from sales of investments went into a reserve fund to increase the value

---

[61] *The Clarion*, III:8 (August, 1931), 245. Baron Ashfield had been "general manager of American electric railways," especially in Detroit, for twelve years, was "chairman and manager" of fourteen transportation businesses (including one in Havana), was a director of Midlands Bank and of a chemical company as well as the "British and German Trust, Ltd." No wonder Davies understood him.

[62] Fabians collected rents on the Society's old building and all their writers collected the usual royalties on their books which received complimentary notice in such organs as *The Clarion*. The Davieses, father and son, were very representative Fabians. The son's reporting had a touch of merriment and irony. He mocked the left-wing to whose gallery he played. The father, a fundamental Capitalist in thought, cherished the Society as the son cherished *The Clarion* for sentiment's sake.

of uninvested money. Investors were offered these inducements : Shares multiplied their value to three times the original price ; their money was invested where the market was known to be the best ; the trust could borrow cheaply at banks and from the public. There is scant evidence that the pure-Socialists understood Davies. Fabian intellectuals undoubtedly connived with his patent Capitalism. If Socialism must liquidate the investing class, there were fruits still to be garnered from the doomed system.

Hinging on fiscal policy was the attitude toward France. Fabians hailed the Hoover Moratorium as the great "creative" statement of the age. At first it was thought France could not refuse to cooperate. It will be recalled that Henderson leaned toward France in the matter of the Austro-German tariff *verein*. In other words, the intellectual attitude toward rationalistic France was at one now with the seasoned loyalty of Neville Chamberlain. Ever since the D'Abernon Commercial Treaty, England was a friend to France who had lost her hegemony in Europe. We have seen how Mrs. Hamilton criticized Snowden for his adherence to the old-fashioned Trade Unionist francophobia. Snowden was once said to have ended the "subservience" of Britain to France. That was after his stubborn resistance to that portion of the Young Plan which was unfavorable to Britain,[63] when for a brief moment Snowden was a hero all over England. But in general the period 1925-1931 was marked by cajoling a recalcitrant France on the part of political Labourites.[64]

France rendered null the Naval Conference and it was known in March of 1930 that so it must be since the Monetary Conference had failed. At this conference Snowden's efforts in favor of Brüning had been checked by MacDonald and Henderson in favor of France. The effect in England was to keep Labour in power longer. Tories were too well schooled in politics to miss the timing of an upward momentum. The failure of these conferences was a Labour boon. The ungrateful work of getting passed the Coal Bill broke the health of the highly respected Fabian economist, William Graham ; but his victory in its final passage resulted from

---

[63] Cf. Snowden, *op. cit.*, II, pp. 777–838.

[64] Feiling, *op. cit.*, p. 193, reveals "the French were anxious to get their hands on our throats as they have on the Germans" in September, 1931.

the fact that Liberals did not vote so as not to defeat the Government. Had there been any hope of success for the coming Naval Conference, the Liberals might have voted with the Tories on Graham's bill in order to throw Labour out so as to procure the prestige of a successful Naval Conference for the Conservatives.[65] At the same date it was reported that Fabian Susan Lawrence, Undersecretary of State for Health, told the Fabian Society at a reception that there would be no dissolution because Snowden needed two budgets to iron out the fiscal disorder inherited from Churchill.[66] So we see the conflict of Fabian present-day francophilism against their history of francophobia had domestic political repercussions. It was all right for France to spoil the Naval Conference under the circumstances.

Fabian Josiah Wedgwood contributed "Pacifists at Odds" in June of 1930. He found Fabian Norman Angell's attitude pro-French and in favor of the *status quo* as against W. H. Dawson, whose *Future of Empire* he advertised, and who was pro-American. Dawson had written that America had been right in rejecting the Versailles Pact which would have meant endorsing the existing treaties and Article 18, all favorable to French hegemony in Europe. Wedgwood was inclined to agree with Dawson and to find Angell, whose view greatly resembled Neville Chamberlain's, responsible for the pro-French attitude whereby the Labour Government missed the opportunity to dictate terms on one of Hoover's proposals to exclude food supplies from capture as contraband and thus to settle one problem of freedom of the seas:[67] The Socialist viewpoint had been divided and the Party had pulled in two directions; so the French had taken this advantage to destroy by delaying tactics the effects of the Hoover Moratorium.

It is not unusual to find divided opinion in political ranks. The

---

[65] *The Clarion,* II:3 (March, 1930), 67.

[66] *Ibid.* Churchill had defended his disorderly exchequers by saying he did not foresee the Strike and increased unemployment. It was simply false to blame Churchill for a budget in disarray which was caused by the American Crash of 1929 after which exports of American capital dropped (cf. Spender, *Great Britain, Empire and Commonwealth,* p. 693) from $1,130 million in 1928 to zero in 1930. Prosperity in 1928–1929 had been admitted, as we have seen; likewise, the break in the U. S. market in 1928.

[67] *The Clarion,* II:6 (June, 1930), 172.

important point is that a Party demanding solidarity and bloc-voting and a " machine that will work " did not make adjustments to political realities. The Labour platform had to allow for fluid political action while its constituent Socialism made demands for solidarity and adherence to a dogmatic creed which it could not define. On France fell the onus of defeating German recovery.

The same division between spokesmen for the Party and for the Government was evident still regarding Russia. While " trade " was the incentive offered rank and file Trade Unionists, it is certain that the supposed Socialism of Russia like the imminent Socialism of France attracted the Socialism in the Labour Government even against the judgment of their political leaders. It is understandable that political laborites alluded to the Acros raid [68] incessantly to embarrass the Tories. No Labour politician admitted that the capture by Soviet-Socialists of the Labour Conference in 1925 [69] led to the Strike of 1926 which prompted passage of the Trade Disputes Act; but in January, 1930, *The Clarion* editor justified Russian illegal propaganda by reminding readers that, while diplomacy was one thing, for another Russia being a " revolutionary country " must be expected to propagandize.[70] This line of thinking surely proved an embarrassment to the Prime Minister.

---

[68] In 1927 the Baldwin Government had discovered machinery for printing propaganda in the Arcos Company premises; and they had broken off relations with Russia. The Labour Government of 1924 had, of course, upon coming into office recognized Russia.

Lansbury had revisited Russia in 1926. There can be no doubt that the good feeling with which he reported his experience stemmed from the cordiality of his reception. (Lansbury, *op. cit.*, pp. 238 f.) Compare this with Ben Turner's story of pilgrimage and association in 1921 with Russian organizers in his *About Myself*, pp. 211–231. The names of fellow pilgrims are interesting: Tom Shaw, Robert Williams, *Mrs. Snowden* (Party); " Alf " Purcell, Harry Skinner, *Miss Bondfield* (TUC); *Clifford Allen* and Dick Wallhead (ILP); *C. R. Buxton* (interpreter) and *Dr. Haden Guest* (medico) and Meakin of the *Daily News* with Mr. George Young. *Ben Turner* was chairman. (Names of then Fabians are italicized. Tom Shaw contributed to *Clarion*, 1929–1931.) The Webbs and Shaw prepared to visit Russia by fortifying themselves with mounds of books and manuals of the Russian language, when the Labour Government went out in 1931.

[69] Cf. Mrs. Cole; *Beatrice Webb*, p. 159.

[70] *The Clarion*, II:1 (January, 1930), 4.

C. Fabians and TUC—Now MacDonald's Mainstay

Two other important divisions loomed large in the misty logic holding the Movement together: The Trade Unions for the sake of whose adherence MacDonald was kept in the leadership, spurned overtures of comradeship from Fabians; on the back-benches the Clydesiders, who were "loud speakers" for Socialism against the Government, were unwilling to be at peace with English Trade Unionism.

The Fabian Society held a reception for MacDonald in December of 1929. The Fabian Reporter said it had been badly arranged. The Fabian Pensions Minister, F. O. Roberts, was Master of Ceremonies. Fabian Susan Lawrence made the welcoming address. When John Beard of the TUC was called upon, he was found to be absent. The same embarrassment followed the calling upon Mr. Moses, M.P., of the Doake Division. The writer noted that at this reception Ishbel MacDonald contended for social success with the Countess of Warwick,[71] and Mrs. Webb was unnoticed. She had "grown old gracefully." The reporter was quite premature in retiring Beatrice so soon. She wished, no doubt, to be unnoticed because she and Sidney did not like Mac-Donald. Evidently the TUC men did not like Fabians. The reception and the Webb's attendance like that of the Fabian editor was designed to hide the rift in Labour's lute. Then the Reporter revealed it in all its delicate splinters of social sensitiveness.

At the mid-point of Labour's second Government, Cole defined the terms of Trade Unionism in relation to the Labour Party. "Trade Unions and the Government" appeared in February of 1930. Taking Cole's aphorisms in their order of appearance can only strengthen the conclusion that Trade Unionism and a Socialist way of life are not miscible elements:[72]

1) The unions must abstain from alliance with employers—"the borderline of negotiation and alliance should not be crossed."
2) Trade Unions and the Labour Movement were "agents for the

---

[71] *The Clarion,* III:8 (August, 1931), 235. Cf. Frances Countess of Warwick, *Life's Ebb and Flow.* She was "*converted*" to Socialism by Blatchford.

[72] *The Clarion,* I:12, n.s. (December, 1929), 5. Also, cf., *The Clarion,* II:2 (February, 1930), 41.

attainment of Socialism." 3) The Trade Unions had thrown in their lot with the Party and therefore were expected to press for Socialism in the industrial field. 4) Their objective therefore was a satisfactory standard of life for everybody and " satisfactory relationship between man and man cannot be got without Socialism." 5) Now he faced realism: A slump was good for the Party with its ability to compromise; bad for Trade Unions, harnessed to the ebb and flow of trade. Conversely a boom was bad for the Party and good for Trade Unionism. 6) But unions must never assent to permanent acceptance of Capitalism: " The politicians must not compromise us so as to damage the strategic position of the Trade Unions, or the Trade Unions so as to hamper the Labour Party." Both aim toward Socialism and the abolition of Capitalist employers for whom there should never be recognition of their " right to exist." Of course, while they exist they must be recognized. 7) Cole did not approve of a Socialist Party based on individual membership; better, a *working-class* basis to " guarantee *devotion* to the interests of the *whole people.*" (The italics indicate the contradiction which Cole did not recognize. Of course, without individual memberships the bloc working-class basis produced artificial homogeneity.) 8) Trade Unionists were to take comfort from the statement that " the Labour Party as constituted " makes the fullest provision for the *internal* expressions of the Trade Union point of view. Whatever the meaning of " *internal expression* " may be, Cole's self-contradictions had a clear meaning: The subjugation of unions to the furtherance of Socialism.[73]

Cole held week-end parties at Easton Lodge where invited guests discussed the problem of credit. Mosley was among them with John Strachey " his ghost." [74] The Labour Members of Parliament were said to be dejected concerning the Government but the group which met at Easton Lodge worried the Fabian Reporter more.[75] Mosley had proposed his " Dictatorship of Five " and

---

[73] *Ibid.,* the fourth point furnishes support to the definition of social democracy as a secular religion.

[74] *The Clarion,* III:1 (January, 1931), 3. The almost worshipful attitude of Strachey toward Mosley is described.

[75] In this period of dejection, Vernon Hartshorn died. Mrs. Hamilton used her pen to influence the selection of Dr. Addison, a recent convert to

eighteen members of the Party signed it. (Their names appear in another connection.) *The Clarion's* writer himself maintained the confidence that one man among those present would save the Movement: Ernest Bevin, the Trade Union leader, had learned his economics on the Macmillan Commission, and on the Banking and Economic Advisory Committee—his minority report had been "deadly orthodox." He would not let his four million union men be divided in a "New Party" Movement. He was likely to be the next Prime Minister.[76]

In a time when it was still thought the Government would last for two or three years—a point which alone indicates the lack of comprehension of the fiscal problem of England and the world— when Labour M.P.'s were still enthusiastic for the Government, the Trade Union body stood forth in distinction from the rest of the Party. A bitter feeling resulted from the success the Trade Unionists achieved in speaking directly in Committee against the abuses sought to be rectified by the Anomalies Bill. The Bill made lawful some means of checking admitted abuses: Printers, for example, who by working three days earned £6 a week were collecting benefits for the other days.[77] Working wives of working husbands created a problem for local poor law administrators.[78] The remedy was devised by TUGC.[79] Against the corrective measure stood the "loud speakers" for Socialism, who were critical of the Government, as Tom Williams wrote in *The Clarion*.[79] He also stated that the Government should not penalize those suffering "the results of the failure of the capitalist system," suggesting as the excuse for "poplarizing," the idea of making reparation for Capitalism in society.[80] In the midst of the success of Trade Unionists in correcting some abuses the "Zip" was founded embodying Cole's ideas, the Society for Socialist Inquiry and

Labour and often singled out for praise by the lady Fabian M.P., to replace Hartshorn—a doctor *vice* a miner. *The Clarion,* III :1 (January, 1931), 11.

[76] Commentators thought an election was at least eighteen months away and again Mrs. Hamilton, (*ibid.*), urged a "restatement of aims." It would not be strange to find a future student willing to entertain the notion that Socialism was put over by a sort of hypnosis caused by reiteration of aims.

[77] *The Clarion,* III :8 (August, 1931), 235.

[78] *The Clarion,* III :7 (July, 1931), 195.

[79] *Ibid.,* (August, 1931), p. 235.

[80] *Ibid.* This psychological device has had wide usage.

Propaganda. The need for such was evinced, said the Fabian reporter, in the apologetic attitude on Socialism taken by Mr. Bevin. "Zip" would lay the conclusions on various aspects of Socialism before "ordinary folks" and publish the results "for the guidance of the Labour Party." This sort of work was that done "quietly and unobtrusively by the Fabian Society to whose Executive Mr. Cole was recently elected." [81] The "guidance of the Labour Party" meant dictation to the Trade Unions by the intelligentsia. The need for guidance was evinced by the apologetic Trade Unionist. [82]

The Trade Unions seem to have annoyed their Party's M.P.'s at times. Mrs. Hamilton wrote in April of 1931, "Nothing to Grouse About," but she scolded: "The Trade Unions can't hand over all their babies to Westminster to carry." [83] This was nothing more than an outburst of petulance for a Socialist society intended indeed to carry all labor's problems to Westminster—or carry all Westminster's to 11 Dartmouth Street. An idea of subsidiarity or automatic welfare within an association unconnected with the State was never countenanced in their system of industrial democracy. So while Trade Unions were not to overburden with their peculiar problems, the political machinery, they were supposed to learn Socialism better and be guided by Fabians in their relations with the Party. Nevertheless, the Trade Union leader saved the Movement from the Mosley "New Party" on one hand and the Maxton impracticalities on the other by disregarding Mosley's pleas and evolving an "anomalies" bill to put a stop to needless relief expenditures. Meantime, the Trade Unions were developing a plan for currency expansion—to be extinguished in its incipiency.

---

[81] *The Clarion,* III:7 (July, 1931), 195. In the same article the Fabian expressed great displeasure with the Dockers who had on a recent occasion appeared quite ignorant of this Socialist vocation and had acted like mere union laborers.

[82] Bevin seems to have become a Fabian only in the re-birth of 1936, as we have learned from Mrs. Cole. His position in the International made it necessary to belong to a Socialist society. Mr. Cole, the moving spirit along with John Parker from these years until the present date, kept the Trade Unionist in the orbit of Fabianism for his "guidance."

[83] *The Clarion,* III:4 (April, 1931), 103.

D. FABIAN FRONT COVERS CONFLICT OF BACK-BENCHERS *versus*
THE REST

While the Fabians tried to contain the forces of Trade Unionism, a rear guard attack was directed against them by the "back-
benchers." In July of 1929, the Fabian advice to the ILP was
that it should do Socialism not politics because ILP in political
action could only duplicate the Labour Party's work. It was
almost a censure for infidelity to add, "we cannot pride ourselves
equally (as upon the programme of the Labour Party) upon the
number of convinced Socialists belonging to the Labour Party."
This could have purported censure of the Trade Unionists, but
it was part of a paragraph dealing with ILP. The latter had
fallen down on its function of producing propaganda.[84] In January, 1930, the ILP back-benchers voted against the Government
on an amendment to the Coal Bill at its second reading. Mrs.
Hamilton reported this with scorn.[85] As she had sponsored Dr.
Addison she now extended recognition to a daring young Welsh
miner, Aneurin Bevan, a man well liked by back-benchers. She
seemed to appeal to pride of association to be shared with her in
the company of William Graham, Tom Williams (a *Clarion*
writer), G. Edwards, and Vernon Hartshorn. She said their
speeches were especially admirable. (The speeches of back-
benchers were less graceful to say the least than those of the
Oxonians of the front bench, and less recondite than those of the
scholars of London University or London School of Economics.)
We know that only when writing his memoirs did Kirkwood repent
of his wild manners. Still, he is rarely named by Fabians.

Mrs. Hamilton was Glasgow-born herself; her literary attainment was marked. At this time, while praising leaders' speeches,
she congratulated Margaret Bondfield who was a noted union
organizer and long a Fabian, for her silent gathering of "collective wisdom" for her "Clause 4"—part of the Unemployment
Insurance Act of 1926, amended 1929, whereby burden of proof
that work had been sought by an applicant for relief or placement
was laid upon the Labour Exchanges. The wise Miss Bondfield

---

[84] *The Clarion,* 1:7 (July, 1929), 4.
[85] "The Session's Work," *The Clarion,* II:1 (January, 1930), 5.

said little, listened to all discussion and made an amalgam of all ideas on the topic. She was offered as a model for talkative ILP backbenchers. When in February, Mrs. Hamilton praised the " classless Parliament " in which the Labour Party was remarkable because " they believe[d] in something," a Party in which there were no " nonentities " (as in the Liberal Party) and no " persons of no occupation " (one supposes this to mean the investor Tories), all the encomiums went to Fabians after the Prime Minister who was said to be " masterly ": Snowden, Henderson (her youth was accountable for her saying Henderson was " growing "), Graham and Morrison. " The Front Bench is far stronger than in 1924." [86] Despite her efforts to smooth the surface, the back-benchers constantly complained of the class and the snobbery of the front benches. " Rebels or Robots " clarioned the editor reporting on an occasion when forty-eight young vigorous rebels listened sympathetically to Maxton's " great speech " and a debate between Mrs. Hamilton, M.P., and John Reckitt, M.P. Then Maxton, M.P., had summed up. Patience made the gradualist; impatience, the Communist; courage and the spirit to do it now, the ILP. *The Clarion* writer wished Henderson and Hugh Dalton, the wise ones, had been present.[87] Instinctively the need for the Fabian emollient revealed itself.

The ILP was reminded there must be no " parting of the ways," and there must be Party discipline. Again, gradualness was the principle opposed to Maxton's " Socialism in Our Time." [88] To placate ILP the Reporter reassured them there would be no agreement with Liberals except that but just then arrived at: Labour would not be turned out until an Electoral Reform Bill was passed.

On the current debates on amending the Trades Disputes Act of 1927, again readers found " ILP Rebels." [89] In the Budget debate, the scene became theatrical. Pethick-Lawrence, who was also a member of ILP but a Fabian and a front-bencher, was more a monetary expert than Snowden and, as Financial Secretary to the Treasury, he had charge of the defense of Snowden's Budget.

---

[86] *The Clarion,* II :2 (February, 1930), 37.

[87] *The Clarion,* II :5 (May, 1930), 139. Reckitt was a Christian (Anglo-Catholic) Socialist.

[88] *Ibid.,* 130.

[89] *Ibid.,* 131.

The House was more impolite to him than to Snowden who, in 1927, had resigned from ILP in a formal letter. The back-benchers led by Maxton—the Reporter said he was "impractical"—protested Snowden's statement that the programme called for no greater taxes next year. They maintained that the Labour Party's Programme called for expenditure rising higher, and increasingly higher taxes. Churchill played the Left against the Party and entertained the House by mimicking, while he was debating, the gestures which Pethick-Lawrence had made in futilely signaling to the back-benchers to cease interrupting. If Lloyd George was dictating the Lab-Lib parliamentary policy, Churchill and the Tories (Baldwin obstructing Neville Chamberlain's rise to the premiership) were preparing the rift in Labour's ranks for their own break-through. When it came and only then, the pleaded-for discipline was, ironically, duly observed; the Labour Party stood together against the MacDonald-Snowden-Bondfield coup, and Fabians devised the tactics.

The Clarion editorial of May, 1930,[90] listed two reasons why Maxton's idea to tax the wealthy out of existence was impractical. This would "clog the wheels" before Socialism replaced Capitalism; this would make matters worse even if it produced a Socialist state. (This was also Shaw's criticism of Lenin's pre-NEP system). He also listed three reasons for resisting the ILP agitation: Labour had only a minority government; industry was not yet in the control of the State, that is, the State did not control the flow of capital. Until then, there should be no higher taxes, for to impose higher taxes would cause a flow of capital abroad and act as a deterrent to industrial development. "First let the state control the use to which the country's capital is put, then higher taxation will be the only means of maintaining the State through a *transition to Socialism.*"

Thus did Professor Laski's former student recite his principles. The hallmark of London University is plain.

"To the Mother of Parliaments"[91] was a rebuke to both the back-benchers and the older Fabians. The young Fabian seemed

---

[90] *Ibid.*, 141.

[91] *The Clarion*, II:9 (September, 1930), 259. This unnoted advice was repeated as blame by Norman Angell after the 1931 collapse.

to wish to blame the sentiments of the Old Gang for the Government's slowness of which the back-benchers complained: Labour had "lost its head"; evidently back-benchers and others pined to be in Opposition. After all, unemployment (a topic upon which speeches made for constituents' attention were repeated over and over again) was not Labour's fault. Admittedly there remained unfulfilled, the election promises; gradualness however inevitable was painfully gradual; the "old brilliant speculations" were missing. Perhaps there was something to be said for the Webbs' plan to reorganize Parliament into two sections, one political and one social; but then, Shaw had said "Capitalism will burst it [Parliament]." Could they not wait? Professor Laski's words were in the editor's memory when he advised they must "*determine*" for the present generation and the future "the kind of civilization that the community desires to maintain." He did not intend to be amusing.

The ILP could hardly take guidance toward Party discipline from such an editorial, so marked by neutralizing positive and negative charges.

Then, there was a wrangle over subsidizing Opera. The back-benchers screamed "luxury" when the Government made available to the BBC a share of the Post Office license money. P. R. Leslie, while he showed that this did not increase the drain on the Treasury, thought the BBC had been "handed over" to the Covent Garden Syndicate and the Beecham (Sir Robert was then a Fabian) Imperial League of Opera.[92] To read in Kirkwood's autobiography the struggle which he maintained to achieve the recommencement of building the Queen Mary in order merely to sustain life in the Clydeside community is to appreciate the attitude of the ILP lawmakers toward increased cultural benefits.[93] They became more "doctrinaire" to press their causes.

---

[92] Beecham called himself, at the Jubilee concert in 1950, a one-time Fabian. Fabian Granville-Barker meantime advocated a subsidy for Drama. *The Clarion*, III:12 (December, 1930), 364.

[93] This term "lawmakers" used in this connection is anomalous; it confounds a social problem with a legal method. Mrs. Webb tried to solve the anomaly by inventing another Chamber. The anomaly was created by the surrender to the legislature on the part of societary units of their own

The " classless parliament " was less classless than Mrs. Hamilton hoped it would be. " Don't Play the Enemy's Game " she admonished in December, 1930. She explained that India and the Round Table Discussion then in progress was the politically important thing. While the Government concentrated upon it there was reason for reassurance in the domestic field: Dr. Addison was handling Land Utilization, and was very efficiently abetted by Major Attlee and Tom Johnston. True, Dr. Drummond Shiels had poor luck in the matter of the Palestine White Paper but MacDonald was doing very well. (She was not specific about MacDonald, generally.) There was some accord with the Liberals on the question of the school-leaving age; and the Liberals had an agreement with the Tories on economizing on governmental expenditures. Mrs. Hamilton hinted that the back-benchers might help preserve the balance.[94] This was but a continuation of her admonitions and encomiums. In August of 1930, she faced the problem which so agitated the back-benchers: The relief machinery, she confessed, was collapsing all along the line; nevertheless, she said, 95% of those applying to the exchanges got help. Comparing the Parliamentary Labour Party to a cricket team, she singled out certain names, the team's boast. They were all Fabians; a few were also ILP: Graham, fighting against hostile and vacillating opinion in the House of Lords on Coal; Morrison working out a traffic bill for the basis of nationalizing this key industry; Henderson, the best ever to hold the Foreign Office, in control of " the machine "; Alexander, who handled questions " beautifully "; the law officers were a tower of strength—Melville and Cripps. Heading the Consultative Committee, Henry Snell, although silent, was the ablest and best informed of men. He could " steady " the " fussers." Drummond Shiels recorded Snell's hard work on Colonial matters, specifically at Geneva on the question of " Forced Labour." [95] There was John Scurr the

---

responsibility for economic welfare, the politicizing, in other words, of social elements having an economic purpose.

[94] *The Clarion*, II : 12 (December, 1930), 346.

[95] Webb's anonymity in the Colonial Office at this time is interesting. *The Clarion* said he was " happy " in the Colonial Office. Mrs. Cole said he was unhappy over the Palestine embarrassment.

admirable chairman of the Standing Committee on Housing.[96]
Mrs. Hamilton mentioned C. R. Buxton, also, (the Buxton and
Scurr families were friends and ILP members, also Fabians).
She mentioned also the " yeoman service " in " briefing " the Party
given by Colonel L'Estrange Malone, and singled out Ernest
Thurtle and Chuter Ede [97] along with a " new man," Philip Noel
Baker—all Fabians. Stephen Sanders and W. B. Taylor, an
" accepted authority " on foreign affairs, were listed. The weakest
part of the machine, she noted, was the back-benchers, always
against the Government by habit, in " arrogant egoism " seeking
" cheap newspaper reputations." Mrs. Hamilton lectured them:
The essence of Socialism, she said, was supporting the Government; for " The Government acted consistently in a Socialist
spirit "; they were laying the foundations for public control and
increasing the consuming power of the masses; the Economic
Advisory Council was effectual to these ends.[98]

There was never any indication that this effort settled the turbulence. In January, 1931, " Certain individuals " garnered publicity from anti-Labour peers. This may have been meant to
indicate Mr. Mosley. Measures to placate the " left-wingers "
were, as usual, offered. At a recent caucus, when the Prime Minister had been present,[99] it was agreed the Party would drive for
the Alternative Vote, would regulate the use of motor cars—that is,
their use in driving persons to the polls; and would, they promised
again, repeal the Trades Dispute Bill.[100] There was some warning
of an attempt to be made to cut unemployment benefits. Throughout the period there was agitation to reorganize Agriculture. Land
Utilization and a Marketing Bill were on the calendar. As to the
School Attendance Bill, Mrs. Hamilton stated positively that no

---

[96] John Wheatley with whom Mrs. Hamilton had disagreed *in toto* was
dead. Scurr fell from Fabian grace over the School Bill and died in 1932
having received a papal blessing through Cardinal Bourne.

[97] Ede was identified with Surrey County Teachers Association, a Fabian
and member of the National Labour Club.

[98] *The Clarion*, II :8 (August, 1930), 277.

[99] This was noted as an " advantage." Webb and Laski were later to
ascribe to MacDonald's " aloofness " blame for the debacle of 1931.

[100] *The Clarion*, III :1 (January, 1931), 11.

religious problem would retard its progress now as in 1929.[101]
The Lords had backed Graham on a Dyestuffs Act aimed at taking
control of production from the textile industry; Shinwell was
overcoming the noble Lords who were " mangling " the Coal Act.
And Mrs. Hamilton found that all these items were " foundation
stones " without which the erection of Socialism was impossible.
The persons singled out for notice were Fabians. The back-
benchers gave no evidence of being mollified.

In July of 1931, the Reporter told of a " raging battle " between
the rebels and the front bench. This was only a month before the
National Government was formed. It gives rise to the question of
how many more of the anti-back-benchers were expected by Mac-
Donald to follow him than actually did.[102] He had come to the
conclusion that it was best to split his Party.[103] The above-mentioned incident so distracted the Reporter that, remembering Shaw
he wished the war games then being practiced might be real and
that bombs might fall on Parliament. He no doubt had seen or read
Shaw's *Heartbreak House,* which ends on lines expressive of such
a wish.[104] As to the cause of his distraction: The ILP was unreasonably seeking to amend the Anomalies Bill; the radical,
Charles Trevelyan, had actually questioned the sincerity of the
Government in introducing this Trade Union measure, accusing

---

[101] Cf. Tom Shaw's opinion against retaining the " conscience clause " in
The Clarion, 21, n.s. (January, 1929), 3. The stand on the School Bill of
1929 by which Catholics evidenced their devotion to conscience above Party
so impressed Mr. Laski that in his *The Constitution and the Crisis* he noted
the need for religious conviction, a " faith " to conduct and impel Socialists
toward their final struggle.

[102] MacDonald said Henderson was about to follow him until TUC
" intervened." Probably Henderson would have liked to carry TUC and the
Party with him behind MacDonald. Certainly the attitude of Webb, Laski,
ILP and Zip forbade it.

[103] Cf. Feiling, *op. cit.,* p. 193.

[104] Undeniably, an element in Socialist ranks felt that only fiscal catastrophe
would bring about their desired end, " Socialism now." They had been
taught by Fabians like Webb and Pethick-Lawrence that the nation could
afford and could find the money for handling the Socialist State just as it
found the money to run the war; hence, they should see no reason why the
Socialist Government could not find the money to handle fiscal (Capitalistic)
collapse. After all, their wise one had preached this and so they were hardly
to be censured for naivety.

them of not really seeking to obviate the anomalies of the dole but to make "a mean little bit of economy"; the Tories were cunningly delighted (Steel Maitland said he was voting for the Bill but wondered what Labour would have said had *he* introduced it) ; and the back-benchers continued in rebellion, sniping against the Government. The Reporter went on: Mosley's followers were returning to the fold. Mosley himself was never really in the Party. (Of course, he came into the Party by the way of becoming a Fabian.) It was the end of the ILP. Now Maxton, the man of "charm," was boycotted by the rest of the ILP. These in turn were "furious" with Jimmy Thomas. (Snowden said Thomas never asked for any funds from the Exchequer which were for an unsound purpose.) This Fabian correspondent hinted that Thomas should have delayed introducing his measures until the back-benchers were all abroad in Vienna attending the Labour and Socialist International.[105]

In the August issue, in contrast with this turbulence, again the lady Fabian spoke of MacDonald as the "best man available for the momentous crisis." The ILP had "stabbed him in the back"—this Prime Minister who possessed a "genuine international viewpoint." Mrs. Hamilton laid claim for thanks to MacDonald and Henderson that British "authority" was highest in the world. She had but just said that France, suspicious regarding the Austro-German tariff union, had spoiled the effect of the "great moratorium proposal" of President Hoover. The ILP and the "New Party" (Mosley's) headed by the former president of the Board of Education (Trevelyan) attacked the Anomalies Bill and worked against the Trade Unions in the amending of the Trades Disputes Act of 1927, which had been "redressed" in 1929, Mrs. Hamilton reminded her readers. Tories had moved a vote of Censure on the Agricultural policy of the Government following the revelation of the Party weakness made by back-bench tactics. Land Utilization, Agricultural Marketing, Rural Housing Bills were about to be put upon the Statute book. The benefits of small holdings allotments, low-cost housing, marketing machinery (price controls), and the providing of "national direction" for large scale farming facilities were listed. Understandably, "the

---

[105] *The Clarion*, III :7 (July, 1931), 227.

Land Lords " Party opposed the agricultural proposition and took advantage of the fissure observable in Labour Party solidarity. " Electoral Reform " having been defeated in Lords, the Peers were labelled " reactionary " and " class-conscious." However, since the Tories were still willing to hand over to Labour the " terrific " problems of the day, there would be no election for at least two years.[106]

Before the next month's issue of the *Clarion* there was a National Government and an Election followed in November. Looking back over the conflict with the back-benchers we see some causes.

The Party in power had been injured by its incongruous parts. Political Fabians cajoled the back-benchers without avail. The raging battle over the anomalies bill had betrayed the Party and the Premier. It was hard enough to counteract the tidal attraction of Mosley on one side and Maxton on the other, without having to contend with the back-benchers' disregard alike for the superior brains of those named to elicit their respect and the self-interest of the English Trade Unionists. In little matters the mentality of the back-benchers was revealed: Their disdain for Liberals and their scorn for custom, costume, and protocol; their philistine attitude toward the great " spiritual " aims of the devisers of the monolithic State such as music and drama. Facts suggest that MacDonald had some reason for believing that he could take the moderates with him.

The all-smoothing *NS* had characterized the Maxton-Cook revolt of 1928 as " not serious." All-understanding and poised, it had pointed out that these young men wanted " Socialism in our time; " they were shocked at the sight of Trade Unions in friendly conference with employers. Illogically, *NS* also said, such " friendly conferences " the Labour Party had " rudely " refused to adopt. Then it went on to state its long view which might well have been MacDonald's:

> That one day a more or less clear cut socialist party will mark itself off from the Labour Party is pretty certain, we think. But that day is not yet, and this manifesto is

[106] *The Clarion*, III : 8 (August, 1931), 228.

likely to prove a futile gesture rather than the first step in a grand new frontal attack on Capitalism.[107]

The Webbs themselves had by 1930 chosen out of the men on all sides, to replace both Passfield and Parmoor in Lords, the one most near to Tory mentality, the man then receiving the ecomiums of the Conservative Press, Philip Snowden. But the Prime Minister must have misread the reason for the apparent agreement of the Webbs with a right-wing policy. In his telling of the story of 1931, Webb touched upon the Party conflicts and passed on to vilify MacDonald. The Webbs were not satisfied, according to Mrs. Cole, with the idea of a Labour Party. Their idea of an Order would perhaps have channelized the energies of the ardent and the staid, if only by repression, or in Cole's phrase, " internal expression." Mrs. Webb saw contradiction in the attempt to solve social problems of an economic nature by a political unit of legal mentality and she invented another kind of Parliament which she explained in the December, 1930, issue of *The Clarion*.[108] In general, it aimed at doing away with the House of Lords and creating two Parliaments or a political and a social section—" The Machine That Will Work " was Lord Ponsonby's expression. Mrs. Webb's Parliament bore no resemblance to the corporative state. Although it showed respect for the products of autonomous associationalism it did not conceive of the existence of unpoliticized associations. In the face of the fiscal realities posed for MacDonald in 1931, such schemes seemed, no doubt, inconsequential. But workers or their vocal leaders were bemused. Citrine in his preface to the *LYB* of 1931, remarked that there was a " stirring of the dry bones of politics " caused by Labour's insistence upon progressive and democratic planning by States where Labour took power, to relieve mankind of the ills of an archaic system.[109] The Labour leader seemed to imagine that politics had long been dead bones which Labour had revived. (Labour had been more like a burr under the saddle of politics.) It is understandable that Labour leaders so recently going into

---

[107] *NS*, XXXI:791 (June 23, 1928), 346.

[108] *The Clarion*, II:12 (December, 1930), 343.

[109] Cf. *LYB* (1931), p. iii. This ascribed to systematic agitation, spontaneity.

politics imagined politics had never been lively until they appeared upon the scene. Not only was the Movement a new force, as evinced by Citrine and the Webbs, it exhibited naive conceptions which MacDonald, now long inured to the realities of politics, failed to comprehend.

E. FABIANS AGAINST THE SYSTEM: EMERGENT IDEA OF DICTATORSHIP

Fabian Hamilton Fyfe wrote " Why Not Get This Peer Business Out of the Way? " The situation he described as " Peers *vs* People " arose from the fact that some of the legislation which had passed the House of Commons had been blocked in the House of Lords.[110] Fyfe found it deplorable that the Party clung to antiquated ways and even created Labour peers. Of course, Labour picked its peers from those who had no sons in order to defeat the hereditary principle.[111] Fyfe now pressed the attack on the Lords made by the former Prime Minister's son, Oliver Baldwin. The latter had contributed to *The Clarion* for a few months in 1929. His ardor for Socialism with a Soviet quality brought him into conflict with most of the political leaders of Labour. He was a Fabian and a Mosley Manifesto signer. Inveighing against the " aged hoary system." he said the Labour Ministers had forgotten their Socialism and had placed belief in Civil Service servants. These permanent officials were running the Government. Oliver Baldwin disapproved of Tom Shaw's acquiescing in the " voluntary " army enlistment system; he complained of "too much Jowittism ";[112] he questioned Clynes about the ban on Russian films (Clynes answered that it was not in the public interest to explain); he found fault with Miss Bondfield for agreeing to strike off the rolls of the Labour Exchanges those " not genuinely seeking work "—the n.g.s.w. cases. He did approve of Susan Lawrence, of Hugh Dalton, and, for his directness and firmness of Charles Trevelyan. Nevertheless, he said, " Yes, Comrades, I

---

[110] Much had become law. Cf. *LYB* (1931), pp. 230–382.

[111] *The Clarion,* III:4 (April, 1931), 107.

[112] He was referring to a convert to Labour, the new Attorney General, A. W. Jowitt K.C., a minister's son, now Viscount Jowitt. Since 1922 he had served as a member of the Royal Commission on Lunacy.

am disappointed ": Bondfield and Thomas had not tackled the problems of currency and credit, due no doubt to the influence of the Bank of England.

We are indebted to Comrade Oliver for a list of backbenchers: the Welsh miner Aneurin Bevan,[113] the Scotsman Fenner Brockway, a Fabian, W. J. Brown, a Fabian, and Fabians Roden Buxton and Somerville Hastings.[114] Young Baldwin also supplied further evidence of contradiction, for while he saw continuity in the Young Plan, the editor pointed out that Snowden had destroyed its continuity with the Dawes Plan. Although Baldwin thought that the restoring of the gold standard had depressed the standard of living, brought on the Strike, increased unemployment and induced Stanley Baldwin's downfall, all the measures he sponsored were social rather than fiscal, except his original one—to nationalize royalties. This would have gone hard on the Fabians.[115] Oliver Baldwin is significant only because so early he started the ever-continuing criticism of the Government: In September, 1929,[116] he began complaining of the Ministry's failure to handle certain relief cases which he had forwarded to them from his vacation place where he, deploring the fact, was obliged to enjoy three months with pay for no work. The puritan strain was strong in some of these Socialists. In November, he came back with " Tackle the Banks ";[117] but far from analyzing the Bank problem he singled out Thomas to accuse him of merely selling coal in Ottawa, while Henderson, he said, was the most effectual of officials at Geneva. Snowden, he said, had showed at the Hague that he would produce no Socialism. More Socialism should come from Noel-Buxton's Agriculture programme but if the " family allowance " scheme went into effect it should only be with provision for information concerning birth control to accompany payments.

Baldwin was the type of the audacious youth that Professor Laski was to call upon to forward Socialism after the fall of 1931.

---

[113] His name appears on a Fabian lecture schedule in 1942. So far his services had not been required on the international scene.

[114] *The Clarion,* I :8, n.s. (August, 1929), 7. Not named was Jenny Lee, very active.

[115] *The Clarion,* I (September, 1929), 2.

[116] *The Clarion,* I :9, n.s. (September, 1929), 7.

[117] *The Clarion,* I :11, n.s. (November, 1929), 7.

His previous attack on the efficiency of Miss Bondfield had been answered by Tom Williams, M.P., in October.[118] Williams was her Parliamentary Private Secretary. Denying that she was subservient to the civil service officers, he showed how impossible it was to do better under a law which was made up of twenty Acts of Parliament, which involved, ordinarily, 45,000 umpire decisions annually, required 700 local officers, and 400 labour exchanges, a court of referees, an insurance officer and an umpire. It was, in the end, those officers who were criticized by the young radical,— Bondfield, Snowden, Thomas—who, with Tom Johnston, followed MacDonald into the National Government.

Baldwin left *The Clarion* staff when Mrs. Hamilton and C. Delisle Burns joined it in January, 1930.[119] The trend toward destructive criticism of Parliament and of ministers and the tendency to countenance the idea of dictatorship did not change. The editor disclosed the latter tendency in his expressions. Although he wished that Shaw would acquire some new ideas or desist from lecturing to the Fabian Society because his ideas on education were twenty years old and he "made a charlatan attack on democracy," this son of Alderman Davies never rebuked his professor, Harold Laski, for his doubts about democracy. As part of the attack on democracy, systems of control or State Planning were contemplated. An Englishman and a Fabian, G. E. C. Catlin, then a professor at Cornell, wrote "Mastering the Machine" for the issue of October, 1930.[120] Quoting Bevin on "conscious control of economic factors and forces" Catlin rejected the Trade Unionist "rationalisation" as a Liberal idea not a Socialist one, and went on to advocate a National Planning Council which would involve, he said, "political rationalisation" and social control. He made the conclusive step in November when again he wrote "crisis in Britain." This time he quoted Maxton, "a Christian martyr," who had said: "If you can't get international socialism, will you take *national socialism* or do you prefer to have nothing?" According to Catlin and Maxton, Russian State Socialism was not for "the glory of the State, but the glory of the Community." No one asked the Cornell pro-

---

[118] *The Clarion*, I :10, n.s. (October, 1929), 9.
[119] *The Clarion*, I :12, n.s. (December, 1929), 7.
[120] *The Clarion*, II :10 (October, 1930), 282.

fessor if by " community " was meant the soviet, the zemstvo, the village, an extension of one of these terms to embrace the idea of Nation, or the reduction of the idea of State to the service-function implied in any of the terms. Catlin followed Maxton in advocating a State Planning Committee for the home market and the dependencies, to eliminate dependence upon foreign markets.[121] The currency given the idea of State Planning made it possible even to ask " Do we want a Dictator? " There was Thomas who needed to be a dictator to achieve anything concrete in the way of increased production for jobs and increased outlet for trade. For once the editor sympathized with the harassed Thomas, now Minister for the Dominions. Nevertheless, he thought Thomas leaned too near the Tories, and he considered Beaverbrook and Rothermere in their Empire Campaign not unlike Mussolini.[122] If he turned to the Thomas critics there was Mosley whose one ideal was Hitler.[123] On the other hand, there was Bertrand Russell, cynical and witty, " destroying faith in Democracy " in favor of his " old love "—Anarchy. Even though *The Clarion* complained that there was no new blood in the Fabian lecture series, it began at this time to print the lectures of Russell, Mrs. Webb, and Laski.[124]

The Mosley problem had been acute in June, 1930, and that scion of wealth had aired his grievance with the Party for hours on end in Parliament. Then the Prime Minister, as the Reporter noted, had been fighting on four fronts [125]—the Naval Conference, the Unemployment problem, the Party imbalance drawing his attention from far-left to near-Tory, the menace of Dictatorship. When in December, 1930, Mosley again came forth with a manifesto demanding a " dictatorship of the five," fifty percent of the

---

[121] *The Clarion*, II:11 (November, 1930), 314.

[122] *The Clarion*, II:6 (June, 1930), 171.

[123] *Ibid.* (November, 1930), 311.

[124] *The Clarion*, II:11 (November, 1930), 311. Thomas paid dearly for his modicum of sympathy. By the following November he was expelled from the Party's Executive, and from the N.U.R., his pension illegally cancelled. Cf. Thomas, *op. cit.*, pp. 196–198. Thomas was convinced that the rank and file had no knowledge of his defence, which was printed but not permitted to be circulated, and that left-wingers hostile to him since 1921 were responsible for his ill treatment.

[125] *The Clarion*, II:6 (June, 1930), 163.

appended names were those of Fabians. The signers of the Mosley Manifesto of December 7, 1930, were these, as given in the *Daily Herald*: Fabians Sir Oswald Mosley, MP, Oliver Baldwin MP, L. Lovat Fraser, MP, J. P. Horrabin, MP, Lady Cynthia Mosley, MP, H. T. Muggeridge, MP, M. Philips Price, MP, (PPS to Graham) E. J. Strachey, MP, S. F. Markham, MP (replaced Weir as PPS to MacDonald); [126] and these Miners, Aneurin Bevan, MP,[127] W. G. Cove, MP (now of the National Executive of the Union of School Teachers), J. Bates, MP, and A. J. Cook; and these ILP Back-benchers W. J. Brown (also a Fabian), Doctor R. Forgan, MP, John McGovern, MP (successor to Wheatley), J. J. McShane, MP, C. J. Simmons, MP.[128]

It helps to understand the Prime Minister's dilemma to consider that the names represented prominent types in his Party: the barrister, the educator, the Maxton-follower, the descendant of some prominent family, the angry coal miner. Idealists, they had made borrowings from the Platonic ideal of an elite; they had more than a hint of fascism in their thinking; and they subscribed to a belief that in order to achieve positive ends social control must involve dictatorship. The Party was not an ordinary political party made up of people of diverse classes, pursuits, vocations, religions, and opinions, who might use Party as a civil implement to call rulers to account. The Labour Party was contrived by collecting the economic coefficients of social units into a quasi-political configuration. An ordinary party shares with its rival party, in the national sum of civil interests—call them political coefficients—[129] inhering in and generated by social units which

[126] Weir, *op. cit.,* p. 435.

[127] Bevan's Fabian lecture in *FN*, 53:6 (June, 1942) noted. An inquiry elicited a very surprised answer from Miss Eve Saville, a clerk in Filson's office, that Fabians had no record of his membership.

[128] *Daily Herald* December 8, 1930, p. 3. Typical Clydesiders' names do not appear.

[129] This writer conceives of politics or civil interest as a sort of electric charge generated in subsidiary social groups—families, businesses, cultural or economic associations. This energy interacts with its like from group to group and unites outside the groups to form the State. An agency of the common good or the common interest, the State is something more, having received the imprint of *majestas* by reason of the divine source of its authority. Within the State society acquires adhesion from the crossing of

are economically or culturally determined and are free of the State though enveloped in the Nation. A State formed by a " Labour " Party must become the usurper of the area of religion because the constituent economic coefficients of men and societies inhere in the realm of ethics. The challenger of the very being of the Labour-State is that capitalism which is defined as voluntary and private enterprise, and is amenable to the private juridical order.[130] Economics, inherent in such capitalism constitutes the prime disputant of the right of the State to usurp the place of religion in ethics, in the family, in enterprise, in association of persons for mutual benefit. The religion of Socialism asks to be allowed to guide economic life toward the material benefit of the community. Material benefit is exactly equivalent to " profit." Religion asks to leave man free to direct within himself by respect for natural law and public statute the profit motive in relation with the common good. The benefits to society of men's being free surpass the description of being mere good feeling arising from allowed or permitted self-will in private persons. These matters had to be learned by the intelligentsia of British Socialism, according to British character, empirically. In 1931, a harassed Prime Minister had to make a choice. It could not be a choice consonant with the quasi-religious socialism he once spoke at Lossiemouth.

The search continues to uncover a single creative idea offered to him as an alternative by his equally harassed mentors. Professor Laski, in debate with Clifford Allen who had been created Lord Allen in 1932, stated that Henderson in the crisis had adduced alternatives; but Laski did not enumerate them.[131] Ideas came but they were all destructive:

A comradely letter from one who signed " Ganzy " referred to Fabian Tom Groom's " Up the Rebels," written to encourage ILP rowdy tactics at a *Clarion* fellowship meeting at Warwick.[132]

---

the horizontal line of socio-economics by the vertical line of politics. To fashion artificial politics out of economics reduces the societary contours to a total horizontal stratification easily manipulated by a Tyrant-State.

[130] The papal expression cited *supra* p. 201 uses " Economics," a word in plural form which implies a nice distinction between the science and its *metier*.

[131] *The Clarion,* IV :2 (February, 1932), 29.

[132] The aristocratic site was the estate of the Countess who wrote of her

" Ganzy " reminded Groom's readers that they ought to 1) show that the church and the present order are interwoven; 2) inculcate the idea that organized religion is Socialism's adversary and must be fought; 3) adopt the Russian five-year plan.[133] Earlier, Fabian Hannen Swaffer, writing of " Religious Persecution," [134] sought to reconcile his readers to the cruelties of Russia's Socialists by equating these to the persecution of Englishmen by Englishmen— the current prosecution of spiritists, and patent discrimination against believers in transubstantiation demonstrated by the point that Anglo-Catholic Bishops could not sit in the House of Lords. This example is not offered because it samples benighted thinking of simple persons of good will. Although Swaffer wrote with a vagabond air, he was nevertheless a noted lecturer and Fabian Summer School teacher. No contradictory reply followed either " Ganzy " or Swaffer. The ecumenical Fabians passed judgment upon moral propositions concerned with the family by approving the rising cult of nudeness practiced in London Parks which were now under the direction of the benevolent Lansbury. " Britannia rules the Heat Waves," it was said and the youth of contemporary demoralized Berlin were presented as exemplars.[135] Irreverence of another kind was evinced by Lord Snell who remarked that bishops should confine their activities to their prayers and not engage in " stabbing Labour in the Back." [136] In the Society, a highly developed microcosm of the Party, the idea of dictatorship was gaining strength and losing its horror, while a tone of irreligion became clearer than ever before.

The conflict with the back-bench mentality heightened the tension because it was so much a conflict within the Fabian Society— 11 Dartmouth Street *versus* Easton Lodge. This conflict was typified in the Webbs themselves. They certainly cared nothing for the Mosley camp or the Ganzy type but they were not sure the Labour Party could produce the effects of an Order. For the

---

conversion to Socialism in *Life's Ebb and Flow.* The use of her good bed, board and automobiles by fatigued workers in the Strike of 1926 is depicted in Susan Lawrence's novel, *Clash.*

[133] *The Clarion,* III :7 (July, 1930), 231.
[134] *The Clarion,* III :5 (May, 1930), 137.
[135] *The Clarion,* I :9, n.s. (September, 1929), 3.
[136] *The Clarion,* III :11 (November, 1931), 311.

Webbs, the Society was becoming too much like the Party. Ideologically, the Party oscillated between the poles of tyranny and anarchy. " Democracy " was impugned by Maxton with his national Socialism, by Mosley abetted by Strachey with the "dictatorship of the Five," by Russell with his anarchy, by Cole with his labour-corps schemes, and by Shaw with his contempt for Parliament. It was not all mischievous : Fabian against Fabian on whether to permeate or abolish the House of Lords ; Fabian in *The Clarion* against Fabian on the back-benches ; ILP Fabians against Fabians in the Government—the more ardent for their Socialism, the less light could they throw on the fiscal perplexity. Yet there was an indefinable common bond ; there were certain agreements, and a common style. Let us call it the " *ubi tendimus* "—that magnetized impulsion toward the new and secular order. (Laski, as cited elsewhere, said the age was " clamant " for a secular way of life.) MacDonald shared the esoteric spirit but his political experience drew him out of the Fabian orbit.

We have said that the challenge of fiscal perplexity produced no creative ideas. The triviality of certain responses would preclude their inclusion here except for the importance they have acquired in later reasoning. For example, at the end of a session in which Mr. Ernest Davies had argued against " rationalisation " and " world price," he fairly shouted " Change the whole system! " For, he averred, he had discovered "where Communists were made "—where this year's debutantes were " presented." [137] Such generalizations provided subterfuge for those unable to present constructive ideas. Once in their past, they had been able to set up a great alternative. They had gathered into Albert Hall a vast crowd unanimous in the insistence that peace, when it came after the first World War, would take the form of a League and a Covenant. Now they were preparing to survey the ruins of an experiment in government, and no great alternative was forthcoming.

F. Fabian Self-Rebuke

In September, the self-analysis following collapse had already begun. Strangely, the materials of the assay were almost entirely

---

[137] *The Clarion,* II :6 (June, 1930), 163.

new. They included a number of fiscal elements hitherto hardly mentioned. There had been a threat to sterling. It was considered to have been manufactured by the Press. It would be suggested that the 'Press had outwitted both the Tories with their ancient Tariff ideas and the Socialists with their hesitations as to tariffs or " cuts." Laski was to write for *The Clarion,* " The Crisis and After " to state that the Socialists considered the maintenance of the whole wage structure to depend upon keeping the floor of insurance benefits under it. Early in September it was being said that it was not due to the May Report that " foreigners " were withdrawing funds; but Lord Passfield declared that such was the case, in his *What Happened.* Without reference to the situation produced by the failure of the proposed Austro-German tariff union, the editor attributed the outflow of gold to the need to replace funds immobilized in Germany. No allusion to the part played by Henderson in favoring France to defeat the *Verein.* " We " had lent money to Germany; Webb refined this to indicate that financial houses in the City had lent money and under the stringency had had to call on the Bank of England when the withdrawal of gold started—as early as 1929. When the Bank rate had been raised before the 1929 election, the Fabian spokesman had objected and cried out that it should be lowered by law; now the Fabian son of Alderman Davies announced that to have borrowed gold and to have raised the Bank rate would have been sufficient to stabilize the financial situation; instead the Press had attacked sterling. At this point the editor did not disclose something which *The Clarion* later boasted was originated by Labourites Bevin and Citrine; the TUC had advocated and agitated, without encouragement from fellow Fabians, the devaluation of the pound sterling to stimulate exports and production.[138] Directly, the Fabian placed the blame for the debacle upon the bankers and financiers of London for loans made to Germany, endangering, he said, the supply of gold in London. A colleague, Tomlinson, M.P., had stated a month before that those loans which had been made to central European States were usurious.[139] Unable to draw conclusions, readers must retain in memory the data previously

---

[138] *The Clarion,* III (November, 1931), 312.
[139] *The Clarion,* III :100 (October, 1931), 288.

presented concerning Alderman Davies' Investment Trusts and the general encouragement given by him to the making of loans to German municipalities and States. It must be recalled at the same time that the Keynes-Lloyd George statement in the financial programme of 1929 campaign pointed to the need to stop this sort of thing, and to develop national assets by putting money to work at home. In the Pethick-Lawrence commentary upon *Labour and the Nation* there had been no objection to Davies' stand expressed weekly in his column " The City " in the *NS*. Nor had a Fabian voice been raised to encourage Pethick-Lawrence in his attack upon the fiscal problem made at the point of the too low prices. *The Clarion* summed up the exhaustion of credit, the precarious state of the budget, the dilemma concerned with economy in payments to the Unemployed, and what it chose to consider Snowden's ineptitude (he had Pethick-Lawrence in his Department) : The collapse had done " immeasurable harm to the Movement." [140]

Two items come up for consideration : 1) There was no general line of hatred for MacDonald reflected in *The Clarion* immediately following the Crisis ; he was considered to have been " heroic " but " unwise," [141] and 2) there is a subtle indication as to why the Webb-Henderson leadership and the far-left stayed together and did not break the Party into two parts, one a moderate-labor faction following MacDonald, and the other a straight Socialist Party. The high tensile common bond of these two ill matched factions is discoverable in the direction taken by the Fabian Socialist mouthpiece : The aim and the job of Socialists must now be not to " get the Capitalists out of the mess," but to exert all energies for Socialism and one day a majority Government. It did not then matter that back in July the Hoover Moratorium had been hailed as so " simple " and so " just " a " miracle " which gave the world back its confidence because it had " given Capitalism a breathing space "—like Russia's Five-Year Plan.[142] Now there was to be no

---

[140] *Ibid.* (November, 1931), 312.

[141] *The Clarion*, III :9 (September, 1931), 254.

[142] *The Clarion*, III :7 (July, 1931), 194. This item had also argued that the Austro-German tariff union had been made necessary by the Versailles inequities and that France must now at least accept the moratorium. But the leadership which now the left-wing followed had sided with France against

quarter for Capitalists. The " floor " of wages was the point upon which the division, MacDonald-Snowden against the rest took place. The rigidity of the wage scale had become a crowbar to wreck Capitalism.

The decision taken by the leadership to repudiate MacDonald— the head but not the leader—was taken to save the Movement. Offered a standpoint of pure Socialism, the left-wing which had really been more critical of the other moderates than of Mac-Donald went with the Fabian leadership. Why did the Trade Unions not break away? The Party leadership knew well by now that they would not. There had been a rehearsal after all. When enticed by the Cole-Mosley novelties, the nearly 4,000,000 Trade Unionists had followed Bevin in solidarity and shunned the " New Party." Why did Bevin follow a lead labelled Socialism, when Trade Unionism is by nature capitalistic? It will be recalled that Bevin had fought the acceptance of Government by the Party when it did not command a majority. It might well be that he preferred to a " Labour " Government the bargaining position of a Party in Opposition, and that a Tory Government suited his purposes by favoring business. The possibility of " the conquest of a mere majority," Laski's step to revolution or civil war was indeed remote in 1931. The Party was saved by a slogan of Socialism. It was saved only in order to save the Movement. If the leadership offered the return to first principles and the re-statement of Social-ism sincerely, in order to shepherd the left-wing flock, it was articu-lating the common bond which would draw them toward the destruction of the " whole system." If it acted with a view presently to keep the segments of the Party together, it aimed at the ultimate rule of the One-Party, by means of the Movement. The British Fabian is not a gradualist without a goal. That goal is not the survival of Capitalism nor the protection of any agency which defends its own right to exist independently of the State. That is why *The Clarion* Fabians did not study fiscal problems, did

---

Austria. Over a year before, Mrs. Hamilton had narrated with complete satisfaction the success of MacDonald in winning American sympathy for the Labour Government and in creating sentiment in the United States against an " isolated war "—presumably against depression. Cf. *The Clarion,* II :3 (March, 1930), 69.

not fall in behind the Prime Minister. The Labourite memoirs of the period are unanimous that the Movement stood firm as a rock. Having counted but 6,000,000 voters, they said this. They had only lost the floating vote and that could be re-won. People could always be induced to imagine that by voting Labour they were voting reform. Six million were enough to form cadres.

Laski complained of " brilliant secrecy." There are some facts which make the need for secrecy understandable. The son of that great financial expert, A. E. Davies, had reported, boastingly, in his monthly that he had a leak from the Cabinet. It seemed a bit imprudent of him since he was an associate of the ex-Prime Minister's Fabian son, Oliver Baldwin.[143] The informant could have been Mr. Weir. Davies revealed that he had this leak at the time when after he had revealed the effort of the Party in Parliament to control the Cabinet through the Consultative Committee, it was said that they had called Thomas' " bluff." Thomas had offered the alternatives: ten percent " cuts "—or tariffs. If the ultimate proposal regarding the fiscal problem had been leaked to the Fabian Socialist publication, the furor would have been astonishing and the results confusing. The Fabian press was not ostensibly backing the Bevin-Citrine devaluation ideas. The Beaverbrook-Rothermere Press, though it was not preaching devaluation was coming near to achieving it by calculated reports. Concerning England's financial state, the Baldwin-MacDonald understanding with George V had to be brilliantly secret. But in October, two months after the Crisis, Davies said MacDonald had believed his duty lay in the direction he had taken.[144] This too might have come from a Cabinet leak, even from a page out of Chamberlain's Diary. Even so, Davies also remarked that MacDonald would now be " unsafe " at the National Labour Club and

---

[143] *The Clarion*, III :10 (October, 1931), 283.

[144] To read the letter which MacDonald sent to Thomas in February 1930, refusing to accept the latter's resignation when Mosley had gone over his head with quasi-fascist schemes, is to learn that the Prime Minister's principal consideration was the national safety—" national interest "—even then. With this motive he obliged Thomas to carry on, and he called Mosley and Strachey to his office for advisement upon their misbehavior. Cf. Thomas, *op. cit.*, p. 172. " None of us is in a position now to follow our feelings; we must endure however hard the road may be."

that at the 1917 Club, the haunt of Intellectuals, discussion about Russia exclusively had ceased. Yet even the revolutionary Jenny Lee, along with Jimmy Maxton, maintained that MacDonald had had no other alternative. He had saved Capitalism from crumbling. Miss Lee stoutly maintained that the only real alternative, was revolutionary Socialism; and, it would seem, they were not ready for it.[145] The need for brilliant secrecy was two-fold: Fabian press agents had a " leak "; wiser heads knew Labour's Left could not be taken into confidence.

This was the time when " Fabians Resolve[d] the Crisis " with a Summer School headed by Lord Passfield; also, when the " opponents of the National Government," Barbara Wootton, A. E. Davies, Norman Angell, S. K. Ratcliffe, H. J. Laski, the youngest, and " of course " G. B. Shaw, the eldest, discussed " Capitalism in Dissolution "—nothing from the Fabians about reassembling the Party, rallying to the political field, adjusting the platform to public opinion. The Fabians went into retreat like religious to study the first principle and foundation of their professed Socialism. That was how they " resolved the Crisis." [146] A very significant note crept into the end of the report: The Reporter had learned, doubtless from his source in the Cabinet or its environs, that the Reverend James Burr,[147] head of the Consultative Committee, had been the one who " called Jimmy's bluff " (by choosing no " cuts " and no tariffs) ; that eight of the Ministers led by Henderson had opposed cuts in unemployment benefits.[148] The story about Burr's interference indicates the attempt to

---

[145] *The Clarion,* III :9 (September, 1931), 255.

[146] *Ibid.*

[147] There were several Protestant ministers who were Labour M.P.'s; Henderson was an ex-minister. Burr replaced the demoted Scurr.

[148] It can be learned from Thomas himself that it was clear that Henderson and his followers had in mind the votes they might lose in an election thought to be imminent. That Thomas was bitterly disliked in a small circle makes it imperative that he be heard. No one worked harder to " rationalize " and to increase both industrial production and colonial trade. No one received less assistance from his colleagues. Lord Snowden testified to the soundness of Thomas' ideas (cf. Snowden, *op. cit.,* II, pp. 775 f) but averred Thomas would need to be a dictator to succeed in getting cooperation from employers or workers.

direct the Cabinet to the ends of the Parliamentary Labour Party.[149]
This would, besides developing a force outside of the machinery
necessary for Liberal cooperation, revolutionize the Parliamentary
system as practiced in Britain since Walpole's day, the system
which supported " Ministerial Responsibility." Lord Ponsonby
had written of a " machine that will work " and currently Shaw
was talking about forces developed outside of Parliament which
were building up strength to reduce to desuetude the negative reactionary thing that Parliament was by its nature.

His informant told Davies that the National Government was
" sprung " without giving time for alternatives to be suggested or
compromise to be reached. But the idea of a National Government could not but have been in the back of the Cabinet Members'
minds. It had been mooted among themselves and in the Press
for some time. It is this question which points to Weir, Mac-
Donald's Parliamentary Private Secretary, as the possible informant of *The Clarion's* reporter; Davies divulged the source
when he told, under the heading " Betraying the PM," [150] that he
was reading the " yet unpublished Memoirs of a friend of mine
well known in London circles." The story here told with argument inspired by animus toward MacDonald is identical with
the story, argument and animus in Weir's *Tragedy of Ramsey
MacDonald.* These memoirs had been written in 1922. Weir
stayed in MacDonald's office until 1931. These memoirs, even as
Weir's later book, traced the history of the idea of a National
Government as far back as 1911. Lord Haldane had been present
when representatives of the Conservative and Liberal Parties had
suggested such a Government and MacDonald had then agreed to
join a Cabinet so formed. The comment does not show that in 1911
the reason for acceptance of such a suggestion was " permeation,"
concerning which there could have been differences as to method.
We have seen how even in 1929 there was a real question as to
whether Labour should join forces with the Conservative or
with the Liberal Party. Chamberlain's part in persuading Mac-
Donald to make the decision he made in 1931 has been noted. It

---

[149] *Ibid.*
[150] *The Clarion,* III :12 (December, 1931), 339 f.

remains to add that Churchill [151] later wrote: " Certainly during the summer I had talked to MacDonald about a national administration and he had shown some interest." Stanley Baldwin, who, as Keith Feiling says, preferred to be in a position to give advice rather than to take action, and who, Churchill says, was the real ruler of England during these years, suggested a National Government to MacDonald and Henderson. The latter refused offhand. It was Baldwin no doubt, of all the advisors, who best knew the King's mind. Henderson doubtless expected a dissolution and an election in which that Party would win the far-left vote which had refused to cut the unemployed benefits. He must have been certain that even if elected with a mandate for Socialism, the Party would have found itself either in conflict with the back-bench mentality or in servitude to it. It was not desirable to win, only to unify or keep the command of the socialist-labour cadre. Henderson, it would seem, did not assume as Harold Laski did that the forces of " property," or the " investing class " would go into revolt and confront an elected Labour Party with civil war. Henderson also had some insight into the King's mind and knew how far he could go after coming into conflict with the King's right to choose a royal favorite to form a Government, the point at which a Socialist majority should logically go into revolt. Henderson's " Party " would get its revolution without either civil war or revolt if it kept " the Movement " intact. His mind is best judged by his action in 1923 when he saw the Baldwin approach to Protection and seized the challenge with, " We'll get an election out of this." The Fabian Society went with Henderson. If he had followed Mac-Donald, England would have reverted to a political complexion half Tory, half Whig. The unions and the agitators would have been liberated, to exert influence on either side at their choice.

In October, Mrs. Hamilton who had written two very friendly biographies of MacDonald broke publicly with him.[152] *The Clarion* readers were told that she who spoke " pure Socialism " and Doctor Addison who was popular with the back-benches were the " only distinguished " Labour M. P.'s now. (The Laski-taught

---

[151] Churchill, *The Gathering Storm*, p. 36.

[152] *The Clarion*, III:10 (October, 1931), 283. Her biographies were patently campaign literature.

editor omitted Fabians Lansbury and Cripps, and also Attlee, who succeeded Lansbury in the leadership.) [153] According to *The Clarion*,[154] the Party had unanimously followed Henderson and its aim had been clarified: Socialism by constitutional means. At the coming pre-election Conference at Scarborough this aim should be implemented. The departure from the gold standard had rendered it easier to attack the *rentier* class by stabilizing the pound at a level below its old parity. Economies would then become unnecessary and control of the Banks would follow speedily. Currently, the depreciated pound was the best thing possible.[155] There would be no need for tariffs, although the Tories would fight the election on the dead Protection issue. (The editor was mistaken. The election was fought as in the autumn of 1924 on the question of Socialism and again fear swayed many voters, the fear raised by the alleged threat to the safety of the Postal Savings fund.)

The Clarion readers saw that Fabians really considered that devaluation was "the best thing possible." The elder Davies thought that the pound should be forthwith stabilized; the younger, that it should be allowed to drop until the *rentier* class should be despoiled.[156] In any case, the stock exchange experienced a boom, export trade revived and a general feeling of optimism pervaded economic life. The "hoarders", (meaning France) had been forced to put money back into circulation. Selling was easier but credit seemed more stringent. Imports were declining and revenue from tariffs was dropping. Living costs were rising. The "poor foreigner" was driven out. (The Davieses tilted with adversaries named "London" and "foreigner." The term, "Germany," cloaked municipalities, States, and industrialists.) The Labour Government, according to the commentator, had not realized that the Party was not in favor of reprieving Capitalism. (The self-

---

[153] The only place where Doctor Addison is to be found associated directly with Fabians is in *FSAR*, May, 1920, p. 11. He was a medical doctor, and an author of books on "politics," for example, *Practical Socialism* (1926), as well as medicine. In 1930, he succeeded C. R. Buxton in the Ministry of Agriculture and Fisheries.

[154] *The Clarion*, III:10 (October, 1931), 282.

[155] *Ibid.*

[156] *The Clarion*, III:11 (November, 1931), 311.

appointed spokesman for the Party had praised the Hoover Moratorium in July which " gave Capitalism a breathing space.") The Labour Government's fall had been inevitable because a point had been reached where " a Government pledged to Socialism could no longer try to save the Capitalist system from the disaster that was overtaking it." [157] Perhaps it must be concluded that the " Party " against the Government stood upon the point of the rigid wage scale and asked for a mandate to rule the ensuing disaster—Davies (*fils*) was close to " Party " councils. Or else this represents reasoning after the fact, and mere " idealism." Ideological motives were not expressed in the Cabinet. Actually, had Henderson won an election his first move would have had to be to follow the Trade Unions' resolution and devalue the pound, to ward off catastrophe.

Now in October, readers were told that the " deserters " had been all along " out of touch with the Movement." To name half of them: MacDonald, Sankey, Thomas,[158] Snowden (of the Cabinet) and Margaret Bondfield, Clifford Allen, Lovat-Fraser, Tom Johnston. Tomlinson indicated in his commentary that he wished to be discreet about their names because the point of view concerning their future treatment was shifting.[159] " No sentiment," said Ernest Davies. They must all be " excommunicated," except Lord Sankey.[160] (There had been no excommunication of Mosleyites.) The ex-Ministers should be presented with bouquets and not asked awkward questions in the House; although they had only " saved their faces " by voting against economies. They had really been " poor Socialists," agreeing to cuts in social services and *not framing a devaluation policy of their own.* (But readers

---

[157] *The Clarion,* III :10 (October, 1931), 282.

[158] It is difficult to call Thomas a Fabian. He was independent of the Society as far as election funds went, having NUR funds at his command; but he had to belong to a Socialist Society of some kind to take his place on the Internationale. He was not ILP.

[159] *The Clarion,* III :10 (October, 1931), 288.

[160] In his judicial character, he had long been above Party; but he was a consistent Fabian. Cf. *FN,* 40 :8 (August, 1929), one of the many instances of association and collaboration in Fabian lecture schedules. Lord Sankey, alone of all those who followed MacDonald, attended the Labour Party conference (Parliamentary) after the National Government was formed. Cf. Williams, *op. cit.,* p. 341.

should have known that, as Tomlinson related, Bevin and Citrine had been " abused " for advocating devaluation.[161])

It seems clear that the National Government went into office with a well-prepared and well-concealed fiscal programme, secretly conceived. The Prime Minister's slogan to " save the Pound " was a political feint. Devaluation must follow upon the " going off the gold standard." The pound was to be " saved " by increasing its purchasing power. Only secrecy could prevent upheaval in the financial world. Actually then, the conflict lay between those who hoped for inevitable destruction of Capitalism by means of gradualness or " erosion," and those whose livelihood and freedom from economic and political dictatorship depended upon Capitalism, particularly the Trade Unions.

A. E. Davies, well known to United States readers, was introduced to *The Clarion* readers in October, 1931, as the noted financial expert he was.[162] In the past as has been said he had given much encouragement to the lending of funds and investing of money in German businesses. " London," he said, (not the Bank of England) had made huge loans to German banks, which were now in trouble. This trouble he did not connect with the rejected Austro-German tariff union or the delaying tactics of the French which destroyed the effects of the moratorium. Austria's Credit Anstalt had collapsed. Davies spoke of it—correctly—as " Rothschild's "; and by doing so transferred the concept of Austria's calamity to a person who could claim little sympathy either in socialist or in anti-semitic circles. He said the high bank rate in England had attracted. " foreign " taking for *short* notice and then the May Report had shown the country to be " living beyond its means " so a run of an alarming kind on the *long* term loans to foreign countries was commenced. The Government's request for a loan from France and America had surrendered English supremacy to France. Davies' pat suggestions were not original: Stabilize the pound (we have seen his son advocated not stabilizing until the *rentier* class should have been despoiled) ; acquire gold by sales; increase exports over imports. It depended, he said, upon the Government whether this would cause living standards to

---

[161] *The Clarion* III :10 (October, 1931), 288.
[162] *Ibid.*, p. 284.

be lowered or not. In this same article Davies justified the allowance to families on the dole which enabled them to recreate at races, and movies and did not limit their right to vote. He charged the Tories with having in the hope of splitting Labour by the dole question revealed the national financial weakness, which revelation had had international repercussions resulting in a drain on gold.[163] The story Keith Feiling supplies shows this statement to be somewhat partisan.[164]

Because they had been defeated by a France whom they dared not now disown, MacDonald and Henderson had gone to Berlin in July of 1931, to try to help Germany out of her financial troubles. But England had to show she could steady her financial course in order to be of any help to Germany. To do so Labour must procure a loan from Paris bankers who demanded that Germany be not the beneficiary of England's gains. From Berlin MacDonald, possibly abetted by Henderson at the time, had signalled to Chamberlain the need to create a National Government. Chamberlain (somewhat francophile) agreed with Baldwin that their Party could not accept the suggestion. At that time the public thought that the alternative to "cuts" was tariff. "Tariff" was impossible because of France. Had Chamberlain and Baldwin accepted the idea of a National Government and "cuts," then the onus for cutting the dole would have fallen equally upon both the Tory and the Labour parties. Two parties would have emerged, Labour and Tory. Since to save the precarious unity of the Labour Party would mean keeping within it the revolutionary element, urgent for "Socialism in our time," Chamberlain and Baldwin could not be expected to desire such an outcome. Since to allay fear of inflicting unreasonable sacrifice Snowden had insisted throughout the stress that the lowered cost of living warranted the adjustment downward of the wage scale, Chamberlain and Baldwin aimed to achieve this effect by another method.[165] When the National Government was formed upon an unspoken programme to devalue, it was acting according to the Trade Unionists' published principle; and MacDonald had good reason to expect them to follow him.

[163] *Ibid.*
[164] Feiling, *op. cit.*, p. 192.
[165] *Ibid.*

That they did not was the work of Henderson and of Bevin; and the effect of the ethos of Socialism in the Labour Movement.[166]

The splitting of the Party in the upper quartile rather than in the center was the result of the Webb-Henderson decision not to stand with MacDonald. The necessity of splitting the Party was produced by its incongruities. Self-criticism followed upon the revelation that the power to form a Government lay still within the province of the Crown. It fell along fiscal lines and only later turned to vindictiveness against MacDonald.

The source of the conflict becomes easy to comprehend as readers contrast with the analysis made by Fabians of *The Clarion* staff, the measured reproaches for example, of Norman Angell meted out to the fanatics who had caused to be aroused in England a phobia about a "predatory" political party. How little the financial problem was understood is now measurable; and silhouetted in the shapeless materia of undefined Socialism is the outline of its inherent catastrophe. The first of the critics to be noted was either very subtle or quite unconscious of the revealing data he furnished. His picture of the degenerative effects of living on the dole was a secondary aim in his "Let Us Take to The Road." [167] A vagabond and sturdy rogue, "Joseph Stamper," as he signed himself, sang out this call to the unemployed. He advocated tramping and suggested that the Government set up "canteens" as in war time to care for those who would follow his advice. Between the lines the reader saw the curse of industrialism and the blight of materialism. Indignation was stirred; but hopelessly. There were many services for the unemployed, much care but nothing to replace the loss of social and moral tone. Stamper told a story of nerves, the social services, and suicide. Industrialism left a vacuum in the civilization once filled by a concept of vocation in craftsmanship and in an agricultural way

---

[166] *The Clarion* mocked the grief and tears of MacDonald when it was learned how the defeat of Labour affected him. The bitter young writer also re-told what he had heard from Lansbury, that MacDonald had met him one day and said, "I'm coming back." "Oh!" had been Lansbury's sarcastic rejoinder. Indeed, the Labour Party was something one was bidden to belong to and bidden to vote with, or formally excommunicated from, and not, as in America, something one might "be" like a Republican or a Democrat.

[167] *The Clarion,* III:10 (October, 1931), 291.

of life; and materialism left wide the gap once filled by charity. "Take to The Road" might have constituted a constructive slogan. It was more a piece of irony than a constructive idea, but nothing more than this vagabond song symbolized the inherent cause of England's dilemma. The analysis of the failure went on, on fiscal and political lines. The great failure of Fabians was a psychological one. They misconstrued the psychology of both workers on the dole and Capitalists.

After the election, "Our Point of View" [168] was stated: "Democracy has given the verdict and we must accept it." Labour would not waste energies in defense but turn to the creation of a programme. This should set forth the conditions of world peace and world cooperation; nothing could restore the purchasing power of Central Europe and Latin America save world cooperation. This was a signal to the left wing to try to get some cooperation from their brother Socialists in Russia and France, with an eye to increased trade.

The Reporter (Davies also, no doubt) [169] took up the question of the threat of revolution. "Are we to believe that Mr. Henderson, Mr. Graham, Lord Passfield, Mr. Lees-Smith and the rest were preparing to overthrow Capitalism by force?" The question was the old begging one. Force was never defined. A revolution of barricades and party coups followed by civil war or oppression would not "overthrow Capitalism," and Fabians, especially the peaceful one cited above knew it. The force they would and did use was that slow erosion which is the effect of "gradualness"; their force was the force of the Root of Unrest. They purposed to obtain the effects of an explosion without its disorder. True, *The Clarion* readers could have agreed that all these studious and laborious Socialists who grappled at the time with political realities were not more revolutionary than Stanley Baldwin. Nevertheless, none of them ever refuted the statements of Harold Laski. *The Clarion* itself had built up a cumulative menace to the order of things by harping on "laying the foundations of Socialism." [170]

---

[168] *Ibid.*, p. 310.

[169] *The Clarion*, III:11 (November, 1931), 310.

[170] Cf. Karl Marx, *The Secret Diplomacy of the 18th Century*, posthumously edited by Eleanor Aveling (London: Sonnenschein and Company,

Clarion readers were reassured: Henderson, Graham, Passfield, Lees-Smith and their associates were not preparing to overthrow Capitalism " by force." But the new Government should have no rest. If this National Government sought to stabilize the pound by " false economy," it would lower the living standard. Employment had increased already (he admitted " general worsening of conditions " during the Labour term) [171] and so had world trade; but it would not last. This, he said, was a Government of a class for a class—the interests of the *rentier* class were not those of the masses.

The only indication of a catastrophic trend in Professor Laski's thought appeared in his commentary of the same date: [172] Faith in constitutional action was to wane in the next few years. At this time, if he entertained the thoughts expressed in 1932, he withheld them from *The Clarion* readers. Many " labour " people had voted Conservative. Laski probably had in mind only the action of the Consultative Committee in attempting to direct the Cabinet when he remarked that " unless a Socialist government, in the full sense of the term, comes soon representative government will have little chance of survival." [173] While Webb was writing in *What Happened* that neither Party had any genius or expert upon whom to call, Professor Laski complained that MacDonald and Snowden had held the rank and file in contempt and had not consulted the " experts at the Party's disposal." Now he called for the marshalling of youth to front the Opposition with " audacity." (It was a pity to overlook the audacious talent of the old back-benchers.)

1899). There were two aspects to Fabian destructionism. One was found in unspoken assumption that the English would always be orderly; Tories were gentlemen and there was always the King. They were perhaps unconscious of the security they felt, warrantedly, despite their prankish irresponsibility. Under this aspect Fabian Socialists played a game of politics and aimed to capture power as a " win." The other aspect was something Karl Marx did not hesitate to uncover, but which this writer will leave to readers to find in recalling certain Fabian misconceptions about the relations of the Catholic Church to fascism, to European politics, to medieval economy, to capitalism, to the Jesuits, to *the present order*. Under this aspect Fabian Socialism was a force as old as Mohammet.

[171] *The Clarion,* p. 311.
[172] *Ibid.,* p. 313.
[173] *Ibid.*

The audacity of Sir Stafford Cripps met Laski's approval and he had the politeness to mention in the same connection George Lansbury (who was to be replaced soon by Clement Attlee).[174]

Evidently the campaigning of Tom Johnston and Margaret Bondfield in explaining to the working people the dangers of continuing in the course set by the Labour Government had been effectual; for, while Mrs. Hamilton's constituents had held to "a genuine socialist and international faith," others were greatly affected so that when Mr. Davies motored slum dwellers to the polls, they avowedly voted conservative. (It is an irony that the House of Lords had vetoed a bill to make it illegal to use motor cars this way.) Mrs. Hamilton unable to be too harsh with her former hero said that MacDonald and Snowden had escaped into the "safe harbourage of the National Government" and had "given the baby to carry to Tom Johnston and Margaret Bondfield."[175]

More and more in this self-criticism there emerges the inference that the Socialism of Britain was a "faith." Here is Mary Agnes Hamilton speaking of the faith of her constituents as if to attest their true discipleship. Above, it has been seen, Laski alluded to "faith" in constitutional action and in the same connection praised Henderson for one in whom "faith in socialism pervaded his whole being."[176] Examples could be multiplied.

It is extremely important from the point of view of the capitalist that Mrs. Hamilton, M.P., believed the "scare" of the threat to Postal Savings Funds was comparable to the scare of the Capital Levy. It was hardly to avoid the incongruity of listing political with economic matters that she omitted the scare of the Zinoviev Letter.[177]

The nadir of self-blame for the disaster to the Party (not the Movement) appeared in *The Clarion* in December. A lecture to the Fabian Society given by Fabian Sir Norman Angell on November 5,[178] was reported as "Cooperation or Dictatorship?" The burden of it was that there should have been cooperation be-

---

[174] *Ibid.*
[175] *Ibid.*, p. 319.
[176] *Ibid.*, p. 313.
[177] *Ibid.*, p. 319.
[178] *The Clarion*, III :12 (December, 1931), 341.

tween Socialism and Capitalism during the "transformation" period. Angell's indictment is concise: "Gradualness" had been obscured by the "platform attitude" of the Party; the words "abolish" and "destroy" had been heard in too many perorations; in the deadlock, facing collapse, too large a segment of Labourite opinion had been "so much the better"; Labour had not made up its mind whether to prevent or to promote breakdown; if bankers met to discuss ways of distributing gold or stabilizing currency, they received no encouragement from Labour—they were "Capitalists"; Labour asked for "Power"—Power might be a "crowbar" held over industry; also, Labour misinterpreted Russia—a simple peasant economy in process of transformation was confused with the intricate British system; they were committed to gradualism yet Party members treated employers as enemies—during wars cooperation had not been inhibited by Labour's threat to annihilate Capital, because cooperation was given then for the sake of the people not for "the benefit of predatory political parties"; Labour oscillated between

> . . . the policy of smashing the present system by producing chaos and the policy of transforming it while it is running smoothly. [They should aim instead at] redistribution of national income by transferring through taxation part of profits to social services, then industry must be allowed and encouraged to make profits; . . . such policy is much easier when profits are being made than when they are not.[179]

Norman Angell fell short of defining the real philosophical basis for cooperation (collaboration in production for the common good, with mutual responsibility) when he said "real opposition of interests between worker and capitalists" existed; but he thought that, even so, cooperation was "not inconsistent." (It was, of course, inherently self-contradictory to imagine that elements having opposite ends could cooperate. Marx was perfectly consistent; if conflict of destiny exists, there can be no truce.) Socialists, Sir

---

179 *Ibid.* The cultivation of certain profitable enterprises to furnish funds for a Welfare State is an idea having contemporary exemplifications which persistently confuse critics who fall into use of the terms "Socialist" or "Fascist."

Norman said, were pledged indeed to *replace* [180] the present order yet there was a point of " common interest " between Labour and Capital. Although he gave no indication of it, Sir Norman may indeed have perceived that the note of *common interest* gave to the " transition " the sign of infinity, like Shaw's figure of railway tracks which seem to converge on the horizon, and never shall meet. When would this underlying common interest cease to exist? He wisely did not say. If many Fabians believed that the stage of " transition " was eternal and if they expected the rest of England to understand that this was their expectation, the Fabian Society certainly behaved toward its tutelary followers as if it expected that inevitably Socialism must come about after a transition.

Even the jests of *The Clarion* Reporter spoke of Dictatorship. " Enter the World Dictator " [181] referred to the suggestions of a Fabian, A. H. Abbati of the self-founded Unclaimed Wealth Utilization Committee of Geneva, to increase the purchasing power of rich countries by desisting from income tax assessment in order to increase sales in poor countries. Outright inflation was his aim and the editor was willing to make him dictator of the world.[182] It is not necessary at this point to consider the implication involved in the mirth of the would-be tax evader and the tremendously earnest founder. The world—and a rich country, England—was straightened by the sanctions of the natural law forbidding usury and menaced by the crowbar of a rigid wage scale. The worried man and the comic editor are almost tragic symbols of the era.

Norman Angell pointed to " cooperation "; another Fabian pointed to " dictatorship," for remedy. Cole of ZIP contributed " Socialism, 1932 Edition." [183] His verdict was that the Labour Party would merit no confidence from the electorate " until we sound as if we knew our job." A Party committed to the bloc vote and Party discipline must have a uniform policy and an agreed interpretation of Socialism. Shaw had said as much much

---

[180] The individual or company having been " replaced " finds the word not unconnotative with " destroy."

[181] *The Clarion,* IV :1 (January, 1932), 3. cf., *How To Pay for the War* for Abbati's idea.

[182] *The Clarion,* IV :11 (February, 1932), 27.

[183] *Ibid.,* p. 7.

earlier; but he showed that this was " only for Marxists," implying that they would have to declare themselves such.

In spite of the general improvement in the economic sphere, Fabians continued to insist that a chaotic situation existed caused by the collapse of the capitalistic machine. The *Clarion* editor pointed everywhere to "mad" nationalism and agreed with the Fabian Society's current exposition of the dissolution of capitalism,[184] while he demanded that Lord Simon become vocal for international co-operation. Laski also pointed to the financial failures in America and generalized about the breakdown of capitalistic organization. Shaw just back from Russia preached " constructive Socialism " and said he had seen Russia in transition to Fabianism—anarchism and syndicalism had given way to evolutionary socialism in USSR. And as to Fabians themselves, " We are either communists or whatever MacDonald and Snowden are— whatever that is." [185] Shaw with his facility for drawing out the conclusions to his colleagues' dangling premises disclosed the common faith shared by Socialists in England and Russia. In juxtaposition with the internationalism advocated by the *Clarion* that faith was seen to demand the sacrifice of national self-interest.

Shaw whom Pease called " always the loyalest of colleagues," [186] summed up 1931 in 1944. Speaking of Ramsay MacDonald's premiership he said it was a colossal success from the plutocratic standpoint:

> The Fabians demonstrated that the possibilities of modern scientific industry are far beyond the resources of old-fashioned private enterprise conducted by little competing partnerships. . . . [They could be realized only by state or municipal authority and revenue.] Whatever Party could capture these would rule the roost. The Fabian Society intended Labor [sic] to capture them . . . what happened was the rise of State-Aided Capitalism which exactly suits both the dominant Conservative Trade Union leaders [Citrine was named] and the high-minded and academically cultivated re-discoverers of the Moralized Capitalism of the now forgotten Positive Philosophy

---

[184] *The Clarion*, III:12 (December, 1931), 338.
[185] *Ibid.*, p. 339.
[186] Pease, *op. cit.*, p. 223.

of Auguste Comte [to Lord Olivier was attributed this
contribution] . . . called Fascism in Italy, National
Socialism in Germany, and Freedom in England, where
we are up to our waist in it . . . [this State-Aided Cap-
italism] is the best arrangement of which we are capable
at present.[187]

Labour's contest with the Conservatives to " rule the roost " and
the inter-Party conflict with Trade Unionism to seize the machinery powered by " Freedom," if grasped in full significance explains
the instinct with which the King and Baldwin, and Chamberlain,
" the pack-horse of all our affairs " as Churchill called him were
able to take advantage of the political momentum. It was necessary to embargo gold, inflate the currency, repudiate the debt to
America. These were measures which counteracted Baldwin's
past performances. They must now be MacDonald's acts. His
" party " did not now embrace the Socialist leadership but the
undistinguished commonality. " State-aided Capitalism " in
Britain did not mean subsidized or State-planned industry, but
only an understanding Government. Goods began to move and
workers to work. MacDonald was given the impossible task of
coping with National Socialism or State-Capitalism in Europe,
where Germany had no King and Italy had no Tories.

Disappointed, yet consistently united still by a deeply recognized assent, the Christian Socialists of the Clyde, the ILP economic
philosophers, the humanitarian atheists, the charitarian Anglicans,
the comtean moralists, the fatalists of Inevitability, those liberals
who taught that no man should serve another yet all should be
served, those liberals whose " *non serviam!* " produced a material
constructed to substitute for theology—all broke ranks, only reform another day.

---

[187] Shaw, *op. cit.,* in *FQ,* 41 (April, 1944), 2 f.

CHAPTER XIII

CONCLUSION

The continuity of the Fabian Society was demonstrated by the re-edition of the *Fabian Essays* in 1948 with a new preface added to the older two and a postscript, both additions having for author the first editor, Shaw.[1] It is necessary to stress this continuity because there is a saying current that Fabianism is no more. Some commentators imagine that it perished in the War of 1914–1918 or that it dissolved in the debacle of 1931. The last postscript of George Bernard Shaw would lead his readers to believe that the old Fabians of the *Essays* had disappeared by 1911. Misunderstanding arises from the fact that little sympathy exists between the new " Webbs," namely, the Coles, and Shaw. Mrs. Cole, as she grew up into revolution, grew toward Mrs. Webb's ideas; and she took the trouble to get the latter's sponsorship and accord when she re-used the name Fabian and reformed the Society in 1938–1939.[2] Taking over the remnant Davies (père) saved through the 1930's, Margaret Cole grafted a new stock onto the parent Society. Shaw aimed to defeat the sense of continuity thus achieved—although he, like Mrs. Cole, professed Communism now—by speaking of " ex-Fabians " filling offices in the Government as of 1948, stating that " *fin de siecle* " Fabianism is now " an old wives' tale." [3] He prodded, goaded, mocked. Even so, he assumed that Fabianism was extant:

Although this volume of essays is sixty years old, and I,

[1] G. B. Shaw, " Sixty Years of Fabianism," a postscript in *Fabian Essays: Jubilee Edition* (London: Allen and Unwin, 1948).

[2] Cf. Margaret Cole, *Growing up into Revolution,* p. 203. Mrs. Cole dislikes Shaw. She considers him a mountebank. This opinion, however, agrees perfectly with his statement, written to this student, that Sidney Webb did more than any other man on earth to bring out George Bernard *Shaw the born actor.* Mrs. Cole imputes irresponsibility to Shaw but she herself finds in retrospect that the Society which the Coles revived provided as the measure of satisfaction " fun and games in politics."

[3] Shaw, " Sixty Years of Fabianism," *loc. cit.,* p. 214.

its editor, am ninety, it is still alive and doing its work, which was and is to rescue Socialism and Communism from the barricades, and from confusion with traditional heterodoxies of anti-clericalism, individualist anti-State republicanism [Americanism], and middle-class Bohemian anarchism [Guild Socialism], in short, to make it a constitutional movement in which the most respectable citizens and families may enlist, without forfeiting the least scrap of their social or spiritual standing [class feeling].[4]

In this series of negatives is discoverable what Fabian "Socialism and Communism" is: It is Statism. Shaw would consider Washington and Madison anti-state republicans in the sense of their being anti-doctrinaire and in favor of that subsidiary which insures liberty. Shaw's summary inculcates the belief that one might even be a Catholic[5] and a Fabian. Although Socialism stood rejected by the Church on account of the very philosophy of society in which Fabians gloried as they gloried in the name of Socialist, Shaw indicates Fabianism was or is to be something else.[6] The other name was and is Social Democracy; tomorrow it

---

[4] *Ibid.*, p. 207.

[5] Cf. Sir Henry Slesser, *Judgment Reserved*. "Our Roman Catholic members . . . were not Socialists in the sense in which the Pope had condemned that creed," p. 151. Sir Henry had not yet become a Catholic. As an Anglican, he discovered the non-Christian basis of Fabian philosophy.

[6] Cf. Leo XIII, *Graves de Communi* [of 1901] entitled *Christian Democracy*, (New York: Paulist Press, 1941). "Social Democracy . . . [holds] there is really nothing existing above the natural order of things, and that the acquirement and enjoyment of corporal and external goods constitutes man's happiness. It aims at putting all government in the hands of the people, reducing all ranks to the same level, abolishing all distinction of class and finally introducing community of goods . . . right of ownership is to be abrogated. . . ." p. 6. Cf. also, *Quadragesimo Anno* (1931), the encyclical letter of Pope Pius XI on *Reconstruction of the Social Order* (New York: Paulist Press), p. 32, "no one can be at the same time a sincere Catholic and a true Socialist." Pius XI sifts all the variants of Socialism and rejects each one: Those who look for nothing else than that certain forms of property must be reserved to the State, that a certain type of social rulership which in violation of all justice has been seized and usurped by owners of wealth be restored where it belongs—to the State; those who seek to contrive that class war abstain from enmity and hatred and that the war against private property be abated, "have no reason for becoming Socialists."

may be " dynamic democracy," where " republic " is a term for
" decadent form of government." Shaw implies that maybe the
name Fabianism will be changed; but that whatever it is that the
Essays taught—and today teach—it is a rescued " Socialism and
Communism." [7] Whatever it is, its original habitat was in the non-

---

Ibid., p. 30. But—and this may well be a description of the British under
Webb's guidance and their influence in the International—" for the most part
they [Socialists] do not reject class warfare and the abolition of property,
but merely are more moderate in regard to them. Now, when false principles
are thus mitigated and in some sense waived, the question arises, or is
unwarrantedly proposed in certain quarters, whether the principles of
Christian truth also could not be somewhat moderated and attenuated, so as
to meet Socialism, as it were, upon common ground. Some are engaged by
the empty hope of gaining in this way the Socialists to our cause, but such
hopes are vain. Those who wish to be apostles among the Socialists should
preach the Christian truth whole and entire, openly and sincerely without
any connivance with error. If they wish in truth to be heralds of the Gospel,
let their endeavor be to convince Socialists that their demands, insofar as
they are just, are defended much more cogently by the principles of Christian
faith, and are promoted much more efficaciously by the *power* of Christian
charity. [Italics inserted.]

" Whether Socialism be considered as a doctrine, or as a historical fact, or
as a movement, if it really remains Socialism, it cannot be brought into
harmony with the dogmas of the Catholic Church, even after it has yielded
to truth and justice in the points we have mentioned [*i.e.,* been mitigated and
amended so that nothing reprehensible regarding class war and private
property remain]; the reason being that *it conceives human society* in a way
utterly alien to Christian *truth.*" *Ibid.,* pp. 30 f. (Italics supplied.)

[7] Shaw lumps together " Socialism and Communism." We have seen how
Lenin asked Lansbury and Tillett how long he would have to wait for them
and how in turn both pointed out to the dictator that his system was not
real Communism—which he admitted. We have seen how Shaw told Stalin
that on Lenin's tomb should be inscribed, " the inevitability of gradualness ";
and how he claimed NEP was pure Fabianism. The influence of Fabianism
upon Russian Communism (now an imperial and national Communism using
national Communist party groups to its own ends) is marked in a document,
the last published proceedings of the All-Russia Communist Party Congress
of 1936. The ruthless expropriation which Shaw disapproved in his letter to
the writer, having been repaired by NEP, " NEPism " is to be foregone.
The drive is set for all-out " Socialism." That the project was laid down
in 1936 to infiltrate through liberals, progressives and persons capable of
being used as foils for penetration and permeation, is indicated by the lack of
a Report or manifesto and the insistence on " Now, Socialism " in newspapers, cited. The efficacy of the example of British Socialism had been

conformist pulpits of England, where having become tolerant of
conflicting theologies it espoused "morals" in substitution for
theology as an integrating social force. "Morals" was in turn
translated into "education" and "respectability," as in the re-
edited *Essays* Lord Oliver reiterated.[8] By writing that "spiritual

---

effective. The fact of its articulation in 1936 leads one to presuppose that the
practice of the "new" system had originated some time before, just as the
announcement of NEP in 1924 was preceded by its having functioned at
least since 1922. The document is in Russian and may be found in the
Library of Congress as HX13.A3V7, 1937. Friends of this writer translated
portions for her.

[8] Cf. "Moral," *Fabian Essays*, pp. 96–102, where the co-founder equated
morality with reason and art with spirituality. He defined the motive for
caring for the social "residuum"—itself a social menace—as benevolence;
the end of man's life, to "identify his life with society"; rent and interest,
as "tribute"; and all property as appropriation. Olivier incidentally re-
produces the dialectical phenomena we have noted in the Webbs and other
Socialists: 1) An historical concatenation which his argument does not need,
i.e., the story of the spoliation of the Catholic Church by Protestantism which
developed ownership of land and a system of rent and destroyed the
"medieval machinery" of charity, producing the factory system from which
necessarily the cooperative system must emerge; 2) the Comtean idea of
progress wherewith he sees Socialism as "but a stage in the unending
progression out of the weakness and the ignorance in which society and
the individual alike are born, toward the strength and the enlightenment in
which they can see and choose their own way forward," (pp. 101 f.). Certainly, the historical causes of emergent cooperation lend nothing to Olivier's
Positivism and do not produce Socialism. The Comtean "progress" to
enlightenment does nothing for the historical sequence, has only accidental
connection with it, and is made to produce Socialism only by Olivier's
introducing "Commonsense" as Socialism. Olivier introduced Socialism
into the elaborate historical structure he built for it, to which it was unnatural. He might have spoken of a common-sense (of right) based on the
virtue, say, of natural justice, without using the special signal, "Socialism"
—that talisman proffered to a certain mentality which intended to remain
outside that sphere wherein "Socialism," because it conceives of man as
subject to society, is rejected by name. Again as to respectability, Olivier's
concept of education equated that which induced men to act in the realm of
"secondary passions"—not crudely under primary instincts such, one imagines, as the urge to fight for right or against injustice directly or with
emotion.

We have given so much space to Lord Olivier, who died in 1942, because
Shaw, in the 1940's, credited Olivier with the introduction of Positivism,
considered by Shaw a great contribution to the Society.

standing " was not forfeited by joining the Society, Shaw meant that possibly Catholics who joined it were not excommunicated. England had no Plenary Council of Baltimore. He also meant that because Fabian Socialism was very moral and very Protestant, it was tame and respectable.

As Shaw said, respectable families had enlisted in the Movement (in fact, only respectable ones, including as of 1950 a daughter of the Chamberlains, now Lady Pakenham and an outstanding Fabian). On this point a psychological factor shows up: Upper class families subjected to excoriation as parasites upon society had even in the 1920's become sensitive to the degree that great hardihood would be required for them to persist in ignoring the monitory and minatory hostility of the " socialist snobs " (to borrow Elizabeth Brandeis' expression). The uses of a genteel contumely have been well understood.

" A constitutional movement," Fabianism, as Shaw boasted, has taught the use of ballots and inculcated the use of Parliamentary acts to effect Socialism. This typical Fabian showed no fear of substituting administrative fiat for the rule of law. (In another connection the urging of ardent Fabians on the eve of the debacle of 1931 to enact Socialism by law has been reported.) Yet Shaw remarks in the same postcript that repealing *in toto* the Trade Disputes Act of 1927, as the Labour Party " drunk with power " did in 1946, was to " betray [the Party's] inexperience and lack of historical sense." We do not, nor does Shaw, confuse the Party and the Society. But the Government which repealed the law, in an act of class legislation,[9] was made up of Fabians (not to quibble about Shaw's " ex-Fabians "—he might as well have written " arch-Fabians "—in the sense that an archbishop is an ex-bishop). Now Shaw was alarmed. He aroused the fear that class legislation should come by way of repeal rather than enactment.

Shaw believed, as did the Webbs, who wrote in substance in the " Epilogue " to their *Local Government* of 1927, that " Votes for Everybody makes democracy impossible." [10] He and they seemed to sense that democracy is not primarily a political system but a

---

[9] Cf. Mrs. Cole, *Growing Up Into Revolution,* p. 125.

[10] Shaw, " Sixty Years of Fabianism," *op. cit.,* p. 222.

social way of life; [11] that large numbers of votes cast on one side of a measure do not make for greater wisdom in the measure. He took refuge in his old idea of government by an élite and, like the Webbs, neglected if he did not cynically refuse to stress the demand for personal opinion, formed, held and voted by the citizen. Although like all the Fabians, he expected the freedom or leisure arising from economic equality which industrial democracy must provide, to result in the development of talent in comfortable families, he nevertheless insisted that only five percent of the proletariat " conceiving the job and pioneering the drive toward its divine [sic] goal " should be educated to govern. Perhaps it is well that Ellen Terry's " Dear Shaw " envisioned the " divine goal " as one unattainable; " like the horizon or the place where parallel lines (say, railways) visibly meet, [the goal] can never be reached. Providence forbid that it ever should." [12] He was about to add that persons living in the new order and governed by the five percent should be required to " prove their social solvency ": We should be warned that " Unless we use the world, producing and replacing as much as we consume, and a bit over for capital *we may not wake up some morning.*" [13] However, there is really nothing to fear; the tracks will never meet: [14]

---

[11] As we have reported, Shaw, Laski, and W. A. Robson, like the Webbs, believed in the rule of an élite, even of an Order. This conceptual Order seemed to be charged not only with political but with economic rule. Conceivably, like the Apostles, they might arrive at the conclusion that deacons should be appointed for the ministry of "serving at tables." Then the élite might remain the agents of the political order—" shepherd Kings " becoming " King." " Democracy " would still serve to mold the contours of society. Under Socialism, by means of the Party or Order, " democracy " would produce totalitarian control. (The same democratic contours infused with creative Charity informing the personality and opinion of individual citizens would produce social justice.)

[12] Shaw, " Sixty Years of Fabianism," *op. cit.,* p. 222.

[13] *Ibid.,* p. 227. (Italics supplied.) But we should mercifully not be told the night before of our imminent liquidation.

[14] Between Shaw's lines we see that Fabian " Socialism " is an esoteric thing—more properly, a carrot held out to the warring sects to corral them into the Party. This writer has no hesitation in calling it a *mystique,* a mystique however suitable to the mentality of very pragmatic people; therefore, the carrot figure is more apropos.

Although Socialist may be substituted for Capitalist Government in twenty-four hours, it by no means follows
that industry and agriculture, *religion and art and their
professions, land and capital,* can be transferred from
private to public ownership and management in twenty-
four hours or completed even within twenty-four years.[15]

So much for the Shavian " constitutionalism " of Fabian Socialism.

The editor of the *Fabian Essays* did not allude to the fact that
Socialists all over the world, especially at Geneva and in Britain,
had since 1919 been cajoled into joining the Second International
or the Labour Party, respectively, by the promise that the tracks
would one day meet and Socialism would evolve from gradualism.
Not reform, not amelioration, not social justice to owners and
workers through collaboration, but Socialism, which connoted
" equality " and " freedom " by abolition of Capitalism and competition, had been promised, with socialization of the means of
production as merely a necessary step.[16] It is plain to see that
pure Socialists in Europe and Politburo Communists have reason
for detesting British Fabianism. On the other hand, this is no
reason why those " damnably otherwise " should love it.

Socialism and Communism equated were not to be confused
with, hence were not by definition, Guild Socialism with its subsidiary and free associations,[17] nor " anti-State " republicanism with

---

[15] *Ibid.,* p. 215. Italics are inserted. This is Shaw in 1948 with the
Society's approval. The Shaw of 1911 or of 1924 did not speak of postpone-
ment.

[16] Cf. " The Congress of the Labour and Socialist International," *ILO
Studies and Reports,* Series A, No. 6 (October, 1920). Bound in the Library
of Congress as HD4813.14, these reports are self-paginated. In this report
occurs the expression " democratic socialism " (specifically rejected by Leo
XIII in 1901). The expressed objective is stated to gather adherents in
opposition to the Third International of Moscow. This report is the work
of Webb aided by Snowden and it expounds the principle that while the immediate resolution as adopted applied only to industrial socialization, in
theory socialization was applicable to all, even professional production and
was a step toward the abolition of private production and competition: the
aim, " To arrive at Socialism by progressive transformation [promising it
would be swift] of national institutions on an international plan and by the
suppression of classes."

[17] Shaw wrote this student that he made it orthodox; Mrs. Cole wrote
that it never was orthodox; Mrs. Webb called it the " bridge " to industrial

its vertically representative political system;[18] nor anti-clerical-ism—avowedly, Fabians are simply not anti-clerical; they are professedly not clerical. Fabianism simply ignores the presence of that which Olivier termed, in apposition to "medieval church," "a socialistic society" which was, he said, destroyed by Protestantism. It is remarkable how unnoticeable was the Catholic Church in England during the 1920's.[19] Fabians spoke of it as defunct.

If at first sight it would seem Shaw was saying that Fabianism rejected Cole's Guild Socialism, nevertheless a point of agreement is to be found in another of Shaw's lines: " Trade Unionism tends to become a dictatorship of skilled labor, *opposed to the State without which basic Communism is impossible.*" [20] For Shaw with

democracy; and Attlee prefaced his studies of 1937 and 1949 with the statement that there was no orthodoxy.

[18] Anti-State republicanism being in Shaw's word "individualist" seems to describe the Jefferson-Jackson ideals of subsidiarity. This student submits that the Statism of *e.g.,* ADA, and of "Fair Deal" centralization, has no right to claim the paternity of Jefferson or Jackson. They do not try to claim Washington or Madison. Incidentally, the figure of speech used by President Roosevelt regarding "driving the money changers from the temple" occurs earlier in the writing of Ben Tillett, *op. cit.,* p. 280.

[19] Cf. the Reverend Gilbert C. Binyon (Fabian), *The Christian Socialist Movement in England* (London: SPCK, 1931), especially XVII, pp. 154 f, where Toynbee points out the omission of Theology. The Coles knew and loved G. K. Chesterton, who had ceased to be a Fabian before the War and before he became a Catholic. He lectured to the Nursery on "Liberty" in 1927 (*FN* XXXVIII January, 1927.) Unmentioned were Belloc, and A.C., and Robert Hugh Benson: occasionally the writings of Father Vincent McNabb are mentioned in passing. Labour Party Catholics (many Irish who thought of the Party as the friend of Ireland) no doubt believed that to seek to procure a municipal sewage system for all, electric light for the poor, national highways and "socially controlled" rails, coal, and water—was hardly "revolution." A learned critic of Socialism, L. von Mises misunderstands the Christian attitude toward material progress, finding it inconsistent in Catholics to "bless" railroads and wires, in his *Socialism,* (New Haven: Yale University Press, 1951), p. 423. Catholic workers in England in the 1920's found the arguments between the Popes and the Webbs far over their heads. Pius XI retorted to *Is the Soviet Socialism a New Civilization?* with a blunt negative: It is a rationalized barbarism, said *Divini Redemptoris.*

[20] Shaw, "Sixty Years of Fabianism," *op. cit.,* p. 222 (italics supplied). This recalls Kingsley Martin's revelation of the reason Fabians disregarded —and destroyed—the Whitley Council system.

his Statism embodied, as he declared time and again, in the perfect
Fabianism of the New Economic Plan,[21] as for Cole, who peers
beyond the monolith that is only the shadow of a political entity,
the State is the servant of Communism, that which sees to it that
worker control and economic equality are sustained.[22] Apparently,

---

[21] Cf. "The Trade Union Movement in Soviet Russia," *ILO (Geneva)
Studies and Reports* (London: King and Son, 1927). Each chapter is
divided into two sections: 1) Under Communism, 2) under NEP, which
represented for Russia a temporary deviation. (*Ibid.*, p. 17.) Herein we
find stated the conclusion that the nationalization of the Trade Unions is
inevitable, and the words which draw Cole and Shaw together: Communistic
Trade Unionism which "is not opposed to the State in the abstract metaphysical meaning of the word." Cf. *ibid.*, p. 5, citing Lozovsky (Secretary,
Red International Labor Union. Cf. Lorwin, *op. cit.*, p. 662).

[22] Nicholas S. Timasheff, *The Great Retreat* (New York: Dutton and
Company, 1946), p. 368 (see also pages 349 and 371), shows that what he
calls the "Great Retreat" began in 1931. Timasheff is so convinced of the
thesis of his book, precisely, that Russia under the second five-year plan,
which was postponed during 1931 to 1934 and altered to the "Retreat"
pattern, resumed the progress interrupted in 1906 or 1914 and that Russia
became an apt partner with the Great Democracies as demonstrated by her
piety of nationalism at Stalingrad, that he cannot possibly perceive that the
"Retreat" was a step in progress in Communistic imperialism—another
great deception of the West by means of declaring "truth" in Russian
semantics.
Russia was the first nation (France reverted to bourgeois rule) to come
through a reign of terror and then to do the next thing: Reset the old
human pattern—religion, family, art, shopkeeping and artisanry—by dictation of the materialistic state to a people made thoroughly obedient. Timasheff could not have seen in 1946 that after aggression upon a land, the
Communist party in the incipient stage fastens upon it not the pattern of
the Russia of 1945 but that of 1918.
The constitution of 1936, which, as Timasheff notes, evoked Sidney Webb's
worshipful amazement, was a description of the *status quo* of 1932 to 1936.
It tuned the Soviet Union into unison with the social democracy of Fabianism and made of Sidney and Beatrice Webb—it is a harsh word—its first
great dupes. The liquidation of Zinoviev would stand as a false oath written
in blood that Communists were only Fabians. The local Communist party
of Britain might become the mere nuisance it appears to be—noisy and
colorful, but without the following, without a message; for the message of
Stalin would be henceforth carried by "Liberals." The Party, calling itself
"the vanguard of labor," would be temporarily feinting. Cf. Maurice
Dobb, "Politics and Party in Russia," *The Clarion*, 26 n.s. (June, 1929), 4;
and Frank Neumann, "Approaches to the Problem of Political Power,"

neither of them knows that the " Queen " State [23] is entombed in the monolithic chimera toward which they press—the All-State which is No-State.

It is this writer's opinion that " fun and games in politics " [24] supplies the key to Fabianism in British political life. This is understandable. Men, especially men so talented, the posterity of Elizabethan sea dogs—not to recall the Vikings—were endowed by their creator with an inalienable right to live gloriously, adventurously.

Political Science Quarterly, LXV (June, 1950), 161–181. The latter's documentation for the idea that the " changes " (*i.e.,* " retreat " or new Constitution) did not imply giving up " Revolution," is valuable; but his interpretation—that the Communist Party embraced " Social Democracy " out of fear of Fascism—is disputable—unless " Fascism " equates Catholicism.

[23] Cf. Pius XI, *On Reconstructing the Social Order (Quadragesimo Anno),* 1931 (Washington, D. C.: NCWC, new translation, 1942), p. 38:

". . . grave evils . . . have resulted from an intermingling and shameful confusion of the functions and duties of public authority with those of the economic sphere—such as, one of the worst, the virtual degradation of the majesty of the State [the Paulist Press translation gives " queenly " position for majesty of the State], which although it ought to sit on high like a queen and supreme arbitress, free from all partiality and intent upon the common good and justice, is become a slave, surrendered and delivered to the passions and greed of men."

These words described the cartelized State, also the execrable dominance of " internationalism of finance," as well as the State which results from the effort to make a *political* system of that " Democracy " which is conceived as a social way of life.

Pius XII in his Christmas Message of 1944 (NCWC) defines Democracy in the light of the *burden* it puts on a citizen, if not positively " a postulate of nature imposed by reason itself " as something which demands *holding* and *expressing personal* opinion for the common good. This means individual, not bloc voting.

A marvelous description of the difference between masses and people, between liberty and false " freedom," between equality and " colorless uniformity," between authority and demogogic tyranny which uses the State to manipulate the masses so as to reduce the State to an instrument of the masses' " whims," is found in the same allocution, pp. 6–11.

[24] Mrs. Cole in 1949 surveyed the success of the Fabianism she had re-created protesting that the Coles were not really the counterpart of the Webbs in the Society. She noted over two hundred Fabians then in Parliament and asked herself if the new generation had been provided with all that had made her youth interesting. She answered affirmatively that the present generation had been indeed provided with " fun and games in politics." Cf. her *Growing Up Into Revolution,* p. 208.

Once they quested upward to trouble the stars with architectural symbols in stone to testify to their high adventure in theology. Then voteless persons shared in the labor and rested in the beauty of the social offering that was made of a cathedral to God. All that is changed. There are no sacraments to house, no trysting places for a man's soul daring the infinite Flame. But men must play as Wisdom plays in Creation. So the modern Anglo-Saxon plays at politics. The game is to capture Power.[25]

---

[25] Igor Bogolepov Mikhailovich, once (1937) a Colonel in the Red Army (in Spain) and (1930–1936) a member of the Soviet Foreign Office, testified before the Internal Security Subcommittee of the Senate Committee on the Judiciary, April 7, 1952, that among others, several American and British writers incorporated in their published works material supplied by the Soviet Foreign Office, a propaganda and infiltrative agency. Referring to the Webbs' *Soviet Socialism, a New Civilisation,* the testimony is as follows:

Mr. Bogolepov: The materials for this book actually were given by the Soviet Foreign Office.

Senator Ferguson: Given to the Webbs?

Mr. Bogolepov: Yes. They had only to remake a little bit for English text, a little bit criticizing, but in its general trend the bulk of the material was prepared for them in the Soviet Foreign Office . . . and I participated myself in part of this work . . . the chapter concerning the very humanitarian way of Soviet detention camps and jails was written by the Soviet secret police itself.

Mr. Morris: You know that?

Mr. Bogolepov: I received it from the Chief of one of the Divisions of the NKVD . . . when he came to my office in the Foreign Office, and then I gave this material to the Vice Chief of the Western Division, Chaim Weinberg, who was attached to the Webbs and who proceeded to translate that material.

Senator Watkins: Did you read the English books after they were published and you have compared the information with what was given out?

Mr. Bogolepov: Yes. When I came to the West I found this book and I read it with much interest. I found that the material which I prepared was so well done that the Webbs didn't change it any.

[N. B. This testimony is privileged matter.]

BIBLIOGRAPHY

PRIMARY MATERIALS

Primary sources in order of importance include *Fabian News,* a monthly of which the writer examined the issue from 1904 to 1950. These sheets supplied names of members of the Fabian Society and lists of subordinate groups such as " Fabian Women," the " Half-Circle Club," " Fabian Nursery," and " Locals." Announcements of lectures, syllabi and reports thereof, and descriptions of social activities, summer schools, and common-room facilities are also to be found there. The *Fabian Society Annual Reports,* used for the period 1919–1932, reveal the markedly constant membership. These contain also rather full obituary notices, accounts of book-box usage—a travelling library service—announcements of new books and pamphlets, and the extent of sales thereof, together with reports on the financial condition of the Society. Such information testifies against those who assume that the society disappeared with the first World War. The writer made use of the *Fabian Quarterly* for assurance as to continuity of membership and ideas. Its dates lie outside the scope of this study. The *New Statesman,* a weekly, established as an organ of Fabianism by Webb and Shaw, was examined and used extensively as evidence of editorial assent, or of signed Fabian opinion, for the period 1920–1932; but the greater weight of evidence of Fabian reaction to and from political life, 1929–1931, was gleaned from *The Clarion.* Blatchford's " Old Expirer " was revived by graduates from the Fabian Nursery. Priceless evidence of Fabian activity in organizing labor for the political front was gathered in the *Labour Year Book,* especially in the issues of 1916, 1919, and 1931. *Studies and Reports Series A* of the International Labour Organization supplied testimony to the action of Fabians on the International Labour and Socialist scene.

Although no effort will be made to publish them, the writer received gracious letters from several Fabians in reply to her inquiries. The late George Bernard Shaw wrote answers in red ink between the lines and around the margin of a letter. Besides the information related in the body of this study, there was revealed Shaw's affection for the recently deceased Webb whose genius Shaw acknowledged having discovered and whose character Shaw confessed he dramatized. He identified Fabianism with that for which Stalin, among a million others, speaks today.

Mrs. Margaret Cole responded to queries on Fabian history with great kindness. She said the answers to the writer's questions would require a book and, indeed, her latest, *Growing Up Into Revolution* written after the correspondence, has been of great assistance. It has been very painful to disagree at times with this excellent pen-woman.

The kindly Alderman A. Emil Davies provided distinctions for defining the Fabian relationships with *New Statesman,* and with the London School of Economics. In line with the general helpfulness of the people at 11 Dartmouth Street, Mr. J. L. Jolley, Home Research Secretary of the Fabian Society, gave information regarding contacts of visiting Fabians in the United States, listing ADA, CIO-PAC, the *Nation,* the *New Republic,* Socialist Party Headquarters, and the League for Industrial Democracy. It was he who stated that J. M. Keynes was a Fabian; but this is not otherwise verifiable. Again, a brief answer from Mr. Andrew Filson verified the continuity of the *Fabian News* and the amicable method by which the New Fabian Research Bureau was amalgamated with the parent Society in 1939. Eve Saville answered for Filson in another brief note and expressed surprise that the names of some whose membership she had taken for granted were not on office lists—e.g., Stephen Spender, and Aneurin Bevan. Also, A. Lockhurst Scott endeavored to explain that Trades Councils are not by definition affiliated with the Labour Party but he showed the connection between the two elements of the movement.

Ernest Davies, M. P., confirmed the writer's findings from internal evidence regarding the Fabianism of *The Clarion* after 1928. The widow of C. Delisle Burns wrote that she was unable to confirm the rumored association of her husband with the Seven of 1923. Ishbel Ridgely née MacDonald sent her reply on the advertisement of her Plough Inn, Flowers Bottom, Speen, Bucks.

She stated that she was out of touch with everything the questions implied, and did not know to whom one might write for information. Barbara Ward, with apologies, wrote that she had turned the inquiry over to the Fabian Society. It cannot be ascertained that this Catholic Labourite and publicist is a Fabian. From Freda White of the Research Department of the *Daily Herald,* and from Odham's Press (which took over *The Clarion*) came the broadsheet *Labour Press Service* (Special Jubilee Edition) along with a letter both of some value for this study.

Harold Laski, since deceased, replied on the stationery of Roosevelt College, Chicago where also are located the headquarters of the League for Industrial Democracy.

American Fabians Stuart Chase and Upton Sinclair answered candidly concerning their rather abortive Fabian activities, as did Harry Laidler of the League for Industrial Democracy.

The American Fabian is represented in the Library of Congress by volume V numbers 7 to 11 with which publication ceased in 1900 when the followers of Bliss threw the torch to the Bellamy National Clubs. Its little masthead rings with words of Mazzini and William Godwin. Judging from some items its message reached, albeit tenuously, from Elm Street in New York to Alhambra, California.

Material of primary importance is also to be found in the numerous memoirs and works authorized by Fabians, and included in the list given below.

BIBLIOGRAPHY

Books

Adams, Martin Ray. *Studies in the Literary Backgrounds of English Radicalism*, Lancaster, Pa.: Franklin and Marshall College Studies, 1947.

Anderson, Benjamin M. *Economics and the Public Welfare*. Toronto and New York: D. Van Nostrand, 1949.

*Attlee, Clement Richard. *The Labour Party in Perspective—And Twelve Years Later*. London: Victor Gollancz, 1949.

Barnes, George N. *From Workshop to War Cabinet*. London: Herbert Jenkins, 1924. Introduction by the Rt. Hon. D. Lloyd George, M. P.

Beaverbrook, Lord. *Politicians and the Press*. London: Hutchinson and Company, 1925.

*Binyon, Rev. Gilbert Clive. *The Christian Socialist Movement in England*. New York and Toronto: The Macmillan Co., 1931.

Blatchford, Robert. *My Eighty Years*. London: Cassell and Company, 1931.

Brand, Carl Fremont. *British Labour's Rise to Power*. California: Stanford University Press, 1941.

*Burns, C. Delisle. *A Short History of the World 1918–1928*. New York: Payson and Clarke, 1928.

Carr, Edward Hallett. *The Soviet Impact on the Western World*. London: Macmillan and Co., 1946.

——*The Twenty Years' Crisis 1919–1139*. London: Macmillan and Co., 1940.

Churchill, Winston. *The Aftermath*. London: Macmillan Company, 1941.

Churchill Winston S. *The Gathering Storm*. Boston: Houghton Mifflin Company, 1948.

Clapham, J. H. *An Economic History of Modern Britain*. Cambridge: The University Press, 1938.

*Cole, George Douglas Howard. *Fabian Socialism*. London: George Allen & Unwin, 1943.

*Cole, Margaret. *Beatrice Webb*. Longmans, Green & Co., 1945.

*Cole, Margaret Isabel (Postgate). *Growing Up Into Revolution*. London: Longmans, Green and Co., 1949.

Clynes, John Robert. *Memoirs: 1869–1924; 1924–1937 (Vol. 1 & 2)*. London: Hutchinson & Co., Ltd., 1937.

D'Abernon, Edgar Vincent. *Rapallo to Dawes, 1922-24*. New York: Doubleday, Doran & Company, Inc., 1930.

————*Dawes to Locarno, 1924–26.* New York: Doubleday, Doran & Company, Inc., 1931.

*Davies, Ernest. *American Labour.* London: George Allen & Unwin, 1943. Preface by Harold J. Laski.

*Dell, Robert ·Edward. *The Geneva Racket 1920–1939.* London: Robert Hale, 1941.

Dundas, Lawrence John Lumley (Ronaldshay). *The Life of Lord Curzon.* London: Ernest Benn, 1928.

Elton, Godfrey (Baron). *Life of James Ramsay MacDonald 1866–1919.* London: Collins, 1939.

Feiling, Keith Graham. *Life of Neville Chamberlain.* London: Macmillan Company, 1946.

*Finer, Herman. *Road to Reaction.* Boston: Little, Brown & Co., 1945.

————*The T. V. A.* Montreal: International Labour Office, 1944.

Flechtheim, Ossip, *Die KPD in der Weimarer Republic.* Offenbach Bollwerk: Verlag K. Drott, 1948.

*Fyfe, Hamilton. *Behind the Scenes of the Great Strike.* London: The Labour Publishing Company, 1926.

*Haldane, Viscount. *Human Experience.* New York: E. P. Dutton & Company, 1926.

*Hall, H. Duncan, and Lowell, A. L. *The British Commonwealth of Nations* in World Peace Foundation Pamphlets X :6, Boston: W.P.F., 1927.

*Hamilton, Mary Agnes. *Arthur Henderson: A Biography.* London: William Heinemann Ltd., 1938.

————*Sidney and Beatrice Webb.* Boston: Houghton Mifflin Company, 1933.

*Hammond, Kenneth G. Brooks. *When Hostilities Cease.* London: Victor Gollancz, Ltd., 1944.

*Hobson, John A. *Free-Thought in the Social Sciences.* London: George Allen & Unwin, Ltd., 1926.

*Hobson, Samuel George. *Pilgrim to the Left.* New York: Longmans, Green & Co., 1938.

Hogg, Quintin McGarel. *The Left Was Never Right.* London: Faber and Faber, 1945.

*Hutchison, Keith. *The Decline and Fall of British Capitalism.* New York: Charles Scribner's Sons, 1950.

*Huxley, Julian; W. Arnold-Forster; H. J. Laski; John Marrack; Aleck Bourne; John Hammond; Kenneth G. Brooks. *When Hostilities Cease.* London: Victor Gollancz Ltd., 1944.

Kirkwood, David. *My Life of Revolt.* London: George G. Harrap & Co., 1935. Forewords by the Rt. Hon. Winston S. Churchill, C. H., M. P. and the Rt. Hon. George Lansbury, M. P.

Knight, William (Collector & Editor). *Memorials of Thomas Davidson, The Wandering Scholar.* Boston & London: Ginn & Co., 1907.

The Labour Party's Aims. London: Allen and Unwin, 1923.

The Labour Year Book of 1919. London: The Co-operative Printing Society, 1919.

*Lansbury, George. *My Life.* London: Constable and Co., 1928.

*Laski, Harold J.; Harold Nicolson; Herbert Read; W. M. Macmillan; Ellen Wilkinson, and G. D. H. Cole. Programme for Victory—*A Collection of Essays prepared for the Fabian Society.* London: The Labour Book Service, 1942.

Lorwin, Lewis L. *Labor and Internationalism.* New York: The Macmillan Co., 1929.

Lynd, Helen Merrell. *England in the Eighteen-Eighties—Toward a Social Basis for Freedom.* London, N. Y., Toronto: Oxford University Press, 1945.

*Martin, Kingsley. *The British Public and the General Strike.* London: Hogarth Press, 1926.

Marx, Karl. *The Eastern Question.* Edited by Eleanor Aveling. London: Sonnenschein & Co., 1899.

———*The Secret Diplomacy of the 18th Century.* Edited by Eleanor Aveling. London: Sonnenschein & Co., 1899.

*Oakeshott, Michael Joseph. *The Social and Political Doctrines of Contemporary Europe.* Cambridge: The University Press, 1942. Foreward by Ernest Barker. American edition, New York: The Macmillan Company, five prefaces by Frederic A. Ogg.

Oldmeadow, Sir J., *Life of Cardinal Bourne.* Burns, Oates & Co., 1948.

*Parker, John. *Labour Marches On.* England: Penguin Books, 1947.

Parmoor, Lord (Charles Alfred Cripps). *A Retrospect.* London: William Heinemann. 1936.

Pearson, Hesketh. *Bernard Shaw—His Life and Personality.* London: Collins, 1942.

*Pease, Edward R. *The History of the Fabian Society.* London: Second Edition, with a Supplementary Chapter; Fabian Society . . & by George Allen & Unwin, Ltd., 1925.

Phelan, Edward J. *Albert Thomas et la crèation du B. I. T.* Paris: *Collection " Les écrits " par* J. Guéhenno. Editions Bernard Grasset, 1936.

*Ponsonby, Arthur Augustus William Harry. *Now is the Time.* London: Leonard Parsons, 1925.

Rommen, Heinrich A. *The State in Catholic Thought.* Missouri: B. Herder Book & Co., 1945.

Samuel, Rt. Hon. Viscount Herbert L., *Grooves of Change.* Indianapolis: Bobbs-Merrill Company, 1946.

*Shaw, G.B.S. *Fabian Essays, Jubilee Edition.* London: Allen and Unwin, 1948.

Shotwell, James Thomson (Editor). *The Origins of the International Labor Organization.* Two volumes. New York: Columbia University Press, 1934.

*Slesser, Henry Herman. *A History of the Liberal Party.* London: Hutchinson & Co., 1944.

——*Judgment Reserved.* London: Hutchinson & Co., 1941.

*Snell, Lord Henry. *Men, Movements, and Myself.* London: J. M. Dent and Sons, 1936.

*Snowden, Philip Viscount. *An Autobiography.* Two Volumes. London: Ivor Nicholson and Watson, 1934.

——*If Labour Rules.* London: The Labour Publishing Co., 1923.

——*Labour and National Finance.* London: Leonard Parsons, 1920.

Spender, John Alfred. *Great Britain Empire and Commonwealth 1886–1935.* London: Cassell and Co., 1936.

——and Asquith, Cyril. *The Life of Herbert Henry Asquith, Lord Oxford and Asquith.* London: Hutchinson and Company, 1931.

Sylvester, A. J. *The Real Lloyd George.* London: Cassell & Co., 1947.

*Tawney, Richard Henry. *Beatrice Webb 1858–1943.* London: Geoffrey Cumberlege, 1945.

——*The British Labor Movement.* New Haven: The Yale University Press, 1925.

——*Equality.* New York: Harcourt, Brace and Co., 1931.

Thomas, Albert: The International Labour Organization. Translated by Monica Curtis. London: George Allen & Unwin, 1931.

——*International Social Policy.* Geneva: International Labour Office, 1948.

*Thomas, James Henry. *My Story.* London: Hutchinson & Co., 1937.

*Tillett, Benjamin. *Memories and Reflections.* London: John Long, 1941.

Tiltman, H. Hessell. *J. Ramsey MacDonald Labor's Man of Destiny.* New York: Frederick A. Stokes Co., 1929.

Timasheff, Nicholas S. *The Great Retreat.* New York: Dutton and Company, 1946.

*Turner, Ben. *About Myself.* London: Cayme Press, 1930.

*Wallas, Graham. *Human Nature in Politics.* London: Constable and Company, 1948.

*Warwick, Frances Evelyn, Countess of. *Life's Ebb & Flow.* New York: William Morrow & Co., 1949.

*Webb, Beatrice. *My Apprenticeship.* New York: Longmans, Green and Co., 1926.

*Webb, Beatrice. *Our Partnership.* New York: Longmans, Green and Co., 1948.

*Webb, Sidney (editor). *How to Pay for the War: Being Ideas Offered to the Chancellor of the Exchequer by the Fabian Research Department.* London: Fabian Society & George Allen & Unwin., Ltd., 1916.

*Webb, Sidney and Beatrice. *English Local Government: English Poor Law History: Part I The Old Poor Law.* London: Longmans Green and Co., 1927.

——*English Poor Law History: Part II: The Last Hundred Years.* London: Longmans Green and Co., 1929.

——*The Decay of Capitalist Civilisation.* Westminster: Fabian Society & George Allen & Unwin, 1923.

——*The History of Trade Unionism.* London: Longmans Green and Company, 1920.

——*Industrial Democracy.* London: Longmans Green and Co., 1902.

*Webb, Sidney; Bernard Shaw; Sidney Ball, and Sir Oliver Lodge. *Socialism and Individualism.* New York: John Lane Co., 1911.

*Wedgwood, Josiah Clement. *Essays and Adventures of a Labour M. P.* New York: Huebsch Inc., 1924.

——*Testament to Democracy.* New York: Religious Emergency Council of Great Britain, 1943.

Weir, Lauchlan Macneill, *The Tragedy of Ramsey MacDonald.* London: Secker and Warburg, 1938.

*Wells, H. G. *After Democracy.* London: Watts and Company, 1932.

*Wilkinson, Ellen. *Clash.* London: Harrap and Co., 1929.

*Williams, Francis. *Fifty Years' March.* London: Odhams, 1949.

Wolfers, Arnold. *Britain and France Between Two Wars.* New York: Harcourt, Brace and Co., 1940.

*Woolf, L. S., *International Government.* New York: Brentano's, 1916.

FABIAN TREATISES AND PAMPHLETS

Barou, Noah, Ph. D. *World Cooperation 1844–1944.* London: Fabian Publications, Ltd., Victor Gollancz, Ltd., 1944.

Cole, Margaret. *The General Election 1945 and After.* London: Fabian Publications, Ltd., Victor Gollancz, Ltd., 1945.

——*The Fabian Society Past and Present.* London: The Fabian Society, 1942.

——*Labour's Second Term.* London: Fabian Publications, 1949.

——*Education for Democracy—A Report Presented to the Fabian Society.* London: George Allen & Unwin Ltd. & The Fabian Society, 1942.

Forty Years of Education. New York: The League for Industrial Democracy, June, 1945.

The International Labour Organization. London: Fabian Publications, Ltd., Victor Gollancz, Ltd., 1944.

Labour and the New Social Order. London: The Labour Party, 1918.

Laski, Harold J. *The Crisis and the Constitution: 1931 and After.* London: Hogarth Press; Fabian Society, 1932.

——*Socialism as Internationalism.* London: Fabian Publications, Ltd., Victor Gollancz, Ltd., 1949.

Mortished, R. J. P. *The World Parliament of Labour—A Study of the I.L.O.* London: Fabian Publications, Ltd., Victor Gollancz, Ltd., 1946.

Shaw, Bernard. *Fabian Failures and Successes.* London: Fabian Publications, Ltd., 1944.

Starr, Mark. *Labour Politics in U.S.A.* London: Fabian Publications, Ltd., Victor Gollancz, Ltd., 1949.

Tawney, P. H. *Labour and the Nation.* London: The Labour Party, 1928.

Thirty-Three Years in the Public Service. Chicago: The Public Ownership League of America, 1946.

Tillett, Ben. *Trades Unionism and Socialism (Labour Press Pamphlet No. 28).* London: Clarion Newspaper Co., Ltd., n. d.

Webb, Sidney & Beatrice. *Is Soviet Communism a New Civilisation?* London: The Left Review, 1936.

Woolf, Leonard. *Foreign Policy—The Labour Party's Dilemma.* London: Fabian Publications, Ltd., Victor Gollancz, Ltd., 1947.

A Word on the Future to British Socialists. London: The Fabian Society, 1942.

Worswick, G. D. N. *The War Material Controls.* London: The Fabian Society, N. D.

TRACTS

Barea, Ilsa and Arturo. *Spain in the Post-War World.* London: Fabian Publications, Ltd., Victor Gollancz, Ltd., 1945.

Cole, George Douglas Hyde. *Guild Socialism* (Fabian Tract No. 192). London: The Fabian Society, 1920.

Davies, Albert Emil, L.C.C. *The London County Council 1889–1937* (Fabian Tract No. 243). London: The Fabian Society, 1937.

——*Public Ownership: Points From Prospectuses* (Fabian Tract No. 224). London: The Fabian Society, 1928.

Fraser, Robert. *A Social Philosophy for Fabians* (Fabian Tract No. 234). London: The Fabian Society, 1930.

Garratt, Geoffrey Theodore. *Agriculture and the Labour Party* (Fabian Tract No. 228). London: The Fabian Society, 1929.

Labour's Next Step—A Wartime Strategy (Tract Series No. 252). London: The Fabian Society, 1940.

Laski, Harold Joseph. *The British Cabinet—A Study of its Personnel 1801–1924* (Fabian Tract No. 223). London: The Fabian Society, 1928.

——*The Limitations of the Expert* (Fabian Tract No. 235). London: The Fabian Society, 1931.

——*Socialism and Freedom* (Fabian Tract No. 216). London: The Fabian Society, 1925.

Lawrence, Frederick William Pethick. *National Finance* (Fabian Tract No. 229). London: The Fabian Society, 1929.

Neep, Edward John. *Seditious Offences* (Fabian Tract No. 220). London: The Fabian Society, 1926.

Oakeshott, Joseph F. *The Humanizing of the Poor Law* (Fabian Tract No. 54). London: Humanitarian League; The Fabian Society (reprint), 1897.

Olivier, Baron Sydney Haldane. *Imperial Trusteeship* (Fabian Tract No. 230). London: The Fabian Society, 1929.

Passfield, Baron Sidney James U. *English Progress Towards Social De-mocracy* (Fabian Tract No. 15). London: The Fabian Society, 1901.

Robson, William A. *Socialism and the Standardized Life* (Fabian Tract No. 219). London: The Fabian Society, 1926.

Sanders, William Stephen. *The Socialist Movement in Germany* (Fabian Tract No. 169). London: Fabian Society, 1913.

Shaw, George Bernard. *The League of Nations* (Fabian Tract No. 226). London: The Fabian Society, 1929.

———*Socialism: Principles and Outlooks; Fabianism* (Fabian Tract No. 233). London: The Fabian Society, 1930.

Slater, Gilbert, D. Sc. *Currency, Credit and the Unemployment Crisis* (Fabian Tract No. 239). London: The Fabian Society, 1932.

Swanwich, Helena Maria. *Labour's Foreign Policy—What Has Been and What Might Be* (Fabian Tract No. 227). London: The Fabian Society, 1929.

Webb, Beatrice. *A New Reform Bill* (Tract No. 236). London: The Fabian Society, 1931.

Webb, Sidney. *National Finance and a Levy on Capital—What the Labour Party Intends* (Fabian Tract No. 188). London: The Fabian Society, 1919.

———*The Labour Party on the Threshold* (Fabian Tract No. 207). London: The Fabian Society, 1923.

———*The Reform of the House of Lords* (Fabian Tract No. 183). London: The Fabian Society, 1917.

———*The Root of Labour Unrest* (Fabian Tract No. 196). London: The Fabian Society, 1920.

———*What Happened in 1931: A Record* (Fabian Tract No. 237). London: The Fabian Society, 1932.

West, Julius. *The Russian Revolution and British Democracy* (Fabian Tract No. 184). London: The Fabian Society, 1917.

ARTICLES

Brandeis, Elizabeth. "Memories of a Socialist Snob." *The Progressive,* 12 (August, 1948), 31.

Burke, Richard V., "A Conception of Ideology for Historians" *The Journal of the History of Ideas,* X:2 (April, 1949).

Chamberlain, John. "Smothered Without Debate." *Plain Talk,* IV:4 (January, 1950), 48–51.

*Clark, William. "The Fabian Society." *The New England Magazine,* X:1 (March, 1894), 89–99.

*Macrae-Gibson, J. H. "The British Civil Service and the Trade Unions Act of 1927." *American Political Science Review,* XXIII (November, 1929), 922–929. (Edited by L. D. White.)

Neumann, Frank L. "Approaches to the Study of Political Power." *The Political Science Quarterly,* LXV (June, 1950), 161–181.

Pigou, A. C. "Mr. and Mrs. Webb on Consumer Co-Operation." *The Economics Journal,* XXXII (March, 1922), 53–57.

Saltau, Roger H. "The British Political Scene Since the General Election." *The American Political Science Review,* XXIII (November, 1929), 892–907.

Schlesinger, Arthur. "Biography of a Nation of Joiners." *American Historical Review,* L (October, 1944), 1–26.

*Slesser, Sir Henry. "Through Anglicanism to the Church." *The London Tablet,* 192 (November 20, 1948), 326 ff.

Asterisks indicate the author is, or was, a Fabian.

ENCYCLICALS AND ALLOCUTIONS

Leo XIII, Pope. *Graves de Communi (Christian Democracy).* New York: The Paulist Press, 1941.

Pius XI, Pope. *Quadragesimo Anno (On Reconstructing the Social Order).* Washington, D. C., N.C.W.C., 1942.

Pius XII, Pope. "Labor and Management Duties as Seen by Pope Pius XII." *U. S. News and World Report,* June 17, 1949, p. 13 f.

———"Address to Congresses of Social Studies and Christian Social Union" (NCWC Press Release, June 5, 1950).

———Christmas Message of 1944 (Washington: NCWC).

———"The Modern State" (Address of August 5, 1950, before the Eighth International Congress of Administrative Sciences), in *The Catholic Mind* (July 1951) 460–462.

———"*Les bases indispensable d'une organisation politique de l'univers*" (Address of April 6, 1951, to the Congress of the *Mouvement universel pour une Confédération mondiale*) in *La Documentation Catholique* XLVIII, (April 1951).

INDEX OF NAMES

579

GENERAL INDEX